A Formal Theory of Commonsense Psychology

Commonsense Psychology refers to the implicit theories that we all use to make sense of people's behavior in terms of their beliefs, goals, plans, and emotions. These are also the theories we employ when we anthropomorphize complex machines and computers as if they had humanlike mental lives. In order to cooperate and communicate successfully with people, these theories will need to be represented explicitly in future artificial intelligence systems.

This book provides a large-scale logical formalization of commonsense psychology in support of humanlike artificial intelligence. It uses formal logic to encode the deep lexical semantics of the full breadth of psychological words and phrases, providing 1,400 axioms of first-order logic organized into 29 commonsense psychology theories and 16 background theories. This in-depth exploration of human commonsense reasoning for artificial intelligence researchers, linguists, and cognitive and social psychologists will serve as a foundation for the development of humanlike artificial intelligence.

Andrew S. Gordon is Research Associate Professor of Computer Science and Director of Interactive Narrative Research at the Institute for Creative Technologies at the University of Southern California. His research advances technologies for automatically analyzing and generating narrative interpretations of experiences. A central aim of his research is the large-scale formalization of commonsense knowledge, and reasoning with these formalizations using logical abduction. He is the author of the 2004 book, *Strategy Representation: An Analysis of Planning Knowledge.*

Jerry R. Hobbs is Chief Scientist for Natural Language Processing at the Information Sciences Institute and a research professor at the University of Southern California. He has numerous publications in computational linguistics, artificial intelligence, knowledge representation, information extraction, and discourse analysis. He was an editor of the book *Formal Theories of the Commonsense World* and author of *Literature and Cognition.* He is a fellow of the Association for the Advancement of Artificial Intelligence, is a past president of the Association for Computational Linguistics, and is a recipient of that organization's Lifetime Achievement Award.

To Cynthia and Margaret

A FORMAL THEORY OF COMMONSENSE PSYCHOLOGY

How People Think People Think

ANDREW S. GORDON
University of Southern California

JERRY R. HOBBS
University of Southern California

CAMBRIDGE
UNIVERSITY PRESS

CAMBRIDGE
UNIVERSITY PRESS

University Printing House, Cambridge CB2 8BS, United Kingdom

One Liberty Plaza, 20th Floor, New York, NY 10006, USA

477 Williamstown Road, Port Melbourne, VIC 3207, Australia

4843/24, 2nd Floor, Ansari Road, Daryaganj, Delhi - 110002, India

79 Anson Road, #06-04/06, Singapore 079906

Cambridge University Press is part of the University of Cambridge.

It furthers the University's mission by disseminating knowledge in the pursuit of education, learning, and research at the highest international levels of excellence.

www.cambridge.org
Information on this title: www.cambridge.org/9781107151000
DOI: 10.1017/9781316584705

© Andrew S. Gordon and Jerry R. Hobbs 2017

First published 2017

Printed in Great Britain by Clays Ltd, St Ives plc

A catalogue record for this publication is available from the British Library.

Library of Congress Cataloging-in-Publication Data
Names: Gordon, Andrew S., author. | Hobbs, Jerry R., author.
Title: A formal theory of commonsense psychology : how people think people think /
    Andrew S. Gordon, University of Southern California, Jerry R. Hobbs, University of
    Southern California.
Description: Cambridge, United Kingdom ; New York, NY : Cambridge University Press, 2017. |
    Includes bibliographical references and index.
Identifiers: LCCN 2017020865 | ISBN 9781107151000 (alk. paper)
Subjects: LCSH: Psychology. | Common sense. | Reasoning.
Classification: LCC BF121 .G645 2017 | DDC 150–dc23
LC record available at https://lccn.loc.gov/2017020865

ISBN 978-1-107-15100-0 Hardback

Contents

Part I Commonsense Psychology

1 Commonsense Psychology and Psychology   *page* 3
   1.1   Explaining the Behavior of Triangles   3
   1.2   Heider's Commonsense Psychology   5
   1.3   Theory of Mind   7
   1.4   Historical Change in Commonsense Psychology   10
   1.5   The Purpose of Psychology as a Science   13
   1.6   Eliminative Materialism   15

2 Commonsense Psychology and Computers   17
   2.1   Anthropomorphism Is Easy and Fun   17
   2.2   Anthropomorphic Computing   18
   2.3   Alan Turing and the Desktop Barrier   20
   2.4   Coping with Discordant Computers   22
   2.5   The Value of a Good Model (to a Computer)   24
   2.6   Computational Modeling of Cognitive Processes   26
   2.7   Inferential Theories in Artificial Intelligence   28
   2.8   Models in the Right Direction   29
   2.9   Jan Smedslund's Psychologic   31

3 Formalizing Commonsense Psychology   36
   3.1   Coverage and Competency   36
   3.2   Successive Formalization   38
   3.3   Strategy Representation   39
   3.4   Psychological Expressions   47
   3.5   Draft Formalizations   53
   3.6   Final Formalizations   54
   3.7   Intermediate Applications   56
   3.8   Repeatability   58

4   Commonsense Psychology and Language   60
   4.1   Knowledge Management   61
   4.2   Similarity Comparisons   62
   4.3   Memory   63
   4.4   Envisioning   64
   4.5   Explanation   65
   4.6   Managing Expectations   66
   4.7   Other-Agent Reasoning   67
   4.8   Goals   67
   4.9   Goal Themes   68
   4.10 Threats and Threat Detection   68
   4.11 Plans   69
   4.12 Goal Management   71
   4.13 Execution Envisionment   71
   4.14 Causes of Failure   72
   4.15 Plan Elements   72
   4.16 Planning Modalities   73
   4.17 Planning Goals   74
   4.18 Plan Construction   75
   4.19 Plan Adaptation   75
   4.20 Design   76
   4.21 Decisions   77
   4.22 Scheduling   78
   4.23 Monitoring   79
   4.24 Execution Modalities   79
   4.25 Execution Control   80
   4.26 Repetitive Execution   82
   4.27 Mind–Body Interaction   82
   4.28 Observation of Plan Executions   83
   4.29 Emotions   84

Part II   Background Theories

Introduction   91

5   Eventualities and Their Structure   93
   5.1   Eventualities and Their Individuation   93
   5.2   The Structure of Eventualities   95
   5.3   Generation   98

6   Traditional Set Theory   100

7   Substitution, Typical Elements, and Instances   105
   7.1   Substitution   105
   7.2   Typical Elements   106
   7.3   Handling Some Thorny Issues   108
   7.4   Functional Dependencies   111
   7.5   Instances   113

8   Logic Reified   116
  8.1   Conjunction   116
  8.2   Negation   117
  8.3   Disjunction and Implication   118

9   Functions and Sequences   121
  9.1   Pairs and Functions   121
  9.2   Sequences   123

10 Composite Entities   126
  10.1   Definitions   126
  10.2   Some Simple Examples   129
  10.3   The Figure–Ground Relation   130
  10.4   Patterns and Their Instances   132

11 Defeasibility   135

12 Scales   139
  12.1   Basics   139
  12.2   Scale-to-Scale Functions   143
  12.3   Constructing Scales   143
  12.4   Qualitative Structure on Scales   145

13 Arithmetic   150
  13.1   Integers   150
  13.2   Rational Numbers   153
  13.3   Measures and Proportions   154
  13.4   Half-Orders of Magnitude   156

14 Change of State   158
  14.1   The change Predicate   158
  14.2   Predicates Derived from change   159

15 Causality   163
  15.1   Causal Complexes and the Predicate cause   163
  15.2   Agents and Agenthood   165
  15.3   Other Causal Predicates   168
  15.4   Ability   170
  15.5   Executability   171
  15.6   Difficulty   173

16 Time   177
  16.1   The Topology of Time: Instants, Intervals, and
         Temporal Sequences   177
  16.2   Relating Eventualities and Time   181
  16.3   Temporal Ordering and Interval Relations   183
  16.4   Durations   187
  16.5   Periodicity   190
  16.6   Rates and Frequency   191

17   Event Structure   196
17.1   Events and Subevents   196
17.2   Event Sequences and Conditionals   197
17.3   Iterations   199

18   Space   202
18.1   Space and Spatial Analogies   202
18.2   Spatial Systems and Distance   203
18.3   Location   205

19   Persons   207

20   Modality   211
20.1   The Predicates Rexist and atTime   211
20.2   Positive Modalities   213
20.3   Possibility and Necessity   213
20.4   Likelihood, or Qualitative Probability   215

Part III   Commonsense Psychology Theories

21   Knowledge Management   223
21.1   Objects of Belief   223
21.2   Belief   224
21.3   Belief Revision   228
21.4   Degrees of Belief   231
21.5   Assuming   235
21.6   Having Things in Mind and in Focus   238
21.7   Inference   239
21.8   Justification   242
21.9   Knowledge   244
21.10   Intelligence   245
21.11   Sentences and Knowledge Domains   246
21.12   Expertise   248
21.13   Mutual Belief   250

22   Similarity Comparisons   256
22.1   Similarity   256
22.2   Similarity of Structured Entities   265
22.3   Cognizing Similarities   267

23   Memory   270
23.1   Storing and Retrieving   270
23.2   Accessibility   271
23.3   Associations and Causing to Remember   273
23.4   The Meanings of "Remember" and "Forget"   274
23.5   Remembering To Do   277
23.6   Repressing   277

24 Envisioning   280
   24.1   Thinking Of   280
   24.2   Causal Systems   283
   24.3   Contiguous Causal Systems   286
   24.4   Envisioned Causal Systems   289
   24.5   Envisionment and Belief   291
   24.6   Other Varieties of Thinking   295

25 Explanation   299
   25.1   Explanations and Mysteries   299
   25.2   The Explanation Process   301
   25.3   Explanation Failures   303

26 Managing Expectations   306

27 Other-Agent Reasoning   309

28 Goals   312
   28.1   Goals, Subgoals, and Plans   312
   28.2   The Content of Goals   315
   28.3   Goals and Multiple Agents   317
   28.4   Trying, Succeeding, and Failing   319
   28.5   Functionality   320
   28.6   Good and Bad   322
   28.7   Value, Cost, and Importance   322

29 Goal Themes   332
   29.1   Thriving   332
   29.2   Pleasure and Pain   333
   29.3   Short-Term versus Long-Term Goals   336
   29.4   Goal Themes   338

30 Threats and Threat Detection   341
   30.1   Threat Situations   341
   30.2   Threat Detection and Management   343
   30.3   Seriousness   345

31 Plans   348
   31.1   Plans as Mental Entities   348
   31.2   The Planning Process   350
   31.3   Strategies and Tactics   355
   31.4   Executability and Complete Plans   356
   31.5   Types of Plans   358
   31.6   Helping   362

32 Goal Management   366
   32.1   Adding, Removing, and Modifying Goals   366
   32.2   Priority   368
   32.3   Assessing and Prioritizing Goals   370

33 Execution Envisionment   373
    33.1   Executions and Their Envisionment   373
    33.2   Envisioning Success and Failure   374
    33.3   Specific and Arbitrary Contexts of Execution   376
    33.4   Envisioned Executions and Time   378

34 Causes of Failure   380
    34.1   Introduction   380
    34.2   Contributing Source Taxonomies   381
    34.3   Taxonomy of Plan Failure Explanation Patterns   381
    34.4   Causal Complexes and Failure   383
    34.5   Applications   385

35 Plan Elements   387

36 Planning Modalities   392
    36.1   The Activity of Planning   392
    36.2   Planning Activity and Other Agents   393
    36.3   Counterfactual Planning   394

37 Planning Goals   397
    37.1   Constraints and Preferences   397
    37.2   Including and Avoiding   400
    37.3   Enabling and Blocking   401
    37.4   Minimizing and Maximizing   402
    37.5   Locating Instances for Plans   403
    37.6   Maintaining Plan Progress   404

38 Plan Construction   407
    38.1   The Planning Activity   407
    38.2   Planning Process Control   408
    38.3   Planning Subprocesses   409
    38.4   Planning Problems   411
    38.5   Selecting among Candidate Plans   412

39 Plan Adaptation   416
    39.1   Tweaking   416
    39.2   Types of Plan Adaptation   418
    39.3   Outcomes of Plan Adaptation   419

40 Design   421
    40.1   Artifacts   421
    40.2   Designs   423
    40.3   Designing   424

41 Decisions   427
    41.1   The Decision-Making Process   427
    41.2   Choices and Choice Sets   430
    41.3   The Process of Deliberation   432
    41.4   Justifications for Decisions   435
    41.5   Consequences of Decisions   436

42   Scheduling   439
   42.1   Simultaneous Actions   439
   42.2   Schedules   440
   42.3   Scheduled and Pending Plans   443
   42.4   Schedule Preferences   446
   42.5   Scheduling Actions   446

43   Monitoring   451
   43.1   Monitoring Processes   451
   43.2   Characteristics of Monitoring Processes   453

44   Execution Modalities   456
   44.1   Executions   456
   44.2   Modalities of Execution   458
   44.3   Plan Execution and Time   460

45   Execution Control   464
   45.1   Beginning Executions   464
   45.2   Executions in Progress and Completed   466
   45.3   Execution Costs and Outcomes   468
   45.4   Abstract Plans and Their Instantiations   469
   45.5   Plans and Aspect   471
   45.6   Distraction   474

46   Repetitive Execution   478

47   Mind–Body Interaction   484
   47.1   Introduction   484
   47.2   Mind and Body   485
   47.3   Awareness and Focusing   485
   47.4   Perception   486
   47.5   Bodily Actions   488
   47.6   Perceiving Bodily Actions   491
   47.7   Controlling Perception   492
   47.8   Levels of Capability and Activity   493
   47.9   States of Consciousness   497

48   Observation of Plan Executions   502
   48.1   Observing the Plan Executions of Other Agents   502
   48.2   Instructions   504
   48.3   Performances and Their Specification   505
   48.4   Skill   506
   48.5   Evaluation   509

49   Emotions   513
   49.1   Emotions in General   513
   49.2   Intensity and Arousal   515
   49.3   Happiness and Sadness   518
   49.4   Shades of Happiness   521
   49.5   The Raw Emotions   524

49.6   Basic Emotions Cognitively Elaborated   528
       49.6.1   Happiness and Sadness for Others   528
       49.6.2   Hope and Fear-2   530
       49.6.3   Reactions to Goals Realized and Frustrated   531
       49.6.4   Reactions to Achievements and Failures   533
49.7   Envy and Jealousy   536
49.8   Liking and Disliking   538
49.9   Emotional States and Tendencies   539
49.10 Appraisal and Coping   541

Appendix A: First-Order Logic   545
A.1   Predicate-Argument Relations   545
A.2   Logical Connectives   546
A.3   Variables and Quantifiers   548
A.4   Rules of Inference   549
A.5   Axioms and Logical Theories   549
A.6   Models   550
A.7   Definition and Characterization   552
A.8   Common Patterns in Axioms   553

References   557
Index   567

PART I

Commonsense Psychology

Commonsense Psychology and Psychology

1.1 EXPLAINING THE BEHAVIOR OF TRIANGLES

In 1944 Fritz Heider and Marianne Simmel published the results of a novel experiment conducted at Smith College in Northampton, Massachusetts. In "An experimental study of apparent behavior" Heider and Simmel (1944) prepared a brief film
depicting the movements of a two triangles and a circle in and around a shape made
to look like a room with a door. The film was shown to 114 undergraduate women
at Smith College divided into three experimental groups. In the first, subjects were
given the general instruction to "write down what happened in the picture." In the
second, subjects were instructed to interpret the movements of the figures as actions
of persons and to answer ten questions in a written questionnaire. The third group
was shown the film in reverse, by running the filmstrip backwards through the pro-
jector, and asked a subset of the same questions.

The Heider–Simmel film, which is today readily viewable on online video web-
sites, is not particularly remarkable as a piece of animated cinematography. Compared to Walt Disney's films of the same era, including *Pinocchio*, *Fantasia*, and
Bambi, the film must have appeared anachronistic even to the original Smith College subjects. Each frame in the film was produced as a photo of geometric shapes
cut from cardboard and placed on a horizontal translucent-glass plate illuminated
from above. The careful placement of the shapes in each frame created a narrative
stream of events, evidenced only by the silent trajectories of each shape and its position in relation to the others. As expected, the subjects in the three experimental
groups interpreted these events as a coherent narrative and described them in terms
of the interrelated behaviors of three intentional characters, in and around a room
defined by four walls and a door. Somewhat surprising is the degree to which these
descriptions attributed mental states to these nondescript shapes. Heider and Simmel provide the following as representative of the descriptions produced by the first
experimental group:

> A man has planned to meet a girl and the girl comes along with another man. The first man
> tells the second to go; the second tells the first, and he shakes his head. Then the two men
> have a fight, and the girl starts to go into the room to get out of the way and hesitates and
> finally goes in. She apparently does not want to be with the first man. The first man follows

her into the room after having left the second in a rather weakened condition leaning on the wall outside the room. The girl gets worried and races from one corner to the other in the far part of the room. Man number one, after being rather silent for a while, makes several approaches at her; but she gets to the corner across from the door, just as man number two is trying to open it. He evidently got banged around and is still weak from his efforts to open the door. The girl gets out of the room in a sudden dash just as man number two gets the door open. The two chase around the outside of the room together, followed by man number one. But they finally elude him and get away. The first man goes back and tries to open his door, but he is so blinded by rage and frustration that he cannot open it. So he butts it open and in a really mad dash around the room he breaks in first one wall and then another. (pp. 246–247)

Nearly every subject in the first group described the events in anthropomorphic terms, typically involving a fight between two men (the triangles) over a woman (the circle). The natural tendency was to describe what happened in terms of human behavior, even without instructions to do so. The narratives of these subjects employ mentalistic phrases: The girl hesitates; she doesn't want to be with the first man; the girl gets worried; man number two is still weak from his efforts to open the door; the girl and man number two finally elude man number one and get away; man number one is blinded by rage and frustration. The second group of subjects further explained these anthropomorphic interpretations: the larger triangle is an aggressive bully, the smaller triangle is heroic, the circle is helpless, and the actions of the smaller triangle and circle lead to their successful escape from the larger triangle, sending him into a rage for being thus thwarted. The third group of subjects, seeing the film in reverse, also interpreted the movements as human actions. Here the variations in narrative were much greater: a man resolved to his fate is disrupted by a woman accompanied by evil incarnate, a prisoner thwarts a murder attempt and then escapes, and a mother chastises a father over the behavior of their child.

In 1944 when this work was published, psychology in the United States was still under the strong influence of Behaviorism and its efforts to eschew mentalistic constructs in explanations of human behavior. Set in this context, Heider and Simmel's experiment might be viewed as a poignant challenge to their contemporaries, highlighting a particular human behavior that seems impossible to understand without appealing to mentalistic causes. Instead, it may be better to view this work as a continuation of the Gestalt psychological traditions that Fritz Heider brought with him from Europe. After receiving his Ph in 1920 from the University of Graz in Austria, Heider spent a decade in Germany working under the intellectual leaders of the Gestalt school of psychology, including Wolfgang Koehler, Max Wertheimer, Kurt Koffka, and Kurt Lewin. The study of visual perception was a major focus of this group of academics, and their use of simple geometric shapes in experimental stimuli was standard practice before and after Heider left Germany for the United States in 1930.

Heider's adoption of film technology was the novelty that shifted the course of his personal research trajectory. Before, Heider had been concerned with a fundamental problem of object perception: How is it that people attribute to objects properties such as color and texture, where these properties exist only as senses of the perceiver? Heider proposed that a cognitive process was at work, attribution, in which people infer invariant properties of objects as the causes of their perceptions. Moving to film from printed experimental stimuli, the subjects in Heider's experiments are faced with the challenge of inferring the causes of animacy of these geometric objects. In attempting to do so, they employ the same rich theory that they use to explain the behavior of other people, which gives rise to the anthropomorphic interpretations of Heider and Simmel's film. When triangles and circles start moving around a screen in trajectories that defy physics-based explanations, then psychological explanations are the next-best candidates.

1.2 HEIDER'S COMMONSENSE PSYCHOLOGY

In Heider's view, the psychological explanations told by the subjects in Heider and Simmel's experiments were not based on scientific theories, but rather on a commonsense theory of psychology. Here the behaviors of the triangles and circle are explained using mentalistic terms for the characteristics attributed to these objects, including their beliefs, goals, plans, and emotions. This was the same theory that people used to explain the behavior of others in everyday interpersonal relations, and that served as the basis for everyday predictions, decisions, and planning that involved other people. Commonsense psychology is not a theory in the scientific sense, meant to describe how our brains actually operate. Instead, it is a commonsense theory of how we think we think.

Heider articulated his conception of a commonsense psychology a decade later with the publication of his most famous work, *The Psychology of Interpersonal Relations* (1958). Heider begins by contrasting scientific theories with commonsense theories, noting that the former focus on findings that are surprising and unintuitive, precisely those results that contradict the latter. However, here the relationship between scientific psychology and commonsense psychology is different than seen in other fields:

> If we erased all knowledge of scientific physics from our world, not only would we not have cars and television sets and atom bombs, we might even find that the ordinary person was unable to cope with the fundamental mechanical problems of pulleys and levers. On the other hand, if we removed all knowledge of scientific psychology from our world, problems in interpersonal relations might easily be coped with and solved much as before. Man would still "know" how to avoid doing something asked of him, and how to get someone to agree with him; he would still "know" when someone was angry and when someone was pleased. He could even offer sensible explanations for the "whys" of much of his behavior and feelings. In other words, the ordinary person has a great and profound understanding of himself and of other people which, though unformulated or only vaguely conceived, enables him to interact with others in more or less adaptive ways. (p. 2)

Heider's interest in commonsense psychology was twofold. First, if commonsense psychology guides the everyday behavior of people in interpersonal situations, then it is an essential part of the phenomenon that is the subject of scientific study. If we are to develop scientific theories with predictive utility, then this essential part of the phenomenon must be adequately described as well. This point is true even if we, as scientists, believe that inferences drawn from commonsense psychology are invalid. Heider notes, "If a person believes that the lines in his palm foretell his future, this belief must be taken into account in explaining certain of his expectations and actions" (p. 5). In contrast, Heider believed that commonsense psychology was not fundamentally flawed. Quite the contrary, his second motivation for studying commonsense psychology was for the truths it contains: "This book defends the opposite point of view, namely, that scientific psychology has a good deal to learn from common-sense psychology. In interpersonal relations, perhaps more than in any other field of knowledge, fruitful concepts and hunches for hypotheses lie dormant and unformulated in what we know intuitively" (pp. 5–6).

Having decided to focus on the role of commonsense psychology in interpersonal relations, there still remains a choice as to which scientific questions are to be pursued. How does the role of this knowledge progress in cognitive development of a normal child? Are there cross-cultural differences in the commonsense psychology explanations that people produce? Are these reasoning abilities the result of evolution, possibly shared by nonhuman primates, or are they the product of human cultural development? What is the relationship between commonsense psychology and mental disorders that impair human social interaction? These are exactly the sorts of questions that continue to be pursued by psychologists more than a half-century after the publication of Heider's book. However, these are not the questions that Heider chose to address. Instead, Heider's research instinct was to focus on describing the contents of the theory itself–to articulate explicitly the intuitive knowledge of human psychology that allows us to interact with each other in more or less adaptive ways.

Heider's specific purpose was "to offer suggestions for the construction of a language that will allow us to represent, if not all, at least a great number of interpersonal relations, discriminated by conventional language in such a way that their place in a general system will become clearer. This task will require identifying and defining some of the underlying concepts and their patterns of combination that characterize interpersonal relations" (p. 9). Drawing from both his own intuitions and insights from previous scientific studies, Heider sought to describe commonsense psychology as a set of interrelated concepts, a system of beliefs that people effortlessly employed when explaining the behavior of others. His methods were strictly analytical, alternating between the semantic analysis of sets of interrelated everyday words and the conceptual analysis of hypothetical situations in order to explore a particular area of commonsense psychology. Heider focused on ten central concepts in his analyses: subjective environment (life spaces), perceiving, causing, can, trying, wanting, suffering, sentiments, belonging, and ought.

In explicating each of these concepts, Heider articulates a set of commonsense beliefs that are meant to capture the essential inferences of interpersonal relations. Here Heider adopts a notation partly fashioned after that of symbolic logic, where the symbol p represents the person whose subjective environment is being considered, o and q represent other persons, and r represents some undetermined person (somebody). The symbols $x, y,$ and z designate impersonal entities, things, situations, or changes. Examples of these commonsense beliefs are as follows, in the discussion of sentiment:

> p dislikes o induces p avoids o, or p withdraws from a disliked o. (p. 191)
> p likes o and p not in contact with o leads to tension, or p is unhappy when the loved o is absent. (p. 191)
> p likes o induces o benefits p, or p will tend to believe that the liked o benefits him. (p. 200)

While these examples are somewhat interpretable to the casual reader, Heider also invented additional notations meant to compactly encode the more complex propositions, described in the book's appendix. In doing so, Heider crafts a subset of second-order predicate logic with infix predicate-argument notation and universal quantification and negation. Heider refrained from using much of this notation in the body of the text, perhaps to the benefit of the majority of his readers. For example, all of the things (x) that a person (p) wants someone (o) not to perceive is compactly represented as (p. 301)

$$\hat{x}(pW : o \text{ not Perc } x).$$

Heider viewed his work as only the beginning of a much larger intellectual enterprise. He aimed only to "clarify some of the basic concepts that are most frequently encountered in an analysis of naive descriptions of behavior." (p. 14). Heider may have hoped that his treatment of these concepts was the first of many, and that his interests and methods would be adopted by scores of psychologists who followed in his footsteps. Instead, Heider's book was the first and last of its kind within the mainstream of psychology research. Heider trained no ambitious graduate students to carry the banner of this work toward new and fruitful areas, and his contemporaries were ill-equipped to replicate the sorts of analytic methods that he employed. Even Heider acknowledged the methodological challenge:

> It would be an impossible task to describe in detail how these concepts were arrived at. Long years of analyses of word meanings of short stories or daily experiences contributed to the belief in the fruitfulness of working with them. The attitude that underlay these analyses was a feeling that there is a system hidden in our thinking about interpersonal relations, and that this system can be uncovered. (p. 14)

"Long years of analyses" driven by beliefs, attitudes, and feelings was not a particularly attractive research methodology in psychology as the Cognitive Revolution began in the 1950s. Instead, the most direct influence of Heider's work was seen in the field of social psychology, where psychologists proposed new theories to account for the nonintuitive findings of interpersonal perception. Here, Heider's account of the attribution of characteristics to people and situations became known as Attribution Theory. Edward Jones and Keith Davis (1965) proposed Correspondent Inference Theory to account for a perceiver's inferences about what an actor was trying to achieve by a particular action. Harold Kelley (1967) proposed the Covariation Model of Attribution, suggesting that people attribute a behavior to whatever it covaries with across the people and situations in which it is engaged. Edward Jones and Victor Harris (1967) described what became known as the Fundamental Attribution Error: the tendency for people to overvalue personality-based explanations of behavior and undervalue situation-based explanations. Edward Jones and Richard Nisbett (1971) argued that there is Actor–Observer Asymmetry in personality-based and situation-based explanations, where people favor situation-based explanations for their own behavior (although see Malle, 2006, for a critical review). Today, Attribution Theory continues to be tweaked in the face of new experimental findings in social psychology. At the very least, this progression of research continues to keep Heider's book on the reading lists of contemporary psychologists, even as the disconnect between Heider's analytical approach and contemporary research in social psychology continues to widen.

1.3 THEORY OF MIND

The vast majority of psychological research related to Heider's commonsense psychology has been conducted in areas other than social psychology. In these areas, a different umbrella term is commonly used to refer to both the commonsense theory and its associated cognitive processes: Theory of Mind. This term itself is problematic, as the "theory" part implies a particular theoretical perspective on how people reason about the "mind" part, namely through the fluid application of theoretical knowledge. The problems with this term have been fortuitous, though, as it has forced decades of psychologists to wrestle with fundamental questions about the role of knowledge (as a classical theoretical construct) in contemporary psychology. The unfolding story has touched on nearly every area of psychology research, which we only briefly summarize here. In doing so, our aim is to highlight the successes that have been garnered in understanding the nature of these reasoning abilities, but as well to highlight a persistent inability for researchers in this area to sufficiently describe the contents of people's commonsense psychology knowledge.

Appropriately enough, the story begins in developmental psychology, where changes in a child's capacity to reason about the mental states of other people has been experimentally observed. One experimental instrument for studying children's abilities to reason about the mental states of others is the false-belief task. In a standard version of this task (Wimmer and Perner, 1983), the child is introduced to two characters, Maxi and his mother. Maxi places an object of interest into a cupboard and then leaves the scene. While he is away, his mother removes the object from the cupboard and places it in a drawer. The child is then asked to predict where Maxi will look for the object when he returns to the scene. Success on this task has been criticized as neither entirely dependent on commonsense psychology abilities nor broadly representative of them (Bloom and German, 2000); however, its utility has been in reliably demonstrating a developmental shift. In a notable meta-analysis, Wellman, Cross, and Watson (2001) analyzed 178 separate studies that employed a version of this task, finding that three-year-olds will consistently fail this task on the majority of trials by indicating that Maxi will look for the object in the location to which his mother has moved it. Four-year-olds will succeed on half the trials, while five-year-olds will succeed on the majority of trials. Call and Tomasello (1999) demonstrate that these results are consistent across verbal and nonverbal versions of this task.

There is a developmental change between three- and five-year-olds, but the question of what develops remains. One school of thought is that this developmental change can best be characterized as the acquisition by children of a better theoretical model of human psychology, a view first referred to as the Theory Theory by philosopher Adam Morton (1980). This view has several ardent advocates among developmental psychologists (Wellman, 1990; Gopnik and Wellman, 1992; Astington, 1993; Bartsch and Wellman, 1995; Gopnik and Meltzoff, 1997), who characterize young children as extremely effective scientists who incrementally adapt their innate knowledge of people to accommodate for their experiences in the world. After years of social interaction, children's developing theories of the mind become more robust in their abilities to predict and explain human behavior, and increasingly include all of the principles of commonsense psychology in Heider's (1958) original characterization. This perspective is consistent with a broader position within developmental psychology that argues that the development of cognitive abilities is best viewed in terms of conceptual change. This perspective follows from the constructivist theories of development advanced by Piaget (1954), and can be contrasted with nativist theories that view the emergence of cognitive abilities as the maturation of innate brain functions.

The conflicting perspectives of nativism and constructivism have sparked many researchers to take interest in developmental disorders associated with deficits in Theory of Mind abilities, mainly autism. Autism in children is characterized by a varied range of symptoms, but generally includes impairments in children's abilities to interact socially with others, delays and impairments in verbal communication, and abnormal displays of repetitive or restricted behavior. Baron-Cohen, Leslie, and Frith (1985) first hypothesized that the main behavioral symptoms of autism could be explained by a deficit in Theory of Mind abilities. In an much-replicated study, Baron-Cohen et al. compared normal children with those diagnosed with autism and Down's syndrome on a variant of false-belief task involving two dolls. Even though the mental age of the autistic children was higher than that of the other groups, they alone failed to correctly ascribe a false belief to the doll in the experiment. The finding sparked a vigorous theoretical debate among the community of developmental psychologists and autism researchers that continues today. Tager-Flusberg (2007) reflects on two decades of research that followed the hypothesis of Baron-Cohen et al. which has upheld the original result: Children with autism have difficulty attributing mental states to themselves or to other people. However, the significance of this finding is in doubt. Deficits in theory of mind abilities are not universal among autistic children, and do not offer an explanation for other typical symptoms such as repetitive and restricted behavior patterns. Tager-Flusberg cautions against a narrow view of the social-cognitive deficits in autism, and draws attention to more recent research on children's perception of mental-state information in faces, voices, and body gestures (Klin et al., 2003). If the connection between Theory of Mind abilities and autism is to be explanatory, then the traditional understanding of Theory of Mind must be broadened to include these social-perceptual skills. As it stands today, the relationship between autism and Theory of Mind abilities is sufficiently complex to preclude this area of research from weighing in on the nativist-constructivist debate.

Cross-cultural psychology research and ethnographic methods in cognitive anthropology have shed some light on which of these two perspectives, constructivism or nativism, best characterizes our abilities to reason about the minds of others. Lillard (1998) reviews the evidence for and against differences between the standard European/American commonsense psychological model and that of non-European/American cultures, and argues that meaningful variations can be found in four areas. First, not all cultures appear to view the mind as equal to the self, as internal to and distinct from the body, or as an important topic of conversation and attention. Second, there are variations in the degree to which other cultures view behavior as a result of mental processes. In some cultures, situational, social, and ethereal factors are seen as playing a more significant role in driving behavior than in the European/American view. Third, whereas the primary way of affecting the mind in the European/American view is through perception of the world, several cultures hold beliefs that the mind is also affected by ritual acts, ethereal forces, or by transgressions of people in their past. Fourth, the characterizations of specific mental processes, particularly perception, emotion, and thinking, can vary widely across cultures, and can include the beliefs that hearing applies to nonacoustic phenomenon, that the cause of sadness is an illness, and that thinking about something is only a superficial means of understanding something. In summarizing the evidenced cultural differences in commonsense psychological theories, Lillard recommends caution: Systematic cross-cultural studies of adult theories of the mind have yet to be completed. Moreover, Lillard is quick to point out that cultural differences should not be seen as proof of cultural relativism in commonsense psychology; underlying the differences seen between cultures is a substantial amount of similarity, with many common beliefs that might be candidates for human universals. As with many findings of cross-cultural studies, the universality of any psychological trait is likely to be a matter of degree. On one hand, Avis and Harris (1991) demonstrated the universality of the human ability to reason about the beliefs and desires of others in their experiments with children of the Baka, a group of pygmies living in the rain forests of southern Cameroon. On the other hand, Wu and Keysar (2007) studied people's ability to take the perspective of another in a visual perception task, and demonstrated significant differences between Chinese and American-raised adults attending the same university on the south side of Chicago. While significant differences such as these suggest a role for enculturation in the development of commonsense psychology, the current cross-cultural evidence does not strongly favor either the constructivist or nativist perspective.

Are Theory of Mind abilities unique to humans? In the title of their 1978 paper, Premack and Woodruff posed the question: Does the chimpanzee have a theory of mind? An affirmative answer would lend weight to nativism over constructivism, as well as downplay the overall significance of culture and enculturation in human Theory of Mind abilities. Reviewing the thirty years of primate experimentation that followed from Premack and Woodruff's provocative paper, Call and Tomasello (2008) provide the definitive answer to their question: yes and no. There is solid experimental evidence that chimpanzees understand the goals and intentions of others, as well as the perception and knowledge of others. The behavioral evidence from chimpanzees suggests understanding that goes beyond the reading of surface behaviors of others, to underlying goals and perceptions – at least to the extent that human infants do in similar experimental designs. In contrast, there is no experimental evidence that chimpanzees can grasp the notion of a false belief, or predict the behavior of another based on what the other knows. If we take a narrow view of the scope of Theory of Mind abilities, focusing on social cognitive reasoning, then our closest biological relatives have nothing like our human abilities. If instead we broaden our scope to include social perception and intentional interaction, then chimpanzees are convincingly competent. This shift in research focus toward social competency has led some researchers consider the question for more distant biological relatives, including domesticated dogs and other highly social animals (Pennisi, 2006). The broad set of social skills that are often associated with human Theory of Mind abilities appear to be widespread throughout the animal kingdom. Birds will hide food far away from potential thieves, and wait to stash food until an onlooker is distracted. Hyenas recognize not only just their own status relative to the pack leader but also the status relationships of other pack members. Domesticated dogs are able to follow a human's eyes or pointing gestures to hidden food. In contrast, not one other species has passed the false belief test, or exhibited anything like the deep social reasoning in which humans effortlessly engage.

1.4 HISTORICAL CHANGE IN COMMONSENSE PSYCHOLOGY

As with other universals, core commonsense psychological beliefs could be the product of our biology, or could be the result of cultural influences that are so saturated throughout the world's societies that they are difficult to separate from our biology.

In either case, an important question to consider is whether commonsense psychological beliefs can change substantially over time, and whether substantial changes have occurred since the advent of tribalism, government, and the beginning of the historical record.

In an effort to investigate these questions, a number of researchers have sought evidence for significant changes in commonsense psychology in the texts of classical antiquity (e.g., Snell, 1953). One of the more provocative of these historical analyses was that of Julian Jaynes (1976) in support of his ideas on the emergence of consciousness. In this work, Jaynes examines references to psychological concepts as they appear in a variety of early narratives, including the Iliad and the Odyssey. Jaynes argues that these texts use terms such as *thumos* (emotional soul), *phrenes* (mind or heart), *kradie* (heart), *etor* (heart or guts), *noos* (conscious mind), and *psyche* (soul or conscious mind) that do not connote conscious mental activity, as implied by contemporary translations. Instead, Jaynes ties the semantics of these words to the "bicameral mind," where volition, planning, and initiative are organized externally and provided to a person, rather than produced through conscious thought. The study of these words advances his claim that there was a shift in the way the people of ancient Greece thought about consciousness. Jaynes's more controversial idea was that these changes were indicative a real change in human psychology: the emergence of human consciousness, just two and a half millennia ago.

Although Jaynes successfully argues that there was a shift in the way that mental concepts were referenced in these early texts, one could argue that these changes can be attributed solely to changes in linguistic convention, rather than to changes in the underlying semantics of the language or the cognitive abilities that are based on these representations. For this criticism, Jaynes makes the controversial retort, "Let no one think these are *just* word changes. Word changes are concept changes and concept changes are behavioral changes" (p. 292, original emphasis). While this comment raises a much larger philosophical debate concerning mental representation, arguments made on either side would be improved if the evidence were stronger. Among other points, it is tempting to argue that the changes exhibited in Jaynes sampling of early texts are not representative of the cultural environment in which these texts were produced.

Rather than looking at early texts for changes in commonsense psychology, it is interesting to consider when the most recent significant change might have occurred. Probably the strongest argument for recent, widespread cultural change in Theory of Mind involves our shared understanding of the relationship between conscious and unconscious thought. As Whyte (1978) argues, our modern conception of unconscious thought is an invention that was conceivable around 1700, topical around 1800, and effective around 1900. While scientific discussion of the unconscious became prevalent in the latter half of the nineteenth century (e.g., von Hartmann, 1931), truly widespread socialization of concepts related to the unconscious can be largely attributed to the impact of the writings of Sigmund Freud. In *The Interpretation of Dreams*, first published in German in 1900 and translated to English in 1913, Freud outlined an understanding of human cognition that involved the influence of subconscious desires in behavior. Although Freud's use of symbolism in explaining dreams is often joked about in everyday conversation, the more central idea of a subconscious desire has become a fundamental part of the way people talk about their goals. It is uncontroversial when a person reports, "I must have wanted to leave my wife all along, but I only recently became aware of this subconscious desire of mine."

In our own previous work (Gordon and Nair, 2003), we investigated whether a corresponding shift in thinking about subconscious desires was evident in the writings of English-language novelists before and after the widespread popularity of Freud's idea. In this work, we authored generalized finite-state transducers for recognizing English expressions related to the idea of a subconscious desire, including phrases like "I am not sure what I want" and "It was a goal that I did not know I had" along with specific references to "unconscious desires" and "subconscious goals." We then applied these transducers to 176 English language novels published between 1813 and 1922, a corpus of more than 20 million words, and analyzed the recognized sentences according to the publication date of each book. Our expectation was that we would see evidence for one of two possibilities. The first was that would find an increase in expressions of unconscious desires after the widespread popularity of Freud's idea (after 1913), suggesting that there had indeed been a widespread change in the way that people thought about human psychology. The second was that there would be no significant change in the relative frequency of these expressions across the time span of our corpus, suggesting that Freud's idea had not fundamentally changed the way that people thought about or talked about the mind. In fact, neither of these expectations was true; instead there was evidence that a significant shift had occurred, but that it had taken place around fifty years before the first publication of Freud's influential book, in the middle of the nineteenth century. Before the late 1850s, few (if any) references to these concepts appear in the corpus. After this point, English language novelists increasingly used the vocabulary that questioned the certainty of one's own desires and the existence of subconscious goals, including this remarkable passage from George Eliot's 1860 novel, *Mill on the Floss*:

> Maggie, in her brown frock, with her eyes reddened and her heavy hair pushed back, looking from the bed where her father lay to the dull walls of this sad chamber which was the centre of her world, was a creature full of eager, passionate longings for all that was beautiful and glad; thirsty for all knowledge; with an ear straining after dreamy music that died away and would not come near to her; with a blind, unconscious yearning for something that would link together the wonderful impressions of this mysterious life, and give her soul a sense of home in it.

In an exercise of conceptual forensics, it is interesting to note that George Eliot was the pen name of English novelist Mary Ann Evans, a leading writer in the Victorian era and the center of literary circles in London and elsewhere. Evans had moved to Germany in 1854, where she was presumably influenced by the people she met in German intellectual circles. As characterized by Whyte (1978), Germany was a hotbed for philosophical investigations of the unconscious mind at the time that Evans was there. Significant figures included Eduard Van Hartmann, who later published an extremely popular and seminal work on the unconscious mind, *Philosophy of the Unconscious*, in 1869. Although we know of no evidence, it is fascinating to consider that Evans's remarkable reference to an unconscious yearning was a product of the cultural dissemination of a new idea in the way that people think the mind works. If we take the suggestion from Jaynes's comment given earlier, and assume that these discourse changes are indicative of conceptual changes, then we should also assume that commonsense psychology is a moving target, a model that is subject to some amount of cultural change.

1.5 THE PURPOSE OF PSYCHOLOGY AS A SCIENCE

The idea that commonsense psychology may be the subject of cultural evolution should be of particular interest to scientists in the field of psychology. Arguably, the purpose of psychology is to change commonsense psychology. The pursuit of science in general is to further our understanding of the natural world (including people), where the word "our" here is not meant to refer only to the scientific community, but rather to all of humanity. Certainly all psychology researchers need to believe that some amount of change is possible to the commonsense psychological views that are more broadly believed, as a principle of their profession. However, the contemporary view of commonsense psychology among psychologists is as a naïve theory, distinct from the best-supported scientific theories of human cognition. The assumption is that there are two psychologies, folk and scientific, and that the aim of science education in psychology is to get more people to swap the former for the latter.

The contemporary view of commonsense psychology as naïve is largely an outgrowth of empirical studies of naïve physics, where the commonsense views that people have about physical phenomenon have been shown to be often wrong in interesting ways. An oft-cited example is the curvilinear momentum error (Clement, 1983; McCloskey, 1983), where subjects erroneously predict that balls traveling in a curvilinear trajectory due to the physical forces of attached strings or the walls of a tube will continue to travel in a curvilinear path when these forces are abruptly removed. The term "roadrunner physics" is often applied to this and other examples of erroneous commonsense physical beliefs, in homage to the cartoon characters of Warner Brothers' *Looney Tunes* and *Merrie Melodies* television programs, where depictions of impossible physical phenomena is commonplace.

Do similar fallacies appear in commonsense psychology? It would be hard to argue that commonsense psychology is complete and indefeasible: People are surprised by the behavior of people around them on a daily basis. It is nearly impossible to reliably predict what someone will say next in any mundane conversation, let alone what he or she would think about any reasonably complex issue. More interesting would be to find evidence for consistently incorrect predictions about the consistent behavior of a population sample. Here too, examples are easy to find. Nichols et al. (1996) describe an experiment that challenges the competency of people to predict the behavior of other people in a psychological experiment. In this work, Nichols et al. begin with a surprising finding of an experiment by Ellen Langer (1975), where it was found that subjects would place a significantly higher buy-back value on a lottery ticket that they had chosen from a set over one that had been randomly given to them. Nichols et al. replicated this earlier finding, but also sought to show that people would not be able to predict these differences in valuations. The experimenters produced a pair of videotapes of a confederate subject participating in a variation of Langer's original experiment, differing only in whether the confederate had chosen the lottery ticket from a set or had been given to them without choice. Two groups of subjects then watched one of the two videotapes, and were asked to predict the price the subject on the tape would set for selling back his lottery ticket. Their finding was that these subjects could not correctly predict Langer's original result, that the lottery ticket selected by choice would be valued significantly higher than the other. Instead, subjects predicted buy-back prices in both cases that were not significantly different.

Nichols et al. (1996) argue that this finding has broader implications in the debate concerning how people engage in commonsense psychological reasoning. As an alternative to Theory Theory, advocates of Simulation Theory argue that inferring the mental states of others involves imagining that you are in the same situation as the target person, and monitoring how your own mind responds – which then is your best guess of what is going on in the other's mind (Goldman, 1989; Gordon, 1986; Harris, 1989; Heal, 1986). However, Nichols et al. viewed the failure of subjects predict the Langer effect as evidence against Simulation Theory: A mind in simulation mode should replicate the same human tendency to inflate the lottery ticket's value. Irrespective of the argument of Nichols et al., the more general observation here is that commonsense psychology may lead to predictions of the reasoning processes of other people that do not match with scientific psychological evidence. It is hardly surprising that there is a difference between commonsense psychology and empirical results; indeed, nearly every published finding in experimental psychology may be similarly surprising to the average nonpsychologist. If these findings were not surprising (counter to commonsense expectations), then they would likely not be published in psychological journals and conferences in the first place.

One view of these findings is that they merely expose the gap between the cutting edge of scientific psychology and the widespread adoption of new findings within the culture at large. Rather than conceiving of two psychologies, folk and scientific, it may be more productive to view the scientific pursuit of psychology as a means of extending, refining, and changing our commonsense understanding. Explicit theories of psychology may find success in the scientific process, communicated explicitly and implicitly throughout the culture, and ultimately adopted as implicit truths in the culture at large. In this view, psychology is at the fringe of commonsense psychology, challenging some aspects of our commonsense knowledge while accepting the rest as given. The Langer effect, as investigated by Nichols et al., could be seen as a fragment of psychological theory that currently falls in the gap between the cutting edge of psychology and commonsense. That is, it is a belief about valuation that is widely held by experimental psychologists, but not by their subjects.

Psychology researchers should hope that their proven theories may one day cross this gap and impact commonsense psychology. However, there is little evidence of this sort of scientific influence beyond a few remarkable historical cases. The Freudian concepts of subconscious desires and repressed memories may be among the few cases in which a strong argument could be made of successful transfer from science to commonsense psychology. Yet this "success" may have been more the product of larger social changes, zeitgeist, and the fashion of the times than the strength of Freud's writing on the matter. Few psychologists conducting research today place much stock in theories that involve subconscious desires and repressed memories, but replacing these aspects of commonsense psychology with a new revised theory would require an equally powerful alignment of social, culture, and scientific factors – an alignment that does not seem eminent. To complicate matters, Freud's ideas continue to have utility in contemporary cognitive psychology, as exemplified by experimental work on the deliberate suppression of unwanted memories (Anderson and Green, 2001).

1.6 ELIMINATIVE MATERIALISM

The gap between scientific psychology and commonsense psychology has received the most attention within the philosophy of mind literature (Fletcher, 1995; Greenwood, 1991), particularly around a philosophical position known as Eliminative Materialism. One definition, put forth by the philosopher Paul Churchland, is as follows:

> Eliminative materialism is the thesis that our common-sense conception of psychological phenomena constitutes a radically false theory, a theory so fundamentally defective that both the principles and the ontology of that theory will eventually be displaced, rather than smoothly reduced, by completed neuroscience. (Churchland, 1981, p. 67)

Eliminative Materialism sees our everyday abilities to reason about the minds of other people as theory driven, that is, based on a flawed commonsense theory of human psychology. Moreover, this theory could be (and should be) replaced with a better one, for example, one that is more in accordance with our best scientific understanding of human psychology, particularly a theory that is based on current functional theories of the brain. Eliminative Materialism argues that there is a significant gap between commonsense psychology and scientific psychology, but does not see it as one that can be overcome by incrementally fixing the aspects of commonsense psychology that are demonstrably wrong. Instead of tinkering with our existing commonsense psychology, perhaps as Freud's impact had done as discussed in the previous section, we should reject it outright and adopt a more valid conceptual framework for reasoning about the mental lives of others and ourselves.

As a philosophical position, Eliminative Materialism is a provocative idea that helps clarify the debate within the philosophy of mind community. As a vision for the future, however, Eliminative Materialism is an extremely radical idea, the stuff of a good science-fiction novel where the course of humanity of forever changed by a singular event. Imagine a world were everyone on the planet, including the children of the Baka pygmies living in the rain forests of southern Cameroon (Avis and Harris, 1991), were to not think of people as thinkers imagining the future and explaining the past, assuming and doubting different beliefs in their mind and memory, coping with their unpleasant emotions, and guided by prioritized goals and scheduled plans. What aspect of human life, all of our political and social institutions, would not be radically changed if this were the case? The philosopher Jerry Fodor takes note of the underlying radicalism in Eliminative Materialism:

> … if commonsense intentional psychology really were to collapse, that would be, beyond comparison, the greatest intellectual catastrophe in the history of our species; if we're that wrong about the mind, then that's the wrongest we've ever been about anything. (Fodor, 1987, p. xii)

It would not take too much effort to convince most people that they have an incorrect understanding of the transmission in their manual-shift automobile. Even those drivers two have performed flawless shifts for decades might be very surprised to see what a real transmission looks like if it were placed on a table in front of them. In reality, an automobile transmission is a very complicated device, with more moving parts than most people would want to bother thinking about while they are driving. If they did, they would surely run the risk of being distracted by its complexity, leading to more automobile accidents and a shrinking of the gene pool. With respect to the task at hand, a driver may prefer a simple but incorrect model of his or her transmission, as long as it has the predictive power to get the job done. The philosopher Daniel Dennett argues the same point with respect to commonsense psychology:

> What I want to stress is that for all of its blemishes, warts, and perplexities, folk psychology is an extraordinarily powerful source of prediction. It is not just prodigiously powerful but also remarkably easy for human beings to use. We are virtuoso exploiters of not so much a theory as a craft. The theory of folk psychology is the ideology about the craft, and there is lots of room, as anthropologists will remind us, for false ideology. (Dennett, 1991, p. 135)

Whether right or wrong, commonsense psychology seems to be working well for us at the moment. In some ways, Eliminative Materialism is ultimately an optimistic message of hope, that one day our species will achieve a greater degree of enlightenment concerning the human mind through scientific exploration. Its failing is in expecting that such a change will could come about any time soon. Although it is possible that significant improvements could be made, it is difficult to imagine how these changes could be so widely distributed and integrated into the reasoning processes of the world's peoples within any reasonable amount of time. Churchland's (1981) enthusiasm for neuroscience as a future successor to commonsense psychology is overly optimistic to the extreme extent; few if any scientific theories of moderate complexity have ever usurped an incumbent commonsense theory in any of the world's cultures, least of all a commonsense theory so entrenched in language, literature, the arts, the law, and economic practices. The commonsense psychology concepts of goals, plans, beliefs, expectations, explanations, threats, opportunities, emotions, decisions, and perceptions will have a secure place in our commonsense theories, our vocabulary, our government, our social institutions, and our scientific pursuits for the duration of our lifetimes, the lifetimes of many future generations, and throughout the lifespan of any technology we build that incorporates these concepts. Given that we are stuck with it, it would be prudent to describe exactly what are the contents of our commonsense psychology theories, and figure out how to put this description to good use.

2

Commonsense Psychology and Computers

ANTHROPOMORPHISM IS EASY AND FUN

Anthropomorphism is a human universal (Brown, 1991). That is, people in every culture naturally anthropomorphize nonhuman things. Like most other human universals with evolutionary utility, anthropomorphism is easy and fun. As every parent knows, contemporary first-world children experience an unending festival of anthropomorphism, where every fish, train, and lunar mass not only has a human face, but is also endowed with human emotions, human goals, and human reasoning abilities. Remarkably, children effortlessly cope with this massive amount of make-believe without too much trouble, and though they may desperately wish that their toys would come to life as they sometimes do in the movies, few seem particularly surprised that they do not.

While it is tempting to view anthropomorphism as simply a fanciful diversion of youth, the fish, trains, and moons that children treat as people are perhaps better viewed as training for the anthropomorphism that pervades the lives of adults. Playful attribution of human intellect to nonhuman physical objects continues as our toys become larger, where automobiles have preferences for high-octane gasoline and lawnmowers can be temperamental. More seriously, anthropomorphism becomes a tool for understanding the complexities of organizations. In adult anthropomorphism, governments easily acquire mental faculties, such that China can be concerned about its future petroleum needs and the United States can assign a higher priority to national security than to civil liberties. In many cases, this style of anthropomorphism is linguistic shorthand for references to the mental states of government officials, such as the concerns of members of the Chinese cabinet or the priorities of the US president. However, it is just as easy to talk about mental states of governments that are in reference to no one specifically among its citizenry, such as California's appetite for litigation.

Serious anthropomorphism by adults is best exemplified by the way that people treat corporations, each with its own corporate mission, values, institutional memories, business plans, and identity as a corporate citizen. As with governments, sometimes these terms are references to the people who direct the practices of the corporation. The corporate mission may be that of the corporation's founders. Institutional memories may be those held by real people in the organization, past or present. Other times, these attributed mental states may be in direct conflict with those of most or all of a corporation's employees, as when corporations are downsized or even completely liquidated in order to maximize shareholder value. Far from linguistic playfulness, the United States has legalized corporate anthropomorphism through judicial action throughout the nineteenth and twentieth centuries. An 1886 US Supreme Court opinion (concerning *Santa Clara County v. Southern Pacific Railroad*) established corporations as "persons" for purposes of Constitutional interpretation of the Fourteenth Amendment, originally penned to secure the rights of emancipated slaves. The 2010 U.S. Supreme Court case of *Citizens United v. Federal Election Commission* established First Amendment protections for corporations, viewing limits on corporate financing of political campaigns as a violation of the freedom of speech.

Nearly any institution or object that exhibits some behavior is subject to the anthropomorphic tendencies of people. The philosopher Daniel Dennett has called this tendency the *intentional stance*, viewing it as a strategy for predicting the behavior of complex things. He writes:

> Here is how it works: first you decide to treat the object whose behavior is to be predicted as a rational agent; then you figure out what beliefs that agent ought to have, given its place in the world and its purpose. Then you figure out what desires it ought to have, on the same considerations, and finally you predict that this rational agent will act to further its goals in the light of its beliefs. A little practical reasoning from the chosen set of beliefs and desires will in most instances yield a decision about what the agent ought to do; that is what you predict the agent will do. (Dennett, 1989, p. 17)

For governments and corporations, the strategy may be a good one, leading to often-correct predictions of their behavior without needing to understand the complexity of multiagent interactions that are involved in these organizations. The downside of the human tendency for anthropomorphism is seen when it leads to predictions that are flat-out wrong. For example, it is a sort of serious anthropomorphic playfulness that leads us to believe that the cells in our immune system have the goal of finding and destroying harmful viruses and bacteria in our bodies, and that viruses have the intention of hijacking the mechanisms of healthy cells in pursuit of their own self-replication mission. But should we also predict that viruses resort to evasive tactics when the immune system's antibodies begin to neutralize them, as any reasonable adversaries would do when their lives were in danger? Thinking about cells and viruses as reasonable agents, where behavior is a causal product of intentional thought, may help people grapple with the complexity of the immune system in the short run, but can just as easily be a barrier to the acquisition of a deeper understanding of immunological complexity as systems of interactions. Of course, most people aren't interested in acquiring a deep understanding of immunological complexity. More often, our relationship with complexity is about simply dealing with it.

2.2 ANTHROPOMORPHIC COMPUTING

When it comes to human-made complexity, computers reign supreme. Personal computers have replaced the automobile as the most complicated device that people willfully bring into their homes. While some modest percentage of automobile owners understand their construction well enough to fix them when they break down, few electrical engineering professors understand the complexity of contemporary computers well enough to undertake the repair of their own personal systems. As with cellular immunology, few people really want to understand how computers actually work. Instead, people are looking for ways of dealing with their increasing pervasiveness in our lives, and anthropomorphism is often the best approach.

In their book, *The Media Equation*, Stanford communications professors Byron Reeves and Clifford Nass describe how people naturally ascribe social roles to computers and other media sources (Reeves and Nass, 1996). The thesis of this book is that people treat computers, television, and new media as real people, and that social science findings concerning the way that people treat each other also are true in human–media interaction. For example, Reeves and Nass describe a series of experiments that examine the principles of politeness that people employ in human–human interaction, specifically the tendency to inflate a judgment of someone else's performance when that person is the ones directly asking for your opinion. In these experiments, human subjects demonstrate this same tendency when judging the performance of a computer program with which they have interacted; they inflate their judgment of its performance when it is the computer itself that asks them for their opinion, as opposed to a different computer on the other side of the room (p. 23). Reeves and Nass argue that this finding and others lends support to the view that people treat computers as social agents, treating them as if they could appropriately fill the role of a person when applying the unconscious, automatic social behaviors that they have developed through their human–human interactions.

The practical implications of this perspective on human–computer interaction concern the alignment of users' social tendencies with the behavior of computational devices. Reeves and Nass view these implications in terms of learnability and enjoyment:

> If human–media interactions are social and natural, then there are a number of unexpected ways to improve the design of media. Many of these applications stem from one important conclusion: Humans are experts on social relationships, and they are experts on how the physical world works. Rules for using media as tools, on the contrary, are often arbitrary and must be learned. When media conform to social and natural rules, however, no instruction is necessary. People will automatically become experts in how computers, television, interfaces, and new media work.

> Because people have a strong positive bias toward social relationships and predictable environments, the more a media technology is consistent with social and physical rules, the more enjoyable the technology will be to use. Conforming to human expectations means that there is instant expertise just because we're human, and there are positive responses, including feelings of accomplishment, competence, and empowerment. (p. 8–9)

The argument here is that if users are naturally going to treat their computers as people, then the computers should be designed in a manner that is in accordance with people's expectations. But which expectations should designers concern themselves with specifically? Recalling Dennett's intentional stance from the previous section, some of these expectations may be about the mental states and processes of people, that is, commonsense psychological models that people apply to nonhumans in an anthropomorphic manner. However, these are not the expectations that Reeves and Nass are talking about, as they note in their dismissal of anthropomorphism:

> Another common assumption about technology is that when people treat media as human, they are guilty of anthropomorphism, a mistaken belief that inanimate objects are human. Anthropomorphism, however, is rare and is not the basis for the media equation. Social responses are commonplace, even when people know that the responses are inappropriate. (p. 10–11)

Instead, the expectations that Reeves and Nass are talking about concern the behavior of participants in social interactions, for example, that it is polite to inflate a judgment of others' performances when they are the ones asking for it directly. However, here Reeves and Nass have the wrong view of anthropomorphism, that is, as a rare and mistaken belief that inanimate objects are human. Far from rare, anthropomorphizing nonhuman objects in our environment (including media) is a pervasive part of all of our everyday lives, a human universal. Anthropomorphism is easy and fun, not an inappropriate or mistaken belief that inanimate objects are human. It is an adaptive means of coping with the complexities of the world. Users are naturally going to anthropomorphize their computers, treating them as rational agents with beliefs, purposes, and desires, in Dennett's terms. Assigning a social role to this personification is a natural, apparently unavoidable part of taking an intentional stance.

Thinking about human–computer interaction in this manner does little to make the findings reported by Reeves and Nass any less interesting, particularly the conclusion that people are ill-equipped to avoid the attribution of social roles to computers. However, adopting anthropomorphism as part of the explanation for these tendencies has a significant impact on Reeves and Nass's prescriptions for the design of computational systems. In addition to conforming to the social expectations of their users, computational systems should be aligned with the cognitive expectations that their users apply to them.

Anthropomorphic computing may be the best term to describe this engineering approach. The central principle of anthropomorphic computing is that computational systems should facilitate the anthropomorphic tendencies of their users by behaving in a manner that is in accordance with users' commonsense psychological models. People are naturally going to treat computational systems as if the latter have plans, goals, beliefs, expectations, and emotions. They are naturally going to predict and explain the reasoning behavior of computational systems using the same commonsense psychological models that are used in predicting and explaining human reasoning behavior, rather than the engineering models that are used in the architectural design of computing hardware and software. By aligning the reasoning behavior of computational systems with commonsense psychological models, human–computer interaction will be facilitated; users can apply their commonsense models to their computers with verisimilitude.

2.3 ALAN TURING AND THE DESKTOP BARRIER

Today, personal computers are designed around a completely different metaphor. Instead of treating computers as people, developers want users to treat computers as office space. The desktop metaphor, first developed at Xerox Palo Alto Research Center in the 1970s and popularized in the operating systems of Apple Computer and Microsoft in the 1980s, creates a user interface based on the manipulation of virtual physical objects that one would find in his or her office: a desktop, a set of documents, an inbox, an address book, a calculator, a calendar, a filing cabinet, and a wastepaper basket. Every one of these virtual objects is lifeless and familiar, facilitating user anthropomorphism no more or less than their real-world counterparts. By turning computers into an extension of office space, the desktop metaphor reduces the ease in which people can see computers as people; people do not typically anthropomorphize their entire offices, so why would they anthropomorphize one corner of it?

The desktop interface creates a barrier to the anthropomorphizing tendencies of computer users. Consider the way that human–computer interaction was envisioned before the popularization of the desktop interface in the 1980s. The late 1960s found *Star Trek*'s Captain Kirk talking with the bridge computer on the starship *Enterprise* and a conflicted HAL 9000 murdering astronauts in Arthur C. Clark's *2001: A Space Odyssey*. These Hollywood portrayals of computers as people were reflections of an inherent anthropomorphism in computer science from its inception, best exemplified by Alan Turing's own fascination with intelligent computation. By the time that Turing wrote the article "Computing Machinery and Intelligence" (1950) and set the field of artificial intelligence in motion, he had spent a decade engineering significant mechanical and electronic computational devices. The Turing Test that he described then defined intelligence as a human judgment: Can a computer fool a person into believing that it is a person itself? Removing the deceptive nature of this definition, we can recharacterize the central question of the Turing Test in commonsense psychology terms: Does this computer operate the way people think they think? Operating the way people think they think, rather than the way they actually think, is central to the judgment of intelligence in the Turing Test. If the difference between the two turns out to be rather significant, we could easily imagine that a computer operating in accordance with commonsense psychology would be judged more humanlike than an actual human, who is operating the way that people actually think.

Today, as it was for Turing a half-century ago, the thought of super-humanlike computation is little more than a theoretical amusement. Any person who judges the intelligence of today's computers by this (or any other halfway reasonable) criterion is going to be sorely disappointed. Outside of a few narrow computational tasks, few people today would attribute more intelligence to a computer than to an infant or even a household pet. If you see your personal computer as a person, then you are not going to be particularly impressed with its intelligence. However, if you see your computer as a collection of office tools and useful devices that extends your actual office environment, then your attributions are going to be much more positive. Anthropomorphizing your computer makes it look like an idiot. The desktop interface makes it look like a collection of magical objects.

The desktop metaphor for human–computer interaction is a barrier that reduces the anthropomorphizing tendencies of users. For three decades it has successfully tempered the expectations of users toward the functional capabilities of desktop computers. In the grand scheme of things, however, it will likely be seen as a historical curiosity, as an artifact of an era when people equated computation with desktop computers in office environments. The desktop metaphor is successful because office workers already know how to interact with things in their office. This approach made perfect sense for the twentieth century, when office workers were exactly the people who bought and used personal computers. But things are now changing; computing power will be a nearly free, ubiquitous resource within decades, available to people who may have never even seen a first-world office building. Anthropomorphic computing will be the successful human–computer interface of the twenty-first century because everyone on the planet will be a user of computing technology, and all of them already know how to interact with people.

Since the early 1970s we have seen a remarkable transition in the way that computation is embodied in real-world objects. Building-sized supercomputers shrank into desktop workstations. Personal computers turned into handheld devices and mobile phones. The trend toward cheaper, faster, smaller computers is not going to end. We will soon be squeezing millions of them out like toothpaste from a tube, or rolling them out like masking tape in the not-too-distant future. When computers look like and cost as much as postage stamps, no one is going to imagine them to be extensions of an office environment. The desktop metaphor for human–computer interaction will be relegated to history; billions of people on Earth will be looking for a more natural means of interacting with computational power.

Anthropomorphism with postage-stamp computers works like this: After you buy a vintage twentieth century toaster for the kitchen of your new apartment, you roll out a stamp from your computer roll and stick it on the side of the toaster. "You're a toaster," you tell it in order to turn it on, and then proceed to give it some instructions: "Let me know if I forget about the toast I'm making, keep an eye out for smoke, save power by shutting down when I'm on vacation." You roll out another one and stick it to the front door: "You're the front door." You instruct it to call the police if someone is trying to break in, check with the windows to make sure the apartment is locked up when no one is home, and send away any solicitors who come knocking. "You're a toy train," you say to the stamp that you put on one of your child's toys. "Let me know when one of your parts comes loose, and look for opportunities to teach my child some conversational Japanese." Anthropomorphism is easy and fun.

Building postage-stamp computers with the necessary sensors, power, and network connectivity to support these functions is not going to be the biggest challenge. The real hurdle will be designing computers that can accommodate this level of user anthropomorphism; if they are going to do the right thing, these computers will need to operate the way that people think an intelligent device should, namely, the way people think they think.

2.4 COPING WITH DISCORDANT COMPUTERS

The desktop metaphor may have been successful over the late twentieth and early twenty-first centuries precisely because it discourages people from exercising their natural anthropomorphic tendencies. The sad truth is that if you are so inclined to playfully take an intentional stance with your computer, you are likely to become annoyed. The behavior of an average early twenty-first century computer is extremely complex, but almost none of it is in accordance with the commonsense psychological models that we apply via anthropomorphism. Even the fish, trains, and lunar objects that we anthropomorphize seem less discordant than computers, simply because their minimal behavior is not rich enough for us to care about the discrepancies. The inability of computers to conform to our commonsense psychological expectations, or even to acknowledge them, is the first major cause of discord. A common criticism that users have of computational systems is that their operation is counterintuitive. It is important to consider exactly which intuitions are being referenced by this phrase, given that generally people do not have any intuitions about computers to begin with. Some of these intuitions are probably about manufactured devices in general, and others about the relationships among information, action, and object. In this chapter we have argued that some of these intuitions are about the intelligent behavior of people. In being counterintuitive, the behavior of computational systems is violating the set of expectations that we have about human psychology.

An example of this type of discordance can be seen in the differences between users' and computers' view of the focus of attention. In the commonsense view, people like to focus on one thing at a time, and have trouble dividing their attention between two or more tasks. We use phrases like "I am concentrating on this right now" to note that our attention is unavailable or "my mind was somewhere else" to explain why attention was not directed. Interestingly, people hold this view even though they, like the computers they are using, are incredibly talented at multitasking. Although computers do not yet have the human ability to drive a car, hold a conversation on a mobile phone, and read a map all at the same time, they are nonetheless efficiently multithreaded. When anthropomorphizing computers, users expect that they will have only a single task or problem in their focus of attention at any given moment. In reality, contemporary operating systems are typically running several dozen different processes and several times as many threads at any one moment, with efficient multithreading policies that ensure that no single one of them is unduly dominant. Asking your computer "What are you up to right now?" poses a difficult question to answer. The real problem that this creates, however, is for users who are trying to predict the behavior of the computer they are using. If I close my email application now, will the messages left in my outbox still be delivered? If I install this new operating system upgrade, will it wait for my web documents to finish downloading before it reboots? If my computer game is using up all of the screen space of the display, then are my background applications going to run faster or slower? Computer scientists who understand multithreading might come up with reasonable answers for these questions, but most computer users can only guess.

A second source of discordance concerns the poverty of understanding that computers have of their users. Although personalization and user modeling are becoming more and more common in contemporary computing systems, few attempt to consider user behavior beyond the observable. Consider the discordant characteristics of word processing applications like the one being used to type this sentence. In many ways, it is a remarkably intelligent application: It corrects many spelling errors as they are typed, it suggests active-voice constructions for passive-voice sentences, and it seems to know when one would be interested in the contents of the automatically saved recovery file when launching the program after a system crash. However, it seems rather oblivious to the mental processes involved in authoring or reviewing a document. Why would it interrupt to ask if you wanted to update your operating system software when you are in the middle of typing a sentence? Why would the screensaver engage when you have had only half the time needed to read the displayed text of the document you just opened? Why is it not at all concerned that you have typed a series of keyboard shortcuts that would delete the chapter you have been working on all week? There is plenty of available evidence for your computer to make a reasonable guess as to what is going on in your mind, and if you are going to interact with your computer in any humanlike manner, that is exactly what you expect it to do.

A third source of discordance is perhaps the most problematic: Computers have almost no capacity for understanding language related to psychology, despite its central importance in human–human interaction. Users who anthropomorphize computers are going to want to discuss their own beliefs, expectations, emotions, goals, or plans in nearly every single interaction that they have with them. Yet the limited natural language understanding capabilities of contemporary human–computer dialogue systems make them ill-equipped to interpret the meaning, intention, or implications of these references. For contemporary users of desktop computing applications, the discordance is even worse in the other direction of communication; applications routinely use references to mental state concepts that lead users toward incorrect inferences. An operating system utility reports that it is checking for new software, a multiplayer computer game is waiting for other network players to join, and a utility program is scheduling to back up the computer hard drive. Each of these expressions has inferential consequences for users: If you are checking for something, then you don't already know that is there. If you are waiting for something, then you are more likely to expect it to happen than not. If you are scheduling to do something, then you may look for opportunities to get it done early if time allows, and you do not do it twice if you indeed manage to fit it in earlier. In almost all computer applications, these words and phrases are simply part of canned statements found in language-specific localization files used by the software. In cases in which statements need to be dynamically generated, software developers tend to be less creative in their use of psychological language, at the expense of comprehension. What does it mean when my computer reports that it is reducing the memory cache size by 128 megabytes to free up space on the hard drive?

2.5 THE VALUE OF A GOOD MODEL (TO A COMPUTER)

In arguing in favor of anthropomorphic computing, we are not advocating the development of machines that are indistinguishable from people in their reasoning behavior. With more than seven billion real people alive on the planet at the time of this writing, there really is no reasonable engineering need to create devices that think exactly the same way that people do (although the scientific value cannot be understated). If you would like to interact with an intelligent person, then you should. Instead, computer science has always been concerned with developing machines with superhuman reasoning abilities: Computers that can perform flawless calculations, explore massive search spaces, process massive data sets, and work tirelessly at repetitive jobs without becoming bored or feeling compelled to organize their own labor unions. The most efficient means of performing these operations rarely looks like anything the human brain seems to be doing. In developing computers that better facilitate the anthropomorphic tendencies of their users, the aim is to support richer forms of human–computer interaction between these superhuman reasoning machines and the human population at large.

Furthermore, we are not really advocating here for the development of machines that operate exactly how people think they think, that is, constructed according to the expectations that people have about the behavior of their own mental processes. Although people's commonsense models of psychology are remarkably rich, they probably do not provide an adequate blueprint to build a working device. That is, commonsense psychology tends to be descriptive of the behavior of human reasoning rather than the method that underlies this behavior. For example, the human memory concepts of repressed memories, false memories, forgetfulness, and photographic memory are all well grounded in commonsense psychological models, but this is not to say that people have any intuitive understanding of the mechanism of human memory that could give rise to these phenomena. But even in cases in which our commonsense intuitions may provide some guidance for computational mechanisms, it may not make any sense to actually adhere to the model in authoring reasoning algorithms. There is no particular reason to believe that our intuitions about reasoning process are going to be efficiently optimized, exhaustive in their performance, or even (computationally) correct.

Instead of mirroring humanlike reasoning in machines, anthropomorphic computing is fundamentally about instilling computers with an explicit awareness of the commonsense psychology model that is being applied to them, along with the ability to reason about this model in support of human–computer interaction. The aim here is to ensure that both parties in the interaction are sharing the same model. For people, this model takes the form of an implicit commonsense theory of human psychology. For computers, it must be explicitly represented in some algorithm-friendly formalism.

The value of this commonsense psychology model for computers is its ability to reduce the discordance caused by the intentional stance of their users. First, it allows computers to make some informed guesses about the expectations that human users have of the computer's computational state. Even if the mechanism by which computers are executing tasks do not resemble human cognition in any way, computers can at least recognize when their behavior is counterintuitive from a user's perspective. In these cases, some mitigating strategy can be employed to explain to the user what is really going on or reduce the importance of consequent user inferences in the success of the interaction.

Second, commonsense psychological models give computers the framework in which to maintain user models that include their mental states and processes. As we discussed in the previous section in reference to word processing applications, it can be extremely important to know what might be in the user's focus of attention. Likewise, computers could benefit from tracking the user's preferences, goals, plans, hopes, and fears throughout sessions of interaction. They need to make predictions and generate explanations about what the user is thinking, wanting, and going to do next. Even further, computers need to be able to dynamically compute the implications of changes in their model of users as they pertain to the current state of the computational task. Mental models of the other person are perhaps the most important factor in governing the flow of control in human–human interactions, determining the direction of conversation and cooperation. The same is going to be true in human–computer interactions when anthropomorphism is encouraged, with significant impact on how user interface programs are designed.

Third, an explicit model of commonsense psychology provides computers with a conceptual framework in which to understand and produce natural language expressions related to mental states and processes. English, along with all other natural languages, is extremely rich in ambiguous words and phrases related to every aspect of commonsense psychology. An explicit commonsense psychology model provides a means of disambiguating the senses of expressions based on the context of the human–computer dialogue, making it easy to know that something "on the tip of my tongue" might refer to the state of the user's memory, even if the topic of conversation is actually about cooking, eating, or some other tongue-related activity. Likewise, a commonsense psychology model can be instrumental in selecting the appropriate word or phrase to use when composing a natural language statement to the user. Instead of reporting that it is reducing the memory cache size by 128 megabytes to free space on the hard drive, an anthropomorphic computer might construct a statement that makes some sense to more than a tiny fraction of its users. "Let me think through this a bit more slowly. I want to make sure I can remember it later."

None of these ideas for exploiting commonsense psychology in support of human–computer interaction are developed any further in this book. Instead, the focus is on a more fundamental problem, namely that of providing an explicit model of commonsense psychology for use in this interaction. Anthropomorphic computing is integrally dependent on the existence and correctness of this model, but the task of actually writing it down in some computer-friendly format is no simple matter.

2.6 COMPUTATIONAL MODELING OF COGNITIVE PROCESSES

It is quite possible that computer scientists, as a group, are more resistant to doing labor than their counterparts in other academic disciplines. If we believe that people end up in careers by following their interests, then this should come as no surprise. Computation is fundamentally about automation; the attraction of computer science is getting the computer to do the work for you. This character flaw has hardly hindered the success of the field, but merely focused creative energies on small algorithms (and big ideas) that produce amazing results. Many of these results seem like magic. Machine-learning algorithms automatically find complex rules for distinguishing between classes by analyzing entries in corpora of millions of training examples. Search algorithms automatically identify sequences of actions that transform hundreds of randomly placed boxes into a single neatly stacked column in a matter of seconds. Genetic algorithms modify other bits of code over thousands of iterations to find a version that best serves an intended function. Most notably, each of these magical algorithms can be written down on single piece of paper, for the most part. Their strength is based on the ingenuity of their design, not the size of their implementation. Optimistically, one might hope that injecting some commonsense psychology into computers could also be done with about a page of computer code.

However, regardless of our own ingenuity as computer scientists, engineering commonsense psychology is going to require a lot of labor. If we succeed in our implementations, they are going to require substantially more than a single page of computer code printout. Certainly our implementations are going to be subject to ingenious optimizations, but the limits of this optimization have less to do with computers and more to do with people. The commonsense psychological models that people have are remarkably complex, cover a broad range of inferences, and are referenced by an enormously rich vocabulary in natural languages. In every case in which computer scientists see a part of this model that may be reducible to something more compact or efficient, they are running the risk of moving their implementation further away from the actual model that is shared among people as commonsense knowledge. There are not going to be any one-page algorithms, magic bullets, or bolts of lightning that will enable us to quickly inject some commonsense psychology into computers. Instead, it is going to require a large-scale engineering effort.

The goal of this engineering effort will be a computational model of commonsense psychology, developed to support the interaction between computational systems and the human users who naturally anthropomorphize them. The term "computational modeling" underscores the desire to engineer something that is both realizable in computational systems and accurately reflects the phenomenon as it appears the natural world. Here the natural phenomena are human inferences about human psychology, and its inherent complexities will preclude any simple computational implementations.

In the natural sciences, computational modeling of phenomena in the natural world is now prevalent across numerous fields of study. Climatologists develop computational models to investigate global climate change. Cellular biologists develop computational models to investigate the dynamics of cell signaling and genetic expression. At the intersection of computer science and psychology research, computational modeling has typically been concerned with implementations of cognitive models. These models are software systems that propose testable hypotheses, highlight the inadequacies of current theories, and predict the behavior of people by simulating their reasoning processes. Computational modeling of this sort plays an important role in the scientific pursuit of a deeper understanding of human psychology, largely by forcing cognitive scientists to articulate their theories so precisely that they can be implemented in software systems. These implementations highlight the inadequacies of a given theory and provide researchers with better means of judging the true differences between competing theories, and more generally support the refinement of theories through the scientific method. For example, an algorithm can be authored to model human similarity judgments and the drawing of analogies (e.g., Falkenhainer et al., 1989) and used to inform a theory about how these cognitive functions are computed in the human brain (e.g., Gentner and Markman, 1997). Similarly, computational cognitive models of this sort exist for emotional appraisal (Gratch, 2000), memory retrieval (Gentner and Forbus, 1991), decision making (Busemeyer and Johnson, 2004), and a broad range of other aspects of human reasoning behavior.

There is substantial disagreement as to how seriously researchers should treat commonsense psychology concepts such as goals, beliefs, and expectations in the development of computational models of cognitive processes. Early contributors to this debate argued that these propositional attitudes have direct correlates in human reasoning (Fodor and Pylyshyn, 1988; Pylyshyn, 1984), so computational models that manipulate representations of these concepts can be informative in advancing our understanding. The opposing argument was that our emerging understanding of human neural architecture undermined accounts of mental processing that appealed to commonsense psychology (Churchland, 1986; Stich, 1983). In this view, researchers who author computational models of cognitive processes are better off if they take seriously what is actually known about the neural wiring of the brain.

Martin Pickering and Nick Chater put a new twist on the debate by arguing that the concerns of commonsense psychology are orthogonal to the areas in which computational modeling has been able to make substantial progress.

> According to our view, folk psychology and cognitive science should be seen neither as cooperative nor as standing in competition. They are, de facto, independent enterprises, since cognitive science simply cannot handle the knowledge-rich phenomena which are the subject matter of folk psychology. [...] The intractability of formalizing folk psychology

explains why there has been a singular lack of success in attempting to provide a cognitive science of knowledge-rich mental processes; and why cognitive science has succeeded only by focusing on knowledge-free aspects of cognition, with which folk psychology is not concerned. (Pickering and Chater, 1995, p. 311)

Pickering and Chater go further to describe examples from research in vision, memory, and language comprehension, arguing that progress in computational modeling in these areas has made progress only when researchers have eschewed approaches that incorporate propositional knowledge. In every attempt to model knowledge-rich processes, researchers have run up against the intractable problem of formalizing this knowledge and the relevant inference mechanisms for manipulating it. As a result, no good scientific explanations of these processes exist, leaving our commonsense psychological theories as the only available tool for understanding these phenomena. Cognitive science should stick to the parts of the human mind that it is equipped to explain, and leave the rest to the more interpretive fields in the social sciences.

In the two decades since voicing their pessimism about knowledge-rich cognitive modeling, the prospects have not improved. Although cognitive modeling is now a well-established methodological tool in psychology research, its main utility has been for the development of psychological theories, not for psychological simulation of knowledge-rich processes. That is, we can develop computational models of memory retrieval, decision making, and emotional appraisal that are defeasible hypotheses for how the human brain performs these tasks, but cannot build one that predicts what people might remember, decide, or feel in any real-world context. Doing so would require that we characterize the actual content of people's knowledge of past experiences, preferences, and desires in ways that interact with the algorithmic models of cognitive processes. This is not the sort of labor in which cognitive psychologists engage.

2.7 INFERENTIAL THEORIES IN ARTIFICIAL INTELLIGENCE

Of course, researchers in the field of artificial intelligence (AI) are also in the business of developing computational systems using terms that evoke human psychology, including planning, decision making, and learning. Although the techniques, concerns, and people in cognitive science and AI are often the same, the differences tend to focus on what exactly is being modeled in these computational systems. Drew McDermott summed it up best in a 1986 interview with Kentaro Toyama:

Q [Toyama]:   What do you think is the difference between AI and biology, or AI and cognitive science?

A [McDermott]: The only difference is that cognitive science is more committed to understanding existing biological cognition, as opposed to all possible cognition, which is what AI studies. So, to cite a well-worn analogy, cognitive science is to AI as ornithology is to aerodynamics. (Toyama and McDermott, 1996, pp. 3–4)

However, there is at least one significant type of computational modeling within AI that is squarely committed to understanding existing biological cognition. In developing inferential theories in AI, the aim is to develop computational models of the knowledge that people use to generate explanations and predictions. The aim is not to develop computational systems that generate all possible inferences, but rather the ones that would actually be produced by real humans.

Whereas computational cognitive models in the cognitive sciences are always directly concerned with human reasoning functions, the content of inferential theories can relate to any topic or subject area that people reason about. There are inferential theories of liquids (Hayes, 1985), the cutting of solid objects (Davis, 1993), and the cracking of eggs (Morgenstern, 2001). In some cases, these inferential theories are about people, for example, an inferential theory of the concept of ownership (McCarty, 2002). Furthermore, some of the theories about people concern their mental states and mental processes, and can collectively be viewed as inferential theories of commonsense psychology. For example, a logical theory of human emotions (e.g., Sanders, 1989) attempts to capture the commonsense inferences that people make about their own emotional state and the emotional states of others.

Computational cognitive models and inferential theories are the products of two very different research pursuits. Cognitive models are authored to advance the study of the way that people think, that is, the processes of human cognition. Inferential theories are authored to describe the way that people think about something, the knowledge that supports the cognitive processes of explanation and prediction.

This distinction becomes particularly confusing when inferential theories are about cognitive processes. Conceptually, inferential theories of commonsense psychology may overlap enormously with a particular computational cognitive model. For example, an inferential theory of human emotions (e.g., Sanders, 1989) may be concerned with exactly the same mental states and processes as a cognitive model of human emotions (Gratch, 2000), and even share much of the same terminology, logic, and constructs. The real difference is in how these two classes of models are evaluated. A cognitive model of human emotions will be evaluated on how well it models the empirical evidence of human emotional behavior. An inferential theory of human emotions will be evaluated on how well it models the predictions and explanations that people generate when reasoning about human emotional behavior. In nearly all cases, these two evaluation criteria are going to be at odds with each other, pushing a given body of research in one direction or the other. To avoid this sort of floundering, it is important that computational modeling research be explicit about which of these two pursuits a theory is targeting. The research that we describe in this book is specifically focused on inferential theories of commonsense psychology. Our aim is to describe the way that people conceptualize mental states and processes, how people think people think.

2.8 MODELS IN THE RIGHT DIRECTION

There are many ways that one could develop inferential theories, including the use of graphical probabilistic inference networks, production rule libraries, or even through the development of large case bases that support analogical inference. In practice, the researchers who actually author commonsense theories in support of automated inference almost always use formal logic. We will discuss the role of logic in commonsense reasoning research further in later chapters, but here we would like to review some of the history and trends of logical formalizations of commonsense psychology.

As any researcher in commonsense reasoning will tell you, there is an enormous variety of knowledge areas that await formalization. A rich commonsense knowledge base will include axioms concerning the weather, the preparation of meals, the organization of corporations, and the nature of basketball games. Given the wide variety of knowledge areas that are going to need some attention, one might find it surprising that the vast majority of knowledge representation research has focused on physical systems, with special attention to time, space, and events. Some will argue that time, space, and events are going to be the foundation of all of the other theories that will one day be developed, so it is critical to devote special attention to these core concerns. A more plausible explanation is simply that researchers focus on the things that they find interesting, and logicians like physics more than psychology. As AI has its academic home in schools of engineering, most graduate students pursuing knowledge representation have been immersed in the physical sciences rather than the humanities. When they look around them for commonsense reasoning problems that need to be solved, problems relating to physical systems are more likely to be readily at hand. As engineers, and with an engineering mindset, AI researchers tend to focus on exploiting the automation that is enabled by intelligent algorithms. However, the culture of automation in engineering schools has had difficulty catching up with the information age, where practical applications of automation are more commonly found in the service sector (dealing with people) than in the manufacturing sector (dealing with widgets).

Logical formalizations of commonsense psychology arguably began in the 1960s and 1970s with interest in epistemic logic, following the original formulation by Jaakko Hintikka (1962). Epistemic logic is a type of modal logic in which the epistemic modal operator (K) is used to explicitly indicate what is known, with a second operator for belief (B). By drawing a distinction among truth, knowledge, and belief, logicians began to explore aspects of introspection (termed the KK principle), logical omniscience, and epistemic necessity. Following Hintikka, researchers have incrementally added additional syntactical notations to adequately represent additional commonsense psychological ideas. Rolf Eberle (1974) added an additional operator (I) to characterize the process of mental inference, that is, that a consequence is inferred from an antecedent. Hector Levesque (1984) formalized the notions of explicit and implicit belief. Ronald Fagin and Joseph Halpern (1988) expanded on Levesque's approach by incorporating a formalization of awareness. The most significant milestone in this line of research occurred in the late 1970s and in the 1980s, when researchers pushed beyond the concerns of knowledge and inference and into the realm of plans, goals, and actions (e.g., Cohen and Perrault, 1979). AI researchers, along with the philosopher Michael Bratman (1987), pursued logical frameworks that linked the beliefs, desires, and intentions of agents. Among the more popular logical formalisms were those of Philip Cohen and Hector Levesque (1990), Anand Rao and Michael Georgeff (1991), Munindar Singh and Nicholas Asher (1993), Kurt Konolige and Martha Pollack (1993), and Michael Wooldridge (2000).

There are a number of remarkable characteristics of this line of research, not the least of which is that it is, indeed, a single line of continuous research that spans four decades. It is also notable that there has been a persistent attraction to syntax in the way that new psychological concepts are treated within these formalizations; new concepts are incrementally introduced by defining a new reasoning modality and a new notational scheme. It cannot be overlooked that the growth in the scope of psychological concepts that are addressed is extremely slow. Researchers have invested decades of research into a handful of commonsense psychological concepts (knowledge, belief, inference, awareness, desire, and intention) to achieve a satisfactory degree of depth in their understanding of their logical properties. Finally, it must be noted that few, if any, researchers attempt to directly utilize these formalizations in implemented commonsense reasoning systems. Instead, as Cohen and Levesque state, "The theory presented here can be regarded as a specification for the design of an artificial agent, and should not be viewed as a logic with which an agent should reason" (1990, p. 257).

It is this last characteristic that has driven other commonsense reasoning researchers to take a markedly different approach, sometimes referred to as the authoring of formal content theories. Content theories typically eschew syntactical considerations, often employing simple first-order logic in which new concepts can be introduced with new predicate-argument forms. The emphases in this approach shift toward the authoring of lists of axioms that define the commonsense consequences of facts that are known. John McCarthy (1979) was an early proponent of this approach, and started the ball rolling by authoring first-order formalizations of ideas in earlier epistemic logic work. Subsequent content theories of commonsense psychology have been sporadic, but mid-sized axiomizations have been authored for commonsense psychological areas that are much broader than seen in belief-desire-intention work. Ernest Davis has been particularly prolific in this pursuit, authoring formalizations for such topics as the knowledge preconditions for plans (Davis, 1994) and the relationship between knowledge and communication (Davis, 2005). With Leora Morgenstern, Davis has tackled the integration of formalizations for action, knowledge, plans, and communication (Davis and Morgenstern, 2005). Morgenstern looked specifically at formalizations of surprise and expectation (Morgenstern, 2005). Also notable is Kathryn Sanders's early content theory of human emotions (Sanders, 1989).

2.9 JAN SMEDSLUND'S PSYCHOLOGIC

One of the observations in reviewing this previous work on formalizations of commonsense psychology is that there is an inverse relationship between notational complexity and conceptual breadth: The less you concern yourself with syntax, the more you can focus on the content. This point is perhaps best illustrated in the interesting work of Norwegian psychologist Jan Smedslund. Smedslund's research focuses on theoretical aspects of psychology as a science, and he makes the controversial argument that much of experimental psychology is not truly empirical. In his view, the root cause of the problem is commonsense psychology.

Smedslund (2002) outlines the argument as follows, using a pair of hypothetical experiments as examples. Consider first an empirical study to determine if the sum of the interior angles of triangles is equal to 180 degrees (the hypothesis), where data are obtained through the measurements of investigators. Suppose the mean result is 181.90 degrees instead of 180 degrees as defined by Euclidean geometry. In interpreting this result, few researchers would choose to reject the null hypothesis. Instead, the appropriate conclusion is that the procedure used to obtain the results was flawed. The hypothesis is, in fact, a tautology that follows a priori from our conceptual system of geometry. Next consider an analogous empirical study in psychology, where the hypothesis is that people become surprised if, and only if, they experience something unexpected. Suppose again that the data find that 97 percent of people who are surprised report experiencing something unexpected. In interpreting this result, researchers should not conclude that 3 percent of people do not actually experience something unexpected, but rather that the procedure they have used to obtain the data is flawed. The hypothesis, again, is a tautology: The meaning of surprise entails experiencing something unexpected in the conceptual system of commonsense psychology. These hypothetical experiments cannot be considered to be empirical because there is a direct conceptual relationship between terms in the hypothesis, as they are commonly understood. Smedslund argues that these problems are not a theoretical curiosity of these two degenerate cases, but rather are pervasive across the vast majority of experimental studies in psychology. That is, it is common to find that the independent and dependent variables in experimental designs are related to each other in the conceptual system of commonsense psychology. As a consequence, these studies are pseudoempirical, in that the data that are obtained do not reveal the truth-value of the hypothesis, only the correctness of the procedure.

Smedslund offers a prescription to remedy these problems: Psychologists need to explicitly consider the relations between their independent and dependent variables within the conceptual system of commonsense psychology. In effect, Smedslund is arguing that some knowledge engineering needs to be done to identify the implicit commonsense theories that people have of mental states and processes. What is remarkable about Smedslund and his research is that he has done two things that set him apart from other theorists in this area. First, he has attempted to execute this knowledge engineering task himself on a reasonably large scale, authoring a library of the concepts, definitions, and axioms of commonsense psychology that he calls Psychologic (Smedslund, 1997). Second, he has attempted to validate the contents of this library of commonsense psychological knowledge by studying the degree to which people within and across cultures are in agreement about the truth of this knowledge (Smedslund, 2002). Smedslund describes Psychologic as follows:

> Psychologic is a project of explicating the implicit conceptual system of psychology embedded in ordinary language, or in other words, the basic assumptions and distinctions underlying our ways of thinking and talking about psychological phenomena. (Smedslund, 1997, p. ix)

Smedslund has revised Psychologic a number of times since it was first introduced (Smedslund, 1988), with the most recent version appearing in the 1997 book, *The Structure of Psychological Common Sense* (Smedslund, 1997). There Psychologic is presented as a language "EL" (for Elements of Psychology), consisting of primitive terms, definitions, axioms, corollaries, theorems, and extensive notes, all written as plain English sentences.

Psychologic identifies twenty-two primitive terms whose meanings are taken to be self-evident, namely terms for psychological states (aware, feel, want, belief, understand, strength), for temporal relationships (when, after, before, now), for action (act, talk, can, try, ability, difficulty, exertion), normative values (right, wrong, good, bad), and a term for people (person). Psychologic elaborates these primitive terms through forty-three definitions, which take the form illustrated by the following examples, where the notation "= df" is taken to mean "is by definition equal to."

Definition 1.2.3 *"Intentional" = df "directed by a preference for achieving a goal."* (p. 5)

Definition 1.2.8 *"X is relevant for achieving a goal G" = df "taking X into account increases the likelihood of achieving G."* (p. 5)

Definition 3.3.15 *"Two wants are compatible" = df "Acting according to one of the two wants can be combined with acting according to the other."* (p. 34)

Using these definitions, Psychologic presents fifty-six axioms to describe the conceptual relationships that exist between these terms, as in the following examples:

Axiom 3.5.1 *The strength of P's belief X is directly proportional to P's estimate of the likelihood that X is the case.* (p. 38)

Axiom 4.1.1 *P's feeling follows from P's awareness of the relationship between P's wants and P's beliefs.* (p. 45)

Axiom 5.3.15 *All understanding depends on relevant pre-understanding.* (p. 66)

Although the language of Psychologic is meant to be articulated wholly by these primitive terms, definitions, and axioms, the contents of Psychologic as a conceptual system are really elaborated in the statements that Smedslund sees as direct consequences of this conceptual system. These consequences are presented in the form of 108 theorems, listed with short proofs written in English, and an additional 135 corollaries that are viewed as direct consequences of the axioms and theorems. Examples of each are as follows:

Theorem 1.2.10 *P takes into account what P takes to be relevant for the achievement of P's goal.* (p. 5)

Theorem 3.3.17 *If the wants W1 and W2, are compatible, then they combine in such a way that W1 & W2 > W1 and W1 & W2 > W2.* (p. 34)

Corollary 3.5.2 *If P's belief A is stronger than P's belief B, then P's estimate of the likelihood of A is higher than P's estimate of the likelihood of A.* (p. 38)

Corollary 3.7.3 *Every person reflectively believes in the possibility of his or her nonexistence.* (p. 42)

Smedslund's project has received a substantial amount of criticism within his own field, with detractors tending to outnumber advocates. A representative collection of counterarguments can be found in the commentaries that follow Smedslund's 1991 presentation of Psychologic in the journal *Psychological Inquiry* (Smedslund, 1991). Given the fair amount of discussion and academic debate of Smedslund's research that exists within this corner of the field of psychology, it is remarkable that this research remains so isolated from the other fields across the cognitive sciences that have a direct interest in commonsense psychology. Smedslund draws no connection between his work and ongoing research on Theory of Mind in philosophy, to research on the acquisition of Theory of Mind in developmental and social psychology, or to work in the formalization of commonsense knowledge within the field of AI. Nearly without exception, the reverse is true as well: Smedslud's project has not received attention within these other fields. Although we can hardly criticize Smedslund for this lack of cross-pollination given the degree to which each of these academic fields are isolated from each other, there are some obvious benefits to be gained from an interdisciplinary treatment of this work. Here we will focus specifically on how Smedslund's formulation of Psychologic should be viewed from the perspective of

AI research on logical formalization of commonsense reasoning. Admittedly, this is far removed from the Smedslund's intended purpose, and should not be interpreted as a criticism of his contribution to psychology.

The first and most obvious criticism of Psychologic from the perspective of artificial intelligence is the lack of formalization. Although Psychologic is presented by Smedslund with all of the trappings of a formal conceptual system, using labels like primitive terms, axioms, corollaries, and theorems, there remains an enormous amount of ambiguity in the English language in which this system is presented. While reducing ambiguity is an explicit goal of the Psychologic project, Smedslund's presentation makes little progress in this regard. The English sentences presented as axioms, corollaries, and theorems could productively be viewed as starting points for logical formalization. However, if this future formalization effort were somehow successful, the necessary set of primitive terms and elaborating definitions would be vastly more numerous than the few dozen that Smedslund suggests.

By eschewing logical formalism, however, Smedslund has demonstrated that a single knowledge engineer can address a very broad range of concepts. Psychologic touches on issues related to awareness, consciousness, intentionality, reflection, communication, learning, acting, trying, wanting, believing, emotions, respect, trust, care giving, understanding, control, self-respect, and ability. In this regard, Psychologic certainly is broader than any previous work in the formalization of commonsense psychology discussed earlier, which is slowly working its way past the concepts of belief, desire, and intentionality. However, there is a real sense that a significantly broader scope could have been obtained given this level of informality. Where, for example, is there any discussion of memories stored or forgotten, of explanations and predictions, of the generation and scheduling of plans, of competing factors in decision making, or in the mechanisms of control that allow people to put their plans into action? All of these ideas have been extremely well studied in the sorts of experimental psychology work that Smedslund criticizes as pseudoempirical. Simply flipping through some of your favorite psychology journals would yield a broader base for outlining a conceptual system of commonsense psychology. This second criticism is ultimately about methodology: Smedslund offers no principled approach to achieving either breadth or depth in the product of his efforts.

A third criticism, if it can be called that, concerns the actual content of the axioms that Smedslund has authored. From the perspective of a knowledge engineer in AI, the platitudes of commonsense psychology in Psychologic lack a certain degree of nuance. Smedslund leans toward prescriptive (even optimistic) rather than descriptive statements, for example, "Every person wants to care for someone," or "P wants everyone to accept what P believes is right and to reject what P believes is wrong." These are two examples of an even larger stylistic concern in Smedslund's work, namely his tendency to overstate the universality of a relationship, for example, that "all understanding depends on relevant preunderstanding," or that "a conscious person is continuously acting," or that "Learning (the impact of experience) is irreversible." Under some interpretations of the meaning of the constituent terms these statements might be considered to be common sense, but in these cases the interpretations probably are not. This stylistic criticism is not to say that these formulations are obviously wrong, but rather that a contemporary knowledge engineer in AI would not have stated them in this manner, even when speaking informally.

The question of whether or not these formulations are correct is another matter entirely. In addition to authoring and updating the conceptual system of Psychologic, Smedslund has conducted a large number of studies to ascertain the degree of consensus in the general population concerning the truth of these propositions. Smedslund (2002) summarizes eight of these consensus studies as following one of two possible methodologies. In the first method, participants are asked to judge a given Psychologic axiom as "always true" or "not always true," and to provide counterexamples in the latter case. In the second method, positive and negative versions of candidate propositions were judged by participants to be either "most likely true" or "most likely false." Across all of these studies, consensus is calculated as the percent agreement between the participants' judgments and Smedslund himself, and in some cases, after he has invalidated some of the participants' judgments or encouraged them to change their responses for the sake of consistency. Although methodologically problematic, these studies do suggest a number of future directions for ascertaining the degree of general consensus concerning commonsense knowledge. Consensus studies like these are completely absent from current AI research on the logical formalization of commonsense knowledge, a criticism that equally applies to our own work as presented in this book.

The real value that we see in Smedslund's work is markedly different than his own aim of changing the practices of experimental psychology. Instead, we view Psychologic as an ambitious attempt to be descriptive of commonsense psychology on a larger scale than any attempt since the initial work of Fritz Heider (1958). However, we have not used Smedslund's Psychologic as a basis for our own research on large-scale formalizations of commonsense psychology. Overall, we expect that the content of Smedslund's theories in its current state would be extremely difficult to formalize in a manner that would support automated reasoning. Likewise, the coverage of Psychologic's content has a number of gaps that would be difficult to fill in a piecemeal manner, the result of an authoring methodology that did not ensure uniform coverage across the broad range of commonsense psychological concerns.

Smedslund's work on Psychologic helps us better understand the inverse relationship between notational complexity and conceptual breadth: The less you concern yourself with syntax, the more you can focus on the content. However, the real promise of anthropomorphic computing cannot not be realized without breaking this relationship in some fundamental way; what is needed is a methodology that will allow us to author inferential theories of commonsense psychology that have the formality of research in automated commonsense reasoning along with a degree of breadth that is even greater than seen in the work of Smedslund. This is the central problem that is addressed in this book, and our solution is in the execution of a novel authoring methodology that achieves both coverage and competency.

3

Formalizing Commonsense Psychology

3.1 COVERAGE AND COMPETENCY

A central problem in artificial intelligence (AI) is the development of large-scale formalizations of commonsense knowledge (McCarthy, 1959). Progress toward this goal has been slow because (1) sufficiently powerful and expressive formal languages need to be developed, (2) the millions of facts that people know and use must be articulated, (3) these facts need to be encoded in a formal language, and (4) reasoning systems that efficiently use this knowledge need to be developed (Davis and Morgenstern, 2004). Put another way, the challenges of formalizing commonsense knowledge are barriers to both breadth and depth. In breadth, researchers are aiming for formalizations of commonsense knowledge that have broad coverage over the concepts in the domains in which commonsense reasoning problems exist. In depth, researchers require that these formalisms have the competency to solve commonsense problems in an automated manner.

Achieving both coverage and competency in the formalization of commonsense knowledge has been an elusive prize. The tradition in this field has been to focus on depth (competency) first, and to leave the problem of breadth (coverage) as somebody else's problem. Today, the field could best be described as a system of interactions between a community of authors and a handful of aggregators. In the general case, the set of authors is made up of academic researchers who simultaneously work on (1) a formal language that is slightly more expressive or powerful than previously published languages, (2) capturing a small handful of facts that people know and reason with, and (3) encoding these facts into the formal language that they have developed. These researchers publish their results in commonsense reasoning symposiums, knowledge representation conferences, and selected academic journals. The aggregators take the best products of these efforts and integrate them into large-scale knowledge bases, typically by rewriting them into their own formal languages. An important example of an aggregator is Cycorp Inc., which maintains the CYC knowledge base (Lenat, 1995), a confederation of thousands of microtheories authored by Cycorp knowledge engineers who base their work, when possible, on the best theories from the commonsense reasoning research community.

By many standards, this strategy of authors and aggregators has been a success. There is little evidence to suggest that this strategy will not, in the limit, lead to formalizations of commonsense knowledge with coverage and competency that satisfy the requirements of the majority of AI commonsense reasoning tasks. Still, in the near term (perhaps the next several decades), there is reason for concern. As a research methodology, the strategy of authors and aggregators has problems.

The first problem with this strategy is that it leads to theories that are predictably spotty in coverage. The best work of knowledge representation researchers is done on domain theories that have few dependencies on other areas of commonsense reasoning. In aiming to develop theories with competency using innovative new representation languages, it is uncommon for researchers to directly incorporate the work of some other researcher who may have tackled a different corner of the commonsense reasoning problem. Doing so might require just as much work as redeveloping this other work within their own framework, and neither of these two pursuits is traditionally valued as publishable research. As a consequence, researchers select a scope of the content theories that they create that has few dependencies to other theories, if any. This set of content theories includes concerns related to time, states, events, space, objects, quantities, taxonomies, and sets, all areas that are relevant to nearly every real-world commonsense reasoning problem, but that can be productively investigated in isolation from one another. Of course, this set of independent theories is only a small fraction of the breadth of commonsense reasoning theories that will need to be developed. Absent from this set are all of the remaining theories that are relevant to nearly every real-world commonsense reasoning problem, but that are highly interdependent with other theories. Most notably, the set of underinvestigated theories includes nearly everything having to do with people, their behavior, and their thoughts.

The second problem with the strategy of authors and aggregators is that the second part of this process, aggregation, is prohibitively expensive for the vast majority of researchers in the field, making it an unrepeatable process that misses out on the innovations that would be the products of academic competition. The CYC knowledge base of Cycorp Inc. is an impressive technical achievement, but there is little evidence to suggest that the methods used in the creation of this knowledge base are superior to alternative approaches, in that they lead to content theories that have a superior degree of coverage and competency in solving commonsense reasoning problems. The methodological questions concerning aggregation will probably never be answered; it is highly doubtful that enough capital resources could ever again be gathered to duplicate Cycorp's efforts, using some alternative aggregation method. Yet, without an ability to experiment with new methods, innovation in this area is going to be extremely limited. Put another way, if a bright graduate student working on a doctoral thesis cannot do this work, then it is going to be difficult to inject radical new ideas into this area of research.

A different strategy is needed. What is needed is an approach in which a small group of researchers can achieve high levels of both coverage and competency within the scope of a single research effort. Rather than simply optimizing the two processes of authoring and aggregating content theories, we propose that the most gains in efficiency can be achieved by changing the development paradigm as a whole. In this chapter, we describe the method that we used to author broad-coverage content theories of commonsense psychology in first-order logic. Our approach is divided into stages in which issues of breadth (coverage) are focused on first, and in which depth (competency) is incrementally achieved through successive formalization. In describing this method, our aim is to enable the repeatability of this process, for the development both of theories of commonsense psychology as well as for the remaining highly interdependent underinvestigated content theories that underlie commonsense reasoning abilities.

3.2 SUCCESSIVE FORMALIZATION

Successive formalization is an approach to large-scale knowledge representation in which the full breadth of the final content theories is identified first, described as a nonformalized collection of concepts. Then this entire set of concepts is incrementally formalized into logical theories through a series of elaborations and refinements. In this approach, coverage is achieved from the very beginning of the process, but the competency of the theories is not achieved until the very end. This approach is markedly different from typical knowledge engineering methods as practiced by members of the commonsense reasoning research community, where coverage is abandoned early in order to achieve theories that have competency in their ability to draw correct inferences in commonsense reasoning problems (Davis, 1998).

In using this approach for the development of large-scale formalizations of commonsense psychology, our efforts were divided into four stages. Here we briefly summarize each of these four stages, and describe each in greater detail in the four sections that follow.

In the first stage, the full breadth of concepts related to commonsense psychology was identified through a large-scale analysis of human planning strategies across a variety of planning domains (Gordon, 2004b). An analysis of the analogies that people naturally make about planning situations, captured as strategies, was used to determine the sorts of conceptual representations that underlie and facilitate these analogies. By conducting this analysis on a very large scale, analyzing hundreds of strategies across ten diverse planning domains, evidence was gathered as to the conceptual scope of the formalization problem. From this analysis, thirty content areas related to human mental states and processes were identified, along with a first draft of the sorts of concepts that populated these content areas – a collection of hundreds of commonsense psychology concepts.

In the second stage, the set of commonsense psychological concepts was further broadened and refined through an analysis of English-language expressions (Gordon and Nair, 2003). In this stage, large-scale thesauri were compiled to catalogue all of the English words and phrases related to each of the representational areas. These references were associated with existing concepts in the set where possible, but additional concepts were catalogued when references were identified that were not judged to be synonymous with existing concepts. Also, in cases where sets of English expressions were judged synonymous with two or more existing concepts, these concepts were combined into a single term. Sets of synonymous words and phrases where then combined into hand-authored finite-state transducers that could be used to automatically annotate English text according to the mental states and processes that were explicitly referenced in the text. This linguistic resource had immediate applicability beyond the knowledge engineering function that it served, and was used in a number of large-scale corpus-analysis investigations. However, its creation helped even out the consistency of the concepts organized into the representational areas of commonsense psychology, filling in obvious gaps that existed as a consequence of the approach taken in the first stage, and eliminating conceptual redundancy in the concept set. At the conclusion of this stage, there remained thirty representational areas of commonsense psychology that organized hundreds of commonsense psychological concepts.

In the third stage, first-draft axiomizations of each of the representational areas were authored in first-order logic (Hobbs and Gordon, 2005). For each representational area, we considered each of the concepts that had been identified in the previous stage, discussing and debating their meaning and their inferential role in the commonsense model that we shared of how people think. Then we authored a set of axioms that encoded these inferential roles in a formal manner. The aim of this authoring process was productivity rather than logical rigor, so we adopted a relaxed style of first-order axiomization. During this phase, we were extremely liberal with the use of undefined and underdefined predicates. In many cases, predicates were used with the expectation that one of the remaining theories would define their meaning. In other cases, predicates were used that had been defined in previous theories, but with differing argument structure than previously used, reflecting a changing conception of the role of the predication in the overall set of theories. Nearly 900 axioms were authored during this stage across the representational areas of commonsense psychology.

In the fourth stage, the first-draft theories were transformed into formal theories with rigorous semantics and consistent predicate-argument relationships. To begin this stage, we created an index of each predicate that was used across the first-draft theories, and used it to further plan where each concept would be defined. Many of these predicates were more general than the identified scope of commonsense psychology, describing concepts related to time, space, events, states, and other core concepts of commonsense reasoning. We then formalized these concepts in sixteen background theories, establishing the representational basis for our formalization of the commonsense psychology. We then authored final versions of each of commonsense psychology areas, collapsing two of our previous theories into one because of their shared underlying semantics. At the end of our efforts, we had logical formalizations of sixteen background theories and twenty-nine commonsense psychology theories.

In the remainder of this chapter, we discuss each of these four stages of successive formalization in detail, followed by a discussion of practical issues related to the repeatability of this method for other researchers.

3.3 STRATEGY REPRESENTATION

Few aspects of human intelligence are more revealing about how we think than the analogies that we come up with in everyday situations. Some people seem to come up with novel analogies all of the time, drawing parallels between their physical medical checkup and a military interrogation, between their marriage and the behavior of the lions of the Serengeti, and between their office jobs and the labor of coal miners beneath the earth. When people tell you an analogy that they see, they are giving you some evidence about the way they conceive of the world around them, telling you that the way they think about one situation has something directly in common with the way they think about the analogous situation.

Likewise, few aspects of human intelligence have received more attention in cognitive science research than the processes of analogical reasoning. Common among all of the most supported theoretical process models of analogical reasoning are some basic assumptions about mental representation, namely that people think of cases as collections of symbolic concepts, and that these collections are structured by various relationships between concepts (e.g., Gentner, 1983; Holyoak and Thagard, 1989). Accordingly, analogy-making is viewed as the identification of some relational structure that is shared between two case representations. A variety of different algorithms have been proposed as computational process models for human analogical reasoning, where each attempts to compute the structural similarity of any two case representations. A common criticism of this area of research is that these approaches are overly general; the results of any evaluation of an analogical reasoning algorithm will be almost entirely dependent on the representational commitments that are made by researchers in describing any two input cases. Different formulations of the same case may yield dramatically different results when comparing any two computational process models of analogy, and there are few research tools available to researchers that produce indisputable evidence in favor of one formulation over another.

For the purpose of analyzing people's mental representations, we can turn these criticisms of process models of analogical reasoning inside out. Instead of looking for knowledge representations that can be used to evaluate process models of analogical reasoning, our understanding of analogical reasoning should be used as an investigative tool to gather evidence in support of how knowledge is represented in the mind. As there is consensus that human analogical reasoning involves the identification of shared relational structure between cases, then analyzing the analogies the people naturally make should provide some evidence for the concepts and relationships that people employ when representing analogous cases. A quote from Albert Einstein and Leopold Infeld summarizes this approach more poetically:

> The association of solved problems with those unsolved may throw new light on our difficulties by suggesting new ideas. It is easy to find a superficial analogy which really expresses nothing. But to discover some essential common features, hidden beneath a surface of external differences, to form, on this basis, a new successful theory, is important creative work. (Einstein and Infeld, 1938, pp. 273)

This passage from Einstein and Infeld was written to justify their presentation of an analogy between a violin string and the wavelike properties of elementary particles. In this analogy, Einstein and Infeld focused on two essential common features relevant to this analogy, the concepts of a standing wave and a moving wave, and the theory that they are referring to is that of probability waves in quantum physics. Although this analogy is interesting in that it tells us a bit about the way that Einstein and Infeld conceive of violins and particles, we could probably learn more about mental representation in general by looking at the analogies that people naturally make in the course of their daily lives, and by conducting this analysis on a large scale. In the idealized version of this methodology, groups of analysts would propose representations for the shared relational structure for each of the pairs of analogous cases that had been collected as a corpus of naturally generated analogies, and this analytic evidence would be aggregated in order to provide some evidence for the sorts of representational structures that people were naturally using to reason about everyday cases and situations. This idealization of the methodology would be nearly impossible to execute in practice, however. Even if the funding for such an investigation could be obtained, researchers would still be left with the problem of collecting a suitably large corpus of naturally occurring analogies made by people in the course of their daily lives. No established method of capturing naturally occurring analogies exists today, even for a single pair of analogous cases.

In 1999, one of us (Gordon) began to consider using planning strategies as a suitable surrogate for naturally occurring analogies. People demonstrate a remarkable agility for recognizing, reasoning about, and applying strategies in their daily lives. Political parties talk about strategies for taking control of the legislature. Physicians talk about strategies of treating infectious diseases. Spouses talk about strategies for maintaining a healthy marriage. Artists talk about strategies for raising their ability for creative expression. When considering the meaning of the word "strategy" in everyday conversation, some commonalities are evident. In each case, the word "strategy" refers to an abstraction over a planning problem and its solution. More specifically, a strategy is a planning problem and solution where all of the specific concepts of the problem and solution are replaced with abstractions of those concepts, leaving a pattern that can usefully characterize a broad variety of planning problems and solutions across a broad variety of planning domains. Strategies typically include four implicit components, namely a set of situational features, a goal that someone is trying to achieve, an imagined possibility of the future, and a plan of actions that will lead to the achievement of the goal. Strategies are the shared relational structure between analogous planning cases, providing evidence for the essential common features that people use to represent everyday planning situations. For use as a subject of analysis, strategies have the advantage over naturally occurring analogies in that they are much easier to collect from people; in many cases, you can simply ask people what strategies they think about in their area of expertise, and they will tell you exactly what you are looking for.

By exploiting the relative ease with which strategies could be collected, one of us (Gordon) conducted a large-scale representational requirements analysis by collecting hundreds of strategies across many different planning domains, and then analyzing each to identify their essential features (Gordon, 2001, 2004a,b). Each analysis produced some weak evidence for the sorts of concepts that participated in the mental representation of everyday planning cases, which was aggregated in order to define the representational breadth of real-world planning problems.

This work began by first creating a corpus of hundreds of strategies across many different planning domains. Here the term "planning domain" is used to refer to some delineation of an area of expertise, for example, professional areas such as politics or education, or subject areas like zoology or immunology. In this work, ten different planning domains were studied: business practice, education, government, warfare, science, artistic performance, personal relationships, object counting, and the anthropomorphic strategies in the domains of animal behavior and immunology. One of three different techniques was used to collect strategies in each planning domain. The first technique was to collect strategies from existing texts that are nearly encyclopedic of strategies within their respective domains. For example, warfare strategies were collected by extracting them from Sun Tzu's *The Art of War* and government strategies were collected from an analysis of Niccolo Machiavelli's *The Prince*. The second strategy collection technique was to conduct directed interviews with experts within a planning domain, asking them directly for descriptions of the strategies they think about when reasoning about planning problems within the domain. This technique was used to collect the strategies of business professionals, educators, artistic performance, and scientists. The third strategy collection technique could be described as interpretive observation, where the practices of people engaged in planning and problem solving within a planning domain were analyzed to see what strategies were evident. Instead of evidencing the strategies that people are actually using in these domains, this technique is useful to determine the strategies that can be seen by the analyst/observer in his or her interpretation of this behavior. For example, this technique was used to identify strategies that are evident in the behavior of people engaged in object-counting tasks, for example, determining the exact number of people currently in a large office building. The decision of which planning domains to investigate was based entirely on the availability of encyclopedic texts, access to subject matter experts, or our own personal interests. Although far from a random sample, the resulting collection of strategies offered a degree of breadth that guaranteed that the resulting set of required representations would be suitably broad as well.

In all, 372 strategies were collected from these ten planning domains using these three collection techniques. Following is a short description of each of these ten planning domains, along with an example of one of the strategies that were collected (from Gordon, 2004a).

- Animal Behavior (37 strategies). An analysis of an introductory zoology text revealed the strategies that people attribute to animals to explain their behavior in an anthropomorphic manner. Example: Cowbirds and cuckoo birds abandon their eggs in the nests of other bird species that will raise the hatchlings along with their own offspring.
- Business (62 strategies). Directed interviews with students of business administration and investment law produced a collection of strategies used in the business areas of marketing, production, and acquisitions. Example: Companies that compete for repeat business from consumers gain customer loyalty by issuing redeemable points (e.g., frequent flyer miles) with each purchase.
- Counting (20 strategies). Interpretive observation was used to identify the ways that people perform various object counting tasks, where variation is determined by characteristics of the situation. Example: When counting identical things organized in a circle, people will mark their starting location to avoid over-counting.
- Education (32 strategies). Directed interviews with former primary and secondary school teachers produced a set of strategies that focused on assessment, teaching methods, and techniques for motivating students. Example: Occasionally delivering an unscheduled "pop quiz" encourages students to study materials in the duration between larger exams.
- Immunology (21 strategies). An analysis of several introductory immunology textbooks produced a set of strategies that anthropomorphically describe the behavior of cells and viruses as goal-directed agents. Example: One way that cells guard against the spread of viruses is to destroy themselves through programmed cell death when an infection is detected.

- Machiavelli (60 strategies). Niccolo Machiavelli's sixteenth-century text *The Prince* was analyzed to collect a set of strategies to be used by government leaders to obtain and maintain their power. Example: If established as a lord by the nobility of a territory, a new prince should work to become popular to establish a power base among the citizenry.
- Performance (39 strategies). Directed interviews with concert pianists were used to collect the strategies that musicians use to manage their performance abilities. Example: To avoid being derailed by distracting events during a performance, musicians will purposefully cause surprising distractions to occur during their practice sessions in order to become accustomed to them.
- Relationships (22 strategies). Interpretive observation of dating couples was used to identify a set of strategies that people use to find, keep, and leave a loving partner. Example: On a first date, a skeptical person may ask a friend to telephone halfway through to give him or her a chance to fabricate an emergency that requires him or her to leave.
- Science (34 strategies). Directed interviews and interpretive observation were used to collect a set of strategies that research scientists use to advance their fields, pursue funding, and garner attention to their work. Example: To moderate the difficulty of obtaining research funds, many researchers tie their work to some application domain that is backed by wealthy interests, such as the military or pharmaceutical companies.
- Warfare (45 strategies). *The Art of War*, written by Chinese military strategist Sun Tzu around the fifth century BC, was analyzed to collect strategies pertaining to waging war against military adversaries. Example: By leaving the enemy a means of retreat, the attacking army prevents the threat of extraordinary heroic defenses on the part of a desperate adversary.

The next step in this process was to author definitions of each of these 372 strategies that would highlight their essential features. These definitions were aimed at capturing all of the common characteristics of any instance of the strategic pattern, regardless of whether or not these instances were in the original planning domain of the strategy. That is, the definition of an artistic performance strategy should be broad enough to characterize planning cases in the domain of scientific discovery, if indeed the same strategy could be applied. In practice, this level of generality was achieved by defining the essential characteristics of instances of the strategy in the most general terms possible, while ensuring that every imagined instance that included these characteristics was indeed an instance of the strategy. These definitions were authored in a preformal style, adapted from earlier work on strategy representation (Collins, 1987). The aim of these definitions was not to create full representations of these strategies in logical notation, but rather to identify the abstract concepts and the relationships between them that are used in human mental representations of planning cases.

Following are three examples of the 372 strategy representations (from Gordon, 2004a). In each case, the representation takes the form of a short descriptive sentence that references the strategy, followed by a paragraph-sized characterization where each reference to an essential common feature of instances of the strategy is italicized and capitalized. As a convention, the term "planner" references the person who is executing the strategy, whereas other people are referred to simply as agents. Agent labels (e.g., "A1" and "A2") were not included in the original strategy representations, but are added here to aid in readability.

◾ Business strategy 59: Macaroni defense
Prevent takeover by issuing bonds to be redeemed at high cost if a takeover occurs.

The planner has a *Leadership role* in an *Organization*, and *Envisions a threat* to goals of the *Organization* that a different agent A1 will execute a plan that includes *Trade* of an *Amount of resources* of the agent A1 for *Portions of ownership* that are a *Majority portion*. The planner executes a plan to *Make an offer* to a different agent A2 where the *Offer requirement* is that the agent A2 *Transfers resources* to the *Organization* of an *Amount of resources*, and the *Offered action* is that the planner will *Schedule* the *Transfer of resources* to the agent A2 of an *Amount of resources* that is greater than in the *Offer requirement*, with the *Offer condition* that If it is the case that if an *Arbitrary agent* executes the plan that is the plan in the *Threat*, the *Organization* will *Enable* the agent A2 in the offer to cause the *Organization* to *Reschedule* the *Offer action* with an *Amount of resources* that is greater. The planner then *Schedules a plan* to *Inform* the agent A1 in the *Threat* of this offer after the *Successful execution* of the plan.

◾ Machiavelli strategy 48: Foster, then crush animosity to improve renown.
"For this reason many consider that a wise prince, when he has the opportunity, ought with craft to foster some animosity against himself, so that, having crushed it, his renown may rise higher."

The planner has a *Role* in a *Power relationship* over a *Community* and has the goal that a set of agents A1 *Believe* that the planner is the *Best candidate* for this role. There exists an agent A2 that has goals that are in *Goal conflict* with the planner, and that has had a *Planning failure* to achieve their goals with a *Cause* of *Lack of resources* or *Lack of agency*. The planner plans and executes for the goal that the agent A2 *Believes* that there exists an *Opportunity* for this agent A2 to achieve their goals, where no *Opportunity* exists. The planner then *Monitors* the agent A2 for the *Start of execution* of plans to achieve the goals. When this occurs, the planner executes a plan to *Destroy* the agent A2, with the goal that the first set of agents A1 have *Event knowledge* of the planner's execution.

◾ Warfare strategy 44: Give false information to enemy spies.
Secretly use enemy spies to send deceptive information to your enemy.

The planner has an *Adversarial relationship* with another agent A1. An agent A2 has a *Cooperative relationship* with the agent A1 to execute *Cooperative plans* that include Informing the agent A1 of *Information* that involves the planner. The agent A2 has the *False belief* that the planner has a *False belief* that the planner has a *Cooperative relationship* with the agent A2. The planner *Monitors planning* for *Adversarial plans* that have a *Threat* that the adversary agent A1 will *Successfully execute* a *Counterplan*. In this case, the planner executes a plan to cause the agent A2 to have a *False belief* about the *Adversarial plan*, and then *Enables* the *Cooperative plan* of this agent A2 that includes *Informing*.

The final step in this process was to aggregate the evidence provided by individual strategy representations into a coherent picture of the scope of the conceptual representations that people use to reason about planning cases. A total of 8,844 words and phrases were highlighted as essential features in the 372 strategy representations that were authored. To begin the process of aggregating this evidence, a controlled vocabulary was created out of these 8,844 terms. This was done by grouping identical and synonymous words and phrases by a single controlled vocabulary term, resulting in a set of 988 unique concepts. Finally, these 988 unique concepts were manually clustered together into groups of related terms. A total of 48 groups of terms were identified through this process, which generally correspond to existing areas of knowledge representation research, or the topic areas in the social and cognitive sciences.

An example of one of these 48 clusters of terms is presented in the list that follows. This set of terms constitutes all of the essential features used in the 372 strategy representations related to concepts of time, including durations and moments. These time concepts are listed alphabetically, along with a short phrase to describe the concept (from Gordon, 2004b).

Time (23 terms)

1. Arbitrary duration: Any duration in a set of unspecified durations
2. Average duration: A duration with a length that is the average length of a set of other durations
3. Before: A moment with a lesser position in an ordered set of moments
4. Current moment: The moment that is now in the real world or in envisioned worlds
5. Disjunctive duration set: A set of durations with no equivalent moments
6. Duration: The ordered set of all moments between two nonequivalent moments
7. Duration end: The last moment in a duration
8. Envisioned duration: A duration that is envisioned by an agent
9. Envisioned end time: The duration end of an envisioned duration
10. Envisioned start time: The duration start of an envisioned duration
11. Every moment: Any moment in a set of moments
12. Greater duration: A duration with a larger set of moments than another duration
13. Immediately after: A moment with a later position in an ordering with none in-between
14. Immediately before: A moment with a lesser position in an ordering with none in-between
15. Indefinite duration: A duration that does not have a duration end
16. Lesser duration: A duration with a smaller set of moments than another duration
17. Maximum duration: The duration in a set that has the greatest length
18. Minimum duration: The duration in a set that has the smallest length
19. Moment: A single point in time
20. Moment in duration: A moment that is a member of the set of moments in a duration
21. Start time: The first moment in a duration
22. Total duration: The additive lengths of a set of durations
23. Variable duration: The length of an arbitrary duration in a set with different lengths

This list of terms should be interpreted as an outline of the required conceptual breadth of any formal theory of time that aims to achieve both coverage and competency in reasoning about everyday planning problems. The representational area of time is among the most well-investigated of all commonsense reasoning content theories, a research history that includes Allen's Temporal Logic (Allen, 1983) and the Ontology of Time for the Semantic Web (Hobbs and Pan, 2004). Not surprisingly, contemporary content theories for commonsense temporal reasoning have excellent coverage over the set of concepts listed above; nearly all of these concepts can be straightforwardly defined through a combination of predications from current logical theories of time.

The same can be said of an additional seven of the forty-eight representational areas, namely the sets of concepts related to states, events, space, physical entities, quantities, classes, and sets. Collectively, these representational areas define the scope of the vast majority of previous commonsense knowledge representation research efforts. The attention that these areas have received in the past is well deserved; concepts and axioms in these areas provide a necessary foundation for nearly every conceivable commonsense reasoning problem in any real-world commonsense reasoning application. However, the same might be said of every one of the additional forty representational areas identified in this investigation. The difference between these additional areas and the first eight is in the degrees of interdependency that theories in these two groups require; these first eight representational areas can be developed in isolation from each other, whereas the latter forty cannot. As a consequence, the commonsense reasoning research community has naturally gravitated toward the first set when authoring content theories, where it has been possible to achieve competency without tackling the problem of coverage.

The remaining forty of the forty-eight representational areas are all concerned with people, in two general ways. Ten of these representational areas can be characterized as having to do with commonsense sociology, or with the external actions of people and groups more generally. These ten areas include concepts related to types of people, their social relationships, and the way they organize into communities and organizations. It includes concepts having to do with resources used by people, the abilities and skills that people possess, and the activities that they engage in as part of their daily lives. Finally, this set includes general clusters of actions that people perform, namely communication actions, information actions, actions taken among groups of people, and the actions that people take in the physical manipulation of the world around them.

However, the most notable result of this analysis of planning strategies was to reveal the central importance of representations related to commonsense psychology. The remaining thirty of the forty-eight representational areas, consisting of 630 of the 988 of the concepts used in strategy representations, were directly related to the mental states and processes of people. Although these areas had each been the focus of research across the cognitive sciences, collectively they are among the least-investigated representational areas in commonsense reasoning research.

This approach of analyzing hundreds of planning strategies constituted the first stage of our four-stage methodology for developing formal commonsense theories that achieved both coverage and competency. At this point, we had a clear understanding of the scope of the representational requirements of commonsense reasoning systems that reasoned about everyday planning situations. It was here that we made the pragmatic decision to scale back the focus of our knowledge engineering efforts. The forty-eight representational areas naturally divide into three parts: eight independent background areas, ten areas of commonsense sociology, and thirty areas of commonsense psychology. We decided to work on only one of these areas at a time, choosing to focus our efforts specifically on commonsense psychology. Our thought was that the background representational areas had already received a disproportionate amount of research attention, and so rehashing this territory would not have the greatest impact on the field. Commonsense sociology, including the social relationships of people and their actions, is as starved for attention as commonsense psychology, but our intuition was that developing satisfying content theories for these representational areas would likely require well-developed theories of commonsense psychology, but not the reverse. Most importantly, commonsense psychology is fascinating stuff, and we decided that if we were going to devote a number of years of our lives formalizing something, it had better be something that was inherently interesting. Commonsense sociology, not without its own interesting mysteries, would have to wait for another day.

3.4 PSYCHOLOGICAL EXPRESSIONS

The starting point for the second stage of this methodology were the 630 concepts organized into 30 representational areas, identified through an analysis of planning strategies. The conceptual scope of these 30 representational areas seemed to catalogue the breadth of research interests in psychology and AI, including memory, explanation, expectation, planning, decision making, and emotion. While the scope of this area list was excellent, the coverage of the lists of concepts within each area was spotty in areas, where the richness of a representational area was only hinted at by the concepts clustered into the group. The best example of this problem was seen in the representational area of human memory. Among all of the 372 strategy representations that were authored, only three concepts related to human memory retrieval were needed, as follows:

1. Memorize: The mental event of storing information in memory so that it can be retrieved later
2. Memory cue: A concept that causes a memory retrieval of information when it comes into the focus of attention
3. Memory retrieval: The mental event of retrieving information from memory

While each of these concepts should certainly be included in any commonsense theory of human memory, so should many other key ideas that are obviously related to this area. At the very least, this list should include the concept of memory storage, which is the commonsense corollary to memory retrieval. It should probably also include the concepts concerning memory items themselves, and the mental events of remembering or forgetting to do something. Indeed, a little bit of brainstorming could yield any number of new concepts that might be appropriately included in this representational area. What was needed was a principled methodology for filling in the conceptual gaps that existed among the thirty representational areas of commonsense psychology, improving the coverage of this conceptual catalogue while retaining the original scope of the thirty areas.

Our solution was to use the English language to elaborate the coverage of the representational areas, using a novel analytic methodology. The English language is full of words and phrases related to commonsense psychological ideas. We talk about the things "long forgotten," the "sense of desperation," "winging it" through a situation, our "secret desires," our "diabolical plans," and our "tough decisions." For every concept that was identified through our initial representational requirements analysis, there are a remarkable number of words and phrases that can be used to reference it. Our intuition was that these words and phrases within the English language had a comparable scope but better coverage than our lists of 630 commonsense psychology terms. Accordingly, we devised a methodology that would allow us to use our existing term lists as a tool for explicating the coverage of the English language over commonsense psychology concepts.

In this second stage of our project, our aim was to identify every possible way of referring to any possible commonsense psychology concept in the English language, and group these references into synonymous sets that reference unique concepts. The 30 representational areas would define the scope of the reference-identification task, with the 630 existing concepts serving as an initial candidate list to be elaborated and refined.

The relation between natural language and mental concepts is the subject of a long and contentious research history in philosophy, linguistics, and the cognitive sciences. In this stage of our project, we adopted a pragmatic set of assumptions concerning this relationship, largely borrowed from the work in the library and information sciences. The first of these assumptions is that words and phrases in natural language are references to concepts that participate in our mental models. The second is that words and phrases can be synonymous with each other, in that they refer to the same concept, and polysemous, in that the same words or phrases may refer to different concepts. Together, these assumptions treat language and mental concepts as separate, but with direct mappings between each other. In a simplification of this view, language understanding can be seen as the correct translation of language into its conceptual form, while language generation is the reverse translation.

Even with these assumptions, one philosophical argument continued to be a cause for concern. There is a reasonable concern that the space of English references and the space of mental concepts have significant nonoverlapping regions, that is, that there are no words and phrases for concepts that participate in our mental models, and possibly vice-versa. This sentiment is perhaps the concern of Wittgenstein's ominous last sentence in *Tractatus Logico-Philosophicus*, "What we cannot speak about we must pass over in silence" (Wittgenstein, 1974). As a consequence, if English words and phrases are used as a tool for explicating concepts that participate in our mental models, then the fear is that significant concepts will be overlooked for lack of an identified linguistic referent. As the old joke warns, a drunk man will foolishly look for his lost keys under a lamppost because that is where the light is better. While we still believe in the merits of this philosophical position, we can safely say that these fears have not been realized in our project. If there existed significant areas of commonsense psychology where mental concepts did not overlap with linguistic expressions, then this would be evident in consideration of the 630 original concepts from our earlier representational requirements analysis. Instead, we found that nearly every one of these concepts had one or more ways of directly referencing the concept in the English language. The point here is that the coverage of the English language is better than our starting point. In looking "under the lamppost" of the English language, the entire space of commonsense psychology concepts is well illuminated.

In executing this stage of the project, we adopted a three-step process that was repeated thirty times, once for each of the thirty representational areas of commonsense psychology. In the first step, huge numbers of candidate references within a representational area were elicited in large-group brainstorming sessions, organized as a type of linguistic party game. In the second step, these candidate references were expanded by consulting a number of existing linguistic resources, including dictionaries, thesauri, and phrase books. Third, these references were grouped into synonymous sets, collectively defining the conceptual coverage of English expressions of commonsense psychology. In addition, these sets of references to commonsense psychology concepts were encoded as finite-state transducers that could be used to automatically annotate the conceptual references that exist in electronic text documents.

In the first step, a large set of candidate references were collected from volunteers in large-group brainstorming sessions. This was certainly among the more lively and entertaining aspects of our project. For this work, we enlisted various staff and students at the University of Southern California to participate in weekly, hour-long meetings held in a small amphitheater. For these meetings, we developed a sort of linguistic party-game, *PsychoPhrase! The Game of Linguistic Creativity*, aimed at eliciting huge numbers of candidate linguistic references to concepts within the scope of a given representational area, one per meeting, over thirty meetings altogether. In a typical meeting, around eight participants would be presented with a series of slides projected onto a screen, each with a target concept, a short definition, and two or three examples of English words or phrases that refer to the concept. Participants would shout out as many words or phrases as they could come up with to reference the concept presented on screen, while the presenter (Gordon) transcribed these phrases directly onto the presentation slides as they were given. An average of twenty-one concepts were presented to participants in the course of a typical hour-long session, leaving less than two minutes for consideration of each one before moving on to the next. While no points or winner was designated for a particular brainstorming session, a competitive atmosphere arose as participants vied to come up with the most creative or most overlooked English references to a given concept. The concepts presented each session were typically taken directly from the subset of 630 commonsense psychology concepts grouped into a given representational area, with definitions that were modified to be more broadly understandable and with examples created by us in preparing the slides before each session. At the beginning of each session, the representational area was introduced with a short description. On this slide, and on each of the individual concept slides that followed, a list of concept names was given in order to remind the participants about the scope of the concepts to be considered, which ones have already been discussed, and which ones are left to be viewed. Twice in each session, at the halfway point and at the very end, a special slide was presented, entitled "Brainstorm! Anything goes!" where participants were asked to shout out any English words or phrases that were related to the series of concepts that they had just considered, but did not seem to be a direct reference to any single one of them.

For example, one group brainstorming session focused on concepts related to the representational area of Threat Detection, concerning the mental abilities that people have to recognize when their goals run the risk of being blocked and their plans are in danger of failing. Fifteen concepts related to Threat Detection were identified through the analysis of planning strategies (Gordon, 2004b), and were presented to participants in this brainstorming session on individual presentation slides. Following are two examples of how these concepts were presented.

Concept: Unrealized threat
Definition: "When something you worried might happen doesn't end up happing after all."
Examples: It was a false alarm. We dodged a bullet on that one. It turned out to be an empty threat.

Concept: Threat assessment
Definition: "When you consider all of the threats at hand, and determine which outcomes would be preferable."
Examples: He thought it was all worth the risk. The threat of jail failed to deter him from a life of crime. He acted only after calculating the risks involved.

Although the words and phrases elicited from participants for each concept cannot be considered exhaustive in any way, they often demonstrated remarkable diversity in the way that people talk about the mind. As an example of the quality of the references that can be obtained using this approach, consider the phrases that were transcribed during the few minutes that participants considered the concepts of an Unrealized threat and a Threat assessment.

Unrealized threat: I was unduly worried about it all. My fears were unfounded. There was no need to panic. We had good timing. We got away with that one. We slipped under the radar / passed that one. It was a narrow escape. I was pleasantly surprised. That was a close one. All's well that ends well. We came through unscathed. I made it through the rain. It was a red herring.

Threat assessment: It was his best bet. She felt it was the best decision. Nothing ventured, nothing gained. No pain, no gain. What would be the best case scenario? She chose the lesser of two evils. He took the path of least resistance. It wasn't worth the gamble, but it was a smart gamble. He put all of his cards on the table. He went with the hand he was dealt. She took a chance. She grabbed the best deal. She hoped for the best. He ventured into the treacherous, dreaded path based on experience.

Importantly, the words and phrases elicited during this first step of the process were commonly outside of the scope of the concept that was presented to the participants, as the preceding examples demonstrate. For this work, these original concepts were intended to be preliminary, to be abandoned later in the process when a better understanding of the concepts in an area could be determined. By collecting words and phrases that spill over into different meanings, and by eliciting additional references from "anything goes" slides, our aim was to begin to fill in the conceptual gaps present in the initial representation of planning strategies.

In the second step in this stage, we further elaborated the data collected through these brainstorming sessions by using existing linguistic resources, including dictionaries, thesauri, and phrase books. Here the aim was to use the words and phrases that were collected as seeds for an exhaustive search of relevant terminology in the English language. Among the most useful of the linguistic resources that we examined were the WordNet lexical reference system (Fellbaum, 1998), Levin's catalog of English verb classes (Levin, 1993), the *Longman Language Activator* production dictionary, and the *Collins Cobuild Dictionary for Advanced Learners*. To complete this work, we enlisted the effort of a total of eight students at the University of Southern California who served as research assistants, seven of whom were master's degree candidates in computer science or computational linguistics. Typically, the product of this step of this stage of the project yielded hundreds of references to commonsense psychology concepts within a given representational area.

The third step in this stage involved clustering all of the collected English references within a representational area by their meaning, and create a new list of unique concepts with broad coverage in the topic area. We executed this step for each of the thirty representational areas in collaboration with the student research assistants who had done the lexical expansion work.

It was not uncommon that this effort resulted in concept lists that were markedly different than the original lists produced during the first stage of our project, the representational requirements analysis using strategy representations. In characterizing the differences, some common transformations were evident that had the effect of reducing the size of the concept lists. The preformal strategy representations frequently included compound concepts and overly specific concepts that were not delineated by English references. For example, the initial term list included the concept of Envisioned decision consequences, referring to the states and events that a person imagines will happen as a result of making a choice in a decision. In analyzing the English references in the representational area of decision making, we saw little if any distinctions between Envisioned decision consequences and the more general concept of Decision consequences. Accordingly, only the more general concept was included in the resulting concept list.

More importantly, the analysis of English references to commonsense psychology concepts in these thirty representational areas identified significant gaps in the coverage of terms from our initial lists. The importance of this linguistic analysis is most evident in the representational area of human memory, mentioned earlier in this section. A total of twelve clusters of English references to memory concepts were identified using this methodology, compared to the initial list of three terms. Following is a list of the twelve memory concepts here, along with a short definition and example English references.

1. Memory ability: The ability that people have to remember things, e.g., he's got a photographic memory
2. Memory item: The contents of people's memory, e.g., he shared his wisdom with us
3. Repressed memory item: A memory item that has been intentionally forgotten, e.g., it was a buried recollection
4. Memory storage: The mental event of putting a memory item into memory, e.g., she learned it by heart
5. Memory retrieval: The mental event of pulling a memory item from memory, e.g., he recalled it exactly
6. Memory retrieval failure: The mental event of failing to pull a memory item from memory, e.g., it was on the tip of her tongue.
7. Memory repression: The mental event of intentionally forgetting a memory item, e.g., he purged it from his mind.
8. Reminding: The mental event where thinking of one thing recalls another from memory, e.g., it was reminiscent of an early time.
9. Memory cue: The thing that causes a person to be reminded of something else, e.g., I'll give you a reminder.

10. Schedule plan retrieval: The mental event of intending to remember to do something, e.g., she made a mental note to do it.
11. Scheduled plan retrieval: The mental event of actually remembering to do the thing that was supposed to be remembered, e.g., he remember to do it.
12. Scheduled plan retrieval failure: The mental event of failing to remember to do the thing that was supposed to be remembered, e.g., it slipped her mind.

This three-step methodology was done for each of the thirty representational areas of commonsense psychology, with two exceptions. First, a slightly different methodology was used for the representational area of human emotions. References to emotion concepts in the English language have one particularly unusual property: There are literally thousands of single words in English that describe different types of emotions that people may feel, including the common words of "love," "hate," and "fear," and more exotic emotion references such as "flabbergasted," "indignation," "jocularity," and "repugnance." Rather than soliciting these terms from volunteers, we compiled existing lists of emotion terms and sorted them into categories. In this effort we were influenced by previous work in "OCC" emotion classes of Ortony, Clore, and Collins (1990) and distinctions made in the WordNet lexicon (Fellbaum, 1998), specifically the full sets of hyponyms for the noun "emotion", the troponyms of the verb "provoke," and the tropynyms of the verb "feel." Each of the items in these sets was then sorted into the OCC emotion classes as a test of the coverage of this taxonomy.

The second exception in using this methodology was in the representational area of Causes of Failure, which includes concepts for the classes of standard explanations that people give for why they failed to achieve their goals. For example, people often say that their failures are the fault of the incompetence of the people with whom they were working. When dealing with concepts at this level of abstraction, several problems prevented us from applying the standard lexical analysis methodology. Like the set of concepts for emotion classes, the number of useful distinctions for classes of failure explanations is potentially very large. However, unlike emotion classes, there are few words or short phrases in the English language that directly reference these classes of explanation. The most direct references seem to be in the form of proverbs and adages, such as "A chain is only as strong as its weakest link," or "A stitch in time saves nine." Collecting, analyzing, and organizing proverbs of this sort into a conceptual taxonomy was the subject of Christopher Owens's doctoral dissertation (1990), where one thousand proverbs yielded a conceptual vocabulary of fifty-nine patterns of explanation. Similarly, Schank and Fano (1992) identified thirty-four patterns of failure explanations in developing a taxonomy of 758 story points in social domains. Both of these previous research efforts complemented the list of explanation classes that we identified in the representational requirements analysis stage of our project, a collection of thirty-one causes of failure. Initially, we attempted to combine all three of these sources to create a unified taxonomy of plan failure explanation patterns to serve as a final taxonomy, consisting of sixty concepts. However, only a handful of conceptual distinctions seemed relevant for the purpose of developing inferential theories. In the end, English words and phrases were collected for only a single concept in this representational area, the concept of a plan failure explanation pattern, with the intention that our attempts to construct a unified taxonomy of plan failure explanation patterns would inform our later formalization work in a more indirect manner.

In applying this lexical analysis methodology to each of the thirty representational areas, a final set of concepts was identified that had broad coverage over the domain of commonsense psychology. This list consisted of more than 500 concepts in all, with large collections of English words and phrases assigned to each.

3.5 DRAFT FORMALIZATIONS

While concept lists have some utility when organized into taxonomies, the aim of our project was to create inferential theories. For this, it was not enough to assert that one concept is a subtype of another. Needed was a means of expressing a relationship between the known and the inferred, for example, if you know something about the emotional state a person, what else could you infer to be true. Furthermore, these relationships needed to be expressed formally, enabling their use in automated reasoning systems. For us, the natural choice was to encode these relationships in first-order logic. There are numerous reasons why logic is both the best and worst possible choice for use as a representational framework (Birnbaum, 1991; Nilsson, 1991). One of us (Hobbs) was a pioneer of logic-based computational linguistics, while the other (Gordon) could hardly tell a quantifier from a Cuisinart. In the end, the decision was made for pragmatic reasons; by authoring our inferential theories in first-order predicate logic form, they could be most easily consumed by the commonsense reasoning research community at large. Few people in this community feel that first-order predicate calculus is better than their own personal variety, but it serves as an effective common denominator for authors of content theories, theoretical logicians, and system builders.

The danger of using logic as a representational framework is that it is hard to be productive when you are worrying about being rigorous. The logical tradition in AI has built up a wide assortment of distractions that pull people away from the job of writing down knowledge, including the model-theoretic semantics of the logic, the frame problem, the various ways of dealing with action and change, and the varieties of modal and default logics. Although there is little doubt that each of these concerns has an important role in knowledge representation research, they too often take priority over the work of actually developing content theories. The culture of knowledge representation research has come to expect that everyone in the field holds these concerns in high regard, making it difficult for any knowledge representation researcher to publish content theories without first addressing these issues. However, all of these concerns are still the focus of active debate, making it impossible to address these issues to everyone's satisfaction. As a result, few researchers enjoy writing papers containing content theories and few of these are actually published in peer-reviewed conferences and journals.

Our approach to large-scale content theory development was to author these theories in two passes. In the first pass, we focused on coverage, ensuring that the axioms that we authored could be used to define and reason over each of the commonsense psychology concepts we identified through strategy representation and language analysis. In this first pass, we ignored nearly all of the traditional concerns of rigorous knowledge representation research. We invented new predicates on-the-fly as needed, and did not attempt to be completely consistent with regard to argument ordering or arity. We freely mixed the use of various approaches to representing temporal, situational, and causal transitions depending on what seemed most natural for expressing a given axiom. We frequently strayed away from strict first-order notation, although it later became clear that we could express everything we needed without employing higher-order logics. We glossed over representational problems that we knew could be easily solved later, focusing our attention on writing down as much content as efficiently as possible.

For these first drafts, we approached each of the thirty representational areas as unique content theories to be formalized as a set of logical axioms. To complete this work, we would begin by discussing the general scope of the concepts in a particular representational area with each other, working directly from the results of the linguistic analysis stage of the project. Then we would examine each of the individual concepts in the area, discussing each to ensure a shared understanding of their meaning, and jotting down some preliminary notes and axioms that would characterize the sorts of inferences that these concepts would support. Most of this work took place over lunch at a pizza restaurant halfway between the USC Institute for Creative Technologies and the USC Information Sciences Institute, which became known to us as the Commonsense Psychology Kitchen (CPK). At the completion of these meetings, one of us (Hobbs) would work individually to complete a full draft of the content theory for the representational area, which would subsequently be critiqued by the other of us (Gordon).

Even after adopting an authoring style that focused on productivity, progress was slow. It took us forty-two months from the time we authored the first content theory (Memory Retrieval in October 2002) to complete the last of these drafts (Emotions in April 2006). The most productive period was during the twelve months beginning October 2004, when we were able to secure some research funding to support this effort. At the completion of this stage of the project, we had authored 892 axioms across 30 content theories, along with the bulk of the text that described the meaning of these axioms in English. An example of one of these draft formalizations can be seen in Gordon and Hobbs (2003), for the representational area of Memory Retrieval.

From the very beginning of this stage of our project, it was clear that a second round of revisions was going to be necessary in order to develop content theories that achieved both coverage and competency in automated reasoning applications. For example, Swanson and Gordon (2005) attempted to use a draft formalization of commonsense memory (Gordon and Hobbs, 2003) in a system for automatically assessing the validity of human memory strategies. Although this attempt was partly successful, it underscored the amount of work that remained in order to produce a full set of commonsense psychology content theories capable of supporting automated inference.

3.6 FINAL FORMALIZATIONS

In the final stage of our project, we completed a full second revision of the content theories of commonsense psychology, with the aim of producing theories that would have high competency for use in automated commonsense reasoning applications. To achieve high competency, it was also necessary to author background content theories to define all of the nonpsychological concepts that were liberally used in our first-draft formalizations.

The central problem that we needed to overcome in authoring our final formalizations was consistency. The draft formalizations commonly included a wide variety of predications for a single concept, used different argument order and arity with the same predicate, and left other predicates undefined. Our strategy was to first take an inventory of the predicates that we were using, reorganize our stock of predicates into the appropriate representational areas or into additional nonpsychological background theories, and then sequentially author a new version of each of these content theories with definitive commitments to the representational forms.

Our inventory of predicates was developed simply by going through each of the thirty draft content theories and recording each unique predicate form that was utilized, where uniqueness was dependent both on the lexical form of the predicate itself and its argument structure. We then created a predicate index that clustered related and synonymous predications into groups. The need for revision is perhaps most evident in considering the variety of predicate forms we used for the concept of instantiation, a relation between a concept and another that is more abstract. Our predicate index included the following nine predicate forms for this single concept, listed with the number and section of the content theories where they were used:

instanceOf(e1,e): 16.6, 27.1, 27.2, 27.3
instance-of(e1,e): 16.6
instances-of(s,e): 16.6, 16.7
instance0(p1,p): 15.9
instance(p1,p): 15.9, 15.10, 15.11
instantiation1(p1,p): 26.8, 26.9
instantiation*(p1,p): 26.9
instantiate0(x,p): 21.1
instantiate(x,s): 21.1, 21.2

After taking inventory of our draft predicates, we divided them into those that were to be defined as part of our final commonsense psychology content theories and those that were nonpsychological in nature, to be defined in a number of background theories. These nonpsychological predicates were sorted into sixteen areas, which were then sequentially addressed as sixteen individual background content theories, presented in this book in Part II. These sixteen background theories were developed over thirteen months, April 2006 to May 2007.

In developing these background theories, a number of strong representational commitments were made that significantly guided the way axioms were to be authored in the final commonsense psychology theories. As elaborated in the first background theory in Part II, a commitment was made to use a style of axiomization that reifies events and states as eventualities, which can then function as arguments of other predications. This, along with a treatment of defeasibility (background theory 7), provided us a framework that permitted a high degree of expressive flexibility without leaving behind a strictly first-order style of logical notation. It was also at this time that we adopted the ISO/IEC 24707 Common Logic standard of logical notation, specifically the Lisp-like style of the Common Logic Interchange Format (International Organization for Standardization, 2007).

In taking inventory of our lists of draft predicates, we decided that two of our commonsense psychology theories – Execution Control and Plan Following – shared much of the same underlying semantics. Accordingly, we merged our formalizations of these two areas into a single theory (Execution Control) that covers the scope of both.

In September of 2007 we began writing the second (final) drafts of each of the twenty-nine commonsense psychology representational areas, this time adhering to the conceptual framework and notational conventions established in the background theories. As in the first drafts of these theories, the task was to develop a system of logical relationships that would enable the definition of each of the concepts identified through the analyses conducted in the first two phases of our overall project, but now in a stronger concern for the competency of these theories in supporting automated commonsense inference. This phase of our project was completed in September of 2016. The most productive period of these years was during 2013, 2014, and 2016, when we received research funding to complete our work from the Office of Naval Research. The results of our efforts are presented in Part III of this book.

3.7 INTERMEDIATE APPLICATIONS

"Successive formalization" is the term we use to characterize the approach that we used to achieve both coverage and competency in authoring our formal theories of commonsense psychology. The term recognizes a recurring strategy that we employed at each stage of this project, namely to favor coverage rather than competency when productivity was the bottleneck, then analyze the authored content to define the scope of the subsequent stage of the project. In each subsequent stage the degree of formality is ratcheted up a notch, until competency is achieved at the last stage of the project. This approach is markedly different from typical practices in the formal knowledge representation community, where the scope of effort is typically defined to be very narrow in order to quickly achieve some degree of competency. In our effort, the scope of commonsense psychology concepts was identified at the very beginning, and remained largely unchanged through the very end.

Practically speaking, this approach can be challenging to execute given the realities of academic funding and scholarship. The primary concern is that this approach delays the utility of the final product until the very end of the process. Over the course of the effort, the approach does not incrementally produce competent formalizations of theories for use in applications or evaluations. Few funding agencies have the stomach to fund multiyear knowledge representation efforts that do not produce any intermediate results, regardless of the potential. Likewise, few journal reviewers or conference program committees want to publish unfinished work, even if they are amenable to the publication of content theories in general. These realities are not likely to change significantly in the years to come, so researchers wishing to utilize a successive formalization approach to large-scale knowledge representation are going to need to be creative with their funding strategies, and learn how to produce useful technologies from the intermediate results of the different stages of their work. Fortunately, the opportunities to produce useful technologies do exist.

The most useful intermediate product of our methodology was the collection of English words and phrases that reference commonsense psychology concepts. In some respects, this collection is not unlike other electronic lexical resources that organize English words and phrases into sets of synonymous concepts, such as the WordNet lexical resource (Fellbaum, 1998). However, our lists of words and phrases had a number of key advantages over this and other available thesauri and dictionaries.

First, we recognized that some concepts are nearly impossible to reference without the use of compound words or phrases, such as "slack time" or "slack in the schedule." In this respect, our lexical resource has greater conceptual breadth than lexical resources that are based primarily on single words. Second, our word and phrase lists largely ignored grammatical and part-of-speech distinctions when grouping synonymous expressions. Although this would generally be considered a disadvantage, the effect was to produce word and phrase groupings that brought together entries that would otherwise be only distantly connected by semantic relations. In WordNet 2.1 for example, the adjective "expected" used in the compound "expected event" has a notably long chain of semantic and derivational relationships to the synonymous noun "expectation," largely due to the scarcity of relationships that span grammatical roles. In ignoring grammatical distinctions in our resource, these synonymous terms can be catalogued under a single concept. Third, in grouping concepts into twenty-nine (final) representational areas, our resource identifies semantic relationships between concepts that are difficult to characterize using the semantic relationships of traditional thesauri and semantic networks, particularly between constituents of (mental) processes.

To exploit these characteristics in natural language processing applications, we invested considerable effort in encoding this lexical resource in a manner that would be more useful than simple word and phrase lists. Instead, each set of synonymous words and phrases was encoded as a finite-state transducer capable of automatically recognizing and tagging the commonsense psychology concepts that appear in English electronic text documents. We utilized the Intex Corpus Processing software application (Silberztein, 1999), which allowed us to quickly author finite-state transducers using a graphical user interface. For each entry in our lists of words and phrases, a generalized linguistic pattern created for recognizing the entry and its derivations, and added to an umbrella transducer that would add a single concept tag into a text document if any of its constituent patterns matched the surface forms of the text. To simplify the specification of linguistic patterns, we relied heavily on a large-coverage English dictionary compiled by Blandine Courtois (2004), allowing us to specify components of these patterns at a level that generalized over noun cardinality and verb inflections. For example, a pattern for an English reference to a memory retrieval event is with a finite-state transducer with four successive transitions to handle both "made him think of" and "makes me think of" by generalizing over the verb and pronoun. Dozens of patterns like this one were authored for each of the commonsense psychology concepts identified during the linguistic analysis stage of our project. When we completed the authoring process in September 2004, we combined each of these individual transducers into a single massive transducer that could be applied to electronic text documents for the purpose of tagging references to all recognized Theory of Mind concepts. The compiled minimal finite-state transducer contained 9,556 states and 85,153 transitions.

Gordon et al. (2003) evaluated the performance of the finite-state transducers that we produced according to traditional information retrieval standards. The transducers for four of the representational areas (Managing knowledge, Memory retrieval, Explanation, and Similarity comparisons) were applied to sentences judged to contain references to each of these areas, elicited from volunteers who participated in a linguistic survey. Results indicated that this approach was effective at identifying 81.5 percent of the expressions associated with these representational areas in

English written text (recall score), and that 95.2 percent of the identified expressions would be judged as appropriate examples in the representation area by a human rater (precision score).

By investing this additional effort into our project, our linguistic analysis work produced a useful technology as an intermediate result. The primarily utility of the finite-state transducers is for large-scale corpus analysis. Any electronic text document written in English could be provided to the transducer as input, producing an annotated document as output where every recognized reference to a commonsense psychology concept was tagged in the text. For example, a passage from William Makepeace Thackeray's 1847 novel *Vanity Fair* is tagged in the following manner.

Perhaps [partially-justified-proposition] she had mentioned the fact [proposition] already to Rebecca, but that young lady did not appear to [partially-justified-proposition] have remembered it [memory-retrieval]; indeed, vowed and protested that she expected [add-expectation] to see a number of Amelia's nephews and nieces. She was quite disappointed [disappointment-emotion] that Mr. Sedley was not married; she was sure [justified-proposition] Amelia had said he was, and she doted so on [liking-emotion] little children.

The capacity to automatically tag large text corpora in this manner is particularly useful in investigating changes in the way that commonsense psychology concepts are referenced over time. Gordon and Nair (2003) used the finite-state transducer for one of the 528 concepts, for recognizing references to unconscious desires, to determine if people changed the way that they referenced this concept before and after it was popularized by the writings of Sigmund Freud. By applying this transducer to 176 English language novels published between 1813 and 1922 and recording frequency counts, Gordon and Nair noted the appearance of a pre-Freudian shift, where no definitive direct references to the concept appeared in this corpus before the middle 1800s. Gordon and Nair (2004) then applied the same corpus analysis techniques to investigate whether young children changed the way that they reference concepts of knowledge and belief over the developmental period in which they acquire abilities to reason about other people's knowledge and belief. For this study, each of the transducers for recognizing thirty-seven concepts in the representational area of Knowledge management were applied to 3001 transcripts in the CHILDES Project corpus of children's speech (MacWhinney, 2000), produced by monolingual English-speaking normally-developing children of ages eleven to eighty-seven months. Evidence indicated that children increasingly produce references to concepts of knowledge and belief throughout childhood, but do not qualitatively change the types or frequency of concepts expressed around the period in which they acquire increased reasoning capabilities related to these concepts. Gordon (2006) reviews both of these investigations and offers a discussion of the relevance of these findings to the evolution of Theory of Mind abilities.

3.8 REPEATABILITY

In referring to the four stages of our project as a methodology, we anticipate that other research will want to repeat all or some of these stages in their own knowledge representation research efforts. Although labor intensive, this methodology could be productively executed again by a single industrious graduate student over the course of a multiyear doctoral thesis research effort, perhaps with an emphasis on nonpsychological representational areas that we were not able to address in our own work. We expect that tenure-track academic professors and industry researchers working in the area of knowledge representation could execute this methodology with moderate funding over three years. With very little research funding, we have demonstrated that two academic research professors can execute this entire methodology in their spare time over the course of fourteen years.

Rather than repeating the entire methodology from strategy representation to final axiomization, it may be more interesting to consider repeating only selective stages of our effort. The centrality of commonsense psychology in AI research ensures that formalizations of these twenty-nine representational areas will continue to be of interest to knowledge representation researchers for the foreseeable future. Accordingly, it will be productive to attempt to formulate alternative axiomizations of these twenty-nine areas using different representational commitments, higher-order or nonclassical logics, and in ways that more obviously support default and probabilistic reasoning. For these future efforts, it makes sense to begin with the concepts identified through strategy representation and elaborated through linguistic analysis (stages 1 and 2 of this project). With identical coverage, these future theories will compete with the ones presented in this book in competency, that is, how well they support automated inference in commonsense problem solving systems, and open the door for the sort of performance competitions that have proven useful in other challenging areas of computer science.

4

Commonsense Psychology and Language

By the time we have become fluent speakers of our native languages, we have learned to use thousands of words and phrases to refer to mental states and processes of ourselves and others. This richness in vocabulary parallels the complexity of the commonsense psychological model that defines the deep lexical semantics of these linguistic expressions. By studying the richness of psychological language, we learn about the various facets of the knowledge representation challenge, and its overall breadth of scope.

In this chapter, we attempt to catalog the full breadth of English words and phrases related to commonsense psychology. We organize this vocabulary into twenty-nine representational areas, and group words and phrases into lists of entries that we consider to be conceptually synonymous. Undoubtedly we have missed quite a few expressions, and we have not attempted to list every synonym or morphological variation. Instead, our goal is specifically about breadth of coverage and granularity of conceptual distinctions. In creating these word lists, we are defining the target of our knowledge representation efforts. Our task is to develop a set of formal theories of commonsense psychology in which all of these words have a referent, and in which the theories themselves are rich enough to distinguish between each enumerated concept. We concede that there are subtle differences between words and phrases that we have grouped into a single enumerated concept. However, we believe that the concept categories capture much of the meaning of each group of expressions, and give us a good starting point for future efforts to articulate (formally) subtle differences in meaning.

In offering this (long) catalog here, we hope to achieve several goals. First and foremost, we can think of no better way to show readers the enormous breadth of commonsense psychology in terms that are already well understood. Second, we see these list as a non-technical index to the topics that are formalized in Part III of this book. Where readers are interested only in certain topics of commonsense psychology, one need only to find the relevant concepts in these lists and consult the corresponding logical formalization. Third, these lists invite alternative formalizations of commonsense psychology, providing a starting point for those that want to pursue radically different approaches with identical conceptual breadth. Fourth, it serves as a new lexical resource for future natural language processing systems, especially those that aim to interpret language using commonsense knowledge.

4.1 KNOWLEDGE MANAGEMENT

Knowledge Management concerns the basic reasoning and inference processes that lie at the core of the commonsense view of human psychology. The conceptual scope of this area, evident in the following linguistic examples, does not veer far from the philosophical concerns in the classical Platonic dialogue *Theaetetus*, which put forth a definition of knowledge as justified true belief, and the field of epistemology that follows from this work. Also included are process-oriented concepts within this representational area, such as the mental actions of adding and removing beliefs and assumptions, checking for inferences, the realization of consequences, and the affirmation of beliefs.

1. Managing knowledge ability: smart, gifted, clever, bright, intelligent, sharp, witty, brilliant, brainy, astute, quick learner, logical, rational, deluded, delusional, retarded, mentally handicapped, not the sharpest knife in the drawer, not the sharpest tool in the shed
2. Bias toward belief: gullible, believer, credulous, tend to believe, easy to convince
3. Bias toward disbelief: doubtful, skeptical, incredulous, naysayer, doubter, not born yesterday
4. True: correct, right, proper, fact, truth, reality, veracity, honest, accurate, verisimilitude, is the case, truly, valid
5. False: wrong, mistaken, incorrect, in error, inaccurate, amiss, awry, falsehood, falsity, fictitious, invalid
6. Truth value: whether or not it is true, true or false, validity, authenticity, credibility
7. Proposition: statement, sentence, position, idea that
8. Belief: think that, believe that, figure that, imagine that, reckon that, opinion, impression, feeling that, hypothesis, sense that, understanding that, estimation
9. Unknown: ambiguous, not known, unsure, uncertain
10. Revealed incorrect belief: mistakenly thought, used to believe that
11. Assumption: presumption, presupposition, premise, supposition
12. Unjustified proposition: hunch, guess, superstition
13. Partially justified proposition: to the best of one's knowledge, as far as one knows, reasonable, not impossible, possible, plausible
14. Justified proposition: logically necessary, logically follows that, no possible objection, justified, proof, fundamental, grounds for, owing to, on account of, validated by, beyond doubt, without a doubt, sure, certain
15. Inference: generalization, inferential, speculative, conjectural, conjecture, judgment
16. Consequence: conclusion, implies that, implication, corollary
17. Justification: rationale, theory behind, pretext for, foundation for, warrant, evidence that
18. Poor justification: does not follow from, not logical, flawed proof
19. Circular justification: circular argument, specious argument, circular reasoning

20. Contradiction: inconsistent, paradox, incongruity, conflicting beliefs, discrepancy, oxymoron, contrary notions
21. Knowledge: info, information, data
22. Knowledge domain: area of knowledge, area of specialization, area of expertise, field of study
23. Partial domain knowledge: some knowledge of, dabbles in, somewhat familiar with, working knowledge of
24. World knowledge: matter of fact, first-hand knowledge, second-hand knowledge, experiential knowledge, experience, hands-on knowledge
25. World model knowledge: theory of, science of, paradigm, world view, way the world works
26. Shared knowledge: commonsense, common thought, widespread belief, general conception, popular opinion, everyone knows that, everyday notion, commonly accepted that
27. Add belief: learn, find out, ascertain, discover, determine, apprehend, accept that, start believing, start to think that, begin to feel that, form the opinion, come to terms with, come around to one's point of view
28. Remove belief: change one's mind, lose faith in, stop thinking that, quit believing in, become unsure
29. Add assumption: assume that, suspect that, postulate, guess that, suppose that
30. Remove assumption: stop counting on, quit assuming, get back to reality
31. Check inferences: consider, think it over, draw inferences, judge, reckon, think about it, reason
32. Ignore inference: never mind that, putting aside that
33. Suppress inferences: without considering, disregarding the fact that, try not to think about, refuse to consider
34. Realize contradiction: conclude a contradiction, realize an inconsistency
35. Realize: conclude, become aware, occur to, dawn on, figure out
36. Knowledge management failure: confused, baffled, puzzled, bewildered, perplexed, mystified, dumbfounded, head in the clouds, lost
37. Reaffirm belief: verify, corroborate, confirm, affirm, reaffirm, make sure that

4.2 SIMILARITY COMPARISONS

Similarity Comparisons concerns the comparison of things, real or imagined, based on their representations. Along with basic notions of similarity and difference, this area includes other mental processes that are based on similarity judgments, specifically the ability to recognize patterns and draw analogies between otherwise dissimilar things.

1. Similarity comparison ability: able to differentiate, good at seeing the differences, be discerning
2. Compared things: comparison set, greater than, more than
3. Make comparison: compare, differentiate, distinguish, tease out the differences, equate, liken
4. Draw analogy: abstract comparison, see a connection, find a similarity
5. Find pattern: like last time, recognize a pattern, see a sequence, notice a trend

6. Comparison metric: dimension by which, variable of interest, distinguishing feature, basis for comparison, range of comparison
7. Same characteristic: have in common, share the feature, common characteristic, similar trait, both share, both have, grouped according to
8. Different characteristic: distinguished by their, both differ in, contrasting feature, different in that, differing in their, same except for, separable by
9. Analogical mapping: corresponds to, maps onto, aligned with, parallels, in the analogy
10. Pattern: trend, tendency, inclination, motif, order
11. Similar: resembles, takes after, has a resemblance to, bears a likeness to, shares features, has much in common, spitting image, chip off the old block, two of a kind, nearly identical, alike, comparable, no difference between
12. Dissimilar: different, contrasting, antithetic, differing, opposite, separable, not the same, bear no resemblance, nothing in common, does not take after
13. Analogous: simile, metaphoric, share an abstraction, the same in the abstract

4.3 MEMORY

In the commonsense view, memory is a metaphorical container for thoughts. Storing and retrieving from memory involve the transfer of thoughts in and out of this store to one's focus of attention. Included are concepts involved in deliberative memory retrieval as well as for passive retrieval, where a memory cue triggers an involuntary reminding.

1. Memory ability: knowledgeable, wise, well-informed, know by heart, know word for word, never forget, have a great memory
2. Memory item: memory, nostalgia, remembrance, recollection, past knowledge, experience, memoir, wisdom, memorable, unforgettable
3. Repressed memory item: repressed memory
4. Memory storage: cause to remember, learn, learn by heart, memorize, learn word for word, commit to memory
5. Memory retrieval: remember, think back, recall, recollect, reminisce, summon up, think of, retain, bear in mind, rings a bell, relive, fresh in one's mind, stick in one's mind, commemorate
6. Memory retrieval failure: no memory of, does not come to mind, lose the memory of, slips the mind, draw a blank, forget, tip of the tongue, rack one's brain
7. Memory repression: repress a memory, bury the thought, clear the thought, purge your mind, forget it
8. Reminding: reminiscent of, evocative, remindful, triggers a memory, reminds one of
9. Memory cue: souvenir, memento, keepsake, memorandum, reminder, cue, hint, help remember
10. Schedule plan retrieval: will not forget to, mental note to, remind one to, remember to, be sure to
11. Scheduled plan retrieval: remembered to, did not forget to
12. Scheduled plan retrieval failure: forget to, did not remember to, slipped one's mind

4.4 ENVISIONING

What are you thinking about? It is a common question that people can easily answer, and one that we will want to pose to robots in the future. Just as with people, we expect that robots should respond with one of handful of types of reports. They might be thinking about the past and how things got to be the way they are now. They might be focused on the present moment and the current state of the world. They might be wondering about the future and what is going to happen next. Perhaps instead they are daydreaming, imagining fictional places and people that have no temporal or causal connection to the world that they are experiencing. These processes all have a few important commonalities. They each involve the manipulation of conceptual models of the world, real or fictional. They each are concerned with events and states within these models that have a temporal and/or spatial extent, and the temporal and causal relationships between them. Each involves the consideration of the possible, freely considering counterfactual events and states as easily as those that are experienced in reality.

The phrase "thinking about" is probably the most commonsense way of referring to the suite of reasoning processes that share these commonalities, but in this book we instead use the term "envisioning." The concepts in this area characterize the infrastructure of causal reasoning, including branching causal timelines of various likelihoods that organize states and events into a system of relationships. Included as well in this area are concepts that pertain to the management of a person's current model of the world, such as advancing this model through the current moment, sending the present to the past and the future to the present, and validating or invalidating the expected model.

1. Envisionment ability: rich imagination, capacity to imagine, capability of foreseeing, imaginative
2. Envisionment failure: have trouble imagining, unimaginable
3. Envisionment preconditions: unforeseeable, before one can think about
4. Envisionment constraint: try not to think about, avoid imagining, keep oneself from thinking
5. Real-world envisionment: actually may happen, really has occurred, in fact will take place, in the real world, actually transpired, nonfiction, in reality
6. Other-world envisionment: fictional, dream, fantasy, fable, fantastical, not reality, only in one's imagination, not really happen, not actually occur
7. Consistent envisionment: both could happen, consistent with the fact that
8. Inconsistent envisionment: cannot both be the case, inconsistent with the fact that
9. Envisioned state: how one imagines it, one's vision of
10. Envisioned current world state: the way the world is, the way things are, present state of things, current view of the world, how one imagines the world to be, current state of affairs, at the current time, state of things now
11. Envisioned past state: view of history, way one thought it was, imagined past, knowledge about what happened
12. Envisioned future state: view of the future, way one thinks it will be, imagined future, beliefs about what will happen
13. Causal relationship: causal connection, causally related to, direct connection between

14. Causal influence: has something to do with, tends to cause, influences, play a role in
15. Causal chain: chain of events, string of events, cascading states, series of causes, domino effect
16. Causal system: scope of feasibility, realm of possibility, conceivable circumstances, network of influences
17. Propagated effects: aftermath, aftereffects, repercussions, in the wake of, consequences of
18. Envisionment branch point: hinges on whether, determining factor
19. Envisionment branch: possible outcome, potential consequence, contingency, fate, potentiality
20. Envisioned likelihood: the odds of, the probability that, the chances of
21. Definite likelihood: inevitable, will definitely happen, in all likelihood
22. Zero likelihood: impossible, will definitely not happen, an impossibility
23. Greater likelihood: more probably, higher chances of
24. Greatest likelihood: the odds are that, most likely
25. Random chance: luck of the draw, pure luck, due to chance, randomness, by hazard
26. Possible causal chain: conceivable fashion, always a way
27. Impossible consequence: no way that, could not have occurred
28. Combined envisioned likelihood: overall odds, joint probability, total chance that
29. Imagine state: imagine, envision, visualize, picture in one's head, once upon a time, in the mind's eye
30. Merge envisionments: dream became reality, fiction turned real
31. Advance envisioned current world state: the moment has arrived, the time is now
32. Correct envisionment: accurately imagined, just as one had imagined
33. Incorrect envisionment: mistaken vision of, had imagined it differently
34. Validate envisioned state: confirmed that, ensured that, checked that
35. Invalidate envisioned state: did not turn out that way

4.5 EXPLANATION

People want to know why. How did the world end up this way? What caused this to happen? The answers to these questions are explanations, the product of the mental process of explanation. Explanation is the side of envisionment that extends models of interconnected events backwards in time, to what came before to cause other events that are considered. The concepts below outline a multistage explanation process that begins with an attempt to explain a mystery, and is followed by the generation and evaluation of candidate explanations that are either adopted or rejected.

1. Explanation ability: critical thinker, deductive ability
2. Cause: induce, give rise to, bring about, lead to, determine, invoke, force, spawn, make happen
3. Mystery: enigma, riddle, conundrum, puzzle, unknown reason, no known cause

4. Explanation criteria: necessary to account for, needed to explain
5. Explanation: be because, owing to, as a result of, due to, by virtue of, on account of, set of factors, be why
6. Candidate explanation: a variety of reasons, another explanation, or because of, perhaps it was because
7. Best candidate explanation: the true reason, the real explanation
8. Factor: part of the reason, be causally involved, due to a combination of
9. Explain: figure out why, imagine why, conceive of why, to account for, elucidate why, come up with an explanation
10. Attempt to explain: consider why, think about why
11. Generate candidate explanations: brainstorm for why, hypothesize that, speculate that
12. Assess candidate explanations: scrutinize the hypothesis, consider the theory that
13. Adopt explanation: accept that the reason, adopt the theory that
14. Explanation failure: for lack of a better explanation, failure to account for, not understanding why
15. Explanation generation failure: no conceivable reason why, heaven only knows why
16. Explanation satisfaction failure: no reasonable explanation, no acceptable reason why
17. Unsatisfying explanation: poor explanation, rejected account of why
18. Explanation preference: prefer explanations that, look for explanations that

4.6 MANAGING EXPECTATIONS

What is going to happen next? Expectations are envisionments of causal consequences, specifically those that are imagined to follow in the future from the current world state. Expectation is the side of envisionment that extends interconnected models of states and events forward in time, toward the temporal and causal consequences of other imagined states. As the world reveals itself, these expectations may be confirmed or violated, the latter of which is the basis for the state of surprise.

1. Expected event: expectation, prediction, anticipated event, be expected
2. Unexpected event: surprise, a twist, out of nowhere, a shock, be unforeseen, fluke, the unimaginable happened
3. Expectation justification: reason for expecting, basis for prediction
4. Add expectation: predict, forebode, foresee, expect, destine, anticipate, envision what happens next
5. Remove expectation: no longer expecting, give up hope that, stop waiting for
6. Expectation ability: prophetic, oracular, visionary, seer, clairvoyant
7. Expectation confirmation: nothing out of the ordinary, just as one had expected, satisfy one's expectations
8. Expectation violation: surprised, astonished, amazed, astounded, dumbfounded, flabbergasted, startled, stunned, taken aback, taken by surprise, shocked, blindsided

4.7 OTHER-AGENT REASONING

Other-Agent Reasoning concerns the imagining of the mental states of other people, as well as introspectively considering one's own mental state. By including these concepts here, we are arguing that a theory of thinking about mental states is itself part of commonsense psychology, that is, that how people think they think includes beliefs about how people think about how people think! This idea is perhaps best understood in consideration of the representational concept of a psychological theory, included below, for which the theory formalized in this book is an instance. Despite the title of this representational area, it is also meant to include the mental processes of self-reflection and introspection, where people think about their own mental processes from the privileged perspective.

1. Other-agent reasoning ability: empathetic, telepathic, inconsiderate, self-centered
2. Psychological theory: psychology, the way people think, theory of mind, way the mind works
3. Other-agent model: know about someone, familiar with someone, acquainted with someone
4. Other-agent envisionment: the way one sees it, from one's perspective, through one's eyes, put oneself in someone's shoes, read someone like a book, see where one is coming from, what is going on in one's head
5. Other-agent envisionment failure: not understand why one would, have the element of surprise
6. Introspection: look inside one's own thoughts, ask oneself what one
7. Introspection failure: not know what I was thinking, surprised oneself

4.8 GOALS

People want a lot of things: a loving partner, a fulfilling career, parents who are well cared for, an attractive physique, a creative outlet, and material possessions. These are the sorts of goals that people target in their pursuit of happiness. The central importance of goals in people's lives is reflected in the richness of language about goals. The list of goal concepts below are abstract goal categories, rather than specific goals that people choose to pursue. A specific instance of a goal may change its class over time. For example, the preservation goal of caring for the health of one's parents may first only be an envisioned future goal when they are young and in good health, a shared goal among siblings when their health needs attention, an auxiliary goal when they are involved in one's plans in some way, and a violated preservation goal when their health turns bad.

1. Goal: ambition, intention, hope, desire, objective, purpose, aim, aspiration, calling, yearning, hunger for, craving, thirst for, aching for, pining for, long for, wish
2. Subgoal: toward the larger goal, waypoint, step along the way to
3. Conflicting goal: impossible to have both, not have one's cake and eat it too
4. Auxiliary goal: be nice as well, also do with, great if also, also if at all possible
5. Shared goal: common aim, shared objective, everybody wants
6. Collaborative goal: goal of the group, team objective, aim of the organization
7. Competitive goal: rivalry for, competition for, compete for, vie for

8. Adversarial goal: fight for, duel for, war against, battle against, thwart, undermine, foil
9. Unknown goal: mysterious objective, unspecified aim
10. Nonconscious goal: sure one wants, know one's own desires, subconscious wish, unconscious desire
11. Achieved goal: get what one wants, accomplishment, victory, achievement
12. Unachieved goal: yet to achieve, still to accomplish, unfulfilled desire, elusive
13. Unachievable goal: pipe dream, vain hope, unrealistic goal
14. Preservation goal: goal to protect, goal to preserve, aim to maintain, aim to uphold
15. Violated preservation goal: failure to protect, failure to preserve, failure to maintain
16. Persistent goal: endeavor, crusade, the movement toward, unending fight against, eternal struggle
17. Envisioned future goal: one day will want, not yet want
18. Envisionment goal: want to imagine, want to dream
19. Planning goal: want to know how to
20. Execution goal: want to do, want to get it done
21. Knowledge goal: desire to understand, curious, curiosity, inquisitive, nosiness

4.9 GOAL THEMES

To capture a commonsense intuition, Schank and Abelson (1977) introduce the term "goal theme," which "contains the background information upon which we base our predictions that an individual will have a certain goal." In their formulation, the attribution of a given goal theme to a person provides a causal account for other goals that would otherwise be senseless if viewed in isolation. Three broad classes of goal themes were described by Schank and Abelson, which can be referred to as role, relationship, and life themes. We include the concept "thrive," the causal antecedent of all of a person's goals.

1. Goal theme: source of one's desires, gives rise to the goal, ought to want, is supposed to want
2. Role theme: want to be a good, one's job to want
3. Relationship theme: want to do right by, for the sake of the relationship
4. Life theme: life's ambition, purpose in life, calling in life
5. Thrive: pursuit of happiness, ultimate purpose, prosper, flourish, make it in this world

4.10 THREATS AND THREAT DETECTION

The commonsense concept of a threat is somewhat remarkable in that it sits at the overlap between so many different ideas in commonsense psychology, particularly those related to one's goals, one's plans, and expectations about the way the world is going to be. Combined, these ideas provide a concise definition: a threat is an expectation that if something is not done, there is some chance that some goals will not be achieved. In everyday English, the term also often refers to the causal antecedents of the expected world state, particularly where these causes are agents, for example, "The rogue state is a threat to world peace."

1. Threat: danger, risk, hazard, ominous, rocky road, thin ice, dangerous ground
2. Goal in threat: be threatened, a threat to, be put in harms way
3. Threat condition: threat hinges on, danger is caused by, ripe for disaster
4. Threat effects: fallout, aftermath, post-apocalyptic, unfortunate consequences, bad outcomes
5. Possible threat: serious threat, prospective danger, not foolproof, danger is real, imminent threat
6. Impossible threat: safe bet, worry over nothing, no fear, nothing to be concerned about
7. Realized threat: not pull it off, fears came true, luck pressed too far, be screwed, not catch a break
8. Unrealized threat: pulled it off, caught a break, came through unscathed, slipped under the radar, dodged a bullet, close call, close one, false alarm, narrow escape, empty threat
9. Threat detection: think of everything, look for chinks in the armor, look before you leap, assessed the risks, considered the pitfalls, thought about the dangers
10. Add threat: raise a red flag, worry about, be concerned with, see the danger, afraid that
11. Remove threat: stop worrying, fears lifted, become unconcerned
12. Threat detection failure: caught off guard, wake up call, caught with one's pants down, sucker punch, not read the writing on the wall, fail to consider the risks
13. Threat assessment: think it is worth it, worth the risk, worth the gamble, venture, calculate the risks
14. Threat detection ability: can judge the risks, can play the odds
15. Bias against risk: paranoid, overly nervous, scaredy-cat, coward, worrywart, cautious, careful, conservative, risk averse
16. Bias toward risk: daring, audacious, adventurous, gambler, reckless, throw caution to the wind

4.11 PLANS

Here the term "plan" is used in the same sense as in this quote from Daniel Burnham (1864–1912), the celebrated American architect and city planner, "Make no little plans. They have no magic to stir men's blood and probably will not themselves be realized" (Moore, 1921). Burnham's quote is emblematic of his design philosophy, as evidenced by his development of the influential Burnham Plan for the city of Chicago, but the quote also directly implies some of the characteristics of plans in general. First, plans are seen as something that are made by people, as Burnham advises the listener to do. Although Burnham's plans often were presented as physical objects (architectural drawings), it is natural as well to view plans as entirely mental constructs, the product of human reason. In the commonsense view, therefore, a plan is a thing that resides in one's head. Second, plans can be small or large. For Burnham, the size of a plan may have been directly correlated to the size of the building, neighborhood, or city that he was envisioning, but a plan's size may also be based on the quantity or severity of the steps involved, or simply the duration that it would take to execute. Third, one person's plan can be communicated to other people for appraisal. When Burnham says that small plans cannot "stir men's blood" he is noting that people can have the plans of other people in their head to appraise their value, without the necessity that those plans be adopted or pursued. The idea that someone could have in his or her head an "un-adopted plan" makes perfect sense in everyday discourse, but much of the theoretical work in artificial intelligence (AI) planning seems to struggle uncomfortably with this notion, leading to a terminology of desires, intentions and commitments that take on nonobvious meanings within the literature. Fourth, plans are either realized in the world or not. For Burnham's realized plans, the world is changed in readily apparent ways: old roads and buildings are demolished, new ones take their place. Other plans may leave no obvious trace of their execution, such as a plan to have a casual conversation with a friend, or to relax at home on a Saturday afternoon. Despite the lack of obvious change to the world, the realization of these plans is dependent on the occurrence of real-world events.

1. Plan: program, scheme, project, plan of action, plot, roadmap, blueprint, agenda, proposal, suggestion, course of action, approach
2. Partial plan: underspecified plan, indeterminate plan, sketchy plan, incomplete plan, half-baked
3. Strategy: tactic, stratagem, abstract plan
4. Strategy instance: example of the strategy, instantiation of the strategy
5. Reusable plan: familiar plan, old trick, procedure, recipe, technique
6. Normal plan: normal thing to do, usual course of action, conventional action, classic approach
7. Adversarial plan: plan of attack, battle plan, diabolical plan
8. Counterplan: plan of defense, counter proposal, defensive stance
9. Assistive plan: plan of assistance, plan of support, plan in support of, aid program
10. Competitive plan: playbook, play, game plan
11. Shared plan: common plan, everyone doing the same thing, everyone had the same idea
12. Collaborative plan: plan to cooperate, plan to work together, partnership, collaboration
13. Envisioned plan: think what one will do, imagine one's plan, one's conceivable plan
14. Unknown plan: not know what the plan is, mysterious plan, the divine plan
15. Nonconscious plan: subconscious plan, unconscious plan, tacit knowledge of how to, force of habit
16. Continuous plan: never-ending plan, endless plan of action, plan to continue indefinitely
17. Periodic plan: routine, regiment, ritual, plan to periodically
18. Repetitive plan: repetitive course of action, plan to repeat
19. Occasional plan: plan to occasionally, plan to sporadically, plan to sometimes
20. Executed plan: completed plan, performed plan, what one did, finished doing, executed as planned

4.12 **GOAL MANAGEMENT**

Goal Management concerns the mental processes involved in managing the lifecycle of one's goals. Goals are seen as entities that can be adopted, suspended, resumed, abandoned, violated, or achieved. A further distinction is made to identify adopted goals that are currently being pursued, that is, the focus of one's planning or execution capacities. People are also viewed as having multiple goals at any given time, with prioritization among them that may be influenced through deliberative assessments.

1. Goal management ability: in touch with one's needs, have one's priorities straight
2. Add goal: resolve to, make up one's mind to, take up the goal of, now want
3. Abandon goal: stop wanting, throw in the towel, call it quits, lose hope, not want anymore
4. Suspend goal: set aside the goal, shelf the desire, put one's goals aside
5. Achieve goal: achieve, accomplish, succeed in, obtain the goal of, cross off one's list
6. Violate goal: be crushed, be vanquished, be foiled, kill one's dreams
7. Modify goal: settle for, try for a different goal, lower the bar, rethink what one wants
8. Specify goal: clarify one's goals, qualify what one wants
9. Generalize goal: pursue a broader goal, broaden one's hopes, be less picky
10. Goal justification: reason for wanting, why one wants, explanation for the desire, underlying motivation
11. Goal assessment: think about what one wants, ask oneself if it is worth it, reevaluate one's intention, rethink one's aim
12. Resolve conflicting goals: decide among goals, sort out contrasting aims
13. Goal preference: most important, more desirable, rather have, better to want
14. Prioritize goals: set one's priorities, prioritize one's goals, order one's intentions
15. Goal set: wish list, set of desires, things that one wants
16. Currently pursued goal: current ambition, latest desire, present aim, what one wants now

4.13 **EXECUTION ENVISIONMENT**

One of the main purposes of envisioning is to imagine how action could change the future, or explain the past. Concepts of Execution Envisionment are fundamental across all envisioning processes, for example, explanation and expectation, but are distinguished in that each of them involves the envisioning of the causal implications of some action of an agent, whether they be one's own or that of others. These concepts form the conceptual foundation for planning one's own actions to achieve goals.

1. Envision execution: imagine doing, rehearse in one's mind, see oneself doing
2. Execution envisionment failure: not imagine how one, not visualize the way one
3. Agency: acting, to act, deed, doing something, a behavior, the act of
4. Side effect: secondary effect, collateral damage, unintentional consequence
5. Opportunity: take advantage of, serendipitously, see an opening, capitalize on

6. Limit of failure: hanging on a thread, breaking point, push one's luck
7. Moment in execution: in the midst of, in the course of
8. Arbitrary moment in execution: any moment while doing, throughout the course of doing
9. Planner: see oneself doing, picture oneself
10. Envisioned execution duration: time needed to, the time it takes to, manhours
11. Envisioned likelihood of success: sure thing, slam dunk, good shot at, odds of succeeding
12. Envisioned failure: appears hopeless, lost cause
13. Arbitrary execution context: could be done anywhere, works in any circumstance, applicable in any situation

4.14 CAUSES OF FAILURE

Try as we might, failure is common. Attributing blame to the root cause of failure is a central challenge in explanation. To simplify our efforts, we often resort to patterns of plan execution explanations that are widely applicable to everyday situations.

1. Poor plan: ignorance, inexperience, naivety, stupidity
2. Poor conditions: perfect storm, bad luck, adverse circumstances
3. Poor execution: ineptitude, impotence, inability, inefficacy

4.15 PLAN ELEMENTS

Plan Elements are those concepts that further elaborate the internal structure of plans, enumerating their component parts. In addition to the concept of a subplan and its varieties, this area includes all of the programmatic control structure that defines a policy for how plans should be executed, including branch points, iterations, repetitions, and preconditions.

1. Subplan: milestone, step, part of the plan, stage in the plan, small part of the plan
2. Partial subplan: step is sketchy, underspecified part of the plan
3. Subplan agency: who does a part, delegated to, part executed by
4. Planned termination: final part of the plan, moment it is finished, close of the plan, after the last step
5. Subplan ordering: series of steps, sequence of actions, ordered steps, chain of actions
6. Precondition: need to first, in order to, before one does
7. Knowledge precondition: need to know first, not do without knowing, necessary knowledge, information needed
8. Resource precondition: need to have first, not do without having, necessary resource, resource needed
9. Conditional branch point: point of divergence, variability in the plan, point of contingency
10. Conditional branch: contingency, option
11. Branch point conditions: at which point it depends on
12. Else conditional branch: the other option, otherwise one plans to, Plan B

13. Termination conditional branch: in that case one is done, otherwise one is finished
14. Iterative subplan: do the same to each, repeat for every
15. Planned iteration quantity: times one planned to
16. Iteration quantity: number of ones one has done
17. Iteration termination condition: reason for leaving ones undone, case one should stop before completing all
18. Repetitive subplan: step over and over, repetitive part of the plan
19. Repetition termination condition: repeat until, keep at it until, do it as long as
20. Repetition quantity: number of times repeated, repetition count
21. Periodic subplan: step repeated every, repeat at regular intervals
22. Periodic subplan period: time between repeating the step, interval between repetitions
23. Reactive subplan: to do in case
24. Reactive subplan condition: while being on the look out for
25. Plan duration: do over a period of, time allotted for
26. Required precondition: need regardless, either way one needs, in any case it is required
27. Required subplan: need to do regardless, either way one needs to, has to be done in any case

4.16 PLANNING MODALITIES

Planning Modalities enumerate the different styles of reasoning that people employ in decided what to do, broadly speaking. The most general concept is that of goal pursuit, an abstraction that includes deliberative plan construction, the adaptation of previous plans, the collaborative negotiation of plans with others, and several other planning modalities. Concepts related to three of these modalities, namely plan construction, plan adaptation, and design, are further elaborated in subsequent representational areas.

1. Goal pursuit: working to achieve, making progress on the goal, working toward
2. Planning: plan to, think of a plan, draft a plan, formulate a plan, map out a plan, lay out a plan, make a plan, devise a plan
3. Planning ability: schemer, crafty, cunning, able to plan
4. Adversarial planning: conspiracy, cabal, devise a battle plan, plan to attack
5. Counterplanning: plan a defense, plan to defend, devise a counterplan
6. Assistive planning: figure out how to help, plan to support, devise a plan to aid
7. Collaborative planning: put our heads together, plan together
8. Competitive planning: devise a game plan, straight out of the playbook
9. Plan construction: figure out the steps, assemble a plan, pull together the parts of the plan
10. Plan adaptation: adapt a plan, salvage a plan, reuse a plan, apply a plan to a situation
11. Modify currently executing plan: change directions, change one's ways, break from the plan
12. Scheduled plan modification: last-minute changes, change at the last minute

13. Single-goal planning: one-track mind, single minded, stay focused on a goal, planning solely to
14. Multiple-goal planning: kill two birds with one stone, plan to get as much done as possible
15. Designing: come up with a design, work out a design, sketch out a design
16. Other-world planning: in that situation one would, if things were different one would
17. Other-agent planning: recommendation, if I were you I would, in your situation I would

4.17 PLANNING GOALS

Planning Goals concerns the goals that a person is trying to achieve in the process of deciding upon a plan of action. Here we are making a distinction between the types of goals that people are devising plans to achieve, and the preferences and priorities that people use to decide between candidate plans. Several of the concepts of planning goals concern the optimization of a resulting plan, such as the search for plans that take the least amount of time (minimize duration) or money (minimize value). Other planning goals prefer plans that include particular actions or events, or create opportunities or obstacles for other people. This area also includes three concepts for the goal of locating something (a person, place, or thing) that will play some other role in the plan.

1. Include action: try to incorporate the step, include in the plan if possible
2. Avoid action: only as last resort, try to avoid doing, streamline the plan
3. Enable event: set the stage for, set the conditions for
4. Block event: prevent against, safeguard against, take preventive measures
5. Enable threat: work toward one's demise, set one up to fail
6. Block threat: take preemptive action, alleviate the risk
7. Enable transfer: clear the path, remove obstacles, clear the way, open the floodgate
8. Block transfer: secure in place, prevent from leaving, keep out, obstruct
9. Enable agency: make it possible to, enable one to
10. Block agency: imprison, paralyze, keep one on a short leash, have someone under one's thumb
11. Enable other-agent goal satisfaction: make someone happy, stay out of one's way
12. Block other-agent goal satisfaction: thwart, derail, undermine, hinder, get in one's way
13. Minimize value: less is more, frugal, thrifty, be conservative with, optimal amount, miserly
14. Maximize value: bigger is better, greed, go for broke, as much as possible, be liberal with
15. Minimize duration: time is of the essence, as fast as possible, not waste time, efficient
16. Maximize duration: prolong, stretch the moment, make it last forever, as long as possible
17. Locate thing: look for, search for, locate, get one's hand on

18. Locate agent: find someone to, search for the person who, fill the job, talent search
19. Locate location: survey, pinpoint, find the place where, scout locations
20. Maintain plan progress: avoid backpedaling, keep moving forward, not undo what one has accomplished

4.18 PLAN CONSTRUCTION

Among the various ways that people decide what to do, Plan Construction is the process of devising plans from scratch. The process involves reasoning about the causal consequences of one's actions, and assembling a plan that would theoretically achieve the goal if correctly executed. This style of planning most closely aligns with the the classical planning paradigm in AI, where operators are selected and ordered through automated means–ends analysis.

1. Suspend planning: hold off on the details, put aside the plan
2. Resume planning: finish the plan, take up the plan again
3. Abandon planning: stop planning, give up on the plan
4. Specify plan: flesh out the details, be specific about the plan
5. Add subplan: add a step, addendum to the plan, put a part in the plan
6. Remove subplan: remove a step, simplify the plan
7. Identify precondition: realize the need to first, see a necessary step
8. Select subplan: choose a step, select an action
9. Order subplans: first things first, figure out the order
10. Obstacle: barrier, impediment, impasse
11. Planning problem: challenge, dilemma, sticky situation, something must be done
12. Planning option: one way to do it, have some leeway
13. Planning decision: decide what to do, choose the best approach
14. Resolved planning problem: get around the problem, solution to the dilemma
15. Planning preference: ideal plan, prefer a course of action that, favor plans that
16. Planning constraint: be constrained by, be under constraints, be limited by
17. Replan: start from scratch, back to the drawing board, try a different approach
18. Replan subplan: patch the plan, fix part of the plan, rework a step
19. Candidate plan: one way to, possible approach, reasonable course of action
20. Assess plan: evaluate the plan, scrutinize the plan, review the plan
21. Select candidate plan: choose the plan, pick the best plan
22. Selected candidate plan: plan one decided on, the original plan, best course of action
23. Unselected candidate plan: Plan B, plan one considered, rejected plan
24. Successful planning: wrap up the plan, finalize the plan, complete the plan
25. Planning failure: at a loss, uncertain what to do, not know what to do, stumped

4.19 PLAN ADAPTATION

Instead of dreaming up new plans to familiar problems, it is often easier just to do the same thing that worked last time. Things are not exactly as they were before, so it may be necessary to adapt to a changed set of circumstances. In the commonsense view of Plan Adaptation, people retrieve old plans that they had for previous situations and modify them in various ways to make them applicable to the current conditions. Sometimes these changes involve the addition or subtraction of plan steps, the modification of magnitudes or parameters, or the assignment of roles in multiperson plans. Some plans are straightforward to adapt, while others take a lot of mental work. In the end, people end up with plans that they like or plans that they reject.

1. Retrieve plan: remember how to, consider an approach, recall a technique, pull from the playbook
2. Modify plan: apply to this situation, adapt to this case, tweak to make it work, rethink the approach
3. Modify plan element: tweak a step, swap an action, substitute a step, amend a part of a plan, change it up a bit
4. Modify plan value: use more, do it with more, try increasing, correct for
5. Modify plan agency: stand in for, play the role of, fill in for, take over for
6. Adaptation cost: difficult to apply, complex application of, straightforward application
7. Successful adaptation: successful application of, thoroughly reworked the plan
8. Failed adaptation: not applicable here, unsalvageable plan, not serve one's purpose

4.20 DESIGN

Design is the planning of a physical configuration, of information to be communicated, or of an object intended to serve some function. The product of this reasoning need not include any actions to be executed, as when we talk about the successful completion of an architectural plan (e.g., the Burnham Plan for the city of Chicago). Instead, the goal is a satisfactory or optimal configuration of some composite entity that adheres to design constraints while supporting an intended use.

1. Design: layout, configuration, invention, model, schematic, arrangement
2. Design constraint: boundary, within limits, design restriction, up to code, limitations, specifications, requirements
3. Intended use: primary use, standard usage, expected application, supposed to be used, function
4. Unintended use: repurposed, nonstandard usage, jury-rigged, unusual application
5. Flawed design: defective design, design failure, engineering failure, bad design, hack
6. Design adherence: precision construction, faithful to the design, fidelity, stick to the design, meet specifications, according to design
7. Generate design: think about the design, working out the layout, imagining the structure, configure, arrange
8. Adapt design: customize the design, modify the design, design inspired by
9. Design failure: unsatisfying design, impossible layout, inconsistent configuration

4.21 DECISIONS

A decision is the selection of a choice among options. The concepts listed in this area take the perspective that decisions should be viewed as a particular class of plan element, usually a part of a larger plan; for example, you'll decide which way to go when we get there, rather than as a distinct planning modality. The process of decision making is compositional, involving the enumeration of a set of choices, deliberation over these choices, selection of the best choice, and (possibly) revision of one's choice after the fact.

1. Decision: decision to make, choice to make, runoff, election
2. Enumerate choice set: identify options, list choices, think of the possibilities
3. Deliberate: ruminate, ponder the choices, mull over one's options, think about the possibilities
4. Selection: make a choice, settle on, go with, pick, decide on, endorse, vote on
5. Decision revision: change one's mind, fickle, renege on, to waffle, vacillate, go back on
6. Suspend decision: sleep on it, leave it on the table, keep one's options open, put off the decision
7. Resume decision: take up the decision, finish deciding
8. Decision series: set of choices, chain of decisions, series of selections
9. Choice set: possible choices, set of options, range of candidates
10. Possible choice: in the running, candidate, prospect, alternative, option
11. Choice characteristic: determining feature, distinguishing characteristic, pros and cons
12. Best choice: frontrunner, favored option, preferred choice, cream of the crop, leading candidate
13. Selected choice: one's pick, one's choice, the one chosen, one's decision
14. Unselected choice: not make the cut, decided against, runner up, rejected choice, not chosen
15. Previously selected choice: the usual, consistent choice, ordinary choice, previous pick
16. Envision choice consequences: consequences of choosing, look before you leap
17. Cost-benefit analysis: evaluate the pros and cons, weight the decision
18. Choice criteria: evaluation metric, yardstick, benchmark, litmus test
19. Choice preference: prefer candidates that, preferential treatment, affirmative action
20. Obvious decision: no brainer, clear choice, clear cut, choice is evident, no deliberation needed
21. Insignificant decision: unimportant decision, inconsequential, immaterial, choice is irrelevant
22. Decision justification: reason for choosing, selection based on, motivation for picking
23. Decision factor: deciding factor, influenced one's decision, play a role in the decision, part of the decision
24. Arbitrary decision justification: random choice, on a whim, impulsive decision, blind choice, crap shoot, luck of the draw
25. Decision consequence: effects of the decision, live with one's choice

26. Positive decision consequence: good choice, excellent pick, decision bears fruit
27. Negative decision consequence: disastrous decision, poor choice, mistake

4.22 SCHEDULING

Scheduling sits at the border between planning and execution, between dreaming and doing, between intention and action. The central concept in this area is that of a schedule, a mental agenda of the plans that one expects be executed at future points in time. The process of scheduling, consequently, is a deliberation concerning the time a plan should be executed.

1. Schedule: one's agenda, to-do list, on one's plate, things that need to be done, stuff to do
2. Schedule capacity: a full plate, full schedule, booked, overbooked, overloaded, busy, stretched thin, packed schedule
3. Unscheduled duration: free time, down time, spare time, nothing to do, idle time
4. Next unscheduled duration: have a moment, have a chance, have a second, have some time, next opening, soonest opportunity
5. Pending plan: wanting to do, wanting to find time for, intend to squeeze into one's schedule
6. Scheduled plan: be slated for, on the schedule, committed to do, appointment
7. Next scheduled plan: up next, next on the agenda, next order of business
8. Scheduled plan duration: time allotment, allotted time, period of performance
9. Scheduled start time: kick off, commencement, will start at, scheduled to begin
10. Scheduled end time: target time, target date, will finish at, scheduled to end, wrap-up time
11. Deadline: time limit, curfew, drop dead date, last possible moment, must be finished by
12. Start time deadline: before it is too late, must start before, strike while the iron is hot
13. Scheduled close to deadline: the eleventh hour, crunch time, down to the wire, time pressure, without a moment to spare, not a moment too soon, by the skin of one's teeth, in the nick of time
14. Scheduled far from deadline: time to spare, breathing room, plenty of time, time to kill
15. Schedule preference: expedite, rush through, rush job, pick up the pace, move it into high gear, as soon as possible
16. Schedule plan: make a date, make an appointment, put on the schedule, fit into the schedule, make time for
17. Schedule periodic plan: set a usual time, schedule regularly, schedule periodically
18. Unscheduled plan: postpone, some other time, put on the back burner, delay, put off, hold off
19. Reschedule plan: reschedule, push back until, push forward to, move up in the schedule
20. Indefinitely postpone: hold off forever, put off one's whole life, do in one's next life

21. Modify schedule: rework the schedule, throw out the agenda, free up some time, rearrange one's schedule
22. Collaborative scheduling: coordinate schedules, arrange schedules, choreograph
23. Scheduling failure: a mix up, double booked, not find time to, dropped the ball

4.23 MONITORING

Plans often include the intentional triggering of some action based on some conditions of the situation. We imagine that stockbrokers would monitor the market for conditions that would prompt them to sell their portfolio. High school students might monitor the wall clock when taking a test to adjust the amount of time that they allot to answering each test question. People driving on an interstate highway might monitor the fuel gauge, the distance to exits, and their own bodies in making decisions about when to stop for gas at a service station. In the list that follows the term "monitor" is used both as a verb referring to the mental event of considering whether a situation matches some trigger conditions, and as a noun referring to a type of mental structure that describes these conditions and the actions that are to be triggered. This latter meaning of monitoring suggests that a stack or set of monitors might be active at any given time for a person, and that the adding and removing of monitors from this stack would be part of any moderately complex plan. It is also within this representational area that we can characterize the concept of waiting, both waiting for and waiting to, as a type of monitor whose conditions trigger the continuation of the remainder of a plan.

1. Monitor: be observant, on the lookout, keep one's eyes peeled, waiting for, await, patrol, check, watchful, vigilant, observant, keep one's eyes open, keep tabs on, guard
2. Monitor thing: not take one's eyes off it, not loose sight of, eyeballing
3. Monitor agent: stakeout, breath down one's back, look over one's shoulder, spy on
4. Monitor self: observe oneself, self conscious, self restraint
5. Terminate monitor: stop waiting, be at ease, let down one's guard
6. Monitor trigger conditions: catch in the act, at first sign of, what one is looking out for
7. Monitoring frequency: how often one checks, time between checking
8. Duration of monitoring: on one's watch, while on patrol
9. Untriggered monitor: detect nothing, nothing alarming
10. Trigger monitor: be alarmed, sound the alarm, see what one is after
11. Monitoring failure: overlook, slip through the cracks, lose sight of, let one's guard down, catch off guard, be right under one's nose

4.24 EXECUTION MODALITIES

There are several ways that people go about doing things. Different execution modalities are distinguished largely by the degree to which the action was planned ahead of time or with respect to temporal factors. In some cases, these modalities are necessarily exclusive, for example, an execution is unlikely to be both planned and spontaneous. In other cases, these modalities simply denote special concerns that an execution system would need to address, that is, the coordination needed for collaborative execution between multiple people.

1. Execution: the doing of, the act of
2. Planned execution: as intended, go according to plan
3. Spontaneous execution: extemporaneous, improvisation, make up as one goes along, wing it, by the seat of one's pants
4. Nonconscious execution: caught up in the moment, could not help oneself, could not control oneself, slipped out of one's mouth, do without thinking
5. Mental execution: using one's brain, put one's head to it, engage the thinking process, mental work
6. Reactive execution: reaction, reflex, deal with it as it happens, play it by ear, putting out fires
7. Repetitive execution: daily grind, bang away at, chip away at, spinning one's wheels
8. Iterative execution: cycle through, page through, cover each, touch on each
9. Periodic execution: do every so often, do from time to time, do regularly
10. Continuous execution: keep cranking out, keep on doing, do indefinitely
11. Triggered execution: do at the right moment, do when the time is right, do as orchestrated
12. Consecutive execution: do in order, follow the steps, do one thing at a time
13. Concurrent execution: do in parallel, juggle at the same time, multitask, do two things at once
14. Simultaneous execution: both do it at the same time, do at exactly the same moment
15. Collaborative execution: synergistic, in synchrony, pitch in, work as a team, combine forces, help each other out, lend a hand, act in unison, teamwork
16. Follow execution rules: walk a fine line, stay on the path, keep within bounds

4.25 EXECUTION CONTROL

Execution Control deals with the mechanisms of putting plans into action, and comprises two halves. First, Execution Control treats plans as sets of instructions and expectations about the effects the instructions will have on the world. It includes the concepts related to the launching and management of these instruction sets, including their starting, stopping, suspension, resumption, and continuation. Along with the basic control functions, this representation area includes concepts pertaining to the execution of particular types of plans with special specifications, including activities, performances, and skills – all of which may have plan representations that are not comprised of explicitly executable sets of instructions.

The best laid plans of mice and men often go awry. The second half of the job of Execution Control is to notice when and where this happens, and to proceed only as long as they are viable. Included here are judgments of when conditions and preconditions in plans are satisfied by the current world state, whether deadlines in plans are met or missed, and the consideration of variables relevant to plans as they are being executed, for example, the elapsed time, the portion of the plan yet to execute, and the accumulated costs of resources that have been expended. This area also includes the key concept of an execution failure, the causes of which are the subject of a pre-vious representational area, Causes of Failure.

1. Execute: launch, actuate, get to it, bring it on, get the show on the road, put it in motion, do it
2. Execute plan: carry out the plan, implement the plan, put the plan into effect
3. Execute explicit plan: carry out as instructed, do as specified, adhere to the plan, conform to the plan, following orders
4. Execute reusable plan: go through the motions, carry out as always, do the same as usual
5. Execute activity: participate in, take part in, engage in, been there done that
6. Execute performance: enact, reenact, perform, recite, exhibit, act out
7. Execute skill: work one's magic, display one's prowess, exhibit one's skills, put one's skills to work, show one's expertise
8. Suspend execution: pause, take a break, take a rest, hold up a moment, hold on a second
9. Suspended execution duration: lull, hiatus, sabbatical, vacation, time off, break time
10. Resume execution: jump back into, back to the job at hand, spin back up, pick up where one left off
11. Continue execution: carry on, continue forward, stay with it, hold steady, hang in there, stick with it, proceed with, never quit
12. Complete execution: wrap up, finish up, close the book, bring it home, put to bed, complete, conclude, close out, finalize, come to fruition, bring to an end, bring to a conclusion
13. Terminate execution: quit, bail out, jump ship, pull the plug, abort, throw in the towel, cease
14. Be distracted: lose focus, be sidetracked, preoccupied, pulled in a different direction, thrown off course
15. Execution rule: regulation, law, ordinance, restriction
16. Delayed execution: delayed start, running late, behind schedule
17. Currently executing plan: be up to, plan in progress, be in the middle of
18. Executed plan portion: progress, headway, work already done
19. Remaining plan portion: yet to be done, more to do, left on one's plate, loose ends, work left to do
20. Execution duration: as long as it takes, the time it took, period of performance
21. Execution start time: commencement, kick off, launch time, time of departure, showtime
22. Execution end time: wrap up time, time of completion, finish time
23. Miss deadline: late, tardy, past schedule, overdue, running behind, be behind on, miss the boat
24. Execution environment: stage, conditions, setting, arena, surroundings
25. Satisfied precondition: stage was set, groundwork, met requirements, ripe for the picking
26. Unsatisfied precondition: conditions not right, not be ready, jump the gun, do too soon
27. Violate precondition: become undone, undo progress, cancel out, unravel
28. Satisfied condition: met the requirement, sufficient, adequate amount, in line with

29. Unsatisfied condition: too little, insufficient, not up to par, inadequate amount, less than required
30. Constant across execution: invariant, steadfast, unaffected, unchanged by
31. Execution costs: running on empty, worth the effort, effortless, difficult, exhausting
32. Successful execution: pull it off, prevail, come to fruition, accomplish
33. Successfully executed plan: feat, achievement, deed, tour de force, stunt
34. Execution failure: botch, blunder, bungle, louse up, come up short, fail, crash and burn, awry
35. Consistently successful plan: standard approach, usual method, best practice, reliable scheme
36. Monitor execution: check progress, status check, watch what one is doing, see how things unfold, see it unfold

4.26 REPETITIVE EXECUTION

Repetitive Execution enumerates the subset of Execution Control concepts involved in the iterative and repetitive execution of plans. Here distinction is made between repetition, which involves doing the same thing over and over again until some condition is met, and iteration, which involves applying some action to every element in some set of definite size. In programming language terms, there is some analogy to the flow-of-control distinction between a while-loop and a for-loop. Here a repetition or iteration in the singular refers to the execution of a subplan that is embedded inside the loop, affording the plural concepts of repetitions or iterations that are already completed or yet to complete. Here we also include the mental events needed for counting repetitions and iterations, affording people both the ability to discover quantity of sets in the world via counting as well as the ability to execute actions a definite number of times.

1. Start repetition: begin repeating, start the cycle, commence orbit
2. Repeat: do again, loop, cycle again
3. Terminate repetition: break the cycle, abandon the routine, cease repeating
4. Increment count: chalk one up, mark one down, tally up
5. Repetitions count: tally, totals, number so far
6. Previous repetition: last time around, earlier cycle, prior loop
7. Current repetition: this time around, ongoing cycle, present loop
8. Next repetition: next time around, next on deck, next one up
9. Completed repetitions: finished cycles, past loops, ones in the bag
10. Remaining repetitions: future cycles, in the pipeline, rounds remaining
11. Start iteration: go through each one, start on the first, start going through
12. Iterate: take up the next one, do the next in line, continue through the series
13. Terminate iteration: quit before all are done, do as many as possible, leave some remaining
14. Complete iteration: exhaust the set, finish the series, no more to do

4.27 MIND–BODY INTERACTION

Mind–body interaction concerns commonsense psychology at its periphery, where mind and body meet. In the commonsense view the mind and the body are distinct, yet have direct means of controlling and informing each other. The actions of the body, from moving one's hand to speaking some word, are seen as the result of some direction on the part of the mind. The directed action may fail or succeed, and in turn provides the mind with the feeling of its doing (body action perception), for example, as awkward or fluent, along with an array of other perceptions enabled by perceptual body parts, for example, one's eyes. These perceptions from the body share with the mind the resource that is one's focus of attention, with a scope that can be limited through concentration.

1. Mind: psyche, intellect, mental life, internal world, head, brain
2. Body: cadaver, carcass, corpse, physique, flesh and blood, figure, frame, remains, physical self, corporeal, earthly being
3. Body action: physical act, bodily movement, motion, gesture, move, budge
4. Body Action Direction: command one's body to move, try to move one's, try to position one's
5. Successful body action direction: gracefully, with dexterity, deftly, nimbly
6. Failed body action direction: awkwardly, one's body was not able, ungracefully, clumsy
7. Coordinated body action direction: align one's motions, move simultaneously, coordinate one's actions
8. Undirected body action: twitch, spasm, convulsion, unintentionally move, slip, stumble, trip, accidental movement
9. Reflex: involuntary response, automatic reaction, instinctively, out of instinct
10. Sense: perceptual organs, sensory modalities, sensory inputs
11. Perception: sensation, stimulus, feeling
12. Body action perception: feel oneself doing, the way it feels to do, sensation of doing
13. Awkward body action: to feel unnatural, strange sensation, uncomfortable action
14. Fluent body action: to feel natural, ergonomic, comfortable motion
15. Perceptual body action: tune out, close one's eyes/ears, shut out
16. Focus of attention: conscious of, on one's mind, in one's thoughts, in one's mind's eye
17. Attend: pay attention to, be aware of, be cognizant of
18. Concentrate: ignore everything but, attend only to, pay attention only to, focus only on
19. Mind–body state: state of mind, out of touch, in tune with, connected with oneself
20. Conscious state: alert, awake, wakeful, waking state
21. Altered state: feeling weird, to not feel normal, screwed up state, intoxicated, be high, inebriated
22. Unconscious state: unconscious, asleep, comatose, in a coma, in a trance, zombie-like

4.28 OBSERVATION OF PLAN EXECUTIONS

Observation of Execution relates to a special case of Plan Following, where a person is following a plan that is being executed by another person. In the general case, the ability to follow the actions of another person is a critical component of collaborative execution, where two or more people attempt to execute a shared plan. However, many of the concepts in this representational area deal specifically with two more specific situations. First is the observation of another person's execution of some performance when the plan is known, for example, for the purpose of assessing their abilities. For example, an Olympic judge follows the performance of a gymnast as they perform their routine, and assesses how well they adhere to some idealized performance specification. Second is the observation of another person's execution when their plan is unknown, for example, for the purpose of learning how to do something. For example, novice surgeons will observe the performance of many surgeries during their medical residency in order to induce the complex plans that they will later execute themselves.

1. Observable execution: open behavior, visible action, outward expression
2. Unobservable execution: invisible action, hidden behavior, inner performance, behind the scenes, private thoughts
3. Observed execution: witness to, caught in the act, audience to, public display
4. Unobserved execution: behind closed doors, covertly, in secret, undetected, done in private, stealthily
5. Performance: recital, demonstration, exhibition, gig, presentation, ceremony, ritual
6. Performance specification: by the book, proper way, traditional way, accepted fashion, procedure, the ropes
7. Candidate performance specification: novice approach, beginner's intuition, assumed technique
8. Generate candidate performance specification: watch and learn, learn by example, mimic, get the hang of, get a feel for
9. Modify candidate performance specification: tweak one's method, adjust one's approach, change one's ways
10. Invalidate candidate performance specification: not see how one, fail to grasp how one, not get it
11. Validate candidate performance specification: catch on, have it down pat, to master, become proficient
12. Assessment: critique, check up, evaluation, judge, rank, assess
13. Assessment criteria: rubric, yardstick, standard, benchmark, baseline, litmus test
14. Assessment result: score, judgment, grade, after action review, progress report, criticism
15. Observe performance adherence: make sure it is done right, watch it being done, oversee, supervise
16. Observe performance divergence: catch a mistake, observe an error, notice a deviation

4.29 EMOTIONS

Emotions play a special role in the commonsense theory of the mind. Indeed, many might not view emotions as part of the mind at all. One might say, "Don't listen to your mind; listen to your heart," or "Don't think too much about it; trust your feelings." Likewise, it is common for people to ascribe emotional reasoning to a spiritual component of their existence, distinct from their body and mind. This perceived dualism between emotional and nonemotional reasoning likely contributed to the widespread popular acceptance of the idea of emotional intelligence during the 1990s, with only tenuous links to psychological research (although see Salovey and Grewal, 2005). However, high-level explicit theories of the role of emotion in reasoning seem to play little or no role in characterizing the lexicon of emotion-related terms in the English language, which is largely dominated to references to specific emotional states.

The use of emotion terms has been studied extensively within the field of linguistics, with particular attention to cross-cultural differences. Good introductions to this line of cross-cultural linguistic research can be found in edited volumes by Athanasiadou and Tabakowska (1998) and Harkins and Wierzbicka (2001), and in the monograph of Wierzbicka (1999). Within computational linguistics there has been recent interest in creating large-scale text corpora where expressions of emotion and other private states are annotated (Wiebe, Wilson, and Cardie, 2005).

In our own analysis of language related to concepts of emotion, we were particularly struck by two characteristics of emotion vocabulary that distinguish them from those of other representational areas. First is the sheer quantity of single words that reference emotion states in the English language; there are hundreds of words that English-speakers use to describe how they are feeling. Second is the low level of polysemy within this set. There are lots of emotion words, and they are unambiguous. In the vocabulary list that follows, we also include feelings and other sensations, and cluster emotion concepts by how they relate to other representational areas of commonsense psychology.

Sensations, or things felt by your skin

1. Cold, Chilly, Frigid
2. Hot, Warm
3. Itchy, Tingling, Prickling, Tickling
4. Numb
5. Pain, Ache, Sore

Body feelings, or things felt mostly by your body

6. Hungry, Famished
7. Thirsty, Parched
8. Nausea, Sick, Disgust, Revulsion, Repulsed, Repugnance, Uncanny, Creepy
9. Aroused, Titillated, Lust, Lechery, Lasciviousness
10. Pleasure, Comfortable, Delight, Ecstasy, Rapture, Ravished
11. Displeasure, Uncomfortable, Discomfort, Awkward
12. Tearful, Weepy
13. Intoxicated, Inebriated, Drunk
14. Sedate
15. Dazed, Stupor
16. Calm, Serene, Peaceful, Tranquil, Relaxed, Repose
17. Stress, Tense, Overwhelmed
18. Tired, Exhausted, Fatigued, Weary, Sleepy
19. Energetic, Sprited, Exhilarated, Excited, Thrilled, Exuberant, Frisson

Knowledge state emotions

20. Certain, Confident, Sure, Conviction
21. Doubt, Uncertain
22. Confused, Bewildered, Perplexed, Puzzled, Disconcert, Discombobulate
23. Interest, Curiosity, Fascination, Wonder, Awe, Intrigue
24. Boredom
25. Amusement, Mirth, Jolly, Jocular, Entertained
26. Crazy, Deranged, Insane
27. Lost, Disoriented

Expectation emotions

28. Anticipation, Expectation, Suspense
29. Trust, Faith
30. Distrust, Suspicion
31. Startled
32. Surprised, Flabbergasted, Dumbfounded, Astonished, Amazed, Stunned
33. Shock, Consternation, Dismay, Stupefy, Appalled
34. Shaken, Rattled, Unnerved, Flustered, Ruffled, Fazed, Traumatized

Threat emotions

35. Fear, Frightened, Scared, Afraid
36. Hope, Encouraged, Optimistic, Sanguine
37. Anxiety, Nervous, Anxious, Worry, Concern, Unease
38. Dread
39. Panic, Frantic, Alarmed
40. Relief, Assuage, Alleviate
41. Terror, Horror
42. Uninhibited, Unrepressed, Unrestrained, Liberated, Free

Execution emotions

43. Apprehensive, Hesitant, Reluctance, Trepidation
44. Cautious, Careful
45. Courageous, Bold
46. Determined, Stubborn, Resolute
47. Eagerness, Enthusiastic, Gusto, Zeal, Zest, Passionate, Vigor, Vehement
48. Frustration, Exasperation, Aggravation
49. Intimidated
50. Shy, Diffident, Timid, Reserved, Self-conscious

Goal emotions, especially with respect to social relationships

51. Want, Desire, Crave, Longing, Yearn, Covet, Wish
52. Admiration, Worship, Reverence, Esteem
53. Respect
54. Humbled, Humility, Modesty
55. Devotion, Loyalty

56. Submissive, Meek
57. Envy, Jealousy, Covetous
58. Contempt, Disdain
59. Love, Infatuation, Adore, Agape, Amorous, Enamored
60. Affection, Fondness, Fancy, Friendliness, Endearment, Kindness, Tenderness
61. Aggressiveness, Belligerent, Bloodthirsty, Hostile, Bellicose, Confrontational, Combative
62. Hate, Loathe, Abhor, Animosity, Despise
63. Spite, Malevolence, Malicious, Malignant, Evil, Vicious

Goal achievement emotions

64. Happy, Pleased, Glad, Jubilant, Merry, Jovial, Cheerful
65. Joy, Elation, Euphoria, Glee
66. Grateful, Thankful, Appreciation
67. Gloating, Schadenfreude, Smug
68. Vindicated, Gratified
69. Pride, Proud, Conceit, Egotistic, Arrogance, Vain, Vanity

Goal failure emotions

70. Sadness, Unhappy, Displeased, Gloomy, Woe, Sorrow, Doleful, Glum, Wretched, Devastated
71. Disappointment, Heartbroken, Brokenhearted, Crushed
72. Disgruntled, Disquiet, Indignant
73. Suffer, Tormented, Misery, Agony, Anguish
74. Depressed, Despondent, Dejection
75. Despair, Hopelessness, Demoralized, Dispirited, Helplessness, Pessimism, Discouraged
76. Distress, Distraught, Upset, Bothered
77. Grief, Grief-stricken, Disconsolate, Mournful, Bereaved
78. Anger, Rage, Furious, Mad, Ire, Livid, Wrath, Outrage, Indignation
79. Annoyed, Irritated, Agitated, Aggravated, Perturbed, Vexed
80. Bitter, Resentment, Vengeful, Vindictive, Pique, Mad
81. Insulted, Offended, Umbrage, Hurt, Huffish
82. Consolation, Solace
83. Pity, Commiserate, Condole, Compassion, Mercy, Empathy, Sympathy
84. Lonely, Homesick
85. Alienated, Isolated, Estranged, Ostracized, Marginalized
86. Embarrassment, Chagrin, Humiliation, Discomfit, Foolish
87. Regret, Remorse, Repent, Rueful, Shame, Ashamed, Guilt

Goal management emotions

88. Satisfied, Satiated, Content
89. Discontent, Restless, Restive
90. Acceptance, Resignation
91. Carefree, Lighthearted, Gay
92. Playful, Whimsy

Decision emotions

93. Like, Inclination, Partiality, Penchant, Predilection, Preference, Bias towards, Taste for
94. Dislike, Disinclination, Aversion, Distaste, Detest
95. Conflicted, Torn
96. Indifferent, Disinterested, Ambivalent, Unconcerned, Apathy

Monitoring states feelings

97. Focused, Attentive, Alert
98. Mesmerized, Transfixed
99. Distracted

Observation of execution emotions

100. Approval
101. Disapproval, Reproach, Deprecate
102. Impressed

Emotion emotions

103. Emotionless, Unmoved, Untroubled, Aloof

Although we do not consider each of these words in Chapter 49 on formalizing emotions, we deal with a large enough illustrative subset of them to give a good idea about how the others would be handled.

Background Theories

Introduction

The rest of this book is heavy on logic; that's what the word "Formal" in the title means. But we believe the book has value beyond the formalization, in the systematic development of the content of the theories, and we would not like to see readers put off by their lack of familiarity or comfort with logic. The logic we use is neither deep nor especially complicated. So we have included an appendix on first-order logic that gives a gentle introduction to all the logic one needs for understanding the axioms in this book.

Even those comfortable and familiar with logic may find it profitable to look over Sections 7 and 8 of the appendix. Section 7 presents our view that commonsense theories are not to be built up by definitions resting ultimately on a set of primitive concepts, in a kind of "Euclidian" program. Rather every predicate is, in a sense, a primitive, but they all occur in axioms that constrain their possible meanings more or less tightly. The most fundamental concepts in commonsense knowledge cannot be *defined* precisely with necessary and sufficient conditions. The most we can hope for is to *characterize* them as precisely as possible with lots of necessary conditions and lots of sufficient conditions. Then Section 8 presents the most common patterns we use in the axioms, and it should reduce their perceived complexity for the reader.

The focus of this book is commonsense psychology. But this is a very complex domain, and it rests on a number of other nonpsychological domains. Before talking about belief, we have to talk about logic. Before doing goals and plans, we need a theory of causality. We can't axiomatize scheduling until we handle time. In Part II we develop these and other background theories.

The theories, one per chapter, fall into two broad categories. Some provide required mathematical infrastructure that will be needed everywhere or argue for fundamental ontological commitments necessary for getting any effort to encode commonsense knowledge off the ground. In Chapter 5 we reify "eventualities", or states and events, by treating them as first-class individuals in the logic. In Chapter 7 we make a similar move with typical elements of sets, or reified universally quantified variables. In Chapter 8 we reify logical connectives. All of this allows us to do in first-order logic what in the past has mostly been done in higher-order logics, or not at all. Our view is that at least the first and third of these moves are mandatory, or any large-scale effort like this one would be dead in the water. In Chapters 6 and 9 we present axiomatizations of sets, functions and sequences in a fairly traditional style. Chapter 11 describes our approach to defeasibility, another absolute must for encoding commonsense knowledge.

The second category of theory, and chapter, is content theories, but content at a very high level of abstraction. It is often said that we understand many domains by analogy with the domain of spatial relationships. But analogies are based on shared properties, and what we have done is identify those properties of space that are most often implicated in analogies, and developed theories of these. The result is a kind of abstract topology. We begin in Chapter 10 with composite entities, or things made of other things; it's hard to think of anything more basic than this. Then in Chapter 12 we build a theory of scales. Arithmetic, in Chapter 13, is seen as an example of a scale, although we axiomatize it in a fairly traditional way. Chapters 14 and 15 deal with change of state and causality, and Chapter 17 with the structure of complex events. Our treatment of time in Chapter 16 rests on the notions of scale and change. The concepts we explicate in Part II are those that we needed for commonsense psychology in Part III. It turned out we required relatively little from a theory of physical space (Chapter 18) and a theory of the physical, noncognitive aspects of persons (Chapter 19), but we have included what we needed. We end with Chapter 20 on modality, or modes of existence, including possibility, probability, and real existence.

With all of this infrastructure, we have what need for axiomatizing commonsense psychology, and probably many other complex domains of commonsense knowledge as well.

5

Eventualities and Their Structure

5.1 EVENTUALITIES AND THEIR INDIVIDUATION

Because commonsense psychology deals with the things people think about and because people think about states and events in the world, we need to maximize the convenience of talking about such things. This is done by making states and events first-class individuals in the logic. That is, states and events are things in the world. They can be referred to by constants and variables in the logic. This enables us to use them as arguments in predications and therefore represent the properties of states and events. We "reify" states and events, from the Latin word "re(s)" for "thing"; we take them to be *things*. We will use the term "eventuality" to cover both states and events, after Bach (1981).

Eventualities may be possible or actual. When they are actual, this will simply be one of their properties. To say that a state e actually obtains in the real world or that an event e actually occurs in the real world, we will write

    (Rexist e)

That is, e really exists in the real world. If I want to fly, my wanting really exists, but my flying does not.

On the other hand, it is often convenient *not* to introduce eventualities, when they are not needed. Therefore, we will have two parallel sets of predicates – primed and unprimed. The unprimed predicates will be the ordinary predicates we are used to in logical representations of language. For example,

    (give a b c)

says that a gives b to c. When we assert this, we are saying that it actually takes place in the real world. The primed predicate is used to talk about the reified eventualities. The expression

    (give' e a b c)

says that e is a giving event by a of b to c. This does not say that the event actually occurs, only that if it did, it would be a giving event. To say the same thing as (give a b c) says, we have to add that e really exists – (Rexist e). Thus, the relation between the primed and unprimed predicates is given by the axiom schema

```
(forall (x)                                                    (5.1)
      (iff (p x)
           (exists (e)(and (p' e x)(Rexist e)))))
```

That is, p is true of x if and only if there is an eventuality e that is the eventuality of p being true of x and e really exists. (We use the term "axiom *schema*" because there will be a different axiom for each predicate p. The variable x here stands for all the arguments of p.)

Note that the prime has no status in the logic. It is simply a notational convention for naming predicates.

The predicate Rexist along with other modalities of existence is explicated further in Chapter 20.

It will be useful to be able to say that something *is* an eventuality. We will use the predicate eventuality for this.

```
(eventuality e)
```

The first question we need to settle about eventualities is how finely they need to be individuated. If John is running, he is also going. If e1 is an eventuality of John's running, there is an eventuality e2 of John's going. Are e1 and e2 the same or different? One possible model of eventualities is chunks of space–time. Under this interpretation John's running would be the chunk of space–time John occupies while he is running. The chunk of space–time he occupies while he is running can be the same as the chunk of space–time he occupies while he is going, so it would look like e1 and e2 should be the same. This model of eventualities is sometimes useful for fueling intuitions about eventualities, and in many cases it is a perfectly adequate way to think about eventualities.

However, when we are modeling cognition, this is not adequate. Mary may believe that John is going but may not believe that he is running. If eventualities are going to be objects of belief – as they are – then there has to be a distinction between the running and the going. So we will take e1 and e2 to be distinct.

Nevertheless, they are closely related. The event e2 occurs precisely because e1 is occurring. The running entails the going. To capture this relation, we introduce the predicate gen, from the philosophical term "generates." We will say that there is a gen relation between e1 and e2. Moreover, we will say that whenever a running event e1 occurs, there is a going event e2 that it generates:

```
(forall (e1 x)                                                 (5.2)
      (if (run' e1 x)
          (exists (e2)
                  (and (go' e2 x)(gen e1 e2)))))
```

We have more to say about the predicate gen in Section 5.3.

Thus, we individuate eventualities very finely. If they can be described differently, they are different though perhaps closely related eventualities. There is a one-to-one correspondence between eventualities and predications in the logic.

Many writers on semantics distinguish between states and events that obtain or occur in the world and the propositions that describe them. We do not. Because we individuate eventualities so finely, there is a one-to-one mapping between eventualities and predications, and we can use only eventualities and attribute to them properties that seem more appropriate for predications, for example, they have predicates, arguments, and arities.

Propositions are more coarse-grained than predications. For example, (p x) and (not (not (p x))) are different predications but the same proposition. Insofar as we need equivalences like this we will capture them in axioms about real existence and other modalities.

One might object that cognitive predicates like believe are more properly applied to propositions or predications than to eventualities. But where this is so, the predicate applied forces the type of argument, and we can view the cognitive predicate as coercing the eventuality argument into a more propositional kind of entity. Thus, one can read (believe John e) as saying John believes *the proposition describing* eventuality e. Because of this deterministic kind of coercion, we can ignore the distinction between propositions and eventualities, and deal only with the latter. We return to this issue in Chapter 21 on Belief.

5.2 THE STRUCTURE OF EVENTUALITIES

It is often necessary to be able to refer to the participants in a state or event, or equivalently the arguments of a predication. For this we introduce a family of predicates. The first, argn, says that some entity is the nth argument of the eventuality. For example,

```
(forall (e x y z)                                              (5.3)
        (if (give' e x y z)(argn x 1 e)))
```

```
(forall (e x y z)                                              (5.4)
        (if (give' e x y z)(argn y 2 e)))
```

```
(forall (e x y z)                                              (5.5)
        (if (give' e x y z)(argn z 3 e)))
```

Note that we start numbering the arguments of primed predicates from 0 and of unprimed predicates from 1, so that a given entity will be the nth argument of both the primed and unprimed predicates. Thus, x is the 1st argument of both (give x y z) and of (give' e x y z).

To complete the picture, we will say the eventuality is the 0th or "self" argument of itself.

```
(forall (e x y z)                                              (5.6)
        (if (give' e x y z)(argn e 0 e)))
```

Axioms like this will in principle have to be written for every predicate. In practice, they would be handled by special mechanisms.

The constraints on the arguments of argn are as follows:

```
(forall (e x n)                                                (5.7)
        (if (argn x n e)(and (nonNegInteger n)(eventuality e))))
```

That is, if x is the nth argument of e, then n is a nonnegative integer and e is an eventuality. There are no constraints on x.

Something is an eventuality if and only if it is the 0th argument of itself.

```
(forall (e)(iff (eventuality e)(argn e 0 e)))                (5.8)
```

Sometimes, we only want to know that an entity is an argument, and don't care which argument it is. The predicate `arg` will express this relation. It is defined as follows:

```
(forall (e x)                                                (5.9)
        (iff (arg x e)(exists (n)(argn x n e))))
```

x is an arg of e if it is the nth argument for some n.

Eventualities can be embedded in other eventualities. So to say that Mary believes John is tall, we might write

```
(and (believe Mary e)(tall' e John))
```

or equivalently,

```
(and (Rexist e1)(believe' e1 Mary e2)(tall' e2 John))
```

John is not directly an argument of the believing event, so `(arg John e1)` does not hold. But it is often convenient to talk about the looser relation that John bears to the believing event. For this we introduce the predicate `arg*`. The statement `(arg* x e)` means that x is an argument of e, or an argument of an argument of e, or an argument of an argument of an argument of e, and so on. We can define it recursively as follows:

```
(forall (x e1)                                               (5.10)
        (iff (arg* x e1)
             (or (arg x e1)
                 (exists (e2)(and (arg e2 e1)(arg* x e2))))))
```

For example, John is an `arg*` of the believing e1 because John is an `arg*` of the being tall e2 and e2 is an `arg` of e1. John is an `arg*` of e2 because John is an `arg` of e2.

It will occasionally be useful to be able to talk about the predicate of an eventuality, or equivalently, of the unique predication that describes the eventuality. The predicate `pred` will express the relation between the predicate and the eventuality. We will use the unprimed predicate for this purpose, and we will simply assume the predicate names are constants in our logic referring to individuals in our domain of discourse. For example,

```
(forall (e x y z)                                            (5.11)
        (if (give' e x y z)(pred give e)))
```

That is, if e is a giving event by x of y to z, then the entity we call give is the pred of e.

The pred of an eventuality is a predicate.

```
(forall (e p)                                                (5.12)
        (if (pred p e)(and (predicate p)(eventuality e))))
```

Predicates, and thus predications, have an arity, that is, a specific number of arguments, so we can also speak about the "arity" of an eventuality as well. Applied to an eventuality as something in the world rather than in a logic, the arity can be thought of as the number of participants in the eventuality that are designated as central. For example, for a giving event, we will designate the giver, the gift and the recipient as central, and say it has an arity of 3. The arity of predicates or eventualities can be described by axiom schemas like those for `argn` and `pred`. For example,

```
(forall (e x y z)                                               (5.13)
        (if (give' e x y z)(arity 3 e)))
```

Note that in the arity we do not count the 0th or self argument.

The arity of an eventuality is a nonnegative integer.

```
(forall (n e)                                                  (5.14)
        (if (arity n e)(and (nonNegInteger n)(eventuality e))))
```

All of Axioms (5.3), (5.4), (5.5), (5.6), (5.11), and (5.13) are instantiations of axiom schemas. There will, in principle, be one set of these for each predicate in the language.

All eventualities have this structure.

```
(forall (e)                                                    (5.15)
        (iff (eventuality e)
             (exists (p n)
                     (and (pred p e)(arity n e)
                          (forall (i)
                                  (if (and (posInteger i)
                                           (leq i n))
                                      (exists (x)
                                              (argn x i e)))))))))
```

That is, if e is an eventuality, then it has a predicate p, an arity n and n arguments. Since the domain of discourse of the logic is the class of *possible* individuals, this axiom does not say anything about whether or not the eventuality or its arguments exist in the real world. That has to be asserted separately with the predicate `Rexist`. Moreover, it is possible to know some properties of an eventuality without knowing its whole structure as given in Axiom (5.15). We may know that something happened and that it was loud, without knowing that it was the event of a bookcase falling over.

The idea of reifying events is usually attributed to the philosopher Donald Davidson (1967), although he was reluctant to reify states as well, and he did not individuate events as finely as we do. The linguist Emmon Bach (1981) recognized the need for a concept that covered both states and events and introduced the term "eventuality." A relatively brief exposition of eventualities as used here can be found in Hobbs (1985) and a more extensive exposition in Hobbs (1998). The latter contains a number of arguments for the need for eventualities, ways of looking at eventualities, and arguments for very fine individuation. Reification of states and events is a common device in artificial intelligence and linguistics. They are called "states of affairs" in the Head-driven Phrase Structure Grammar of Pollard and Sag (1994). They are called "situations" in the Cyc knowledge base, and at least resemble the situations of the Situation Semantics of Perry and Barwise (1983), though both of these differ substantially from the situations of the situation calculus of McCarthy and Hayes (1969) and Reiter (2001). The latter relate not to a characterization of a possible chunk of space–time, but rather describe the entire state of the world at a given instant. The next instant is another situation. This formalism is good for applications in which a single agent is the only thing that is effecting changes in the world, but it is extremely clumsy for representing natural language or expressing a rich theory of common-sense psychology.

5.3 GENERATION

In Section 5.1 we introduced the gen relation without explicating it. It is useful for distinguishing between two eventualities that are *almost* identical but not quite. The relation could hold between what are intuitively the same event under different descriptions, such as running and going. In (gen e1 e2), someone might believe or desire e2 without believing or desiring e1. The running might be fast but the going slow. Perhaps the running caused one to trip, but the going didn't. We can't *define* gen with necessary and sufficient conditions, but we can state several axioms that constrain how we interpret gen, some involving predicates we have not yet explicated.

The gen relation is between two eventualities.

```
(forall (e1 e2)                                              (5.16)
    (if (gen e1 e2)(and (eventuality e1)(eventuality e2))))
```

It is weaker than equality. In particular, an eventuality does not generate itself. The gen relation is antireflexive.

```
(forall (e) (not (gen e e)))                                 (5.17)
```

It obeys a kind of modus ponens rule with respect to Rexist.

```
(forall (e1 e2)                                              (5.18)
    (if (and (gen e1 e2)(Rexist e1))
        (Rexist e2)))
```

Nevertheless it is stronger than implication. Pat's running implies Pat is going, and also generates it. But Pat's running also implies Pat is alive, but the running does not generate the being alive.

```
(exists (e1 e2) (and (imply e1 e2)(not (gen e1 e2))))        (5.19)
```

The predicate imply is explicated in Chapter 8 on Logic Reified, but it has the obvious meaning.

If (gen e1 e2) holds, then e1 and e2 occupy the same chunk of space–time. We can express this with the predicates atTime, explicated in Chapter 16 on Time, and atLoc, from Chapter 18 on Space.

```
(forall (e1 e2 t)                                            (5.20)
    (if (gen e1 e2)(iff (atTime e1 t)(atTime e2 t))))
```

```
(forall (e1 e2 x s)                                          (5.21)
    (if (gen e1 e2)(iff (atLoc e1 x s)(atLoc e2 x s))))
```

Again, the meaning of these two predicates should be obvious.

PREDICATES INTRODUCED IN THIS CHAPTER

(eventuality e)
  e is an eventuality.

(Rexist e)
  e really exists in the real world.

(gen e1 e2)
  e1 generates the existence of e2.

(argn x n e)
  x is the nth argument of e.

(arg x e)
  x is an argument of e.

(arg* x e)
  x is an argument of e or an arg* of an argument of e.

(pred p e)
  p is the predicate of e.

(predicate p)
  p is a predicate.

(arity n e)
  n is the arity or the number of arguments of e.

In addition, we used but have not yet explicated the following predicates:

(nonNegInteger n)
  n is a nonnegative integer.

(posInteger n)
  n is a positive integer.

(leq n1 n2)
  n1 is less than or equal to n2.

(imply e1 e2)
  e1 implies e2.

(atTime e t)
  e happens or holds at time t.

(atLoc e x)
  e happens or holds at location x.

The first three will be explicated in Chapter 13 on Arithmetic, and the last three in Chapter 8 on Logic Reified, Chapter 16 on Time, and Chapter 18 on Space, respectively. We also used the constants 0, 1, 2, and 3, explicated in Chapter 13. The predicates give, run, go, believe, and tall were only for illustrative purposes.

6

Traditional Set Theory

In this chapter we give axioms and definitions from traditional set theory. What we present is a notational variant of standard Zermelo–Fraenkel set theory (e.g., Cohen, 1966), without the Axiom of Infinity. We are simply silent on whether entities of infinite cardinality exist. We will have no occasion in this book to use them.

Sets will be treated as first-class individuals in the logic. They are viewed as entities in the world that can be referred to by constants and variables in the logic. To assert that something is a set, we use the predication (set s). The fundamental relation between sets and their members will be expressed with the predication (member x s). A set is completely defined by its members.

```
(forall (s1 s2)                                              (6.1)
    (if (set s1)
        (iff (equal s1 s2)
            (and (set s2)
                (forall (x)
                    (iff (member x s1)(member x s2)))))))
```

That is, sets can be equal only to other sets, and they are equal when they contain exactly the same members.

The second argument of the predicate member is necessarily a set. There are no constraints on the first argument.

```
(forall (x s)                                                (6.2)
    (if (member x s)(set s)))
```

This is the first use we have seen of the predicate equal. It will be applied to a number of other kinds of entities as well as we go along. Its principal properties are the familiar reflexivity, symmetricity, and transitivity.

```
(forall (x) (equal x x))                                     (6.3)

(forall (x y) (iff (equal x y)(equal y x)))                  (6.4)

(forall (x y z)                                              (6.5)
    (if (and (equal x y)(equal y z))(equal x z)))
```

It is easily verified that equal sets satisfy these properties.
We will use the predicate nequal for pairs of entities that are not equal.

```
(forall (x y)(iff (nequal x y)(not (equal x y))))            (6.6)
```

The null set is the set with no members.

```
(forall (s)                                                  (6.7)
   (iff (null s)
        (and (set s)(forall (x)(not (member x s))))))
```

Sets can be constructed recursively by adding one element at a time. We will use the predicate addElt for this concept.

```
(forall (s s1 x)                                             (6.8)
   (iff (addElt s s1 x)
        (and (set s)(set s1)
             (forall (y)
                (iff (member y s)
                     (or (equal y x)(member y s1)))))))
```

This says that s is constructed by adding the element x to s1 exactly when the members of s are the members of s1, together with x. It is possible that x is already in s1, in which case s and s1 are equal.

A singleton set consisting of an entity x is defined as follows:

```
(forall (s x)                                                (6.9)
   (iff (singleton s x)
        (exists (s1)
           (and (addElt s s1 x)(null s1)))))
```

This is equivalent to saying that x is the only member of s.

We will also have frequent occasions to refer to sets with exactly two members, so for this we will introduce a parallel term.

```
(forall (s x y)                                              (6.10)
   (iff (doubleton s x y)
        (exists (s1)
           (and (nequal x y)(addElt s s1 x)
                (singleton s1 y)))))
```

This is equivalent to saying that x and y are the only members of s.

The predication (deleteElt s s1 x) says that the set s is obtained from set s1 by deleting an element x.

```
(forall (s s1 x)                                             (6.11)
   (iff (deleteElt s s1 x)
        (and (set s)(set s1)
             (forall (y)
                (iff (member y s)
                     (and (member y s1)(nequal y x)))))))
```

That is, the members of s are those members of s1 not equal to x. Note that we do not require x to be a member of s1. If it is not, s and s1 will be equal.

The predication (replaceElt s s1 x y) says that set s is obtained from set s1 by replacing element x with element y.

```
(forall (s s1 x y)                                                    (6.12)
    (iff (replaceElt s s1 x y)
        (exists (s2)
            (and (deleteElt s2 s1 x)
                 (addElt s s2 y)))))
```

That is, to get s, we delete x from s1 and add y to the result. If x is not a member of s1, replaceElt amounts to adding y. If y is already in s1, replaceElt amounts to deleting x.

The union of two sets is defined in the standard way.

```
(forall (s s1 s2)                                                     (6.13)
    (iff (union s s1 s2)
        (and (set s)(set s1)(set s2)
            (forall (x)
                (iff (member x s)
                    (or (member x s1)(member x s2)))))))
```

That is, set s is the union of sets s1 and s2 if its members are members of either s1 or s2.

We will sometimes have occasion to take the union of three sets, so we define a predicate for this.

```
(forall (s s1 s2 s3)                                                  (6.14)
    (iff (union3 s s1 s2 s3)
        (exists (s4)
            (and (union s s1 s4)(union s4 s2 s3)))))
```

That is, we perform two unions.

Set difference is defined similarly to union.

```
(forall (s s1 s2)                                                     (6.15)
    (iff (setdiff s s1 s2)
        (and (set s)(set s1)(set s2)
            (forall (x)
                (iff (member x s)
                    (and (member x s1)
                         (not (member x s2))))))))
```

Set s is the set difference between s1 and s2 exactly when the members of s are the members of s1 less the members of s2.

The definition of intersection is similar.

```
(forall (s s1 s2)                                                     (6.16)
    (iff (intersection s s1 s2)
        (and (set s)(set s1)(set s2)
            (forall (x)
                (iff (member x s)
                    (and (member x s1)(member x s2)))))))
```

The definition of the subset relation is as follows:

```
(forall (s1 s2)                                                    (6.17)
    (iff (subset s1 s2)
         (and (set s1)(set s2)
              (forall (x)(if (member x s1)(member x s2))))))
```

A proper subset is a subset which is not equal.

```
(forall (s1 s2)                                                    (6.18)
    (iff (properSubset s1 s2)
         (and (subset s1 s2)(nequal s1 s2))))
```

Two sets are disjoint if they have no members in common.

```
(forall (s1 s2)                                                    (6.19)
    (if (and (set s1)(set s2))
        (iff (disjoint s1 s2)
             (not (exists (x)
                     (and (member x s1)(member x s2)))))))
```

We have conditioned this definition on the arguments being sets because in Chapter 12 we will extend it to cover scales as well.

The power set of a set is the set of all its subsets.

```
(forall (s0 s)                                                     (6.20)
    (iff (powerSet s0 s)
         (forall (s1)(iff (member s1 s0)(subset s1 s)))))
```

Finally, we define cardinality recursively with the set construction predicate addElt. We assume addition of integers; (sum n n1 n2) means that n is the sum of n1 and n2. We also assume the numbers 0 and 1 and the predicate nonNegInteger.

```
(forall (n s)                                                      (6.21)
    (iff (card n s)
         (and (nonNegInteger n)(set s)
              (or (and (null s)(equal n 0))
                  (exists (s1 x m)
                      (and (addElt s s1 x)
                           (not (member x s1))
                           (card m s1)
                           (sum n m 1)))))))
```

That is, the cardinality of the null set is zero. The cardinality of a set s obtained by adding a new element x to a set s1 is one more than the cardinality of s1.

It will occasionally be useful to talk about sets of eventualities.

```
(forall (s)                                                       (6.22)
    (iff (eventualities s)
         (and (set s)
              (forall (e)
                  (if (member e s)(eventuality e))))))
```

The predicate eventualities is true of sets all of whose members are eventualities.

PREDICATES INTRODUCED IN THIS CHAPTER

(set s)
    s is a set.

(member x s)
    x is a member of s.

(equal x y)
    x is equal to y.

(nequal x y)
    x is not equal to y.

(null s)
    s is the null set or empty set.

(addElt s s1 x)
    s is obtained from s1 by adding x.

(singleton s x)
    s consists of the single element x.

(doubleton s x y)
    s consists of the two elements x and y.

(deleteElt s s1 x)
    s is obtained from s1 by deleting x.

(replaceElt s s1 x y)
    s is obtained from s1 by replacing x with y.

(union s s1 s2)
    s is the union of s1 and s2.

(union3 s s1 s2 s3)
    s is the union of s1, s2, and s3.

(setdiff s s1 s2)
    s is the set difference of s1 and s2.

(intersection s s1 s2)
    s is the intersection of s1 and s2.

(subset s1 s2)
    s1 is a subset of s2.

(properSubset s1 s2)
    s1 is a proper subset of s2.

(disjoint s1 s2)
    For sets, s1 and s2 are disjoint.

(powerSet s0 s)
    s0 is the set of all of s's subsets.

(card n s)
    n is the cardinality of s.

(eventualities s)
    s is a set of eventualties.

In addition, we used the predicates sum and nonNegInteger and the constants 0 and 1, which will be discussed in Chapter 13 on Arithmetic.

7

Substitution, Typical Elements, and Instances

7.1 SUBSTITUTION

We will frequently have occasion to talk about eventualities that exhibit the same pattern, are similar, or are tokens of the same type. Thus, we need predicates for describing this similarity in structure.

The first predicate we will need expresses what we get in ordinary logics by substitution. We need to axiomatize substitution. We would like to be able to say that if John believes he is successful and Mary believes she is successful, then John plays the same role in his belief as Mary plays in hers. Thus, suppose we know the following:

```
(believe' e1 J e3), (successful' e3 J)
(believe' e2 M e4), (successful' e4 M)
```

We would then like to be able to say that if you substitute M for J in e1, you get e2. Alternatively, J plays the same role in e1 that M plays in e2. The way we say this is

```
(subst J e1 M e2)
```

The definition of subst is a bit complex, but the reader should be able to work through the axiom and see why it holds for the above example. (Ignore the fifth line for now.)

```
(forall (x e1 y e2)                                                    (7.1)
    (iff (subst x e1 y e2)
        (exists (p n)
            (and (pred p e1)(pred p e2)(arity n e1)(arity n e2)
                 (noSubstTypelt x e1 y e2)
                 (forall (i z1 z2)
                     (if (and (posInteger i)(leq i n)
                             (argn z1 i e1)(argn z2 i e2))
                         (and (iff (eventuality z1)
                                   (eventuality z2))
```

```
            (if (not (eventuality z1))
                (and (if (nequal z1 x)
                         (equal z2 z1))
                     (if (equal z1 x)
                         (equal z2 y))))
                (if (eventuality z1)
                    (subst x z1 y z2)))))))))))
```

This defines what it is for x to play the same role in e1 as y plays in e2. Both e1 and e2 have to be eventualities; this follows from the fact that they have predicates and arities. They have the same predicate p and the same arity n (line 4). Then we look at all the corresponding pairs of non-self arguments z1 and z2 of e1 and e2 (lines 6–8). z1 and z2 are either both eventualities or both not eventualities (lines 9–10). If z1 is not an eventuality and is not the same as x, then it remains unchanged; z2 is equal to z1 (lines 11–13). If z1 is the same as x, then z2 is y; this is where y is substituted for x (lines 14–15). If z1 (and hence, z2) is an eventuality, then we recurse and substitute x for y in those corresponding arguments; x plays the same role in the argument z1 that y plays in argument z2 (lines 16–17).

Two substitutions can be done by doing one at a time.

```
(forall (x1 x2 e1 y1 y2 e2)                                    (7.2)
   (iff (subst2 x1 x2 e1 y1 y2 e2)
        (exists (e3)
            (and (subst x1 e1 y1 e3)
                 (subst x2 e3 y2 e2)))))
```

For example, if Mary loves John and Sue loves Bill, then we want to say that the pair <Mary, John> plays the same role in the first loving event as the pair <Sue, Bill> plays in the second.

```
(love' e1 M J), (love' e2 S B)
```

We express this by first substituting Sue for Mary in e1 to get e3:

```
(love' e3 S J)
```

and then substituting Bill for John in e3 to get e2. Of course, the existence or nonexistence of e1 and/or e2 says nothing about whether or not e3 holds.

Note that by definition (7.1), the expression (subst e1 e1 e2 e2) means that the predications in which e1 and e2 are the self arguments have the same predicates and the same non-self arguments. That is, the only distinguishing features they have will be external to the predications in which they are self arguments.

7.2 TYPICAL ELEMENTS

Among the things we can think about are both specific eventualities, like "Fido is barking," and general or abstract types of eventualities, like "Dogs bark." We do not want to treat these as radically different kinds of entities. We would like both, at some level, to be treated simply as eventualities that can be the content of thoughts.

For this it is convenient, although nonstandard, to reify the universally quantified variable in statements about all elements of sets. We would like to go from the standard set theoretic notation

```
s = { x | p(x) }
```

or its logical equivalent,

```
(forall (x) (iff (member x s)(p x)))
```

to a simple statement that p is true of a "typical element" of s by reifying typical elements. We use the term "typical element," although "reified universally quantified variable" might be a more precise name for it (cf. McCarthy, 1977). The predication

```
(typelt x s)
```

will say that x is a typical element of the set s. The second argument is constrained to be a set, and conversely, every set has a typical element.

```
(forall (s) (iff (set s)                                    (7.3)
                 (exists (x) (typelt x s))))
```

There is no assumption of uniqueness of typical elements.

The principal property of typical elements is that all properties of typical elements are inherited by the real members of the set.

```
(forall (x s y e1 e2)                                        (7.4)
        (if (and (typelt x s)(member y s)(subst x e1 y e2)
                 (Rexist e1))
            (Rexist e2)))
```

The term "typical element" has been used in previous papers (Hobbs, 1983, 1995, 1998). Some have complained that the term "typical element" is too close to the term "prototype" and in any case suggests defeasibility, that is, that there may be properties of typical elements that are not inherited by all of the real members. The reader may overcome this feeling by thinking of typelt as meaning "type element," the entity that represents the type defined by membership in the set. Indeed we will sometimes use this term. We have also considered using the term "any element" (anyelt). However, this leads to frequent recourse to the barbarism "the any element" or "an any element" to indicate that we are talking about that entity rather than any real member of the set. The intent of typelt is that all of its properties are inherited by all of the real members, as indicated in Axiom (7.4).

One reason for distinguishing between a set and its typical element is to capture the distinction between the two sentences

The men ran.
The men met.

In the first, each individual man runs, so the running would be predicated of a typical element. In the second, it is the set of men that met. Meeting is not something individual men can do by themselves.

A related but stronger concept is represented by the predicate dset. This says that a set s with typical element x contains just those elements for which some eventuality e really exists.

```
(dset s x e)
```

The d is for "defined"; the set s is defined by the property e. The first argument of dset is a set, the second one is its typical element, and the typical element occurs somewhere, perhaps embedded, in the eventuality.

```
(forall (s x e)                                              (7.5)
        (if (dset s x e)
            (and (set s)(typelt x s)(arg* x e))))
```

For example, s might be the set of things Mary believes to be red.

```
(dset s x e), (believe' e M e1), (red' e1 x)
```

If (p' e x), holds, that is, if e is the eventuality of p being true of x, then (dset s x e) is just a way of saying s = {x | p(x)}.

An entity is a member of a defined set if and only if the property e holds for it. (Ignore the third line for now.)

```
(forall (s x e y e1)                                         (7.6)
    (if (and (dset s x e)(subst x e y e1)(Rexist e)
            (notSubsetTypelt y s))
        (iff (member y s)(Rexist e1))))
```

The rightward implication of the iff clause follows immediately from Axioms (7.4) and (7.5). The leftward implication is new and what the concept dset adds over and above typelt.

A typical element of a set exists in the real world exactly when all the real elements exist in the real world. For some eventuality involving a typical element of a set to exist in the real world is just for the corresponding eventualities involving the real elements to exist in the real world.

Axioms (7.4) and (7.6) are useful but they bring with them some thorny technical problems. Essentially, we have to be careful about applying them to eventualities whose predicates are typelt and member. The reader who is willing to take these axioms on faith and believe that in this book they will be used appropriately can skip the next section, where these issues are discussed.

7.3 HANDLING SOME THORNY ISSUES

As they are stated, Axioms (7.4) and (7.6) and the use of typical elements more generally raise some difficult problems.

In Axiom (7.4), suppose (typelt' e x s) holds, that is, that e is the property of x being a typical element of s. Then it seems that each real member of s will inherit that property and thus be a typical element of the set as well. Applying this axiom again, that says that anything true of any of the members would be true of all the other members as well.

In Axiom (7.6), consider what happens when we let y be equal to x and e1 to e. Trivially, (subst x e x e) holds. If e is a property that really exists, then it follows that x, a typical element of s, is a member of s as well as all the real members. When we combine this with the definition of cardinality in Chapter 6, we see that a set {a, b, c}, if x is different from a, b, and c, would have at least four members: a, b, c, and that typical element of the set.

The Law of the Excluded Middle says that a property either is true or is not true of an entity. Suppose we have a set of pencils, some but not all of which are red. Is a typical element red or not red? It would seem that if typical elements are red, then all of the real members are red, and if a typical element is not red, then none of the real members are red.

To get around this family of problems, in Hobbs (1995) a scheme of predicate indexing was introduced. This was fairly complicated, but the essentials of the idea can be described without too much difficulty. Base-level predicates, applying to real entities, were subscripted with 0. If a predicate was applied to a typical element of a set, it was subscripted with the name of the set and defined to be true exactly when the base-level predicate was true of all the real members of the set.

```
(forall (x s)
   (if (typelt x s)
       (iff (p-s x)
            (forall (y) (if (member y s)(p-0 y))))))
```

In a sense, we are transforming the predicate `red` into the predicate `all-red`. Then if a typical member of the set is `all-red`, all the real members are `red`, and conversely.

This solves the problem of the Law of the Excluded Middle. The predicate `red` (or `red-0`) is not true of typical elements, because base-level predicates don't apply to typical elements. The predicate `all-red` (or `red-s`) does apply to typical elements, and it is false, because not all the pencils are red.

It might seem that we could take this `not all-red` property of the typical element and pass it down to all the real members, so that they would all be not red. But that would be a scoping error, a confusion between `not all-red` and `all not-red`. These are not equivalent.

The subscripts on the predicates can be ignored in almost all cases. For example, consider the inference that if x believes p, then x is a person.

```
(forall (x p) (if (believe x p)(person x)))
```

This holds true as well of typical elements. If a typical element x of a set `believes-s` p, then that means all members of the set believe p, so all members of the set are persons, so `person-s` is true of the typical element. The inference holds for typical element predicates as well as base-level predicates.

This is the normal case. We will have a predication about a typical element involving a predicate from some non–set-theoretic content theory, and we will want all the real members of the set to inherit that property.

For this reason, we will reintroduce the unsubscripted predicate, now as a cover term for all the subscripted predicates. An unsubscripted predicate p is true of an entity exactly when some subscripted version of that predicate is true of the entity.

```
(forall (x)
        (iff (p x)
             (exists (i) (p-i x))))
```

Then suppose (p x) holds. If x is an individual, that is, not a typical element of a set, then (p-0 x) will hold. If x is a typical element of s, then (p-s x) will hold.

This means that we will be operating at a less specific level than if we used subscripted predicates. If we are only told (red x), we don't immediately know whether (red-0 x) or (red-s x). But this will almost never get us into trouble, and results in a much simpler formalism.

Returning to the problem of the Law of the Excluded Middle, there are three predicates we need to consider. The predicate red-0 is false of a typical element of the set of pencils because base-level predicates are always false of typical elements. The predicate red-s is false of the typical element because not all the real members of the set are red-0. The unsubscripted predicate red is false of the typical element because none of the subscripted predicates are true of it.

Where the unsubscripted predicates do get us into trouble is with set-theoretic predicates, because of the problems with Axioms (7.4) and (7.6) described previously. In Hobbs (1995) it is noted, as a warning for future development, that "set-theoretic axioms have to be formulated carefully." We are now at that point.

In this book, all but two of the predicates used will be the unsubscripted predicates, and thus can apply to real elements and typical elements. The two predicates are typelt and member. These predicates are closely related. The predicate member, as we are using it, is the base-level predicate member-0, because that is what we need in Chapter 6 in formulating traditional set theory. The predication (member-s x s) is then true of typical elements of s just in case every member of s is a member of s. So the predicate member-s has exactly the same properties as the predicate typelt. They are equivalent; typelt is in fact just another name for member-s.

As we are using the (implicitly) subscripted predicates member (member-0) and typelt (member-s), we cannot allow real members to be freely substituted for typical elements in Axiom (7.4), and we have to be careful about concluding membership in Axiom (7.6). Failure to do these things is what resulted in the problems. To avert these problems and yet retain the power and utility of Axioms (7.4) and (7.6), we have introduced a condition into the definition of substitution (subst), namely (noSubstTypelt x e1 y e2) in the fifth line of (7.1). We are doing a kind of surgery on the definition of subst on just those cases that cause trouble for typical elements – when e1 itself is a typical element relation between x and s and y is a member of s.

```
(forall (x e1 y e2)                                           (7.7)
   (iff (noSubstTypelt x e1 y e2)
        (exists (s) (and (typelt' e1 x s)(member y s)))))
```

Now Axiom (7.4) will not allow us to conclude that a real member is also a typical element, because (subst x e1 y e2) will not be true if e1 is the property of x being a typical element of a set of which y is a member.

The problem with Axiom (7.6) is that the problematic conclusion (member y s) involves the implicitly subscripted predicate member. We will thus run into problems whenever y is a typical element of s or of a subset of s. Without line 3, all the antecedents of the leftward implication can be satisfied, yet y, being a typical element, will be the wrong sort of entity to have the base-level predicate member true of it. To get around this problem, we do surgery on Axiom (7.6) and rule out the problematic cases with the condition (notSubsetTypelt y s).

```
(forall (y s)                                                        (7.8)
   (iff (notSubsetTypelt y s)
        (not (exists (s1)(and (typelt y s1)(subset s1 s))))))
```

Note that the `dset` predication does not necessarily guarantee the existence of the set; that is, there is no Axiom of Comprehension. If e is the eventuality that x is not a member of s, then we would have the Russell paradox: An entity y is member of the set if and only if it is not a member of the set. Such a set s does not exist in the real world.

Note also that the typical element of one set may be a legitimate member of another set. None of its properties are inherited by the other members of the latter set.

7.4 FUNCTIONAL DEPENDENCIES

Every person has a mother. The usual way to express this in logic is

```
(forall (x)
   (if (person x)
       (exists (y) (mother y x))))
```

This is a general situation or eventuality in the world, and it can be the content of a thought. Therefore we would like to reify it. This means we have to reify its parts: the x and the y. We already know how to reify the x. It is a typical element of the set of entities defined by the property e where (person' e x), that is, the set of persons. Here we discuss how to reify the y.

Not all the mothers are the same, so we can say that the mother is "functionally dependent" on the person, with respect to the property of being a mother. We will abbreviate this predicate to `fd`. The predication (fd y x e) says that y is functionally dependent on x with respect to property e. The argument x must be a typical element of a set, and both x and y must be involved somehow in e.

```
(forall (x y e)                                                      (7.9)
   (if (fd y x e)
       (and (arg* x e)(arg* y e)
            (exists (s) (typelt x s)))))
```

In the preceding example, e is the eventuality such that (mother' e y x), that is, the property of y being the mother of x.

The principal property of `fd` is that when e holds and a real entity instantiates x, then there is a real entity that instantiates y and the corresponding eventuality holds.

```
(forall (x y e s x1)                                                 (7.10)
   (if (and (fd y x e)(Rexist e)(typelt x s)(member x1 s))
       (exists (y1 e1)
           (and (subst2 x y e x1 y1 e1)(Rexist e1)))))
```

For example, Charles is a person, so he is a member of s. The predication (Rexist e) holds because it really is true that every person has a mother. Suppose Elizabeth is Charles's mother. Then Elizabeth is y1 and e1 is the eventuality such that (mother' e1 Elizabeth Charles) holds, that is, the eventuality of Elizabeth being Charles's mother.

The y1's constitute a set too, and thus have a typical element. It would be pleasant if we could assume that the functionally dependent entity y was the same as that typical element. (This was suggested in Hobbs (1983).) But this is not possible because, in this case, it would imply that every mother is the mother of everyone.

```
(mother y x) ⇒ (mother y1 x)        for some y1, by (7.10)
             ⇒ (mother y1 x1)       for every x1, by (7.4)
```

Corresponding to the functional dependency, there is a function (normally called a "skolem function") that maps any element x1 of the set s into the corresponding y1, and that function has a range. We will define these here.

```
(forall (x x1 y y1 e)                                              (7.11)
    (iff (skfct y1 y x1 x e)
         (and (fd y x e)
              (exists (e1)
                  (and (subst2 x y e x1 y1 e1)
                       (if (Rexist e)(Rexist e1)))))))
```

The expression (skfct y1 y x1 x e) says that y1 is the value of the function defined by the functional dependency (fd y x e) applied to x1.

The range of the functional dependency is then the set of all values of the skolem function.

```
(forall (s1 x y e)                                                (7.12)
    (iff (rangeFd s1 y x e)
         (forall (y1)
             (iff (member y1 s1)
                  (exists (x1) (skfct y1 y x1 x e)))))))
```

The predicates typelt, dset, and fd are enough for reifying universally quantified propositions. It is well known that any logical expression can be rewritten in "prenex" form, in which all the universal quantifiers outscope all the existential quantifiers. All of the existentially quantified variables will then have fd relations with universally quantified variables.

With the device of skolemization, functions are introduced for every existentially quantified variable; their arguments are all the universally quantified variables, and their values are the existentially quantified variables. For example, if we were to express the statement that any point <x, y> on a horizontal grid, oriented in the cardinal directions, has a latitude, a longitude, and an elevation, the prenex form would be

```
(forall (x y)
    (exists (a b c)
        (and (lat a x y)(long b x y)(elev c x y))))
```

(a is the latitude of <x,y>, b is the longitude of <x,y>, and c is the elevation at <x,y>.) After skolemization, this would be

```
(forall (x y)
    (and (lat (f x y) x y)(long (g x y) x y)(elev (h x y) x y)))
```

Our fd predicate captures these functional relations f, g, and h.

But in fact we know that longitude depends only on x, latitude depends only on y, and elevation depends on both. So rather than represent the functional dependencies in the mechanical way skolemization does, involving all the universally quantified variables, we would just have the following fd relations:

(fd a y e1), (fd b x e2), (fd c x e3), (fd c y e3)

where e1, e2, and e3 are the lat, long, and elev relations, respectively.

When a functionally dependent entity depends on more than one typical element, that is, when an existentially quantified variable depends on more than one universally quantified variable, we can instantiate the functionally dependent entity one step at a time. In the elevation example, we would first instantiate the x to a specific x-value x1 using Axiom (7.10), giving us (elev c1 x1 y). The c1 is then functionally dependent on y, and we can use Axiom (7.10) again to give us (elev c2 x1 y1). The entity c2 is now a real elevation, rather than a functionally dependent entity.

But to get this to work, we need a rule that passes functional dependence relations down to partial instantiations. The following axiom does this.

$$
\begin{array}{ll}
\text{(forall (c1 c x1 x y e e1)} & \text{(7.13)} \\
\quad \text{(if (and (skfct c1 c x1 x e) (fd c y e) (nequal x y)} & \\
\qquad \quad \text{(subst2 c1 x1 e1 c x e))} & \\
\quad \text{(fd c1 y e1)))} &
\end{array}
$$

The relation (fd c1 y e1) is inherited from (fd c y e) whenever some other universally quantified variable x induces a partial instantiation of c.

In the elevation example, c1 will range over all the elevations for points whose longitude is x1. The exact real elevation will depend on the latitude y.

We will say that an entity that is a typical element of a set or functionally dependent on a typical element of a set is nonspecific.

$$
\begin{array}{ll}
\text{(forall (x)} & \text{(7.14)} \\
\quad \text{(iff (nonspecific x)} & \\
\qquad \text{(or (exists (s) (typelt x s))} & \\
\qquad \quad \text{(exists (y s e) (and (typelt y s) (fd x y e)))))))} &
\end{array}
$$

An entity is specific if and only if it is not nonspecific.

(forall (x) (iff (specific x) (not (nonspecific x))))   (7.15)

7.5 INSTANCES

If x is a typical element of a set and x1 is a member of the set, we can say that x1 is an instance of x. We would like to extend this notion to eventualities.

First let us define the set of parameters in an abstract eventuality e.

$$
\begin{array}{ll}
\text{(forall (s e)} & \text{(7.16)} \\
\quad \text{(iff (parameters s e)} & \\
\qquad \text{(forall (x)} & \\
\qquad \quad \text{(iff (member x s)} & \\
\qquad \qquad \text{(exists (s1)} & \\
\qquad \qquad \quad \text{(and (arg* x e)(typelt x s1)))))))))} &
\end{array}
$$

The parameters of an abstract eventuality e are those typical elements of sets that are somehow involved in e; arg* is a precise characterization of "somehow involved in."

A partial instantiation results from instantiating some of the parameters of the abstract eventuality either with real members of their sets or with typical elements of subsets. We can define a partial instance in this way.

```
(forall (e1 e)                                                    (7.17)
    (iff (partialInstance e1 e)
        (forall (s x)
            (if (and (member x s)(parameters s e))
                (exists (x1 s1)
                    (and (subst x e x1 e1)(typelt x s1)
                        (or (member x1 s1)
                            (exists (s2)
                                (and (typelt x1 s2)
                                    (subset s2 s1))))))))))
```

That is, e1 is a partial instance of e exactly when for every parameter x in e, there is a corresponding entity x1 in e1 which is either a member of the set that x ranges over or is a typical element of a subset of that set. Note that we use the predicate subset rather than properSubset, so one limiting case of a partial instance of e is e itself. Moreover, it admits some parameters being instantiated while others are not.

Also, we could exercise the option of line 7 in the axiom and use only real members, in which case we have a complete instantiation. In this case, there are no remaining typical elements and thus no parameters. So we can define a complete instantiation as a partial instantiation with no remaining parameters.

```
(forall (e1 e)                                                    (7.18)
    (iff (instance e1 e)
        (and (partialInstance e1 e)
            (forall (s1)
                (if (parameters s1 e1) (null s1))))))
```

Equivalently, we could have used Axiom (7.17) without the last three lines.

We can say that a eventuality type e1 holds for an entity y as its x parameter if when the entity is substituted for x in the eventuality type, the resulting instantiation really exists.

```
(forall (e1 y x)                                                  (7.19)
    (iff (holdsFor e1 y x)
        (exists (s e2)
            (and (subst y e2 x e1)(typelt x s)(member y s)
                (Rexist e2)))))
```

For example, if e1 is the eventuality type of a person being tall, then e1 holds for John if John is tall, that is, if his tallness really exists.

Predicates Introduced in This Chapter

(subst x e1 y e2)
   x plays the same role in e1 that y plays in e2.

(subst2 x1 x2 e1 y1 y2 e2)

The pair <x1,x2> plays the same role in e1 that the pair <y1,y2> plays in e2.

(typelt x s)
   x is a typical element of s.

(dset s x e)
   s is the set with typical element x defined by the property e.

(noSubstTypelt x e1 y e2)
   It is not the case that e1 is a typical element relation between x and some set
   s and y is a member of s; this blocks using subst when e1 is a typical element
   property.

(notSubsetTypelt y s)
   y is not a typical element of a subset of s; this blocks problematic applications of
   Axiom (7.6).

(fd y x e)
   y is functionally dependent on x by a function described by e.

(skfct y1 y x1 x e)
   y1 is the value of the function corresponding to the functional dependency of y
   on x with respect to e when applied to x1.

(rangeFd s y x e)
   s is the range of the values of the entity y that is functionally dependent on x with
   respect to e.

(nonspecific x)
   x is a typical element or functionally dependent on a typical element.

(specific x)
   x is not nonspecific.

(parameters s e)
   s is the set of typical elements that appear somewhere in e as arguments.

(partialInstance e1 e)
   e1 is a partial instantiation of e; nonspecific arguments are either instantiated or
   specialized.

(instance e1 e)
   e1 is a complete instantiation of e; all nonspecific arguments are instantiated.

(holdsFor e1 y x)
   The eventuality type e1 holds for entity y; substituting y for a nonspecific argument x of e1 yields an eventuality that really exists.

8

Logic Reified

8.1 CONJUNCTION

Since we are reifying eventualities and identifying them with propositions, we need as well to reify combinations of eventualities. In particular, we need to be able to talk about the conjunction and disjunction of two eventualities/propositions, about their negation, and about conditionals or implications.

We will use the name of the logical operator as the name of the predicate, and as with all predicates there is a primed version of the predicate that is basic. We will generally, although not always, use the primed version. Confusion with the logical operators should not arise. A good rule of thumb is that if the arguments of and, or, and not are predications, then and, or, and not are the logical operators; if the arguments are variables, then and, or, and not are predicates in our "Logic Reified" theory. Thus, in (and (p x)(q x)), and is the logical operator, and in (and e1 e2), and is the predicate explicated below. In any case, if a confusion does arise, the meaning of the two expressions will be the same.

Conjunction is the most straightforward. The and of two eventualities is itself an eventuality, and it exists when its two constituent eventualities exist.

```
(forall (e e1 e2)                                          (8.1)
    (if (and' e e1 e2)
        (and (eventuality e) (eventuality e1) (eventuality e2)
            (iff (Rexist e)
                (and (Rexist e1)(Rexist e2))))))
```

This says that if e is the conjunction of e1 and e2, then all of e, e1, and e2 are eventualities, and e really exists exactly when e1 and e2 both really exist.

It does not matter whether the arguments of and' are eventuality types or eventuality tokens.

It is often convenient to apply the Rexist predicate and similar predicates to sets of eventualities. When this is done, it will be interpreted as conjunction. In fact,

116

existence of a set in the real world is always true whenever all its members exist in the real world, so we need not restrict the axiom to eventualities.

```
(forall (s)                                                        (8.2)
    (if (set s)
        (iff (Rexist s)
            (forall (e)
                (if (member e s)(Rexist e))))))
```

8.2 NEGATION

The simplest way to characterize negation is analogous to Axiom (8.1). The negation of an eventuality really exists if and only if the eventuality doesn't.

```
(forall (e1 e2)                                                    (8.3)
    (if (not' e1 e2)
        (and (eventuality e1)(eventuality e2)
            (iff (Rexist e1)
                (not (Rexist e2))))))
```

If e1 is the eventuality of e2's not obtaining, then e1 really exists exactly when e2 does not really exist.

However, a problem arises with negation. Generally, what is negated is not an eventuality token but an eventuality type. Consider the situation where e2 is an eventuality token of the door being opened. Then we want e1 to be the negation of that, and expect its existence to mean that the door is not being opened. Suppose in e2 the door is opened two feet; being an eventuality token, it can have properties this specific that are not represented in the eventuality structure. Then e1 could be the eventuality token of the door being opened one foot. Axiom (8.3) would hold; if the door is opened two feet, it's not opened one foot, and if it's opened one foot, it's not opened two feet.

We could define a stronger concept – call it nott' – which says that there is an eventuality type of which e2 is an instance, and the negation is the negation of that eventuality type.

```
(forall (e1 e2)                                                    (8.4)
    (if (nott' e1 e2)
        (exists (e3)
            (and (instance e2 e3)(not' e1 e3)))))
```

In the door opening example, e2 is the eventuality token of opening the door two feet, e3 could be the eventuality type of opening the door in general, and e1 would be the eventuality type that negates the latter.

This may seem highly underspecified, as we are not demanding that e3 encompass all openings of the door. It could be the eventuality type of opening the door today, or within the last half hour, or only from the inside of the room. But in fact in natural language, we always must determine from context what the set of eventuality tokens is that is being ruled out. The sentence "John didn't open the door" usually does not mean that he never in the past opened the door. It is usually very highly contextually constrained. That is, part of the interpretation process is exactly to find the appropriate eventuality type e3 that is being negated.

In this book, when we use the predicate not', we will generally apply it to eventuality types. For example, one person might have a goal of e2 while another person has a conflicting goal of e1 where (not' e1 e2) holds. Goals are generally eventuality types rather than tokens, so the negation presents us with no problem.

The other context in which negation appears is in changes of state where some eventuality exists before the change and does not exist after the change. For this, we will define predicates changeFrom and changeTo that will hide the complexities in dealing with types and tokens. This is done in Chapter 14.

A weaker version of Axiom (8.3) is

```
(forall (e1 e2)                                              (8.5)
    (if (and (not' e1 e2)(Rexist e1))
        (and (eventuality e1) (eventuality e2)
             (not (Rexist e2)))))
```

If a negation really exists, the thing negated doesn't.

8.3 DISJUNCTION AND IMPLICATION

Disjunctions and implications also generally take eventuality types as arguments. We will not insist on it in the definitions, but we will use the predicates in this book in this fashion.

Disjunction can be defined analogous to conjunction.

```
(forall (e e1 e2)                                           (8.6)
    (if (or' e e1 e2)
        (and (eventuality e) (eventuality e1) (eventuality e2)
             (iff (Rexist e)
                  (or (Rexist e1)(Rexist e2))))))
```

If eventuality e is the disjunction of eventualities e1 and e2, then e really exists exactly when one of e1 and e2 really exists.

Disjunction can be applied to a whole set of eventualities. We will say that the disjunction of a set really exists exactly when one of the members of the set really exists.

```
(forall (e s)                                               (8.7)
    (if (disjunction e s)
        (and (eventuality e)(eventualities s)
             (iff (Rexist e)
                  (exists (e1)
                      (and (member e1 s)(Rexist e1)))))))
```

Implication is defined similarly to or', except that in addition to a single eventuality as the antecedent, we will allow a set of eventualities as well. The set will be interpreted as the conjunction.

```
(forall (e e1 e2)                                           (8.8)
    (if (imply' e e1 e2)
        (and (eventuality e) (eventuality e2)
             (or (eventuality e1) (eventualities e1)))))
```

The implication really exists provided the consequent really exists whenever the antecedent really exists.

```
(forall (e e1 e2)                                          (8.9)
   (if (imply' e e1 e2)
       (iff (Rexist e)
            (if (Rexist e1)(Rexist e2)))))
```

A set of eventualities really exists exactly when each of the eventualities exists, so this definition covers the case of e1 being a set of eventualities as well as the case of its being a single eventuality.

The most important rule of inference involving implication is Modus Ponens. It can be stated as follows:

```
(forall (e e1 e2)                                          (8.10)
   (if (and (imply' e e1 e2)(Rexist e)(Rexist e1))
       (Rexist e2)))
```

That is, if e is the implication from e1 to e2, and e and e1 really exist, then e2 also really exists. This is an immediate consequence of Axioms (8.9) and (8.2).

Implication is transitive. If e1 implies e2 and e2 implies e3, then e1 implies e3. This follows from Axioms (8.9) and (8.2).

```
(forall (e1 e2 e3 i1 i2 i3)                                (8.11)
   (if (and (imply' i1 e1 e2)(imply' i2 e2 e3)(imply' i3 e1 e3)
            (Rexist i1)(Rexist i2))
       (Rexist i3)))
```

Two sets of eventualities are inconsistent if one implies an eventuality and the other implies its negation. That is, they have inconsistent consequences.

```
(forall (s1 s2)                                            (8.12)
   (iff (inconsistent s1 s2)
        (and (eventualities s1) (eventualities s2)
             (exists (e1 e2)
                (and (imply s1 e1)(imply s2 e2)(not' e2 e1))))))
```

We can say that some set s1 of eventualities minimally proves an eventuality e2 if s1 implies e2 but no proper subset of s1 proves e2, and furthermore e2 is not itself a member of s1.

```
(forall (s1 e2)                                            (8.13)
   (iff (minimallyProves s1 e2)
        (and (not (member e2 s1))
             (imply s1 e2)
             (not (exists (s2)
                      (and (properSubset s2 s1)
                           (imply s2 e2)))))))
```

Ruling out e2 in s1 is a way of eliminating the trivial case where {e2} minimally proves e2.

Quantifiers are also a part of logic, but these were dealt with in Chapter 7. The reification of a universally quantified proposition is an eventuality that involves typical elements.

PREDICATES INTRODUCED IN THIS CHAPTER

(and' e e1 e2)
   e is the eventuality of both e1 and e2 existing.

(not' e1 e2)
   e1 is the eventuality of e2 not existing.

(nott' e1 e2)
   e1 is the eventuality of nothing of e2's type existing.

(or' e e1 e2)
   e is the eventuality of either e1 or e2 existing.

(disjunction e s)
   e is the eventuality of some member of s existing.

(imply' e e1 e2)
   e is the eventuality of an implicational relation between e1 and e2 existing.

(inconsistent s1 s2)
   s1 and s2 are inconsistent sets of eventualities.

(minimallyProves s1 e2)
   s1 proves e2 and no subset of s1 proves e2.

9

Functions and Sequences

9.1 PAIRS AND FUNCTIONS

It will be useful to have two predicates labeling something as an ordered pair, or more simply, a "pair." The expression (pair0 p) says that p is a pair, while the expression (pair p x y) says that p is the pair <x,y>.

```
(forall (p)                                                    (9.1)
    (iff (pair0 p)
         (exists (x y) (pair p x y))))
```

The distinguishing feature of pairs is that they have a first and a second element.

```
(forall (p x y)                                                (9.2)
    (if (pair p x y)
        (and (first x p)(second y p))))
```

We could define pairs in the traditional way in set theoretic terms. The pair <x,y> is defined as the set {x, {{y}}. This is certainly a model of the axioms involving pair, but it would be pedantic to call this the definition.

Two pairs are equal exactly when their first elements are equal and their second elements are equal.

```
(forall (p1 x1 y1 p2 x2 y2)                                    (9.3)
    (if (or (pair p1 x1 y1)(pair p2 x2 y2))
        (iff (equal p1 p2)
             (and (pair p1 x1 y1)(pair p2 x2 y2)
                  (equal x1 x2)(equal y1 y2)))))
```

That is, if either p1 or p2 is a pair, then they are equal if and only if they are both pairs, their first elements are equal, and their second elements are equal.

The first and second elements of a pair are unique.

```
(forall (p x1 x2 y1 y2)                                        (9.4)
    (if (and (pair p x1 y1)(pair p x2 y2))
        (and (equal x1 x2)(equal y1 y2))))
```

A function f from a set s1 onto a set s2 is a set of pairs in which each element of s1 occurs exactly once as the first element in a pair, and every element of s2 occurs as a second element of at least one pair. We will call this predicate function0 because in Chapter 12 we will extend it to scale-to-scale functions as well.

```
(forall (f s1 s2)                                                  (9.5)
    (iff (function0 f s1 s2)
        (and (set s1)(set s2)(set f)
            (forall (p)
                (if (member p f)
                    (exists (x y)
                        (and (member x s1)(member y s2)
                            (pair p x y)))))
            (forall (x)
                (if (member x s1)
                    (exists (p)
                        (and (member p f)(first x p)))))
            (forall (p1 p2 x)
                (if (and (first x p1)(first x p2)
                        (member p1 f)(member p2 f))
                    (equal p1 p2)))
            (forall (y)
                (if (member y s2)
                    (exists (p)
                        (and (member p f)(second y p)))))))))
```

Lines 4–8 of this definition say that a function is a set of pairs, the first elements of which come from s1 and the second elements of which come from s2. Lines 9–12 say that there is a value of the function for every element of s1. Lines 13–16 say that that value is unique. Lines 17–20 say that every element of s2 is a value of some member of s1 under the function f.

We won't use these terms formally, but we can call s1 the domain of the function and s2 the range.

```
(forall (f s1 s2) (if (function0 f s1 s2)(domain s1 f)))           (9.6)
```

```
(forall (f s1 s2) (if (function0 f s1 s2)(range s2 f)))            (9.7)
```

If f is a function from s1 to s2, we will say that f maps an element x of s1 to an element y of s2 when the pair <x,y> is a member of f.

```
(forall (f x y)                                                    (9.8)
    (iff (map f x y)
        (exists (s1 s2 p)
            (and (function0 f s1 s2)(member p f)
                (first x p)(second y p)))))
```

That is, (map f x y) means $f(x) = y$.

As an aside, we note that when we have a Skolem function, or a functional dependency, we have a corresponding function.

```
(forall (y1 y x1 x e s1 s2)                                    (9.9)
    (if (and (skfct y1 y x1 x e)(typelt x s1)(rangeFd s2 y x e))
        (exists (f)
            (and (function0 f s1 s2)
                (forall (p)
                    (iff (pair p x1 y1)(member p f)))))))))
```

9.2 SEQUENCES

Here we will assume we have the positive integers, as described in Chapter 13. The expression (posInteger n) says that n is a positive integer. The expression (leq n1 n2) says that n1 is less than or equal to n2.

The expression (ints s n1 n2) says that s is the set of all positive integers from n1 to n2, including n1 and n2.

```
(forall (s n1 n2)                                             (9.10)
    (iff (ints s n1 n2)
        (and (posInteger n1)(posInteger n2)(set s)
            (forall (n)
                (iff (member n s)
                    (and (posInteger n)(leq n1 n)(leq n n2)))))))
```

A sequence of length n is a function whose domain is the first n positive integers.

```
(forall (s)                                                  (9.11)
    (iff (sequence s)
        (exists (s1 s2 n)
            (and (function0 s s1 s2)(ints s1 1 n)))))
```

There are no constraints on s2.
We define length as follows:

```
(forall (n s)                                               (9.12)
    (if (sequence s)
        (iff (length n s)
            (exists (s1 s2)
                (and (function0 s s1 s2)(ints s1 1 n))))))
```

The nth element in a sequence is the entity in the range of the function that n is mapped into.

```
(forall (s n y)                                             (9.13)
    (if (sequence s)
        (iff  (nth y n s)(map s n y))))
```

The first element of a sequence is the nth element where n is 1.

```
(forall (s y)                                              (9.14)
    (if (sequence s)
        (iff (first y s)(nth y 1 s))))
```

Note that first is the same predicate we used for the first element of a pair. Formally, there is no confusion because all axioms involving the predicate first are conditioned on its second argument being either a pair or a sequence. Intuitively, any confusion is harmless, because the set of pairs is isomorphic to the set of sequences of length two.

The rest of a sequence is the sequence that remains after the first element is removed.

```
(forall (s1 s)                                              (9.15)
    (iff (rest s1 s)
        (and (sequence s)(sequence s1)
            (forall (i x)
                (iff (map s1 i x)
                    (exists (j)
                        (and (posInteger i)(successor j i)
                        (map s j x)))))))))
```

The expression (rest s1 s) says that s1 is the rest of s (after the first is removed). For example, the sequence <a,b,c> viewed as a function maps 2 to b. Then the sequence <b,c> maps 1 to b.

The last element of a sequence is the nth element where n is the length of the sequence.

```
(forall (s y n)                                             (9.16)
    (if (and (sequence s)(length n s))
        (iff (last y s)(nth y n s))))
```

An entity is in a sequence if it is the nth element of the sequence for some n.

```
(forall (x s)                                               (9.17)
    (iff (inSeq x s)
        (exists (n) (nth x n s))))
```

If one element's n is less than another's, it is before the other in the sequence.

```
(forall (x y s)                                             (9.18)
    (iff (beforeInSeq x y s)
        (exists (n1 n2)
            (and (sequence s)(nth x n1 s)(nth y n2 s)
                (lt n1 n2)))))
```

It will be useful to define the relation between two successive elements of a sequence.

```
(forall (x1 x2 s)                                           (9.19)
    (iff (successiveElts x1 x2 s)
        (exists (n1 n2)
            (and (successor n2 n1)(nth x1 n1 s)(nth x2 n2 s)))))
```

We won't need infinite sequences.

PREDICATES INTRODUCED IN THIS CHAPTER

(pair0 p)
 p is an ordered pair.

(pair p x y)
 p is the ordered pair <x,y>.

(first x p)
   x is the first element of a pair or sequence.

(second y p)
   y is the second element of a pair.

(function0 f s1 s2)
   f is a function from s1 onto s2.

(domain s1 f)
   s1 is the domain of function f.

(range s2 f)
   s2 is the range of function f.

(map f x y)
   The function f maps x to y; $f(x) = y$.

(ints s n1 n2)
   s is the set of positive integers from n1 to n2, including n1 and n2.

(sequence s)
   s is a sequence.

(length n s)
   n is the length of the sequence s.

(nth y i s)
   y is the ith element of sequence s.

(rest s1 s)
   s1 is the rest of the sequence s after the first element of s.

(last y s)
   y is the last element of sequence s.

(successiveElts x1 x2 s)
   Entities x1 and x2 are successive elements of sequence s.

(inSeq y s)
   y is an element of the sequence s.

(beforeInSeq x y s)
   x comes before y in the sequence s.

In addition, the following predicates will be explicated in Chapter 13.

(posInteger n)
   n is a positive integer.

(leq n1 n2)
   n1 is less than or equal to n2.

(successor n1 n)
   n1 is the successor of n; $n1 = n+1$.

(lt n1 n2)
   n1 is less than n2.

The constant 1 will also be explicated there.

10

Composite Entities

10.1 DEFINITIONS

A composite entity is a thing composed of other things. It is one of the most basic concepts in a knowledge base of commonsense knowledge. It is hard to think of anything that is not a composite entity, and much of our everyday vocabulary is for talking about composite entities.

Under the concept of "composite entity" we mean to include complex physical objects, such as a door, a cup, a telephone, a chair, and an automobile; living beings, such as a tree, a honey bee, and a person; complex events, such as a hike, the process of erosion, and a concert; and complex information structures, such as an equation, a sentence, a theory, and a schedule. Some entities, such as books, have both physical and informational components. In this theory of composite entities, we do not make any distinctions among the types of components an entity might have. From the standpoint of the theory of composite entities, the physical-abstract distinction is of no interest.

A composite entity is characterized by a set of components, a set of properties, and a set of relations.

```
(forall (x)                                              (10.1)
    (iff (compositeEntity x)
        (exists (s1 s2 s3)
            (and (componentsOf s1 x)(propertiesOf s2 x)
                (relationsOf s3 x)))))
```

The set of components of a composite entity is nonempty.

```
(forall (s1 x)                                           (10.2)
    (if (componentsOf s1 x)
        (and (set s1)(compositeEntity x)(not (null s1)))))
```

There are no further constraints on the components.

A component of a composite entity is one of the components. That is, the predicate componentOf gives us a quick way to say a single entity is a component.

126

```
(forall (y x)                                             (10.3)
   (iff (componentOf y x)
        (and (compositeEntity x)
             (exists (s)
                (and (componentsOf s x)(member y s))))))
```

An aggregate of two entities is a composite entity with those two entities as its components.

```
(forall (x y z)                                           (10.4)
   (iff (aggregate x y z)
        (and (compositeEntity x)
             (exists (s)
                (and (componentsOf s x)(doubleton s y z))))))
```

We define a predicate componentOrWhole as the disjunction of componentOf and being equal to the whole.

```
(forall (x1 x)                                            (10.5)
   (iff (componentOrWhole x1 x)
        (or (equal x1 x)(componentOf x1 x))))
```

An entity y is external to a composite entity x if neither it nor any of its components is equal to x or one of x's components.

```
(forall (y x)                                             (10.6)
   (iff (externalTo y x)
        (not (exists (y1 x1)
                (and (componentOrWhole y1 y)
                     (componentOrWhole x1 x)
                     (equal y1 x1))))))
```

The constraints on the properties of a composite entity are that they are properties, that is, that they have one argument, and that that argument be the whole or one of the components. For example, a window x has a pane of glass y as its component, and we may want to say that the pane is transparent. The property is the e such that (transparent' e y). But we may want embedded properties as well. For example, suppose we want the property that y is either transparent or translucent. This would be the property e such that

```
(and (or' e e1 e2)(transparent' e1 y)(translucent' e2 y))
```

This is still a property because once we recurse through the eventuality arguments e1 and e2, we bottom out in a single entity y.

We will capture this property of complex expressions with the predicate onlyarg*. Its definition recurses through eventuality arguments and bottoms out in a single entity y.

```
(forall (y e)                                               (10.7)
    (iff (onlyarg* y e)
        (and (eventuality e)(nequal y e)
            (forall (y1)
                (if (arg y1 e)
                    (or (equal y1 y)
                        (onlyarg* y y1)))))))))
```

Then all the elements in the properties of a composite entity have an `onlyarg*` that is either a component of the composite entity or the whole.

```
(forall (s2 x)                                              (10.8)
    (if (propertiesOf s2 x)
        (and (set s2)(compositeEntity x)
            (forall (e)
                (if (member e s2)
                    (exists (y)
                        (and (componentOrWhole y x)
                            (onlyarg* y e)))))))))
```

The set of relations of a composite entity are relations between a component or the whole, and something else.

```
(forall (s3 x)                                              (10.9)
    (if (relationsOf s3 x)
        (and (set s3)(compositeEntity x)
            (forall (e)
                (if (member e s3)
                    (exists (y z)
                        (and (componentOrWhole y x)(arg* y e)
                            (nequal z y)(arg* z e)))))))))
```

Note that z, the thing the component or whole y is related to, can be another component, the whole if y is not the whole, or something external. So the set of relations can include relations between two components, between a component and the whole, or between a component or the whole and something external. The axiom is also silent about whether or not entities other than y and z are involved; the relation could be among three or more entities.

A relation is a relation of a composite entity if it is in the `relationsOf` set.

```
(forall (e x)                                               (10.10)
    (iff (relationOf e x)
        (exists (s)
            (and (relationsOf s x)(member e s)))))
```

It will be useful to be able to say something is a property or a relation of a composite entity.

```
(forall (e x)                                               (10.11)
    (iff (propOrRelOf e x)
        (exists (s)
            (and (member e s)
                (or (propertiesOf s x)(relationsOf s x))))))
```

10.2 SOME SIMPLE EXAMPLES

Some of the kinds of entities we have previously introduced can be viewed as composite entities.

A set is probably the simplest kind of composite entity. As a composite entity, its components are its members, its only property is that it is a set, and there are no relations.

```
(forall (e s s1 s2 s3)                                        (10.12)
   (if (and (set' e s)(Rexist e)(not (null s))
            (singleton s2 e)(null s3))
       (and (compositeEntity s)(componentsOf s s)
            (propertiesOf s2 s)(relationsOf s3 s))))
```

Alternatively, we could call the `member` relations between its elements and the whole the relations.

Ordered pairs can also be viewed as composite entities, where the components are the first and second elements, there are no properties other than the whole being a pair, and the relations are the `first` and `second` relations between the components and the whole.

```
(forall (p x y e1 e2 e3)                                      (10.13)
   (if (and (pair0' e1 p)(first' e2 x p)(second' e3 y p)
            (Rexist e1)(Rexist e2)(Rexist e3))
       (exists (s1 s2 s3)
          (and (compositeEntity p)
               (doubleton s1 x y)(componentsOf s1 p)
               (singleton s2 e1)(propertiesOf s2 p)
               (doubleton s3 e2 e3)(relationsOf s3 p)))))
```

A sequence can be viewed as a composite entity, whose components are the elements of the sequence and whose relations are the ordering relations in the sequence.

```
(forall (e s)                                                 (10.14)
   (if (and (sequence' e s)(Rexist e)
            (exists (x)(inSeq x s)))
       (exists (s1 s2 s3)
          (and (compositeEntity s)
               (forall (x)(iff (member x s1)(inSeq x s)))
               (componentsOf s1 s)
               (singleton s2 e)(propertiesOf s2 s)
               (forall (e1)
                  (iff (member e1 s3)
                       (exists (x y)
                          (and (beforeInSeq' e1 x y s)
                               (Rexist e1)))))
               (relationsOf s3 s)))))
```

Line 3 of this axiom says that the sequence is not empty. Lines 6 and 7 say that the components are the elements of the sequence. Line 8 says that the only property is (sequence s). Lines 9–14 say that the relations are all the `beforeInSeq` relations.

10.3 THE FIGURE–GROUND RELATION

The figure–ground relationship is of fundamental importance in language and cognition. We encode this with the predication (at x y s), saying that a figure x is at a point y in the ground s.

To prime our intuitions about the figure–ground relation, consider the following examples of the uses of the preposition "at."

■ Spatial location:
    John is at the back of the store.
    Ground: Physical space
■ Location on a scale:
    Nuance closed at 57 3/8.
    Ground: Scale of numbers/prices
■ Membership in an organization:
    Chris is now at a competing company.
    Ground: Set of organizations
■ Location in a text:
    At this point, we should provide some background.
    A table is attached at the end of the article.
    Ground: The text (One might argue that this is simply spatial, the location in the physical object that is the text, or temporal, the time in the reading of the text, but it is true of every copy of the text and every reading of it.)
■ Time of an event:
    At that moment Pat stood up.
    Ground: Time scale
■ Event at an event:
    Let's have the discussion at lunch.
    Ground: Set of events
■ At a predication:
    His intonation was at variance with his words.
    Mary is at work.
    Emily was at ease in his company.
    Ground: Set of predications

We cannot simply locate a figure at some isolated point, not viewed as part of a larger system or composite entity, because that would tell us nothing. In any given instance, what counts as a ground and what counts as a possible location are context dependent. The background structure s of which y is a component may differ in different circumstances. Sometimes s will be a loose organization of vague locations; sometimes it will be a coordinate system.

If x is at y in s, then y must be a component of s and x must be external to s.

        (forall (x y s)   (10.15)
            (if (at x y s)(and (componentOf y s)(externalTo x s))))

To be a ground, s must at least be a composite entity. (This follows from (componentOf y s).) But the elements of s must be sufficiently similar to support the same interpretation of the at relation in every case. Thus, we would not have a single space consisting of organizations and times, where "at an organization" means membership and "at a time" means the time of occurrence of an event.

Or consider a book as a composite entity consisting of pages, a cover, a binding, and content. The first three are sufficiently similar that they can support some inter- pretations of "at," for example, a bookworm at the cover, the binding, or one of the pages. The pages themselves are similar enough that they can support more complex relationships; for example, "John is at page 235" may mean that John has read from the beginning to page 235. But there is probably no property common to all four components, including the content, that would support a single interpretation of the at relation.

The parts of a bicycle are all similar in that they are parts of a bicycle or in that they are physical objects. This will support a spatial at relation. But the at relation cannot be something that is conditional on further properties of the parts, such as "holding the handlebars if the part is the handlebars, turning the chain if the part is the chain, and leaning over the front wheel if the part is the front wheel."

Thus, a ground is a composite entity whose parts are all uniform in that they all share some property. We will take this to be a sufficient condition as well and define a potential ground as follows:

$$
\begin{array}{ll}
\text{(forall (s)} & \text{(10.16)} \\
\quad \text{(iff (ground s)} & \\
\qquad \text{(and (compositeEntity s)} & \\
\qquad\quad \text{(exists (e y)} & \\
\qquad\qquad \text{(and (arg* y e)} & \\
\qquad\qquad\quad \text{(forall (y1)} & \\
\qquad\qquad\qquad \text{(if (componentOf y1 s)} & \\
\qquad\qquad\qquad\quad \text{(exists (e1)} & \\
\qquad\qquad\qquad\qquad \text{(and (subst y e y1 e1)} & \\
\qquad\qquad\qquad\qquad\quad \text{(if (Rexist s)} & \\
\qquad\qquad\qquad\qquad\qquad \text{(Rexist e1)))))))))))}
\end{array}
$$

Something is a potential ground if it is a composite entity and there is some prop- erty type e that holds when its parameter y is instantiated with any component y1 of s. That is, there is some property e that all the components share.

This could also be written as

$$
\begin{array}{ll}
\text{(forall (s)} & \text{(10.17)} \\
\quad \text{(iff (ground s)} & \\
\qquad \text{(and (compositeEntity s)} & \\
\qquad\quad \text{(exists (e y s1)} & \\
\qquad\qquad \text{(and (componentsOf s1 s)(typelt y s1)(arg* y e)} & \\
\qquad\qquad\quad \text{(if (Rexist s)(Rexist e)))))))}
\end{array}
$$

The real existence of e ensures the real existence of all of its instantiations.

Then we can say that the third argument of an at relation must be a ground.

$$
\text{(forall (x y s)(if (at x y s)(ground s)))} \qquad \text{(10.18)}
$$

The predicate ground means that its argument is a potential ground for some figure and some at relation.

This figure–ground relation is central in the development of scales and in the characterizations of many verbs of change of state.

10.4 PATTERNS AND THEIR INSTANCES

A pattern is a composite entity that contains type elements among its components.

```
(forall (x)                                        (10.19)
   (iff (pattern x)
        (exists (y s1)
            (and (componentOf y x)(typelt y s1)))))
```

The parameters of a pattern are the components that are type elements.

```
(forall (x)                                        (10.20)
   (if (pattern x)
       (iff (patternParameters s x)
            (forall (y)
                (iff (member y s)
                     (exists (s1)
                         (and (componentOf y x)(typelt y s1))))))))
```

Line 2 restricts this definition to the case where its second argument is a pattern. Lines 3–7 define the set s of parameters to be the set of componenets y of x that are also type elements of some set s1.

An instance of a pattern is a composite entity in which all parameters have been replaced by entities that are members of the set the parameter is the type element of.

```
(forall (x x1 s)                                   (10.21)
 (if (and (pattern x)(patternParameters s x))
     (iff (patternInstance x1 x)
          (forall (y s1)
              (if (and (member y s)(typelt y s1))
                  (exists (y1)
                      (and (member y1 s1)(componentOf y1 x1)
                          (forall (p)
                              (if (and (propOrRelOf p x)(arg* y p))
                                  (exists (p1)
                                      (and (subst y1 p1 y p)
                                          (propOrRelOf p1 x1)))))))))))))
```

Line 2 restricts this definition to the case where x is a pattern and s its set of parameters. Lines 3–12 give the definition for an entity x1 being an instance of pattern x. Lines 4–7 say that for every parameter y in x, x1 has a component y1 taken from the set for which y is the type element. Lines 8–12 moreover say that all the properties and relations p in which y participates in the pattern x have a corresponding relation p1 in x1.

Suppose we want to guard a building, so we make up a pattern, or drawing, of a large square to represent the building and two small human figures at opposite corners. That drawing is the pattern x. The square and human figures constitute the set s of parameters y. The square represents the type element of a set s1 of possible buildings and the human figures represent the type element of a set s1 of trained security guards. An instance x1 of this pattern has an actual building y1 and two actual security guards y1. The atOppositeCornersOf relation p among the building and security guards in the pattern has a corresponding relation p1 in the instance.

We can define an "incomplete instance" to be a composite entity in which at least one parameter is instantiated and some but not all of the properties and relations are instantiated.

```
(forall (x x1 s)                                          (10.22)
   (if (and (pattern x)(patternParameters s x))
       (iff (incompleteInstance x1 x)
           (and (exists (y y1 s1 p p1)
                   (and (member y s)(typelt y s1)
                        (componentOf y1 x1)(member y1 s1)
                        (propOrRelOf p x)(arg* y p)
                        (subst y1 p1 y p)(propOrRelOf p1 x1)))
                (exists (p y)
                   (and (propOrRelOf p x)(arg* y p)
                        (forall (y1 p1)
                           (if (subst y1 p1 y p)
                               (not (propOrRelOf p1 x1)))))))))))
```

Lines 4–8 say that at least one of the parameters and at least one of its properties or relations is instantiated. Lines 9–13 say that at least one of the properties or relations is not instantiated.

Patterns are sometimes stipulated to be norms, either by frequency or by social convention. When a pattern is a norm, we can talk about an instance of it being complete or perfect.

PREDICATES INTRODUCED IN THIS CHAPTER

```
(compositeEntity x)
```
   x is a composite entity.

```
(componentsOf s1 x)
```
   s1 is the set of components of composite entity x.

```
(componentOf y x)
```
   y is a component of x.

```
(aggregate x y z)
```
   x is a composite entity whose components are y and z.

```
(componentOrWhole y x)
```
   y is either a component of x or x itself.

```
(externalTo y x)
```
   Neither y nor any of its components is equal to x or one of its components.

```
(onlyarg* y e)
```
   y is the only arg* of e, after recursing through all the eventuality arguments.

```
(propertiesOf s2 x)
```
   s2 is the set of properties of composite entity x.

```
(relationsOf s3 x)
```
   s3 is the set of relations of composite entity x.

```
(relationOf e x)
```
   e is one of the relations of x.

(propOrRelOf e x)
   e is one of the properties or relations of x.

(at x y s)
   x is at component y in composite entity s.

(ground s)
   The components of s are sufficiently similar for it to be a potential ground in an
   at relation.

(pattern x)
   x is a pattern.

(patternParameters s x)
   s is the set of parameters of x

(patternInstance x1 x)
   Composite entity x1 is an instance of pattern x in which all parameters of x are
   instantiated.

(incompleteInstance x1 x)
   Composite entity x1 is a partial instance of pattern x in which not all parameters
   of x are instantiated.

11

Defeasibility

So far, all of the axioms we have written are always true. It is always the case, for example, that two sets with exactly the same members are equal. But we cannot get very far in axiomatizing commonsense knowledge if we insist on this everywhere. Most of our everyday knowledge is only approximately correct. It is defeasible, in that we can draw a conclusion with it and later have the conclusion be defeated by new, more precise information.

The classic example is the knowledge we have that birds fly.

```
(forall (x) (if (bird x)(fly x)))                          (11.1)
```

When we hear that Tweety is a bird, we conclude that Tweety can fly. But later we may learn that Tweety is an emu. In that case, Tweety doesn't fly. Our knowledge that birds fly is only defeasible. This is not to say it is useless. It just means that we need to be somewhat more careful in stating and using the knowledge.

In logic, the technical term for this property is "nonmonotonic." Classical logic is "monotonic" in the sense that once we conclude something, nothing we learn subsequently can change that conclusion. Commonsense knowledge is nonmonotonic.

One way to deal with this problem is to add another proposition to the antecedent of implications.

```
(forall (x)                                                (11.2)
    (if (and (bird x)(etc1 x))
        (fly x)))
```

This says that if x is a bird and x has other unspecified properties encoded as etc1, then x can fly.

There are a number of ways the etc predicates can enter into the inference process. In weighted abduction (Hobbs et al., 1993), one tries to prove something by standard deductive means, but one can, at cost, make assumptions where the knowledge is lacking. The preferred proof is then the lowest-cost proof, for example, the one that minimizes the number of assumptions. Hobbs et al. (1993) describe various criteria for determining costs and choosing the best proof.

In the bird example, we want to know whether x flies. All we know is that x is a bird. So we assume (etc1 x), and conclude that x can fly.

Suppose later we learn that x is an emu, and we have the knowledge that emus are birds but don't fly.

```
(forall (x) (if (emu x)(bird x)))                    (11.3)
```

```
(forall (x) (if (emu x)(not (fly x))))               (11.4)
```

There is no contradiction in the knowledge base consisting of these three axioms. If x is an emu, then (etc1 x) is not true, and we can't assume it.

The best known version of this way of representing defeasible knowledge is McCarthy's (1980) circumscriptive logic. Rather than using etc, he uses ab for "abnormal." So Axiom (11.2) becomes

```
(forall (x)                                          (11.5)
    (if (and (bird x)(not (ab1 x)))
        (fly x)))
```

If x is a bird and x is not abnormal in a way specific to the predicate ab1, then x can fly.

We might further know that being an emu is one way of being abnormal in this respect.

```
(forall (x) (if (emu x)(ab1 x)))                     (11.6)
```

In the framework of Hobbs et al. (1993), there are no axioms that allow one to conclude explicitly that the etc predicates are true or false. They are simply carriers for the costs of using defeasible knowledge. In circumscriptive logic one may use axioms like (11.6) to state explicit properties that make something abnormal in some respect. (In fact, (11.6) follows from (11.5), (11.3) and (11.4).)

We have subscripted the etc and ab predicates because the extra conditions they encode are different for every axiom. It is also defeasibly true that birds have two legs.

```
(forall (x)                                          (11.7)
    (if (and (bird x)(etc2 x))
        (twoLegged x)))
```

But the extra conditions under which a bird can fly and the extra conditions under which a bird has two legs are different. We can't have a single etc or ab predicate do all the work. There has to be a separate one for every axiom.

It may be that there are inferential relations among the defeasibility predicates. For example, defeasibly all birds have feathers.

```
(forall (x)                                          (11.8)
    (if (and (bird x)(etc3 x))
        (feathered x)))
```

This is only defeasible because a plucked chicken lacks feathers.

This axiom assures us that (etc3 x) includes *all* the extra properties that entail that birds have feathers. But it doesn't assure us that (etc3 x) includes *all and only*

the extra properties that entail that birds have feathers. For that we need the biconditional axiom

```
(forall (x) (if (bird x)(iff (etc3 x)(feathered x))))
```
(11.9)

Now suppose it is the case that a bird without feathers cannot fly. We could then
state an explicit relation among the etc predicates, as follows:

```
(forall (x) (if (and (bird x)(etc1 x))(etc3 x)))
```
(11.10)

That is, if the extra conditions that enable a bird to fly are true, then so are the extra
conditions that make it feathered. But in fact this could be derived from Axioms
(11.2) and (11.9) and the following axiom:

```
(forall (x) (if (and (bird x)(fly x))(feathered x)))
```
(11.11)

In our treatment of defeasible knowledge we will not explicitly relate etc conditions to each other. Whatever relations there are will only be derivable from other
axioms with more intuitive content.

The arguments of the etc propositions need to include all the universally
quantied variables that scope over the etc predication. For example, consider the
defeasible knowledge that mothers love their children.

```
(forall (x y)(if (and (mother x y)(etc4 x y))(love x y)))
```
(11.12)

The unspecified conditions etc4 that make the conclusion certainly true could be
properties of the mother alone or the child alone, or a relation between the two of
them.

Now for an abbreviation: We could introduce a different etc predicate into every
defeasible axiom. For example, we might index them with the number of the chapter
and the number of the axiom within that chapter. So for example, a defeasible Axiom
(11.14) in Chapter 11 would have the predicate etc.11.14.

The arguments of the etc predicate in a Horn clause or other axiom in implicative normal form would in general have to be all the univerally quantified variables
that scope over the predication. In principle, the extra conditions they encode could
depend on any of these variables. Thus, a defeasible axiom might look like the following:

```
(forall (x y)
    (if (and (p x y)(etc.11.14 x y))
        (exists (z) (q x z))))
```
(11.13)

But all this notation is redundant. The index can be recovered from the chapter
and axiom numbers, and the arguments can be recovered from the universal quantifier. Moreover, the notation is useless for the reader, because this particular etc
predicate will appear in no other axiom. Its sole function is to indicate the defeasibility of the one axiom it appears in.

Thus, we will abbreviate all etc predications to simply (etc). Axiom (11.13) would be abbreviated to

```
(forall (x y)                                                        (11.14)
    (if (and (p x y)(etc))
        (exists (z) (q x z))))
```

It is straightforward to recover the real meaning of this expression.

A caveat is in order, however. The purpose of this abbreviation is to lighten the visual load on the reader from axioms that are often already quite burdensome. The axioms with (etc) cannot simply be given to a theorem-prover as is; it might assume (etc) in one axiom and then apply it in another. The abbreviations have to be expanded out before the axiom is given to the reasoning engine.

NOTATION INTRODUCED IN THIS CHAPTER

(etc)

An abbreviation for (etc<index> x y...), where <index> is unique to the axiom in which the (etc) appears and x y... are the universally quantified variables that scope over the (etc).

12

Scales

12.1 BASICS

A scale is a set of entities with a partial ordering among them. Thus, it is a composite entity where the components are the members of the set and one of the relations is the partial ordering. It is of course possible for particular scales to have other properties and other relations.

```
(forall (s)                                                    (12.1)
   (if (scale s)
       (and (compositeEntity s)
            (exists (s1 e x y s2 s3)
                (and (componentsOf s1 s)
                     (partialOrdering e x y s)
                     (subset s2 s3)(relationsOf s3 s)
                     (forall (e1)
                         (if (member e1 s2)
                             (exists (x1 y1)
                                 (and (member x1 s1)(member y1 s1)
                                      (subst2 x1 y1 e1 x y e)))))))))))
```

The fifth line says there is a set s1 of components or elements of the scale. Line 6 says there is a partial ordering e. Line 7 says there is a subset s2 of the relations of s, and lines 8–12 say that the members of s2 are instances of the partial ordering.

In more conventional notation, we can think of e as a lambda expression and x and y as its two bound variables. However, because the subst2 predicate we defined in Chapter 7 works equally well on types and tokens, we don't need to specify that x and y are variables, or types, or typical elements, or anything else.

Note that we allow other relations in the scale besides the partial ordering ones; s2 is a subset of the relations of s. It can be the entire set, so that the ordering relations are the only relations. It is also possible for s2 to be the empty set, giving us the uninteresting limiting case of a scale with no ordering relations among its elements.

We can state the conditions on the arguments of `partialOrdering` as follows:

```
(forall (e x y s)                                          (12.2)
   (if (partialOrdering e x y s)
       (and (scale s)(arg* x e)(arg* y e))))
```

That is, s is a scale and e is a relation between x and y.

We will use `inScale` as an abbreviation for being a component of a scale.

```
(forall (y s)                                              (12.3)
   (iff (inScale y s)
        (and (scale s)(componentOf y s))))
```

We will frequently refer to the components of a scale as being "points" on that scale.

It is generally more convenient to speak directly of the partial ordering relation among elements. We can define a "less than" relation as follows, using the predicate name `lts` to indicate that it is relative to a particular scale s.

```
(forall (e x1 y1 s)                                        (12.4)
   (iff (lts' e1 x1 y1 s)
        (exists (e x y e1)
           (and (partialOrdering e x y s)
                (subst2 x y e x1 y1 e1)))))
```

Then the standard properties of partial orderings can be defined in terms of the predicate `lts`. The partial ordering is antireflexive.

```
(forall (x s) (not (lts x x s)))                           (12.5)
```

It is antisymmetric.

```
(forall (x y s) (if (lts x y s)(not (lts y x s))))         (12.6)
```

It is transitive.

```
(forall (x y z s)                                          (12.7)
   (if (and (lts x y s)(lts y z s))
       (lts x z s)))
```

We can define a "greater than" relation in the obvious way.

```
(forall (x y s)                                            (12.8)
   (iff (gts y x s)(lts x y s)))
```

In Axiom (12.4) we did not state any restrictions on the arguments x and y of the `lts` relation. It may seem that they should be points on, or components of, the scale. But in fact we will just as often be making comparisons between entities that are *at* points on the scale. Suppose someone gets up at 7 A.M. and goes to work at 8 A.M. It will be true that 7 A.M. is before 8 A.M., but it will also be true that the getting up is before the going to work, and that the getting up is before 8 A.M., and that 7 A.M. is before the going to work. Therefore, we will allow the arguments of lts to be either points on the scale or entities that are *at* points on the scale.

```
(forall (x y s)                                        (12.9)
    (if (lts x y s)
        (and (or (inScale x s)
                 (exists (x1) (and (at x x1 s)(inScale x1 s))))
             (or (inScale y s)
                 (exists (y1) (and (at y y1 s)(inScale y1 s)))))))
```

The at relation preserves the partial ordering.

```
(forall (x1 x2 y1 y2 s)                                (12.10)
    (and (if (at x1 y1 s)
             (iff (lts x1 y2 s)(lts y1 y2 s)))
         (if (at x2 y2 s)
             (iff (lts y1 x2 s)(lts y1 y2 s)))
         (if (and (at x1 y1 s)(at x2 y2 s))
             (iff (lts x1 x2 s)(lts y1 y2 s)))))
```

It is convenient to have a predicate onScale both for points in a scale and for entities at points in a scale.

```
(forall (x s)                                          (12.11)
    (iff (onScale x s)
         (or (inScale x s)
             (exists (y) (and (inScale y s)(at x y s))))))
```

We can now define "less than or equal" and "greater than or equal" relations.

```
(forall (x y s)                                        (12.12)
    (iff (leqs x y s)
         (or (lts x y s)
             (and (onScale x s)(equal x y)))))
```

```
(forall (x y s)                                        (12.13)
    (iff (geqs x y s)
         (or (gts x y s)
             (and (onScale x s)(equal x y)))))
```

The antisymmetric property for leqs follows from (12.6) and (12.12).

```
(forall (x y s)                                        (12.14)
    (if (and (leqs x y s)(leqs y x s))
        (equal x y)))
```

The onScale condition was necessary to restrict the effect of these axioms when x equals y.

The top of a scale is the highest point in the scale.

```
(forall (x s)                                          (12.15)
    (iff (top x s)
         (and (inScale x s)
              (forall (y) (if (inScale y s)(leqs y x s))))))
```

The bottom of a scale is the lowest point in the scale.

```
(forall (x s)                                                    (12.16)
    (iff (bottom x s)
        (and (inScale x s)
            (forall (y) (if (inScale y s)(leqs x y s))))))
```

As the scale is only a partial ordering, it may not have a top and/or a bottom.

A subscale of a scale has as its components a subset of the components of the scale and its partial ordering relation is the partial ordering of the scale restricted to that subset.

```
(forall (s1 s)                                                  (12.17)
    (iff (subscale s1 s)
        (and (scale s1)(scale s)
            (forall (x) (if (inScale x s1)(inScale x s)))
            (forall (x y)
                (iff (lts x y s1)
                    (and (inScale x s1)(inScale y s1)
                        (lts x y s)))))))
```

The reverse of a scale is one in which the partial ordering is reversed.

```
(forall (s1 s)                                                  (12.18)
    (iff (reverse s1 s)
        (and (scale s1)(scale s)
            (forall (x y)
                (and (iff (inScale x s)(inScale x s1))
                    (iff (lts x y s)(lts y x s1)))))))
```

Two scales are disjoint if their sets of components are disjoint.

```
(forall (s1 s2)                                                 (12.19)
    (if (and (scale s1)(scale s2))
        (iff (disjoint s1 s2)
            (exists (s3 s4)
                (and (componentsOf s3 s1)(componentsOf s4 s2)
                    (disjoint s3 s4))))))
```

A total ordering is a partial ordering in which of any two elements, one is either less than, equal to, or greater than the other.

```
(forall (e x y s)                                               (12.20)
    (if (lts' e x y s)
        (iff (totalOrdering e x y s)
            (forall (x1 y1)
                (if (and (inScale x1 s)(inScale y1 s))
                    (or (lts x1 y1 s)(equal x1 y1)
                        (lts y1 x1 s)))))))
```

A scale is potentially a ground, and very frequently we speak of entities being located "at" some point on a scale.

```
(forall (s) (if (scale s)(ground s)))                          (12.21)
```

12.2 SCALE-TO-SCALE FUNCTIONS

We can extend the notion of function to scales by saying that for a scale to be the domain or range of a function is for its set of components to be the domain or range.

```
(forall (f s1 s2)                                          (12.22)
   (iff (function f s1 s2)
        (exists (s3 s4)
           (and (if (set s1)(equal s3 s1))
                (if (scale s1)(componentsOf s3 s1))
                (if (set s2)(equal s4 s2))
                (if (scale s2)(componentsOf s4 s2))
                (function0 f s3 s4)))))
```

In lines 4–7, s3 and s4 are assigned to the appropriate set, and in the last line function on sets and scales both is defined as function0 on the corresponding sets.

A scale-to-scale function is monotone-increasing if the mapping preserves the domain scale's "less than" ordering.

```
(forall (f s1 s2)                                          (12.23)
   (if (and (function f s1 s2)(scale s1)(scale s2))
       (iff (monotoneIncreasing f)
            (forall (x1 x2 y1 y2)
               (if (and (map f x1 y1)(map f x2 y2)(lts x1 x2 s1))
                   (lts y1 y2 s2))))))
```

In Chapter 10, we defined functions as "onto." A function f is "into" a set or scale s3 if there is a subset or subscale s2 for which f is a function "onto."

```
(forall (f s1 s3)                                          (12.24)
   (iff (functionInto f s1 s3)
        (exists (s2) (and (or (subset s2 s3)(subscale s2 s3))
                          (function f s1 s2)))))
```

12.3 CONSTRUCTING SCALES

We will have frequent occasion to define particular scales. This is done by specifying the set of entities that are the components of the scale, and the relation that is the partial ordering of the scale.

```
(forall (s s1 e)                                           (12.25)
   (iff (scaleDefinedBy s s1 e)
        (and (scale s)(componentsOf s1 s)
             (exists (x y) (partialOrdering e x y s)))))
```

For example, we can say that a sequence is a scale whose partial ordering is the beforeInSeq relation. The bottom element is the first element.

```
(forall (s s1 e x y)                                       (12.26)
   (if (and (sequence s)(componentsOf s1 s)
            (beforeInSeq' e x y s))
       (and (scaleDefinedBy s s1 e)
            (forall (z)(if (first z s)(bottom z s))))))
```

Similarly, a set of sets under the subset relation is a scale. If it contains the null set, that is the bottom element.

```
(forall (s1 e x y)                                           (12.27)
    (if (and (forall (s2)(if (member s2 s1)(set s2)))
             (subset' e x y))
        (exists (s)
            (and (scaleDefinedBy s s1 e)
                 (forall (z) (if (and (member z s1)(null z))
                                  (bottom z s)))))))
```

We will see many scales defined in this fashion.

We will often be faced with the problem of characterizing scales that we cannot define precisely but wish to place some constraints on their interpretations. Frequently, the entities we are placing at points on the scale are associated with sets, and we would like the ordering on the scale to be consistent with the subset relation on the associated sets. For example, in Chapter 15 we analyze the notion of task A being "more difficult than" task B. Something is difficult to the extent that there is a set of obstructions that tend to prevent it from happening. We would like to capture the idea that the more obstructions there are, the more difficult the task is. At the very least, the difficulty ordering for tasks should be consistent with the subset ordering on their associated sets of obstructions. If task B has all the obstructions of task A and then some, task B is at least as difficult as task A.

In the following definition, s is a scale, and e is an abstract relation between a set (line 4) and the kind of entities that are placed at points on the scale (line 5). In lines 6–10, s1 is the set associated with x1, and s2 is the set associated with x2. If s1 is a subset of s2 (line 11), then x1 is less than or equal to x2 on the scale s (line 12).

```
(forall (s e)                                                (12.28)
    (iff (subsetConsistent s e)
         (and (scale s)(eventuality e)
              (forall (s0)(if (argn s0 1 e)(set s0)))
              (forall (x)(if (argn x 2 e)(exists (y)(at x y s))))
              (forall (e1 e2 s1 s2 x1 x2)
                  (if (and (instance e1 e)(argn s1 1 e1)
                                          (argn x1 2 e1)
                           (instance e2 e)(argn s2 1 e2)
                                          (argn x2 2 e2)
                       (subset s1 s2))
                      (leqs x1 x2 s))))))
```

Alternatively, we can, and often do, simply state a mapping r from sets to points on a scale s and stipulate the monotonicity condition between the subset relation and the partial ordering on s, in an axiom of the following form:

```
(forall (s1 s2 x1 x2 s)                                      (12.29)
    (if (and (subset s1 s2)(r s1 x1)(r s2 x2))
        (leqs x1 x2 s)))
```

That is, given some mapping r, if set s1 is a subset of s2 and r maps s1 to x1 and s2 to x2, then x1 is less than or equal to x2 on the scale.

New scales can also be constructed out of existing scales.

Suppose we have two scales with the same set of components. Then we can define a composite scale that is consistent with the two original scales. For example, suppose the set is points in the United States, in the first scale the partial ordering (in this case total) is northOf, and in the second scale the partial ordering is eastOf. Then in the composite scale the partial ordering is at least consistent with the northAndEastOf relation. We may in addition impose further structure on the composite scale, for example, by saying that the northOf relation takes precedence, giving us a kind of lexicographic ordering, or alternatively we could order the points by distance from the southwest corner, another partial ordering consistent with northAndEastOf.

The loose constraints on a composite scale are as follows:

```
(forall (s s1 s2)                                                    (12.30)
    (if (compositeScale s s1 s2)
        (and (exists (s3)
                (and (componentsOf s3 s1)(componentsOf s3 s2)
                     (componentsOf s3 s)))
             (forall (x y)
                (if (and (lts x y s1)(leqs x y s2))
                    (lts x y s)))
             (forall (x y)
                (if (and (leqs x y s1)(lts x y s2))
                    (lts x y s))))))
```

That is, the same set is the set of components of the two original scales and the composite scale (lines 3–5). If an entity x is less than an entity y on one of the original scales and less than or equal to y on the other, then it is less than y on the composite scale (lines 6–11).

12.4 QUALITATIVE STRUCTURE ON SCALES

There is a range of structures we can impose on scales. These map complex scales into simpler scales. For example, in much work in qualitative physics the actual measurement of some parameter may be anything on the real line, but this is mapped into one of three values: positive, zero, and negative. Where the parameter is vertical velocity, this means we are interested only in whether something is going up, staying at the same elevation, or going down.

An even simpler scale is one with only two points, where one is less than the other. Any predication defines such a scale, where the two points are the predication being false and the predication being true, and where the former is less than the latter.

When we axiomatize arithmetic in Chapter 13, it will also be a scale, and of course it imposes a very common kind of structure on other scales, namely, measurements of quantities. In addition, we will define a "half-order of magnitude" structure for scales that is frequently useful in making approximate judgments.

Here we will define another sort of structure on scales, one reflected in language. What we have defined so far is adequate for characterizing the comparative and superlative forms of adjectives –"taller" and "tallest" – but not for the absolute form of adjectives: "tall." In natural language and in qualitative reasoning we often characterize something as being in the high or low region of a scale, or somewhere in the middle, with no more precise characterization of its location. We will call these regions the Hi, Md, and Lo regions of the scale. Each of these predicates is a relation between a scale s and one of its subscales s1; (Hi s1 s) says that s1 is the Hi region of s.

The Hi, Md, and Lo regions of a scale are subscales.

$$(\text{forall } (s1\ s)\ (\text{if } (\text{Hi } s1\ s)(\text{subscale } s1\ s))) \tag{12.31}$$

$$(\text{forall } (s1\ s)\ (\text{if } (\text{Md } s1\ s)(\text{subscale } s1\ s))) \tag{12.32}$$

$$(\text{forall } (s1\ s)\ (\text{if } (\text{Lo } s1\ s)(\text{subscale } s1\ s))) \tag{12.33}$$

There are certain purely scalar properties of these regions. The top of the scale is in the Hi region of the scale, and in fact is the top of the Hi region.

```
(forall (s1 s)                                              (12.34)
   (if (Hi s1 s)
      (forall (x) (iff (top x s)(top x s1)))))
```

Similarly, the bottom of a scale is the bottom of its Lo region.

```
(forall (s1 s)                                              (12.35)
   (if (Lo s1 s)
      (forall (x) (iff (bottom x s)(bottom x s1)))))
```

The bottom of the Hi region and the top of the Lo region, as well as the top and bottom of the Md region, will rarely be known exactly, and the Hi and Md region will generally overlap, as well as the Lo and Md regions. Nevertheless, we can say that if a point is in the Lo region, then it is less than all the points in the Hi region.

```
(forall (s s1 s2 x y)                                       (12.36)
   (if (and (Hi s1 s)(Lo s2 s)(inScale x s1)(inScale y s2))
      (lts y x s)))
```

It is often useful to go from the absolute form of an adjective to its underlying scale, for example, from "tall" to the height scale. We will use the predicate scaleFor for this relation.

```
(forall (s e)                                               (12.37)
   (iff (scaleFor s e)
      (exists (s1)
         (and (Hi s1 s)
            (forall (e1 x y)
               (if (and (at' e1 x y s1)(argn x 1 e))
                  (iff (Rexist e)(Rexist e1)))))))))
```

For example, suppose we have (tall' e x), that is, e is the property of x's being tall. Then s is the height scale, s1 is the Hi region of the height scale, and whenever we have a relation e1 of x being at a point y in that Hi region, then e1 holds exactly when e holds. That is, some entity x is tall exactly when x is at a point in the Hi region of the height scale. The height scale is the scaleFor the property tall. In line 6 we specify that x must be the first argument of e, because if there are multiple arguments, we need to say which one is the relevant argument placed on the scale.

There are two primary external theories that a theory of the qualitative structure on scales should link to. The first is a theory of distributions and the second is a theory of functionality.

The real distribution of a collection of entities along some scale is often Gaussian. But Gaussian curves are not something that people can reason with very well in their everyday lives. We will not develop a commonsense theory of distributions here. But one can imagine going about it by approximating the Gaussian by means of a step function. The coarsest approximation would have three steps: the highest around the mean and two lower steps to approximate the two tails. Perhaps the middle step goes from one standard deviation before to one standard deviation after the mean. Given such a theory, we could stipulate that, defeasibly, when an entity falls into the region corresponding to the leftmost step, it is in the Lo region of the scale, and when it falls into the region corresponding to the rightmost step, it is in the Hi region. Exactly how such step functions would approximate the Gaussian would have to be worked out.

A more naive theory might simply sat that entities in the Hi region are defeasibly above the average.

A theory of functionality is precisely what we work out in our theory of goals in Part III of this book. Often when we say that an entity is tall, we mean that it is tall *enough* for something or *too* tall for something. Discovering that something is recognizing the connection between qualitative scalar judgments and functionality. A similar observation is made by Graff (2000), who states that the extensions of vague predicates depend crucially on "interest relative" properties.

More specifically, we can say that, defeasibly, if something is in the Hi region of a scale, then that property plays a causal or enabling role in some agent's goal being achieved or not being achieved. We can state this as follows:

```
(forall (e x y s1 s)                                        (12.38)
    (if (and (at' e x y s1)(Hi s1 s)(etc))
        (exists (c a g g1)
            (and (member e c)(goal g a)
                (or (causalComplex c g)
                    (and (not' g1 g)(causalComplex c g1)))))))))
```

That is, if e is the property of x being in the Hi region of some scale, then defeasibly e is part of a causal complex that will bring about some agent's goal or its negation. Causal complexes are explicated in Chapter 15.

This axiom does not tell us what the goal is. That has to be determined from context. But it does alert us to the possible relevance of such a goal, and indeed in text the goal is often to be found nearby. For example, in

The getaway car was fast.

the car was probably fast enough to get away.

PREDICATES INTRODUCED IN THIS CHAPTER

(scale s)
   s is a scale.

(partialOrdering e x y s)
   e is a partial ordering on the components of s, where x is less than y.

(inScale y s)
   y is a component of the scale s.

(lts x y s)
    x is less than y in the partial ordering for scale s.

(gts x y s)
    x is greater than y in the partial ordering for scale s.

(onScale x s)
    x is a point on scale s or at a point on s.

(leqs x y s)
    x is less than or equal to y in the partial ordering for scale s.

(geqs x y s)
    x is greater than or equal to y in the partial ordering for scale s.

(top x s)
    x is the highest element in the scale s.

(bottom x s)
    x is the lowest element in the scale s.

(subscale s1 s)
    s1 is a subscale of scale s.

(reverse s1 s)
    s1 is the reverse of scale s.

(disjoint s1 s2)
    For scales, the component sets of scales s1 and s2 are disjoint.

(totalOrdering e x y s)
    e, the partial ordering on the components of s, where x is less than y, is in fact total.

(function f s1 s2)
    f is a function from a set or scale s1 onto a set or scale s2.

(monotoneIncreasing f)
    Function f is monotone-increasing scale-to-scale function preserving the scales' "less than" ordering.

(functionInto f s1 s2)
    f is a function from a set or scale s1 into a set or scale s2.

(scaleDefinedBy s s1 e)
    s is the scale with components s1 and partial ordering defined by relation e.

(subsetConsistent s e)
    s is a scale whose ordering is consistent with the subset ordering among sets associated by the relation e with entities placed at points in s.

(compositeScale s s1 s2)
    s is a composite scale with the same components as scales s1 and s2 and a partial ordering consistent with the partial orderings of s1 and s2.

(Hi s1 s)
    s1 is the high region of scale s.

(Md s1 s)
    s1 is the middle region of scale s.

(Lo s1 s)
    s1 is the low region of scale s.

(scaleFor s e)
   The property e corresponds to being in the Hi region of scale s.

In addition, we used the two following predicates that have not yet been defined, the first from Chapter 15 and the second from Chapter 28.

(causalComplex c e)
   The collection c of eventualities is a causal complex for effect e.

(goal g a)
   Eventuality type g is a goal for agent a.

We also used the constants 1 and 2.

13

Arithmetic

13.1 INTEGERS

In a practical reasoning system, one would not try to solve arithmetic problems by automatic theorem-proving from basic axioms. One would simply use the procedural attachment capabilities of the theorem-prover and utilize the computer's much more efficient arithmetic operations. Nevertheless, for conceptual completeness, we will axiomatize basic arithmetic here, following the standard Peano axiomatization, in terms of a successor predicate.

For consistency, we will treat arithmetic operations via predicates rather than via functions and use prefix notation rather than the conventional infix notation. However, the integers will be constants, the only constants we will use in this book. We could treat them as properties true only of unique individuals, but that would be altogether too pedantic.

Zero is a nonnegative integer.

```
(nonNegInteger 0)                                              (13.1)
```

Every nonnegative integer has a successor which is also a nonnegative integer.

```
(forall (n)                                                    (13.2)
    (if (nonNegInteger n)
        (exists (n1)
            (and (nonNegInteger n1)(successor n1 n)))))
```

The arguments of successor are nonnegative integers.

```
(forall (n1 n)                                                 (13.3)
    (if (successor n1 n)
        (and (nonNegInteger n1)(nonNegInteger n))))
```

Besides zero, the only other specific numbers we will need are one, two, and ten. However, to define ten, we need to define three through nine.

```
(and (successor 1 0)(successor 2 1)(successor 3 2)             (13.4)
     (successor 4 3)(successor 5 4)(successor 6 5)
     (successor 7 6)(successor 8 7)(successor 9 8)
     (successor 10 9))
```

A positive integer is any nonnegative integer except zero.

```
(forall (n)                                                    (13.5)
    (iff (posInteger n)(and (nonNegInteger n)(nequal n 0))))
```

No nonnegative integer has zero as its successor.

```
(not (exists (n) (and (nonNegInteger n)(successor 0 n))))     (13.6)
```

Successors are unique.

```
(forall (n n1 n2)                                              (13.7)
    (if (and (successor n1 n)(successor n2 n))
        (equal n1 n2)))
```

We will define addition recursively in terms of the successor relation. The predication (sum n1 n2 n3) means that n1 is the sum of n2 and n3. The sum of a number n and zero is n.

```
(forall (n)                                                    (13.8)
    (if (nonNegInteger n)(sum n n 0)))
```

The recursive step is as follows:

```
(forall (n n1 n2 n3 n4)                                        (13.9)
    (if (and (successor n3 n2)(sum n4 n1 n2))
        (iff (sum n n1 n3)(successor n n4))))
```

The more conventional and more succinct way of saying this is n1+S(n2) = S(n1+n2).

We won't constrain the arguments of sum to be nonnegative integers because we can extend sum to other kinds of numbers. But we can say that the nonnegative integers are closed under addition.

```
(forall (n1 n2 n3)                                             (13.10)
    (if (and (nonNegInteger n2)(nonNegInteger n3)(sum n1 n2 n3))
        (nonNegInteger n1)))
```

Addition is associative.

```
(forall (n n1 n2 n3 n4 n5)                                     (13.11)
    (if (and (sum n4 n2 n3)(sum n5 n1 n2))
        (iff (sum n n1 n4)(sum n n5 n3))))
```

In more conventional notation, n1+(n2+n3) = (n1+n2)+n3.

Addition is commutative.

```
(forall (n n1 n2)                                              (13.12)
    (iff (sum n n1 n2)(sum n n2 n1)))
```

More conventionally, n1+n2 = n2+n1.

We will not need multiplication in other chapters, but we need to introduce it here because we will need it in defining proportions and half-orders of magnitude.

Multiplication is defined in a manner similar to addition. The predication (product n1 n2 n3) means that n1 is the product of n2 and n3.

The product of a number n and zero is zero.

```
(forall (n)                                              (13.13)
    (if (nonNegInteger n)(product 0 n 0)))
```

The recursive step is as follows:

```
(forall (n n1 n2 n3 n4)                                  (13.14)
    (if (and (successor n3 n2)(product n4 n1 n2))
        (iff (product n n1 n3)(sum n n4 n1))))
```

The more conventional way of saying this is n1*S(n2) = (n1*n2)+n1.
The nonnegative integers are closed under multiplication.

```
(forall (n1 n2 n3)                                       (13.15)
    (if (and (nonNegInteger n2)(nonNegInteger n3)
            (product n1 n2 n3))
        (nonNegInteger n1)))
```

We will not place constraints on the arguments of product because we want to extend it to rational numbers as well.

One is the identity under multiplication. This follows from (13.13) and (13.14).

```
(forall (n)                                              (13.16)
    (if (nonNegInteger n)(product n n 1)))
```

Multiplication is associative.

```
(forall (n n1 n2 n3 n4 n5)                               (13.17)
    (if (and (product n4 n2 n3)(product n5 n1 n2))
        (iff (product n n1 n4)(product n n5 n3))))
```

In more conventional notation, n1*(n2*n3) = (n1*n2)*n3.
Multiplication is commutative.

```
(forall (n n1 n2)                                        (13.18)
    (iff (product n n1 n2)(product n n2 n1)))
```

Or, n1*n2 = n2*n1.
Multiplication and addition are related by the distributive law.

```
(forall (n n1 n2 n3 n4 n5 n6)                            (13.19)
    (if (and (sum n4 n2 n3)(product n5 n1 n2)(product n6 n1 n3))
        (iff (product n n1 n4)(sum n n5 n6))))
```

More conventionally, n1*(n2+n3) = n1*n2 + n1*n3.
A "less than" relation can be defined for nonnegative integers as follows:

```
(forall (n1 n2)                                          (13.20)
    (if (and (nonNegInteger n1)(nonNegInteger n2))
        (iff (lt n1 n2)
            (exists (n3)(and (posInteger n3)(sum n2 n1 n3))))))
```

That is, n1 is less than n2 if and only if there is some positive integer n3 such that n2 is the sum of n1 and n3. We condition this on n1 and n2 being nonnegative integers because we will extend it to rational numbers as well.

The relations leq, gt, and geq can be defined in the obvious ways.

(forall (n1 n2)(iff (leq n1 n2)(or (lt n1 n2)(equal n1 n2))))   (13.21)

(forall (n1 n2)(iff (gt n1 n2)(lt n2 n1)))   (13.22)

(forall (n1 n2)(iff (geq n1 n2)(or (gt n1 n2)(equal n1 n2))))   (13.23)

A nonnegative integer is a number.

(forall (n) (if (nonNegInteger n)(number n)))   (13.24)

13.2 RATIONAL NUMBERS

Fractions will be characterized by a nonnegative integer (the numerator) and a positive integer (the denominator). The predication (fraction f a b) says that f is the fraction a/b. Such fractions exist.

(forall (a b)   (13.25)
    (if (and (nonNegInteger a)(posInteger b))
        (exists (f) (fraction f a b))))

Two fractions are equal under the usual conditions.

(forall (f1 f2 a1 a2 b1 b2 c1 c2)   (13.26)
    (if (and (fraction f1 a1 b1)(fraction f2 a2 b2)
            (product c1 a1 b2)(product c2 a2 b1))
        (iff (equal f1 f2)(equal c1 c2))))

That is, a1/b1 = a2/b2 exactly when a1*b2 = a2*b1.
  The nonnegative integers can be embedded in the set of rational numbers.

(forall (n) (if (nonNegInteger n)(fraction n n 1)))   (13.27)

That is, n = n/1.
  The lt relation can be extended to rational numbers.

(forall (f1 f2 a1 a2 b1 b2 c1 c2)   (13.28)
    (if (and (fraction f1 a1 b1)(fraction f2 a2 b2)
            (product c1 a1 b2)(product c2 a2 b1))
        (iff (lt f1 f2)(lt c1 c2))))

That is, a1/b1 < a2/b2 exactly when a1*b2 < a2*b1. This also extends the other ordering relations, leq, gt, and geq.
  We won't need to add two fractions. The product of two fractions is defined as follows:

(forall (f f1 f2 a1 a2 b1 b2 c1 c2)   (13.29)
    (if (and (fraction f1 a1 b1)(fraction f2 a2 b2)
            (product c1 a1 a2)(product c2 b1 b2))
        (iff (product f f1 f2)(fraction f c1 c2))))

That is, if f1 = a1/b1 and f2 = a2/b2, then f1*f2 = (a1*a2)/(b1*b2). This definition works if the numerators and denominators are fractions as well as if they are integers. Thus, product can take fractions for any of its arguments.

We will say that a fraction is a number, and that product requires a number and a nonzero number for its numerator and denominator.

(forall (f a b)(if (fraction f a b)(number f)))   (13.30)

(forall (f a b)   (13.31)
    (if (fraction f a b)(and (number a)(number b)(nequal b 0))))

All of this leaves open the possibility of defining the product of numbers other than the nonnegative rational numbers we have defined. But we will not need irrational or negative numbers in this book.

13.3 MEASURES AND PROPORTIONS

Sets of rational numbers, and hence sets of nonnegative integers, are very important examples of scales. We will focus on sets in which 0 is the smallest element.

If e is the lt relation between x and y and s1 is a set of numbers containing 0 but no smaller number, then there is a nonnegative numeric scale s with s1 as its set and e as its partial ordering.

(forall (s1 e x y)   (13.32)
    (if (and (lt' e x y)
             (forall (n)(if (member n s1)
                            (and (geq n 0)(number n))))
             (member 0 s1))
        (exists (s)
          (and (scaleDefinedBy s s1 e)(nonNegNumericScale s)))))

Conversely, a nonnegative numeric scale has the lt relation for its ordering and a set of numbers, including zero, as its set.

(forall (s)   (13.33)
    (if (nonNegNumericScale s)
        (exists (s1 e x y)
          (and (lt' e x y)
               (forall (n)(if (member n s1)
                              (and (geq n 0)(number n))))
               (member 0 s1)
               (scaleDefinedBy s s1 e)))))

It follows that a nonnegative numeric scale is a scale.

A measure is a monotone increasing function from a scale into a nonnegative numeric scale in which the bottom of the domain scale, if there is one, maps into zero.

(forall (m s1)   (13.34)
    (iff (measure m s1)
         (exists (s2)
           (and (scale s1)(nonNegNumericScale s2)
                (functionInto m s1 s2)
                (monotoneIncreasing m)
                (forall (x)(if (bottom x s1)(map m x 0)))))))

For example, if s1 is the scale whose set is a set of sets including the null set and whose partial ordering is subset, then cardinality is a measure.

```
(forall (e x y s1 s m n u)                                    (13.35)
    (if (and (forall (z) (if (member z s1) (set z)))
             (exists (w) (and (member w s1) (null w)))
             (subset' e x y)
             (scaleDefinedBy s s1 e)
             (card' m n u))
        (measure m s)))
```

Line 2 says that s1 is a set of sets. Line 3 says that the null set w is one of those sets. Line 4 defines e as the subset relation. Line 5 says s is the scale defined by s1 and e. Line 6 defines m as the cardinality relation. Under these conditions, m is a measure on s.

Suppose we have two points x and y on a scale s1 that has a measure. Then the proportion of x to y is the fraction whose numerator and denominator are the numbers the measure maps x and y into, respectively.

```
(forall (f x y m s1)                                          (13.36)
    (if (and (measure m s1) (inScale x s1) (inScale y s1))
        (iff (proportion f x y m)
             (exists (n1 n2)
                 (and (map m x n1) (map m y n2)
                      (fraction f n1 n2))))))
```

In more conventional notation, if m is a measure function mapping s1 into a nonnegative numeric scale, then the proportion f of x to y is given by $f = m(x)/m(y)$.

The constraints on the arguments of proportion are as follows:

```
(forall (f x y m)                                             (13.37)
    (if (proportion f x y m)
        (exists (s1)
            (and (measure m s1) (inScale x s1) (inScale y s1)))))
```

The identity function is the function that maps every entity into itself.

```
(forall (f s)                                                 (13.38)
    (iff (identityFunction f s)
         (and (function f s s)
              (forall (x) (if (member x s) (map f x x))))))
```

The identity function on a nonnegative numeric scale is a measure.

```
(forall (f s)                                                 (13.39)
    (if (and (nonNegNumericScale s) (identityFunction f s))
        (measure f s)))
```

Thus, we can talk about the proportion of one point on a numeric scale to another, via the identity measure.

Frequently, when an entity is measured on a numeric scale, we say that that entity is at that point on the scale. For example, we might say

The temperature is at 90 now, but it's going to fall this evening.

When two scales are disjoint, we can define the measure relation as an at relation, thereby tapping into the rich vocabulary language has for talking about changes in such relations, such as the word "fall." If an entity is mapped into a point by a measure, it is at that point.

```
(forall (m s1 s2 x y)                                           (13.40)
    (if (and (measure m s1)(function m s1 s2)(disjoint s1 s2)
             (map m x y))
        (at x y s2)))
```

The scale s2 is a possible ground by virtue of the fact that all its elements are numbers.

13.4 HALF-ORDERS OF MAGNITUDE

In Hobbs (2000) and Hobbs and Kreinovich (2001) it was argued that measurements in terms of half-orders of magnitude constitute a very important coarse-grained qualitative mode of judgment in commonsense reasoning. Increasing or decreasing the linear size of something by a factor of around three changes the way we interact with it. A box four inches square can be carried in one hand. If it is one foot square, we will carry it with two hands. If it is three feet square, we will get help in carrying it. We approach meetings differently if we know they will last twenty minutes, one hour, or three hours. The most common American coins and bills come in half-orders of magnitude – $0.01, $0.05, $0.10, $0.25, $1.00, $5.00, $10.00, and $20.00. The words "about," "approximately," and "nearly," when applied to quantitative measures, typically have some half-order of magnitude as their implied precision, and add a fuzz around the judgment the width of that half-order of magnitude. The word "several" usually indicates a half order of magnitude; we could state this succinctly as "Several squared equals ten." Although we rarely know the precise measure of something on a scale, we often can say what a half-order of magnitude it is.

In this book we will need only a predicate saying when two entities are the same half order of magnitude. This is straightforward to define. The proportion of the smaller to the larger is less than the square root of 10. Because we lack irrational numbers, we will square the proportion.

```
(forall (x y s1 m)                                              (13.41)
    (if (and (leqs x y s1)(measure m s1))
        (iff (sameHOM x y s1 m)
            (exists (f f2)
                (and (proportion f y x m)(product f2 f f)
                     (leq f2 10))))))
```

```
(forall (x y s1 m)                                              (13.42)
    (if (and (gts x y s1)(measure m s1))
        (iff (sameHOM x y s1 m)(sameHOM y x s1 m))))
```

The constraints on the arguments of sameHOM are as follows:

```
(forall (x y s1 m)                                              (13.43)
    (if (sameHOM x y s1 m)
        (and (inScale x s1)(inScale y s1)(measure m s1))))
```

CONSTANTS INTRODUCED IN THIS CHAPTER

The constants introduced were the integers 0, 1, 2, 3, 4, 5, 6, 7, 8, 9, and 10.

PREDICATES INTRODUCED IN THIS CHAPTER

(nonNegInteger n)
    n is a nonnegative integer.

(successor n1 n)
    n1 is the successor of n; $n1 = n+1$.

(posInteger n)
    n is a positive integer.

(sum n1 n2 n3)
    n1 is the sum of n2 and n3; $n1 = n2+n3$.

(product n1 n2 n3)
    n1 is the product of n2 and n3; $n1 = n2*n3$.

(lt n1 n2)
    n1 is less than n2; $n1 < n2$.

(leq n1 n2)
    n1 is less than or equal to n2.

(gt n1 n2)
    n1 is greater than n2.

(geq n1 n2)
    n1 is greater than or equal to n2.

(number n)
    n is a number.

(fraction f a b)
    f is the fraction whose numerator is a and whose denominator is b; $f = a/b$.

(nonNegNumericScale s)
    s is a scale whose elements are nonnegative numbers, including 0, and whose partial ordering is lt.

(measure m s)
    m is a monotone increasing mapping from a scale s into a nonnegative numeric scale, mapping the bottom of s into 0.

(proportion f x y m)
    f is the proportion or ratio of m(x) to m(y), where m is a measure on the scale containing x and y.

(identityFunction f s)
    f is the function that maps every element of s into itself.

(sameHOM x y s1 m)
    Two elements x and y of a scale s1 are of the same half-order of magnitude under measure m.

14

Change of State

14.1 THE change PREDICATE

It is hard to imagine a universe without change. It is even harder to imagine cognition in such a universe. Change of state is very nearly the most basic concept human beings are equipped with. We could not survive very long without recognizing the changes in our environment. Our very sense of time arises from our awareness of change.

We will represent change of state with the predicate change relating two eventualities. The expression (change e1 e2) says that eventuality e1 changes into eventuality e2. Moving is a change from being at one place to being at another. Growing up is a change from being small to being larger. Learning is a change from not knowing something to knowing it. And so on, for all the processes we are familiar with.

We cannot define change. It is too basic a concept in our minds. But there are a number of constraints we can express concerning the eventualities that are the arguments to change.

The arguments of change are eventualities.

```
(forall (e1 e2)                                            (14.1)
    (if (change e1 e2)(and (eventuality e1)(eventuality e2))))
```

They can be eventuality types or eventuality tokens. For example, the change may be from the door being open three inches to the door being open two inches, where both are eventuality tokens of the door being open. There is no assumption in the change predicate that the eventualities e1 and e2 precisely define the conditions before and after the change; we will see later that the two derivative predicates changeFrom and changeTo will incorporate this assumption, and hence will apply primarily to eventuality types.

One might think there could be a magical change of a person into a cat, and this would be a change relation between entities that are not eventualities. But we view this as a change in properties of a single individual. There is an x such that first x is a person and then x is a cat.

A change of state is a change of state of something. It would be strange to say that there was a change from Bill Clinton's being president to the Red Sox winning the World Series. They have nothing to do with each other. So a further constraint on change is this.

```
(forall (e1 e2)                                              (14.2)
    (if (change e1 e2)
        (exists (x)(and (arg* x e1)(arg* x e2)))))
```

The eventualities e1 and e2 have to involve some common entity x.

Change is defeasibly transitive. If e1 changes into e2 and e2 changes into e3, then generally we can say there is a change from e1 to e3.

```
(forall (e1 e2 e3)                                           (14.3)
    (if (and (change e1 e2)(change e2 e3)(etc))
        (change e1 e3)))
```

One reason change is only defeasibly transitive is that the first change may involve one entity and the second another. For example, suppose e1 is John's being married to Mary, e2 is John's being married to Susan, and e3 is Susan's being married to Bill. It seems strange to say that there is a change from John's being married to Mary to Susan's being married to Bill. Part of the etc condition for this axiom is that the two changes involve the same entity.

We would like to say that when e1 changes into e2, they are somehow contradictory or inconsistent with each other. Something has actually changed. We should not get direct changes from an eventuality e into itself. However, this cannot be expressed as a constraint on the arguments of change, because cyclic change is possible. We can have a change from state e1 to state e2 and then a change back to state e1 again. By transitivity, there defeasibly has been a change from e1 to itself. But the only reason this has been possible is because there was an intermediate state that was different. We can state this by saying that if the states are not inconsistent, then the change must be a composite of two changes, one to and the other from an inconsistent state.

```
(forall (e e1 e2)                                            (14.4)
    (if (change' e e1 e2)
        (or (inconsistent e1 e2)
            (exists (e3 e4 e5 e6)
                (and (change' e4 e1 e3)(change' e5 e3 e2)
                     (and' e6 e4 e5)(gen e6 e))))))
```

Because change is not normally cyclic, we can make it a defeasible inference that the start and end states are inconsistent, by thinking of the negation of the second disjunct of Axiom (14.4) as an "et cetera" condition.

```
(forall (e e1 e2)                                            (14.5)
    (if (and (change e1 e2) (etc))
        (inconsistent e1 e2)))
```

14.2 PREDICATES DERIVED FROM change

It will be useful in avoiding verbosity later to introduce here several predicates defined in terms of change.

We will say that there is a changeIn something when there is a change in its properties.

```
(forall (e x)                                                    (14.6)
   (iff (changeIn' e x)
        (exists (e1 e2 e3)
           (and (arg* x e1)(arg* x e2)(change' e3 e1 e2)(gen e3 e)))))
```

We know from Axiom (14.2) that there is at least one such x in every change.

Very often we are interested not in both the start and end states of a change, but only in one. For this, we will define changeFrom and changeTo predicates. We would like these to be more powerful than the change predicate, however. We would like it to be the case that when there has been a changeFrom some eventuality e1, where (p' e1 x) holds, then after the change, (p x) is not true. That is, no eventuality corresponding to (p x) really exists. The following axiom accomplishes this.

```
(forall (e e1 e3)                                               (14.7)
   (if (subst e3 e3 e1 e1)
       (iff (changeFrom' e e1)
            (exists (e2 e5)
               (and (change' e5 e1 e2)(gen e5 e)(inconsistent e3 e2))))))
```

Recall from Chapter 7 that the expression (subst e3 e3 e1 e1) means that e1 and e3 have the same predicate and same arguments, other than the self argument. So (open' e1 d) and (open' e3 d) may be two distinct instances of the door d being open, but if there is a changeFrom e1, it can't be into e3 or any other situation in which the door is still open.

The changeTo predicate is defined similarly.

```
(forall (e e2 e4)                                               (14.8)
   (if (subst e4 e4 e2 e2)
       (iff (changeTo' e e2)
            (exists (e1 e5)
               (and (change' e5 e1 e2)(gen e5 e)(inconsistent e4 e1))))))
```

Here the start state of the change must exclude any other instance of the type which e2 instantiates. We can't changeTo a state of the door being open from a state in which the door is already open.

If we want to make the arguments of the change more specific, we can do so by having them be explicitly conjunctive. Thus, we can have a changeFrom a state of the door being open two inches by saying something like

```
(and (changeFrom' e e1)(and' e1 e2 e3)
     (open' e2 d)(measure' e3 e2 2in))
```

In Chapter 10 we introduced the notion of an external figure being at a location in a structured ground. We can combine this with the notion of "change" to get a very abstract sense of "move." An entity x moves from y to z exactly when there is a change from x's being at y to its being at z.

```
(forall (e x y z)                                    (14.9)
    (iff (move' e x y z)
        (exists (e1 e2 e3 s)
            (and (at' e1 x y s)(at' e2 x z s)(change' e3 e1 e2)
                (gen e3 e)))))
```

As we introduce various specializations of the at relation, we will inherit corresponding specializations of the move event. For example, a change in the measure of something is a move.

Among the many possible scales, some are conceived of as being really or metaphorically vertical. Altitude is obviously vertical in reality. The scale of numbers is viewed metaphorically as vertical, and resident on this, the scale of probabilities is viewed as vertical. Scales that provide values for human concerns tend to be viewed as vertical. Two scales that are not normally viewed as vertical in our culture are horizontal distance and time.

We will not attempt to analyze why some scales are vertical and others are not. We will simply stipulate of the appropriate scales that they are vertical. For example, a nonnegative numeric scale is vertical.

```
(forall (s) (if (nonNegNumericScale s)(vertical s)))    (14.10)
```

The argument of vertical has to be a scale.

```
(forall (s) (if (vertical s) (scale s)))               (14.11)
```

If an entity moves from a point on vertical scale to a higher point, we say that there has been an increase.

```
(forall (e x y z s)                                    (14.12)
    (iff (increase x s)
        (exists (y z e1 e2)
            (and (at' e1 x y s)(at' e2 x z s)(lts y z s)
                (vertical s)(change e1 e2)))))
```

Similarly, if an entity moves from a point on a vertical scale to a lower point, there has been a decrease.

```
(forall (e x y z s)                                    (14.13)
    (iff (decrease x s)
        (exists (y z e1 e2)
            (and (at' e1 x y s)(at' e2 x z s)(lts z y s)
                (vertical s)(change e1 e2)))))
```

PREDICATES INTRODUCED IN THIS CHAPTER

(change e1 e2)
   There is a change from eventuality e1 to eventuality e2.

(changeIn x)
   There is a change in some property of x.

(changeFrom e1)

There is a change out of eventuality e1.

(changeTo e2)

There is a change into eventuality e2.

(move x y z)

x moves from y to z.

(vertical s)

Scale s is a real or metaphorical vertical scale.

(increase x s)

x increases on scale s.

(decrease x s)

x decreases on scale s.

15

Causality

CAUSAL COMPLEXES AND THE PREDICATE cause

The account of causality we use here is that of Hobbs (2005b). This distinguishes between the monotonic, precise notion of "causal complex" and the nonmonotonic, defeasible notion of "cause." The former gives us mathematical rigor; the latter is more useful for everyday reasoning and can be characterized in terms of the former. We begin with an abbreviated account of these concepts.

When we flip a switch to turn on a light, we say that flipping the switch caused the light to turn on. But for this to happen, many other factors had to be in place. The bulb had to be intact, the switch had to be connected to the bulb, the power had to be on in the city, and so on. We will use the predicate cause for flipping the switch, and introduce the predicate causalComplex to refer to the set of all the states and events that have to hold or happen for the effect to happen. Thus, the states of the bulb, the wiring, and the power supply would all be in the causal complex.

The predicate causalComplex has two arguments, a set of eventualities (the cause and the various preconditions) and an eventuality (the effect). We will also allow the first argument to be a single eventuality.

```
(forall (s e)                                          (15.1)
    (if (causalComplex s e)
        (and (eventuality e)
            (or (eventualities s)
                (eventuality s)))))
```

That is, if s is a causal complex for effect e, then e is an eventuality, and s is either an eventuality or a set of eventualities.

Because we can view a single eventuality as a singleton set of eventualities, the expressions (causalComplex e1 e) and (and (causalComplex s e) (singleton s e1)) are equivalent. Because a set of eventualities really exists exactly when their conjunction really exists, then, for example, the expressions (and (causalComplex s e) (doubleton s e1 e2)) and (and (causalComplex e0 e) (and' e0 e1 e2)) are equivalent. These equivalences will allow us to be sloppy in referring to causal complexes as eventualities, sets of eventualities, or conjunctions of eventualities.

Causal complexes have two primary features. The first is that if all of the eventualities in the causal complex obtain or occur, then so does the effect. This property interacts with time, so we will state the axiom in Chapter 16 on Time.

The second property is that each of the members of the causal complex is relevant, in the sense that if it is removed from the set, the remainder is not a causal complex for the effect.

```
(forall (s s1 e1 e)                                        (15.2)
    (if (and (causalComplex s e)(member e1 s)(deleteElt s1 s e1))
        (not (causalComplex s1 e))))
```

It may be that we can still achieve e in another manner, but that would involve adding other eventualities to the causal complex; we would no longer have s1. For example, flipping the switch e1 may be part of a causal complex s for turning a light off e. If I remove this from the set of eventualities that really exist, the remaining set s1 is not a causal complex for turning the light off. I could add another eventuality, say, unscrewing the light bulb. But that would be a different causal complex, neither s nor s1.

A common approach to causality is to treat it in terms of counterfactuals (e.g., Lewis, 1973). The sentence "Flipping a switch causes the light to go on" is true, so goes the first attempt at this reduction, exactly when the counterfactual sentence "If the switch hadn't been flipped, the light would not have gone on" is true. The standard counterexample to this is illustrated in the movie *Gosford Park*. A woman knows her son is going to kill his father, so she gets there first and poisons him. When the son approaches, the father is slumped over dead. The son thinks he is sleeping, and stabs him. Did the woman's poisoning the father cause him to die? In this case, the counterfactual is not true. If the woman had not poisoned the father, he would have died anyway, at the hand of the son. This sort of example forces one to tinker with the account of causality in terms of counterfactuals. But in terms of causal complexes, there is nothing paradoxical about this example, and there is no violation of Axiom (15.2). The son's stabbing of his father was not in the causal complex for his father's dying. All he did was stab his father's corpse. Without that stabbing, the death would still have occurred, so Axiom (15.2) tells us that the stabbing was not part of the operative causal complex. If we remove the poisoning from the causal complex, the remainder of the causal complex would not have brought about the death. If we add the stabbing to that remainder, the death would have occurred, but that is a different causal complex.

In practice, we can never specify all the eventualities in a causal complex for an event. So although the notion gives us a precise way of thinking about causality, it is not adequate for the kind of practical reasoning we do in planning, explaining, and predicting. For this, we need the defeasible notion of "cause."

In a causal complex, for most events we can bring about, the majority of the eventualities are normally true. In the light bulb case, it is normally true that the bulb is not burnt out, that the wiring is intact, that the power is on in the city, and so on. What is not normally true is that someone is flipping the light switch. Those eventualities that are not normally true are identified as causes (cf. Kayser and Nouioua, 2009). They are useful in planning, because they are often the actions that the

planner or some other agent must perform. They are useful in explanation and prediction because they frequently constitute the new information.

In Hobbs (2005b) the interpretation of the predicate cause is constrained by
axioms involving the largely unexplicated notion of "presumable," among others;
most elements of a causal complex can be presumed to hold, and the others are
identified as causes. We won't repeat that development here, but we will place some
looser constraints on causes. We will use the predicate cause0 here, because in the
next section we will introduce a cause predicate that will also allow agents as well as
eventualities to be causes.

First, a cause is an eventuality in a causal complex.

```
(forall (e1 e2)                                                     (15.3)
    (if (cause0 e1 e2)
        (exists (s)(and (causalComplex s e2)(member e1 s)))))
```

This allows only single eventualities to be causes, and of course many events have
multiple causes. But this is not a limitation because we can always bundle the multiple
causes into a single conjunction of causes. So if e1 is pouring starter fluid onto a
pile of firewood and e2 is lighting a match, then the cause of the fire starting is e3
where (and' e3 e1 e2) holds.

This notion of cause0 as the conjunction of the nonpresumable eventualities in
a causal complex fails to cover the case illustrated by "Gravity is the cause of my
desk staying on the floor." Perhaps the predicate "presumable" should be replaced by
"nonproblematic"; in making the statement about gravity, we are "problematizing"
the effect of gravity. In any case, the explication of the predicates "presumable" and
"problematic" would require the kind of theories of human cognition and action that
we present in Part III of this book.

The principal useful property of cause is a kind of causal modus ponens. When
the cause happens or holds, then, defeasibly, so does the effect. This interacts with
time, so we defer stating the axiom until Chapter 16.

Causality is not strictly speaking transitive. Shoham (1990) gives as an example
that making a car lighter causes it to go faster, and taking the engine out causes the
car to be lighter, but taking the engine out does not cause the car to go faster. In
the second action, we have undone one of the presumable conditions in the causal
complex for the first action. The two causal complexes are inconsistent. However,
when they are consistent, cause is transitive, so we can say that cause is defeasibly
transitive.

```
(forall (e1 e2 e3)                                                  (15.4)
    (if (and (cause0 e1 e2) (cause0 e2 e3) (etc))
        (cause0 e1 e3)))
```

15.2 AGENTS AND AGENTHOOD

There are some entities in the world that are viewed as being capable of initiating a
causal chain. This is a scientifically inaccurate view; when a dog stands up and walks
across a room, there are events in its brain that caused it to do so. But the idea pervades commonsense reasoning. We say that the dog's walking was caused by the dog,
and don't necessarily expect to find anterior causes.

We will call such entities agents. People are the prime examples of agents, but the class also includes robots and other intelligent software, higher animals, organizations, and a variety of fictional entities such as gods, ghosts, and goblins. Frequently, when we use a person metaphor for some other type of entity, agenthood is what motivates us.

In this book we will use the predicate agent to describe this broader class of entities. Much in the cognitive theories in Part III describe abstract properties that would be true of anything capable of what might be called cognition, and those elements of the theories will be attributed to agents in general. Properties that are specific to persons, such as emotions and human perceptual organs, will be attributed only to persons.

We defined cause0 as applying only to eventualities. We can now introduce cause as a predicate like cause0 except that it also allows agents as its first argument. In Chapter 31 we will talk about the process by which plans become actions. This can be subsumed under the predicate will. The expression (will a e) means that agent a wills to carry out eventuality e, and then e happens with no intermediate causes. Then for an agent a to cause an event e is for a's willing e to function as a cause0. The following axiom defines cause to be cause0 when the first argument is an eventuality. When the first argument is an agent, that agent's willing is the cause0 of the second argument.

```
(forall (a e2)                                              (15.5)
    (and (if (eventuality a)
             (iff (cause a e2)(cause0 a e2)))
         (if (agent a)
             (iff (cause a e2)
                  (exists (e1)
                      (and (will' e1 a e2)(cause0 e1 e2)))))
         (if (not (or (eventuality a)(agent a)))
             (not (cause a e2)))))
```

The chief property of agents is that they, defeasibly, are capable of causing some events.

```
(forall (a)                                                 (15.6)
    (if (and (agent a)(etc))
        (exists (e) (cause a e))))
```

Case roles common in linguistics can be defined in terms of core theories. In particular, the agent of an event is an agent that causes it.

```
(forall (a e)                                               (15.7)
    (iff (agentOf a e)
        (and (agent a)(cause a e))))
```

In this formulation, we are silent about whether there are prior causes for the willing of the event. There may or may not be a prior cause.

The word "action" will not be a technical term in this theory, but for convenience we will use it informally to refer to events that have an agent.

Doing an action can be defined as follows:

```
(forall (a e)                                              (15.8)
    (iff (do a e)
         (and (agentOf a e)(Rexist e))))
```

Agent a has done an action e if and only if a is the agent of the action and the action really takes place.

Although we will not deal with other "case labels," it would perhaps be of interest to define some of the others in this framework, specifically, `instrumentOf`, `objectOf`, `sourceOf`, and `goalOf`, as they can be characterized in terms of the causal structure of the event. What we are calling the "object" of an action has also been called the "patient," and also, more bizarrely, the "theme." It is the entity that goes through a change in the final stage of the causal chain.

```
(forall (x e)                                              (15.9)
    (iff (objectOf x e)
         (or (changeIn' e x)
             (exists (e1 e2)
                (and (and' e e1 e2)(cause e1 e2)(objectOf x e2))))))
```

That is, x is the object of an event if the event is a change in x, or recursively if the event is a causal chain of subevents, the final event of which has x as its object.

An instrument is an entity that the agent causes to go through a change of state, broadly construed, where this change plays an intermediate role in the causal chain.

```
(forall (y e)                                              (15.10)
    (iff (instrumentOf y e)
         (exists (a e1)
            (and (agentOf a e1)(changeIn' e1 y)
                 (or (cause e1 e)
                     (exists (e2)
                        (and (cause e1 e2)(and' e e1 e2))))))))
```

That is, y is an instrument of an event e if the agent causes a change in y, and that causes e or the end state in e.

When the property that changes in the object is a real or metaphorical at relation, say, from (at x z s) to (at x w s), for some s. then we can call z the "source" and w the "goal." However, because the predicate goal with a different meaning plays such a huge role in this book, we will call this case label the `terminusOf` the action or event.

```
(forall (z e)                                              (15.11)
    (iff (sourceOf z e)
         (exists (x w e1 e2 s)
            (and (at' e1 x z s)(at' e2 x w s)(change' e e1 e2)))))
```

```
(forall (w e)                                              (15.12)
    (iff (terminusOf w e)
         (exists (x z e1 e2 s)
            (and (at' e1 x z s)(at' e2 x w s)(change' e e1 e2)))))
```

Agents frequently work together. When they do, we can call the set of agents a "collective." So far, we can state that collectives are sets of agents.

```
(forall (s)                                                  (15.13)
    (if (collective s)
        (forall (a) (if (member a s)(agent a)))))
```

We will introduce further properties of collectives in Part III, namely, that they have mutual beliefs and common goals.

15.3 OTHER CAUSAL PREDICATES

The predicate cause is important in planning, explanation, and prediction, but for many cognitive acts, we will rely on a much looser notion – that of being simply causally involved. An eventuality e1 is causally involved in bringing about some effect e if it is in some causal complex for e.

```
(forall (e1 e2)                                              (15.14)
    (iff (causallyInvolved e1 e2)
        (exists (s) (and (causalComplex s e2) (member e1 s)))))
```

A causal complex consists of causes and other, presumable or nonproblematic, eventualities. The latter are frequently referred to as enabling conditions or preconditions. For these, we will introduce the predicate enable. One eventuality e1 enables another e2 if it is a noncause part of a causal complex s for e2. In the preliminary predicate enable0 we include the causal complex s as one of the arguments, because there may be many ways to achieve the effect, only some of which require e1 to hold.

```
(forall (e1 e2 s)                                            (15.15)
    (iff (enable0 e1 e2 s)
        (and (causalComplex s e2) (member e1 s)
            (not (cause e1 e2)))))
```

The expression (enable0 e1 e2 s) says that e1 is an enabling condition for e2 provided it is in the causal complex s that will be used to bring about e2, but is not the cause of e2.

If an eventuality e1 is required for any way of bringing about e2, then we can use the two-argument predicate enable – (enable e1 e2).

```
(forall (e1 e2)                                              (15.16)
    (iff (enable e1 e2)
        (forall (s) (if (causalComplex s e2)(enable0 e1 e2 s)))))
```

If an enabling condition does not hold, then the effect will not occur. Because the enabling condition is presumable, its negation is not presumable. We thus have a causal complex for the negation of the effect in which the negation of the enabling condition is not presumable, and hence a cause. More succinctly, if e1 enables e2, then (not e1) causes (not e2).

```
(forall (e1 e2)                                                    (15.17)
    (iff (enable e1 e2)
        (forall (e3)
            (if (not' e3 e1)
                (exists (e4) (and (not' e4 e2)(cause e3 e4)))))))
```

That is, e1 enables e2 just in case any negation of e1 causes some negation of e2.

In the STRIPS model of Fikes and Nilsson (1971), the enabling conditions correspond to the preconditions and the body corresponds to the cause. The added and deleted states correspond to the effect.

Two related notions are "allow" and "prevent." An eventuality e1 allows an eventuality e2 if e1 does not cause (not e2).

```
(forall (e1 e2)                                                    (15.18)
    (iff (allow e1 e2)
        (forall (e4) (if (not' e4 e2) (not (cause e1 e4))))))
```

An eventuality e1 prevents e2 if e1 is the cause of (not e2).

```
(forall (e1 e2)                                                    (15.19)
    (iff (prevent e1 e2)
        (exists (e4) (and (not' e4 e2) (cause e1 e4)))))
```

There are two weaker varieties of the predicate cause that are occasionally useful. The first is partiallyCause. An eventuality e1 partially causes another eventuality e2 if e1's conjunction with another eventuality e3 causes e2.

```
(forall (e1 e2)                                                    (15.20)
    (iff (partiallyCause e1 e2)
        (exists (e3 e4)
            (and (not (cause e1 e2))(not (cause e3 e2))
                (and' e4 e1 e3) (cause e4 e2)))))
```

The second predicate is tcause. The expression (tcause e1 e2) means that e1 tends to cause e2. Very often in planning we can't be sure our actions will actually cause the desired outcome. We only know that they will increase its probability, and we proceed on this basis.

In Hobbs (2005b) the following beginning of an account of probabilistic causality is given. Suppose s is the only causal complex for an effect e. Suppose we are certain that a subset s1 of s actually holds. Then when we say that s1 will bring about e with probability p, we are simply saying that p is the joint probability of the eventualities in s − s1.

If the probabilities are high enough to be called "likely," that is, they are, distributionally and/or functionally, in the high region of the "likelihood" scale, then we can use the predicate tcause. If (cause e1 e2) holds, then the other eventualities in the causal complex for e2 can be presumed to hold. If (tcause e1 e2) holds, then the other eventualities in the causal complex for e2 are merely likely. Both cause and tcause are only defeasible, but tcause is more defeasible. It is more likely to be defeated.

```
(forall (e1 e2)                                              (15.21)
    (iff (tcause e1 e2)
        (exists (s c)
            (and (causalComplex s e2) (member e1 s)
                (deleteElt s1 s e1) (likely s1 c)
                (if (Rexist s)(cause e1 e2))))))
```

That is, e1 tends to cause e2 if e1 is in a causal complex s for e2, if the rest of s is likely, and if e1 would be singled out as a cause of e2 provided s actually obtains.

It may also be useful to have a predicate that makes the value of the likelihood explicit. Its definition is very similar to that of tcause.

```
(forall (e1 e2 q c)                                          (15.22)
    (iff (tcauseq e1 e2 q c)
        (exists (s)
            (and (causalComplex s e2) (member e1 s)
                (deleteElt s1 s e1) (likelihood q s1 c)
                (if (Rexist s1)(cause e1 e2))))))
```

That is, e1 tends to cause e2 with likelihood q, given constraints c, if e1 is in a causal complex for e2, if the likelihood of the rest of s is q, and if e1 would be singled out as a cause of e2 provided the rest of s actually obtains.

The predicates likelihood and likely are explicated in Chapter 20 on Modality.

The notion cause is stronger than the notion tcause, in the sense that if e1 causes e2 then it tends to cause e2.

```
(forall (e1 e2)                                              (15.23)
    (if (cause e1 e2)(tcause e1 e2)))
```

15.4 ABILITY

The concept of "ability" is difficult to characterize. It is closely related to possibility. We will see in Chapter 20 that possibility is characterized with respect to a set of constraints. Something is possible if those constraints do not rule it out.

Ability is also with respect to an implicit set of constraints. Suppose Joan is sleeping when we ask, "Is Joan able to play tennis?" The answer is clearly no if we include her sleeping as one of the constraints. If we don't, it may well be yes.

But when we speak of an agent's ability to do something, we generally remove from consideration eventualities that are beyond the agent's control. For example, is Joan able to play tennis if all the tennis courts within reach are already occupied. In that case, it would not be *possible* for her to play tennis, but she is still *able* to play tennis. A person's ability to perform an action is normally viewed as the action being possible provided all the eventualities not under his or her control go the right way.

First we define the eventualities beyond an agent a's control as the subset s1 of eventualities in a set s that a cannot bring about by a's efforts alone. That is, a is not the agent of actions in s1 nor the agent of an action that causes events in s1.

```
(forall (s1 s a)                                              (15.24)
    (iff (evsBeyondControl s1 s a)
         (and (eventualities s)(subset s1 s)(agent a)
              (forall (e)
                  (iff (member e s1)
                       (and (not (agentOf a e))
                            (not (exists (e1)
                                 (and (agentOf a e1)
                                      (cause e1 e)))))))))))
```

Now we can say that an agent a is able to do e, given a set of constraints c, if the agent's causing e is possible with respect to c whenever the set s1 of all the events in a causal complex s for e that are beyond a's control really exist independently.

```
(forall (a e c)                                               (15.25)
    (iff (able a e c)
         (exists (s s1 e1)
             (and (causalComplex s e)(cause' e1 a e)(member e1 s)
                  (evsBeyondControl s1 s a)
                  (if (Rexist s1)(possible e1 c))))))
```

That is, a is able to do e with respect to constraints c whenever there is a causal complex s for effecting e, a's causing e is a member of that causal complex, s1 is the subset of s beyond a's control, and if s1 really exists, then a's causing e is possible with respect to constraints c.

If the set of constraints c does not include Joan's sleeping, then it is possible for Joan to play tennis, so she is able to play tennis. If Joan herself has all the requisite skills for playing tennis, that is, if the constraints c do not rule out events under Joan's control in the causal complex for playing tennis, she is able to play tennis with respect to constraints c.

Ability is the state of being able.

```
(forall (e1 a e c)                                            (15.26)
    (iff (ability e1 a e c)(able' e1 a e c)))
```

That is, e1 is a's ability to do e given constraints c if e1 is the state of a's being able to do e given constraints c.

Our analysis of ability is consistent with that of Heider (1958, Chapter 4). He analyzes ability into two components: the agent's power, or the actions the agent is capable of bringing about, and the difficulty inherent in environmental factors, or in our terms, the events beyond the agent's control.

15.5 EXECUTABILITY

In computational settings, it is relatively easy to say what "executable" means. An action is executable if it is directly implemented in the underlying software and its preconditions are satisfied. But more generally, the notion of "executable" is a matter of perspective. From one perspective, one can view driving home from work as an executable action. From a finer-grained perspective, one has to decompose this into actions such as drive a block and turn right. At an even finer granularity, we can take as the executable actions such things as maintaining a certain pressure on the accelerator and turning the steering wheel by a certain amount. There is no limit in principle to how fine-grained the decomposition can be, although when talking about human plans, we are generally satisfied calling something executable if it is an automatic action that does not require conscious thought.

We can posit a notion of "directly causes" (dcause) as a relation between an agent or event and an event, which is true when there are no intermediate, mediating events.

```
(forall (e1 e2)                                            (15.27)
   (iff (dcause e1 e2)
        (and (cause e1 e2)
             (not (exists (e3)
                    (and (cause e1 e3)(cause e3 e2)))))))
```

Whether or not this is possible in reality is irrelevant; we certainly have the idea in our commonsense thinking. If a vase breaks on being dropped, we think of its hitting the ground as the direct cause of the breaking, without imagining internal stresses in the ceramic material between the hitting and the breaking. Many bodily and mental actions are seen as directly caused by the person. So when a man moves his arm, he directly causes the arm to move.

If an agent can will an event to happen, then this willing is a direct cause of the event.

```
(forall (e1 a e)                                            (15.28)
   (if (and (will' e1 a e)(cause e1 e))
       (dcause e1 e)))
```

Here, e1 is the action of a's willing e to happen. If e1 really causes e, then it is a direct cause of e.

An agent directly causes an event if and only if the agent's willing it to happen directly causes it.

```
(forall (a e)                                               (15.29)
   (if (agent a)
       (iff (dcause a e)
            (exists (e1)(and (will' e1 a e)(dcause e1 e))))))
```

This axiom provides the coercion from events to agents as direct causes.

In Chapter 19 on Persons and in Part III on Commonsense Psychology, we will see several examples of events that persons are able to cause directly by willing.

Next we need the concept of an eventuality being "enabled" at a particular time. In Section 15.3 we defined enable0, enablement with respect to a particular causal complex, being a noncause element of the causal complex. We will say that a causal complex for an eventuality is enabled at time t if all its preconditions hold at time t.

```
(forall (s e t)                                          (15.30)
    (iff (enabled s e t)
        (forall (e1)
            (if (enable0 e1 e s)(atTime e1 t)))))
```

We use the predicate atTime, explicated in Chapter 16, meaning that an eventuality occurs or holds at a particular time.

If an agent can directly cause an action that is enabled, then it is executable. Moreover, if the action can be caused by another executable action, then it is executable. Thus, Mary's driving a nail into a board is executable if the enabling conditions hold – she has the hammer, the nail, and the board – because she can directly cause her hand to grasp the hammer and her arm to swing, this will cause the hammer to hit the nail, and that will cause the nail to go into the board.

```
(forall (e a c t)                                        (15.31)
    (iff (executable e a c t)
        (exists (s)
            (and (enabled s e t)
                (or (exists (e1)
                        (and (dcause' e1 a e)(possible e1 c)))
                    (exists (e2)
                        (and (cause e2 e)
                            (executable e2 a c t))))))))
```

The expression (executable e a c t) says that action e is executable by agent a given constraints c at time t. For this to hold, there must be a causal complex s that brings e about and s must be enabled at time t. Moreover, either the agent can directly cause e, or recursively, something that causes e must be executable.

In Chapter 33 on Execution Envisionment, we will deepen the analysis of executability in the context of planning.

15.6 DIFFICULTY

If an action is difficult for an agent, it is because there are states and events, that is, eventualities, that tend to cause the action not to happen. We will attempt to capture this intuition in a predicate called difficult that takes an action and its agent as arguments.

```
(forall (a e)                                            (15.32)
    (if (difficult e a)(and (agent a)(agentOf a e))))
```

The expression (difficult e a) says action e is difficult for agent a.

First, we define the set of difficulties associated with an action as the set of eventualities that tend to cause the action not to happen.

```
(forall (s e)                                                    (15.33)
    (iff (difficultiesWith s e)
        (forall (e1)
            (iff (member e1 s)
                (exists (e2) (and (not' e2 e)(tcause e1 e2)))))))
```

The predicate `difficultiesWith` is a relation between a set of eventualities and an eventuality. Thus, it may be used with the predicate `subsetConsistent` from Chapter 12 on Scales to constrain the ordering on a scale of difficulty. In a move that will be common in Part III of this book, we will not define the scale of difficulty; we will only constrain it by subset consistency. If the set of difficulties associated with achieving e1 contains the set of difficulties associated with achieving e2, then e1 is more difficult than e2. This fact does not specify the complete structure on the scale, but it does provide a minimal condition on the ordering.

```
(forall (s s1 e)                                                 (15.34)
    (if (and (difficultyScale s e)(difficultiesWith' e1 s e))
        (subsetConsistent s e1)))
```

What we are beginning to capture here is the observation that the more obstructions there are, the more difficult something is. It is often hard to judge whether one action is more or less difficult than another, but when we analyze the issue, we often consider what obstructions there are to each action's achievement.

Finally, we can say that something is difficult if it is in the `Hi` region of a difficulty scale, or in other words, the difficulty scale is the `scaleFor` the `difficult` property.

```
(forall (e1 e a)                                                 (15.35)
    (iff (difficult' e1 e a)
        (and (agent a)(agentOf a e)
            (exists (s)
                (and (difficultyScale s e)(scaleFor s e1))))))
```

This completes our analysis of "difficult," such as it is. An action is difficult if it is in the functionally or distributionally high region of a scale whose ordering is consistent with the subset ordering on sets of obstructions involved in performing the action.

PREDICATES INTRODUCED IN THIS CHAPTER

(causalComplex c e)
    The collection c of eventualities is a causal complex for effect e.

(cause0 e1 e2)
    Eventuality e1 causes eventuality e2.

(cause e1 e2)
    Eventuality or agent e1 causes eventuality e2.

(agent a)
    a is an agent.

(agentOf a e)
    Agent a is the agent or cause of eventuality e.

(do a e)
    Agent a does action e.

(objectOf x e)
    x is the entity undergoing change in e.

(instrumentOf x e)
    x is an instrument used in e.

(sourceOf x e)
    e is a change in an "at" relation and x is the location of the initial "at" relation.

(terminusOf x e)
    e is a change in an "at" relation and x is the location of the final "at" relation.

(collective s)
    s is a collective of agents.

(causallyInvolved e1 e2)
    e1 is in some causal complex for e2.

(enable0 e1 e2 s)
    Eventuality e1 is a member of a causal complex s for eventuality e2 but not the cause of e2.

(enable e1 e2)
    Eventuality e1 is a member of every causal complex for eventuality e2 but not the cause of e2.

(allow e1 e2)
    e1 doesn't cause not e2.

(prevent e1 e2)
    e1 causes not e2.

(partiallyCause e1 e2)
    e1 together with something else causes e2.

(tcause e1 e2)
    e1 tends to cause e2.

(tcauseq e1 e2 q c)
    e1 tends to cause e2 with likelihood q given constraints c.

(evsBeyondControl s1 s a)
    s1 is the subset of eventualities in s that are not under agent a's control.

(able a e c)
    Agent a is able to do e under constraints c.

(ability e1 a e c)
    e1 is agent a's ability to do e under constraints c.

(dcause e1 e2)
    Eventuality or agent e1 directly causes eventuality e2 without any intermediate causes.

(enabled s e t)
    All the enabling conditions for causal complex s resulting in eventuality e hold at time t.

(executable e a c t)
    Action e is executable by agent a under constraints c at time t.

(difficultiesWith s e)
    s is the set of obstructions tending to prevent action e from being performed.

(difficultyScale s e)
    s is a scale for measuring the difficulty of actions of type e.

(difficult e a)
    Action e is difficult for agent a.

In addition, we used the five following predicates that have not yet been defined, the first from Chapter 16 on Time, the next three from Chapter 20 on Modality, and the last from Chapters 19 on Persons and 31 on Plans.

(atTime e t)
    e occurs or holds at time t.

(possible e c)
    e is possible with respect to constraints c.

(likelihood q e c)
    q is the likelihood of e, given constraints c.

(likely e)
    e is likely.

(will a e)
    Agent a does e by an act of will.

16

Time

16.1 THE TOPOLOGY OF TIME: INSTANTS, INTERVALS, AND TEMPORAL SEQUENCES

This development of an ontology of time is a condensation and abridgment of OWL-Time (Hobbs and Pan, 2004), with some minor differences.

There are two kinds of temporal entities: instants and intervals.

```
(forall (t) (if (instant t) (temporalEntity t)))                 (16.1)
```

```
(forall (t) (if (interval t) (temporalEntity t)))                (16.2)
```

No assumptions are made about whether intervals *consist* of instants. Rather one can specify relations between the two, such as that an instant begins or ends or is inside an interval. Later in this section we will introduce the idea of the time span of an eventuality. The predicates begins, ends, insideTime and several others will allow temporal sequences and eventualities as well as temporal entities in their second argument positions. Axioms presented below will specify the coercion from eventualities to their time spans. We thus include eventualities in the constraints on the arguments of these predicates.

```
(forall (t1 t2)                                                  (16.3)
    (if (begins t1 t2)
        (and (instant t1)
            (or (temporalEntity t2)(tseq t2)(eventuality t2)))))
```

```
(forall (t1 t2)                                                  (16.4)
    (if (ends t1 t2)
        (and (instant t1)
            (or (temporalEntity t2)(tseq t2)(eventuality t2)))))
```

```
(forall (t1 t2)                                                  (16.5)
    (if (insideTime t1 t2)
        (and (instant t1)
            (or (temporalEntity t2)(tseq t2)(eventuality t2)))))
```

The beginning and end of an instant is itself.

```
(forall (t1 t2)                                             (16.6)
    (if (and (instant t2)(begins t1 t2))
        (equal t1 t2)))
```

```
(forall (t1 t2)                                             (16.7)
    (if (and (instant t2)(ends t1 t2))
        (equal t1 t2)))
```

An interval t between two instants t1 and t2 is an interval that begins at t1 and ends at t2. It will be useful to extend this to intervals and define it as the interval from the end of t1 to the beginning of t2.

```
(forall (t t1 t2)                                           (16.8)
    (iff (intervalBetween t t1 t2)
        (exists (t3 t4)
            (and (ends t3 t1)(begins t4 t2)
                 (begins t3 t)(ends t4 t)))))
```

A positively infinite interval is one that has no end.

```
(forall (t)                                                 (16.9)
    (iff (posInfInterval t)
        (and (interval t)(not (exists (t2) (ends t2 t))))))
```

A positively infinite interval may or may not have a beginning. In the full OWL-Time, negatively infinite intervals are also defined, but they will not be needed here.

The ontology is silent about whether there can be intervals of zero length, but when the beginning and end of an interval are distinct, we will call it a proper interval. Positive infinite intervals are regarded as proper intervals; we ignore negative infinite intervals here.

```
(forall (t)                                                 (16.10)
    (iff (properInterval t)
        (or (exists (t1 t2)
                (and (begins t1 t)(ends t2 t)(nequal t1 t2)))
            (posInfInterval t))))
```

Time is ordered by a before relation that we explicate in Section 16.3. It is basically a relation between instants, but we can extend it to intervals in the obvious way. We will use it here in defining temporal sequences.

A temporal sequence is a set of nonoverlapping temporal entities. In Hobbs and Pan (2004) we allowed concatenations to be temporal sequences, and then defined the minimal temporal sequence in which no two intervals in the set meet. Here we will shortcut past that wrinkle and define temporal sequences to be minimal.

Concatenations are not allowed. Thus, between any two distinct members of the set there is another interval or instant that is not in the set.

```
(forall (s)                                                          (16.11)
   (iff (tseq s)
        (and (forall (t) (if (member t s)(temporalEntity t)))
             (forall (t1 t2)
                (if (and (member t1 s)(member t2 s))
                    (and (or (equal t1 t2)(before t1 t2)
                             (before t2 t1))
                         (if (before t1 t2)
                             (exists (t3)
                                (and (not (member t3 s))
                                     (before t1 t3)
                                     (before t3 t2)))))))))))
```

Line 3 of this definition says that the members of a temporal sequence are instants or intervals. Lines 5–7 say they are nonoverlapping. Lines 8–12 say they have a temporal entity between them that is not in the temporal sequence.

If there is an element of the temporal sequence before all its other elements, this is called the "first" element.

```
(forall (s t)                                                        (16.12)
   (if (tseq s)
       (iff (first t s)
            (and (member t s)
                 (forall (t1)
                    (if (member t1 s)
                        (or (equal t1 t)(before t t1))))))))
```

If there is an element of the temporal sequence after all its other elements, this is called the "last" element.

```
(forall (s t)                                                        (16.13)
   (if (tseq s)
       (iff (last t s)
            (and (member t s)
                 (forall (t1)
                    (if (member t1 s)
                        (or (equal t1 t)(before t1 t))))))))
```

Note that these axioms do not imply that there really is a first or last element.

Two elements of a temporal sequence are "successive elements" if there is no element between them.

```
(forall (s t1 t2)                                                    (16.14)
   (iff (successiveElts t1 t2 s)
        (and (member t1 s)(member t2 s)(before t1 t2)
             (not (exists (t)
                    (and (member t s)(before t1 t)
                         (before t t2)))))))
```

If the temporal sequence is finite, it can be viewed as a (finite) sequence in the sense of Chapter 9. In this case, the predicates first, last, and successiveElts defined here and in Chapter 9 are consistent.

The predicate before is a partial ordering on the elements of a temporal sequence.

```
(forall (e t1 t2 s)                                              (16.15)
    (if (and (tseq s)(before' e t1 t2))
        (partialOrdering e t1 t2 s)))
```

A temporal sequence is a scale whose ordering relation is before.

```
(forall (s e t1 t1)                                              (16.16)
    (if (and (tseq s)(before' e t1 t2))
        (scaleDefinedBy s s e)))
```

The convex hull of a temporal sequence is the smallest interval spanning all the members of the temporal sequence. We will define it here only for the finite case.

```
(forall (s t1 t2 t3 t4)                                          (16.17)
    (if (and (tseq s)(first t1 s)(begins t3 t1)
             (last t2 s)(ends t4 t2))
        (forall (t)
            (iff (convexHull t s)
                 (intervalBetween t t3 t4)))))
```

The three basic relations, begins, ends, and insideTime, can be extended to cover temporal sequences as well as instants and intervals.

```
(forall (t s)                                                    (16.18)
    (if (tseq s)
        (iff (begins t s)
             (exists (t1) (and (first t1 s)(begins t t1))))))
```

```
(forall (t s)                                                    (16.19)
    (if (tseq s)
        (iff (ends t s)
             (exists (t1) (and (last t1 s)(ends t t1))))))
```

```
(forall (t s)                                                    (16.20)
    (if (and (tseq s)(insideTime t s))
        (and (not (begins t s))(not (ends t s)))
            (exists (t1)
                (and (member t1 s)
                     (or (equal t1 t)(insideTime t t1)
                         (begins t t1)(ends t t1)))))))
```

```
(forall (t s)                                              (16.21)
   (if (tseq s)
       (if (exists (t1)
              (and (member t1 s)
                   (or (equal t1 t)(insideTime t t1))))
           (insideTime t s))))
```

There are two axioms for insideTime to stay neutral about the beginnings and ends of intervals in the temporal sequence. Axiom (16.20) says that if instant t is inside temporal sequence s, it may be the beginning or end of one of its intervals (but not the beginning or end of the temporal sequence as a whole). Axiom (16.21) guarantees being inside the temporal sequence only if it is *inside* one of the intervals; the endpoints of the interval may or may not be inside the temporal sequence.

16.2 RELATING EVENTUALITIES AND TIME

There are four predicates that relate eventualities to instants and intervals. The first is atTime and it relates an eventuality to an instant, saying that that eventuality really exists or obtains at that instant. We state the constraints on its arguments, but we do not attempt to define it.

```
(forall (e t)                                              (16.22)
   (if (atTime e t)(and (eventuality e)(instant t))))
```

The predicate during says that the eventuality really exists or obtains throughout an interval.

```
(forall (e t)                                              (16.23)
   (iff (during e t)
        (and (eventuality e)(properInterval t)
             (forall (t1) (if (insideTime t1 t)(atTime e t1))))))
```

The theory is silent on whether the eventuality really exists or obtains at the end points of the interval.

The "time span of" an eventuality encompasses all the instants and intervals for which it really exists or obtains. The time span may be an instant, an interval, or a temporal sequence.

```
(forall (t e)                                              (16.24)
   (iff (timeSpanOf t e)
        (or (and (instant t)(atTime e t)
                 (forall (t1)
                    (if (nequal t1 t)(not (atTime e t1)))))
            (and (interval t)(during e t)
                 (forall (t1)
                    (if (atTime e t1)
                        (or (insideTime t1 t)(begins t1 t)
                            (ends t1 t)))))
```

```
        (and (tseq t)
             (forall (t1)
                 (if (and (member t1 t)(instant t1))
                     (atTime e t1)))
             (forall (t1)
                 (if (and (member t1 t)(interval t1))
                     (during e t1)))
             (forall (t1)
                 (if (and (instant t1)(atTime e t1))
                     (or (member t1 t)
                         (exists (t2)
                             (and (interval t2)(member t2 t)
                                  (or (begins t1 t2)
                                      (insideTime t1 t2)
                                      (ends t1 t2)))))))))))
```

This definition is complicated only because there are several cases to capture. In lines 3–5, if the time span is an instant, then the eventuality really exists at that instant and no others. In lines 6–10, if the time span is an interval, the eventuality really exists at every instant inside the interval and at no instants that are outside it. Lines 11–25 cover the case in which the time span is a temporal sequence. The eventuality is happening at every instant in the temporal sequence (lines 12–14), and during every interval in the temporal sequence (lines 15–17). Lines 18–25 say that any instant at which the eventuality is happening (line 19) must be an instant in the temporal sequence (line 20) or in an interval in the temporal sequence (lines 21–25).

We will say that an eventuality "happens in" a temporal entity or sequence if its time span is entirely included in the temporal entity or sequence.

```
    (forall (e t)                                                        (16.25)
        (iff (happensIn e t)
             (exists (t1)
                 (and (timeSpanOf t1 e)
                      (forall (t2)
                          (if (or (begins t2 t1)(insideTime t2 t1)
                                  (ends t2 t1))
                              (or (begins t2 t)(insideTime t2 t)
                                  (ends t2 t)))))))))
```

The three basic relations of Section 16.1 can now be extended to eventualities as well.

```
    (forall (t e)                                                        (16.26)
        (if (eventuality e)
            (iff (begins t e)
                 (exists (t1)(and (timeSpanOf t1 e)(begins t t1))))))
```

```
    (forall (t e)                                                        (16.27)
        (if (eventuality e)
            (iff (insideTime t e)
                 (exists (t1)
                     (and (timeSpanOf t1 e)(insideTime t t1))))))
```

```
(forall (t e)                                              (16.28)
    (if (eventuality e)
        (iff (ends t e)
            (exists (t1)(and (timeSpanOf t1 e)(ends t t1))))))
```

The predicate `posInfIntervalEv` says that its argument is either a positive infinite interval or an eventuality whose time span is a positive infinite interval.

```
(forall (e)                                                (16.29)
    (iff (posInfIntervalEv e)
        (or (posInfInterval e)
            (exists (t)
                (and (timeSpanOf t e)(posInfInterval t))))))
```

The predicate `properIntervalEv` says that its argument is either a proper interval or an eventuality whose time span is a proper interval.

```
(forall (e)                                                (16.30)
    (iff (properIntervalEv e)
        (or (properInterval e)
            (exists (t)
                (and (timeSpanOf t e)(properInterval t)))
            (posInfIntervalEv e))))
```

It will be useful to have a category for the relations `atTime`, `during`, `timeSpanOf`, `happensIn`, and several other predicates when we are axiomatizing scheduling. We will call them `temporal`.

```
(forall (e0 e t)(if (atTime' e0 e t)(temporal e0)))        (16.31)
```

```
(forall (e0 e t)(if (during' e0 e t)(temporal e0)))        (16.32)
```

```
(forall (e0 e t)(if (timeSpanOf' e0 t e)(temporal e0)))    (16.33)
```

```
(forall (e0 e t)(if (happensIn' e0 e t)(temporal e0)))     (16.34)
```

A nontemporal eventuality is one that isn't temporal.

```
(forall (e) (iff (nontemporal e)(not (temporal e))))       (16.35)
```

Temporal properties are ones that say something about when an eventuality occurs.

16.3 TEMPORAL ORDERING AND INTERVAL RELATIONS

Instants are at least partially ordered by a `before` relation. The `before` relation will also be extended to intervals, temporal sequences, and eventualities, so the constraints on its arguments are as follows:

```
(forall (t1 t2)                                            (16.36)
    (if (before t1 t2)
        (and (or (temporalEntity t1)(tseq t1)(eventuality t1))
             (or (temporalEntity t2)(tseq t2)(eventuality t2)))))
```

The ontology is silent about whether time is linearly ordered. In the full OWL-Time, one can assert a single proposition to enable the axiom for linear ordering. We will not require linear ordering in this book.

The beginning of a proper interval is before the instants inside, which are before the end.

```
(forall (t1 t2 t3 t)                                              (16.37)
   (if (properIntervalEv t)
       (and (if (and (begins t1 t)(ends t3 t))
                (before t1 t3))
            (if (and (begins t1 t)(insideTime t2 t))
                (before t1 t2))
            (if (and (insideTime t2 t)(ends t3 t))
                (before t2 t3)))))
```

The beginning of a positive infinite interval, if there is one, is before all the instants inside it.

```
(forall (t1 t2 t)                                                 (16.38)
   (if (and (posInfInterval t)(begins t1 t)(insideTime t2 t))
       (before t1 t2)))
```

The before relation is antireflexive.

```
(forall (t) (not (before t t)))                                  (16.39)
```

It is antisymmetric.

```
(forall (t1 t2)                                                   (16.40)
   (if (before t1 t2)
       (not (before t2 t1))))
```

It is transitive.

```
(forall (t1 t2 t3)                                                (16.41)
   (if (and (before t1 t2)(before t2 t3))
       (before t1 t3)))
```

Allen and Kautz (1985) and Allen and Ferguson (1997) describe an algebra of relations between intervals. We will use four of them, and define them in terms of begins, ends and before. These relations hold only between proper intervals or eventualities that have proper intervals as time spans. The predicate intMeets means that the end of one interval is the beginning of the other.

```
(forall (t1 t2)                                                   (16.42)
   (iff (intMeets t1 t2)
        (and (properIntervalEv t1)(properIntervalEv t2)
             (exists (t) (and (ends t t1)(begins t t2))))))
```

Two intervals overlap if the beginning of one is inside the other.

```
(forall (t1 t2)                                           (16.43)
    (iff (intOverlap t1 t2)
        (and (properIntervalEv t1)(properIntervalEv t2)
            (exists (t)
                (or (and (begins t t1)(insideTime t t2))
                    (and (begins t t2)(insideTime t t1)))))))
```

Note that this predicate subsumes both Allen's "overlaps" relation and its inverse.

One interval finishes the other if it begins inside and ends the same place. We have to complicate this relation a bit to accommodate positive infinite intervals.

```
(forall (t1 t2)                                           (16.44)
    (iff (intFinishes t1 t2)
        (and (properIntervalEv t1)(properIntervalEv t2)
            (exists (t3 t4)
                (and (begins t3 t1)(begins t4 t2)(before t4 t3)))
            (or (exists (t)
                    (and (ends t t1)(ends t t2)))
                (and (posInfIntervalEv t1)
                     (posInfIntervalEv t2))))))
```

One interval t1 is during another t2 if t1 begins after t2 and ends before t2. The conditional in the last line of the definition is to accommodate positive infinite intervals.

```
(forall (t1 t2)                                           (16.45)
    (iff (intDuring t1 t2)
        (and (properIntervalEv t1)(properIntervalEv t2)
            (exists (t3 t4)
                (and (begins t3 t1)(begins t4 t2)(before t4 t3)))
            (exists (t5)
                (and (ends t5 t1)
                    (forall (t6)
                        (if (ends t6 t2)(before t5 t6))))))))
```

We can also extend the before relation from instants to intervals, temporal sequences, and eventualities; one of them is before another if the first's end is before the second's beginning.

```
(forall (t1 t2)                                           (16.46)
    (iff (before t1 t2)
        (exists (t3 t4)
            (and (ends t3 t1)(begins t4 t2)(before t3 t4)))))
```

This axiom allows us to use instant, interval, temporal sequence, and eventuality arguments in the before relation and to reduce all before judgments to judgments about instants.

We will sometimes have occasion to talk about one temporal entity being before or meeting another. We will define the predicate beforeOrMeets as follows:

```
(forall (t1 t2)                                                    (16.47)
    (iff (beforeOrMeets t1 t2)
        (exists (t3 t4)
            (and (ends t3 t1)(begins t4 t2)
                (or (before t3 t4)(equal t3 t4))))))
```

Note that this also covers the case where t1 is the instant that begins t2.

Time is a scale whose ordering relation is before and whose components are instants and intervals.

```
(forall (t)                                                        (16.48)
    (iff (timeScale t)
        (exists (s e t2 t3)
            (and (forall (t1)
                    (iff (member t1 s)
                        (or (instant t1)(interval t1))))
                (before' e t2 t3)
                (scaleDefinedBy t s e)))))
```

Because all the elements in a time scale are temporal entities, a time scale can be viewed as a possible ground.

```
(forall (t) (if (timeScale t)(ground t)))                          (16.49)
```

Then atTime can be viewed as an at relation.

```
(forall (s e t)                                                    (16.50)
    (if (and (timeScale s)(atTime e t))
        (at e t s)))
```

It is because of this metaphor that we can, for example, speak of moving a meeting from one time to another.

The notions of change and causality are probably prior to time in evolution and in individual development, and our ideas about time probably arise out of these prior notions. In a way, we can think of time as an idealized sequence of events or changes, say, the ticks of a clock in some Platonic National Bureau of Standards in the sky. It is not necessary to adopt this view of time, but it is important to relate the fundamental notions of "change" and "cause" with the notion of "before." The constraint for change is that final states can't happen before initial states.

```
(forall (e1 e2)                                                    (16.51)
    (if (change e1 e2)(not (before e2 e1))))
```

An effect cannot happen before its cause.

```
(forall (e1 e2)                                                    (16.52)
    (if (cause e1 e2)(not (before e2 e1))))
```

A similar rule holds for enablement

```
(forall (e1 e2)                                                    (16.53)
    (if (enable e1 e2)(not (before e2 e1))))
```

These axioms leave open the possibility of instantaneous change and causality.

We can state stronger relations between causal predicates and before. In fact, we are now able to state one of the two principal properties of causal complexes, that if all the eventualities in the causal complex happen or hold, then the effect will happen or hold. Moreover, the effect is not before the elements of the causal complex.

```
(forall (s e t1)                                                (16.54)
    (if (and (causalComplex s e)
                (forall (e1)(if (member e1 s)(atTime e1 t1))))
        (exists (t2)
            (and (not (before t2 t1))(atTime e t2))))))
```

There is a similar, defeasible, rule for cause.

```
(forall (e1 e2 t1)                                              (16.55)
    (if (and (cause e1 e2)(atTime e1 t1)(etc))
        (exists (t2)
            (and (not (before t2 t1))(atTime e2 t2))))))
```

This axiom is a kind of causal modus ponens; if e1 happens and e1 causes e2, then e2 happens. The etc condition is that all the other, presumable or nonproblematic, eventualities in the causal complex happen or hold.

The relation before is temporal.

```
(forall (e t1 t2)(if (before' e t1 t2)(temporal e)))           (16.56)
```

16.4 DURATIONS

There are two ways we could introduce measures of the duration of intervals.

The first is to map the time scale directly to the real numbers, and define duration in terms of the difference between the numbers that the beginning and end of the interval are mapped to.

The second is to introduce a relation of sameDuration between intervals and to stipulate that certain intervals are standard durations, called "temporal units." Then any hour-long interval has the same duration as the standard hour. Durations of arbitrary intervals are then defined in terms of concatenations of unit-duration intervals.

We will take the second approach since it is probably closer to the way the notion of duration arose in evolution and arises in individual development.

We will assume that people can make the judgment that two intervals are of the same duration. The predicate sameDuration basically applies to intervals, but trivially every instant is of the same duration, namely, zero. So the constraints on the argument of sameDuration are that its arguments are temporal entities.

```
(forall (t1 t2)                                                (16.57)
    (if (sameDuration t1 t2)
        (and (temporalEntity t1)(temporalEntity t2))))
```

```
(forall (t1 t2)                                                (16.58)
    (if (and (instant t1)(instant t2))
        (sameDuration t1 t2)))
```

The predicate sameDuration is reflexive, symmetric, and transitive.

```
(forall (t)                                              (16.59)
    (if (temporalEntity t)(sameDuration t t)))
```

```
(forall (t1 t2)                                          (16.60)
    (iff (sameDuration t1 t2)(sameDuration t2 t1)))
```

```
(forall (t1 t2 t3)                                       (16.61)
    (if (and (sameDuration t1 t2)(sameDuration t2 t3))
        (sameDuration t1 t3)))
```

We will take temporal units to be arbitrary intervals on the time scale. In a sense, the standard hour will be some hour-long interval, but we will never know exactly which hour-long interval it is. We will then say another interval has a duration of an hour if it has the same duration as the standard hour. The only property of temporalUnit that we can state is that it is an interval.

```
(forall (u)                                              (16.62)
    (if (temporalUnit u)(interval u)))
```

The full OWL-Time ontology describes the relations among different temporal units, for example, that a minute is sixty seconds. But we will not need that knowledge here.

A proper interval is a concatenation of a set of proper intervals if every instant inside the interval is inside, the beginning or the end of some interval in the set and the intervals in the set are nonoverlapping. We will deal only with concatenation of finite intervals.

```
(forall (t s)                                            (16.63)
    (iff (concatenation t s)
        (and (properInterval t)
            (forall (t1)(if (member t1 s)(properInterval t1)))
            (exists (t1 t2)
                (and (begins t1 t)(member t2 s)(begins t1 t2)))
            (exists (t1 t2)
                (and (ends t1 t)(member t2 s)(ends t1 t2)))
            (forall (t1)
                (if (insideTime t1 t)
                    (exists (t2)
                        (and (member t2 s)
                            (or (insideTime t1 t2)(begins t1 t2)
                                (ends t1 t2))))))
            (forall (t1 t2)
                (if (and (member t1 s)(member t2 s))
                    (or (equal t1 t2)(not (intOverlap t1 t2)))))))))
```

Line 4 says that s is a set of proper intervals. Lines 5–6 say that one of those intervals begins with the beginning of t. Lines 7–8 say that one of those intervals ends with the end of t. Lines 9–14 say that any instant inside t is inside some member of s. Lines 15–17 say that the members of s are nonoverlapping.

The predication (durationOf d t u) says that t is made up of d intervals having the same duration as u. We will allow the second argument to be an instant, an
interval, a temporal sequence, or an eventuality.

```
(forall (d t u)                                               (16.64)
    (if (durationOf d t u)
        (and (nonNegInteger d)(temporalUnit u)
            (or (temporalEntity t)(tseq t)(eventuality t)))))
```

The duration of an instant is zero.

```
(forall (d t u)                                               (16.65)
    (if (instant t)(durationOf 0 t u)))
```

The duration of an interval is determined by concatenation.

```
(forall (d t u)                                               (16.66)
    (if (interval t)
        (iff (durationOf d t u)
            (exists (s)
                (and (concatenation t s)
                    (forall (t1)
                        (if (member t1 s)(sameDuration t1 u)))
                    (card d s))))))
```

The duration of a temporal sequence is the sum of the durations of its members.
We define this recursively.

```
(forall (s u)                                                 (16.67)
    (if (null s)(durationOf 0 s u)))
```

```
(forall (s s1 t u d d1 d2)                                    (16.68)
    (if (and (tseq s)(tseq s1)(not (member t s1))(addElt s s1 t)
            (durationOf d1 s1 u)(durationOf d2 t u)(sum d d1 d2))
        (durationOf d s u)))
```

The duration of an eventuality is the duration of its time span.

```
(forall (d e u)                                               (16.69)
    (if (eventuality e)
        (iff (durationOf d e u)
            (exists (t)
                (and (timeSpanOf t e)(durationOf d t u))))))
```

We have stipulated that the relevant intervals are integer multiples of the temporal unit u. This is harmless. In Hobbs and Pan (2004) we define the arithmetic relations among the various temporal units, allowing us to convert from one to the other
and thus to talk about fractional durations. We can always pick our original unit to
be small enough (e.g., microsecond) that for all practical purposes the intervals *are*
integer multiples of the unit. We can then apply the arithmetic relations among units
to get a fractional duration in a more convenient unit.

The predicate `durationOf` is temporal.

```
(forall (e d t u)                                                    (16.70)
    (if (durationOf' e d t u)(temporal e)))
```

In terms of `durationOf` we can define a `shorterDuration` partial ordering.

```
(forall (t1 t2)                                                      (16.71)
    (iff (shorterDuration t1 t2)
         (and (interval t1)(interval t2)
              (exists (d1 d2 u)
                  (and (durationOf d1 t1 u)(durationOf d2 t2 u)
                       (lt d1 d2))))))
```

Then we can define a `scaleOrderedByDuration`.

```
(forall (s)                                                          (16.72)
    (iff (scaleOrderedByDuration s)
         (exists (s1 e t1 t2)
             (and (forall (t) (if (member t s1)(interval t)))
                  (shorterDuration' e t1 t2)
                  (scaleDefinedBy s s1 e)))))
```

16.5 PERIODICITY

A temporal sequence is periodic if there is a constant duration between any two successive temporal entities in the temporal sequence.

```
(forall (s)                                                          (16.73)
    (iff (periodicTseq s)
         (and (tseq s)
              (exists (d u)
                  (forall (t1 t2)
                      (if (successiveElts t1 t2 s)
                          (exists (t)
                              (and (intervalBetween t t1 t2)
                                   (durationOf d t u)))))))))
```

The constant duration in a periodic temporal sequence can be called the "gap duration."

```
(forall (s d t1 t2 t n1 n2 u)                                        (16.74)
    (if (and (periodicTseq s)(successiveElts t1 t2 s)
             (temporalUnit u)(intervalBetween t t1 t2))
        (iff (gapDuration d s u)(durationOf d t u))))
```

Sometimes in commonsense reasoning, it is too stringent a requirement that the gap between two elements of a temporal sequence be exactly equal. It is enough that they be roughly equal, that is, that they be of the same half-order of magnitude. We define the notion of "roughly periodic temporal sequences" to cover this case. This has to be with respect to a granularity defined by a temporal unit.

```
(forall (s)                                                    (16.75)
    (iff (roughlyPeriodicTseq s u)
         (and (tseq s)(temporalUnit u)
              (exists (s0 d)
                  (and (scaleOrderedByDuration s0)
                       (forall (t1 t2 t3 t4)
                           (if (and (successiveElts t1 t2 s)
                                    (successiveElts t3 t4 s))
                               (exists (t12 t34 e d)
                                   (and (intervalBetween t12 t1 t2)
                                        (intervalBetween t34 t3 t4)
                                        (durationOf' e d t12 u)
                                        (sameHOM t12 t34 s0 e)))))))))))
```

In line 5 s0 is the scale of intervals ordered by duration. Lines 6–11 pick out the intervals between two arbitrary pairs of successive elements of the temporal sequence. Line 12 says that they will be measured by the durationOf function with respect to u. Line 13 says that they are of the same half-order of magnitude under this function.

16.6 RATES AND FREQUENCY

We would like to define a notion of "rate" that will cover the following cases, among others:

He was driving 60 miles per hour.
We have 3 meetings every 4 1/2 months.
I see 4 students a day.
We discuss three topics every meeting.

In the most primitive case, there is a set S of events. In our four examples, the event types are driving a mile, having a meeting, seeing a student, and discussing a topic. There is also a set T of time intervals that may or may not be all of equal duration. In the first three examples, the durations are one hour, 4 1/2 months, and one day. In the fourth example, the lengths of the meetings may differ. There is a function mapping the intervals into a subset of S, namely, those events that occur during that interval. If the concept of "rate" applies truly, the cardinalities of all these subsets are the same. This analysis provides us with all we need to define the primitive case. The concept of "rate" will be extended beyond this in the text that follows, so here we use if rather than iff.

```
(forall (s s0 t f n)                                           (16.76)
    (if (and (eventualities s)(set t)(powerSet s0 s)
             (forall (t1)
                 (if (member t1 t)(interval t1)))
```

```
                (function f t s0)
                (forall (t1 s1)
                    (if (map f t1 s1)
                        (and (forall (e)
                                (if (member e s1)(happensIn e t1)))
                            (card n s1)))))
        (rate n s t)))
```

Lines 3–4 say that t is a set of intervals. Lines 5–10 say that the same number n of events in s happen during each of those intervals. Line 11 says that n is the rate of the events happening in the intervals in t.

Next we extend the definition to the case where the third argument of rate is a temporal unit, by assuming that the members of t all have a duration of one in that unit.

```
(forall (n s t u)                                                      (16.77)
    (if (and (eventualities s)(temporalUnit u)
            (forall (t1)(if (member t1 t)(durationOf 1 t1 u)))
            (rate n s t))
        (rate n s u)))
```

Finally, we extend rate to units that are not the duration of the temporal intervals on which the events were measured, allowing us to say "He was driving 60 miles per hour," even though he was driving at that rate only for 5 minutes.

```
(forall (r1 r2 s u1 u2 j)                                             (16.78)
    (if (and (rate r1 s u1)(product r2 j r1)
            (forall (t n1 n2)
                (iff (and (durationOf n1 t u1)(durationOf n2 t u2))
                    (product n1 j n2))))
        (rate r2 s u2)))
```

Lines 3–5 define j as the ratio between the two units. For example, if u1 is minutes, u2 is hours, and n2 is 10, that is, t is 10 hours, then n1 is 600, and j is 60. Thus, if someone is going 4 miles a minute ($r1 = 4$), then they are going 240 miles an hour ($r2 = 60 \times 4 = 240$).

Rate defines a scale, whose elements are the sets of events whose rate is being measured and whose ordering is the "less than" relation between rates.

```
(forall (s s0)                                                        (16.79)
    (iff (rateScale s s0)
        (and (forall (s1)(if (member s1 s0)(eventualities s1)))
            (exists (u e s1 s2)
                (and (temporalUnit u)(lts' e s1 s2 s0)
                    (forall (s3 s4)
                        (iff (and (lts' e s3 s4 s0)(Rexist e))
                            (exists (r1 r2)
                                (and (rate r1 s3 u)(rate r2 s4 u)
                                    (lt r1 r2)))))
                    (scaleDefinedBy s s0 e))))))
```

Here, s is a "rate scale" for the set s0 of sets of eventualities. Line 3 says that s0 is a set of sets of eventualities. Lines 4–10 define e as the ordering relation on sets of eventualities in terms of their rates. Line 11 says that s is the scale whose elements are s0 and whose ordering relation is e.

A set of events is "frequent" if it is in the Hi region of a rate scale.

```
(forall (s1)                                                    (16.80)
   (iff (frequent s1)
        (exists (s s0 s2)
           (and (member s1 s0)(rateScale s s0)(Hi s2 s)
                (inScale s1 s2)))))
```

Here, s1 is a set of eventualities. It is being compared with other sets of eventualities with respect to rate. The entire set of these sets of eventualities is s0. The scale s is the rate scale for s0. The subscale s2 is the Hi region of s. The set s1 of eventualities is frequent if it is in s2.

Recalling the discussion of Section 12.4, by saying that some set of eventualities is in the Hi region of a rate scale, we are defeasibly implying that it lies in the upper end of a distribution of such rates, and that its high rate plays some causal role in someone's goals.

PREDICATES INTRODUCED IN THIS CHAPTER

(instant t)
   t is an instant of time.

(interval t)
   t is an interval of time.

(temporalEntity t)
   t is an instant or an interval.

(begins t1 t2)
   Instant t1 is the beginning of t2.

(ends t1 t2)
   Instant t1 is the end of t2.

(insideTime t1 t2)
   Instant t1 is inside t2.

(intervalBetween t t1 t2)
   t is the interval between t1 and t2.

(posInfInterval t)
   t is a positive infinite interval.

(properInterval t)
   The beginning and end of interval t are distinct.

(tseq s)
   s is a sequence of temporal entities.

(first t s)
   For temporal sequences, t is the first temporal entity in temporal sequence s.

(last t s)
   For temporal sequences, t is the last temporal entity in temporal sequence s.

(successiveElts t1 t2 s)

For temporal sequences, t1 is immediately followed by t2 in temporal sequence s.

(convexHull t s)
  Interval t is the convex hull of temporal sequence s.

(atTime e t)
  Eventuality e is occurring at instant t.

(during e t)
  Eventuality e is occurring at every instant inside interval t.

(timeSpanOf t e)
  Temporal entity or sequence t is all the instants and intervals for which eventuality e really exists or obtains.

(happensIn e t)
  t subsumes the time span of e.

(posInfIntervalEv e)
  e is a positive infinite interval or an eventuality whose time span is a positive infinite interval.

(properIntervalEv e)
  e is a proper interval or an eventuality whose time span is a proper interval.

(temporal e)
  e is a temporal property, that is, atTime, during, timeSpanOf, happensIn, before, or durationOf.

(nontemporal e)
  e is not a temporal property.

(before t1 t2)
  t1 is before t2.

(intMeets t1 t2)
  Interval t1 meets interval t2.

(intOverlap t1 t2)
  Intervals t1 and t2 overlap.

(intFinishes t1 t2)
  Interval t1 begins inside interval t2, and their ends are the same.

(intDuring t1 t2)
  Interval t1 begins after and ends before interval t2.

(beforeOrMeets t1 t2)
  The end of t1 is before or equal to the beginning of t2.

(timeScale t)
  t is a scale whose elements are temporal entities and whose ordering is before.

(sameDuration t1 t2)
  Temporal entities t1 and t2 have the same duration.

(temporalUnit u)
  Interval u is a temporal unit.

(concatenation t s)
  Interval t is the concatenation of the intervals in the set s.

(durationOf d t u)
  The duration of t is d units u.

(shorterDuration t1 t2)
  Interval t1 has shorter duration than interval t2.

(scaleOrderedByDuration s)
  Scale s is a scale whose elements are intervals ordered by duration.

(periodicTseq s)
  Temporal sequence s is periodic, in that the gaps between successive elements are all equal.

(gapDuration d s u)
  d is the duration of the equal gaps in periodic temporal sequence s measured in units u.

(roughlyPeriodicTseq s u)
  Temporal sequence s is roughly periodic, in that the gaps between successive elements are all the same half order of magnitude; u is a unit of duration.

(rate n s t)
  Eventualities in s occur n times in every element of t, if t is a set of intervals, or in every interval of duration t if t is a temporal unit.

(rateScale s s0)
  s is a scale whose elements are the sets of eventualities in s0 and whose ordering is the rate of the sets.

(frequent s1)
  Set s1 of eventualities is in the high region of a rate scale.

17

Event Structure

17.1 EVENTS AND SUBEVENTS

An event is an eventuality that involves a change of state. We will cash out the word "involves" by taking it to be the subevent or equality relation. That is, an event is a change of state or an eventuality that has a change of state as a subevent. But this means that we must, counterintuitively, first explicate "subevent," or at least explicate them in tandem. We will start off with a couple of general properties of the subevent relation, and then enrich the concept as we define event and various event structures.

The subevent relation is antisymmetric.

$$(\text{forall } (e1\ e2)\ (\text{if } (\text{subevent } e1\ e2)\ (\text{not } (\text{subevent } e2\ e1)))) \quad (17.1)$$

It is thus also antireflexive.
The subevent relation is transitive.

```
(forall (e1 e2 e3)                                              (17.2)
    (if (and (subevent e1 e2)(subevent e2 e3))
        (subevent e1 e3)))
```

We now define event:

```
(forall (e)                                                     (17.3)
    (iff (event e)
        (or (exists (e1 e2)
                (and (nequal e1 e2)(change' e e1 e2)))
            (exists (e0 e1 e2)
                (and (nequal e1 e2)(change' e0 e1 e2)(gen e e0)))
            (exists (e1)
                (subevent e1 e)))))
```

Lines 3–4 take care of the case where e is directly a change of state. Lines 5–6 are for cases where e *generates* a change of state e0; for example, we might not want to *identify* a running event with the change of location it effects, but the relation is strong enough between the running and the change for it to be thought of as a change. Lines 7–8 take care of the case in which the change is embedded in some subevent.

We have specified that the change must be from a state e1 to a distinct state e2. This rules out circular changes at the base of an event. But a circular change can be decomposed into a change from an initial state to a distinct state and then back to the initial state. We do mean to rule out "changes" where nothing happens.

As we explicate the predicate subevent, we will do so in a way that respects the constraint that an event is an eventuality. In the base case, where the event is itself a change of state, this holds because e in the above axiom is the self argument of a primed predicate. Where e generates the change of state, e is an eventuality because that's what the arguments of gen are.

```
(forall (e) (if (event e)(eventuality e)))                    (17.4)
```

Now we can say that the arguments of subevent are events.

```
(forall (e1 e2)                                               (17.5)
    (if (subevent e1 e2) (and (event e1)(event e2))))
```

We can build up events that are not directly changes of states, but somewhere in chains of subevents of subevents of subevents, we must bottom out in changes of state.

In the next two sections we will detail some of the ways one event can be a subevent of another. The internal structure of events can be analyzed in terms familiar from control structures in programming languages, but applied not just to intentional actions, but to events in general. In a sense, we view the world as a computer executing its own history.

There can be sequences of events, conditionals, and iterations, among other structures. In the rest of this chapter, we axiomatize some of these possibilities.

17.2 EVENT SEQUENCES AND CONDITIONALS

The aggregate, or conjunction, of two events is an event. Moreover, if even one of the conjuncts is an event, the aggregate is an event. Thus, the sentence "The day was warm and Pat jogged down the beach" describes an event.

```
(forall (e e1 e2)                                             (17.6)
    (if (and (and' e e1 e2)(event e1))
        (and (subevent e1 e)(event e))))
```

Since and' is essentially commutative, we can also say

```
(forall (e e1 e2)                                             (17.7)
    (if (and (and' e e1 e2)(event e2))
        (and (subevent e2 e)(event e))))
```

The and' events, when applied to programming languages, cover the loosest case of parallel processes, where no temporal overlap between the processes is required.

Two events are in sequence if one is before the other, and the aggregate of the two events is just their reified conjunction.

```
(forall (e e1 e2)                                              (17.8)
    (iff (eventSequence e e1 e2)
         (and (event e1)(event e2)
              (and' e e1 e2)(beforeOrMeets e1 e2))))
```

From (17.6) and (17.7) we see that the components of an event sequence are subevents and that the event sequence is itself an event.

```
(forall (e e1 e2)                                              (17.9)
    (if (eventSequence e e1 e2)
        (and (event e)(subevent e1 e)(subevent e2 e))))
```

The definition of eventSequence can be extended to event sequences of arbitrary length by letting e1 and/or e2 be an event sequence. We could but won't relate eventSequence to sequence.

One of the most basic control structures in programming languages is the conditional, so we would like to consider conditional events, such as "If something is denser than water, it sinks." One way to deal with conditional events is to factor out the implication. We would not say that there was a conditional event. Rather we would say that if the condition holds, there is an event, the consequent of the conditional. This decision would propagate to more complex events, however. Rather than being able to talk about two sequential events,

The object rolls into the water; if it is denser than water, it sinks.

we would have to talk about two possible events or event sequences,

If the object is denser than water, it rolls into the water and it sinks.
If the object is not denser than water, it rolls into the water.

This expansion would be vastly exacerbated in cases of conditionals embedded in iterations and other conditionals. A programming language designed along these lines would be a nightmare to work in. All possible combinations of potentially relevant conditions would have to be stated up front, each with a different sequence of steps of the corresponding execution following it. As is usually the case, the best strategy is to allow our ontological garden to flourish and simply accept conditional events as events.

We will take a conditional event to be the implicational relation between some eventuality – a state or an event – and an event, with a further relation that the first eventuality must obtain at the beginning of the second.

```
(forall (e e1 e2)                                             (17.10)
    (iff (cond e e1 e2)
         (and (imply' e e1 e2)(event e2)
              (forall (t)
                  (if (begins t e2)(atTime e1 t))))))
```

The conditions on the real existence of e follow from the conditions on the real existence of implication relations stated in Axiom (8.8).

The event e2 is a subevent of e and hence e is also an event.

```
(forall (e e1 e2)                                            (17.11)
    (if (cond e e1 e2)(and (subevent e2 e)(event e))))
```

More complex conditionals can be constructed by having event sequences of conditionals and by having the consequent itself be a conditional.

17.3 ITERATIONS

Some processes in nature seem to us to be pure iterations, with no termination condition and no set of entities the iteration is over. The sun rising and setting is like this. Every day we see a new instance of that event type.

We can define iteration recursively.

```
(forall (e e1)                                               (17.12)
    (iff (iteration e e1)
         (exists (e2 e3)
             (and (eventSequence' e e2 e3)(instance e2 e1)
                  (or (iteration e3 e1)(instance e3 e1))))))
```

Here e1 is an event type, the e2's instantiate e1, and e is the event that consists of the succession of e2's. That e2 is a subevent of e and that e and the e2's are events follow from the properties of eventSequence.

As we have defined it, an iteration has to have at least two elements, and that seems appropriate.

Some iterative processes have a termination condition. In an hourglass the grains of sand fall from the upper chamber to the lower chamber until the upper chamber is empty. We define a predicate whileDo that says one event type e2 is instantiated by successive instances as long as eventuality e1 happens or holds.

```
(forall (e e1 e2)                                            (17.13)
    (iff (whileDo e e1 e2)
         (exists (e3 e4 e5)
             (and (cond e e1 e3)(eventSequence' e3 e4 e5)
                  (instance e4 e2)
                  (or (whileDo e5 e1 e2)(instance e5 e2))))))
```

That is, the whileDo event is a conditional whose condition is e1 and when the condition holds, the consequent occurs, where the consequent is a sequence e3 of the events e4 and e5. Event e4 is an instance of e2, and e5 is also an instance of e2 or it is another whileDo event with e1 as its condition and the event type e2 as its consequent.

It again follows from the properties of eventSequence and cond that the e4's are subevents of e and that e and the e4's are events.

A repeatUntil event can be defined similarly.

```
(forall (e e1 e2)                                            (17.14)
    (iff (repeatUntil e e1 e2)
         (exists (e3 e4 e5)
             (and (eventSequence' e e3 e4)(instance e3 e1)
                  (cond e4 e2 e5)
                  (or (repeatUntil e5 e1 e2)(instance e5 e1))))))
```

The only difference between this and a whileDo event is that an instance e3 of the
body e1 occurs before the condition e2 is checked. The e3's are subevents of e, and
e and the e3's are events.

Sometimes we want to talk about the same event type happening to all the elements in a sequence in turn. That is, there is a parameter x in the event type e1, and
for every member y of the set s, an instance e2 of e1 occurs, in which y plays the role
of x. If s is a sequence of one element, the forAllOfSeq event is just the instance
for that element. If the sequence s is longer, the forAllOfSeq event e is the event
sequence. The first event in the event sequence is an instance e2 of e1, where the first
element y of the sequence s plays the same role in e2 that x plays in e1. The second
event in the event sequence is another forAllOfSeq event, where the sequence s1
is the rest of the sequence s after its first element has been removed.

```
(forall (e s e1)                                                  (17.15)
    (iff (forAllOfSeq e s x e1)
        (exists (y e2 l e3 s1)
            (or (and (length 1 s)(first y s)(subst y e2 x e1)
                     (equal e e2))
                (and (length l s)(gt l 1)(first y s)
                     (subst y e2 x e1)(eventSequence e e2 e3)
                     (forAllOfSeq e3 s1 x e1)(rest s1 s))))))
```

Again, the instances e2 are subevents of e, and e and the e2's are events.

We can obviously do an iteration over the first n integers by letting the sequence
s be the sequence <1,...,n>.

A complex event is a composite entity whose components are its subevents,
among whose properties are the event properties, and among whose relations are
the subevent relations.

```
(forall (e1 e)                                                   (17.16)
    (if (subevent e1 e)
        (exists (s1 s2 s3)
            (and (compositeEntity e)
                 (componentsOf s1 e)(propertiesOf s2 e)
                 (relationsOf s3 e)
                 (forall (e2)(iff (member e2 s1)(subevent e2 e)))
                 (forall (e2)
                     (if (member e2 s1)
                         (exists (e3)
                             (and (event' e3 e2)(member e3 s2)))))
                 (forall (e2)
                     (if (member e2 s1)
                         (exists (e3)
                             (and (subevent' e3 e2 e)
                                  (member e3 s3)))))))))
```

The antecedent in line 2 is (subevent e1 e) because this is a necessary and sufficient
condition for e to be a complex event. Lines 5–6 label the components, properties
and relations. Line 7 says the components are the subevents. Lines 8–11 say that the
event properties are among the composite entity's properties. Lines 12–16 say that
the subevent relations are among its relations.

PREDICATES INTRODUCED IN THIS CHAPTER

`(event e)`
    e is an event.

`(subevent e1 e2)`
    Event e1 is a subevent of event e2.

`(eventSequence e e1 e2)`
    Event e is a sequence consisting of event e1 followed by event e2.

`(cond e e1 e2)`
    e is the conditional event of event e2 occurring if eventuality e1 happens or holds.

`(iteration e e1)`
    e is the event consisting of iterations of event type e1.

`(whileDo e e1 e2)`
    e is the event consisting of iterations of event e2 as long as eventuality e1 happens or holds.

`(repeatUntil e e1 e2)`
    e is the event consisting of iterations of event type e1 happening until e2 happens or holds.

`(forAllOfSeq e s x e1)`
    e is the event consisting of iterations of event type e1 where in successive iterations the role of x is played by the successive members of sequence s.

18

Space

PREDICATES INTRODUCED IN THIS CHAPTER

18.1 SPACE AND SPATIAL ANALOGIES

Many "top-level" ontologies begin with a distinction between physical objects and abstract entities. By contrast, we have made it through thirteen background theories without ever mentioning the distinction. The reason for this is that the core of language doesn't seem to care much about this distinction. We can be *in* a building, and we can be *in* politics and *in* trouble. We can *move* a chair from the desk to the door, and we can *move* the debate from politics to religion and *move* money from one bank account to another. Ontologies that begin with this distinction, or similar ones like Cyc's tangible–intangible distinction (Lenat and Guha, 1990), fail to capture important generalizations in language and as a result very nearly make themselves irrelevant in linguistic applications at the outset.

It has frequently been observed that we understand many abstract domains by analogy with spatial relations (e.g., Vico, 1744; Richards, 1937). A relatively recent rediscovery of this old truth was by Lakoff and Johnson (2008). We operate in space from the moment we are born and thus build up very rich spatial models. By setting up a mapping between a new domain and space, we are able to commandeer these rich models for the new domain and think about it in more complex ways.

This would seem to indicate that the very first theory one should develop in an enterprise such as ours is a very rich theory of space, and then set up some mechanism for analogical reasoning. But what does analogical reasoning involve? It is a matter of identifying common properties of the things being compared, reasoning about them in the familiar domain, and then transferring the results to the new domain. But what is typically transferred from space to new domains in spatial analogies is not just any property. Very rarely, for example, do we transfer the properties of hardness or color or precise distance. The common properties that are transferred are usually topological properties.

In these background theories we have identified some of the most important underlying properties of the spatial domain that are most frequently utilized in analogies – such things as complex structure, scalar concepts, change of state, and so on. We have constructed theories of these abstract properties. The content of these theories is very similar to proposals in work in cognitive linguistics (e.g., Croft and Cruse, 2004) on the "image schemas" that seem to underlie much of our thought.

If one were inclined to make innateness arguments, one position would be that we are born with an instinctive ability to operate in spatial environments. We begin to use this immediately when we are born, and when we encounter abstract domains, we tap into its rich models. The alternative, more in line with our development here, is that we are born with at least a predisposition toward instinctive abstract patterns – composite entities, scales, change, and so on – which we first apply in making sense of our spatial environment, and then apply to other, more abstract domains as we encounter them. This has the advantage over the first position that it is specific about exactly what properties of space might be in our innate repertoire. For example, the scalar notions of "closer" and "farther" are in it; exact measures of distance are not. A nicely paradoxical coda for summing up this position is that we understand space by means of a spatial metaphor.

It is also a curious and perhaps surprising fact about our efforts to construct the cognitive theories of Part III that very few purely spatial concepts turned out to be necessary. We occasionally need to make reference to physical objects, to one physical object being *at* another, and to a physical object being *near* another. And that is all.

18.2 SPATIAL SYSTEMS AND DISTANCE

We will use the predicate physobj – (physobj x) – to say that something is a physical object. We will not explicate this notion, because it would take us deeply into commonsense physics rather than commonsense psychology. We would have to talk about properties of color, weight, and malleability. Instead we will simply stipulate that something is a physical object, and not attempt to constrain the possible interpretations of the predicate physobj by means of further axioms.

The key notion in our treatment of space will be spatialSystem. A spatial system is a composite entity whose components are physical objects and among whose relations are a distance relation.

```
(forall (s)                                                          (18.1)
    (iff (spatialSystem s)
        (and (compositeEntity s)
             (exists (s1)
                 (and (componentsOf s1 s)
                      (forall (x) (if (member x s1)(physobj x)))))
             (exists (s2 s3)
                 (and (relationsOf s2 s)(subset s3 s2)
                      (forall (e)
                          (if (member e s3)
                              (exists (d x1 x2 u)
                                  (distance' e d x1 x2 u s)))))))))
```

Line 3 says that a spatial system s is a composite entity. Lines 4–6 say that its components are physical objects. Lines 7–12 say that some (s3) of the relations (s2) of s are distance relations e between two components x1 and x2 of s with respect to some spatial unit u.

In the predicate distance, we take d to be a nonnegative number dependent upon the spatial unit u that is used, rather than reifying distances as distinct entities. We won't say what a spatial unit is, but it can be characterized in the same way temporal units were characterized in Chapter 16. The constraints on the arguments of distance are as follows:

```
(forall (d x1 x2 u s)                                    (18.2)
    (if (distance d x1 x2 u s)
        (and (nonNegInteger d)(spatialSystem s)
             (componentOf x1 s)(componentOf x2 s)
             (spatialUnit u))))
```

We will constrain the predicate distance by the usual mathematical properties. The distance between an entity and itself is zero.

```
(forall (x u s)                                          (18.3)
    (if (and (componentOf x s)(spatialUnit u)(spatialSystem s))
        (distance 0 x x u s)))
```

The distance between two entities is symmetric.

```
(forall (d x1 x2 u s)                                    (18.4)
    (iff (distance d x1 x2 u s)(distance d x2 x1 u s)))
```

The triangle inequality holds.

```
(forall (d1 d2 d3 d4 x1 x2 x3 u s)                       (18.5)
    (if (and (distance d1 x1 x2 u s)(distance d2 x2 x3 u s)
             (distance d3 x1 x3 u s)(sum d4 d1 d2))
        (leq d3 d4)))
```

We will get to the definition of near by three steps: define a shorterDistance relation, define a "near-ness" scale, and define near as in the Hi region of that scale.

A distance d1 is a shorter distance than d2 in a spatial system s under the obvious conditions.

```
(forall (d1 d2 s)                                        (18.6)
    (iff (shorterDistance d1 d2 s)
         (exists (u x1 x2 x3 x4)
             (and (distance d1 x1 x2 u s)(distance d2 x3 x4 u s)
                  (lt d1 d2)))))
```

A scale for "near-ness" for a spatial system is the reverse of a scale whose elements are the distances between elements of s and whose ordering function is shorterDistance. We reverse the scale so that shorter distances end up in the Hi region.

```
(forall (s1 s)                                                  (18.7)
    (iff (nearnessScale s1 s)
         (exists (u s2 s3 e d1 d2)
             (and (scaleDefinedBy s2 s3 e)
                  (forall (d)
                      (if (member d s3)
                          (exists (x1 x2)(distance d x1 x2 u s))))
                      (shorterDistance' e d1 d2 s)(reverse s1 s2)))))
```

In this definition, s3 is a set of distances in s, s2 is the scale of these distances, and s1 is the reverse of that scale. The eventuality type e is a shorterDistance relation in s, d1 and d2 are its parameters, and u is an arbitrary spatial unit.

Finally, for x1 to be near x2 is for the distance between them to be in the Hi region of a near-ness scale.

```
(forall (x1 x2 s)                                                (18.8)
    (if (and (componentOf x1 s)(componentOf x2 s))
        (iff (near x1 x2 s)
             (exists (s1 s2 d u)
                 (and (nearnessScale s1 s)(Hi s2 s1)
                      (distance d x1 x2 u s)(inScale d s2))))))
```

Since we have defined near between two entities in terms of the Hi region of a scale, we can draw inferences about the distributional and functional properties of the distance between them, as indicated in Section 12.4.

18.3 LOCATION

In Section 10.3 we introduced the figure–ground relation (at x y s), meaning that external entity x is at component y of composite entity s. A spatial system is a possible ground by virtue of the fact that all its components are physical objects. That is the common property they have that makes a unitary interpretation of the at relation possible (cf. Axiom 10.14).

```
(forall (s) (if (spatialSystem s)(ground s)))                    (18.9)
```

We can now characterize the predicate atLoc, for "at a location" as at where s is specialized to spatial systems.

```
(forall (x y s)                                                  (18.10)
    (if (atLoc x y s)
        (and (spatialSystem s)(at x y s))))
```

Since s is a spatial system and x is at y in s, y must be a physical object. We are silent about what kinds of things x can be. Certainly physical objects can be at another physical object – Jill is at her desk. Events involving physical objects can also be at physical objects – Jill is typing at her desk. Not all the arguments of an event need to be at the location. We can say that a telecon is going on at a point in Jill's office, but not all the participants of the telecon need to be at that location. We do not say anything about whether abstract eventualities or abstract entities can be at physical locations.

Two entities that are at locations in a spatial system are near if their locations are near.

```
(forall (s y1 y2 x1 x2)                                    (18.11)
    (if (and (componentOf y1 s)(componentOf y2 s)
             (atLoc x1 y1 s)(atLoc x2 y2 s))
        (iff (near x1 x2 s)(near y1 y2 s))))
```

PREDICATES INTRODUCED IN THIS CHAPTER

(physobj x)
    x is a physical object.

(spatialSystem s)
    s is a composite entity whose components are physical objects related by distance.

(distance d x1 x2 u s)
    d is the distance in units u between x1 and x2 in spatial system s.

(spatialUnit u)
    u is a spatial unit.

(shorterDistance d1 d2 s)
    d1 and d2 are distances between components of spatial system s, and d1 is less than d2.

(nearnessScale s1 s)
    s1 is a scale whose components are distances between pairs of entities in spatial system s.

(near x1 x2 s)
    x1 is near x2 in s.

(atLoc x y s)
    x is at y in spatial system s.

19

Persons

Finally we arrive at people. The theories of Part III are intended to some extent to apply to other kinds of agents than just people, such as robots and organizations, and some aspects of the cognitive theories, such as goals, plans, and beliefs, we would expect to find in any cognitive agent in some form. But many aspects are idiosyncratic to people – accidents of evolution, in a sense. For example, there is probably no reason a robot or an organization should be thought of as having emotions. In Part III, when we are talking about aspects of cognition that apply to all cognitive agents, we will call the agent simply an "agent." When we are talking about particularities of people, we will condition the axioms on the relevant arguments being persons.

A person is a kind of agent.

```
(forall (p) (if (person p)(agent p)))                        (19.1)
```

A person is also a kind of physical object.

```
(forall (p) (if (person p)(physobj p)))                      (19.2)
```

A person has a body and a mind.

```
(forall (p)                                                  (19.3)
    (if (person p)
        (exists (b m)(and (body b p)(mind m p)))))
```

In this axiom, b is person p's body, and m is p's mind. We won't restrict p, as an argument of body and mind, to being a person, because animals have bodies and other cognitive agents can be viewed as having minds.

All we need to know of the mind right now is that it is a composite entity.

```
(forall (m p)                                                (19.4)
    (if (mind m p) (compositeEntity m)))
```

Thus, we can talk about entities external to the mind.
A body is a physical object.

```
(forall (b p) (if (body b p)(physobj b)))                    (19.5)
```

A body is a composite entity whose components are body parts. In fact, it is a spatial system, because all the body parts are physical objects.

```
(forall (b p)                                                    (19.6)
    (if (body b p)
        (and (spatialSystem b)
            (exists (s)
                (and (componentsOf s b)
                    (forall (x)
                        (iff (member x s)(bodyPart x p))))))))))
```

A person p has a set of body parts, namely, the components of the body.

```
(forall (p s)                                                    (19.7)
    (iff (bodyPartsOf s p)
        (exists (b)
            (and (person p)(body b p)(componentsOf s b)))))
```

We won't explicate what the various body parts are. This would be a job for commonsense anatomy. But there are two distinguished subsets of body parts that are significant to our concerns – sense organs and body parts that can be directly and voluntarily controlled. A person is capable of perception and action, and both of these require interaction between the body and the mind. These two subsets of body parts are what mediate perception and action.

For now, we will simply posit a predicate perceive, which is a relation between an agent and an entity or eventuality external to the mind.

```
(forall (a x m)                                                  (19.8)
    (if (and (perceive a x)(mind m a))
        (and (agent a)(externalTo x m))))
```

Ultimately, we will want to say how perception tracks reality. But this involves interaction with belief, inference, and action, and will be dealt with in Part III.

Something being near a person is an enabling condition for perceiving it.

```
(forall (p x e2)                                                 (19.9)
    (if (perceive' e2 p x)
        (exists (e1 s)
            (and (near' e1 x p s)(enable e1 e2)))))
```

In Chapter 18 we defined near in terms of the Hi region of a scale based on distance. Hi regions are related to functionality, and frequently perception is the relevant function. Something is near because it is near enough to perceive.

The sense organs are a subset of the body parts.

```
(forall (p x)                                                    (19.10)
    (if (and (person p)(bodyPartsOf s1 p))
        (exists (s2)
            (and (subset s2 s1)
                (forall (o)
                    (iff (member o s2)(senseOrgan o p)))))))
```

It follows that sense organs are body parts.

```
(forall (o p)                                                   (19.11)
    (if (senseOrgan o p)(bodyPart o p)))
```

When something is perceived, there is a sense organ whose "intact-ness" enables the perception.

```
(forall (p x e2)                                                (19.12)
    (if (and (person p)(perceive' e2 p x))
        (exists (o e1)
            (and (senseOrgan o p)(intact' e1 o)(enable e1 e2)))))
```

The predicate intact will be explicated in Chapter 28 on Goals, in the discussion of functionality.

Another subset of body parts can be directly controlled by a person's will. That is, the person's willing an event is the direct cause of the motion of the body part.

```
(forall (p s1)                                                  (19.13)
    (if (and (person p)(bodyPartsOf s1 p))
        (exists (s2)
            (and (subset s2 s1)
                (forall (x)
                    (if (member x s2)
                        (exists (e1 e2 y z)
                            (and (move' e2 x y z)(will' e1 p e2)
                                (dcause e1 e2)))))))))
```

In this axiom, s1 is the set of all of person p's body parts. The set s2 is the body parts p can voluntarily control. That is, for every body part x in s2, there is an eventuality e2 in which x is moved from someplace y to another place z, and this moving is directly caused by p willing it.

In a more detailed account of human physical action, we could state in axioms specific facts about what actions are voluntarily and directly controlled by a person. For example, suppose we wish to state that a person can voluntarily lift his or her arm. The axiom would be as follows:

```
(forall (p)                                                     (19.14)
    (if (person p)
        (exists (e1 e2 x)
            (and (lift' e2 p x)(arm x p)(will' e1 p e2)
                (dcause e1 e2)))))
```

By contrast, we can move our hair by shaking our head or lifting our hair with our hands, but we cannot *directly* cause our hair to move.

We will explicate the concept of will in Chapter 31, when we discuss how intentions are converted into actions.

PREDICATES INTRODUCED IN THIS CHAPTER

(person p)
  p is a person.

(body b p)
  b is p's body.

(mind m p)
    m is p's mind.

(bodyPart x p)
    x is one of p's body parts.

(bodyPartsOf s p)
    s is the set of p's body parts.

(perceive a x)
    Agent a perceives x.

(senseOrgan o p)
    o is one of p's sense organs.

The predicates lift and arm were used strictly for illustrative purposes and will play no further role.

In addition, we used but have not yet explicated the following predicates:

(intact x)
    x is intact and able to fulfill its function.

(will a e)
    Agent a wills event e to occur.

The predicate intact is explicated in Chapter 28. The predicate will is further explicated in Chapter 31.

20

Modality

20.1 THE PREDICATES Rexist AND atTime

Eventualities exist in a Platonic universe of possible (and impossible) individuals – entities, states, and events. If they happen to actually occur in the real world, that is one of their properties, and we express it with the predicate Rexist. Real existence can be thought of as one possible mode of existence. There are others. An eventuality could be part of someone's beliefs but not occur in the real world. It could exist in someone's imagination. It could exist in some fictional universe. It could be merely possible rather than real. It could be likely. It could be unlikely, or not real, or impossible. An especially important modality is "happening at a particular time" or atTime.

We have gone to some effort in this book to simplify the logical formulas as much as possible. Using unprimed predicates when possible and primed predicates only when necessary has been one way of doing this. Another issue we debated was whether to include time arguments in every predication, and we decided against it in order to keep the notation relatively simple. But that raises the question: Just what is the relation among unprimed predicates, Rexist, atTime, and temporal arguments?

The relation between unprimed predicates and Rexist is straightforward, as expressed in Axiom Schema (5.1), repeated here.

```
(forall (x)                                                          (20.1)
        (iff (p x)
             (exists (e)(and (p' e x)(Rexist e)))))
```

That is, p is true of x if and only if there is an eventuality e that is the eventuality of p being true of x and e really exists. The expression (p x) is really an abbreviation for

```
(and (p' e x)(Rexist e))
```

The relation between atTime and temporal arguments is similarly straightforward. Suppose p' is a predicate taking an eventuality argument e and some sequence of other arguments x – (p' e x) – and p-t is a corresponding predicate with no eventuality argument but with an extra time argument t, saying that p is true of x at time t. Then the equivalence of the two representation styles would be captured by the following axiom schema.

```
(forall (x t)                                              (20.2)
   (iff (exists (e) (and (p' e x)(atTime e t)))
        (p-t x t)))
```

The relation between `Rexist` and `atTime` is trickier to describe. The predicate `Rexist` is fine for describing a world that does not change. The expression (`Rexist` e) simply means that the eventuality holds or is happening in that world. But in a world that changes, it is not obvious what `Rexist` means. Let's work into it with an example. Suppose we want to write an axiom that says that if someone smiles, they are happy.

```
(forall (x) (if (smile x)(happy x)))                       (20.3)
```

The smiling and the happiness have to be true at the same time. The implication does not hold if x smiles in April and is happy in July.

We can relate `Rexist` to time if we say that it means that the eventuality exists at some stipulated instant we call Now. We will say that an instant is *Now* by means of the expression (`Now` t). Now exists and is unique.

```
(exists (t) (Now t))                                       (20.4)
```

```
(forall (t2 t2) (if (and (Now t1)(Now t2))(equal t1 t2)))  (20.5)
```

Then for something to really exist is for it to happen or hold Now.

```
(forall (e t)                                              (20.6)
   (if (Now t)
       (iff (Rexist e)(atTime e t))))
```

Then the illustrative axiom (20.3) says that if x smiles now, x is happy now. The two times have to be the same.

But since any time can be Now, the expression of the axioms in terms of `Rexist` or, equivalently, unprimed predicates, is merely a way of anchoring all the predications in a single moment of time. Axiom (20.3) holds for any possible Now, and hence for any possible instant. Thus, we can go from

```
(forall (x) (if (smile x)(happy x)))
```

to

```
(forall (e1 x)
   (if (and (smile' e1 x)(Rexist e1))
       (exists (e2)(and (happy' e2 x)(Rexist e2)))))
```

by Axiom Schema (20.1); and then to

```
(forall (e1 x t)
   (if (and (Now t)(smile' e1 x)(atTime e1 t))
       (exists (e2)(and (happy' e2 x)(atTime e2 t)))))
```

by Axiom (20.6); and then to

```
(forall (x t)
   (if (smile-t x t)(happy-t x t)))
```

by Axiom Schema (20.2) and because any time t can be Now.

For linguistic purposes, a more perspicuous treatment of "now" would be to view it as a relation between a point in time and an act of uttering. But we will not pursue that idea here.

20.2 POSITIVE MODALITIES

Of the various modalities, the most important are what can be called "positive modalities." Generalizations can be captured at this level, and we could do so by introducing the predicate PosMod as a cover term for all positive modalities. PosMod takes two arguments. Although we will only use PosMod applied to eventualities, there is no reason it cannot be applied to other entities as well. Its second argument will be a predicate that labels the modality.

```
(forall (e p)                                              (20.7)
        (if (PosMod e p)
            (predicate p)))
```

For example, Rexist is a positive modality.

```
(forall (e) (if (Rexist e)(PosMod e Rexist)))             (20.8)
```

The predicate Rexist as the second argument of PosMod labels the modality as real existence.

The principal property of positive modalities is that modus ponens can be applied within the modality. If an eventuality exists in some modality, and that eventuality implies another eventuality, the second eventuality also exists in that modality.

```
(forall (e1 e2 m)                                          (20.9)
        (if (and (PosMod e1 m)(imply e1 e2))
            (PosMod e2 m)))
```

Thus, if e1 really exists and e1 implies e2, then e2 also really exists. Possibility and likelihood are also positive modalities. If e1 is possible and e1 implies e2, then e2 is also possible. If e1 is likely and e1 implies e2, then e2 is also likely.

Negation is clearly not a positive modality. Flying implies moving, but the fact that someone is not flying does not mean that they are not moving.

An agent's belief is also not a positive modality, in this strict sense. The agent may not believe the implication, although we could define a notion of a positive epistemic modality, of which knowledge and belief would be instances.

20.3 POSSIBILITY AND NECESSITY

Possibility is with respect to a set of constraints. For example, is it possible to put an X in the central square in tic-tac-toe if your opponent has already put an O there? No, if you accept the rules of the game. But if the only constraints you accept are the laws of physics, then, yes, you can. It is possible.

Thus, the predicate possible has two arguments, an eventuality and a set of constraints.

```
(forall (e c)                                              (20.10)
  (if (possible e c) (and (eventuality e)(eventualities c))))
```

For something to be possible with respect to a set of constraints is for those constraints not to rule it out. An eventuality is possible if and only if the constraints do not imply a negation of the eventuality.

```
(forall (e c)                                                    (20.11)
   (iff (possible e c)
        (forall (e1)
            (if (not' e1 e)
                (not (imply c e1))))))
```

That is, e is possible with respect to a set of constraints c just case whenever e1 is some negation of e, then it is not the case that c's real existence implies e1's real existence.

When we hear a statement that something is possible, part of the job of interpreting it is deciding from context what the set of constraints is, and in discourse statements of possibility are frequently accompanied by an indication of the constraints.

Possibility is a positive modality.

```
(forall (e c) (if (possible e c)(PosMod e possible)))           (20.12)
```

Necessity is similarly with respect to a set of constraints. An eventuality is necessary if the set of constraints implies it. If my king is in check in chess, is it necessary for me to move it out of the way or interpose another piece? Yes, if I accept the rules of chess. But if I accept only the laws of physics, no. I don't have to play the game at all.

The predicate necessary has two arguments, an eventuality and a set of constraints.

```
(forall (e c)                                                    (20.13)
    (if (necessary e c) (and (eventuality e)(eventualities c))))
```

An eventuality e is necessary with respect to a set of constraints c if and only if c implies e.

```
(forall (e c)                                                    (20.14)
   (iff (necessary e c)(imply c e)))
```

Necessity is a positive modality because of the transitivity of imply.

```
(forall (e c) (if (necessary e c)(PosMod e necessary)))         (20.15)
```

It is a theorem that if an eventuality is possible, its negation is not necessary.

```
(forall (e c e1)                                                 (20.16)
    (if (and (possible e c)(not' e1 e))
        (not (necessary e1 c))))
```

Impossibility is the negation of possibility.

```
(forall (e c)                                                    (20.17)
    (iff (impossible e c)
         (and (eventuality e)(eventualities c)
              (not (possible e c)))))
```

Impossibility is obviously not a positive modality.

20.4 LIKELIHOOD, OR QUALITATIVE PROBABILITY

Possibility is one common judgment we make about eventualities in situations of uncertainty. Another is probability or likelihood. But we have a terminological problem in developing a qualitative theory of probability, namely, what to call it. "Qualitative probability" is too cumbersome. "Probability" by itself means something else very precise to a large number of people, the mathematical theory of probability, and it would be too confusing to use the term for something different. The term "likelihood" is also a very precise technical term – the probability not of the output of a model but of the parameters of the model given its output, for example, the probability that a coin is fair given the results of a series of tosses – although this technical term has the advantage of being less widely known. The ad hoc nominalizations "probable-ness" and "likely-ness" are barbarisms. The words "chance" and "chances" seem to have more to do with opportunities and good outcomes. "Odds" is a technical, mathematical term that is very widely known. We will make the best of a bad set of options and use the term "likelihood," but it should be understood that it is not the same as what is meant in statistics by the term. We mean not the cleaned-up, mathematical version, but the qualitative, vague judgments we make in everyday life, as when we say it is likely to rain without having any real mathematical basis for the judgment. We might be able to make a rough guess, such as "a 60% chance of rain," but we'd have no basis for deciding between a 60% chance and a 59% chance.

When ordinary people talk about the likelihood of some event occurring, they do not have in mind one of the set of real numbers between 0 and 1. For us, likelihoods will be elements of a scale, but rather than being totally ordered, they will be only partially ordered. We might wonder what the likelihood is of our favorite television show presenting a new episode this week, and we might wonder what the likelihood is of the Alpha Centauri system having more than ten planets, but we'll rarely have to decide which is more likely, and if we did have to make that decision, we'd be hard-pressed to find a basis for it. The Likelihood Scale will have a top and a bottom, where the top means the event is certain to happen and the bottom means it is certain not to happen, but the top and bottom will not be identified with the real numbers 1 and 0. Since likelihoods are not numbers, we cannot apply arithmetic operations like addition and multiplication to them. We can only state some fairly weak ordering relations. Nevertheless, all the axioms we state will be true in the mathematical theory of probability. Probability will be one model of our qualitative theory, just not the only one. The predicate likelihood will express a relation between these likelihoods and eventualities. In addition, like possibility, likelihood is with respect to an implicit set of constraints that in a sense defines the sample space. Making the constraints an argument allows us to relate likelihood to possibility and to entailment.

```
(forall (d e c)                                                    (20.18)
    (if (likelihood d e c)(and (eventuality e)(eventualities c))))
```

The expression (likelihood d e c) says that d is the likelihood of eventuality e occurring, given constraints c. Normally, e will be an eventuality type, but we will not require this.

The d values will be elements on a scale. For now we will assume we have a lowerLikelihood relation. Then the scale will be the scale with likelihoods as its elements and the `lowerLikelihood` relation as its partial ordering. We will call this the `likelihoodScale`.

```
(forall (s)                                                         (20.19)
    (iff (likelihoodScale s)
        (exists (s1 e r d1 d2)
            (and (forall (d)
                    (iff (member d s1)
                        (exists (e c) (likelihood d e c))))
                (lowerLikelihood' r d1 d2)
                (scaleDefinedBy s s1 r)))))
```

We have introduced three predicates, `likelihood`, `likelihoodScale`, and `lowerLikelihood`, but these are really only ways of referring to different aspects of likelihoods. We have not yet begun to nail down the content of the notion. We will take some initial steps now.

If something has a likelihood that is neither the top nor the bottom of the likelihood scale, then it is possible. That is, we cannot prove from the constraints that the eventuality does not occur. However, we also cannot prove from the constraints that it does occur. Either possibility is consistent with the constraints. Given an eventuality e and a set of constraints c, we can ask what other set s of eventualities would have to obtain in order to entail that e also obtains. Let's call this set `alsoRequired`. The expression (`alsoRequired s e c`) says that s is a set of eventualities that will entail the real existence of e, over and above c. Our use of the word "Required" in the predicate name indicates that we want the set to be minimal.

```
(forall (s e c)                                                     (20.20)
    (if (eventuality e)
        (iff (alsoRequired s e c)
            (and (eventualities s)(eventualities c)
                (exists (s1 c1)
                    (and (union s1 c1 s)(subset c1 c)
                        (minimallyProves s1 e)))))))
```

The expression (`alsoRequired s e c`) says that the set of eventualities s is also required, over and above the set of eventualities c, to make e follow. Lines 5–6 say that adding s to a relevant subset c1 of c turns e from a likelihood to a certainty. Lines 6–7 say that s is a minimal such set.

Now suppose whenever we add a set of eventualities to get e1 to exist it also gets e2 to exist. Then we can say that e2 is at least as likely as e1. That is, the more we have to assume will happen, the less likely it is.

```
(forall (s1 e1 d1 s2 e2 d2 c s)                                     (20.21)
    (if (and (alsoRequired s1 e1 c)(alsoRequired s2 e2 c)
            (subset s2 s1)
            (likelihood d1 e1 c)(likelihood d2 e2 c)
            (likelihoodScale s))
        (leqs d1 d2 s)))
```

This development could be recast in terms of possible worlds, had we developed an approach to possible worlds. If the set of possible worlds in which e2 occurs is a proper subset of the set of possible worlds in which e1 occurs, e1 is more likely. We have presented the propositional equivalent of this.

The second set of constraints on determining likelihoods comes from combining likelihoods for component eventualities to determine likelihoods of composite eventualities. In particular, we can say something about how likelihoods operate under "and," "or," and "not." We cannot be as precise about this as we can in probability theory, but we can say that the likelihood of the conjunction e of two eventualities e1 and e2 is less than or equal to the likelihood of each of them.

```
(forall (s e e1 e2 d d1 d2 c)                              (20.22)
    (if (and (likelihoodScale s)
             (likelihood d1 e1 c)(likelihood d2 e2 c)
             (and' e e1 e2)(likelihood d e c))
        (and (leqs d d1 s)(leqs d d2 s))))
```

The likelihood of the disjunction e of two eventualities e1 and e2 is greater than or equal to the likelihood of either of them.

```
(forall (s e e1 e2 d d1 d2 c)                              (20.23)
    (if (and (likelihoodScale s)
             (likelihood d1 e1 c)(likelihood d2 e2 c)
             (or' e e1 e2)(likelihood d e c))
        (and (leqs d1 d s)(leqs d2 d s))))
```

If the likelihood of an eventuality is the top of the likelihood scale given constraints c, then it is entailed by c.

```
(forall (d e c s)                                          (20.24)
    (if (and (likelihood d e c)(likelihoodScale s))
        (iff (top d s)(necessary e c))))
```

If the likelihood of an eventuality is the bottom of the likelihood scale, then it is impossible given the constraints.

```
(forall (d e c s)                                          (20.25)
    (if (and (likelihood d e c)(likelihoodScale s))
        (iff (bottom d s)(impossible e c))))
```

If something has a likelihood above the bottom of the likelihood scale with respect to a set of constraints, it is possible with respect to those constraints.

```
(forall (d e c s)                                          (20.26)
    (if (and (likelihood d1 e c)(likelihoodScale s)(bottom d s))
        (iff (lts d d1 s)(possible e c))))
```

A word about the interaction of likelihood and time: We make likelihood judgments about past, present and future eventualities.

It is likely that John Wilkes Booth acted alone.
It is likely that Kim secretly loves Pat.
It is likely that the Democrats will win the next presidential election.

But usually it is the likelihood of future events that is at issue. To say that it is likely to rain tomorrow we do not say that it is likely that the rain really exists – that would be now – but that the "tomorrow-ness" of the rain really exists. It is the atTime or other temporal proposition to which we assign a likelihood.

A likelihood scale consists of elements that are all likelihoods and hence have a common property; the scale can then be a potential ground.

```
(forall (s) (if (likelihoodScale s)(ground s)))                (20.27)
```

If the likelihood of an eventuality e is d, we can say that e is *at* d on the likelihood scale, if c holds.

```
(forall (d e c s e1)                                           (20.28)
    (if (and (likelihood d e c)(likelihoodScale s)
            (at' e1 e d s))
        (imply c e1)))
```

The likelihood scale is conceptually vertical. We talk about likelihoods being higher or lower.

```
(forall (s) (if (likelihoodScale s)(vertical s)))              (20.29)
```

Thus, we can talk about the likelihood of something increasing.

One eventuality is more likely than another with respect to a set of constraints if its likelihood is higher.

```
(forall (e1 e2 c)                                              (20.30)
    (iff (moreLikely e1 e2 c)
        (exists (s d1 d2)
            (and (likelihoodScale s)
                (likelihood d1 e1 c)(likelihood d2 e2 c)
                (lts d2 d1 s)))))
```

An eventuality is likely with respect to constraints c if its likelihood d is on the high end of the scale of likelihoods.

```
(forall (e c)                                                  (20.31)
    (iff (likely e c)
        (exists (s d s1)
            (and (likelihood d e c)(likelihoodScale s)
                (Hi s1 s)(inScale d s1)))))
```

If an eventuality is likely, its negation is not likely.

```
(forall (e e1 c)                                               (20.32)
    (if (and (likely e c)(not' e1 e))
        (not (likely e1 c))))
```

The predicate likely is a positive modality for a given c.

It will be useful to have a predicate for "lower or equal likelihood."

```
(forall (d1 d2)                                                (20.33)
    (iff (leqLikelihood d1 d2)
        (or (lowerLikelihood d1 d2)(equal d1 d2))))
```

Many other properties of probability depend on its numerical nature and do not carry over to our qualitative notion of likelihood.

PREDICATES INTRODUCED IN THIS CHAPTER

(Now t)
> t is an instant stipulated to be Now.

(PosMod e p)
> The positive modality p holds of eventuality e.

(possible e c)
> e is possible with respect to a set of constraints c.

(necessary e c)
> e is necessary with respect to a set of constraints c.

(impossible e c)
> e is impossible with respect to a set of constraints c.

(likelihood d e c)
> d is the likelihood of e really existing, given constraints c.

(likelihoodScale s)
> s is a scale of likelihoods.

(lowerLikelihood d1 d2)
> d1 is a lower likelihood than d2.

(alsoRequired s e c)
> s is a set of eventualities which when added to constraints c entails e.

(moreLikely e1 e2 c)
> e1 is more likely than e2 given constraints c.

(likely e c)
> e is likely, given constraints c.

(leqLikelihood d1 d2)
> d1 is of lower or equal likelihood than d2.

The predicates smile and happy were used only for illustrative purposes, although happiness is explicated in Chapter 49.

Commonsense Psychology Theories

21

Knowledge Management

21.1 OBJECTS OF BELIEF

A fundamental concept in a theory of knowledge management is "belief." Traditionally, theories of belief concern propositions, agents, certain relations among propositions, and certain relations between agents and propositions. However, in Chapter 5,
we rejected the distinction between propositions and eventualities as at best super-
fluous. At worst, propositions do not divide the world up in a sufficiently fine-grained
fashion to be the objects of belief.

If, as is often taken to be the case, two propositions are identical whenever they
are logically equivalent, then it is not adequate to take the objects of belief to be
propositions. Suppose e1 and e3 are eventualities such that

(p' e1 x), (not' e2 e1), and (not' e3 e2)

That is, e3 is the eventuality of the negation of the negation (e2) of e1 holding.
The eventuality e3 is the eventuality of it not being the case that the eventuality e1
does not really exist. We do not take e1 and e3 to be identical. Their corresponding propositions are, in standard logical notation, $p(x)$ and $\neg\neg p(x)$. These are logically equivalent, and hence in such accounts are identical propositions. That is, under
this account of propositions, there is a many-to-one mapping from eventualities to
propositions.

Such a view of propositions is not adequate for a theory of cognition. It is quite
possible to know, believe, or understand "not not P" without knowing, believing, or
understanding P, because we have not yet computed their equivalence. (This is what
makes reading Michel Foucault so hard.) If we were to adopt that view, then all mathematical truths would be the same proposition as any true statement. Sadly, we do
not know all of mathematics simply by learning one true thing.

Belief can be viewed as a relation between an agent and an eventuality. However, it is mediated by something that can be in the head. Most eventualities are in
the world, not in the head. We can say that an agent has a concept of an eventuality, and that is what is believed, directly. We can say that this concept "represents"

an eventuality. The predicate `represent` is a three-part relation among an agent, a concept, and an eventuality.

```
(forall (c e a)                                                    (21.1)
    (if (represent c e a)
        (and (concept c) (eventuality e) (agent a))))
```

The expression (`represent c e a`) says that concept c represents eventuality e for agent a. The predicate `eventuality` is explicated in Chapter 5. The entire book can be viewed as an explication of the predicate `agent`. We will not attempt to define `concept`; occasionally in this book we will say that something is a concept. Its chief property is that it can in some sense be "in" the mind. Besides the concepts of eventualities, we might have concepts of individual entities; images are another example of concepts.

Representations of an eventuality inherit from the eventuality a predicate, an arity, and zero or more arguments.

Now we can posit a belief predicate – call it `believe0` – between an agent and a concept of an eventuality. The expression (`believe0 a c`) says that agent a believes the concept c. If `believe0` holds between a and c, then there is an eventuality e that c represents for a.

```
(forall (a c)                                                      (21.2)
    (if (believe0 a c)
        (exists (e) (represent c e a))))
```

Now that we have made the distinction between eventualities and their concepts, we can, as we have done before, introduce a predicate that glosses over the distinction. The predicate `believe` will take an agent as its first argument, and as its second argument an eventuality or the concept representing an eventuality.

```
(forall (a e)                                                      (21.3)
    (iff (believe a e)
        (or (and (concept e)(believe0 a e))
            (and (eventuality e)
                (exists (c)
                    (and (represent c e a)(believe0 a c)))))))
```

In a sense, we are coercing the eventuality into the corresponding concept when we see it in a belief or other cognitive context.

In the rest of this book we will use the predicate `believe` because the distinction between eventualities and their representations will not be significant. If we need to make the distinction between concepts in the mind and things in the world, we can talk about concepts related to eventualites by the relation (`represent c e a`) and take the set of such concepts for a given agent to be isomorphic to the set of eventualities.

21.2 BELIEF

There are three primary properties of belief that must be captured, all of them defeasible. First, we can do logic inside belief contexts. Defeasibly, we believe the consequences of our beliefs, though there can be notable lapses. Second, perceiving is, at least defeasibly, believing. Third, our beliefs influence our actions.

First logic: We believe a conjunction exactly when we believe the conjuncts.

```
(forall (a e1 e2 e3)                                        (21.4)
    (if (and' e1 e2 e3)
        (and (if (and (believe a e1)(etc))
                 (and (believe a e2)(believe a e3)))
             (if (and (believe a e2)(believe a e3)(etc))
                 (believe a e1)))))
```

Note that the corresponding property does not hold for disjunction. Someone could have believed Osama bin Laden was either in Pakistan or in Afghanistan without either believing that he was in Pakistan or believing that he was in Afghanistan.

To believe a set of eventualities or propositions is to believe each of the members of the set.

```
(forall (a s)                                               (21.5)
    (if (and (agent a)(eventualities s))
        (iff (believe a s)
             (forall (e)(if (member e s)(believe a e))))))
```

There is no Law of the Excluded Middle with belief. It is possible to neither believe nor disbelieve a proposition. But it is reasonable to assume that people defeasibly do not believe in contradictions. We may believe both a proposition and its negation, but when our attention is called to the fact, we generally try to resolve the conflict. We return to this in Section 21.3.

```
(forall (a e1 e2)                                           (21.6)
    (if (and (believe a e1) (not' e2 e1) (etc))
        (not (believe a e2))))
```

Defeasibly, we can do modus ponens in belief contexts. If someone believes P and believes that P implies Q, then he or she will generally believe Q.

```
(forall (a e1 e2 e3)                                        (21.7)
    (if (and (imply' e1 e2 e3) (believe a e2)
             (believe a e1) (etc))
        (believe a e3)))
```

This is only a defeasible inference, because otherwise it would entail logical omniscience. Logical omniscience is knowing all the logical consequences of what is known, clearly a radical idealization that fails often in reality. An agent knowing the axioms of set theory would know all mathematical truths. Later in this chapter and in subsequent chapters we will explicate circumstances under which the conclusion can be drawn more reliably.

Other logical equivalences can be expressed as axioms the agent believes, so Rules (21.5) and (21.7) about belief allow us to conclude that the agent can do propositional logic. For example, consider the situation of an agent knowing that ¬¬P implies P. This situation is described in our theory as follows:

```
(not' e2 e1), (not' e3 e2), (imply' e4 e3 e1), (believe a e3),
    (believe a e4)
```

The eventuality e1 corresponds to P, e2 to ¬P, and e3 to ¬¬P. The first `believe` proposition says that agent a believes ¬¬P. The second one says that a believes that ¬¬P implies P. Axiom (21.7) allows us to conclude – defeasibly because of the `(etc)` condition – that a believes e1, that is, P. Of course, if a does not know e4, that ¬¬P implies P, then we cannot conclude that a can draw the inference.

To do first-order logic inside belief contexts, we need an axiom that says agents can do universal instantiation. In Chapter 7, we developed a treatment of general eventualities, for example, the eventuality that all dogs are mammals, in terms of "type elements" of sets. We also defined the notion of a partial instance of such an eventuality, namely, an eventuality all of whose parameters are either subsets or elements of the parameters of the original eventuality. Thus, someone who believes all dogs are mammals and believes beagles constitute a subset of dogs believes all beagles are mammals. Someone who believes all dogs are mammals and that Rex is a dog believes Rex is a mammal. This property of belief can be stated as follows:

```
(forall (a e1 e2 e3)                                          (21.8)
    (if (and (partialInstance' e1 e2 e3)(believe a e3)
             (believe a e1) (etc))
        (believe a e2)))
```

The first conjunct in the antecedent says that e1 is the condition of e2 being a partial instance of e3, the second conjunct says the agent a believes the generalization e3, and the third conjunct says a believes the partial instance relation. The defeasible conclusion is that a believes the specialization e2.

An `instance` is also a `partialInstance`, so this axiom covers the case of completely instantiated generalizations as well.

The second facet of belief we wish to capture is the idea that seeing is believing, or more precisely, perceiving is defeasibly believing. We introduced the predicate `perceive` in Chapter 19 on Persons. One can perceive entities that are external to one's mind. Now we can state its effect on belief.

```
(forall (a e)                                                 (21.9)
    (if (and (perceive a e) (etc)) (believe a e)))
```

Beliefs are also influenced by communication. We often believe what we are told, although sometimes after assessing the motives and expertise of the speaker, as well as its implications for what we already believe. Hearing from a reliable source is, defeasibly, believing. The explication of this link would require a theory of commonsense communication and microsociology, and is beyond the scope of this book.

The third facet of belief is that belief influences action. Specifically, we tend to act in a way that would maximize the satisfaction of our goals, given what we believe. We will go into greater detail in subsequent chapters about this process, after developing our theories of goals and plans. But for now we will simply make the very general statement that there are beliefs that will make someone "will" different actions.

```
(forall (a)                                                  (21.10)
    (if (agent a)
        (exists (e1 e2)
            (and (if (believe a e1)(will a e2))
                 (if (not (believe a e1))(not (will a e2)))))))))
```

That is, there exist a belief e1 and an action e2 such that if agent a believes e1, a will will to do e2, and if a does not believe e1, a will not will to do e2. We can make the first half of this axiom stronger by saying that the belief plays a causal role in the willing of the action.

```
(forall (a)                                                         (21.11)
    (if (agent a)
        (exists (e1 e2 e3 e4)
            (and (if (and (believe' e3 a e1)(will' e4 a e2))
                     (cause e3 e4))
                 (if (not (believe a e1))(not (will a e2))))))))
```

Here, e3 is the believing of e1, e4 is the willing of e2, and the believing causes the willing. The negative case remains the same; causality rather than implication is probably too strong.

We have not made this axiom defeasible. It is hard to imagine an agent all of whose beliefs are inconsequential.

It will be useful to refer to the set of someone's beliefs. For this, we will use the predicate beliefs.

```
(forall (s a)                                                       (21.12)
    (iff (beliefs s a)
         (forall (e)
             (iff (member e s)(believe a e)))))
```

Here s is the set of a's beliefs.

Every agent has a set of beliefs.

```
(forall (a)                                                        ·(21.13)
    (if (agent a) (exists (s) (beliefs s a))))
```

In our empirical studies of how belief functions in strategies and in texts, we have determined several other useful properties of beliefs.

Every agent believes some eventualities and disbelieves others.

```
(forall (a)                                                         (21.14)
    (if (agent a)
        (exists (e) (believe a e))))
```

```
(forall (a)                                                         (21.15)
    (if (agent a)
        (exists (e1 e2) (and (not' e1 e2)(believe a e1)))))
```

We can define an eventuality to be unknown to an agent if the agent believes neither it nor its negation.

```
(forall (a e)                                                       (21.16)
    (iff (unknown e1 a)
         (and (agent a)(eventuality e1)
              (forall (e2)
                  (if (not' e2 e1)
                      (and (not (believe a e1))
                           (not (believe a e2)))))))))
```

For every agent, some propositions are unknown.

```
(forall (a)                                                    (21.17)
   (if (agent a)
       (exists (e) (unknown e a))))
```

Every agent changes beliefs.

```
(forall (a)                                                    (21.18)
   (if (agent a)
       (exists (e1 e2 e3 t)
          (and (changeFrom' e1 e2)(believe' e2 a e3)
               (atTime e1 t)))))
```

That is, for every agent a, there is some belief e3 and some time t such that a changes from believing e3, that is, ceases to believe e3 at time t.

We have not made Axioms (21.13) through (21.18) defeasible. It is difficult to imagine someone who believes nothing, someone who believes or disbelieves everything, someone who knows everything, or someone who never changes his or her mind.

21.3 BELIEF REVISION

Changing beliefs, or belief revision, is a topic on which there has been a great deal of research in artificial intelligence. We will examine one important issue, without, however, trying to address all of the extensive literature.

First some straightforward concepts: Agents can add or delete beliefs. These changes are defined as follows.

```
(forall (a e)                                                  (21.19)
   (iff (addBelief a e)
        (exists (e1) (and (changeTo e1)(believe' e1 a e)))))
```

```
(forall (a e)                                                  (21.20)
   (iff (deleteBelief a e)
        (exists (e1) (and (changeFrom e1)(believe' e1 a e)))))
```

An agent has the ability to manage knowledge, by adding and deleting beliefs. The predicate able, recall from Section 15.4, is with respect to a set of constraints. We won't try to explicate those constraints here. We only state that agents have the ability.

```
(forall (a)                                                    (21.21)
   (if (agent a)
       (exists (e1 e c)
          (and (able a e1 c)(addBelief' e1 a e)))))
```

```
(forall (a)                                                    (21.22)
   (if (agent a)
       (exists (e1 e c)
          (and (able a e1 c)(deleteBelief' e1 a e)))))
```

The conditions under which these knowledge-management operations are possible may be quite complex. For example, we probably don't want to say that someone who knows no physics is capable of adding a belief concerning string theory. Similarly, if someone is asleep or merely fatigued, we may not want to say they have the ability to add a belief.

Individual people have greater or lesser tendencies to add new beliefs and perform other knowledge-management actions. For example, some people are more gullible than others, believing the statements of others without further justification; others are more skeptical, and more likely to doubt the statements of others. More on this in the next section.

In most work on belief revision (Peppas, 2008), one is assumed to have a consistent set of beliefs. A new fact, generally certain, is learned that is inconsistent with the belief set. The belief set then has to be restored to consistency. A number of methods and criteria have been proposed for this operation, but usually the intuition is that we try to make as few changes as possible in our existing belief set.

One usually assumes logical omniscience; the belief set is taken to be deductively closed. This is not realistic; we don't know all the logical consequences of what we know. But the operations for restoring consistency in that framework when an inconsistency *exists* are going to be the same as the operations in our framework when an inconsistency is *discovered*. Thus, the assumption of logical omniscience does not make that work irrelevant.

It is also usually assumed that the new fact that triggers the inconsistency is something we are certain of, and it is thus the prior belief set that must be altered. This is not always the case. If we see a colleague flying down the hallway, we may decide simply to disbelieve what we saw, rather than make the massive changes in our commonsense knowledge that would be required to remove the inconsistency. But when we discover that we "believe" both P and ¬P, we have to withdraw belief in one of the two, and the process for doing so will be the same. So we can frame the problem as one of restoring a belief set to consistency by withdrawing belief in ¬P and whatever would imply it.

Most often when we revise our beliefs, we do so not by withdrawing assent to some belief but by complicating or otherwise modifying the beliefs. Where the belief set consists mostly of implicative rules, we will generally try to find rules where we can tighten the antecedent or loosen the consequent to escape the contradiction. For example, suppose we believe that whales live in water and that things that live in water are fish. We then learn that whales are not fish, and we restore our belief set to consistency by tightening the antecedent of the second rule to something like "lives in water and has gills." A child with limited experience with dogs may believe all dogs are brown.

```
(forall (x) (if (dog x)(brown x)))
```

On encountering a white dog, the child experiences an inconsistency and weakens the consequent of the rule.

```
(forall (x) (if (dog x)(or (brown x)(white x))))
```

Moreover, when we change an axiom, ideally we should also check all of our beliefs that resulted from the use of that axiom. This problem has been extensively studied in the literature on truth-maintenance systems (Doyle, 1995). Typical solutions involve associating beliefs with their justifications. We say a bit about justifications in Section 21.8.

But all these modifications can be viewed as deleting the original belief and adding the modified belief.

Choosing which rules to delete or modify is a challenging problem. A classic treatment of belief revision is that of Alchourrón, Gärdenfors, and Makinson (1985). They propose a set of eight postulates for any theory of belief revision. The axioms say that the revision on adding a consistent P to a consistent set of beliefs is a consistent set of beliefs including P. If P triggered no inconsistency, the revision is only the addition of P. In addition, whatever changes are made to the belief set interact with logical structure in the right way. But beyond this, the eight so-called AGM postulates give no guidance concerning what prior beliefs need to be changed.

Several general methods for altering the set of prior beliefs have been proposed. Winslett (1991) takes the intersection of all the maximal subsets of the prior beliefs consistent with P, with P added in. This is the cautious strategy of "When in doubt, leave it out." A similarly timid strategy is that of Fagin, Ullman, and Vardi (1983), in which one takes the disjunction of the subsets. This has the advantage of not losing the information in the prior belief set, just bracketing it inside disjunction. Bolder approaches (e.g., Nebel, 1994) posit priorities on beliefs and favor retracting beliefs of lower priority.

Here we only encode a weak form of the general principle that one makes the fewest, least consequential changes to the knowledge base possible, essentially keeping maximal subsets not known to be inconsistent.

To recognize an inconsistency is to consciously believe a proposition at the same time as believing one's beliefs imply its negation.

```
(forall (a so)                                              (21.23)
    (iff (recogInconsist a s0)
        (exists (e1 e2 e3)
            (and (beliefs s0 a)(thinkThat a e1)(imply' e2 s0 e3)
                (not' e3 e1)(thinkThat a e2)))))
```

The expression (recogInconsist a s0) says that agent a recognizes that belief set s0 is inconsistent. The predicate thinkThat is defined in Section 21.6; it means to have a belief in the focus of attention. In lines 3–5 e1 is the new certain fact, e3 is the negation of e1, and e2 means that the belief set s0 implies that negation.

Recognizing an inconsistency will usually cause an agent to have the goal of having a belief set with no recognizable inconsistency.

```
(forall (e0 a s0)                                           (21.24)
    (if (and (recogInconsist' e0 a s0)(etc))
        (exists (e1 e2 e3 s1)
            (and (not' e2 e1)(recogInconsist' e1 a s1)
                (goal' e3 e2 a)(cause e0 e3)))))
```

Here e0 is the recognition that triggers the goal. The set s0 is the offending belief set. Set s1 is the desired new belief set. Eventuality e2 is the negation of a recognition e1 of an inconsistency in s1. e3 is the eventuality of e2 being a goal of a's, and that is caused by e0. The predicate goal is explicated in Chapter 28.

To change a belief set is for there to be a change from one's beliefs being a set s0 to them being a set s1.

```
(forall (a s0 s1)                                          (21.25)
    (iff (changeBeliefSet a s0 s1)
        (exists (e0 e1)
            (and (beliefs' e0 s0 a)(beliefs' e1 s1 a)
                (change e0 e1)))))
```

If an agent recognizes an inconsistency in the belief set, that will cause the agent to have the goal of changing the belief set to one in which there is no recognizable inconsistency.

```
(forall (e0 a s0)                                          (21.26)
    (if (and (recogInconsist' e0 a s0)(etc))
        (exists (e1 e2 s1)
            (and (changeBeliefSet' e1 a s0 s1)(goal' e2 e1 a)
                (not (recogInconsist a s1))(cause e0 e2)))))
```

Finally we give a rule saying that in changing one's beliefs, one retains as much of the prior belief set as possible.

```
(forall (a s0 s1 s2 a1 a2 d1 d2)                           (21.27)
    (if (and (recogInconsist a s0)(not (recogInconsist a s1))
            (not (recogInconsist a s2))
            (setdiff a1 s1 s0)(setdiff a2 s2 s0)
            (setdiff d1 s0 s1)(setdiff d2 s0 s2)
            (properSubset a1 a2)(properSubset d1 d2)(etc))
        (and (changeBeliefSet a s0 s1)
            (not (changeBeliefSet a s0 s2)))))
```

The situation in the antecedent (lines 2–6) is that the agent a has recognized an inconsistency in belief set s0. Belief sets s1 and s2 are two belief sets in which no inconsistency is recognized. Set a1 is the set of beliefs added to s0 to get to set s1, and similarly for a2. Sets d1 and d2 are the deletions. If all the additions and deletions required to turn s0 into s1 were also required to turn s0 into s2 and then some (line 6), then s1 is a better revised belief set than s2, and that's what a will generally adopt.

21.4 DEGREES OF BELIEF

There are many issues where we believe neither a proposition nor its negation with absolute certainty. Rather we sort of believe it, or sort of don't believe it, or we view it as a toss-up. In a treatment of commonsense psychology, we need not just a theory of belief but also a theory of "graded" belief. We need the notion of believing something to some degree.

For this, we will introduce the predicate gbel, expressing a relation between an agent, an eventuality, and a degree.

```
(forall (a e d)                                            (21.28)
    (if (gbel a e d) (and (agent a)(eventuality e))))
```

We will next examine what the degree d should be.

One can argue that to believe P to degree d is to believe the probability of P is d. That is, the degree of belief in P is an absolute belief about the likelihood of P. We will develop this in terms of likelihoods as laid out in Section 20.4.

To have a graded belief in eventuality e of degree d is to believe the likelihood of e to be d. Likelihood is relative to a set of constraints. For graded beliefs, the constraints will be the set of the agent's beliefs.

```
(forall (a e d)                                                        (21.29)
   (if (gbel a e d)
       (exists (s s1 e1)
          (and (beliefs s a)(deleteElt s1 s e1)
               (likelihood' e1 d e s1)(believe a e1)))))
```

That is, if an agent a has a graded belief in e of degree d, then a believes the likelihood of e is d, given everything else a believes.

Just as with belief, we need to examine the relation between graded belief on the one hand and inference, perception, and action on the other.

There have been many detailed proposals for how one should do reasoning in systems for graded belief. Rather than adopting one of these frameworks, we will state some general properties that any theory of graded belief should have. With belief, we considered conjunction, disjunction, negation, modus ponens, and universal instantiation. We will do the same here. These rules are derivable from similar properties in the treatment of likelihood.

The graded belief in a conjunction is less than or equal to the graded belief in each of its conjuncts.

```
(forall (a e1 e2 e3 d1 d2 d3)                                          (21.30)
   (if (and (and' e1 e2 e3)(gbel a e1 d1)(gbel a e2 d2)
            (gbel a e3 d3))
       (and (leqLikelihood d1 d2)(leqLikelihood d1 d3))))
```

If one of the conjuncts is "believed" rather than believed to a degree, the graded belief in the conjunction is the same as the graded belief in the uncertain conjunct.

```
(forall (a e1 e2 e3 d1 d2)                                             (21.31)
   (if (and (and' e1 e2 e3) (gbel a e1 d1) (gbel a e2 d2)
            (believe a e3))
       (equal d1 d2)))
```

Similarly, the graded belief in a disjunction is greater than or equal to the graded belief in all the disjuncts.

```
(forall (a e1 e2 e3 d1 d2 d3 s1)                                       (21.32)
   (if (and (or' e1 e2 e3)(gbel a e1 d1)(gbel a e2 d2)
            (gbel a e3 d3))
       (and (leqLikelihood d2 d1)(leqLikelihood d3 d1))))
```

It follows from the fact that an eventuality and its negation cannot both be "likely," that is, in the Hi region of a likelihood scale, that one cannot have a high graded belief in both an eventuality and its negation. We will not develop this observation formally, as we won't need it.

A somewhat stronger statement is that if one proposition has a higher degree of belief than another, then the ordering is reversed for their negations.

```
(forall (a e1 d1 e2 d2 e3 d3 e4 d4)                          (21.33)
    (if (and (gbel a e1 d1)(not' e3 e1)(gbel a e3 d3)
             (gbel a e2 d2)(not' e4 e2)(gbel a e4 d4)
             (leqLikelihood d2 d1))
        (leqLikelihood d3 d4)))
```

Implication increases graded belief; the belief in the consequent is at least as high as the belief in the antecedent.

```
(forall (a e1 d1 e2 d2 e)                                    (21.34)
    (if (and (gbel a e1 d1)(gbel a e2 d2)
             (imply' e e1 e2)(believe a e))
        (leqLikelihood d1 d2)))
```

The behavior of universal instantiation under graded belief follows from all this. If an agent believes a general principle to degree d1, then the agent will believe each instance of that principle to at least that degree.

```
(forall (a e1 e2 e3 d2 d3)                                   (21.35)
    (if (and (partialInstance' e1 e2 e3)(believe a e1)
             (gbel a e2 d2)(gbel a e3 d3))
        (leqLikelihood d3 d2)))
```

The first conjunct in the antecedent says that e1 is the condition of e2 being a partial (or complete) instance of a generalization e3; the second conjunct says that the agent a believes this to be the case; the last two conjuncts label the agent's degree of belief in e2 and e3. The conclusion is that the degree of belief in the generalization is no higher than the degree of belief in any of the instances or partial instances.

In the previous section, we linked belief and perception. Should we similarly link graded belief and perception? Perception results in full belief of what is perceived, so that leaves no room for graded belief. But one might think of having a theory of partial perception and saying that partial perception to some degree results in graded belief to a corresponding degree. For example, if a person sees someone who from the back looks like Al Gore, one would say there was a partial perception of Al Gore and that induces a corresponding graded belief that Al Gore is there.

It seems to us more perspicuous to say that there is no partial perception of Al Gore, but rather there is complete perception of someone who from the back looks like Al Gore. Then the resulting graded belief is a result of inference based on this narrower absolute belief. In this approach, there is nothing to say about the relation between perception and graded belief.

Graded belief does interact with action. Very often the higher our degree of belief in something, the more likely we are to engage in a particular action. When a person believes to some degree that there is a mugger in the next block, he or she may or may not go that way. But when the degree of belief is high enough, generally still short of certainty, a different route will be chosen.

Exactly how graded belief interacts with action, however, is very dependent on the details of how belief, graded belief, and goals get turned into action. We will explicate this process in subsequent chapters.

One suspects something if one's graded belief in it is greater than one's graded belief in its negation.

```
(forall (a e1 e2)                                          (21.36)
    (iff (suspect a e1)
        (exists (e2 d1 d2)
            (and (not' e2 e1)(gbel a e1 d1)(gbel a e2 d2)
                (lowerLikelihood d2 d1)))))
```

One's graded belief in a proposition can increase or decrease. We will define a predicate only for increasing.

```
(forall (a e d1 d2)                                        (21.37)
    (iff (increaseBelief a e)
        (and (change e1 e2)(gbel' e1 a e d1)(gbel' e2 a e d2)
            (lowerLikelihood d1 d2))))
```

That is, there is a change from the graded belief in e being d1 to its being d2, and d1 is less than d2.

In some cases, graded belief becomes high enough that it becomes absolute belief. Belief and graded belief are related in one obvious way. Believing the probability of something is 1 is equivalent to believing it. We will use the top of the Likelihood scale rather than 1.

```
(forall (a e d s)                                          (21.38)
    (if (and (gbel a e d)(top d s)(likelihoodScale s))
        (believe a e)))
```

More generally, we could say there is a threshold, perhaps changing, above which a graded belief becomes a belief. If that threshold is high, one has a bias toward disbelief. If it is low, one's bias is toward belief. This is the difference between being skeptical and credulous. The threshold is a value on the likelihood scale, and is specific to an agent.

```
(forall (t a)                                              (21.39)
    (iff (thresholdOfBelief t a)
        (exists (s)
            (and (likelihoodScale s)(inScale t s)(agent a)
                (forall (e d)
                    (if (and (gbel a e d)(leqLikelihood t d))
                        (believe a e)))))))
```

That is, t is agent a's threshold of belief on likelihood scale s if and only if a believes everything whose graded belief is higher than t.

We can define a "threshold of belief scale" as one whose elements are thresholds of belief for arbitrary agents and whose partial ordering is lowerLikelihood.

```
(forall (s)                                                      (21.40)
   (iff (thresholdOfBeliefScale s)
        (exists (s1 e t1 t2)
           (and (forall (t)
                   (iff (member t s1)
                        (exists (a)(thresholdOfBelief t a))))
                (scaleDefinedBy s s1 e)
                (lowerLikelihood' e t1 t2)))))
```

We can then say that an agent has a bias toward belief if the agent's threshold of belief is in the low region of the scale.

```
(forall (a)                                                      (21.41)
   (iff (biasTowardBelief a)
        (exists (s s1 t)
           (and (thresholdOfBeliefScale s)(Lo s1 s)
                (thresholdOfBelief t a)(inScale t s1)))))
```

Similarly, an agent with a threshold of belief in the high region has a bias toward disbelief.

```
(forall (a)                                                      (21.42)
   (iff (biasTowardDisbelief a)
        (exists (s s1 t)
           (and (thresholdOfBeliefScale s)(Hi s1 s)
                (thresholdOfBelief t a)(inScale t s1)))))
```

As always, the Hi and Lo regions of the scale have to be determined from functionality and distribution.

21.5 ASSUMING

Agents are able to assume propositions. Generally the reason for doing this is that reasoning can be done within assumption. We assume a proposition, do some reasoning, and determine what else would be true.

One function of assuming is hypothesis testing. We assume a hypothesis and examine the consequences. If a consequence is false, we know the hypothesis is false. If all the consequences we draw are true, it will strengthen our belief in the hypothesis.

Indirect proof is a variety of hypothesis testing. We assume a proposition is false and we prove that a falsehood results, thereby demonstrating that the proposition is true.

A proof by cases involves successively assuming the full range of possible values for some variable and proving the proposition in question for each of them. When we combine that with the fact that the cases are exhaustive, we have a proof.

We make assumptions also to suppress certain reasoning processes and their consequent actions. Suppose a student offers a teacher a bribe for a grade, and the teacher replies, "I'm going to assume you didn't say that." The alternative is to follow the consequences of the offer, which may result in more serious difficulties than either of them wants.

When we assume something for the sake of the discussion, we are pretending that the proposition is true in order for our partner in the conversation to express consequences that depend on it, without committing ourselves to belief in the proposition. We are able to reason about that assumption. For example, we can judge whether an argument is coherent, given the assumption.

Assumptions function in language in the form of accommodation. Assuming a proposition will allow us to make sense out of what the speaker says, so we assume that proposition, on no more warrant than that it yields a sensible interpretation. For example, in interpreting

> There's a pile of inflammable trash next to your car. You'll have to get rid of it.

we assume "it" refers to the trash rather than the car, as the interpretation of the second sentence is more sensible in that case.

Finally, there are cases in social life in which something may or may not be true, but if everyone makes the assumption that it is true, then it will be true. Money is like that. The proposition that a dollar bill can be traded for a dollar's worth of goods is just an assumption, but because everyone assumes it, it becomes true.

Assumption is like belief in that one can reason inside assumption, but it is unlike belief in that perception does not cause assumption – it causes belief – and in that one does not act on pure assumptions without them first being converted into some degree of belief.

The ability to do reasoning inside assumption is captured in a manner similar to belief.

We assume a conjunction exactly when we assume the conjuncts (simultaneously).

```
(forall (a e1 e2 e3)                                    (21.43)
   (if (and' e1 e2 e3)
      (iff (assume a e1)
         (and (assume a e2)(assume a e3)))))
```

It is possible at different moments to assume contradictory propositions as two different alternatives to ponder. But we will take these to be different acts of assumption. It is also possible to assume contradictory propositions simultaneously, but the result of reasoning about these assumptions will be the recognition that they are contradictory.

Propositions can enter into reasoning under assumptions either if they are assumed or if they are believed. It will thus be convenient to have a predicate that covers both propositional attitudes.

```
(forall (a e)                                           (21.44)
   (iff (believeOrAssume a e)
      (or (believe a e)(assume a e))))
```

Defeasibly, we can do modus ponens in assumption contexts. If someone assumes P and believes or assumes that P implies Q, then he or she will assume Q as well.

```
(forall (a e1 e2 e3)                                        (21.45)
    (if (and (imply' e1 e2 e3)(assume a e2)
            (believeOrAssume a e1) (etc))
        (assume a e3)))
```

Universal instantiation for assumption is stated similarly to Axiom (21.8).

```
(forall (a e1 e2 e3)                                        (21.46)
    (if (and (partialInstance' e1 e2 e3)(assume a e3)
            (believeOrAssume a e1) (etc))
        (assume a e2)))
```

Assumptions in general do not have to be justified in the same way as beliefs. Typically, the motive for assuming is rather the reasoning process it will trigger or suppress.

Assumptions are not directly caused by perception. We may utilize assumptions to come to the best explanation for what we perceive, and we may thereby come to believe those assumptions, but this process is mediated by reasoning. Nor do we act on our assumptions in the same way as we act on our beliefs. People might assume for the sake of discussion that there is no car coming toward them in the other lane on the other side of the hill, but they are unlikely to act on that assumption. Assumptions may ultimately result in action, but only if the strength of belief in the propositions is increased sufficiently in the course of reasoning.

One way assumption can lead to belief is when we compute the consequences of our assumptions and verify those against our beliefs. When this succeeds, the strength of belief in the proposition may increase.

```
(forall (a e1 e2 e3)                                        (21.47)
    (if (and (assume a e1)(believe a e3)(imply' e3 e1 e2)
            (believe a e2) (etc))
        (increaseBelief a e1)))
```

Sometimes the increase in graded belief results in absolute belief.

Abduction, named and explored by Peirce (1955) but going back at least to Wolff (1963, p. 67) in 1728, is a mode of reasoning in which one tries to find the best or most plausible explanation for a set of evidence. Essentially, one tries to prove the occurrence of the evidence from the general and specific facts that one knows, and one makes assumptions where the knowledge is lacking. If the proof works out, this itself is taken as an indication that the assumption is true. In the case of this axiom, e1 is the assumption, e2 is the evidence, and e3 is the general knowledge. Thus, this axiom begins to capture the role of assumptions in hypothetical reasoning, language and scene interpretation, and other abductive mental processes.

Just as agents can add or delete beliefs, they can make or retract assumptions.

```
(forall (a e)                                               (21.48)
    (iff (makeAssumption a e)
        (exists (e1) (and (changeTo e1)(assume' e1 a e)))))
```

```
(forall (a e)                                                    (21.49)
    (iff (retractAssumption a e)
         (exists (e1) (and (changeFrom e1)(assume' e1 a e)))))
```

These axioms define the actions. The following axioms state that agents are able to perform the actions under some set of constraints c.

```
(forall (a)                                                      (21.50)
    (if (agent a)
        (exists (e1 e c)
            (and (able a e1 c)(makeAssumption' e1 a e)))))
```

```
(forall (a)                                                      (21.51)
    (if (agent a)
        (exists (e1 e c)
            (and (able a e1 c)(retractAssumption' e1 a e)))))
```

21.6 HAVING THINGS IN MIND AND IN FOCUS

In Chapter 19 on Persons, we said that a person has a mind. The mind of a person, as conceived by commonsense psychology, is a complex entity with at least two parts – a memory and a focus of attention. In people, we think of these two parts as distinct and nonoverlapping. But agents need not be persons, and such agents may not have such a clear distinction between the focus of attention and the memory; there may be nothing in the structure of such agents' minds that corresponds to these concepts. Yet in the text that follows we define a number of important concepts for agents in general in terms of the focus of attention. For that reason, we will not put tight constraints on these two components of the mind; in some classes of agents, we may have to simply stipulate that they exist and take them both to be coterminous with the mind itself.

```
(forall (m a)                                                    (21.52)
    (if (mind m a)
        (exists (f) (and (focusOfAttention f a)(componentOf f m)))))
```

```
(forall (m a)                                                    (21.53)
    (if (mind m a)
        (exists (m1) (and (memory m1 a)(componentOf m1 m)))))
```

We will go into greater detail concerning this division in Chapter 23 and subsequent chapters. But the nature of these components will be explicated as we state various axioms about them, including the ones in this section. The focus of attention is where we consciously entertain or think about concepts.

The predicate inm will represent the mental version of "being in." Something can be in an agent's mind, or in any component of the mind.

```
(forall (x y)                                                    (21.54)
    (if (inm x y)
        (exists (a)
            (or (mind y a)
                (exists (m)(and (mind m a)(componentOf y m)))))))
```

As with the objects of belief, we will not constrain the first argument of inm to be a concept, because we can always coerce the entity or eventuality to the corresponding concept.

If something is believed, it is in the mind of the believer.

```
(forall (a e)                                               (21.55)
   (if (believe a e)
      (exists (m) (and (mind m a)(inm e m)))))
```

If one has a graded belief about something or if one makes an assumption, one has it in mind.

```
(forall (a e d)                                             (21.56)
   (if (gbel a e d)
      (exists (m) (and (mind m a)(inm e m)))))
```

```
(forall (a e)                                               (21.57)
   (if (assume a e)
      (exists (m) (and (mind m a)(inm e m)))))
```

It will be convenient to have a shorthand for something being in an agent's focus of attention.

```
(forall (x a)                                               (21.58)
   (iff (inFocus x a)
      (exists (f)(and (focusOfAttention f a)(inm x f)))))
```

If an agent has something e he believes in focus, we will say that the agent "thinks that" e.

```
(forall (a e)                                               (21.59)
   (iff (thinkThat a e)
      (and (believe a e)(inFocus e a))))
```

"Thinking that" is thus defined as conscious belief.

21.7 INFERENCE

When an agent a infers an eventuality e from a set s of eventualities, there is a causal relation from a's belief in s to a's conscious belief in e.

```
(forall (a e s)                                             (21.60)
   (if (infer a e s)
      (exists (e1 e2)
         (and (believe' e1 a s)(thinkThat' e2 a e)
            (cause e1 e2)))))
```

The expression (infer a e s) says that a infers e from s, and implies that a's belief in s causes a to think that e holds.

This is a weak constraint on infer. We leave open the possibility that there are other ways besides inference that a's belief in s can cause a to think that e holds. But the three classical modes of inference – deduction, abduction, and induction – cover many of the examples that one might come up with. We now define these.

Deduction is as follows:

```
(forall (a e s)                                                   (21.61)
   (iff (deduce a e s)
        (exists (e1 e2 e3 e4)
            (and (believe' e1 a s)(imply' e2 e3 e)(member e2 s)
                 (or (member e3 s)(deduce a e3 s))
                 (thinkThat' e4 a e)(cause e1 e4)))))
```

The agent a deduces e from s if s contains some general rule e2 from which e can be inferred, and either s contains the premises e3 of the rule or they can be deduced from s. Then belief in e is caused by belief in s.

One abduces the missing premises of a general rule when they would imply a believed consequent. That is, in abduction, from e2 and (imply e1 e2), one infers e1, under certain circumstances.

```
(forall (a e s)                                                   (21.62)
   (iff (abduce a e s)
        (exists (e1 e2 e3 e4)
            (and (believe' e1 a s)(imply' e2 e e3)
                 (doubleton s e2 e3)(thinkThat' e4 a e)
                 (cause e1 e4)))))
```

In this definition, we have not tried to specify the other circumstances that lead to the abduction, for example, that e is the best explanation of e2, or the most plausible, or the most economical in some sense. We merely state that if one does infer the premise from the conclusion, for whatever reason, then it is an instance of abduction.

In induction, the agent thinks that a general principle holds because of a belief that a number of its instances hold.

```
(forall (a e s)                                                   (21.63)
   (iff (induce a e s)
        (exists (e1 e3)
            (and (believe' e1 a s)
                 (forall (e2)(if (member e2 s)(instance e2 e)))
                 (thinkThat' e3 a e)(cause e1 e3)))))
```

The set s is a set of instances e2 of a general principle e. The agent a's belief in the instances causes a conscious belief in the general principle. As with abduction, we don't attempt to specify the conditions under which such an induction results in good inferences.

This definition leaves the door open for the limiting case in which one believes *all* of the instances in the general principle, and hence believes in the general principle, which would also be an example of deduction.

Note that in the definition of deduce, by the recursive reference to deduce, we allow the inference process to have multiple steps. In the definitions of abduce and induce we restricted the mode of inference to a single step. One can embed these operations as steps in a larger inference process, but we wanted to focus on the specific abduction or induction step.

Deduction, abduction, and induction are all modes of inference.

```
(forall (a e s) (if (deduce a e s)(infer a e s)))            (21.64)
```

```
(forall (a e s) (if (abduce a e s)(infer a e s)))            (21.65)
```

```
(forall (a e s) (if (induce a e s)(infer a e s)))            (21.66)
```

While we have not provided necessary and sufficient conditions for the predicate `infer`, we have listed three ways an action can be an `infer`, and we have placed a necessary constraint on `infer`.

People can manipulate their inference processes, by considering possible inferences, ignoring them, suppressing the inference process, recognizing contradictions, and reaffirming already held beliefs.

Checking inferences is a composite event made up of individual `inFocus` events of possible inferences from a set of premises. In the following axiom, e1 is the "checking inferences" composite event, a is the agent, s is the set of premises, the e2's are the individual `inFocus` events, and the e's are the inferences following from s that a considers.

```
(forall (s1 a s)                                             (21.67)
    (iff (checkInferences' e1 a s)
        (forall (e)
            (if (infer a e s)
                (exists (e2)
                    (and (inFocus' e2 e a)(subevent e2 e1)))))))
```

To suppress inferences from a set s of premises is to not check inferences.

```
(forall (a s)                                                (21.68)
    (iff (suppressInferences a s)
        (not (checkInferences a s))))
```

To ignore an inference is to draw the inference, have it in focus, and then not check inferences involving it.

```
(forall (a e s)                                              (21.69)
    (iff (ignoreInference a e s)
        (and (infer a e s)(inFocus e a)
            (forall (s1)
                (if (member e s1)(suppressInferences a s1))))))
```

To conclude a contradiction is to infer something whose negation is already consciously believed.

```
(forall (a s)                                                (21.70)
    (iff (concludeContradiction a s)
        (exists (e1 e2)
            (and (infer a e1 s)(not' e2 e1)(thinkThat a e2)))))
```

To reaffirm a belief is to find another independent set of premises from which it can be inferred. We capture independence as follows: The two sets of premises are s1 and s2. They are not equal, and they are both minimal in the sense that no subset of either would lead the agent a to conclude the belief e. (This is similar to the `minimallyProves` predicate of Chapter 8, but applies to inference in general and not just deduction.)

```
(forall (a e)                                                    (21.71)
    (iff (reaffirmBelief a e)
        (exists (s1 s2 e1)
            (and (infer a e s1)(infer' e1 a e s2)(believe' e2 a e)
                 (cause e1 e2)(nequal s1 s2)
                 (forall (s3)
                     (if (subset s3 s1)(not (infer a e s3))))
                 (forall (s4)
                     (if (subset s4 s2)(not (infer a e s4)))))))))
```

There are a number of ways to be confused. One is to infer something that is inconsistent with one's beliefs.

```
(forall (a s e1 e2)                                              (21.72)
    (if (and (infer a e1 s)(believe a s)(believe a e2)
             (not' e2 e1))
        (confused a)))
```

21.8 JUSTIFICATION

Justification is closely related to inference. A set s of premises justifies something e for an agent a if a believes e as a result of inferring e from s.

```
(forall (s e a)                                                 (21.73)
    (iff (justify s e a)
        (exists (e1)
            (and (infer' e1 a e s)(believe' e2 a e)(cause e1 e2)))))
```

The predication (justify s e a) is read "s justifies e for a."

Sometimes the belief is warranted by the inference; sometimes it is not. Justifications can be sound, partial, circular, poor, and just plain missing.

A set of propositions soundly justifies a proposition for an agent if the set minimally proves the proposition and the agent believes all the propositions in the set.

```
(forall (s e a)                                                 (21.74)
    (iff (soundlyJustify s e a)
        (and (justify s e a)(minimallyProves s e))))
```

There are several types of partial justifications.

A set s of propositions partially justifies something e for an agent a if s minimally proves the proposition and the agent at least suspects each of the members of s, that is, that the agent believes them more strongly than their negations.

```
(forall (s e a e0)                                              (21.75)
    (if (and (minimallyProves' e0 s e)(believe a e0)
             (forall (e1)
                 (if (member e1 s)(suspect a e1))))
        (partiallyJustify s e a)))
```

Abductions and inductions always only provide partial justifications, because both are fallible.

```
(forall (s e a e0)                                              (21.76)
    (if (and (minimallyProves' e0 s e)(believe a e0)
            (exists (e1 e2)
                (and (abduce' e1 a e s)(believe' e2 a e)
                    (cause e1 e2))))
        (partiallyJustify s e a)))
```

```
(forall (s e a e0)                                              (21.77)
    (if (and (minimallyProves' e0 s e)(believe a e0)
            (exists (e1 e2)
                (and (induce' e1 a e s)(believe' e2 a e)
                    (cause e1 e2))))
        (partiallyJustify s e a)))
```

It is not sufficient for partial justification for the agent to believe only some of the premises. That Porky flies can be proved from the propositions that Porky is a pig and that pigs fly, but one's belief that Porky is a pig would not be a partial justification for a belief that Porky flies.

We do not attempt to catalogue exhaustively the ways in which a justification can be only partial.

A circular justification is one in which the conclusion is one of the premises.

```
(forall (s e a)                                                 (21.78)
    (iff (circularlyJustify s e a)
        (and (justify s e a)(member e s))))
```

A poor justification is a set of premises which cannot be extended to a set that minimally proves the conclusion.

```
(forall (s e a)                                                 (21.79)
    (iff (poorlyJustify s e a)
        (and (justify s e a)
            (not (exists (s1)
                (and (subset s s1)
                    (minimallyProves s1 e)))))))
```

A poor justification cannot be a partial justification.

```
(forall (s e a)                                                 (21.80)
    (if (poorlyJustify s e a)(not (partiallyJustify s e a))))
```

Something is unjustified for an agent if there is no justification for it.

```
(forall (e a)                                                   (21.81)
    (iff (unjustified e a)
        (not (exists (s) (justify s e a)))))
```

21.9 KNOWLEDGE

Beliefs can be true or false. We can define "true" and "false" in terms of real existence, as follows:

```
(forall (e) (iff (true e)(Rexist e)))                          (21.82)
```

```
(forall (e) (iff (false e)(not (Rexist e))))                   (21.83)
```

But we will not use these in this development. The predicates Rexist and not will suffice.

Knowledge is at least true belief. An agent who knows something believes it, and it is true.

```
(forall (a e)                                                  (21.84)
    (if (know a e)
        (and (believe a e)(Rexist e))))
```

But it more than simply this; the belief also has to be justified. Suppose someone believes Al Gore, wherever he is, is standing up right now. Suppose it is also true. This should not count as knowledge if the person has no justification for this belief. It is just a lucky guess. Thus, the expanded axiom is as follows:

```
(forall (a e)                                                  (21.85)
    (if (know a e)
        (and (believe a e)(Rexist e)
            (exists (s) (soundlyJustify s e a)))))
```

The implication in this axiom still only goes to the right. Gettier (1963) came up with a class of examples to show that these three conditions are not sufficient to define knowledge. Justification, truth, and belief are necessary but not sufficient conditions for knowledge. An agent may believe a true proposition for reasons that aren't true. We can strengthen Axiom (21.85) by insisting that the justification s is true as well.

```
(forall (a e)                                                  (21.86)
    (iff (know a e)
        (and (believe a e)(Rexist e)
            (exists (s)
                (and (soundlyJustify s e a)(Rexist s))))))
```

There is a rich literature investigating the further conditions that would be necessary in order to have a definition of knowledge, but we will not pursue this any further. This axiom provides a definition that is sufficient for most purposes.

Knowledge is not a different kind of mental act from belief. It is just belief that happens to be justified and happens to be true (and happens to have whatever other properties are required for true knowledge).

Knowledge happens when truth and belief agree. When they don't agree, we have false positives and negatives. A false positive for an agent is something that is believed that is not true.

```
(forall (e a)                                                  (21.87)
    (iff (falsePositive e a)
        (and (believe a e)(not (Rexist e)))))
```

A false negative for an agent is something that is true but is believed not to hold.

```
(forall (e a)                                                    (21.88)
    (iff (falseNegative e a)
         (and (Rexist e)
              (exists (e1)(and (not' e1 e)(believe a e1))))))
```

Learning is a change into a state of knowledge.

```
(forall (a e)                                                    (21.89)
    (iff (learn a e)
         (exists (e1)
              (and (know' e1 a e)(changeTo e1)))))
```

Realizing something is a kind of learning. We can realize something because of perception.

I just realized that woman has a dog in her purse.

We can realize something by inference.

I just realized that Grant was a truly great general.

But we can't realize something by reading it. So the statement

I just realized Grant was elected president in 1868.

is not appropriate if we learned that fact by reading the sentence in a history book, "Grant was elected president in 1868."

Thus, to realize something is to learn it by inference or perception.

```
(forall (a e)                                                    (21.90)
    (iff (realize a e)
         (and (learn a e)
              (exists (e1 s e2)
                   (and (or (perceive' e1 a e)(infer' e1 a e s))
                        (know' e2 a e)(cause e1 e2))))))
```

Because realizing happens as a result of perceiving or inferring, what is realized is usually the size of a sentence or two, rather than a whole body of knowledge.

Sometimes an agent realizes a belief is false.

```
(forall (a e)                                                    (21.91)
    (iff (realizeBeliefFalse a e)
         (exists (e1 e2 e3)
              (believe' e1 a e)(not' e2 e)(believe' e3 a e2)
              (change e1 e3))))
```

21.10 INTELLIGENCE

The intelligence of agents is extremely difficult to characterize. It has a great many components. One of these components is the ability to draw inferences, and here we introduce the intelligence scale and constrain its interpretation in terms of this ability.

Other factors in determining intelligence are the ability to think of analogies, creativity or the ability to come up with new ideas, and the speed of drawing inferences. But we will not attempt to characterize these factors or to present a general theory of intelligence.

We will not attempt to give necessary and sufficient conditions for the partial ordering moreIntelligent. But it is consistent with the ability to draw inferences. If Pat is able to draw all the correct inferences from a set of premises that Chris can draw and then some, then defeasibly Pat is more intelligent than Chris. Indeed, this is precisely how we often compare the intelligence of two people – seeing how well they solve the same problem set. The rule is defeasible because Chris may outperform Pat on other criteria for intelligence.

```
(forall (a b)                                                        (21.92)
   (if (and (forall (e s)
              (if (and (infer b e s)(minimallyProves s e))
                  (infer a e s)))
          (exists (e s)
            (and (infer a e s)(minimallyProves s e)
                 (not (infer b e s))))
          (etc))
      (moreIntelligent a b)))
```

Lines 2–4 say that a legitimately infers everything that b infers. Lines 5–7 say that a legitimately infers things that b does not. In line 9 this means a is more intelligent than b.

Intelligence is a scale, that is, a *partial* ordering, on people where the partial ordering relation is moreIntelligent, as constrained above and by whatever other constraints one can legitimately posit.

```
(forall (s)                                                          (21.93)
   (iff (intelligence s)
        (exists (s1 e x y)
           (and (forall (a)
                  (iff (member a s1)(agent a)))
                (moreIntelligent' e x y)
                (scaleDefinedBy s s1 e)))))
```

For an agent to be intelligent is for the agent to be in the Hi region (functionally and/or distributionally) of the intelligence scale.

```
(forall (a)                                                          (21.94)
   (iff (intelligent a)
        (exists (s s1)
           (and (intelligence s)(Hi s1 s)(inScale a s1)))))
```

An agent's knowledge-management ability is the agent's place on the intelligence scale.

21.11 SENTENCES AND KNOWLEDGE DOMAINS

A natural language sentence differs from propositions in a way that has caused much confusion in the philosophy of language. A sentence can be thought of as having a set of propositions, its "propositional content," and this propositional content may be true or false. But in sentences there is a distinction between the "claim" made by a sentence and the rest of its propositional content. We will view a sentence as a composite entity with an associated set of propositions that is its propositional content and an associated claim. One of the propositions is the claim, and the conjunction of all of them is the propositional content. As usual, we will use eventualities rather than propositions.

```
(forall (s)                                                    (21.95)
    (iff (sentence s)
         (exists (s1 e1)
             (and (propContent s1 s)(claim e1 s)
                  (eventualities s1)(member e1 s1)))))
```

We can always speak of the truth or falsity of sentences as propositions, but as sentences, they can only be true or false if all the nonclaim propositions are true. The old philosophical nugget, "The king of France is bald," has the associated propositional content (or conjunction of propositions)

```
(exists (x y)(and (king x y)(France y)(bald x)))
```

The claim of the sentence is (bald x).

The following axiom defines when sentences are true and false:

```
(forall (s)                                                    (21.96)
    (if (and (sentence s)(propContent s1 s)(claim e s)
             (deleteElt s2 s1 e)(Rexist s2))
        (and (iff (true s)(Rexist e))
             (iff (false s)(not (Rexist e))))))
```

Here, s1 is the propositional content of sentence s, e is s's claim, s2 is all of the propositional content except the claim, and all of that really obtains. Under these conditions, the sentence can be true or false, and it is so depending on whether the claim e really obtains or not.

The Law of the Excluded Middle is not true for sentences. There are sentences, such as "The king of France is bald," that are neither true nor false, because the nonclaim propositional content is not all true.

A fact is a true sentence:

```
(forall (s)                                                    (21.97)
    (iff (fact s)
         (and (sentence s)(true s))))
```

Believing a sentence is believing its propositional content.

```
(forall (s s1 a)                                               (21.98)
    (if (and (sentence s)(propContent s1 s)(agent a))
        (iff (believe a s) (believe a s1))))
```

A knowledge domain is a set of sentences "about" a particular kind of thing. Knowledge domains have a certain coherence to them. Because we are not presuming the sentences to be true, they might be better called "belief domains," but we will stick with the term "knowledge domain."

It is difficult to characterize what this coherence is. Here we propose one particular notion of a knowledge domain, wherein a knowledge domain is simply characterized by a set of predicates. A knowledge domain is a set of sentences all of whose claims have predicates in that set. The predicate predicatesOf will pick out that set of predicates.

```
(forall (d)                                                    (21.99)
    (if (knowledgeDomain d)
        (exists (s)
            (and (predicatesOf s d)
                (forall (p) (if (member p s)(predicate p)))))))
```

That is, a knowledge domain has a set of predicates.

Then a knowledge domain is a set of sentences, all of whose claims are in the predicatesOf set.

```
(forall (d s)                                                  (21.100)
    (if (and (knowledgeDomain d)(predicatesOf s d))
        (forall (s1 e p)
            (if (and (member s1 d)(claim e s1)(pred p e))
                (member p s)))))
```

For example, the knowledge domain "Baseball" might have the appropriately specialized associated predicates pitch, hit, base, and homer, but it probably would not have the predicates grass, dirt, and round, even though they will be useful in describing facts about baseball.

21.12 EXPERTISE

The expertise s of an agent a in knowledge domain d is the set of sentences in that domain that the agent knows (or rather, believes).

```
(forall (s a d)                                                (21.101)
    (iff (expertise s a d)
        (and (agent a)(knowledgeDomain d)
            (forall (s1)
                (iff (member s1 s)
                    (and (member s1 d)(believe a s1)))))))
```

An agent can know a knowledge domain to a greater or lesser degree. Expertise in a domain thus has a scalar quality, rather than being an absolute notion. One agent can have more expertise than another. We will call this partial ordering moreExpert. It is difficult to decide between two people who know different areas of a knowledge domain who is the greater expert. But if agent a knows every fact that agent b knows in the knowledge domain and then some, agent a is more expert than agent b in the domain. This places one constraint on the interpretation of moreExpert, albeit a loose one.

```
(forall (a b d)                                               (21.102)
   (if (and (forall (s)
               (if (and (member s d)(believe b s))(believe a s)))
            (exists (s)
               (and (member s d)(believe a s)(not (believe b s))))
            (etc))
      (moreExpert a b d)))
```

The expression (moreExpert a b d) says that agent a is more expert than agent b in knowledge domain d.

We often make judgments about two people's relative expertise on the basis of their answers to the same set of questions.

Note that this does not account for the case where a believes lots of false things. We could add a condition to the statement of (21.102) that a knows fewer false things.

The moreExpert ordering is a relation among two agents and a knowledge domain

```
(forall (a b d)                                               (21.103)
   (if (moreExpert a b d)
      (and (agent a) (agent b) (knowledgeDomain d))))
```

The expertise scale for a knowledge domain d can then be identified, as the scale defined by a set of agents and the partial ordering moreExpert.

```
(forall (s d)                                                 (21.104)
   (iff (expertiseScale s d)
      (exists (s1 e a b)
         (and (forall (x)(if (member x s1)(agent x)))
              (moreExpert' e a b d)
              (scaleDefinedBy s s1 e)))))
```

It is a quite complex and largely domain-dependent problem to spell out what constitutes greater expertise in any specific domain, and in fact it is often a matter of great dispute. There is probably very little to be said about the relation in general beyond what we have axiomatized here.

For an agent to be an expert in a domain is for the agent to be in the Hi region (functionally and/or distributionally) of the expertise scale for that domain.

```
(forall (a)                                                   (21.105)
   (iff (expert a d)
      (exists (s s1)
         (and (expertiseScale s d)(Hi s1 s)(inScale a s1)))))
```

This is a fuzzy notion, and the most we can ever hope to do is to state some sufficient conditions for an agent to be an expert in some particular context.

It is possible to be an expert in something other than a knowledge domain. We may know all the facts about pole vaulting that a professional pole vaulter knows, and yet not be the expert in pole vaulting that he or she is.

21.13 MUTUAL BELIEF

Members of a community, from a conversational pair to the set of those who share Western culture, not only know a certain set of facts. They know that the other members of the community also know the facts, and know that the others know that they know them, and so on. This is the concept of "mutual belief." Mutual belief is a relation between a set or community of agents and a proposition or eventuality. The constraints on the arguments of the mutual belief predicate mb are thus as follows:

```
(forall (c e)                                              (21.106)
    (if (mb c e)
        (and (set c)(forall (a) (if (member a c)(agent a)))
            (eventuality e))))
```

The two principal axioms characterizing mutual belief relate it to individual belief and to mutual belief in the mutual belief. The first says that if a community of agents mutually believe something, then each member of the community believes it.

```
(forall (c e a)                                            (21.107)
    (if (and (mb c e)(member a c))
        (believe a e)))
```

The second principal property of mutual belief is that if a community mutually believes something, they mutually believe that they mutually believe it. This axiom allows us to step up from one level of mutual belief to a higher one.

```
(forall (c e)                                              (21.108)
    (if (mb c e)
        (exists (e1)
            (and (mb c e1)(mb' e1 c e)))))
```

We will take these two axioms to be mutually believed by all agents. Furthermore, it is mutually believed by all agents that all agents can do logic, for example, apply modus ponens. Then it is possible to show that if an agent a is a member of a community c, a believes e is mutually believed by c, and a believes agent b is a member of c as well, then a can conclude a range of complex embeddings of belief and mutual belief. For example, it follows that a believes that b believes that a and b mutually believe e. From mutual belief we can draw complex inferences about the beliefs of other members of the community.

These axioms do not allow us to conclude mutual belief from a set of premises, and it has sometimes been a criticism against the notion of mutual belief that one would require an infinite number of such premises involving the predicate believe. In fact, in everyday life, we shortcut this problem all the time. Clark (1992) proposed the heuristic of copresence. If we both perceive something in a situation where we are aware of each other's presence, then we mutually believe that it has occurred.

We can state a definition for a collection c of agents being copresent at an event e, as follows:

```
(forall (c e)                                                    (21.109)
    (iff (copresent c e)
         (forall (a)
             (if (member a c)
                 (and (perceive a e)
                      (forall (a1)
                          (if (and (member a1 c)(nequal a1 a))
                              (exists (e1)
                                  (and (perceive' e1 a1 e)
                                       (perceive a e1)))))))))))
```

That is, all the members of c are copresent at event e if they all perceive it and they all perceive that the others perceive it.

Copresence defeasibly entails mutual belief.

```
(forall (c e)                                                    (21.110)
    (if (and (copresent c e) (etc))
        (mb c e)))
```

To conclude mutual belief absolutely from statements of belief would require an infinite number of premises of the form

```
(believe' e1 a e), (believe' e2 b e), (Rexist e1), (Rexist e2),
(believe' e3 a e2), (believe' e4 b e1), (Rexist e3), (Rexist e4),
(believe' e5 a e1), (believe' e6 b e2), (Rexist e5), (Rexist e6),
(believe' e7 a e4), (believe' e8 b e3), (Rexist e7), (Rexist e8),
....
```

But in fact, as we move down this list, the probability that a line is false when all the previous lines have been true becomes vanishingly small. It is possible to think up exceptions at every level, but the deeper we get, the rarer such occurrences are. In fact, very often we make the assumption that if we know something, so does everyone else. Just going two levels deep, we get a fairly reliable, defeasible inference of mutual belief. Sometimes there will be breakdowns, but we rarely need to reason about levels of belief deeper than that.

```
(forall (c a b e e1 e2)                                         (21.111)
    (if (and (doubleton c a b)
             (believe' e1 a e)(Rexist e1)
             (believe' e2 b e)(Rexist e2)
             (believe a e2)(believe b e1) (etc))
        (mb c e)))
```

In fact, Clark's copresence heuristic follows from this approximation and from the principal that perceiving is believing.

We can extend the notion of mutual belief from propositions to sentences in the natural way.

```
(forall (s c)                                                    (21.112)
   (if (sentence s)
       (iff (mb c s)
            (exists (s1)(and (propContent s1 s)(mb c s1))))))
```

We can thus extend mutual belief to entire knowledge domains.

```
(forall (d c)                                                    (21.113)
   (if (knowledgeDomain d)
       (iff (mb c d)
            (forall (s)(if (member s d)(mb c s))))))
```

One of the most important sorts of knowledge we have is knowledge about who knows what. This can be encoded in the form of axioms about mutual belief by certain communities about certain knowledge domains. For example, we know that if someone is an American he or she is likely to know the basic facts about the American government. People who live in a neighborhood are likely to know where its grocery stores are. Computer scientists are likely to know about hash tables, linguists are likely to know about noun phrases, and researchers in artificial intelligence are likely to know about the frame problem.

PREDICATES INTRODUCED IN THIS CHAPTER

(concept c)
   c is a concept.

(represent c e a)
   Concept c represents eventuality e for agent a.

(believe0 a c)
   Agent a believes concept c.

(believe a e)
   Agent a believes concept or eventuality e.

(beliefs s a)
   s is the set of a's beliefs.

(unknown e a)
   Agent a believes neither e nor its negation.

(addBelief a e)
   Agent a adds e to a's set of beliefs.

(deleteBelief a e)
   Agent a deletes e from a's set of beliefs.

(recogInconsist a s0)
   Agent a recognizes that belief set s0 is inconsistent.

(changeBeliefSet a s0 s1)
   Agent a's belief set changes from s0 to s1.

(gbel a e d)
   Agent a believes e to degree d.

(suspect a e)
    Agent a has a higher graded belief in e than in its negation.

(increaseBelief a e)
    Agent a's graded belief in e increases.

(thresholdOfBelief t a)
    t is the likelihood above which agent a will commit to believing something.

(thresholdOfBeliefScale s)
    s is the scale of thresholds of belief.

(biasTowardBelief a)
    Agent a has a bias toward belief.

(biasTowardDisbelief a)
    Agent a has a bias toward disbelief.

(assume a e)
    Agent a assumes e.

(believeOrAssume a e)
    Agent a believes or assumes e.

(makeAssumption a e)
    Agent a begins to assume e.

(retractAssumption a e)
    Agent a ceases to assume e.

(focusOfAttention f a)
    f is agent a's focus of attention.

(memory m a)
    m is agent a's memory.

(inm x y)
    x is mentally in y, which is a mind or component of a mind.

(inFocus x a)
    x is in agent a's focus of attention.

(thinkThat a e)
    Agent a has belief e in focus.

(infer a e s)
    Agent a infers e from premises s.

(deduce a e s)
    Agent a deduces e from premises s.

(abduce a e s)
    Agent a abduces e from premises s.

(induce a e s)
    Agent a induces e from premises s.

(checkInferences a s)
    Agent a entertains the possible inferences one can conclude from premises s.

(suppressInferences a s)
    Agent a does not check the inferences from premises s.

(ignoreInference a e s)
    Agent a infers e from premises s but does no further reasoning with e.

(concludeContradiction a s)
    Agent a infers e from s where e is inconsistent with a's beliefs.

(reaffirmBelief a e)
    Agent a infers an already held belief in a new way.

(confused a)
    Agent a is confused, for example, by entertaining inconsistent beliefs.

(justify s e a)
    Premises s justify e for agent a.

(soundlyJustify s e a)
    Premises s soundly justify e for agent a.

(partiallyJustify s e a)
    Premises s partially justify e for agent a.

(circularlyJustify s e a)
    Premises s constitute a circular justification for e by agent a.

(poorlyJustify s e a)
    Premises s constitute a poor justification for e by agent a.

(unjustified e a)
    Agent a has no justification for e.

(true e)
    Eventuality e really exists.

(false e)
    Eventuality e does not really exist.

(know a e)
    Agent a knows e.

(falsePositive e a)
    Agent a believes e but e does not hold.

(falseNegative e a)
    e holds but agent a believes e does not hold.

(learn a e)
    Agent a learns e.

(realize a e)
    Agent a realizes e.

(realizeBeliefFalse a e)
    Agent a realizes e does not hold.

(moreIntelligent a b)
    Agent a is more intelligent than agent b.

(intelligence s)
    s is the scale of intelligence.

(intelligent a)
    Agent a is intelligent.

(sentence s)
> s is a sentence, that is, a set of propositions one of which is its claim.

(propContent s1 s)
> s1 is the set of propositions associated with a sentence s.

(claim e s)
> e is the claim of sentence s.

(fact s)
> s is a true sentence.

(knowledgeDomain d)
> d is a coherent set of sentences.

(predicatesOf s d)
> s is the set of predicates that characterizes a knowledge domain d.

(expertise s a d)
> s is the set of sentences in knowledge domain d that agent a believes.

(moreExpert a b d)
> Agent a is more of an expert in knowledge domain d than agent b.

(expertiseScale s d)
> s is the scale whose set is the set of agents and whose partial ordering is moreExpert in knowledge domain d.

(expert a d)
> Agent a is an expert in knowledge domain d.

(mb c e)
> Members of the set c of agents mutually believe e.

(copresent c e)
> Members of the set c of agents are copresent at eventuality e.

In addition, we have used but have not yet explicated the following predicates:

(will a e)
> Agent a wills event e to occur.

(goal e a)
> Eventuality e is a goal of agent a's.

22

Similarity Comparisons

22.1 SIMILARITY

People are very good at determining when and in what ways two things are
similar. In this chapter we introduce several notions of similarity, of increasing
complexity.

Two things are similar if they have a property in common. A dialog expanding on
similarity might go as follows:

> A: Bush was similar to Reagan.
> B: How so?
> A: They were both conservative Republicans.

A normal adjunct on a similarity statement is introduced with "in that," specifying
the common property:

> Bush was similar to Reagan in that both were conservative Republicans.

Being a conservative Republican is the property (or properties) they have in common. At the same time they differ in that Reagan was from California and Bush is
from Texas.

We can define this simple notion of similarity and difference as follows:

```
(forall(x y e1 e2)                                                      (22.1)
   (iff(similarInThat x y e1 e2)
      (and(arg* x e1)(arg* y e2)(subst x e1 y e2)(Rexist e1)(Rexist e2))))
```

They differ if there is a property that holds for one but not the other.

```
   (forall (x y e1 e2)                                                  (22.2)
      (iff (differentInThat x y e1 e2)
         (and (arg* x e1)(arg* y e2)(subst x e1 y e2)(Rexist e1)
              (not (Rexist e2)))))
```

Similarity in general is more complex than this. Two entities are more similar the more inferentially independent properties they have in common. Suppose we have three blocks with the following properties:

A: Red, square, large
B: Red, round, large
C: Red, square, small

Then we can say block A is more similar to block C than block B is. A and C share two properties – red and square – whereas B and C share only one property – red.

Treatments of similarity by cognitive psychologists are frequently in terms of shared features. "Feature" is just a pretheoretic version of a monadic predicate (if "red" is a feature) or family of predicates (if "color" is a feature), so such approaches involve counting common properties.

A frequent computational approach to similarity is to represent the entities by feature vectors, with a 1 or 0 as each component depending on whether the entity has or doesn't have the feature, and to take the dot product of the vectors as the measure of similarity. This again is the number of the features or properties the entities have in common.

For quantitative measurements, it is harder to see similarity as shared properties. If Pat is 181 cm tall and Chris is 179 cm tall, then we might say that Pat and Chris are of similar heights, and we would be tempted to treat the difference between the two values as a measure of the similarity. But we can view such measurements in terms of shared properties. For example, our properties could be "less than 178 cm tall," "less than 179 cm tall," "less than 180 cm tall," "less than 181 cm tall," "less than 182 cm tall," and so on, together with their negations. If Kim is 182 cm tall, then Pat shares more of these properties with Kim than Chris does. So Pat is more similar in height to Kim than Chris is. More generally, Pat and Kim share more "height-relevant" properties than Chris and Kim, such as "able to reach the top shelf."

If we are measuring only similarity of one kind of quantitative measurement, then a derived quantitative measurement of similarity may be appropriate. But if we are concerned with abstract similarity of any kind of entity, judgments of the sort people make every day, then we are better off treating it in terms of shared properties, so it is useful to see how quantitative measurements can be reduced to shared properties, even at the expense of greater complexity.

Similarity is a scalar notion, but once we get away from quantitative measurements, the ordering among elements is not always defined. Suppose John and Bill are both similar to George in that all three are fathers. John and George are similar in that both live in Los Angeles. Bill and George are similar in that both were born in Alabama. Is John or Bill more similar to George? If we can answer this at all, it is because of contextual factors.

However, if for every property Bill shares with George, John also shares that property with George, and then some, we can say that John is more similar to George than Bill is. That is, similarity has the property of subset consistency. Similarity is an imprecise scale with a partial ordering, but it is constrained to be subset-consistent over sets of shared properties.

When the shared properties have further arguments, these arguments should also be similar. Suppose, for example, we want to know if John and Bill are similar. If John loves his wife and Bill loves his car, we might not want to say that John and Bill are similar in that both love something, because a wife and a car are themselves insufficiently similar.

When we are dealing with complex systems with complex structure, similarity is strengthened by recursion through properties and arguments. John and Bill are similar in that they are both men. They are more similar if they are both fathers. They are more similar if they are fathers of two children. They are even more similar if they each have two boys. They are even more similar if the boys all play soccer. They are even more similar if the boys' soccer teams are in the same league. And so on.

Consider an example from text – the first sentence of a physics problem.

> A ladder weighs 100 lb with its center of gravity 10 ft from the foot, and a 150-lb man is 10 ft from the top.

The "and" linking the two clauses indicates a similarity in the situations described; "and similarly" is the most frequent sense of "and" in discourse, with "and then" a close second. We can recognize this similarity by recursing through eventualities and their arguments. Since this is a problem in mechanics, both clauses convey something about forces acting on objects with magnitudes in a direction at a point in the object.

```
(force ladder 100lb down x)
(force man    150lb down y)
```

The predicates of these eventualities are the same, so they are similar situations if or insofar as their arguments are similar. The ladder and the man are similar in that both are physical objects. 100 lb and 150 lb are similar in that both are measurements of weight. The third arguments of each eventuality are identical, so they are similar. Now consider x and y. They are similar to the extent that their properties are similar. The distance from x to the foot of the ladder is 10 feet, and the distance of y from the top of the ladder is 10 feet. We know no other properties of x and y.

```
(distance 10ft x f)
(distance 10ft y t)
```

The predicates of these properties are the same. The first arguments are the same, hence are similar. To see whether f and t are similar, we need to look at their properties. We know that f is the foot of the ladder and t is the top of the ladder, and feet and tops are both ends. Hence, we have a common property.

```
(end f ladder)
(end t ladder)
```

The predicates are the same. The second arguments are identical, hence similar. At this point we have bottomed out, and can conclude that the original force situations were similar. (In Hobbs (1979) this example was used to show how forcing similarity results in the implicit argument of "top" being interpreted as the ladder. In Hobbs and Kehler (1997) it was used to illustrate the process of recognizing similarity as a preliminary to a treatment of verb phrase ellipsis.)

We will first define a relatively simple notion of similarity, though complex enough to handle the physics problem example. Two entities are similar0 if they have similar properties or if they are eventualities with similar structure. The latter two notions will be defined co-recursively. Properties are similar by virtue of the similarity of their arguments, which in turn are similar by virtue of their properties. Thus, we introduce the predicates simStr0 for similar structures and simPr0 for similar properties, and define each in terms of the other.

This co-recursion is already complex enough. But a further complication is introduced by the need to avoid looping. In the physics example, when we are trying to judge the similarity of the distance properties by recursing on its arguments, we don't want to recurse on x and y, as we are already in the process of checking on their similarity. If we did, it would result in an infinite loop. Similarly, when we are examining all the properties of x and y, we don't want to examine the force properties, because, again, we are already in the process of checking their similarity.

This problem necessitates a certain amount of bookkeeping in the axioms that follow. The principal predicates will have an argument m, in addition to the entities being compared, where m is the set of pairs we have matched already. Before recursing on a pair of properties or arguments, we check to make sure it is not already in the set m.

The predicate similar0 is defined as follows:

```
(forall (x1 x2)                                              (22.3)
   (iff (similar0 x1 x2)
        (exists (m p)
           (and (null m)
                (or (simPr0 x1 x2 m)
                    (and (eventuality x1)(eventuality x2)
                         (simStr0 x1 x2 m)))))))
```

The expression (similar0 x1 x2) says that the entities x1 and x2 are similar (in this simple sense). Line 4 sets the list of matches so far to null. Line 5 checks whether x1 and x2 have similar properties. Lines 6–7 check whether they have similar structure if they are eventualities.

Two eventualities are similar if they are equal, or if they have the same predicate and similar arguments.

```
(forall (e1 e2 m)                                            (22.4)
   (iff (simStr0 e1 e2 m)
        (or (equal e1 e2)
            (exists (p d m1)
               (and (pair d e1 e2)(addElt m1 m d)
                    (pred p e1)(pred p e2)
                    (forall (n x1 x2 d1)
                       (if (and (argn x1 n e1)(argn x2 n e2)
                                (pair d1 x1 x2)(not (member d1 m)))
                           (simPr0 x1 x2 m1)))))))))
```

Line 3 checks for equality. Line 5 adds the current pair of eventualities to the list of matches being considered. Line 6 checks that the predicates of the eventualities are the same. Lines 7–10 iterate through the corresponding pairs of arguments and determine whether they are similar by virtue of shared properties. In line 9 we make sure we have not already considered this pair.

Two entities are `similar0` if they are equal, or if there is a property that they both share.

```
(forall (x1 x2 m)                                                    (22.5)
   (iff (simPr0 x1 x2 m)
        (exists (d m1)
           (and (pair d x1 x2)(addElt m1 m d)
                (or (equal x1 x2)
                    (exists (e3 e4 p n d1)
                        (and (pred p e3)(pred p e4)
                             (argn x1 n e3)(argn x2 n e4)
                             (pair d1 e3 e4)(not (member d1 m))
                             (simStr0 e3 e4 m1)))))))))
```

Line 5 tests for equality. Lines 6 introduces the candidate common properties e3 and e4. Lines 7–8 check whether they have the same predicates and corresponding arguments. Line 9 makes sure we are not already dealing with this pair of properties. Line 10 checks whether these eventualities have similar structure.

The predicate `similar0` gives us a binary notion of similarity. Two things are either similar or not. This is because of the existential quantifier in line 6 of the definition of `simPr0`. We insist on only one shared property. But as we saw in the three blocks example earlier, the more properties two things have in common, the more similar they are. We can get a graded or scalar notion of similarity by modifying the preceding definitions somewhat. In particular, we will have them accumulate the properties the entities share and then use that to constrain a partial ordering on a similarity scale.

The definition of this somewhat more complex notion of similarity, `similar1`, is almost the same as that of `similar0`.

```
(forall (x1 x2 s)                                                    (22.6)
   (iff (similar1 x1 x2 s)
        (exists (m p)
           (and (null m)
                (or (simPr1 x1 x2 m s)
                    (and (eventuality x1)(eventuality x2)
                         (simStr1 x1 x2 m s)))))))
```

The only difference is that the three predicates now have an extra argument s which will be the set of properties of x2 that match properties of x1, found in the course of the co-recursion.

The predicate `simStr1` holds when the eventualities are equal, or the predicates are the same and the corresponding arguments have similar properties.

```
(forall (e1 e2 m s)                                                  (22.7)
   (iff (simStr1 e1 e2 m s)
        (or (and (equal e1 e2)(singleton s e2))
            (exists (p d)
                (and (pair d e1 e2)(addElt m1 m d)
                     (pred p e1)(pred p e2)
                     (iterArgs e1 e2 1 m1 s1)
                     (addElt s s1 e2))))))
```

Line 3 checks whether e1 and e2 are equal, and if so, contributes property e2 to
the set s of matches. Line 6 checks whether the predicates are the same. In line 7
we invoke the predicate iterArgs to iterate through all the corresponding pairs of
arguments and build up the set s1 of matches found in this process. If all this succeeds
in establishing similarity, the final set s of matching properties is s1 with e2 added in
(line 8).

The predicate iterArgs iterates by recursion through the arguments of e1 and
e2. Employing this predicate enables us to build up the set s one argument at a time.

```
(forall (e1 e2 n m s)                                           (22.8)
    (iff (iterArgs e1 e2 n m s)
        (exists (x1 x2 d1 s1 s2 n1 n0)
            (and (argn x1 n e1)(argn x2 n e2)
                 (pair d1 x1 x2)(addElt m1 m d1)
                 (if (member d1 m)(null s1))
                 (or (member d1 m)(simPr1 x1 x2 m s1))
                 (successor n1 n)(arity n0 e2)
                 (if (leq n1 n0)(iterArgs e1 e2 n1 m1 s2))
                 (if (gt n1 n0)(null s2))
                 (union s s1 s2)))))
```

The variable n is the number of the argument we are dealing with, and n1 is the next
number. Lines 3–4 pick out the nth arguments x1 and x2 of e1 and e2. The "(if ...
(or ..." in lines 6–7 effect an "if ... then ... else ..." structure. Line 6 blocks a check
for similar properties if we are already dealing with these entities. Otherwise in line
7 we check for similar properties. In line 9, if we have not already dealt with all the
arguments of e1 and e2, we go on to the next pair of arguments. In line 11 we combine
the matches we found from the nth argument (s1) and the matches we found from
subsequent arguments (s2), to form s.

The predicate simPr1 tells us whether two entities x1 and x2 are similar by virtue
of having the same properties, and if so, tells us what those properties are, in the
set s.

```
(forall (x1 x2 m s)                                            (22.9)
    (iff (simPr1 x1 x2 m s)
        (or (and (equal x1 x2)(eventuality x2)(singleton s x2))
            (and (equal x1 x2)(not (eventuality x2))(null s))
            (exists (d m1 t)
                (and (pair d x1 x2)(addElt m1 m d)(null t)
                     (iterProps x1 x2 t m1 s)
                     (not (null s)))))))
```

Lines 3–4 check for the limiting case of equality; if it succeeds and they are eventualities, we'll say that e1 and e2 are similar by virtue of property e2; for noneventualities,
nothing is added to s. The predicate iterProps invoked in line 7 iterates through the
properties of x1 and x2 and accumulates the set s of common properties. If this set
is not empty, in line 8, the predication is true; otherwise it is false – x1 and x2 have
no common properties.

The predicate iterProps enables us to look at inferentially independent properties of x1 and x2 and construct a set of the matches.

```
(forall (x1 x2 t m s)                                          (22.10)
   (iff (iterProps x1 x2 t m s)
        (or (exists (e3 e4 p n t1 d1)
                (and (pred p e3)(pred p e4)
                     (argn x1 n e3)(argn x2 n e4)
                     (not (imply t e4))
                     (addElt t1 t e4)
                     (pair d1 e3 e4)(addElt m1 m d1)
                     (if (member d1 m)(singleton s1 e4))
                     (or (member d1 m)(simStr1 e3 e4 m s1))
                     (iterProps x1 x2 t1 m1 s2)
                     (union s s1 s2)))
            (null s)))))
```

In lines 3-5 we are looking for a property e3 of x1 and a property e4 of x2 with the same predicate p, where x1 and x2 play the same role. In line 9 we check whether we have already dealt with this pair and if so, we add e4 to s. This will ensure that interProps does not fail because of this pair of properties. In line 10, if we haven't already dealt with this pair, we check it for similarity of structure. In line 11 we check for further matching properties. In line 12 the set s combines the eventualities we found from this property (s1) with the eventualities we found from subsequent properties (s2).

In the definition of iterArgs we knew the arity of the predicate, so we knew when we were through iterating. For iterProps, we don't know in general how many properties we have to examine, and we need a way of making sure we do not loop on the same property. This is the role of the variable t. It is the set of properties of x2 that we have already tried. We could prevent looping by having in line 6 the test (not (member e4 t)). But by having what we have, we subsume this and also capture the requirement that the common properties we find be inferentially independent. We do not want to discover the similarity of John and Bill by virtue of their both being men, and then "strengthen" that similarity by virtue of their both being humans, mammals, animals, and physical objects.

The only conjunct in lines 4–12 that can fail is line 6, and this means we have run out of inferentially independent properties of x1 and x2, and we are done. This iteration makes no contribution to the set s of matches.

To summarize, the expression (similar1 x1 x2 s) says that the entities x1 and x2 are similar by virtue of the properties of x2 in s and the corresponding properties of x1. In the physics example, this would include the force relation, the physical object property, the weight property, the distance relation, and the end relation.

The predicates similar0 and similar1 are essentially equivalent. It is a theorem that

```
(forall (x1 x2)                                               (22.11)
   (iff (similar0 x1 x2)
        (exists (s)
           (and (similar1 x1 x2 s)(not (null s))))))
```

The difference between them is that similar0 requires only one property in common, whereas similar1 tells us in the set s all the properties the entities have in common. This gives us a graded or scaler notion of similarity that we can use to construct a similarity scale.

For a similarity scale we need a partial ordering. We cannot define it precisely. If faced with the question of whether South Korea is more or less similar to China than North Korea, we would consider the various properties we know about each of the countries and look for overlaps, But there simply may be incommeasurabilities. But we can constrain the partial ordering by subset consistency. For example, if Taiwan is similar to China by virtue of the properties in set s1, South Korea is similar to China by virtue of the properties in set s2, and s2 is a proper subset of s1, then we can say that Taiwan is more similar to China than South Korea is. We can state this as an axiom.

```
(forall (x y z)                                            (22.12)
    (if (and (similar1 x z s1)(similar1 y z s2)
             (properSubset s2 s1))
        (moreSimilar x y z)))
```

The expression (moreSimilar x y z) says that x is more similar to z than y is. This axiom does not *define* (iff) the partial ordering, but it does help to characterize it (if).

In practice, in trying to establish that two entities are similar, one tries to find as many inferentially independent properties as possible that they have in common. In text understanding, for example, this is not as formidable as it sounds. As we saw in the physics example earlier, the text generally tells you only a few properties of the entities it introduces. We can't take into account the color of the man's hair because we don't know it.

For the purposes of defining similarity scales, we will turn moreSimilar into a relation on pairs <x,z> and <y,z>.

```
(forall (p1 p2 e)                                          (22.13)
    (iff (moreSimScale p1 p2)
         (exists (x y z)
             (and (pair p1 x z)(pair p2 y z)
                  (moreSimilar x y z)))))
```

The relation "more similar to z" is a partial ordering for any z. Thus, we can define a corresponding similarity scale.

```
(forall (s)                                                (22.14)
    (iff (similarityScale s)
         (exists (s1 e p1 p2)
             (and (forall (p)(if (member p s1)(pair0 p)))
                  (moreSimScale' e p1 p2)
                  (scaleDefinedBy s s1 e)))))
```

Note that the partial ordering is undefined for any pairs that do not have a common standard z with respect to which the comparison is made. Thus, we could not express that England is more similar to the United States than North Korea is to China. Perhaps this could be handled by positing an abstract entity to which both the United States and China could be compared, but we will not pursue that here. The predicate moreSimScale is a partial ordering, and as it stands, if the pairs don't have the same z, the relation doesn't hold.

Finally, for x and z to be similar is for the pair to be in the functionally and distributionally high region of the similarity scale.

```
(forall (x z)                                          (22.15)
   (iff (similar x z)
        (exists (s s1 p)
           (and (similarityScale s)(Hi s1 s)(inScale p s1)
                (pair p x z)))))
```

What and how many shared properties are sufficient for similarity is a very context-dependent judgment. In the physics example earlier, the man and the ladder were sufficiently similar by virtue of their both being physical objects. That is because in the mechanics problems domain, the only thing that matters is that they both have mass.

The adjectives "similar" and "different" are antonyms. This means that "different" is stronger than just "not similar" in the same way that "short" is more specific than just "not tall." The adjective "different" like "similar" is a qualitative judgment on a similarity scale. Two things are different if their similarity is in the functionally and distributionally low region of the similarity scale.

```
(forall (x z)                                          (22.16)
   (iff (different x z)
        (exists (s s1 p)
           (and (similarityScale s)(Lo s1 s)(inScale p s1)
                (pair p x z)))))
```

These definitions mean that two things cannot be both similar and different. However, we can use the predicates similarInThat and differentInThat to assert specific similarities and differences, and both of these can hold at once for the same pair.

As we have defined it, similarity is symmetric. If x is similar to z then z is similar to x. But one of the classic treatments of similarity in cognitive science was that of Tversky (1977), and one of his key observations was that similarity is not symmetric. The following example (circa 1977) illustrates this.

North Korea is similar to the People's Republic of China.
* The People's Republic of China is similar to North Korea.

We would have been much more likely to assent to the first of these statements than to the second. This has to do with the fact that most of us know much more about China than about North Korea. It would be strange for most people to use North Korea as a standard of comparison to explicate China.

But it is not clear whether the strangeness of the second example is a fact about the similarity relation or about the structure of sentences in discourse. To say "x is similar to z" is to focus on the subject x and to attempt to convey a whole package of properties of x very succinctly. For this to work, one would have to know more about z than about x, making the second example strange. In any case, the concept of similarity we have defined here is symmetric between its two arguments.

```
(forall (x y)                                          (22.17)
   (iff (similar x y)(similar y x)))
```

22.2 SIMILARITY OF STRUCTURED ENTITIES

When the entities being compared are composite – that is, when they have components, properties of components, and relations among components – then special cases of similarity are possible. The first case happens when there is a subset of the components, properties, and relations of two composite entities that are the same. In this case we say that the two entities have a common pattern.

First we define a mapping between two composite entities as one that maps components of one into the components of the other in a way that preserves properties and relations.

```
(forall (m x1 x2)                                               (22.18)
    (iff (ceMapping m x1 x2)
        (exists (u1 s11 s12 s13 u2 s21 s22 s23)
            (and (union3 u1 s11 s12 s13)(componentsOf s11 x1)
                 (propertiesOf s12 x1)(relationsOf s13 x1)
                 (union3 u2 s21 s22 s23)(componentsOf s21 x2)
                 (propertiesOf s22 x2)(relationsOf s23 x2)
                 (function m u1 u2)
                 (forall (y1)
                    (if (member y1 s11)
                        (exists (y2)
                            (and (member y2 s21)(map m y1 y2)))))
                 (forall (y1 y2 e1 e2 n p)
                    (if (and (member y1 s11)
                             (or (member e1 s12)(member e1 s13))
                             (map m y1 y2)(map m e1 e2))
                        (and (iff (argn y1 n e1)(argn y2 n e2))
                             (iff (pred p e1)(pred p e2)))))))))
```

Lines 3–8 say that m is a mapping from the entities, properties and relations of x1 to the entities, properties and relations of x2. Lines 9–12 say that components are mapped to components. Lines 13–18 say that the mapping preserves the structure of x1, by mapping predicates into the same predicate and the arguments of the source property or relation into the corresponding arguments of the target.

In Chapter 10 we defined a pattern as a composite entity with parameters. We can say a composite entity exhibits a pattern when it is an instance of the pattern.

```
(forall (x p)                                                   (22.19)
    (iff (exhibitPattern x p)
        (exists (m)
            (and (pattern p)(patternInstance x p)
                 (ceMapping m p x)))))
```

Then two composite entities have a common pattern if there is a pattern that they both exhibit.

```
(forall (x1 x2)                                                 (22.20)
    (iff (commonPattern x1 x2)
        (exists (p)
            (and (exhibitPattern x1 p)(exhibitPattern x2 p)))))
```

Entities exhibiting a common pattern do so by virtue of the similarity of their components, properties and relations, which are properties of the composite entity. Because ceMapping preserves predicates, this is a specific case of similarity as defined in the previous section.

In a ceMapping properties and relations are mapped into properties and relations with the same predicates. More complex comparisons are possible if we allow systematic mappings of the predicates as well. We will call the combination of these a "structure mapping." We follow Gentner (1983) in taking analogies to depend on structure mappings. This means that an analogy is similar to a pattern except that the mapping between components needs to be extended to a mapping between the predicates of properties and relations as well.

We will define structure mappings in two steps. First we will construct a composite entity in which only the predicates of the properties and relations have been replaced according to a mapping p. Then we will apply ceMapping.

```
(forall (m p x1 x2)                                              (22.21)
    (iff (cePredReplace m p x1 x2)
        (exists (s12 s13 u1)
            (and (propertiesOf s12 x1)(relationsOf x13 x1)
                 (union u1 s12 s13)
                 (forall (e1 e2 q1 q2)
                     (if (and (member e1 u1)(map m e1 e2)
                              (pred q1 e1)(map p q1 q2))
                         (pred q2 e2)))))))
```

The expression (cePredReplace m p x1 x2) says that m maps composite entity x1 into composite entity x2, changing the predicates according to mapping p. Lines 6–9 effect the predicate replacement.

Now we can define a structure mapping by positing an intermediate composite entity in which only the predicates have been changed.

```
(forall (m p x1 x2)                                             (22.22)
    (iff (structureMapping m p x1 x2)
        (exists (x3)
            (and (cePredReplace m1 p x1 x3)
                 (ceMapping m2 x3 x2)
                 (iff (map m x y)
                     (exists (z)
                         (and (map m1 x z)(map m2 z y))))))))
```

Lines 6–8 define mapping m as the composition of m1 and m2.

Two things are analogous if there is a structure mapping between them.

```
(forall (x1 x2)                                                (22.23)
    (iff (analogous x1 x2)
        (exists (m p) (structureMapping m p x1 x2))))
```

Because a structure mapping does not preserve predicates, the resulting analogy may not be a case of similarity. But normally when m maps one predicate into another, it is because of some more general predicate they are both specializations of. Consider the analogy of the planets orbiting around the Sun and a charismatic professor surrounded by his graduate students. The reason a mapping from "orbits" to "is a graduate student of" works is because both imply that the Sun/professor to some extent controls the behavior of the planet/student. Thus the two entities (planet and student) do have properties in common.

22.3 COGNIZING SIMILARITIES

We can compare entities with respect to their similarities and differences. To do so is to think about those properties that they share and fail to share.

```
(forall (a x y)                                          (22.24)
    (iff (compare a x y)
        (exists (e1 e2 e3 e4)
            (and (thinkOf a e1)(thinkOf a e2)
                 (similarInThat x y e1 e2)
                 (thinkOf a e3)(thinkOf a e4)
                 (differentInThat x y e3 e4)))))
```

Comparisons defeasibly cause one to think that the entities compared are either similar or different.

```
(forall (e0 a x1 x2)                                     (22.25)
    (if (and (compare' e0 a x1 x2) (etc))
        (exists (e e2 e3 e4)
            (and (cause e0 e)(changeTo' e e2)
                 (or (thinkThat' e2 a e3)(thinkThat' e2 a e4))
                 (similar' e3 x1 x2)(different' e4 x1 x2)))))
```

The similarity scale constitutes a comparison metric.

```
(forall (s) (iff (comparisonMetric s)(similarityScale s)))    (22.26)
```

To find a pattern in two things is to come to think that that pattern holds in them.

```
(forall (e0 a x1 x2)                                     (22.27)
    (iff (findPattern' e0 a x1 x2)
        (exists (e e2 e3)
            (and (changeTo' e e2)(thinkThat' e2 a e3)
                 (commonPattern' e3 x1 x2)(gen e e0)))))
```

To draw an analogy between two things is to think that a structure mapping holds between them.

```
(forall (e0 a x1 x2)                                     (22.28)
    (iff (drawAnalogy' e0 a x1 x2)
        (exists (e e2 e3 m)
            (and (changeTo' e e2)(thinkThat' e2 a e3)
                 (structureMapping' e3 m x1 x2)))))
```

PREDICATES INTRODUCED IN THIS CHAPTER

(similarInThat x y e1 e2)
   x and y are similar in that e1 holds for x and e2 holds for y.

(differentInThat x y e1 e2)
    x and y are different in that e1 holds for x and e2 holds for y.

(similar0 x1 x2)
    x1 is similar to x2 by virtue of a single property.

(simStr0 e1 e2 m)
    e1 has structure similar to e2, other than matched pairs in m.

(simPr0 x1 x2 m)
    x1 has properties similar to x2's, other than matched pairs in m.

(similar1 x1 x2 s)
    x1 is similar to x2 by virtue of the common properties in s.

(simStr1 e1 e2 m s)
    e1 has structure similar to e2, other than matched pairs in m, where s is the similar properties.

(iterArgs e1 e2 n m s)
    s is the set of similarities of e1 and e2 in e2's nth and subsequent arguments, other than matched pairs in m.

(simPr1 x1 x2 m s)
    x1 has properties similar to x2's, other than matched pairs in m, where s is the similar properties.

(iterProps x1 x2 t m s)
    s is the set of similarities of x1 and x2 in x2's set t of properties, other than matched pairs in m.

(moreSimilar x1 x2 x)
    x1 is more similar to x than x2 is.

(moreSimScale p1 p2)
    The elements of pair p1 are more similar to each other than the elements of pair p2.

(similarityScale s)
    s is a scale of similarity.

(similar x z)
    x is similar to z.

(different x z)
    x is different from z.

(comparisonMetric s)
    Scale s is a comparison metric.

(ceMapping m x1 x2)
    Function m is a mapping from the components, properties, and relations of composite entity x1 to those of composite entity x2, preserving structure.

(exhibitPattern x p)
    Composite entity x exhibits or instantiates pattern p.

(commonPattern x1 x2)
    Composite entities x1 and x2 exhibit a common pattern.

(cePredReplace m p x1 x2)

Composite entities x1 and x2 differ only in that the predicates of x1 have been replaced in x2 according to mapping p; m maps x1 to x2.

(structureMapping m p x1 x2)

Function m is a mapping from the components, properties, relations, and predicates of composite entity x1 to those of composite entity x2, preserving structure, where p maps predicates to predicates.

(analogous x1 x2)

x1 and x2 are analogous.

(compare a x1 x2)

Agent a compares x1 and x2.

(findPattern a x1 x2)

Agent a finds a common pattern in x1 and x2.

(drawAnalogy a x1 x2)

Agent a draws an analogy between x1 and x2.

23

Memory

23.1 STORING AND RETRIEVING

Recall from Section 21.6 that we said an agent has a mind, and that a mind has at least two components, a memory and a focus of attention. Intuitively, the focus of attention is where conscious thought takes place, and the memory is where concepts, or memories, are stored. As in Chapter 21, we will allow objects of thought to be concepts or the entities and eventualities the concepts are of. That is, when an entity or eventuality is treated as an object of thought, we intend the corresponding concept, as explicated in Chapter 21.

An agent stores a concept in memory when there is a change from a state in which the concept is in the person's focus of attention but not in the memory to one in which it is in the memory.

```
(forall (a m)                                                    (23.1)
    (if (and (agent a)(memory m a))
        (forall (e c)
            (iff (store' e a c)
                (exists (e1 e2)
                    (and (inFocus c a)(changeTo' e1 e2)
                         (inm' e2 c m)(gen e1 e)))))))
```

For storing to happen the concept must be in focus at the same time, but the axiom is silent about whether the concept is still in focus after storing has occurred.

Similarly, to retrieve a concept from memory is to change from a state in which the concept is in memory and not in focus to one in which it is in focus.

```
(forall (a m)                                                    (23.2)
    (if (and (agent a)(memory m a))
        (forall (e c)
            (iff (retrieve' e a c)
                (exists (e1 e2)
                    (and (inm c m)(changeTo' e1 e2)
                         (inFocus' e2 c a)(gen e1 e)))))))
```

The chapter contains revisions of material published previously in (Gordon and Hobbs, 2003, 2004).

Storing and retrieving are actions by agents.

```
(forall (a c)(if (store a c)(agent a)))                      (23.3)
```

```
(forall (a c)(if (retrieve a c)(agent a)))                   (23.4)
```

The only way for a concept to get into an agent's memory is for it to be stored.

```
(forall (e c m a)                                            (23.5)
    (if (and (inm' e c m)(memory m a))
        (exists (e1)(and (store' e1 a c)(cause e1 e)))))
```

Note that this rules out preexisting Platonic ideals in the memory, contra *Meno*.

23.2 ACCESSIBILITY

Concepts in memory have an "accessibility" which is an element in a partial ordering.

```
(forall (m a c)                                              (23.6)
    (if (and (memory m a)(inm c m))
        (exists (x) (accessibility x c m))))
```

Accessibility is a function mapping a concept and an agent's memory into an element of a partial ordering.

```
(forall (x c m)                                              (23.7)
    (if (accessibility x c m)
        (exists (a) (memory m a))))
```

```
(forall (x1 x2 c m)                                          (23.8)
    (if (and (accessibility x1 c m)(accessibility x2 c m))
        (equal x1 x2)))
```

Accessibilities are partially ordered; they are elements in the agent's accessibility scale.

```
(forall (x c m a)                                            (23.9)
    (if (and (accessibility x c m)(memory m a))
        (exists (s)
            (and (scale s)(inScale x s)
                (accessibilityScale s a)))))
```

```
(forall (s a)                                                (23.10)
    (if (accessibilityScale s a)
        (and (agent a)(scale s))))
```

There is no assumption that accessibility is comparable across agents.

For any given agent, there is an accessibility value below which concepts are not retrieved from memory; we can call this the "memory threshold." In other words, a concept's accessibility being above the memory threshold enables retrieval.

```
(forall (m a s)                                              (23.11)
    (if (and (memory m a)(accessibilityScale s a))
        (exists (x0)
            (and (memoryThreshold x0 a)(inScale x0 s)))))
```

```
(forall (m a s)                                              (23.12)
    (if (and (memory m a)(accessibilityScale s a))
        (forall (x0)
            (iff (memoryThreshold x0 a)
                (forall (x1 c e e1)
                    (if (and (accessibility x1 c m)(gts' e x1 x0 s)
                            (retrieve' e1 a c))
                        (enable e e1)))))))))
```

If a concept's accessibility is above the memory threshold, then it is accessible.

```
(forall (c a)                                                (23.13)
    (iff (accessible c a)
        (exists (m x1 s x0)
            (and (memory m a)(accessibility x1 c m)
                (accessibilityScale s a)(memoryThreshold x0 a)
                (lts x0 x1 s)))))
```

Our theory of goals in Chapter 28 includes an explication of a partial ordering of importance. A concept is more or less important to an agent, depending on the relation of the concept to the agent's goals.

There is an at least defeasible monotonic relation between the importance of a concept and its accessibility.

```
(forall (c1 c2 i1 i2 x1 x2 s1 s2 a)                          (23.14)
    (if (and (importanceScale s1 a)(accessibilityScale s2 a)
            (importance i1 c1 a)(importance i2 c2 a)
            (accessibility x1 c1 a)(accessibility x2 c2 a)
            (lts i1 i2 s1)(etc))
        (leqs x1 x2 s2)))
```

This relation is a key part of an explanation for why John's forgetting their anniversary might cause Mary to get angry.

The theory of memory is silent on how long a particular concept retains a particular accessibility value, but we do explicate some features of the causal structure underlying changes in accessibility, in the next section.

23.3 ASSOCIATIONS AND CAUSING TO REMEMBER

One concept can remind an agent of another concept. This occurs when the first concept being in focus causes the second to be remembered.

```
(forall (e1 c1 a c2)                                          (23.15)
    (iff (remind' e1 c1 a c2)
        (exists (e2 e3)
            (and (inFocus' e2 c1 a)(cause e2 e3)(retrieve' e3 a c2)
                (gen e3 e1)))))
```

That is, c1's being in focus causes the agent to retrieve c2.

Concepts can be associated with each other, and this interacts with accessibility. There are many ways for things to be associated, and the things that are associated are not necessarily eventualities. The expression (associated x y a) means that the concepts, entities, or eventualities x and y are associated in a's mind. The third argument of associated is an agent; there are no constraints on the other arguments.

```
(forall (x y a)                                              (23.16)
    (if (associated x y a)(agent a)))
```

The relation associated is defeasibly symmetric in x and y.

```
(forall (x y a)                                              (23.17)
    (if (and (associated x y a)(etc))(associated y x a)))
```

There are many ways two things can be associated for an agent. Causes and effects are associated, and so are antecedents and consequents in implicative rules.

```
(forall (a e1 e2 e3)                                         (23.18)
    (if (and (cause' e1 e2 e3)(believe a e1))
        (associated e2 e3 a)))
(forall (a e1 e2 e3)                                         (23.19)
    (if (and (imply' e1 e2 e3)(believe a e1))
        (associated e2 e3 a)))
```

Eventualities are associated with their arguments.

```
(forall (a e x e1)                                           (23.20)
    (if (and (believe a e1)(arg' e1 x e))
        (associated e x a)))
```

Thus, for example, conjunctions and their conjuncts are associated. Thinking of one will defeasibly cause an agent to think of the other. The same is true for disjunctions and their disjuncts.

Other specific kinds of association would be partially explicated in a theory of the structure of information.

In this treatment of memory we will not use any deeper analysis of association; rather we will concern ourselves with the causal consequences of concepts' being associated. In particular, a concept being in focus raises the accessibility of associated concepts.

```
(forall (c1 c2 a e e3)                                          (23.21)
    (if (and (associated c1 c2 a)(changeTo' e e3)
            (inFocus' e3 c1 a))
        (exists (e0 e1 e2 x1 x2 s)
            (and (change' e0 e1 e2)(accessibility' e1 x1 c2 a)
                (accessibility' e2 x2 c2 a)(lts x1 x2 s)
                (accessibilityScale s a)(cause e e0)))))
```

That is, if concept c1 is associated with concept c2 for agent a and there is a change e to a state in which c1 is in focus for a, then e causes an increase in the accessibility of c2 for a. This accessibility increase may or may not be enough to enable a to retrieve c2.

It is a part of our theory of envisionment (or thinking) in Chapter 24 that agents can sometimes cause themselves to have a concept in their focus of attention. Then because of associations among concepts, agents have a causal structure they can manipulate to bring about retrievals from memory. This gives rise to strategies for remembering that involve calling to mind related concepts. For example, we might try to remember someone's name by running through the letters of the alphabet and hoping that the first letter of the name will cause the name to be retrieved. One might place a box of dishwasher detergent next to the front door as a reminder to start the dishwasher before leaving for work; the association between the detergent and the action of turning on the dishwasher makes this a good strategy (Swanson and Gordon, 2005).

23.4 THE MEANINGS OF "REMEMBER" AND "FORGET"

The English word "remember" can refer to a range of notions. At the simplest level, it can mean that the agent has the concept in memory and that it is accessible, but not necessarily in focus. In this sense, you remembered twenty minutes before encountering this sentence that Columbus discovered America in 1492.

```
(forall (c a)                                                   (23.22)
    (iff (remember1 a c)(accessible a c)))
```

Even though the concept is not in focus, it is accessible in memory.

A somewhat stronger notion of remembering is when there has actually been a retrieval from memory. For a concept to be retrieved is for it to be remembered.

```
(forall (c a)                                                   (23.23)
    (iff (remember2 a c)(retrieve a c)))
```

This rule was deliberately glossed in the passive. There is no notion of a's agency in the retrieval of a concept as we have defined retrieve. Thus, this notion of remembering covers cases where a fact simply pops into an agent's head, with no prior effort or intention.

A stronger sense of "remember" is one in which the agent plays a causal role in the remembering.

```
(forall (c a)                                                    (23.24)
    (iff (remember3 a c)
        (exists (e) (and (cause a e)(retrieve' e a c)))))
```

This happens when someone is told to remember who the president of the United States is, and somehow immediately they do. This sense of "remember" is what is conveyed in imperatives like

Remember that bears are unpredictable.

(Often such sentences are used to invite the hearer to draw an inference rather than retrieve something from memory, but in these cases it is an implicature that it was already in memory.)

Rule (23.24) is silent about whether the causality is immediate or there are intermediate actions on the agent's part designed to jog his or her memory. A stronger notion of remembering involves the latter. There is a distinct attempt to retrieve something from memory, and it succeeds. Since succeed as defined in Chapter 28 entails trying, we can state this simply as follows:

```
(forall (c a)                                                    (23.25)
    (iff (remember4 a c)
        (exists (e) (and (succeed a e)(retrieve' e a c)))))
```

It is a theorem that each of these senses implies the previous. All of these types of remembering are senses of "remember."

```
(forall (c a) (if (remember2 a c)(remember1 a c)))              (23.26)
```

```
(forall (c a) (if (remember3 a c)(remember2 a c)))              (23.27)
```

```
(forall (c a) (if (remember4 a c)(remember3 a c)))              (23.28)
```

```
(forall (c a) (if (remember1 a c)(remember a c)))              (23.29)
```

Because people can cause concepts to be in their focus of attention and this may cause them to remember other concepts, people have an ability to remember things.

```
(forall (a m c)                                                  (23.30)
    (if (and (person a)(memory m a)(inm c m)(etc))
        (exists (e s) (able a e s)(remember' e a c))))
```

That is, if a person a has a concept c in memory, then defeasibly there exists a set of constraints s such that the person is able to remember c, modulo those constraints.

There are other senses of "remember," for example, in WordNet, that are beyond the scope of this book, such as to remember or memorialize the war dead, and to remember someone in your will.

There are at least three levels of forgetting. In the simplest, the accessibility of a concept in memory has fallen below the memory threshold. To forget a concept is for the accessibility of the concept to change from being above the memory threshold to being below it, or more simply, to change from the situation in which it is accessible.

```
(forall (e a c)                                              (23.31)
    (iff (forget1' e a c)
        (exists (e1 e2)
            (and (changeFrom' e1 e2)(accessible' e2 c a)
                (gen e1 e)))))
```

This includes the agent's no longer having the concept in mind at all. It might be that someone once read what year Michigan was admitted to the Union but that nothing short of reading it again could jog this fact back into accessibility.

It is a theorem that if an agent a forgets something in this sense at a particular time, a does not remember it at that time, under any notion of remembering.

```
(forall (a c)                                                (23.32)
    (if (forget1 a c)(not (remember1 a c))))
```

A weaker sense of "forget" is when some concept is accessible, but it just is not accessed at the appropriate time. A man who forgets his wife's birthday will probably be able to say what day that is if asked, but just doesn't call it to mind at the right time. Or someone dashes into the surf, is pulled out to sea, is rescued, and says, "I forgot about the undertow." The concept was accessible; it just wasn't accessed. Thus to forget in this sense is to not retrieve when such a retrieval would have been good for you in some way. (The predicate goodFor is defined in Chapter 28.)

```
(forall (e a c)                                              (23.33)
    (iff (forget2' e a c)
        (exists (e1 e2)
            (and (retrieve' e1 a c)(goodFor e1 a)(not' e2 e1)
                (gen e2 e)))))
```

There is a sense of "forget" in which the agent intentionally ceases to have the concept in focus, as in "Forget about the possibility of failure; just do your best." There is a change from the concept being in focus, and the agent causes that.

```
(forall (e a c)                                              (23.34)
    (iff (forget3' e a c)
        (exists (e1 e2 e3)
            (and (cause' e1 a e2)(changeFrom' e2 e3)
                (inFocus' e3 c a)(gen e1 e)))))
```

This action is of course not always possible, but when it happens, forget3 describes it.

There are four senses of forget in WordNet. The first is our forget3. The second is our forget1. The last two are syntactic variations on forget1.

This section illustrates the relation between core theories and the lexicon. The core theory of some domain is constructed in a careful, coherent way, and the predicates explicated in the core theory can then be used to characterize the various uses of the relevant lexical items.

23.5 REMEMBERING TO DO

Our plans for achieving goals spread across time. For example, the goal of eating dinner tonight might involve stopping at the grocery store on the way home. The timely performance of an action requires us to be consciously aware of the need to perform the action at the time of its performance. Since things cannot be retained continuously in the focus of attention, it is necessary to remember to do actions before doing them. Thus, as a precondition for doing an action, remembering to do it must also be a part of the plan of which the action is a part.

```
(forall (a e t e1)                                          (23.35)
    (if (and (agentOf a e)(atTime e t)(inFocus' e1 e a))
        (exists (e2) (and (atTime' e2 e1 t)(enable e2 e)))))
```

That is, if a is the agent in an event e that takes place at time t, then e is enabled by being in a's focus of attention at time t. Thus, remembering to do something can become part of a plan, and hence an intention. As with all actions, a person can succeed or fail at remembering to do something.

It may be useful to have an explicit predicate for the important notion of remembering to do an action. An agent remembers to do something if that action was part of a plan of the agent's, and hence a goal, and if this action's being remembered at some time prior to (or not after) the time of the action causes the action to be in focus at the designated time of the action.

```
(forall (a e)                                               (23.36)
    (iff (rememberTo a e)
        (exists (e1 t e2 e3 e4)
            (and (atTime' e1 e t)(goal e1 a)(agentOf a e)
                 (retrieve' e2 a e1)(cause e2 e3)(atTime' e3 e4 t)
                 (inFocus' e4 e1 a)))))
```

That is, agent a remembers to do e if a has the goal of doing e at time t, and retrieving e causes a to have that goal in focus at time t.

This definition does not presume that the action was completed. Factors other than forgetting could have prevented it.

23.6 REPRESSING

At least since the time of Freud, memories can be repressed. The passive predicate repressed requires less in the way of ontology than the active action of "repressing," so we will consider that first.

If a concept c is repressed for an agent a, then c is in a's memory but it is not accessible.

```
(forall (c a)                                               (23.37)
    (if (repressed c a)
        (exists (m)
            (and (memory m a)(inm c m)(not (accessible c a))))))
```

If a concept is repressed, it is unpleasant to the agent. Moreover, the unpleasantness of the concept defeasibly plays a causal role in the concept's being repressed. We won't be explicating the concept "unpleasant," so rather than state these principles, we will state as an axiom that if something is repressed, then it is probably because thinking about it causes one to be unhappy.

```
(forall (a x)                                                       (23.38)
    (if (and (repressed' e x a)(etc))
        (exists (e0 e1 e2)
            (and (thinkOf' e1 a x)(unhappy' e2 a)(cause' e0 e1 e2)
                 (cause e0 e)))))
```

In this axiom x is the memory or thought that is repressed, e1 is the state of a's thinking of x, e2 is the state of a's being unhappy, e0 is the causal relation between the thinking and the unhappiness, and that causal relation causes a's repression e of the memory. The predicate thinkOf is explicated in Chapter 24 on Envisioning; the predicate unhappy is dealt with in Chapter 49 on Emotions.

The converse of this rule would be way too strong. All too often we remember things that make us unhappy.

It is problematic to say that an agent represses a memory. We may want to say in a theory of envisionment, or thinking, or consciousness, that agents are aware of what they are doing. But to store something in memory in a way that it can't be accessed is as contradictory as being told not to think of an elephant. There are two ways around this problem. The first is to say that there are some actions that an agent may do without being conscious of them. The second, the Freudian approach, is to say that agents have within them subagents that can perform actions the superagent is not aware of. These two approaches are probably equivalent.

PREDICATES INTRODUCED IN THIS CHAPTER

(store a c)
  Agent a stores concept c in memory.

(retrieve a c)
  Agent a retrieves concept c from memory.

(accessibility x c m)
  x is the accessibility of concept c in memory m.

(accessibilityScale s a)
  s is the scale of accessibilities of concepts in memory for agent a.

(memoryThreshold x0 a)
  x0 is the threshold of accessibility below which concepts are not accessible for agent a.

(accessible c a)
  Concept c is accessible from agent a's memory.

(remind c1 a c2)
  Concept c1 reminds agent a of concept c2.

(associated c1 c2 a)
  Concept c1 is associated with concept c2 for agent a.

(remember1 a c)
  Concept c is accessible to agent a.

(remember2 a c)
   Agent a retrieves concept c from memory.

(remember3 a c)
   Agent a causes the retrieval of concept c from memory.

(remember4 a c)
   Agent a causes the retrieval of concept c from memory with some effort.

(remember a c)
   Agent a remembers concept c in any of the above senses.

(forget1 a c)
   Concept c is not accessible for agent a.

(forget2 a c)
   Agent a does not access concept c at the appropriate time.

(forget3 a c)
   Agent a causes concept c to no longer be in focus.

(rememberTo a e)
   Agent a remembers to do e.

(repressed c a)
   Concept c is repressed for agent a.

In addition, we used the following six predicates that have not yet been defined. The first four are from Chapter 28 on Goals, the next from Chapter 24 on Envisioning, and the last one is from Chapter 49 on Emotions.

(goodFor e a)
   e aids in the achievement of one of agent a's goals.

(importanceScale s a)
   s is the scale of importance for agent a.

(importance i c a)
   i is the measure of importance of concept c for agent a.

(succeed a e)
   Agent a succeeds in doing e.

(thinkOf a x)
   Agent a thinks of something x.

(unhappy a)
   Concept c is unpleasant for agent a.

24

Envisioning

24.1 THINKING OF

In this chapter we address the very difficult issue of what it is to think about something. There are many varieties of thinking about something, but they all involve having concepts in the focus of one's attention, that is, being conscious of them.

To think of some concept, entity, or eventuality is to have it in the focus of attention and for that to cause other concepts, entities, and eventualities that it is associated with to come to be in the focus of attention as well. We will refer to the state of having something in the focus of attention as "thinking of" it.

```
(forall (a c)                                              (24.1)
    (iff (thinkOf a c)
        (exists (f)
            (and (focusOfAttention f a)(inm c f)))))
```

Recall from Chapter 21 that to think something, or to "think that" some eventuality obtains, is to consciously think of it at the same time as one believes it.

If we perceive an eventuality, then defeasibly this causes us to think that it holds – we are conscious of it and we believe it.

```
(forall (a e e1)                                           (24.2)
    (if (and (eventuality e)(perceive' e1 a e)(etc))
        (exists (e2) (and (thinkThat' e2 a e)(cause e1 e2)))))
```

It follows from the properties of "cause" that if e1 really exists, then defeasibly e2 will really exist starting at a time not earlier than the start of e1.

If we perceive anything, eventuality or not, then defeasibly this causes us to think that it really exists.

```
(forall (a x e1)                                           (24.3)
    (if (and (perceive' e1 a x)(etc))
        (exists (e e2)
            (and (Rexist' e x)(thinkThat' e2 a e)(cause e1 e2)))))
```

The chapter contains revisions of material published previously in Hobbs and Gordon (2005).

Associations are important in thinking. If two entities are associated for an agent, then thinking of one will defeasibly cause the agent to think of the other.

```
(forall (x y a e1)                                           (24.4)
    (if (and (associated x y a)(thinkOf' e1 a x)(etc))
        (exists (e2)
            (and (thinkOf' e2 a y)(cause e1 e2)))))
```

This is similar to Axiom (23.21) on the way associations interact with accessibilities.

It is of course not possible to predict with precision the directions someone's thoughts may take, but if we have an account of the progression they did take, we can often understand the causal basis of that.

If we specialize the associated relation to causality and thinkOf to thinkThat, then we get prediction and explanation. To predict an eventuality is to believe it will occur at some time that is not before the time of the prediction.

```
(forall (a e e1)                                            (24.5)
    (iff (predict' e1 a e)
        (exists (t1 e2 t2 e3)
            (and (atTime e1 t1)(atTime' e2 e t2)
                (not (before t2 t1))
                (thinkThat' e3 a e2)(gen e3 e1)))))
```

Note that for a to predict e is for a to believe that e will occur at some unspecified time in the future. For the agent to predict that e will occur at a specific time t in the future, the relation (atTime e t) has to be part of the eventuality that is believed. That is, to represent that a believes the sun will set at 6 P.M., we would write something like

```
(and (predict a e2)(set' e1 SUN)(atTime' e2 e1 6pm))
```

If an agent believes in a causal relation and thinks that the cause holds, then defeasibly the agent will predict the effect.

```
(forall (x y a e e1 e2 e3)                                  (24.6)
    (if (and (cause' e e1 e2)(thinkThat a e)(thinkThat' e3 a e1)
            (etc))
        (exists (e4)
            (and (predict' e4 a e2)(cause e3 e4)))))
```

If a predicted eventuality actually happens at some future time, then the prediction is validated.

```
(forall (a e e1 t1)                                         (24.7)
    (if (and (predict' e1 a e)(atTime e1 t1))
        (iff (validated e1)
            (exists (t2)
                (and (atTime e t2)(not (before t2 t1)))))))
```

If it does not happen at some future time, the prediction is invalidated.

```
(forall (a e e1 t1)                                          (24.8)
    (if (and (predict' e1 a e)(atTime e1 t1))
        (iff (invalidated e1)
            (forall (t2)
                (if  (not (before t2 t1))(not (atTime e t2)))))))
```

More about this later in this chapter.

If we specialize the associated relation to the inverse of causality, from effect to cause, and specialize thinkOf to thinkThat, then we get explanation. To explain an eventuality is to think that some specific eventuality caused it. In the following axiom, (explain a e e1) means that agent a explains eventuality e with eventuality e1. That is, e1 is the cause of the effect e.

```
(forall (a e e1)                                            (24.9)
    (iff (explain a e e1)
        (exists (e2)
            (and (thinkThat a e2)(cause' e2 e1 e))))))
```

A given eventuality might have one of several different causes, and this often makes an agent consider the alternative causes. This would follow just from two applications of Axiom (24.9). But in addition, it may make an agent think of the disjunction of the alternative causes.

```
(forall (a e e1 e2 e3 e4 e5)                                (24.10)
    (if (and (believe a e3)(cause' e3 e1 e)
            (believe a e4)(cause' e4 e2 e)(thinkOf' e5 a e)(etc))
        (exists (e6 e7)
            (and (thinkOf' e6 a e7)(or' e7 e1 e2)(cause e5 e6)))))
```

That is, if agent a believes e1 can cause e and e2 can cause e, and a thinks of e, then that will defeasibly cause a to think of the disjunction of e1 and e2.

An agent's knowledge is generally incomplete, making it unclear what the effects of a given eventuality will be. In these circumstances, thinking of the eventuality may cause one to think of the alternative possible effects. That is, if the agent believes that an eventuality e could be a partial cause for eventuality e1 or could be a partial cause of eventuality e2, this defeasibly will cause the agent to think of the disjunction of e1 and e2.

```
(forall (a e e1 e2 e3 e4 e5)                                (24.11)
    (if (and (believe a e3)(causallyInvolved' e3 e e1)
            (believe a e4)(causallyInvolved' e4 e e2)
            (thinkOf' e5 a e)(etc))
        (exists (e6 e7)
            (and (thinkOf' e6 a e7)(or' e7 e1 e2)(cause e5 e6)))))
```

The activity of thinking of something is independent of truth and belief. Nothing in these axioms rules out an agent thinking of something that is not true, thinking of something that the agent does not believe, thinking of something that is true but not believed, or thinking of something that is believed but does not hold. One can also think of things one does not currently believe but will come to believe. It is consistent to think of something regardless of what its likelihood is, including a likelihood of zero.

24.2 CAUSAL SYSTEMS

In Chapter 15 we defined a causal complex for an effect as all of the eventualities that have to obtain for the effect to occur. An eventuality is "causally involved" in an effect if it is in a causal complex for that event. An eventuality "causes" an effect if it is the critical element in a causal complex for the effect in the sense that all the other elements of the causal complex normally obtain, but it does not. Of the three notions, "causally involved" is the weakest.

In this chapter we wish to define a "causal system" as the sort of thing people have in mind when they think causally. It will be weaker than a causal complex, because people never have in mind all the relevant eventualities. It will be based on the "causally involved" relation. Essentially we want a directed graph where the nodes are eventualities and the arcs are "causally involved" relations.

In addition, people often have disjunctive branches in mind when they think causally. One of two eventualities might result, or one of two eventualities might have been the cause. These disjunctions constitute branches in the directed graph. So we first define a "branch" and then define causal system arcs to include branches.

```
(forall (e e1 e2 s)                                    (24.12)
    (iff (branch e e1 e2 s)
         (and (member e s)(member e1 s)(member e2 s)
              (or (or' e e1 e2)(or' e e2 e1)))))
```

This says that e is a branch to e1 and e2 in s exactly when e, e1 and e2 are all members of s and e is a disjunction of e1 and e2.

It follows that branch is symmetric in its middle two arguments.

```
(forall (e e1 e2 s)                                    (24.13)
    (iff (branch e e1 e2 s)(branch e e2 e1 s)))
```

These disjunctive branches are binary; an n-ary branch can be modeled as a sequence of binary branches.

Next we reify the disjunct relation, so it can function as an arc in a graph.

```
(forall (e e1 e2)                                      (24.14)
    (iff (or' e e1 e2)
         (exists (e3 e4)
              (and (disjunct' e3 e1 e)(disjunct' e4 e2 e)))))
```

Here e3 is the relation of e1's being a disjunct in the disjunction e, and similarly for e4 and e2.

We can then define a causal system arc as either a "causally involved" relation or a relation between a disjunction and one of its disjuncts, that is, in a branch.

```
(forall (r e1 e2 s)                                              (24.15)
   (if (eventualities s)
       (iff (csArc r e1 e2 s)
           (or (and (causallyInvolved' r e1 e2)
                    (member e1 s)(member e2 s))
               (exists (e3)
                   (and (member e1 s)(member e2 s)(member e3 s)
                        (branch e1 e2 e3 s)
                        (disjunct' r e2 e1)))))))
```

There are two cases in this definition. In the first case, lines 4–5, there is a csArc from e1 to e2 if e1 is causally involved in e2. The second case, lines 6–9, is for a branch from disjunctions to their disjuncts.

We can define a causal system as a set of eventualities together with a set of such causal system arcs among them. That is, it is a composite entity whose components are eventualities and whose relations are csArc.

```
(forall (c)                                                      (24.16)
   (iff (causalSystem c)
       (exists (v s)
           (and (componentsOf v c)(relationsOf s c)
                (eventualities v)
                (forall (r)
                    (if (member r s)
                        (exists (e1 e2)
                            (csArc r e1 e2 v))))))))
```

That is, c is a causal system if and only if c is a composite entity whose components are eventualities, and whose relations are causal links among these eventualities.

Essentially, a causal system is a directed AND–OR graph where the nodes are eventualities, the disjunction eventualities are the OR nodes, and the nondisjunctive directed links are causallyInvolved relations. We don't need an explicit representation of AND nodes because if (and e1 e2) is causally involved in e, then so are e1 and e2, although it is certainly possible for a conjunctive eventuality to be one of the nodes.

We will call the components of a causal system its eventualities.

```
(forall (c v)                                                    (24.17)
   (if (causalSystem c)
       (iff (eventualitiesOf v c)
            (componentsOf v c))))
```

We could similarly define the relations of c to be the causalRelationsOf c, but the predicate relationsOf is already sufficiently mnemonic.

It will be convenient to allow csArc to take causal systems as its fourth argument as well as sets of eventualities.

```
(forall (r e1 e2 c)                                              (24.18)
    (if (causalSystem c)
        (iff (csArc r e1 e2 c)
            (exists (v)
                (and (eventualitiesOf v c)(csArc r e1 e2 v))))))
```

Two eventualities e1 and e2 are "causally linked" in a causal system c if there is a chain of csArc relations in c between e1 and e2, regardless of direction.

```
(forall (e1 e2 c)                                               (24.19)
    (iff (causallyLinked e1 e2 c)
        (exists (r v s)
            (and (eventualitiesOf v c)(relationsOf s c)
                (member r s)
                (or (csArc r e1 e2 c)(csArc r e2 e1 c)
                    (exists (e3 c0 s0)
                        (and (or (csArc' r e1 e3 c)
                                 (csArc' r e3 e1 c))
                            (deleteElt s0 s r)
                            (causalSystem c0)
                            (eventualitiesOf v c0)
                            (relationsOf s0 c0)
                            (causallyLinked e3 e2 c0)))))))))
```

That is, e1 and e2 are causally linked in c if there is a direct csArc relation between them (line 6) or there is a csArc relation between e1 and some e3 which is causally linked with e2 in the rest of c once r is removed. Causal system c0 is what results from removing r.

Next we define a connected subsystem c1 of a causal system c containing eventuality e. (In graph theory this is usually called a "component" of the graph, but we won't use that term here because of the confusion it would cause with the components (i.e., eventualities) of the causal system.)

```
(forall (c1 e c)                                                (24.20)
    (iff (connSubCS c1 e c)
        (exists (v1 v)
            (and (eventualitiesOf v c)(eventualitiesOf v1 c1)
                (member e v)(member e v1)
                (forall (e1)
                    (iff (member e1 v1)
                        (and (member e1 v)
                            (or (equal e1 e)
                                (causallyLinked e e1 c)))))))))
```

A "connected causal system" is a causal system in which all eventualities are causally linked by relations in the causal system.

```
(forall (c)                                                    (24.21)
   (iff (connectedCausalSystem c)
        (exists (v s)
           (and (causalSystem c)(eventualitiesOf v c)
                (relationsOf s c)
                (forall (e1 e2)
                   (if (and (member e1 v)(member e2 v))
                       (causallyLinked e1 e2 c)))))))
```

A "branchless causal system" is a causal system all of whose arcs are causallyInvolved relations, rather than disjunctions.

```
(forall (c)                                                    (24.22)
   (iff (branchlessCausalSystem c)
        (exists (s1 s2)
           (and (causalSystem c)(eventualitiesOf v c)
                (relationsOf s c)
                (forall (r)
                   (if (member r s)
                       (exists (e1 e2)
                          (and (member e1 v)(member e2 v)
                               (causallyInvolved' r e1 e2)))))))))
```

A node e is isolated with respect to a causal system c if there are no arcs into it and no arcs out of it.

```
(forall (e c)                                                  (24.23)
   (iff (isolated e c)
        (exists (v)
           (and (eventualitiesOf v c)(member e v)
                (not (exists (r e1)
                   (or (csArc r e1 e c)(csArc r e e1 c))))))))
```

We will say that the members of the eventualities of a causal system are the eventualities in it.

```
(forall (e c)                                                  (24.24)
   (iff (eventualityIn e c)
        (exists (v) (and (eventualitiesOf v c)(member e v)))))
```

24.3 CONTIGUOUS CAUSAL SYSTEMS

In causal thinking we move incrementally from one envisioned causal system to another, in a sense, by growing or pruning one node at a time. For "causally involved" arcs, we can subsume adding and deleting causes and effects under one relation between two causal systems. The relation oneArcDiff says that the two causal systems c and c0 differ by only one arc, the arc r from e1 to e2. Causal system c will be the larger one, the one that is obtained by adding arc r to c0. If e1 is already in c0 and e2 is not, then this relation captures the operation of adding or deleting an effect. If e1 is not in c0 and e2 is, then the relation amounts to an operation to add or delete a cause. But the relation oneArcDiff is more general in that it also covers the case in which both e1 and e2 are in c0 and the case where neither e1 nor e2 is in c0.

```
(forall (c e1 r e2 c0)                                          (24.25)
    (iff (oneArcDiff c e1 r e2 c0)
        (exists (v0 s0 v s d)
            (and (causalSystem c0)(causalSystem c)
                 (eventualitiesOf v0 s0)(relationsOf s0 c0)
                 (eventualitiesOf v c)(relationsOf s c)
                 (union v v0 d)(doubleton d e1 e2)
                 (causallyInvolved' r e1 e2)(not (member r s0))
                 (addElt s s0 r)))))
```

Causal system c has an arc r from e1 to e2 that c0 lacks. Lines 5 and 6 label the eventualities and causal relations of c0 and c. Line 7 puts e1 and e2 into the eventualities of c, if they are not already there. Line 8 stipulates that r is a causallyInvolved relation not already part of c0. Line 9 says the causal relations of c0 and c differ only by arc r.

The other incremental operations we would like to be able to do on causal systems are introducing and resolving disjunctive branch nodes.

The next definition will make it somewhat easier to define resolveBranch.

```
(forall (c2 c0 d)                                               (24.26)
    (iff (delCSRel c2 c0 d)
        (exists (v0 s0 s2)
            (and (eventualitiesOf v0 c0)(relationsOf s0 c0)
                 (eventualitiesOf v0 c2)(relationsOf s2 c2)
                 (deleteElt s2 s0 d)))))
```

The expression (delCSRel c2 c0 d) says that causal system c2 results from deleting the relation d from causal system c0.

This brings us to one of the most complex axioms in the book. However, the idea behind it is fairly simple. We are changing one causal system c0 into another c. In c0 we have a branch <e0,e1,e2>, and we want to eliminate e0 and the disjunct relation d between e0 and e2. Other arcs feeding into and out of e0 in c0 will be reset to feed into and out of e1 in c. We would also like to eliminate e2 and everything that depends on it. However, if e2 is still causally linked to e1 after d has been removed, no nodes can be eliminated. If they are not causally linked, the connected causal subsystem containing e2 can be eliminated.

```
(forall (c e0 e1 e2 c0)                                         (24.27)
    (iff (resolveBranch c e0 e1 e2 c0)
        (exists (d c2 c1 v0 v v1)
            (and (causalSystem c0)(causalSystem c)
                 (eventualitiesOf v0 c0)(eventualitiesOf v c)
                 (branch e0 e1 e2 v0)(disjunct' d e2 e0)
                 (delCSRel c2 c0 d)(connSubCS c1 e2 c2)
                 (or (and (causallyLinked e1 e2 c2)(null v1))
                     (and (not (causallyLinked e1 e2 c2))
                          (eventualitiesOf v1 c1)))
```

```
(forall (e)
    (iff (member e v)
        (and (member e v0)(nequal e e0)
            (not (member e v1)))))
(forall (r e3 e4)
    (iff (csArc r e3 e4 c)
        (and (or (and (equal e4 e1)
                    (or (csArc r e3 e0 c0)
                        (csArc r e3 e1 c0)))
                (and (equal e3 e1)
                    (or (csArc r e0 e4 c0)
                        (csArc r e1 e4 c0)))
                (and (nequal e3 e1)(nequal e4 e1)
                    (csArc r e3 e4 c0)))
            (nequal r d)
            (not (member e3 v1))
            (not (member e4 v1)))))))))))
```

The expression (resolveBranch c e0 e1 e2 c0) says that causal system c results from taking the branch from e0 to e1 and e2 in causal system c0 and resolving it to e1. Line 4 says that c0 and c are causal systems. Line 5 labels their sets of eventualities. Line 6 identifies <e0,e1,e2> as a branch and labels as d the link from e0 to e2. Line 7 constructs causal system c2, which is c0 without arc d, and the connected subsystem c1 containing e2. Lines 8–10 is where we check whether e1 and e2 are causally linked other than through d; the set v1 is the set of nodes or eventualities that will be deleted as we resolve the branch. If they are causally linked only through d we can delete the entire connected subsystem c1; if there are other links, we can't delete any nodes. Lines 11–14 specify which eventualities are in c, namely, those in c0 except e0 and those in v1. Lines 17–24 reset arcs into and out of e0 to point into and out of e1 instead, leaving other arcs unchanged. Lines 25–27 eliminate the disjunctive arc d and arcs into or out of set v1.

We have called this predicate resolveBranch, but it can just as easily be thought of as introducing a branch by reversing the roles of c0 and c.

Branches give us a way of exploring alternatives in causal systems. There can be different likelihoods associated with the different alternatives, including a likelihood of zero; these would simply be properties of the eventualities. Some branches are more likely than others.

The relations oneArcDiff and resolveBranch define a set of incremental changes on causal systems. Together, they characterize what it is for two causal systems to be "contiguous." Two causal systems are contiguous if they stand in one of these two relations.

```
(forall (c1 c2)                                                    (24.28)
    (iff (contigCS c1 c2)
        (or (exists (e1 r e2)
                (or (oneArcDiff c1 e1 r e2 c2)
                    (oneArcDiff c2 e1 r e2 c1)))
            (exists (e0 e1 e2)
                (or (resolveBranch c1 e0 e1 e2 c2)
                    (resolveBranch c2 e0 e1 e2 c1))))))))
```

The contigCS relation is obviously symmetric.

```
(forall (c1 c2)                                              (24.29)
    (iff (contigCS c1 c2)(contigCS c2 c1)))
```

24.4 ENVISIONED CAUSAL SYSTEMS

When we are thinking causally, we have a contiguous succession of causal systems in mind. Here we first define what it is to envision a causal system (ecs). We then define a contiguous sequence of them (ecsSeq).

The easiest way to define it would be to say that it is a causal system that the agent has in focus, or is thinking of. But we will give a somewhat weaker definition. The agent a is (consciously) thinking of every eventuality in the causal system. But a may or may not be thinking of all the causal relations. They may be merely believed and not in focus, or not even necessarily accessible. For example, when we rapidly assess a situation by intuition, we are using causal knowledge we may not even be aware of. On the other hand, the agent may be consciously thinking of and considering the consequences of a causal rule that is not believed. So we will stipulate that the arcs in the causal system are either believed or in focus.

```
(forall (c a)                                               (24.30)
    (iff (ecs c a)
         (exists (v s)
             (and (causalSystem c)(eventualitiesOf v c)
                  (relationsOf s c)
                  (forall (e)
                      (if (member e v)(thinkOf a e)))
                  (forall (r)
                      (if (member r s)
                          (or (thinkOf a r)(believe a r)))))))))
```

We can relativize the envisioned causal system to a set b of background beliefs that are never challenged, by adding a stipulation that negations of eventualities in b are never in v and if the background beliefs are negations of causallyInvolved relations, those relations are never among the arcs.

```
(forall (b a c)                                             (24.31)
    (if (ecs c a)
        (iff (backgroundBeliefs b a)
             (exists (v s)
                 (and (eventualitiesOf v c)(relationsOf s c)
                      (forall (e1 e2)
                          (if (and (member e1 b)(not' e2 e1))
                              (not (member e2 v))))
                      (forall (r e1 e2 e3)
                          (if (and (causallyInvolved' r e1 e2)
                                   (not' e3 r)(member e3 b))
                              (not (member r s)))))))))
```

The expression (backgroundBeliefs b a) says that b is the set of agent a's background beliefs. Lines 6–8 check that the negation of a background belief is not one of the eventualities in the causal system. Lines 9–12 do the same for the relations.

Now we can define an envisioned causal system sequence (ecsSeq) as a sequence of envisioned causal systems in which the successive causal systems are contiguous and where there is a change of state from each causal system being envisioned to the next one in the sequence being envisioned. Thus there are two sequences – s, whose elements are causal systems linked by a contigCS relation, and s0, whose elements are "thinkings of" ecs's linked by a change relation.

```
(forall (s a)                                                        (24.32)
    (iff (ecsSeq s a)
        (and (sequence s)
            (forall (c1)
                (if (inSeq c1 s)(ecs c1 a)))
            (forall (n n1 l c1 c2)
                (if (and (gt n 0)(length l s)(lt n l)
                        (successor n1 n)
                        (nth c1 n s)(nth c2 n1 s))
                    (contigCS c1 c2)))
            (exists (s0)
                (and (sequence s0)
                    (forall (e1 n)
                        (iff (nth e1 n s0)
                            (exists (c1)
                                (and (nth c1 n s)
                                    (ecs' e1 c1 a)))))
                    (forall (n n1 l e1 e2)
                        (if (and (gt n 0)(length l s0)(lt n l)
                                (successor n1 n)
                                (nth e1 n s0)(nth e2 n1 s0))
                            (change e1 e2)))))))))
```

Lines 3–5 say that s is a sequence of ecs's. Lines 6–10 say that successive causal systems in s are contiguous. Lines 11–17 say that s0 is the sequence of corresponding envisionments of the causal systems. Lines 18–22 say that successive elements of s0 are linked by a change-of-state relation.

Because a conjunction of eventualities is an eventuality, a causal system sequence itself can be viewed as an eventuality. Thus, it can happen in incrementing an envisioned causal system sequence, the agent can tap into a complex, previously constructed causal system sequence, and add it to the sequence in one move. Essentially, the agent is reusing an already constructed causal system sequence; one explains or predicts one's way into that causal system sequence and then adopts it wholesale.

We will say that an eventuality in any element of an envisioned causal system sequence is an envisioned eventuality.

```
(forall (e s a)                                                      (24.33)
    (iff (envisionedEv e s a)
        (exists (c) (and (ecsSeq s a)(inSeq c s)(eventualityIn e c)))))
```

It will be useful to have the notion of envisioning a sequence from one causal system to another.

```
(forall (a e1 e2)                                                    (24.34)
   (iff (envisionFromTo a e1 e2)
        (exists (s)
             (and (ecsSeq s a)(first e1 s)(last e2 s)))))
```

It will also be useful to have less specific versions of this predicate.

```
(forall (a e1)                                                       (24.35)
   (iff (envisionFrom a e1)
        (exists (e2) (envisionFromTo a e1 e2))))
```

```
(forall (a e2)                                                       (24.36)
   (iff (envisionTo a e2)
        (exists (e1) (envisionFromTo a e1 e2))))
```

People have an ability to envision causal system sequences.

```
(forall (a)                                                          (24.37)
   (if (person a)
       (exists (s e1 c)
            (and (ecsSeq' e1 s a)(able a e1 c)))))
```

This is a weak axiom. It only says that for every person, there is some causal system he or she can envision, providing constraints c do not rule it out. It does not say a person can envision any causal system.

As with all abilities, a person can try to envision something but fail.

There are many ways one can think about something, but among them is thinking about it causally. We can say that if every element of an ecsSeq includes a property of x among its eventualities, then the agent is thinking about x.

```
(forall (s a)                                                        (24.38)
   (if (and (ecsSeq s a)
            (forall (c v)
                 (if (and (inSeq c s)(eventualitiesOf v c))
                     (exists (e) (and (member e v)(arg* x e))))))
       (thinkAbout a x)))
```

24.5 ENVISIONMENT AND BELIEF

In Chapter 21 we said that believing a set of eventualities is believing their conjunction. To believe a causal system is to believe the conjunction of the set of eventualities and the set of causallyInvolved relations that characterize the causal system.

```
(forall (a c v s)                                                    (24.39)
   (if (and (causalSystem c)
            (eventualitiesOf v c)(relationsOf s c))
       (iff (believe a c)
            (and (believe a v)(believe a s)))))
```

An agent's graded belief in a set of eventualities is less than or equal to the agent's belief in any member of the set. A graded belief in a causal system is the graded belief in the union of the eventualities and the causal relations of the causal system. The details of how the degree of belief in a causal system arises out of the degrees of belief in its parts are complex and largely unknown. But we are able to say a few things in the text that follows about how graded belief interacts with the process of envisionment.

New envisioned causal systems may be initiated by thinking of an eventuality unconnected with any current envisionment. It may or may not be connected to what is going on in the world for the agent. Many times an envisioned causal system is not intended to correspond to reality. We might imagine what we would do with lottery winnings, or how we should have retorted when we were put down, or what we would say to the president if we had a chance, or what we would talk about with Thomas Jefferson if we could go back in time.

Some envisionments are about events and states that happen in the real world at a particular time.

```
(forall (a)                                              (24.40)
   (if (person a)
      (exists (s t)
         (and (ecsSeq s a)(during s t)))))
```

Some envisionments are about fictional worlds, as in fiction and dreams, and have never happened and never will.

```
(forall (a)                                              (24.41)
   (if (person a)
      (exists (s)
         (and (ecsSeq s a)
              (forall (t) (not (during s t))))))))
```

It is possible for some of the elements of an envisioned causal system to contradict each other, and this often happens as we are trying to diagnose a situation.

However, a very important use of envisioned causal systems is to discover correspondences with reality. We want to predict what will happen from what we know to be true now. Or we want to figure out what brought about what we know to be true now. Or we want to figure out what *is* true now by coming up with plausible explanations and valid predictions and then checking them. That is, we want rules for increasing our degree of belief in an envisioned causal system.

For convenience, we define a predicate expressing a change in degree of graded belief. It says that agent a's belief in e changes from d1 to d2.

```
(forall (a e d1 d2)                                      (24.42)
   (iff (changeGBel a e d1 d2)
      (exists (e1 e2)
         (and (gbel' e1 a e d1)(gbel' e2 a e d2)
              (nequal d1 d2)(change e1 e2)))))
```

Then we can say that defeasibly increasing or decreasing the belief in an element of a causal system causes an increase or decrease in the belief in the causal system as a whole.

```
(forall (a e d1 d2 c v)                                          (24.43)
    (if (and (ecs c a)(eventualitiesOf v c)(member e v)
             (changeGBel a e d1 d2)(gt d1 d2)(etc))
        (exists (d3 d4)
            (and (changeGBel a c d3 d4)(gt d3 d4)))))
```

```
(forall (a e d1 d2 c v)                                          (24.44)
    (if (and (ecs c a)(eventualitiesOf v c)(member e v)
             (changeGBel a e d1 d2)(lt d1 d2)(etc))
        (exists (d3 d4)
            (and (changeGBel a c d3 d4)(lt d3 d4)))))
```

```
(forall (a r d1 d2 c s)                                          (24.45)
    (if (and (ecs c a)(relationsOf s c)(member r s)
             (changeGBel a r d1 d2)(gt d1 d2)(etc))
        (exists (d3 d4)
            (and (changeGBel a c d3 d4)(gt d3 d4)))))
```

```
(forall (a e d1 d2 c s)                                          (24.46)
    (if (and (ecs c a)(relationsOf s c)(member r s)
             (changeGBel a e d1 d2)(lt d1 d2)(etc))
        (exists (d3 d4)
            (and (changeGBel a c d3 d4)(lt d3 d4)))))
```

If a prediction or explanation is verified, that defeasibly increases the agent's degree of belief in the causal system. That is, if agent a changes from entertaining causal system c1 to entertaining causal system c2, where c2 introduces a new eventuality that a believes is true, then that will tend to cause an increase in a's graded belief in the original causal system. The first axiom is for the case of finding a possible cause that is believed to be true. The belief in the causal system increases because an explanation has been found.

```
(forall (a c c0 e1 e2 r e3 e4 v0)                                (24.47)
    (if (and (ecs' e3 c0 a)(ecs' e4 c a)
             (oneArcDiff c e1 r e2 c0)
             (eventualitiesOf v0 c0)(not (member e1 v0))
             (believe a e1)(change' e0 e3 e4)(etc))
        (exists (e)
            (and (changeGBel' e a c0 d1 d2)(gt d2 d1)
                 (cause e0 e)))))
```

That is, there is a change from a's entertaining causal system c0 to a's entertaining causal system c, where c includes a new possible cause, and that new cause is already believed. In this case, that change in what is entertained will defeasibly cause a change in degree of belief in c0, the original causal system.

The next axiom concerns predictions that are verified. There is a change in which the agent thinks of a new possible effect and already believes that to be true. This causes the agent's belief in the original causal system to increase.

```
(forall (a c c0 e1 e2 r e3 e4 v0)                               (24.48)
   (if (and (ecs' e3 c0 a)(ecs' e4 c a)
            (oneArcDiff c e1 r e2 c0)(member e1 v0)
            (eventualitiesOf v0 c0)(not (member e2 v0))
            (believe a e2)(change' e0 e3 e4)(etc))
       (exists (e)
          (and (changeGBel' e a c0 d1 d2)(gt d2 d1)
               (cause e0 e)))))
```

Like all graded beliefs, the degree of belief can increase enough that it becomes a belief, and hence is validated.

Predictions can also be falsified, and this decreases the degree of belief in the original causal system.

```
(forall (a c c0 e1 e2 r e3 e4 v0)                               (24.49)
   (if (and (ecs' e3 c0 a)(ecs' e4 c a)
            (oneArcDiff c e1 r e2 c0)(eventualitiesOf v0 c0)
            (member e1 v0)(not (member e2 v0))
            (not' e5 e2)(believe a e5)
            (change' e0 e3 e4)(etc))
       (exists (e)
          (and (changeGBel' e a c0 d1 d2)(lt d2 d1)
               (cause e0 e)))))
```

Here, e5 is a negation of e2 that a believes.

It often happens in this case that the degree of belief decreases so much that it becomes disbelief. This is what falsification of theories is all about. But to frame this as a nondefeasible axiom, we would have to be very much stricter about what causal relations were captured by the causal system.

Suppose a causal system has a branch in it, and a false proposition is found in the connected subsystem of one of the disjuncts. Then defeasibly there is an increased graded belief in the causal system with that branch resolved to the other disjunct.

```
(forall (c c0 c1 c2 v1 e0 e1 e2 e3 e4 e5 e6 e7 d)               (24.50)
   (if (and (ecs' e3 c0 a)(ecs' e4 c a)
            (resolveBranch c e0 e1 e2 c0)
            (disjunct' d e2 e0)(delCSRel c2 c0 d)
            (connSubCS c1 e2 c2)(eventualitiesOf v1 c1)
            (member e5 v1)(not' e6 e5)(believe a e6)
            (change' e7 e3 e4)(etc))
       (exists (e)
          (and (changeGBel' e a c d1 d2)(gt d2 d1)
               (cause e7 e)))))
```

In this axiom c0 is the causal system with a branch from e0 to the disjuncts e1 and e2, and d is the disjunct relation between e2 and e0. Causal system c2 results from deleting d from c0, and c1 is the connected subsystem of e2 in c2. Suppose a proposition e5 which a believes to be false is in c1, and a changes from entertaining c0 to entertaining c. Then this defeasibly causes an increase in a's degree of belief in c. That is, the belief in the other disjunct increases.

These moves all depend on one's beliefs, and thus whether or not they lead to success, that is, to beliefs more in accord with the world, depends on whether the original beliefs are correct. That is, successful envisionment requires knowledge.

How these changes in degree of belief in the causal system as a whole propagate down to the degrees of belief in its elements is a complex and largely unsolved problem.

If the causal system includes all the eventualities that the agent perceives and the causal system is believed, then the envisioned causal system is the agent's current world understanding (cwu). First we define a time-dependent version of cwu0.

```
(forall (a c t)                                              (24.51)
    (iff (cwu0 c a t)
         (exists (e1 v)
             (and (ecs' e1 c a)(atTime e1 t)
                  (eventualitiesOf v c)
                  (forall (e2)
                      (if (and (eventuality e2)
                               (perceive' e3 a e2)(atTime e3 t))
                          (member e2 v)))))))
```

Time advances, so necessarily one's current world understanding advances with it, as new things are perceived. That is why t is an argument of cwu0. However, many axioms with unprimed predicates and Rexist are anchored in specific times, and it will be convenient to define a two-argument version of the predicate, by stipulating that t is Now. This has the effect of anchoring the current world understanding to the same time as the rest of the axiom.

```
(forall (c a)                                               (24.52)
    (iff (cwu c a)(exists (t) (and (cwu0 c a t)(Now t)))))
```

An envisioned state could be one that occurred in the past or will occur in the future. It is consistent to envision a causal system that is inconsistent with one's current world understanding. It is consistent to envision an eventuality that you believe has a zero likelihood.

24.6 OTHER VARIETIES OF THINKING

Our account of envisioning is an attempt to capture what it is to think causally. But there are many other varieties of thinking. We will not go into any of these in detail, but it may be useful to sketch out how one would approach characterizing them. In every case, we would characterize them as a sequence of sets of eventualities and entities that are in the focus of attention, together with other properties, for example, whether or not they are believed or whether or not they are unpleasant or by what kind of relations they are linked to each other.

There are many varieties of thinking that can be viewed as specializations of envisioned causal system sequences, and some of these are discussed in subsequent chapters, such as planning, explanation, and monitoring the execution of one's plans. Also similar to envisioned causal systems is mathematical thinking, where we are tracing out implicational networks, trying to determine whether eventualities we introduce into the system are necessary or sufficient, and trying to determine everything that must be included. Another example is where we are trying to categorize something we perceive – is that a cat or a raccoon? – by running over diagnostic properties in our mind. This is often important for predicting behavior. A kind of meta-causal reasoning occurs when we ponder whether some aspect of our belief system needs revision; we consider our beliefs and the good and bad consequences of having those beliefs. In all these cases, we are trying to keep an ordered succession of ideas in focus. In defining envisioned causal system sequences, we proposed one common kind of ordering.

Another kind of ordering is similarity. Often episodes of thought linked by similarity are only mental play, as when we see the shape of a dog in a cloud. But similar things often behave similarly, so such similarity reasoning is often functional. We often are able to surmise how to behave in a new situation because it reminds us of a situation we are familiar with.

Another variety of thinking occurs when we are very much engaged in the moment, and mostly what we are consciously thinking is the perceptible situation immediately before us and what our next action should be. For example, an orienteer racing through the very uneven terrain of a forest must be very alert to obstacles and ready to respond to anything that might suddenly appear. Someone performing a new and complex dance is in a similar situation, as is a boxer.

By contrast, fantasizing is disengaged from the current immediate situation. Many of one's beliefs are suspended, while many beliefs are maintained as background assumptions. For example, one might counterfactually imagine having been a child prodigy while holding fixed one's beliefs in what is interesting. A formal characterization would need to deal with both what beliefs are held fixed and what beliefs are up for grabs. Dreaming is a similarly not apparently functional mode of thinking. One would have to characterize the kind of awareness that occurs in sleep, for example, as having much the feel of perception, but with only a narrow window on the world and coupled with an inability to act.

There are also compulsive dysfunctional episodes of thought, for example, in mental fussing where we think of the same problems or irritations over and over again with no hint of problem-solving activity. Another example is when we cannot get the image of a gruesome accident out of our mind. These kinds of thinking seem to involve a high degree of repetition and no apparent progress toward the achievement of our goals.

We leave the characterization of these and other varieties of thinking to future work.

PREDICATES INTRODUCED IN THIS CHAPTER

(thinkOf a c)
  Agent a thinks of concept c.

(predict a e)
  Agent a predicts that e will happen.

(validated e)
  e is a prediction that is validated.

(invalidated e)
  e is a prediction that is invalidated.

(explain a e e1)
> Agent a explains e with e1.

(branch e e1 e2 s)
> e is a disjunction of e1 and e2 and all three are in set s.

(disjunct e2 e)
> e is a disjunction of e2 and something else.

(csArc r e1 e2 s)
> r is a causallyInvolved relation or a disjunct relation and e1 and e2 are members of set s.

(causalSystem c)
> c is a causal system.

(eventualitiesOf v c)
> v is the set of eventualities in causal system c.

(eventualityIn e c)
> e is one of the eventualities in causal system c.

(causallyLinked e1 e2 c)
> There is a path of csArc's between nodes e1 and e2 in causal system c.

(connSubCS c1 e c)
> c1 is the connected subsystem of causal system c containing e.

(connectedCausalSystem c)
> All nodes in causal system c are causally linked.

(branchlessCausalSystem c)
> There are no disjunctive branch nodes in causal system c.

(isolated e c)
> Node e in causal system c has no causal links with any other node.

(oneArcDiff c e1 r e2 c0)
> Causal systems c and c0 differ only in that c has an arc r from e1 to e2.

(delCSRel c2 c0 d)
> c2 is the causal system that results from deleting arc d from causal system c0.

(resolveBranch c e0 e1 e2 c0)
> Causal systems c and c0 differ only in that disjunctive branch e0-e1-e2 in c0 is resolved to e1 in c.

(contigCS c1 c2)
> Causal systems c1 and c2 differ only by oneArcDiff or by resolveBranch.

(ecs c a)
> Agent a has causal system c in focus.

(backgroundBeliefs b e)
> b is a set of beliefs that are not negated in the envisioning e of a causal system.

(thinkAbout a x)
> Agent a thinks about x.

(ecsSeq s a)
> s is a sequence of contiguous causal systems being envisioned by agent a.

(envisionedEv e s a)

 e is an eventuality in a causal system in an envisioned causal system sequence s by agent a.

(envisionFromTo a e1 e2)

 Agent a envisions a sequence from causal system e1 to causal system e2.

(envisionFrom a e1)

 Agent a envisions a sequence from causal system e1 to some other causal system.

(envisionTo a e2)

 Agent a envisions a sequence from some causal system to some other causal system e2.

(changeGBel a e d1 d2)

 Agent a changes the degree of belief in e from d1 to d2.

(cwu0 c a t)

 Causal system c is agent a's current world understanding at time t

(cwu c a)

 Causal system c is agent a's current world understanding now.

Explanation

25.1 EXPLANATIONS AND MYSTERIES

In Chapter 24 on Envisioning we defined what it is for an agent a to explain an eventuality e with eventuality e1. The agent believes that e1 caused e. Our notion of
explanation pertains only to those eventualities e the agent believes actually happened. In this chapter we discuss explanations more fully, including what it means
for one explanation to be better than another, an idealized account of the process of
explanation, and how explanations can fail. Abilities and possibilities are constrained
by the agent's current world understanding.

There are some eventualities that agents are able to explain, with respect to a set
of constraints c.

```
(forall (a c)                                            (25.1)
    (if (and (agent a)(cwu c a))
        (exists (e0 e e1)
            (and (able a e0 c)(explain' e0 a e e1)))))
```

Defeasibly, for any given person a, there are eventualities e that a really does
explain.

```
(forall (a)                                              (25.2)
    (if (and (person a)(etc))
        (exists (e e1)(explain a e e1))))
```

Something is a mystery for an agent a if a is not able to explain it.

```
(forall (e a c)                                          (25.3)
    (iff (and (mystery e a)(cwu c a))
        (and (agent a)(eventuality e)
            (not (exists (e1 e0)
                    (and (able a e0 c)
                        (explain' e0 a e e1)))))))
```

For any given person a, there are eventualities that are mysteries.

```
(forall (a)                                              (25.4)
    (if (person a)
        (exists (e) (mystery e a))))
```

Defeasibly, for any given agent a, there are eventualities that a has the goal of explaining.

```
(forall (a)                                              (25.5)
    (if (and (agent a) (etc))
        (exists (e0 e e1)
            (and (goal e0 a)(explain' e0 a e e1)))))
```

Note that there is a *de re-de dicto* ambiguity in the natural gloss of this axiom. In the de re reading, a wants to explain e with something – anything – e1. In the de dicto reading, a wants to explain e with some specific thing e1. The first is the correct interpretation of the axiom. The second would require in addition a statement that a know the identity of e1.

Goals are explicated in Chapter 28.

For any agent a, there are eventualities that have multiple possible explanations.

```
(forall (a c)                                            (25.6)
    (if (and (agent a)(cwu c a))
        (exists (e e1 e2 e3 e4)
            (and (explain' e3 a e e1)(explain' e4 a e e2)
                (nequal e1 e2)(possible e3 c)(possible e4 c)))))
```

Here, e3 is the eventuality of explaining e with e1, e4 is the eventuality of explaining it with e2, and both are possible. The set c is the set of constraints possibility is with respect to, viz., a's current world understanding.

In such cases, one explanation can be better than another for an agent a. One possible reason for one explanation being better than another is that the agent's graded belief in it is higher.

```
(forall (a e e1 e2 d1 d2)                                (25.7)
    (if (and (agent a)(explain a e e1)(explain a e e2)
            (gbel a e1 d1)(gbel a e2 d2)(gt d1 d2))
        (betterExplanationFor e1 e2 e a)))
```

The predication (betterExplanationFor e1 e2 e a) says that e1 is a better explanation than e2 of e for agent a. Section 24.5 explicates various ways graded belief can increase or decrease.

This does not exhaust the criteria for being a good explanation. Other factors will also come into play in making one explanation better than another. An agent may have preferences for one class of explanation over another. For example, one may prefer explanations in terms of moral rewards rather than in terms of chaotic processes. One may prefer explanations in the theological vocabulary of intelligent design rather than the biological vocabulary of natural selection.

To capture this notion of explanation preferences, we will use the notion of knowledgeDomain introduced in Chapter 21. Recall that a knowledge domain is characterized by a set of predicates, and a sentence is in a knowledge domain if its

claim can be expressed in terms of the predicates. Then agents defeasibly have a preferred class of explanations in that there is a knowledge domain d such that possible
explanations in d are better explanations of e for a than possible explanations that
are not in d.

```
(forall (a)                                                    (25.8)
   (if (and (agent a)(etc))
       (exists (d)
          (and (knowledgeDomain d)
               (forall (e e1 e2)
                  (if (and (member e1 d)(not (member e2 d))
                          (explain a e e1)(explain a e e2))
                      (betterExplanationFor e1 e2 e a)))))))
```

Both graded belief and explanation preferences can vary among agents, and that
is why betterExplanationFor has the agent a as one of its arguments.

The relation (betterExplanationFor e1 e2 e a) is a partial ordering on e1
and e2, and therefore there may be a best explanation in a set s. When there is, this
fact will defeasibly cause the agent to adopt that explanation.

```
(forall (a e e1 s)                                             (25.9)
   (if (and (explain a e e1)(member e1 s)
           (forall (e2)
              (if (and (member e2 s)(explain a e e2)
                      (nequal e1 e2))
                  (betterExplanationFor e1 e2 e a))))
       (bestExplanationFor e1 e a s)))
```

```
(forall (a e e1 e3 e4 s)                                       (25.10)
   (if (and (bestExplanationFor' e3 e1 e a s)(believe a e)
           (forall (e2) (iff (member e2 s)(explain a e e2)))
           (cause' e4 e1 e)(believe' e5 a e4)(etc))
       (cause e3 e5)))
```

That is, if e1 is a's best explanation for e out of the set s of all explanations of e, where
a believes e to hold, then defeasibly that will cause a to believe e1 causes e.

25.2 THE EXPLANATION PROCESS

An idealized picture of the process by which an agent comes up with an explanation
is as follows: First the agent recognizes the need to explain an eventuality. Candidate
explanations are then generated. The candidates are evaluated to see which one is
the best. The inferior candidate explanations are rejected, and the winning candidate
explanation is adopted and becomes part of the agent's beliefs. In this section, we
define a predicate for each of these steps, in part to show that we have developed the
vocabulary required for characterizing this process.

First, we break down the entire process. This axiom is defeasible because the picture of the process is idealized.

```
(forall (a e e1)                                              (25.11)
    (if (and (explain a e e1)(etc))
        (exists (e2 e3 e4 e5)
            (and (adoptGoalToExplain' e2 a e)
                 (generateExplanations' e3 a e s)
                 (assessExplanations' e4 a s e)
                 (adoptExplanation' e5 a e1 e)
                 (before e2 e3)(before e3 e4)(before e4 e5)))))
```

To adopt a goal to explain e is to change into a state where one has that goal.

```
(forall (a e)                                                (25.12)
    (iff (adoptGoalToExplain a e)
        (exists (e1 e2 e3)
            (and (changeTo e2)(goal' e2 e3 a)
                 (explain' e3 a e e1)))))
```

A common reason for adopting a goal to explain something is that it had not been predicted.

```
(forall (a e)                                                (25.13)
    (if (and (agent a)(learn a e)(not (predict a e))(etc))
        (adoptGoalToExplain a e)))
```

To generate candidate explanations is to think of a set of eventualities that possibly cause the effect, given one's current world understanding.

```
(forall (a e s)                                              (25.14)
    (iff (generateExplanations a e s)
        (and (thinkOf a s)
             (forall (e1)
                 (if (member e1 s)
                     (and (explain a e e1)(possible e1 c)
                          (cwu c a)))))))
```

That is, agent a generates a set s of explanations for e if and only if a thinks of s and every member of s is a possible explanation for e, given a's current world understanding c.

To assess the candidate explanations is to determine among various pairs of candidate explanations which ones are better. The assessing is the aggregate of all these comparisons.

```
(forall (e0 a s e)                                           (25.15)
    (iff (assessExplanations' e0 a s e)
        (forall (e2)
            (if (member e2 e0)
                (exists (e3 e4 e5 e6)
                    (and (changeTo' e2 e3)(believe' e3 a e4)
                         (betterExplanationFor' e4 e5 e6 e a)))))))
```

To adopt e1 as an explanation for e is to come to believe that e1 is the cause of e.

```
(forall (a e1 e)                                              (25.16)
   (iff (adoptExplanation a e1 e)
        (exists (e2 e3)
           (and (changeTo e2)(believe' e2 a e3)
                (cause' e3 e1 e)))))
```

The most common reason for an agent to adopt an explanation is that it is the best explanation among those the agent was able to generate. This was encoded in Axiom (25.10).

To reject an explanation e1 for e is to change into a state where one believes that e1 does not cause e.

```
(forall (a e1 e)                                              (25.17)
   (iff (rejectExplanation a e1 e)
        (exists (e2 e3 e4)
           (and (changeTo e2)(believe' e2 a e3)(not' e3 e4)
                (cause' e4 e1 e)))))
```

Defeasibly, but not necessarily, adopting one explanation causes an agent to reject other explanations.

```
(forall (a e s e1 e2 e3)                                      (25.18)
   (if (and (agent a)(generateExplanations a e s)
            (adoptExplanation' e3 a e1 e)(member e1 s)
            (member e2 s)(nequal e2 e1)(etc))
       (exists (e4)
          (and (rejectExplanation' e4 a e2 e)(cause e3 e4)))))
```

25.3 EXPLANATION FAILURES

The notions of trying, success, and failure are explicated in Chapter 28 on Goals. Suffice it to say here that to try to do something is for one to have it as a goal and for that to cause one to carry out some actions in a causal complex that would lead to it. One succeeds when the goal is achieved, and one fails when it is not.

An explanation failure is a failure to explain.

```
(forall (a e)                                                 (25.19)
   (iff (explanationFailure a e)
        (forall (e1 e2)
           (if (and (try a e2)(explain' e2 a e e1))
               (fail a e2)))))
```

That is, a's failure to explain e occurs exactly when every explanation a tries for e fails.

Now we look at the points in the process of explanation at which the attempt to explain may fail. There cannot be a failure to adopt a goal to explain something, because failure implies the attempt, which implies the goal.

If the agent adopts the goal to explain something but is unable to generate any possible candidate explanations, there is an explanation failure.

```
(forall (a e s)                                          (25.20)
    (if (and (adoptGoalToExplain a e)
             (generateExplanations a e s)(null s))
        (explanationFailure a e)))
```

If the agent adopts the goal to explain something and generates possible candidates, but does not assess them, there is an explanation failure.

```
(forall (a e s)                                          (25.21)
    (if (and (adoptGoalToExplain a e)
             (generateExplanations a e s)
             (not (assessExplanations a s e)))
        (explanationFailure a e)))
```

If the agent adopts the goal to explain something, generates possible candidates, and assesses them, but does not adopt an explanation as a result, there is an explanation failure.

```
(forall (a e s)                                          (25.22)
    (if (and (adoptGoalToExplain a e)
             (generateExplanations a e s)
             (assessExplanations a s e)
             (not (adoptExplanation a e1 e)))
        (explanationFailure a e)))
```

PREDICATES INTRODUCED IN THIS CHAPTER

(mystery e a)
Eventuality e is an unexplained mystery for agent a.

(betterExplanationFor e1 e2 e a)
Eventuality e1 is a better explanation for e than e2 is, for agent a.

(bestExplanationFor e1 e a s)
Eventuality e1 is the best explanation for e out of the set s of possible explanations, for agent a.

(adoptGoalToExplain a e)
Agent a adopts the goal of explaining e.

(generateExplanations a e s)
Agent a generates a set s of candidate explanations for eventuality e.

(assessExplanations a s e)
Agent a assesses the set s of candidate explanations for eventuality e.

(adoptExplanation a e1 e)
Agent a adopts e1 as an explanation for e.

(rejectExplanation a e1 e)
Agent a rejects e1 as an explanation for eventuality e.

(explanationFailure a e)
Agent a tries but fails to explain eventuality e.

The predicates goal, try, and fail are explicated in Chapter 28.

(goal e a)
  Eventuality e is a goal of agent a's.

(try a e)
  Agent a tries to achieve e.

(fail a e)
  Agent a fails to achieve e.

26

Managing Expectations

In the chapter on Envisioning, we defined an "envisioned causal system" (ecs) as a set s of eventualities entertained by an agent a with a particular set of causal connections among the eventualities. We defined the "current world understanding" (cwu) to be the ecs s that an agent a believes to be currently the case at time t0 – (cwu0 s a t0). We defined what it is for two causal systems to be contiguous – (contigCS s1 s2). In terms of that, we defined an "envisioned causal system sequence" (ecsSeq) to be a sequence of contiguous ecs's. This provides us with the background we need to formalize expectations and their justifications.

To expect eventuality e to happen or hold at some time t1 in the future generally results from having an envisioned causal system sequence, one of whose elements is the current world understanding and one of whose downstream elements contains the eventuality e. By "downstream" we mean that the time t1 of e must be after the "Now" time t0 that anchors the expectation. That is, e occurs in the future with respect to the expectation. However, we first define expectation only in terms of belief and then use envisioned causal systems to justify the expectation.

```
(forall (e0 a e t1 t0)                                          (26.1)
    (iff (expect' e0 a e t1 t0)
         (exists (e1 e2)
            (and (atTime' e1 e t1)(believe' e2 a e1)
                 (atTime e2 t0)(before t0 t1)(gen e2 e0)))))
```

The expression (expect' e0 a e t1 t0) says that e0 is the eventuality of agent a, at time t0, expecting that e will happen or hold at time t1. The belief e2 that e will happen or hold at t1 constitutes the expectation.

We could also define a graded belief version of this notion, where the graded expectation is equal to the graded belief.

It is possible to fail to believe some event will occur at some future time. We can define "unexpect" to mean this.

```
(forall (a e t1 t0)                                            (26.2)
    (iff (unexpect a e t1 t0)
         (exists (e1 e2)
            (and (atTime' e1 e t1)(believe' e2 a e1)
                 (not (atTime e2 t0))))))
```

When an event is expected, it is justified if there is an envisioned causal system that supports it, and that ecs is its justification.

```
(forall (s a e t1 t0)                                              (26.3)
    (iff (expectationJustification s a e t1 t0)
         (exists (e0 e1 s1 e2)
             (and (expect' e0 a e t1 t0)(cwu0' e1 s a t0)
                  (eventualitiesOf s1 s)(atTime' e2 e t1)
                  (member e2 s1)(cause e1 e0)))))
```

The expression (expectationJustification s a e t1 t0) says that agent a's current world understanding s at time t0 includes e being true at time t1. The fact e1 that s is the current world understanding causes the expectation e0.

To add a justified expectation e is to extend an envisioned causal system to the point where e is predicted.

```
(forall (a e t1)                                                  (26.4)
    (iff (addExpectation a e t1 t0)
         (exists (s0 s1 e0 e1 t2)
             (and (ecs' e0 s0 a)(ecs' e1 s1 a)
                  (not (expectationJustification s0 a e t1 t2))
                  (expectationJustification s1 a e t1 t0)
                  (change e0 e1)))))
```

To remove a justified expectation is just the opposite.

```
(forall (a e t1)                                                  (26.5)
    (iff (removeExpectation a e t1 t0)
         (exists (s0 s1 e0 e1 t2)
             (and (ecs' e0 s0 a)(ecs' e1 s1 a)
                  (expectationJustification s0 a e t1 t2)
                  (not (expectationJustification s1 a e t1 t0))
                  (change e0 e1)))))
```

People have an ability to add and remove expectations.

```
(forall (a)                                                      (26.6)
    (if (person a)
        (exists (e0 c e t1 t0)
            (and (able a e0 c)(addExpectation' e0 a e t1 t0)))))
```

```
(forall (a)                                                      (26.7)
    (if (person a)
        (exists (e0 c e t1 t0)
            (and (able a e0 c)(removeExpectation' e0 a e t1 t0)))))
```

Our abilities depend on a number of factors. Expertise is one. Some people are better at predicting the stock market or elections, because of their expertise or experience. They have more knowledge of the domain and its probabilities. Some people have a better general ability at prediction than others because they are better at projecting further forward and/or are better at calling to mind all the relevant factors.

When the future time of an expectation arrives, the expectation is either confirmed or violated.

$$(\text{forall } (a \ e \ t1) \tag{26.8}$$
$$\quad (\text{iff } (\text{expectationConfirmation } a \ e \ t1)$$
$$\qquad (\text{exists } (t0)$$
$$\qquad\quad (\text{and } (\text{expect } a \ e \ t1 \ t0)(\text{atTime } e \ t1)))))$$

$$(\text{forall } (a \ e \ t1) \tag{26.9}$$
$$\quad (\text{iff } (\text{expectationViolation } a \ e \ t1)$$
$$\qquad (\text{exists } (t0)$$
$$\qquad\quad (\text{and } (\text{expect } a \ e \ t1 \ t0)(\text{not } (\text{atTime } e \ t1))))))$$

Expectation violation differs from out-of-the-blue surprises. If someone is walking along a sidewalk and suddenly a man tackles him, this is a surprise, but it is not an expectation violation if he had no expectations one way or the other about whether such an event would happen. An expectation violation happens when someone predicts one outcome in a causal system and another outcome occurs.

PREDICATES INTRODUCED IN THIS CHAPTER

(expect a e t1 t0)
  Agent a at time t0 expects e to happen at time t1.

(unexpect a e t1 t0)
  Agent a at time t0 does not expect e to happen at time t1.

(expectationJustification s a e t1 t0)
  Envisioned causal system s is a justification at time t0 for agent a for expecting e to happen at time t1.

(addExpectation a e t1 t0)
  Agent a at time t0 adds an expectation that e will happen at time t1.

(removeExpectation a e t1 t0)
  Agent a at time t0 removes an expectation that e will happen at time t1.

(expectationConfirmation a e t1)
  Agent a's expectation that e will happen at time t1 is confirmed.

(expectationViolation a e t1)
  Agent a's expectation that e will happen at time t1 is disconfirmed.

27

Other-Agent Reasoning

People have the ability to reason about the mental state of other people. It presents no new difficulties for us to represent this, because mental events are just a particular kind of event and our notion of causality covers causal relations between mental events and other events. We have treated reasoning as envisioning within a causal system. Thus we can define what it is to reason about someone's mental state in terms of this.

```
(forall (a b e)                                               (27.1)
    (iff (envisionMentalState a b e)
         (exists (s s1 x)
             (and (ecs s a)(thinkOf' e b x)(eventualitiesOf s1 s)
                  (member e s1)))))
```

That is, a envisions b's mental state e if a envisions a causal system s, and if e is b's thinking of something, x, and e is a member of s's set of eventualities.

People are defeasibly able to perform this action.

```
(forall (a b e)                                               (27.2)
    (if (and (person a)(person b)(etc))
        (exists (e1 c)
            (and (able a e1 c)(envisionMentalState' e1 a b e)))))
```

Here, c is the set of implicit constraints the ability is with respect to.

Other-agent reasoning is envisioning the mental state of someone other than the envisioning agent.

```
(forall (a b e)                                               (27.3)
    (iff (otherAgentReason a b e)
         (and (nequal a b)(envisionMentalState a b e))))
```

People sometimes fail to envision the mental state of other people.

```
(forall (a b e)                                              (27.4)
   (iff (otherAgentReasonFail a b e)
        (exists (e1)
           (and (fail a e1)(otherAgentReason' e1 a b e)))))
```

The predicate fail is explicated in Chapter 28 on Goals.

Introspection happens when one envisions one's own mental states:

```
(forall (a e)                                               (27.5)
   (iff (introspect a e)(envisionMentalState a a e)))
```

People have a "cognaesthetic sense;" that is, they have partial observation or perception of their own thought processes. This follows from Axiom (27.2).

Introspection failure happens when an agent fails to introspect:

```
(forall (a b e)                                             (27.6)
   (iff (introspectFail a e)
        (exists (e1)
           (and (fail a e1)(introspect' e1 a e)))))
```

People have models of how people in general think. That is, one agent a has a belief in a causal system, some eventualities of which involve another agent b's thinking of something.

```
(forall (a b)                                               (27.7)
   (if (and (person a)(person b))
       (exists (s s1 e x)
          (and (causalSystem s)(eventualitiesOf s1 s)(member e s1)
               (thinkOf' e b x)(believe a s)))))
```

More specifically, people have models of how members of certain groups think.

```
(forall (a b)                                               (27.8)
   (if (person a)
       (exists (g)
          (forall (b)
             (if (member b g)
                 (exists (s s1 e x)
                    (and (causalSystem s)(eventualitiesOf s1 s)
                         (member e s1)(thinkOf' e b x)
                         (believe a s)))))))))
```

People can take cognitive advice. This is an agent's adopting a belief in a causal system some of whose eventualities are mental acts by the agent.

PREDICATES INTRODUCED IN THIS CHAPTER

(envisionMentalState a b e)
   Agent a envisions a causal system of which a mental event e by b is part.

(otherAgentReason a b e)
   Agent a envisions a mental state e by some other agent b.

(otherAgentReasonFail a b e)
  Agent a fails to envision a mental state e by another agent b.

(introspect a e)
  Agent a envisions a's own mental state e.

(introspectFail a e)
  Agent a fails to envision a's own mental state e.

The predicate fail is explicated in Chapter 28 on Goals.

(fail a e)
  Agent a fails to achieve e.

28

Goals

28.1 GOALS, SUBGOALS, AND PLANS

Human beings are intentional agents. We have goals, we develop plans for achieving these goals, and we execute the plans. We monitor the executions to see if things are turning out the way we anticipated, and when they don't, we modify our plans and execute the new plans. A theory of goals and planning can be applied not just to people but also to other entities that can be conceived of as agents, such as organizations and complex artifacts. In fact, it is a not uncommon cognitive move among people to attribute agency even to natural phenomena such as volcanos and hurricanes. Anything that seems to exploit and manipulate the causal structure of the world as a means toward some end can be viewed as a planning mechanism.

The key concept in modeling intentional behavior is that of an agent a having some eventuality type e as a goal.

```
(forall (e a)                                          (28.1)
    (if (goal e a)(and (eventuality e)(agent a))))
```

The expression (goal e a) says that eventuality e is a goal of agent a. Normally, e will be an eventuality type that can be satisfied by any number of specific eventuality tokens, but it is entirely possible in principle for an agent to have an eventuality token as a goal, where there is only one satisfactory way for things to work out. We won't belabor the distinction here.

Agents know facts about what causes or enables what in the world, that is, facts of the form

```
(forall (e1 x)                                         (28.2)
    (if (p' e1 x)
        (exists (e2)(and (q' e2 x)(cause e1 e2)))))

(forall (e1 x)                                         (28.3)
    (if (p' e1 x)
        (exists (e2)(and (q' e2 x)(enable e1 e2)))))
```

The chapter contains revisions of material published previously in Hobbs and Gordon (2010, 2014).

That is, if e1 is the eventuality of p being true of some entities x, then there is an eventuality e2 that is the eventuality of q being true of x and e1 causes or enables e2. Or stated in a less roundabout way, p causes or enables q.

The agent uses these rules to plan to achieve goals, and also uses them to infer the goals and plans of other agents. A plan is an agent's way of manipulating the causal properties of the world to achieve goals, and these axioms express the causal properties of the world.

We will work step by step toward a characterization of the planning process. The first version of the axiom we need says that if agent a has a goal e2 and e1 causes e2, then a will also have e1 as a goal.

```
(forall (a e1 e2)                                          (28.4)
    (if (and (goal e2 a)(cause e1 e2))(goal e1 a)))
```

This is not a bad rule, and certainly is defeasibly true, but it is of course necessary for the agent to actually believe in the causality. Moreover, if the agent believes a causal relation that does not hold, e1 may nevertheless be adopted as a goal. The causal relation needn't be true.

```
(forall (a e0 e1 e2)                                        (28.5)
    (if   (and (goal e2 a)(cause' e0 e1 e2)(believe a e0))
          (goal e1 a)))
```

We can say furthermore that the very fact that a has goal e2 causes a to have goal e1. We do this by reifying the eventuality g2 that e2 is a goal of a's, and similarly g1. (The e's in this axiom are the eventualities of having something; the g's are the eventualities of wanting it.)

```
(forall (a e0 e1 e2 g2)                                     (28.6)
    (if (and (goal' g2 e2 a)(cause' e0 e1 e2)(believe a e0))
        (exists (g1)(and (goal' g1 e1 a)(cause g2 g1)))))
```

That is, if agent a wants e2 and believes e1 causes e2, that wanting will cause a to want e1. (The belief is also in g1's causal complex, but that would not normally be thought of as the cause.)

Note that while the antecedent and the consequent no longer assert the real existence of having the goal (i.e., g2 and g1), if we know that g2 really exists, then the real existence of g1 follows from the properties of cause.

Note also that the predicate goal reverses causality. For example, because flipping a light switch causes a light to go on, having the goal of the light being on causes one to want to flip the switch.

The eventuality e1 is a subgoal of e2, and we can encode this in the axiom as well.

```
(forall (a e0 e1 e2 g2)                                     (28.7)
    (if (and (goal' g2 e2 a)(cause' e0 e1 e2)(believe a e0))
        (exists (g1)
            (and (goal' g1 e1 a)(cause g2 g1)(subgoal e1 e2)))))
```

Finally, this axiom is not always true. There may be many ways to cause the goal condition to come about, and the mystery of the agent's free choice intervenes. The axiom is only defeasible. We can represent this by means of an "et cetera" proposition in the antecedent.

```
(forall (a e0 e1 e2 g2)                                    (28.8)
    (if (and (goal' g2 e2 a)(cause' e0 e1 e2)(believe a e0)(etc))
        (exists (g1)
            (and (goal' g1 e1 a)(cause g2 g1)(subgoal e1 e2)))))
```

That is, if agent a has a goal e2 (where g2 is the eventuality of wanting e2) and a believes e1 causes e2, then defeasibly this wanting e2 will cause a to want e1 as a subgoal of e2 (where g1 is the eventuality of wanting e1).

A similar succession of axioms could be written for enablement.

```
(forall (a e1 e2)                                          (28.9)
    (if (and (goal e2 a)(enable e1 e2))(goal e1 a)))
```

```
(forall (a e0 e1 e2)                                       (28.10)
    (if  (and (goal e2 a)(enable' e0 e1 e2)(believe a e0))
        (goal e1 a)))
```

```
(forall (a e0 e1 e2 g2)                                    (28.11)
    (if (and (goal' g2 e2 a)(enable' e0 e1 e2)(believe a e0))
        (exists (g1)(and (goal' g1 e1 a)(cause g2 g1)))))
```

```
(forall (a e0 e1 e2 g2)                                    (28.12)
    (if (and (goal' g2 e2 a)(enable' e0 e1 e2)(believe a e0))
        (exists (g1)
            (and (goal' g1 e1 a)(cause g2 g1)(subgoal e1 e2)))))
```

The last axiom says that if g2 is a's having a goal e2 and a believes that e1 enables e2, then there will be a g1 that is a's having a goal e1, e1 will be a subgoal of e2, and a's having goal e2 causes a to have goal e1.

We don't need to introduce defeasibility into the axiom for enablement because all the enabling conditions need to be satisfied for a goal to be achieved, whereas only one of the causes needs to be true.

In the STRIPS terminology of Fikes and Nilsson (1971), the enabling conditions are the prerequisites of the plan operator, and the cause is the body.

The subgoal relation is a relation between two goals, and implies the agent's belief that the subgoal is in a causal complex for the goal.

```
(forall (e1 e2)                                            (28.13)
    (if (subgoal e1 e2)
        (exists (a e3 e4 e5 s)
            (and (goal e2 a)(goal e1 a)
                (causalComplex' e3 s e2)(member' e4 e1 s)
                (and' e5 e3 e4)(believe a e5)))))
```

In lines 5 and 6, e3 is the proposition that s is a causal complex for e2, e4 is the proposition that e1 is a member of s, e5 is the conjunction of these two propositions, and that's what agent a believes.

The subgoal relation is transitive.

```
(forall (e1 e2 e3 a)                                    (28.14)
   (if (and (subgoal e1 e2)(subgoal e2 e3))
       (subgoal e1 e3)))
```

It will be useful below to state that if one believes he or she has a goal, then defeasibly he or she really does have the goal. We are usually pretty reliable about knowing what we want.

```
(forall (e e1 a)                                        (28.15)
   (if (and (goal' e e1 a)(believe a e)(etc))
       (Rexist e)))
```

However, it is possible for an agent to have a goal without knowing it.

28.2 THE CONTENT OF GOALS

There are a number of types of goals, characterized by their content and the agents who have them, that figure large in strategies, and in this section we define a number of these classifications to show that we have built up machinery adequate for describing them.

Any eventuality can be a goal. A particularly important kind of goal is a goal of knowing something, because most actions have knowledge prerequisites.

```
(forall (e a)                                           (28.16)
   (iff (knowledgeGoal e a)
        (exists (e1) (and (goal e1 a)(know' e1 a e)))))
```

Similarly, you can have a goal to envision a situation in a certain manner. You can have a goal to plan in a certain manner. You can have a goal to execute a plan in a certain manner.

Several categories of goal involve the interaction of goals and time. A preservation goal is a goal that some state that is true now remain true in the future, over some time period.

```
(forall (e a t)                                         (28.17)
   (iff (preservationGoal e a t)
        (exists (e1 t1)
           (and (goal e1 a)(during' e1 e t)
                (begins t1 t)(atTime e t1)))))
```

The expression (preservationGoal e a t) says that eventuality e is a goal that holds at the beginning (t1) of time interval t and that agent a wants to be true throughout the interval.

It is possible for a preservation goal to be violated.

```
(forall (e a t)                                         (28.18)
   (iff (preservationGoalViolation e a t)
        (exists (e1 t1)
           (and (preservationGoal e a t)(not' e1 e)(atTime e1 t1)
                (insideTime t1 t)))))
```

A goal can be persistent in that it remains a goal even after it is achieved. An agent's desire to be rich is like this; once people become rich, normally they want that state to be preserved. A shell collector has a goal of finding beautiful shells, and this will persist even after it has been satisfied once.

```
(forall (e a t)                                                    (28.19)
    (iff (persistentGoal e a t)
         (exists (e1)
             (and (goal' e1 e a)(during e1 t)))))
```

Here the condition e1 is e's being a goal of agent a, and it holds all through time interval t, regardless of whether e itself holds or does not hold.

Some goals are envisioned to be desired only at some point in the future. For example, you might not want to retire right now, but you believe or sometimes entertain the idea that someday you will want to retire.

```
(forall (e a t1 t2)                                                (28.20)
    (iff (envisionedFutureGoal e a t1 t2)
         (exists (e1 e2 e3)
             (and (thinkOf' e1 a e3)(atTime' e3 e2 t2)(goal' e2 e a)
                  (atTime e1 t1)(before t1 t2)))))
```

The expression (envisionedFutureGoal e a t1 t2) says that e is a goal that agent a imagines at time t1 having at some subsequent time t2. In line 4 of this definition, e1 is a's thinking (at time t1) that a will have the goal at time t2.

Sometimes goals are achieved. A goal that has been achieved is an eventuality that was once a goal and now really exists. Furthermore, its once having been a goal should have played a causal role in its current real existence.

```
(forall (e a t1 t2)                                                (28.21)
    (iff (achievedGoal e a t1 t2)
         (exists (e1 e2 e3)
             (and (goal' e1 e a)(atTime e1 t1)
                  (instance e3 e)(atTime' e2 e3 t2)
                  (before t1 t2)(cause e1 e2)))))
```

The expression (achievedGoal e a t1 t2) says that e is a goal that a had at time t1 and it actually holds at time t2, in part because it was a goal.

Sometimes goals are not achieved.

```
(forall (e a t1 t2)                                                (28.22)
    (iff (unachievedGoal e a t1 t2)
         (exists (e1 e2)
             (and (atTime' e2 e t2)(goal' e1 e2 a)
                  (atTime e1 t1)(before t1 t2)
                  (not (exists (e3)
                           (and (instance e3 e)
                                (atTime e3 t2)))))))))
```

The expression (unachievedGoal e a t1 t2) says that eventuality e was a goal of a's at time t1 and it (or an instance of it) does not really exist at time t2.

Sometimes goals are never achieved.

```
(forall (e a t1)                                                    (28.23)
    (iff (neverAchievedGoal e a t1)
         (forall (t2)
             (if (before t1 t2)(unachievedGoal e a t1 t2)))))
```

The expression (neverAchievedGoal e a t1) says that eventuality e that agent a had as a goal at time t1 has never subsequently happened.

Goals can be classified with respect to each other. The relation subgoal, for example, does this. It is also possible for goals to conflict with each other.

```
(forall (e1 e2 a)                                                  (28.24)
    (iff (conflictingGoals e1 e2 a)
         (and (goal e1 a)(goal e2 a)
              (forall (e3 t)
                  (if (and (instance e3 e1)(atTime e3 t))
                      (exists (e4)
                          (and (not' e4 e2)(atTime e4 t)))))))))
```

That is, both e1 and e2 are goals of a's, but if an instance of one holds at some time t, then the negation of the other holds at time t as well.

A goal can be auxiliary to another goal, in the sense that the agent wants both goals, but in case of conflict between the goals, the auxiliary goal is the one that is abandoned.

```
(forall (e1 e2 a)                                                  (28.25)
    (iff (auxiliaryGoal e1 e2 a)
         (exists (e0 e3 e4 e5 e6 e7)
             (and (goal' e0 e1 a)(goal e2 a)
                  (if (and (changeTo' e3 e4)(believe' e4 a e5)
                           (conflictingGoals' e5 e1 e2 a))
                      (and (cause e3 e6)(changeFrom' e6 e0)))))))
```

Line 4 says that e2 is a goal of a's and labels as e0 the eventuality of e1 being a goal of a's. Lines 5–7 say that if a comes to believe e1 and e2 are in conflict, then a will cease to have e1 as a goal, as a result of believing this conflict.

28.3 GOALS AND MULTIPLE AGENTS

Individual persons are not the only kind of intentional agent. Sufficiently complex devices of various sorts can be viewed as intelligent agents. So can collectives of agents, whether collectives entirely of people, or assemblages of people and devices. These collectives can have goals. For example, General Motors has the goal of selling cars. They can devise plans for achieving goals. General Motors' plan involves manufacturing and marketing cars. These plans must bottom out in the actions of individual persons or devices, or in things that will be true at the appropriate time anyway.

For example, we can have a plan to get your car started by pushing it a short distance to the top of a hill and then letting it pick up speed on the downhill side until it is fast enough that you can pop the clutch. This plan bottoms out in my individual action of pushing on the back of the car and your individual action of pushing on the frame of the open left door. Of course these actions have to be synchronized, but these are properties of the individual actions. The plan also bottoms out in the event of the car rolling down the hill from the top. This is something that will happen anyway at the appropriate time, and doesn't have to be carried out by any member of the collective.

A shared or collaborative goal is a goal in which the agent having the goal is a collective. Moreover, the members of the collective mutually believe the collective has the goal.

$$
\begin{aligned}
&\text{(forall (e s e1)} \hspace{6.5cm} \text{(28.26)}\\
&\quad \text{(iff (sharedGoal' e e1 s)}\\
&\qquad \text{(exists (e0)}\\
&\qquad\quad \text{(and (goal' e0 e1 s)(mb s e0)(gen e0 e)}\\
&\qquad\qquad \text{(forall (x)(if (member x s)(agent x)))))))))}
\end{aligned}
$$

Because mutual belief implies belief and because if you believe you have a goal then you do really do have the goal, it follows that the individual members of s have e1 as a goal.

$$
\begin{aligned}
&\text{(forall (x s e1)} \hspace{6.5cm} \text{(28.27)}\\
&\quad \text{(if (and (sharedGoal e1 s)(member x s))}\\
&\qquad \text{(goal e1 x)))}
\end{aligned}
$$

Note that the e1 is the same in the antecedent and the consequent, and thus if e1 is that some property be true of the collective, that will be the individual's goal as well – that the collective have that property.

The goals of different agents can conflict. One way is for the goals to be competitive, in the sense that more than one agent has the goal of the same property being true of himself.

$$
\begin{aligned}
&\text{(forall (e1 e2 a1 a2)} \hspace{5.5cm} \text{(28.28)}\\
&\quad \text{(iff (competitiveGoals e1 e2 a1 a2)}\\
&\qquad \text{(exists (e3)}\\
&\qquad\quad \text{(and (subst a1 e1 a2 e2)(goal e1 a1)(goal e2 a2)}\\
&\qquad\qquad \text{(and' e3 e1 e2)}\\
&\qquad\qquad \text{(not (exists (e4 t)}\\
&\qquad\qquad\qquad \text{(and (instance e4 e3)}\\
&\qquad\qquad\qquad\quad \text{(atTime e4 t)))))))))}
\end{aligned}
$$

That is, a1 plays the same role in e1 as a2 plays in e2 (subst), a1 has e1 as a goal, a2 has e2 as a goal, and they can't both hold at once. (More properly, there can't be an instance of both holding at once.) A race is an example of this; each agent wants the property of "wins the race" to be true of himself or herself.

In competitive goals, the goals are similar and it is a property of the situation that they are mutually exclusive. In adversarial goals, the goals are in direct conflict.

One agent wants a goal and the other agent wants its negation. An attack and the self-defensive response are like this.

```
(forall (a1 a2 e1)                                              (28.29)
    (iff (adversarialGoals e1 a1 a2)
        (exists (e2)
            (and (goal e1 a1)(goal e2 a2)(not' e2 e1)))))
```

An agent may or may not know the goals of others.

28.4 TRYING, SUCCEEDING, AND FAILING

When we try to bring about some goal, we devise at least a partial plan to achieve it, including subgoals of the original goal which are actions on our part, and we execute some of those subgoals. Moreover, our executing those actions is a direct result of our having those actions as subgoals. We can take this as a definition of "trying."

```
(forall (e a e1)                                               (28.30)
    (iff (try' e a e1)
        (exists (e0 e2 e3 e4)
            (and (goal e1 a)(subgoal' e3 e2 e1)(instance e4 e2)
                (agentOf a e4)(cause e3 e4)(gen e4 e)))))
```

In this definition, e is the eventuality of an agent a trying to do e1. The eventuality (or eventuality type) e1 is a goal of a's; it's what a tries to do. The eventuality type e2 is a subgoal of e1, and a is the agent in action e4 which is an instance of e2. The expression (cause e3 e4) says that a's having the subgoal e2 causes a to actually do e4. The expression (gen e4 e) says that the actual doing (e4) constitutes the trying (e). That is, a tries to do e1 exactly when a executes a subgoal e2 of e1 precisely because it is a subgoal.

For example, suppose you want to pass a course. An important subgoal would be to sudy for the final. If you study for the final precisely because it will help you pass the course, then you are trying to pass the course.

It follows that if you try to do something e1, then you perform some action or actions that you believe are causally involved in effecting an instance of e1.

```
(forall (a e1)                                                 (28.31)
    (if (try a e1)
        (exists (e2 e3 e4)
            (and (instance e3 e1)(causallyInvolved' e4 e2 e3)
                (believe a e4)(agentOf a e2)))))
```

This is not sufficient as a definition of trying. The causal role of having e2 as a subgoal is necessary in the definition of try. Suppose Pat wants to meet Chris. One way for that to happen is for them to run into each other someday. Now Pat is driving to the grocery store where Chris, unbeknownst to Pat, is currently shopping. Pat's driving to the grocery store is an element of a causal complex leading to the two of them meeting. But we wouldn't say that Pat's driving to the grocery store constitutes an attempt to meet Chris. That wasn't his intent in driving.

Note that this explication of trying allows for an agent to try to achieve conflicting goals. The student who studies for a final and then goes out drinking the whole night before the final may be doing just that.

To succeed at some goal is to try to do it and to have that trying cause the goal to actually occur.

```
(forall (e a e1)                                              (28.32)
    (iff (succeed' e a e1)
        (exists (e2 e3)
            (and (try' e2 a e1)(instance e3 e1)
                (cause e2 e3)(gen e3 e)))))
```

Here, e2 is the attempt, e1 is ultimate goal, e3 is the specific instance of e1 that occurs, and e is the success in achieving the goal. The expression (gen e3 e) says that the instance e3 constitutes the event e of succeeding.

Succeeding implies trying. The converse, sadly, is not true.

To fail at some goal is to try to do it and for it not to actually occur.

```
(forall (a e1)                                               (28.33)
    (iff (fail a e1)
        (and (try a e1)
            (not (exists (e2)
                (and (instance e2 e1)(Rexist e2)))))))
```

There is space between succeeding and failing. One can try to achieve something and that something can come about but not because of one's efforts. In that case, the agent has lucked out, rather than having succeeded. So a student who studied for the final but nevertheless got a 0 on it, but passed the course because the professor gave everyone an A as a political protest, wouldn't be said to have succeeded at passing the course.

28.5 FUNCTIONALITY

Complex artifacts are generally constructed for some purpose. Some real or hypothetical agent has a goal in mind, and the artifact achieves that goal. Cars, for example, have at least the purpose of moving us from place to place. The structure of complex artifacts typically reflects a plan to achieve the goal, where the various components are involved in some subgoal. For example, the steering wheel of a car is involved in the subgoal of having the car go in particular directions. We will call such a subgoal the functionality of the component. Organizations and their components can be analyzed similarly.

In fact natural objects can too, if we associate a hypothetical agent having as a goal the normal behavior the natural object tends to engage in. We can stipulate that the "goal" associated with a tree is to grow and reproduce, and we can analyze the structure of the tree as an instantiation of a plan to achieve that goal. We can then talk about the function of the various parts of the tree. We can even view volcanos, for example, as composite entities that have the associated "goal" of erupting, and talk about the functions of its parts to this end.

In general, almost any composite entity can be associated with a goal by some hypothetical agent, and where components are causally involved with the behavior of the whole, we can view the relation between an action by the component and the behavior of the whole as a subgoal relation. We can then define the functionality of the component as that subgoal relation. (We use the elevated term "functionality" rather than "function" because we have already used the latter to refer to mathematical functions.)

Plans to achieve goals are just a way of exploiting the causal structure of the world to achieve some end, so "goal talk" can be imported into any domain where the manipulation of causal structure is involved.

A composite entity that goes through changes can be viewed as having as an associated goal some element or subset of those changes. We will define that "goal" as the functionality of the whole. We call this predicate functionality0 because it is absolute functionality, not the functionality of a component relative to the behavior of the whole.

```
(forall (x e)                                                    (28.34)
    (if (and (compositeEntity x)(changeIn' e x))
        (iff (functionality0 e x)
            (exists (e2 e3 a)
                (and (goal' e2 e a)(agent' e3 a)(imply e3 e2))))))
```

Line 2 says that x is a composite entity and e is one of x's behaviors. Under these conditions, e is a functionality of x if and only if there is some possible agent a whose existence would imply that e is a goal of a's. The roundabout formulation in line 5 is a way of allowing hypothetical agents. In any positive modality in which a exists, a will have goal e.

If a component has some property or engages in some behavior that is in a causal complex for the functionality of the composite entity as a whole, we can say that property or behavior is the functionality of the component with respect to the functionality0 of the whole.

```
(forall (e1 y e x)                                               (28.35)
    (iff (functionality e1 y e x)
        (exists (s)
            (and (functionality0 e x)(causalComplex s e)
                (member e1 s)(arg* y e1)(componentOf y x)))))
```

The expression (functionality e1 y e x) says that e1 is the functionality of y with respect to behavior e by composite entity x, of which y is a component. Because of the close connection between the subgoal relation and causal complexes expressed in Axiom (28.13), functionality can be viewed as a close analog of the subgoal relation.

A component is intact if it is able to fulfill its functionality. That is, there are no properties of the component that would cause the functionality not to occur.

```
(forall (x)                                                      (28.36)
    (iff (intact x)
        (forall (e1 y e)
            (if (functionality e1 y e x)
                (not (exists (e2 e3)
                        (and (arg* y e2)(not' e3 e1)
                            (cause e2 e3)))))))))
```

28.6 GOOD AND BAD

An eventuality is good for us if it contributes causally somehow to the achievement of one of our goals.

$$
\begin{array}{ll}
\text{(forall (e a)} & \text{(28.37)} \\
\quad \text{(iff (goodFor e a)} \\
\qquad \text{(exists (e1 s)} \\
\qquad\quad \text{(and (goal e1 a)(causalComplex s e1)(member e s)))))}
\end{array}
$$

An eventuality is bad for us if it contributes causally somehow to the nonachievement of one of our goals.

$$
\begin{array}{ll}
\text{(forall (e a)} & \text{(28.38)} \\
\quad \text{(iff (badFor e a)} \\
\qquad \text{(exists (e1 e2 s)} \\
\qquad\quad \text{(and (not' e2 e1)(goal e1 a)(causalComplex s e2)} \\
\qquad\qquad \text{(member e s)))))}
\end{array}
$$

There are of course great controversies around the issues of what is good for or bad for someone in various particular circumstances. The function of these axioms is to reset these disputes to debates about what goals one has or ought to have. As we will see in Chapter 29, this amounts to disputes about what it is for any particular individual "to thrive."

We will remain silent on the contentious issue of whether there are notions of absolute good and absolute bad – monadic predicates rather than dyadic predicates – independent of the agent or agents for whom the eventuality is good or bad. Most if not all moral precepts can be viewed as statements about what is good or bad for some group, and these can be stated in terms of the goodFor and badFor predicates.

28.7 VALUE, COST, AND IMPORTANCE

The concepts of value and cost, in modern society, are often, if not usually understood in terms of money. This has the advantage of turning what is inherently a partial ordering in the commonsense understanding into a total ordering, allowing any two things to be compared. We will not take that approach here. Instead we will try to characterize the more basic concepts of value and cost in terms of the partial ordering. Cost and value are scalar notions, and for all scalar notions we need to introduce a partial ordering relation – moreValuable and moreCostly. As with many commonsense concepts, we cannot define these relations precisely, but we can constrain their interpretations by means of axioms relating them to theories we have developed independently, in this case the theory of goals. Then we can define a valueScale and a costScale in terms of the partial ordering. The predicates valuable and costly identify the Hi region of the scale, the value of something is its location on the valueScale, and the cost of something is its place on the costScale. An interpretation of cost and value in terms of money will be one possible interpretation consistent with our axioms, but not the only one.

The key idea we develop here is that achieving a subgoal is not as valuable as achieving its supergoal, and sacrificing a subgoal is not as costly as sacrificing its supergoal. This is consistent with the monetary view of value and cost because generally money enables goals to be achieved, and more money means more goals can be achieved.

Importance is less often monetized, although winning $10,000 in the lottery is a more important event in your life than winning $10. But importance is closely related to value and cost. The more valuable something is, the more important its acquisition. The more costly a sacrifice, the more important. Value is a positive notion about what is gained; cost is a negative notion about what is lost. In a sense, importance is a neutral notion that generalizes over these two. Valuable acquisitions and costly sacrifices are both important.

Here we will first characterize these concepts for eventualities in terms of their effects on goals. Then we will extend the concepts to entities in general, as anything can have a value, a cost, and an importance.

A concept, entity or eventuality is more or less valuable, costly, or important to an agent depending it's relation to the agent's goals. Thus the three predicates have the agent as an argument. What is important to one agent may be of no consequence to another. Moreover, the entities being compared are distinct.

```
(forall (x1 x2 a)                                             (28.39)
    (if (moreValuable x1 x2 a)(and (nequal x1 x2)(agent a))))
```

```
(forall (x1 x2 a)                                             (28.40)
    (if (moreCostly x1 x2 a)(and (nequal x1 x2)(agent a))))
```

```
(forall (x1 x2 a)                                             (28.41)
    (if (moreImportant x1 x2 a)(and (nequal x1 x2)(agent a))))
```

The expression (moreValuable x1 x2 a) says that something x1 is more valuable than something else x2 to agent a. We place no constaints on the things x1 and x2 whose value is being compared. They can be anything. Similarly for the other two predicates.

Being partial orderings, the three relations are transitive.

```
(forall (x1 x2 x3 a)                                          (28.42)
    (if (and (moreValuable x1 x2 a)(moreValuable x2 x3 a))
        (moreValuable x1 x3 a)))
```

```
(forall (x1 x2 x3 a)                                          (28.43)
    (if (and (moreCostly x1 x2 a)(moreCostly x2 x3 a))
        (moreCostly x1 x3 a)))
```

```
(forall (x1 x2 x3 a)                                          (28.44)
    (if (and (moreImportant x1 x2 a)(moreImportant x2 x3 a))
        (moreImportant x1 x3 a)))
```

An agent proceeds through the world by continually developing, executing and modifying a plan to achieve the top-level goal "To Thrive." All of the agent's actions can be seen as subgoals in this plan; when the actions are dysfunctional, we can see them as part of a plan based on false beliefs about what will result in thriving. A plan can be thought of as a tree-like structure representing the subgoal relation. The higher a goal is in a plan, the more valuable, costly, and important it is, because of the greater amount of replanning that has to be done if the goal is not to be achieved. So the principal constraint we can place on the three scales is that they are consistent with the subgoal relation.

However, this is a bit tricky to specify because an eventuality can be a subgoal of a number of different higher-level goals in the same plan, and we do not want to say an eventuality is of little importance simply because one of its supergoals is of little importance. So we first need to define the notions of an "upper bound supergoal" and a "least upper bound supergoal." An eventuality e1 is an upper bound supergoal of e2 if every path from the top-level goal down to e2 passes through e1. Thus, every reason for doing e2 is in service of e1. Any supergoal e3 of e2's must either be e1, be a subgoal of e1, or if it is a supergoal of e1 then it is a supergoal of e2 only because it is a supergoal of e1. This last condition can be captured by stating that if we remove the subgoal relation between e1 and e2, we also remove the subgoal relation between e3 and e2.

It will be convenient to define the upper bound for a set of subgoals.

```
(forall (e1 s a)                                                    (28.45)
    (iff (ubSupergoal e1 s a)
        (and (agent a)(goal e1 a)(not (member e1 s))
            (forall (e2) (if (member e2 s)(subgoal e2 e1)))
            (forall (e2 e3)
                (if (and (member e2 s)(subgoal e2 e3))
                    (or (subgoal e3 e1)(equal e3 e1)
                        (exists (g1 g3)
                            (and (subgoal' g1 e2 e1)
                                (subgoal' g3 e2 e3)
                                (if (changeFrom g1)
                                    (changeFrom g3)))))))))))
```

The expression (ubSupergoal e1 s a) says that e1 is an upper bound supergoal of all the goals of agent a in set s. Lines 3–4 specify the conditions on the arguments of the predicate; e1 is not itself a member of s. The predicate holds if and only if any eventuality e3 which is a supergoal of a member e2 of s is either a subgoal of e1, or e1 itself, or is a supergoal of e2 only by virtue of being a supergoal of e1. In the last case, there are no paths from e3 down to e2 that don't go through e1.

A goal e1 is a least upper bound supergoal if it is an upper bound supergoal and a subgoal of all other upper bound supergoals.

```
(forall (e1 s a)                                                    (28.46)
    (iff (lubSupergoal e1 s a)
        (and (ubSupergoal e1 s a)
            (forall (e)
                (if (ubSupergoal e s a)
                    (or (equal e e1)(subgoal e1 e)))))))
```

Because every goal is ultimately in the service of the top-level goal "To Thrive," every set of goals has a least upper bound supergoal, except the top-level goal.

Now we can say that if eventuality e1 dominates eventuality e2 on every path in the agent's plan that includes e2, then e1 is more valuable, more costly, and more important than e2. Every reason for wanting e2 is in the service of e1.

```
(forall (s e1 e2 a)                                        (28.47)
    (if (and (singleton s e2) (lubSupergoal e1 s a))
        (moreValuable e1 e2 a)))
```

```
(forall (s e1 e2 a)                                        (28.48)
    (if (and (singleton s e2) (lubSupergoal e1 s a))
        (moreCostly e1 e2 a)))
```

```
(forall (s e1 e2 a)                                        (28.49)
    (if (and (singleton s e2) (lubSupergoal e1 s a))
        (moreImportant e1 e2 a)))
```

More generally, we can say that the least upper bound supergoal of a set of goals is more important than the whole set, as all the members of the set are in the service of the supergoal.

```
(forall (s e a)                                            (28.50)
    (if (lubSupergoal e s a) (moreValuable e s a)))
```

```
(forall (s e a)                                            (28.51)
    (if (lubSupergoal e s a) (moreCostly e s a)))
```

```
(forall (s e a)                                            (28.52)
    (if (lubSupergoal e s a) (moreImportant e s a)))
```

We can apply notions of value, cost, and importance not only to an agent's goals, but also to eventualities that affect those goals. For value, we need a predicate for positive goal relevance.

```
(forall (e a)                                              (28.53)
    (iff (posGoalRelevant e a)
        (exists (e1)
            (and (goal e1 a) (imply e e1)))))
```

That is, an eventuality e is positively goal-relevant to an agent a if its occurrence implies the satisfaction of some goal e1 of a's.

For cost, we need a predicate for negative goal relevance.

```
(forall (e a)                                              (28.54)
    (iff (negGoalRelevant e a)
        (exists (e1 e2)
            (and (goal e1 a) (not' e2 e1) (imply e e2)))))
```

That is, an eventuality e is negatively goal-relevant to an agent a if its occurrence implies the satisfaction of the negation e2 of some goal e1 of a's.

Importance doesn't care about polarity; if passing a course is important to you, so is not passing the course. Thus, we define an eventuality as "goal-relevant" to an agent if its existence implies the existence or nonexistence of one of the agent's goals.

```
(forall (e a)                                                    (28.55)
    (iff (goalRelevant e a)
         (or (posGoalRelevant e a)(negGoalRelevant e a))))
```

The "goal consequences" of an eventuality are those goals of the agent's whose existence or nonexistence is implied by the eventuality. Again we will define a positive version, a negative version, and a neutral version.

```
(forall (s e a)                                                  (28.56)
    (iff (posGoalConsequences s e a)
         (forall (e1)
             (iff (member e1 s)
                  (and (goal e1 a)(imply e e1))))))
```

That is, the positive goal consequences of an eventuality are those goals that are positively impacted by e.

```
(forall (s e a)                                                  (28.57)
    (iff (negGoalConsequences s e a)
         (forall (e1)
             (iff (member e1 s)
                  (and (goal e1 a)
                       (exists (e2) (not' e2 e1)(imply e e2)))))))
```

```
(forall (s e a)                                                  (28.58)
    (iff (goalConsequences s e a)
         (exists (s1 s2)
             (and (posGoalConsequences s1 e a)
                  (negGoalConsequences s2 e a)
                  (union s s1 s2)))))
```

Then we can say the value, cost, and importance of an eventuality depend on the value, cost, and importance of its goal consequences. The first of the following three pairs of axioms says that if something x is more valuable, costly, or important than the goal consequences of eventuality e, then it is more valuable, costly, or important than e. The second axiom in each pair says the opposite.

```
(forall (x s e a)                                                (28.59)
    (if (and (moreValuable x s a)(posGoalConsequences s e a))
        (moreValuable x e a)))
```

```
(forall (x s e a)                                                (28.60)
    (if (and (moreValuable s x a)(posGoalConsequences s e a))
        (moreValuable e x a)))
```

```
(forall (x s e a)                                                (28.61)
    (if (and (moreCostly x s a)(negGoalConsequences s e a))
        (moreCostly x e a)))
```

```
(forall (x s e a)                                                    (28.62)
    (if (and (moreCostly s x a)(negGoalConsequences s e a))
        (moreCostly e x a)))


(forall (x s e a)                                                    (28.63)
    (if (and (moreImportant x s a)(goalConsequences s e a))
        (moreImportant x e a)))


(forall (x s e a)                                                    (28.64)
    (if (and (moreImportant s x a)(goalConsequences s e a))
        (moreImportant e x a)))
```

In a more complete theory of importance, we would relate the importance of an eventuality to its effect on the likelihood of the agent's goals obtaining or not.

We have extended the three partial orderings from goals to eventualities in general. Now we extend it more broadly to any kind of entity. The value, cost, and importance of an entity depends on the value, cost, and importance of its properties and of the events it participates in. Thus, we define the set of "goal-relevant properties," in positive, negative, and neutral versions.

```
(forall (s x a)                                                      (28.65)
    (iff (posGrProps s x a)
         (forall (e)
             (iff (member e s)
                  (and (arg* x e)(posGoalRelevant e a))))))


(forall (s x a)                                                      (28.66)
    (iff (negGrProps s x a)
         (forall (e)
             (iff (member e s)
                  (and (arg* x e)(negGoalRelevant e a))))))


(forall (s x a)                                                      (28.67)
    (iff (grProps s x a)
         (forall (e)
             (iff (member e s)
                  (and (arg* x e)(goalRelevant e a))))))
```

The next three pairs of axioms say that the value, cost, and importance of an entity depend on the value, cost, and importance of its goal-relevant properties. We thereby have extended the three partial orderings to entities in general.

```
(forall (s x1 x2 a)                                                  (28.68)
    (if (and (moreValuable x1 s a)(posGrProps s x2 a))
        (moreValuable x1 x2 a)))


(forall (s x1 x2 a)                                                  (28.69)
    (if (and (moreValuable s x1 a)(posGrProps s x2 a))
        (moreValuable x2 x1 a)))
```

```
(forall (s x1 x2 a)                                          (28.70)
    (if (and (moreCostly x1 s a)(negGrProps s x2 a))
        (moreCostly x1 x2 a)))


(forall (s x1 x2 a)                                          (28.71)
    (if (and (moreCostly s x1 a)(negGrProps s x2 a))
        (moreCostly x2 x1 a)))


(forall (s x1 x2 a)                                          (28.72)
    (if (and (moreImportant x1 s a)(grProps s x2 a))
        (moreImportant x1 x2 a)))


(forall (s x1 x2 a)                                          (28.73)
    (if (and (moreImportant s x1 a)(grProps s x2 a))
        (moreImportant x2 x1 a)))
```

To summarize, x1 is more valuable than x2 to agent a if x2 is, or affects something that is, or has properties that affect something that is, in the service of x1. Similarly for cost and importance.

We can now define a value scale as a scale whose components are any arbitrary set and whose partial ordering is moreValuable.

```
(forall (s a)                                                (28.74)
    (iff (valueScale s a)
        (exists (s1 e x1 x2)
            (and (scaleDefinedBy s s1 e)(moreValuable' e x1 x2 a)
                (agent a)(member x1 s1)(member x2 s1)))))
```

We can define a predicate corresponding to the absolute form of the adjective. Something is valuable to an agent a if it is in the Hi region of a's value scale.

```
(forall (x a)                                                (28.75)
    (iff (valuable x a)
        (exists (s s1)
            (and (valueScale s a)(Hi s1 s)(inScale x s1)))))
```

We often talk about the value of something. We could have restricted the components of a value scale to be just those eventualities that are goals of the agent. Then the value of an eventuality that is not a goal would be the highest-level goal that the eventuality enabled. The value of a noneventuality entity would be the highest level goal enabled by its positive goal relevant properties. However, we characterized the moreValuable partial ordering for *all* eventualities and other entities; they are already in the scale. Thus, the value of something, its place in a value scale, is just itself, as an element in that scale.

```
(forall (x y a)                                              (28.76)
    (iff (value y x a)
        (exists (s)
            (and (valueScale s a)(inScale y a)(equal x y)))))
```

The expression (value y x a) says that y is the value of x to agent a. This holds if y simply *is* x and it has a place in a value scale.

For completeness we can similarly define corresponding concepts for cost and importance.

$$(\text{forall } (s \ a) \hspace{10em} (28.77)$$
$$\hspace{2em}(\text{iff } (\text{costScale } s \ a)$$
$$\hspace{4em}(\text{exists } (s1 \ e \ x1 \ x2)$$
$$\hspace{6em}(\text{and } (\text{scaleDefinedBy } s \ s1 \ e)(\text{moreCostly' } e \ x1 \ x2 \ a)$$
$$\hspace{8em}(\text{agent } a)(\text{member } x1 \ s1)(\text{member } x2 \ s1)))))$$

$$(\text{forall } (s \ a) \hspace{10em} (28.78)$$
$$\hspace{2em}(\text{iff } (\text{importanceScale } s \ a)$$
$$\hspace{4em}(\text{exists } (s1 \ e \ x1 \ x2)$$
$$\hspace{6em}(\text{and } (\text{scaleDefinedBy } s \ s1 \ e)(\text{moreImportant' } e \ x1 \ x2 \ a)$$
$$\hspace{8em}(\text{agent } a)(\text{member } x1 \ s)(\text{member } x2 \ s)))))$$

$$(\text{forall } (x \ a) \hspace{10em} (28.79)$$
$$\hspace{2em}(\text{iff } (\text{costly } x \ a)$$
$$\hspace{4em}(\text{exists } (s \ s1)$$
$$\hspace{6em}(\text{and } (\text{costScale } s \ a)(\text{Hi } s1 \ s)(\text{inScale } x \ s1)))))$$

$$(\text{forall } (x \ a) \hspace{10em} (28.80)$$
$$\hspace{2em}(\text{iff } (\text{important } x \ a)$$
$$\hspace{4em}(\text{exists } (s \ s1)$$
$$\hspace{6em}(\text{and } (\text{importanceScale } s \ a)(\text{Hi } s1 \ s)(\text{inScale } x \ s1)))))$$

$$(\text{forall } (x \ y \ a) \hspace{10em} (28.81)$$
$$\hspace{2em}(\text{iff } (\text{cost } y \ x \ a)$$
$$\hspace{4em}(\text{exists } (s)$$
$$\hspace{6em}(\text{and } (\text{costScale } s \ a)(\text{inScale } y \ a)(\text{equal } x \ y)))))$$

$$(\text{forall } (x \ y \ a) \hspace{10em} (28.82)$$
$$\hspace{2em}(\text{iff } (\text{importance } y \ x \ a)$$
$$\hspace{4em}(\text{exists } (s)$$
$$\hspace{6em}(\text{and } (\text{importanceScale } s \ a)(\text{inScale } y \ a)(\text{equal } x \ y)))))$$

PREDICATES INTRODUCED IN THIS CHAPTER

(goal e a)
Eventuality e is a goal of agent a.

(subgoal e1 e2)
Eventuality e1 is a subgoal of e2.

(knowledgeGoal e a)
e is something a has a goal of knowing.

(preservationGoal e a t)
e is an eventuality that a has the goal of preserving during time interval t.

(preservationGoalViolation e a t)
e is a preservation goal of a's for interval t that does not obtain for the entire interval.

(persistentGoal e a t)
e is a goal of a's that persists during time interval t.

(envisionedFutureGoal e a t1 t2)
  e is a eventuality that a envisions at time t1 that a will have as a goal at time t2.

(achievedGoal e a t1 t2)
  e is a goal that a has at time t1 and achieves by time t2.

(unachievedGoal e a t1 t2)
  e is a goal that a has at time t1 that does not obtain by time t2.

(neverAchievedGoal e a t1)
  e is a goal that a has at time t1 that is never achieved.

(conflictingGoals e1 e2 a)
  e1 and e2 are goals of a that cannot both be achieved.

(auxiliaryGoal e1 e2 a)
  e1 and e2 are goals of a, where if a learns they are conflicting, a will drop e1 as a goal.

(sharedGoal e s)
  e is a goal shared by members of collective s.

(competitiveGoals e1 e2 a1 a2)
  e1 and e2 are the same property instantiated by agents a1 and a2 respectively, and only one of them can really exist.

(adversarialGoals e1 a1 a2)
  e1 is a goal of a1's, and the negation of e1 is a goal of a2's.

(try a e)
  Agent a tries to achieve e.

(succeed a e)
  Agent a succeeds in achieving e.

(fail a e)
  Agent a fails to achieve e.

(functionality0 e x)
  Behavior e is the real or hypothetical functionality of x.

(functionality e1 y e x)
  Behavior e1 by y is the functionality of y as a component of x, with respect to behavior e by x.

(intact x)
  x is intact.

(goodFor e a)
  Eventuality e is good for agent a.

(badFor e a)
  Eventuality e is bad for agent a.

(moreValuable x1 x2 a)
  x1 is more valuable to agent a than x2.

(moreCostly x1 x2 a)
  x1 is more costly to agent a than x2.

(moreImportant x1 x2 a)
  x1 is more important to agent a than x2.

(ubSupergoal e s a)
  e is an upper bound supergoal for all the goals of agent a in set s.

(lubSupergoal e s a)
  e is the least upper bound supergoal for all the goals of agent a in set s.

(posGoalRelevant e a)
  Eventuality e implies the existence of some goal of agent a.

(negGoalRelevant e a)
  Eventuality e implies the nonexistence of some goal of agent a.

(goalRelevant e a)
  Eventuality e implies the existence or nonexistence of some goal of agent a.

(posGoalConsequences s e a)
  s is the set of goals of agent a whose existence is implied by e.

(negGoalConsequences s e a)
  s is the set of goals of agent a whose nonexistence is implied by e.

(goalConsequences s e a)
  s is the set of goals of agent a whose existence or nonexistence is implied by e.

(posGrProps s x a)
  s is the set of properties of x that are positively goal-relevant to a.

(negGrProps s x a)
  s is the set of properties of x that are negatively goal-relevant to a.

(grProps s x a)
  s is the set of properties of x that are goal-relevant to a.

(valueScale s a)
  s is the value scale for agent a.

(costScale s a)
  s is the cost scale for agent a.

(importanceScale s a)
  s is the importance scale for agent a.

(valuable x a)
  x is valuable to agent a.

(costly x a)
  x is costly to agent a.

(important x a)
  x is important to agent a.

(value y x a)
  y is the value of x to agent a.

(cost y x a)
  y is the cost of x to agent a.

(importance y x a)
  y is the importance of x to agent a.

29

Goal Themes

29.1 THRIVING

It is formally convenient to assume that agents have one plan that they are always developing, executing, monitoring, and revising, and that that plan is in the service of a single goal. We will call this goal "Thriving."

```
(forall (a)                                                    (29.1)
    (if (agent a)
        (exists (e)(and (goal e a)(thrive' e a)))))
```

```
(forall (e a)                                                  (29.2)
    (if (thrive' e a)(agent a)))
```

More specific goals arise out of the planning process using the agents' beliefs about what will cause them to thrive.

The main reason for positing this top-level goal is that now instead of worrying about the mysterious process by which an agent comes to have goals, we can address the planning problems of what eventualities the agent believes cause other eventualities, including the eventuality of thriving, and of what alternative subgoals the agent should choose to achieve particular goals. We are still left with the problem of when one goal should be given priority over another, but this becomes a part of the plan construction problem.

We will not attempt to say what constitutes thriving in general, because there are huge differences among cultures and individuals. For most of us, thriving includes staying alive, breathing, and eating, as well as having pleasurable experiences. Or in the words of Spock, "Live long and prosper." But it could well be that agents could decide that they thrive best when their social group thrives, and that may involve agents sacrificing themselves. This is a common view in all cultures, as seen in suicide bombers, soldiers willing to go into battle in defense of their country, and people risking death to rescue accident victims. So thriving does not necessarily imply surviving.

Similarly, a man may decide that he is in so much pain that the best way to thrive is to kill himself. In contrast, a religious ascetic may decide that the best way to achieve the long-term goal of eternal life is to live in pain.

A good theory of commonsense psychology should not attempt to define thriving, but it should provide the materials out of which the beliefs of various cultures and individuals can be stated in a formal manner.

We could define a scalar notion of thriving in terms of the satisfaction of the subgoals of the top-level goal of thriving. First, we would introduce the set of subgoals of the plan to thrive that are currently satisfied. We could then define a moreThriving relation on the possible plans of a given agent. The interpretation of this relation would be constrained by the condition that the satisfied goals of the more thriving plan be more important than the satisfied goals of the less thriving plan. A thriving scale would be defined as the scale whose elements are possible plans of the agent and whose partial ordering is moreThriving. The predicate thriving would correspond to the Hi region of this scale, which would generally be interpreted distributionally as "more thriving than usual" or functionally as "thriving enough for some purpose."

29.2 PLEASURE AND PAIN

Pleasure is sometimes taken as the motive for all action. We do things because we believe they will lead to pleasurable feelings. We will not take that approach, because we are characterizing intentional action as arising out of agents' goals and the plans they develop to achieve these goals. But there is indeed a close relationship between pleasure and goals. If something is pleasurable, we are likely to pursue it as a goal. In fact, this is probably its primary property. A Martian or a robot who did not experience pleasure could go a long way in understanding the role of pleasure in people's lives just by knowing this rule. In terms of evolution, we can see the utility of a mechanism that would impel us toward actions that would generally be good for us, but at the same time can be overridden when we know better, for example, when we refrain from eating a decadent dessert. Like many mechanisms developed in evolution, pleasure is rough and ready, working most of the time, but subject to error.

We will take the expression (pleasure e p) to mean that the eventuality e is the experience of person p feeling pleasure.

```
(forall (e p)                                               (29.3)
    (if (pleasure e p)(person p)))
```

When someone feels pleasure, they know it, and that fact is in their focus of attention.

```
(forall (e0 e p)                                            (29.4)
    (if (and (pleasure' e0 e p)(Rexists e0))(know p e0)))
```

```
(forall (e p)                                               (29.5)
    (if (pleasure e p)(inFocus e p)))
```

Moreover, if someone believes he or she feels pleasure, they really do. It is not something one can be mistaken about.

```
(forall (e0 e p)                                              (29.6)
    (if (and (pleasure' e0 e p)(believe p e0))
        (Rexist e0)))
```

Pleasure is a private experience. If two distinct persons p1 and p2 have experiences of pleasure e1 and e2, the experiences are distinct.

```
(forall (p1 p2 e1 e2)                                         (29.7)
    (if (and (pleasure e1 p1)(pleasure e2 p2)(nequal p1 p2))
        (nequal e1 e2)))
```

A closely related concept identifies the cause of the pleasure.

```
(forall (e1 a)                                                (29.8)
    (iff (pleasurable e1 p)
        (exists (e) (and (pleasure e p)(cause e1 e)))))
```

That is, eventuality e1 is pleasurable to person p if e1 causes the experience e of pleasure in p.

We normally know the causes of our feelings of pleasure, but not always.

```
(forall (e0 e1 p)                                             (29.9)
    (if (and (pleasurable' e0 e1 p)(Rexists e0)(etc))
        (know p e0)))
```

The principal property of pleasure, for our purposes, is that if we believe something is pleasurable, it will often cause us to adopt it as a goal.

```
(forall (e0 e1 e2 p)                                          (29.10)
    (if (and (pleasurable' e0 e1 p)(believe' e2 p e0)(etc))
        (exists (g0)
            (and (goal' g0 e1 p)(cause e2 g0)))))
```

When we feel pleasure, that normally causes us to believe we are thriving.

```
(forall (e p)                                                 (29.11)
    (if (and (pleasure e p)(etc))
        (exists (e1 e2)
            (and (thrive' e1 p)(believe' e2 p e1)(cause e e2)))))
```

Pleasure is a scalar notion. One experience can be more pleasurable than another. This is almost an entirely subjective experience. But we can help out the Martian and the robot a bit here. Defeasibly, the more valuable a goal is to us, the more pleasurable its achievement should be.

```
(forall (e1 e2 p)                                             (29.12)
    (if (and (moreValuable e1 e2 p)(etc))
        (morePleasurable e1 e2 p)))
```

A pleasure scale could then be constructed in the usual way.

An enterprise at the boundary between commonsense physiology and commonsense psychology would be to write axioms capturing the regularities in what kinds of experiences cause pleasure. We could also detail the physiological effects of pleasure, such as smiling and laughing. We won't do either of these here.

We take a similar approach to pain. A simple theory of pain and pleasure would say we seek pleasure and avoid pain. But this can be overridden by our goals. The saying "no pain, no gain" encourages those who are trying to get into shape to continue exercising after it becomes painful. So we will take goals and plans to be the basis for intentional action and relate pain to them. We can see the evolutionary advantage the mechanism of pain gives us. Physical pain generally indicates damage is being done to our body. The principal property of pain is that it, defeasibly, causes us to do something to make the pain stop, and hence make the damage stop. But like pleasure it is a very rough and ready mechanism. Sometimes we feel pain when no damage is being done, as in the phantom limb phenomenon. We sometimes feel pain when there is no way to to relieve it; we'd like to be able to register the warning about damage and then turn the pain off. Sometimes it is in our long-term interest to soldier through the pain, as in exercise or athletic competitions.

We will take the expression (pain e p) to mean that the eventuality e is the experience of person p feeling pain.

```
(forall (e p)                                              (29.13)
    (if (pain e p)(person p)))
```

When someone feels pain, they know it, and that fact is in their focus of attention. It is not something they can be mistaken about.

```
(forall (e0 e p)                                           (29.14)
    (if (and (pain' e0 e p)(Rexists e0))(know p e0)))
```

```
(forall (e p)                                              (29.15)
    (if (pain e p)(inFocus e p)))
```

In these axioms the pain itself (e) is in focus. The fact (e0) that the person is in pain is what is known.

Pain is a private experience. If two distinct persons p1 and p2 have experiences of pain e1 and e2, the experiences are distinct.

```
(forall (p1 p2 e1 e2)                                      (29.16)
    (if (and (pain e1 p1)(pain e2 p2)(nequal p1 p2))
        (nequal e1 e2)))
```

A closely related concept identifies the cause of the pain.

```
(forall (e1 a)                                             (29.17)
    (iff (painful e1 p)
        (exists (e) (and (pain e p)(cause e1 e)))))
```

That is, eventuality e1 is painful to person p if e1 causes the experience e of pain in p. Stubbing your toe is painful. The feeling in your toe is pain.

We normally know the causes of our feelings of pain, but not always.

```
(forall (e p)                                              (29.18)
    (if (and (painful' e0 e1 p)(Rexists e0)(etc))
        (know p e0)))
```

More than pleasure, pain tends to be associated with a particular body part and indicates that damage is being done to that body part.

```
(forall (e p)                                                        (29.19)
   (if (and (pain e p)(etc))
       (exists (x e1 e2)
           (and (bodyPart x p)(changeFrom' e1 e2)(intact' e2 x)
                (cause e1 e)))))
```

Breaking your arm is painful, and the pain is telling you that your arm is broken.

The principal property of pain, for our purposes, is that if we believe something is painful, it will often cause us to adopt as a goal causing the pain to stop.

```
(forall (e0 e1 e2 p)                                                 (29.20)
   (if (and (painful' e0 e1 p)(believe' e2 p e0)(etc))
       (exists (g0 e3)
           (and (goal' g0 e3 p)(not' e3 e1)(cause e2 g0)))))
```

When we feel pain, that normally causes us to believe we are not thriving.

```
(forall (e p)                                                        (29.21)
   (if (and (pain e p)(etc))
       (exists (e1 e2 e3)
           (and (thrive' e1 p)(not' e3 e1)(believe' e2 p e3)
                (cause e e2)))))
```

Like pleasure, pain is a scalar notion along several dimensions. Pain has a volume – your toe hurting versus your whole body hurting. It has intensity; we return to the notion of intensity in Chapter 49. And pain has duration; long-lasting pains are worse than brief pains, other things being equal. These dimensions are independent, and it is often difficult to say whether one pain is worse than another. But just as we did with pleasure, we can help out Martians and robots by saying that there is a correlation between how painful something is and the cost of the goals we are willing to sacrifice to eliminate the pain.

```
(forall (x y p)                                                      (29.22)
   (if (and (moreCostly e1 e2 p)(etc))
          (morePainful e1 e2 p)))
```

A pain scale could then be constructed in the usual way.

As with pleasure, we could develop a rich theory about what kinds of experiences cause pain, and the physiological indications of pain, such as grimacing and crying. But that is beyond the scope of this book.

29.3 SHORT-TERM VERSUS LONG-TERM GOALS

A very common conflict when we are trying to decide what to do is between satisfying short-term goals and pursuing long-term goals. In Aesop's fable of the ant and the grasshopper, the grasshopper pursues the short-term goal of enjoying summer, while the ant pursues the long-term goal of surviving the winter.

The terms "short" and "long" are relative to each other. In absolute terms the relevant delays can be minutes – "Don't fill up on bread before the main course comes" – to years – should you get a good-paying job now or should you go to medical school? The only constraint on the times is that one is before the other.

The goals have to be conflicting; otherwise we'd just satisfy the short-term goal now and the long-term goal a little later. Eating the bread now will spoil your appetite for the main course, and it's nearly impossible to have a full-time job and succeed in medical school.

Finally, the long-term goal has to be more valuable to the agent than the short-term goal. Otherwise we would always simply pursue the short-term goal.

We will abbreviate this situation with the unpronounceable predicate stvslt. Its arguments are an agent a, two desired eventualities e1 and e2, and two times t1 and t2. The constraints on the arguments are given in the following axiom.

```
(forall (a e1 t1 e2 t2)                                        (29.23)
    (if (stvslt a e1 t1 e2 t2)
        (exists (e3 e4)
            (and (agent a)(before t1 t2)
                (atTime' e3 e1 t1)(goal e3 a)
                (atTime' e4 e2 t2)(goal e4 a)
                (conflictingGoals e3 e4 a)
                (moreValuable e2 e1 a)))))
```

Eventuality e3 is e1's happening at t1, and e4 is e2's happening at t2. These two are in conflict. What is to be achieved at time t2, namely, e2, is more valuable to the agent than e1.

To pick the short-term goal e1 is to be in this situation and to change from having e2 as a goal.

```
(forall (e a e1)                                               (29.24)
    (iff (pickST' e a e1)
        (exists (t1 e2 t2 e4 g2 e5)
            (and (stvslt a e1 t1 e2 t2)
                (atTime' e4 e2 t2)(goal' g2 e4 a)
                (changeFrom' e5 g2)(gen e5 e)))))
```

Line 5 says that e4 is the eventuality of e2 happening at time t2, and g2 is that being a goal of a's. Line 6 says that picking the short-term option is equivalent to abandoning e4 as a goal.

The definition of picking the long-term option e2 is similar.

```
(forall (e a e2)                                               (29.25)
    (iff (pickLT' e a e2)
        (exists (e1 t1 t2 e3 g1 e5)
            (and (stvslt a e1 t1 e2 t2)
                (atTime' e3 e1 t1)(goal' g1 e3 a)
                (changeFrom' e5 g1)(gen e5 e)))))
```

We can call the interval between t1 and t2 the "gratification delay."

```
(forall (t e1 e2 a)                                            (29.26)
    (iff (gratificationDelay t e1 e2 a)
        (exists (t1 t2)
            (and (stvslt a e1 t1 e2 t2)
                (intervalBetween t t1 t2)))))
```

Much of the issue in the choice between short-term and long-term goals is that there is usually a cost to the delay.

```
(forall (t e1 e2 a)                                         (29.27)
   (if (and (gratificationDelay t e1 e2 a)(etc))
       (exists (y) (cost y t a))))
```

The conflict between short-term and long-term goals is not unrelated to pleasure and pain. Frequently the short-term goals are the experience of pleasure or the avoidance of pain.

29.4 GOAL THEMES

In general our knowledge is tagged by who else believes it. Academics generally assume that their fellow academics don't believe in parapsychology or flying saucers. Americans believe in democracy. A computer scientist will believe that other computer scientists, but not laymen, will know what the P=NP problem is. Christians believe fellow Christians believe in the resurrection of Jesus, but don't believe that Jews and Muslims believe it. One of us was rather taken aback when he met a nun who didn't believe in God.

The mutual belief predication (mb s e), introduced in Chapter 21, says that a particular set of agents s mutually believes an eventuality or proposition e. That eventuality can be a general rule. Suppose for example that we want a rule that says

```
(forall (x) (if (p x)(q x)))                                (29.28)
```

We can make the implication relation between the eventualities explicit and write

```
(forall (e1 x)                                              (29.29)
   (if (p' e1 x)
       (exists (e2)(and (q' e2 x)(imply e1 e2)))))
```

Now we can reify the implication and treat it as an object of mutual belief by a particular set S of agents.

```
(forall (e1 x)                                              (29.30)
   (if (p' e1 x)
       (exists (e2 e3)
          (and (q' e2 x)(imply' e3 e1 e2)(mb S e3)))))
```

This says that if e1 is the eventuality of p being true of x, then there is an e2 that is the eventuality of q being true of x such that agents in set S mutually believe that e1 implies e2. (This is not quite a statement that S mutually believes the universal rule; that would require us to introduce type elements and would take us too far afield.)

Thus, tagging our knowledge by who knows it is something we can do in the formalism developed so far, by using the believe and mb predicates.

Some things are known by everybody (or at least by all competent adults). We view the axioms in this book to be expressing knowledge that everyone can be assumed to believe.

Among the kinds of knowledge that is mutually believed by groups of agents is knowledge of what sorts of things cause what other sorts of things. Since causal knowledge is used in planning, this is what gives us a basis for reasoning about the goals and plans of others, and consequently for predicting their behavior.

The set s of agents in a mutual belief predication can be defined in any way that turns out to be useful. Often a single predicate defines the set, as in the preceding examples with the predicates `academic`, `American`, `computerScientist`, and `Christian`. This is useful because it means that by making a judgment about membership on the basis of one property, we can make reasonably good predictions about other agents' knowledge, including causal knowledge, and hence behavior. It is useful to a soldier in war, for example, to know that when you see an enemy soldier, he intends to kill you. Of course, such broad generalizations lead to positive and negative stereotypes that, although useful in many cases, can lead us to make significant mistakes in particular instances.

We can define a "goal theme" as a relation between a set of agents and a set of goals from which we can conclude those agents have those goals. We can infer goals of individual agents from the goal themes of the groups they belong to.

```
(forall (s t)                                                    (29.31)
    (iff (goalTheme t s)
         (forall (a e)
             (if (and (member a s)(member e t))
                 (exists (e1) (and (instance e1 e)(goal e1 a)))))))
```

That is, if t is a goal theme among the group s, then t is a set of eventuality types and the members of s are likely to have as goals instances of the eventuality types in set t.

Agents have goals because they believe they will contribute ultimately to the goal of thriving. Thus, we can characterize goal themes in terms of mutual belief in causal knowledge. We will use the weak relation `causallyInvolved` here.

```
(forall (s t e a)                                                (29.32)
    (if (and (goalTheme t s)(member e t)(member a s))
        (exists (e0 e1 e2)
            (and (mb s e0)(causallyInvolved' e0 e1 e2)
                 (instance e1 e)(thrive' e2 a)))))
```

The set s of agents in a goal theme can be defined in many ways. The goal theme could result from their nationality or ethnicity. It could derive from their role in an organization, as for example a waiter, a receptionist, or a professor. It could derive from a relationship they are in, as for example someone who wants to be a good father. It could result from life style choices, such as a puritan, a thrill-seeker, or a hedonist. It could be linked to a personality type such as risk-averse, or to a political inclination such as liberal or conservative.

A belief that it is a goal theme of a group defined by property p that q be true would be expressed by axioms of the following form:

```
(forall (s t x e1 e y)                                          (29.33)
    (if (and (dset s x e1)(p' e1 x)(singleton t e)(q' e y))
        (goalTheme t s)))
```

Self-identity properties are often expressed in terms of goal themes. For example, an American may not merely believe in voting. She may believe, "As an American, I vote." That is, she believes that voting is a goal theme of Americans, and that she is an American.

Following up on our discussion of pleasure and pain, we can define a hedonist (or a set of hedonists) as someone who chooses goals that are pleasurable experiences.

(29.34)

```
(forall (s)
    (iff (hedonists s)
        (exists (t)
            (and (goalTheme t s)
                (forall (e a)
                    (if (and (member e t)(member a s))
                        (pleasurable e a)))))))
```

PREDICATES INTRODUCED IN THIS CHAPTER

(thrive a)
> An agent a's top-level goal, to thrive.

(pleasure e p)
> Eventuality e is person p's experience of pleasure.

(pleasurable e1 p)
> Eventuality e1 causes pleasure in person p.

(morePleasurable e1 e2 p)
> Eventuality e1 is more pleasurable to person p than eventuality e2.

(pain e p)
> Eventuality e is person p's experience of pain.

(painful e1 p)
> Eventuality e1 causes pain in person p.

(morePainful e1 e2 p)
> Eventuality e1 is more painful to person p than eventuality e2.

(stvslt a e1 t1 e2 t2)
> Agent a has a conflict between short-term goal e1 at time t1 and long-term goal e2 at time t2.

(pickST a e1)
> Agent a picks short-term option e1.

(pickLT a e2)
> Agent a picks long-term option e2.

(gratificationDelay t e1 e2 a)
> Time interval t is the time between satisfaction of short-term goal e1 and long-term goal e2 for agent a.

(goalTheme t s)
> Set t of eventualities is a goal theme of set s of agents, that is, agents in s have instances of eventualities in t as their goals.

(hedonists s)
> The members of set s are hedonists.

30

Threats and Threat Detection

30.1 THREAT SITUATIONS

A threat situation is one in which the agent sees that things could turn out badly. To formalize this notion, we need to assume there is a causal system s that is envisioned by the agent a. The threat is somewhere downstream causally from some situation e0, perhaps the present situation in the agent's current world understanding, but perhaps not. Threats are generally not inevitable. Thus, there is in the causal system a branch e between e1 and e2, where one of the alternatives, say e1, leads to one of a's goals being negated and the other alternative does not lead to that goal being negated.

The definition of a threat situation is as follows:

```
(forall (s a e0 e e1 e2 g)                                          (30.1)
    (iff (threatSituation s a e0 e e1 e2 g)
         (exists (s1 e3)
             (and (ecs s a)(member e0 s1)(eventualitiesOf s1 s)
                  (causallyInvolved e0 e)(branch e e1 e2 s)
                  (imply e1 e3)(not' e3 g)(goal g a)
                  (not (imply e2 e3))))))
```

The expression (threatSituation s a e0 e e1 e2 g) says that s is a threat situation for agent a with respect to situation e0, involving an envisioned branch e to alternatives e1 and e2, where one of the alternatives e1 leads to the negation e3 of a goal g of agent a's and the other alternative e2 does not. Line 4 says that s is an envisioned causal system containing e0. Line 5 says that e0 is causally upstream from the branch point e, where e1 and e2 are the two alternatives. Line 6 says that alternative e1 implies the negation of a goal g of a's, and line 7 says that alternative e2 does not. This last condition is a stipulation that a threat is only a possibility, not an inevitability. We generally refer to something as a threat when some evasive action is still possible.

The participating entities in a threat situation can be labeled by their role. The undesirable alternative e1 is the threat.

```
(forall (s a e0 e e1 e2 g)                                         (30.2)
    (if (threatSituation s a e0 e e1 e2 g)(threat e1 a s)))
```

That is, e1 is the threat to agent a in situation s.

For convenience below, we define threat0 to be the predicate threat without the threat situation argument.

```
(forall (e1 a)                                                     (30.3)
    (iff (threat0 e1 a)(exists (s)(threat e1 a s))))
```

The goal that would be violated we can call the "goal in threat."

```
(forall (s a e0 e e1 e2 g)                                         (30.4)
    (if (threatSituation s a e0 e e1 e2 g)(goalInThreat g a s)))
```

That is, g is the goal of a's that is threatened by situation s.

The envisioned branch point is the threat condition.

```
(forall (s a e0 e e1 e2 g)                                         (30.5)
    (if (threatSituation s a e0 e e1 e2 g)
        (threatCondition e a s)))
```

As it stands, a threat situation carries with it no implication of reality. The agent could be imagining what might happen to him if he were transported back to the time of dinosaurs. But there are various modalities that can characterize threat situations, and we will define several such concepts in part to demonstrate that we have built up adequate machinery to do so.

A threat situation is real if the envisioned causal system is the current world understanding and the anchor e0 really exists.

```
(forall (s a e0 e e1 e2 g)                                         (30.6)
    (iff (realThreatSituation s a e0 e e1 e2 g)
        (and (threatSituation s a e0 e e1 e2 g)(cwu s a)
            (Rexist e0))))
```

A possible threat is one which arises in a real threat situation in which the threat e1 is possible, with respect to some set of constraints c.

```
(forall (e1 a c)                                                   (30.7)
    (iff (possibleThreat e1 a c)
        (exists (s e0 e e2 g)
            (and (realThreatSituation s a e0 e e1 e2 g)
                (possible e1 c)))))
```

An impossible threat is one which arises in a real threat situation where the threat e1 is impossible, with respect to some set of constraints c.

```
(forall (e1 a c)                                                   (30.8)
    (iff (impossibleThreat e1 a c)
        (exists (s e0 e e2 g)
            (and (realThreatSituation s a e0 e e1 e2 g)
                (not (possible e1 c))))))
```

Sometimes threats are realized. In this case there was a threat situation at time t1 and at a subsequent time t2, the threat e1 actually occurred.

```
(forall (e1 a)                                                    (30.9)
    (iff (realizedThreat e1 a)
         (exists (s a e0 e e2 g e3 t1 t2)
             (and (realThreatSituation' e3 s a e0 e e1 e2 g)
                  (atTime e3 t1)(atTime e1 t2)(before t1 t2)))))
```

Here, e3 is the eventuality of s being a threat situation for agent a. This was true at time t1. The threat e1 in the threat situation actually occurs at a later time t2.

A threat is unrealized if there is no subsequent time t2 at which the threat actually occurs.

```
(forall (e1 a)                                                   (30.10)
    (iff (unrealizedThreat e1 a)
         (exists (s a e0 e e2 g e3 t1)
             (and (realThreatSituation' e3 s a e0 e e1 e2 g)
                  (atTime e3 t1)
                  (not (exists (t2)
                           (and (atTime e1 t2)(before t1 t2)))))))))
```

30.2 THREAT DETECTION AND MANAGEMENT

To detect a threat is to change into a state in which a situation s is envisioned as a threat situation. Threat detection is often thought of as a more active process. The agent goes through an envisioning process in which the final envisioned causal system is a threat situation. This may be real or hypothetical depending on whether the envisioned causal system is the current world understanding or not.

```
(forall (s1 s a)                                                 (30.11)
    (iff (threatDetection s1 s a)
         (exists (e0 e e1 e2 g)
             (and (ecsSeq s1 a)(last s s1)
                  (threatSituation s a e0 e e1 e2 g)))))
```

The expression (threatDetection s1 s a) says that s1, a sequence of envisioned causal systems, is the process of detecting threat situation s by agent a. This happens when the sequence leads to the recognition of a threat situation.

People have an ability to detect a threat.

```
(forall (a)                                                      (30.12)
    (if (person a)
        (exists (s1 s c)
            (and (able a s1 c)(threatDetection s1 s a)))))
```

People can fail to identify a threat.

```
(forall (a s1 s)                                                 (30.13)
    (iff (threatDetectionFailure a s1 s)
         (and (fail a s1)(threatDetection s1 s a))))
```

To try to detect a threat is to engage in envisioning from a particular anchor situation e0, with the goal of reaching a threat. A failure occurs when this process does not lead to the envisionment of a threat situation.

To be concerned about something is to believe there is a possible threat involving it.

```
(forall (x a)                                                (30.14)
    (iff (concern x a)
         (exists (e3 e1 c)
             (and (believe a e3) (possibleThreat' e3 e1 a c)
                  (arg* x e1)))))
```

The expression (concern x a) says that entity x concerns agent a. This happens when a believes the proposition e3 that eventuality e1 is a threat to a that is possible given constraints c, where e1 somehow involves x.

In particular, threats concern agents.

People vary in their responses to their concerns or perceived risks. One has a bias against risk if a concern is likely to cause one to refrain from performing some action.

```
(forall (a)                                                  (30.15)
    (iff (biasAgainstRisk a)
         (forall (e3 s e0 e e1 e2 g)
             (if (and (threatSituation s a e0 e e1 e2 g)
                      (concern' e3 e1 a) (agentOf a e0))
                 (exists (e4 e5 c)
                     (and (likely e4 c) (cwu c a) (cause' e4 e3 e5)
                          (not' e5 e0)))))))
```

The expression (biasAgainstRisk a) says that agent a has a bias against taking risks. Lines 4 and 5 specify conditions in which there is a concern that some action e0 of the agent might lead to a threat. Lines 7 and 8 say that in these conditions it is likely that the concern will cause a not to do the action.

One has a bias toward taking risks if in this situation one is not likely to refrain from the action.

```
(forall (a)                                                  (30.16)
    (iff (biasTowardRisk a)
         (forall (e3 s e0 e e1 e2 g)
             (if (and (threatSituation s a e0 e e1 e2 g)
                      (concern' e3 e1 a) (agentOf a e0))
                 (exists (e4 e5 c)
                     (and (not (likely e4 c)) (cwu c a)
                          (cause' e4 e3 e5) (not' e5 e0)))))))
```

The concepts of "cautious," "risk-averse," and "adventurous" can be defined in terms of these concepts.

When threats are identified, they are added to those that the agent is concerned with.

```
(forall (a e1)                                               (30.17)
    (iff (addThreat a e1)
         (exists (e3)
             (and (changeTo e3) (concern' e3 e1 a)))))
```

When threats are no longer a concern, they are removed.

```
(forall (a e1)                                           (30.18)
    (iff (removeThreat a e1)
         (exists (e3)
             (and (changeFrom e3)(concern' e3 e1 a)))))
```

Worry is being concerned about a threat and experiencing a low-grade fear about it. We return to this in Chapter 49.

30.3 SERIOUSNESS

A threat can be more or less serious to an agent. Seriousness is a composite scale that depends on importance and likelihood. Of two equally likely threats, the more important one is more serious. Of two equally important threats, the more likely is more serious. This composition of scales is captured in the predicate compositeScale introduced in Chapter 12. The likelihood scale was introduced in Chapter 20. The importance scale was introduced in Chapter 28. Hence, the definition of "seriousness" is as follows:

```
(forall (s a)                                            (30.19)
    (iff (seriousnessScale s a)
         (exists (s1 s2)
             (and (likelihoodScale s1)(importanceScale s2 a)
                  (compositeScale s s1 s2)
                  (forall (e1 x)
                      (if (at e1 x s)(threatO e1 a)))))))
```

Lines 4 and 5 say that the seriousness scale is a composite of the likelihood scale and the importance scale. Lines 6 and 7 say that the elements on the scale are threats. In terms of this we can define the partial ordering "more serious."

```
(forall (e e1 e2 a)                                      (30.20)
    (iff (moreSerious' e e1 e2 a)
         (exists (s s1)
             (and (seriousnessScale s a)(scaleDefinedBy s s1 e)))))
```

The expression (moreSerious' e e1 e2 a) says that e is the eventuality of one threat e1 being more serious than threat e2 to agent a. The predicate scaleDefinedBy, defined in Chapter 12, relates a scale to its set of elements and its partial ordering.

We can define the qualitive predicate serious in terms of the Hi region of the scale.

```
(forall (e e1 a)                                         (30.21)
    (iff (serious' e e1 a)
         (exists (s)
             (and (seriousnessScale s a)(scaleFor s e)))))
```

The expression (serious' e e1 a) says that e is the eventuality of threat e1 being serious to agent a. The predicate scaleFor, defined in Chapter 12, relates a scale to the qualitative predicate of something being in the Hi region of the scale.

The seriousness of a threat is its place in the scale.

```
(forall (x e1 a)                                                (30.22)
    (iff (seriousness x e1 a)
         (exists (s)
             (and (seriousnessScale s a)(at e1 x s)))))
```

To assess a threat is to try to come to know the seriousness of the threat.

```
(forall (a e1)                                                  (30.23)
    (iff (assessThreat a e1)
         (exists (x e3 e4 d)
             (and (try a e3)(changeTo' e3 e4)(know' e4 a d)
                  (seriousness' d x e1 a)))))
```

PREDICATES INTRODUCED IN THIS CHAPTER

(threatSituation s a e0 e e1 e2 g)
  s is a threat situation for agent a viewed from anchor situation e0, where there is a branch e to situations e1 and e2 and e1 conflicts with a's goal g.

(threat e1 a s)
  e1 is the threat to a in threat situation s.

(threat0 e1 a)
  e1 is a threat to a in some threat situation.

(goalInThreat g a s)
  g is the goal of a's that is at risk in threat situation s.

(threatCondition e a s)
  e is the branch point in a threat situation s for agent a.

(realThreatSituation s a e0 e e1 e2 g)
  s is a threat situation for agent a and the anchor e0 really exists.

(possibleThreat e1 a c)
  e1 is a threat to a that is possible given constraints c.

(impossibleThreat e1 a c)
  e1 is a threat to a that is impossible given constraints c.

(realizedThreat e1 a)
  e1 is a threat that is realized.

(unrealizedThreat e1 a)
  e1 is a threat that is not realized.

(threatDetection s1 s a)
  s1 is the process of agent a's detecting a threat situation s.

(threatDetectionFailure a s1 s)
  Agent a's process s1 of threat detection fails to detect threat situation s.

(concern x a)
  x concerns a.

(biasAgainstRisk a)
  Agent a has a bias against taking risks.

(biasTowardRisk a)
   Agent a has a bias toward taking risks.

(addThreat a e1)
   Agent a adds threat e1 to the list of concerns.

(removeThreat a e1)
   Agent a removes threat e1 from the list of concerns.

(seriousnessScale s a)
   s is the seriousness scale for agent a.

(moreSerious e1 e2 a)
   Threat e1 is more serious than threat e2 for agent a.

(serious e1 a)
   Threat e1 is serious for agent a.

(seriousness x e1 a)
   x is the "measure" of the seriousness of threat e1 to agent a.

(assessThreat a e1)
   Agent a assesses the seriousness of threat e1.

31

Plans

31.1 PLANS AS MENTAL ENTITIES

We saw in Chapter 28 on goals how plans result from the use of causal knowledge in trying to achieve goals. In this chapter we discuss plans as mental constructs, something that can be remembered, can be applied many times, may not be completely thought out, can be shared among agents, and so on.

To define this, we first need to define the reflexive transitive closure of the subgoal relation between two eventualities e1 and e2. In addition, we want all of the eventualities to be in a specified set s1 and all of the pairwise subgoal relations to be in a specified set s2. This will insure that the plan is connected.

```
(forall (a e2 e1 s1 s2)                                              (31.1)
    (iff (connectedSubgoal* e2 e1 a s1 s2)
         (or (and (equal e1 e2)(member e1 s1))
             (exists (e3 r)
                 (and (member e3 s1)(subgoal e3 e1)
                      (subgoal' r e3 e1)(member r s2)
                      (connectedSubgoal* e2 e3 a s1 s2))))))
```

That is, e2 is a connectedSubgoal* of e1 for agent a with respect to set s1 of eventualities and set s2 of subgoal relations, if e2 and e1 are identical and in s1, or if there is a subgoal e3 of e1 for a in s1 whose subgoal relation r is in set s2, and e2 is a connectedSubgoal* of e3 for a with respect to sets s1 and s2.

A plan is relative to an agent and a top-level goal. It is a composite entity whose components are the top-level goal, its subgoals, the subgoals of the subgoals, and so on. The relations of the composite entity are the subgoal relations between pairs of subgoals.

```
(forall (p a e)                                                      (31.2)
   (iff (plan p a e)
        (exists (s1 s2)
              (and (compositeEntity p)
                   (componentsOf s1 p)(relationsOf s2 p)
                   (member e s1)
                   (forall (e1)
                        (if (member e1 s1)
                            (connectedSubgoal* e1 e a s1 s2)))
                   (forall (r)
                        (if (member r s2)
                            (exists (e2 e3)
                                 (and (member e2 s1)(member e3 s1)
                                      (subgoal' r e2 e3)))))))))
```

The expression (plan p a e) says p is a plan by agent a to bring about eventuality
e. This holds exactly when p is a composite entity whose components are subgoals of
e (or subgoals of subgoals, etc.), and whose relations are subgoal relations between
pairs of elements in s1.

It will be convenient to define a "subgoal in" relation between eventualities and
plans.

```
(forall (p e1)                                                       (31.3)
   (iff (subgoalIn e1 p)
        (exists (a e s)
              (and (plan p a e)(componentsOf s p)(member e1 s)))))
```

It is also convenient to define a "subgoals of" relation:

```
(forall (s p)                                                        (31.4)
   (iff (subgoalsOf s p)
        (exists (a g) (and (plan p a g)(componentsOf s p)))))
```

A subplan is a plan to achieve a subgoal, and it is a plan as well.

```
(forall (p1 p)                                                       (31.5)
   (iff (subplan p1 p)
        (exists (a e e1 s1 s2 s3 s4)
              (and (plan p a e)(plan p1 a e1)
                   (componentsOf s1 p)(componentsOf s2 p1)
                   (subset s2 s1)
                   (relationsOf s3 p)(relationsOf s4 p1)
                   (subset s4 s3)))))
```

Plans are thus recursively composed of smaller subplans.

Our plans change as we develop them from a top-level goal into something executable and modify them in response to new beliefs about the world. Thus, it is useful
to define the notion of a "plan sequence." A plan sequence is a sequence of plans of
a given agent where there is a change relationship between any two successive elements of the sequence. That is, plan p1 was the agent's plan for achieving e, and now
p2 is such a plan.

```
(forall (s a e)                                                    (31.6)
   (iff (planseq s a e)
        (exists (n)
            (and (sequence s)(length n s)
                 (forall (i1 i2 p1 p2)
                     (if (and (posInteger i1)(successor i2 i1)
                              (lt i1 n)(nth p1 i1 s)(nth p2 i2 s))
                         (exists (e1 e2)
                             (and (plan' e1 p1 a e)(plan' e2 p2 a e)
                                  (change e1 e2)))))))))
```

That is, a plan sequence is a sequence of plans where there has been a change from
each element of the sequence being a's plan to achieve e to the next element in the
sequence being a's plan to achieve e. We assume all elements in the plan sequence
have the same top-level goal. Otherwise, we could move up one level and define the
plan sequence as having that supergoal as its constant top-level goal. An agent's very
top-level goal is always "to thrive," and never changes.

Two eventualities come to be in a subgoal relation because the agent believes
there is a causal or enablement relation between them. That is, the subgoal is causally
involved in the goal.

```
(forall (a e1 e2 p g)                                              (31.7)
   (if (and (subgoal e2 e1)(subgoalIn e1 p)(subgoalIn e2 p)(plan p a g))
       (exists (e)
           (and (believe a e)(causallyInvolved' e e2 e1)))))
```

Therefore, a plan can be thought of as an envisioned causal system.

```
(forall (p a e)                                                    (31.8)
   (if (plan p a e)(ecs p a)))
```

Planning is then a variety of envisioning.

```
(forall (s a e)                                                    (31.9)
   (if (planseq s a e)(ecsSeq s a)))
```

Plan sequences will allow us to talk about agents' changing plans, but tell us nothing about what kinds of changes occur or for what reasons. We will address some of
these issues in subsequent chapters.

31.2 THE PLANNING PROCESS

We think and we act. We often think without acting, and we often act without thinking. In commonsense psychology, these two capacities are viewed as distinct. We
will do that here by dividing cognition crudely into a belief system and a planning
module. A creature with only a belief system would do nothing, however rich its
model of the world. A creature with only a planning module without beliefs about the
state of the world would not survive long. We can view a belief system as a large network of interconnected beliefs, including beliefs about what causes or enables what,
but with no impulse to action. The planning module has goals and uses causal beliefs
to develop plans to achieve these goals. The belief system concerns what agents know;

the planning module concerns what they try to accomplish. The first is about knowledge; the second is about action.

Thus, we can identify three realms in which causality figures. The first is the world with its causal complexes linking ensembles of events.

The second is an agent's belief system, including beliefs about what kinds of things cause what other kinds of things. Desires can be viewed as a particularly important kind of causal belief, a belief about what will contribute to one's thriving.

Desires are usually viewed as weaker than goals. A woman might desire a million dollars, but not work for it, whereas if she has the goal of acquiring a million dollars, it is reasonable to assume she is performing actions that lead in that direction. In a move that is certainly open to considerable debate, we will assign goals to the planning module and desires to the belief system. In a way, we will take "desire" to be what in the belief system corresponds to "goal" in the planning module. Desire will be modeled as a belief, possibly contradicting other beliefs, about what will cause one to thrive at a particular instant. Desires can thus be seen as a variety of beliefs about causes.

```
(forall (a e)                                           (31.10)
    (if (desire a e)
        (exists (e0 e1)
            (and (believe a e1)(causallyInvolved' e1 e e0)
                (thrive' e0 a)))))
```

That is, if agent a desires a state or event e, then a believes e plays a causal role in a's thriving.

This is only a necessary condition for desires, not a sufficient one. If a man believes working at a job he doesn't like is necessary for him to thrive, we wouldn't say he desires to work at the job. Sometimes we judge that we have to do things contrary to our desires.

We certainly desire things that we know are bad for us in the long run. But this is an example of short-term vs. long-term thriving discussed in Chapter 30.

Desires often conflict. A man who desires both good health and a candy bar may be said to believe both that the candy bar will contribute to thriving in the short term and that good health will contribute to thriving in the long term. Often we use the word "desire" to indicate that there is no good causal story for the action, as in "Add salt as desired." But we can view this as merely an indication that our belief about the causal link between the action and thriving is fairly direct and not mediated by more extensive causal reasoning.

In Chapter 24 on Envisioning, we discussed the the conscious cognitive processes of working through the causes and effects of causal relationships to construct envisioned causal systems. By envisioning causal systems an agent can elaborate "atomic" causal beliefs into larger-scale causal beliefs. Where these have as an effect an eventuality that is a frequent goal of the agent's and where the entities involved are appropriately parameterized, we often refer to them as plans. But they exist in the belief system, as "plans in waiting," rather than in the planning module, as "plans in execution."

Beliefs about causality enter into the belief system the same way all beliefs do, by perception in combination with various kinds of valid and invalid reasoning processes.

The third realm in which causality figures is the planning module. The planning module manipulates the causal structure of the world according to one's beliefs to achieve one's goals.

We can view agents as having a single goal – to thrive – and all other goals are subgoals of this in an ever-changing plan to achieve continual thriving. Agents use their causal knowledge to figure out how to achieve their goals; this is the process of planning. They put plans into execution, by carrying out the actions that the plans dictate. They monitor the world as they execute the plan to determine whether the expected results occur. When they don't, or if their goals change for some other reason, they change their plan as appropriate.

We can use the predicate `thePlan` to describe the plan devised by the planning module. It is the plan the agent is executing at any given moment for achieving the goal of thriving, and the agent's actions are defeasibly caused by that action being a subgoal in the Plan.

$$
\begin{array}{ll}
\text{(forall (p a)} & \text{(31.11)} \\
\quad\text{(if (thePlan p a)} & \\
\qquad\text{(exists (e) (and (plan p a e)(thrive' e a)))))} &
\end{array}
$$

That is, the Plan is a plan to thrive.

$$
\begin{array}{ll}
\text{(forall (p a e1)} & \text{(31.12)} \\
\quad\text{(if (and (thePlan p a)(agentOf a e1)(Rexist e1)(etc))} & \\
\qquad\text{(exists (e2) (and (subgoalIn' e2 e1 p)(cause e2 e1)))))} &
\end{array}
$$

That is, actions e1 of a's that really occur are defeasibly caused by a's having the action as a subgoal in the Plan. We do things because we intend to.

The agent's Plan is constantly changing, so the successive versions of the Plan constitute a plan sequence, which we may call "the Plan sequence."

$$
\begin{array}{ll}
\text{(forall (s a)} & \text{(31.13)} \\
\quad\text{(iff (thePlanseq s a)} & \\
\qquad\text{(and (planseq s a e0)(thrive' e0 a)} & \\
\qquad\quad\text{(forall (p i)} & \\
\qquad\qquad\text{(iff (nth p i s)} & \\
\qquad\qquad\quad\text{(exists (e t)} & \\
\qquad\qquad\qquad\text{(and (thePlan' e p a)(atTime e t))))))))} &
\end{array}
$$

That is, a plan p is in the Plan sequence of agent a if and only if there is some time t at which p was the Plan of a's.

Since the Plan sequence is a plan sequence, for any two successive elements of the Plan sequence, there is a change from the first to the second, and the first is thus before the second.

Plans go through a number of stages from conception to execution. If the agent's top-level goal is to thrive, the use of causal knowledge of how to bring about thriving results in the agent's deciding to pursue desires as goals. But because each desire is only one bit of causal knowledge, the planning module will not necessarily adopt every desire as a goal to pursue actively.

An intention is a subgoal in the Plan of an agent that is an action by the agent.

```
(forall (a e)                                                     (31.14)
   (iff (intend a e)
        (exists (p)
           (and (thePlan p a)(subgoalIn e p)(agentOf a e)))))
```

A desire or other eventuality becomes a goal when the agent decides to achieve it. That is, to decide to do something is to effect a change of state from one in which that something is not a goal in the Plan to one in which it is.

```
(forall (a e)                                                     (31.15)
   (if (eventuality e)
       (iff (decideTo a e)
            (exists (e1)
               (and (changeTo e1)(subgoalIn' e1 e p)
                    (thePlan p a))))))
```

We can also decide to execute entire plans.

```
(forall (p1 a g)                                                  (31.16)
   (if (plan p1 a g)
       (iff (decideTo a p1)
            (exists (p e1)
               (and (changeTo e1)(subplan' e1 p1 p)
                    (thePlan p a))))))
```

The decideTo predicate is a bridge from the belief system to the planning module. Just as perception and reasoning transform causes in the world into causal beliefs in the belief system, "deciding to" transforms these causal beliefs, including desires, into intentions.

To plan to achieve a goal is to reason about causes that will bring about the goal and then to decide to adopt as subgoals the actions and eventualities in that plan.

```
(forall (g a p s)                                                 (31.17)
   (if (and (goal g a)(planseq s a g)(last p s)
            (decideTo a p))
       (planTo a g p)))
```

That is, if agent a has goal g, a envisions a plan sequence s for achieving g, plan p is the last element in the sequence s, and a decides to add p as a subplan of thePlan, then a plans to achieve g by means of plan p.

Generally when a goal is decomposed into subgoals, the subgoals are entered into the Plan simultaneously. If we want to retrieve a book from a shelf, we plan to stand up, walk over to the shelf, and reach for the book. It is not the case that we first decide to stand up, then at some later time decide to walk over to the shelf, and so on. Thus, when an agent is observed executing the earlier actions in a decomposition of a goal, the agent can be presumed to have the later actions in the decomposition already in the Plan, as intentions. Similarly, if an agent is executing the preconditions of some planning operator, the agent can be presumed to be planning to execute the body of the operator.

Planning, deciding, and intending all take place in the mind. They initiate actions that take place in the external, physical world. How the gap between the mind and the external world is bridged has until recently been a deep philosophical conundrum. It has only been with the advent of the computer metaphor for mind that we have understood that "thought is computation" (Hobbes, 1651), that computation can be done by physical systems, and that these physical systems can initiate actions in the physical world. But this account is not a part of our everyday commonsense theories. In our commonsense view we simply accept that mental events can effect physical events. If I will my arm to rise, and I'm not otherwise restrained, my arm will rise.

In our framework, we bridge the mind–world gap with the predicate will. The expression (will a e) says that an agent a wills event e to happen. We can will various bodily actions, such as lifting an arm. We can will various mental actions, such as concentrating on some aspect of the environment, or doing mental arithmetic, or planning a party. The actions we will initiate causal chains that can have far-reaching consequences. But it is only a relatively small set of physical and mental actions we can will.

In Chapter 13 we allowed coercions from agents to their acts of will as arguments of the predicate cause, so we could talk about agents causing events. An agent causes an event when the agent's act of will causes it. In Chapter 17 we gave an example of an action that can be willed – lifting one's arm. In Chapter 47 on Mind–Body Interaction we discuss acts of will and voluntary actions in a little more detail. Here we only relate will to the planning and deciding process.

The constraint on the first argument of will is that it is an agent.

$$(\text{forall } (a\ e)\ (\text{if } (\text{will } a\ e)(\text{agent } a))) \tag{31.18}$$

The second argument can take a very limited set of eventualities. One can't will a car to start, although one can will actions that in turn cause the car to start, such as inserting the key into the ignition. The only constraint we will stipulate here is that a must be the agent of e.

$$(\text{forall } (a\ e)\ (\text{if } (\text{will } a\ e)(\text{agentOf } a\ e))) \tag{31.19}$$

If agent a wills e and e actually occurs as a result, then the willing has directly caused e, that is, there are no intermediate eventualities in the causal chain initiated by the willing.

```
(forall (e1 a e)                                                    (31.20)
   (if (and (will' e1 a e)(cause e1 e))(dcause e1 e)))
```

The condition that e1 cause e is in the antecedent because, for example, one could be paralyzed and the act of will fails. Or e could happen right on time, but for other reasons than the willing.

Generally, when someone wills to do something, it is because he or she intends to do it. That is, the action is the next action in thePlan.

```
(forall (a e p)                                                     (31.21)
   (if (and (thePlan p a)(will a e))(subgoalIn e p)))
```

In a weak sort of converse, if some action by the agent is in the Plan, it is possible for a to will the action, and the action occurs, then defeasibly its being in the plan is causally involved in the occurrence.

```
(forall (p a e0 e e1 c)                                             (31.22)
   (if (and (thePlan p a)(subgoalIn' e0 e p)(agentOf a e)
              (will' e1 a e)(possible e1 c)(etc))
       (causallyInvolved e0 e)))
```

31.3 STRATEGIES AND TACTICS

Causal knowledge can be used on an ad hoc basis to develop plans for specific goals. However, we also ruminate about how to achieve general classes of goals, developing general "strategies" for achieving them at some later time. Consider the strategy of securing customer loyalty by giving coupons (Gordon, 2004). The causal basis of this strategy is the following:

1. Giving a coupon to someone enables him or her to use it.
2. The use of a coupon causes the price of the item to be less.
3. The less the price of an item, the more a person prefers to buy the item at the business that sells it for that price.
4. People tend to do what they prefer to do.

We could further unpack the third rule in terms of a person's maximizing available resources. The broad-scale characterization of this strategy is the rule, "Secure customer loyalty by issuing coupons."

A strategy can be seen as a large-scale structure of causal knowledge that can in principle be unpacked into individual causal rules, and rests on these rules, but is generally used as a whole. Moreover, it is knowledge about types that can be instantiated in any number of tokens. For example, we can instantiate the above rule for any number of specific stores, kinds of coupons, and classes of customers.

A strategy like this is a plan, in the sense that it is a way of exploiting the causal structure of the world to achieve certain goals. The term "strategy," however, is usually reserved for very general classes of circumstances. We would not normally call something a strategy if it was a plan that could be employed only once and only with a specific individual. Not all of the entities involved in the strategy need be general. A man may have a strategy for persuading his wife, and only her, of something. But generally if we are to call this a strategy, then the class of situations in which it would be applied would be general

Thus a rather weak constraint on a strategy is that it is a plan whose top-level goal is an eventuality type. Recall from Chapter 7 that an eventuality with parameters is an eventuality type.

```
(forall (p e)                                              (31.23)
    (if (strategy p e)
        (exists (a s)
            (and (plan p a e)(parameters s e)(not (null s))))))
```

Not much would be gained by further specifying that the subgoals in the plan or strategy are eventuality types. The fact that they are subgoals of a top-level eventuality type goal would very nearly force some of them to be eventuality types.

A tactic is also some agent's general plan.

```
(forall (p e)                                              (31.24)
    (if (tactic p e)
        (exists (a s)
            (and (plan p a e)(parameters s e)(not (null s))))))
```

However, it is usual to distinguish strategies and tactics, especially in military and government contexts. The principal difference between these is that strategies tend to be longer-term and aimed at achieving higher-level goals; tactics are shorter-term and aim at achieving lower-level goals. For example, a strategy in Iraq might be to win the hearts and minds of the people by sending in American troops, protecting them, and establishing order, to enable civilian life and commerce to flourish there. Responding to an attack by a sniper in a mosque by blowing up the mosque would be a tactic that achieved the lower-level goal of protecting the troops at the expense of the higher-level strategic goal of winning the hearts and minds of the people. Of course, tactics do not always run counter to strategic goals; normally they are in service of strategic goals. But when they do run counter, it is especially easy to identify them as tactics.

Other features of strategies and tactics derive from the fact that strategies are in the service of longer-term, higher-level goals. Strategies tend to involve more agents than tactics. Strategies, being longer-term, provide the possibility of creative preparation and building capabilities for future circumstances, whereas tactics normally are responses to specific events with available, bounded resources.

A very weak axiom that at least begins to capture the distinction between strategies and tactics is the following:

```
(forall (p1 e1 p2 e2)                                    (31.25)
    (if (and (strategy p1 e1)(tactic p2 e2))
        (not (subplan p1 p2))))
```

That is, a strategy is not a subplan of a tactic. Strategies can contain tactics, but tactics do not contain strategies.

A stronger rule would be that a tactic has some strategic goal it is ultimately in the service of, so we can say that if something is a tactic, it is the subplan of some strategy.

```
(forall (p e)                                            (31.26)
    (if (and (tactic p e)(etc))
        (exists (p1)
            (and (strategy p1 e1)(subplan p p1)))))
```

We make this rule defeasible for cases where the so-called tactic is entirely a response to the immediate situation with no concern for long-term consequences.

31.4 EXECUTABILITY AND COMPLETE PLANS

The definition for plan allows plans to be incomplete. In fact, a single goal with no subgoals is a limiting case of a plan. So what makes a plan "complete"?

A plan is a way of manipulating the causal structure of the world to achieve one's goals. It must bottom out in events that are assured to occur at the proper time. There are three sources for this assurance:

1. The event is an action on the part of the agent that the agent is capable of carrying out at the required time.
2. The event will happen anyway at the required time, because of external causes.
3. The event is an action on the part of another agent, who is committed to performing the action at the required time.

For example, a trapeze artist has the plan to swing out on her trapeze, fly through the air, and be caught by her partner. She knows that she can swing out on her trapeze because this is an action that is executable by her. She knows that she will fly through the air; the laws of physics will take care of that. She knows her partner will catch her because he is committed to doing so. Thus, her plan is complete.

In Chapter 15 we defined the predication (executable e a c t) to mean that action e is executable by agent a given constraints c. Here we will extend this to the concept of executable1, which also covers the cases of physics and committed others taking care of the events. We also make the definition recursive, so an event is executable1 if all its subgoals are executable1.

```
(forall (e a c)                                              (31.27)
    (iff (executable1 e a c t)
        (or (executable e a c t)
            (atTime e t)
            (exists (b) (and (agent b)(committed b e)
                (executable e b c t)))
            (forall (e1)
                (if (subgoal e1 e)(executable1 e1 a c t))))))))
```

This says that event e is executable1 by agent a given constraints c if it is executable by a, or if it will happen anyway, or if some other agent b is committed to making sure e occurs, or if its subgoals are all executable1.

Executability interacts with time in complex ways. Most of a plan will occur not immediately, but at some future time, and later subgoals may become executable because of the satisfaction of earlier subgoals. However, this is accommodated by making e the conjunction of the event and its occurrence at a particular time. So if the event is b's catching a at time t1, the e in the axiom would be an e for which the following hold:

```
(and (catch' e1 b a)(and' e e1 e2)(catch' e1 b a)
    (atTime' e2 e1 t1))
```

That is, b is committed to the conjunction of catching a and having that catch be at time t.

The concept of committed is central to a theory of social relationships and joint action, and is explicated in other work by Hobbs, Sagae, and Wertheim (2012). But its principal property is that if someone is committed to an event occurring and is the agent of that event, then defeasibly that event will occur.

```
(forall (a e e1)                                             (31.28)
    (if (and (committed a e1)(atTime' e1 e t)(agentOf a e)(etc))
        (atTimo o t)))
```

We are now in a position to say what makes a plan complete. A plan is complete when its top-level goal is executable1 now (given constraints c).

```
(forall (p a e c)                                            (31.29)
    (iff (completePlan p a e c)
        (exists (t) (and (Now t)(executable1 e a c t)))))
```

A partial plan is a plan that is not complete.

(forall (p a e c)   (31.30)
    (iff (partialPlan p a e c)
        (and (plan p a e)(not (completePlan p a e)))))

31.5 TYPES OF PLANS

Since a plan can be viewed as a set of subgoals and subgoalOf relations among them, it can be viewed as a conjunction of these subgoals and relations, and hence as a logical expression. Thus, we can substitute values for parameters just as we would in any logical expression, and the result will be an instance of the original plan.

(forall (p1 p)   (31.31)
    (iff (planInstance p1 p)
        (exists (a g) (and (plan p a g)(instance p1 p)))))

An planInstancePlus is a plan instance that has possibly been extended by elaborating some of the subgoals into subplans for achieving them.

(forall (p1 p)   (31.32)
    (iff (planInstancePlus p1 p)
        (exists (a g p0)
            (and (plan p1 a g)(plan p0 a g)(planInstance p0 p)
                (subplan p0 p1)))))

That is, we first construct an instance p0 of p, instantiating the parameters of p. Then we extend p0 to p1, so that p0 is a subplan of p1 with the same agent and the same top-level goal.

Some goals have expected or normal plans associated with them in an agent's knowledge base. Where this is the case, there will be an axiom of the form

(forall (g x a)
    (if (and (goal g a)(q' g x))
        (exists (p) (and (normalPlan p a g) ...))))

where the dots would represent the further specification of the details of the plan and where q is a characterization of the goal. We won't attempt here to specify what normal means, except to say that it has a distributional aspect – normal plans are frequently employed – and a social aspect – normal plans are what communities of agents expect to be executed.

A normal plan is a plan.

(forall (p a g)   (31.33)
    (if (normalPlan p a g) (plan p a g)))

Some plans involve a relationship among agents, including adversarial plans and counterplans, assistive plans, collaborative plans, and shared plans.

Adversarial plans are aimed at preventing or violating the goals of other agents.

```
(forall (p1 a1 a g1)                                              (31.34)
   (iff (adversarialPlan p1 a1 a g1)
        (exists (p g)
           (and (nequal a a1)(plan p a g)(plan p1 a1 g1)
                (not' g1 g)))))
```

That is, p1 is an advesarial plan by agent a1 to achieve goal g1 which is the negation of a goal g another agent a is trying to achieve.

Some plans are aimed at blocking an adversarial plan.

```
(forall (p2 p1 a a1 g1)                                           (31.35)
   (iff (counterplan p2 p1 a a1 g1)
        (exists (e1 e2)
           (and (nequal a a1)(adversarialPlan p1 a1 a g1)
                (cause' e1 p1 g1)(not' e2 e1)
                (plan p2 a e2)))))
```

Here p1 is an adversarial plan of agent a1's to block agent a's goal. Plan p2 is a counterplan by agent a to block plan p1 of a1's. Eventuality g1 is the negation of some goal of a's, eventuality e1 is plan p1's causing that negation, and eventuality e2 is the negation of e1. Counterplan p2 is a plan by agent a for achieving that negation e2, that is, for achieving the failure of a1's adversarial plan p1.

Some plans, although not being exactly adversarial, are competitive in the sense that only one agent can achieve his or her goal. The aim is not to actively defeat the other agents' achievement of their goals, but because of the mutual exclusivity of the set of goals, that would be a side effect of one agent's success. Furthermore, each agent's goal is an instance of a common type.

```
(forall (g a1 a2)                                                 (31.36)
   (iff (competitiveGoal g a1 a2)
        (exists (g1 g2)
           (and (nequal a1 a2)(instance g1 g)(instance g2 g)
                (goal g1 a1)(goal g2 a2)
                (inconsistent g1 g2)))))
```

That is, a competitive goal is one that can be instantiated for each of the competing agents, but it cannot hold for both agents. Then a competitive plan is a plan that is aimed at achieving a competitive goal.

```
(forall (p a1 a2 g)                                               (31.37)
   (iff (competitivePlan p a1 a2 g)
        (exists (g1)
           (and (plan p a1 g1)(instance g1 g)
                (competitiveGoal g a1 a2)))))
```

The other agent a2 will probably also have a competitive plan for achieving an instance of g.

Some plans are assistive in the sense that they aim at achieving a goal for another agent.

```
(forall (p a a1 g)                                            (31.38)
    (iff (assistivePlan p a a1 g)
         (exists (e e1)
              (and (nequal a a1)(goal' e g a)(goal' e1 g a1)
                   (cause e1 e)(plan p a g)))))
```

Here e is the eventuality of g's being a goal of a's, e1 is the eventuality of g's being a goal of a1's, and the latter causes the former. That is, agent a has adopted the goal g precisely because it was a goal of agent a1's. Then p is a's plan for achieving g.

A group s of agents shares a plan p just in case

1. The group itself has the top-level goal.
2. Defeasibly the members of the group mutually believe the subgoal structure of the plan.
3. If members of the group are involved in an action in the plan, then the members are committed to performing their part in that action.

Then we can define a shared plan as follows:

```
(forall (p s g)                                              (31.39)
    (iff (sharedPlan p s g)
         (and (forall (a)(if (member a s)(agent a)))
              (goal g s)(plan p s g)
              (forall (e g1 g2)
                   (if (and (subgoal' e g1 g2)(subgoalIn g1 p)
                            (subgoalIn g2 p)(etc))
                       (mb s e)))
              (forall (a e)
                   (if (and (member a s)(subgoalIn e p)(arg* a e))
                       (committed a e)))))))
```

The expression (sharedPlan p s g) says that p is a shared plan by a group s of agents to achieve goal g. Line 3 says that all members of s are agents. Line 4 says that the group has g as a goal and p is a plan for achieving the goal, where s is viewed as the agent having the goal. The latter establishes that the causal connections are believed to be adequate for achieving the goal. Lines 5–8 say that the members of s mutually believe in the structure of the plan; this implication is only defeasible because each member of the group may not know the entire plan. Lines 9–11 say that the members of s are committed to performing their parts in the plan.

Joint action, or doing something together, is executing a shared plan. For a shared plan to be executable, it must bottom out in the actions of individual agents.

Further explication of commitment and shared plans can be found in Hobbs et al. (2012), where it is used as the basis of a commonsense theory of interpersonal relations and other microsociological concepts.

An agent can take a variety of cognitive stances to his or her own plans or to the plans of other agents. For example, one agent can envision the plan of another agent, the plans of others can be unknown, and an agent's plan can even be unknown to the agent himself or herself.

An envisioned plan is a plan that is envisioned by another agent. A plan is a causal system, and the expression (ecs p a1) says that p is a causal system envisioned by agent a1.

```
(forall (p a a1 g)                                      (31.40)
    (iff (envisionedPlan p a a1 g)
         (and (plan p a g)(ecs p a1))))
```

An unknown plan is a plan by one agent that is not known by another agent.

```
(forall (p a a1 g)                                      (31.41)
    (iff (unknownPlan p a a1 g)
         (and (plan p a g)(nequal a a1)(not (know a1 p)))))
```

A nonconscious plan is one that is not known to the planning agent himself or herself.

```
(forall (p a g)                                         (31.42)
    (iff (nonconsciousPlan p a g)
         (and (plan p a g)(not (know a p)))))
```

Plan types can also be described in terms of when and how often they are executed, or done. As we defined it in Chapter 15, for an agent to do an action is for the agent to be the agent of the action and for the action to really exist. Here we add a further, defeasible constraint, viz., that the agent's goal to do the action causes its occurrence. We also weaken the condition of being the agent of the action to being somehow involved in the event (arg*).

```
(forall (a e)                                           (31.43)
    (if (and (do a e)(etc))
        (exists (e1)
            (and (arg* a e)(Rexist e)(goal' e1 e a)(cause e1 e)))))
```

Here e really happens. Eventuality e1 is e's being a goal of a's, and e1 causes e.

Because a plan is a structured set of eventualities, we can also speak of plans being executed, or done.

```
(forall (p a g)                                         (31.44)
    (if (plan p a g)
        (iff (do a p)
            (forall (e)
                (if (and (subgoalIn e p)(arg* a e))(do a e))))))
```

Plan types can be executed never, only once, or multiple times. Reusable plans will be defined in Chapter 45 on Execution Control as having at least two instances. If these instances are actually executed, we can call the plan a "reused plan."

```
(forall (p a g)                                         (31.45)
    (iff (reusedPlan p a g)
        (exists (p1 p2)
            (and (planInstancePlus p1 p)(planInstancePlus p2 p)
                 (nequal p1 p2)(do a p1)(do a p2)))))
```

The different times of execution of the two plan instances can be built into the description of p1 and p2.

Some plan types are executed occasionally and some are executed repeatedly. To distinguish between these two cases would require a commonsense theory of distributions, which we do not yet have. But at least we can say that both are reused plans.

```
(forall (p a g)                                          (31.46)
    (if (occasionalPlan p a g)(reusedPlan p a g)))
```

```
(forall (p a g)                                          (31.47)
    (if (repeatedPlan p a g)(reusedPlan p a g)))
```

Some plans are executed periodically. A periodic plan is one whose instances constitute a periodic temporal sequence, that is, where the intervals between successive instances are all equal. For the definition, we use the predicate periodicTseq from Chapter 16.

```
(forall (p a g)                                          (31.48)
    (iff (periodicPlan p a g)
        (exists (s)
            (and (reusedPlan p a g)
                (forall (p1)
                    (iff (member p1 s)(planInstancePlus p1 p)))
                (periodicTseq s)))))
```

That is, p is a periodic plan if its instantiations constitute a periodic temporal sequence.

Some plans are to be executed continuously for some interval of time.

```
(forall (p a g t)                                        (31.49)
    (iff (continuousPlan p a g t)
        (exists (e)(and (do' e a p)(timeSpanOf t e)
            (interval t)))))
```

That is, a plan that is continuous over interval t is one whose execution has a time span of t.

31.6 HELPING

The simplest notion of "help" is that one event helps another event to happen if it is in its causal complex. In this sense of "help," if we drop a lighted match in a forest, we are helping to start a forest fire, even though it is no one's goal to start a forest fire. The joke about helping an elderly lady across the street when she doesn't want to cross the street is helping in this sense.

```
(forall (e1 e2)                                          (31.50)
    (iff (help0 e1 e2)(causallyInvolved e1 e2)))
```

In a slightly stronger sense, one agent a helps another agent a1 achieve e if e is a goal of a1's and a does actions in the causal complex for e. In this sense, one might say that John McCain helped Barack Obama become president by choosing Sarah Palin as his running mate. Similarly, if you lose a $20 bill, it may help the person who finds it buy Christmas presents for his children. You have done something that helps someone buy Christmas presents, and that is someone's goal, but there was

no intention on your part that that causal connection obtain. We will call this sense
help1.

(forall (a a1 e)   (31.51)
    (iff (help1 a a1 e)
        (exists (e1)
            (and (goal e a1)(causallyInvolved e1 e)(do a e1)))))

That is, agent a helps agent a1 achieve a1's goal e if a does something e1 that is in
the causal complex for e. Note that a and a1 need not be distinct, as you can help
yourself.

In a stronger sense, agent a has the intention that his actions bring about the goal
e. For example, I might take away your car keys so you can't drive home drunk from
a party. In this way, I help you live and thrive, even though my actions are no part of
a plan you have to live and thrive.

(forall (a a1 e)   (31.52)
    (iff (help2 a a1 e)
        (exists (e1 e2)
            (and (goal' e2 e a1)(causallyInvolved e1 e)
                (do a e1)(cause e2 e1)))))

Here e2 is the condition of e being a goal of a1's, and it functions as a cause of a's
doing e1. Because you want (e2) to live (e), I'll take your keys away (e1). I've thereby
helped you continue to live.

The strongest sense of "help" is when agents a and a1 construct a shared plan in
which a performs some of the actions required to bring about a1's goal e. If I pick up
one end of a sofa to help you carry it across the room in your plan to rearrange your
furniture, I am becoming part of a shared plan we have now adopted for achieving
the rearrangement.

(forall (a a1 e)   (31.53)
    (iff (help3 a a1 e)
        (exists (p s e1)
            (and (sharedPlan p s e)(doubleton s a a1)(goal e a1)
                (subgoalIn e1 p)(arg* a e1)))))

Here p is the shared plan by agents a and a1 to achieve a1's goal e, and e1 is a subgoal
in that plan that a plays a role in.

PREDICATES INTRODUCED IN THIS CHAPTER

(connectedSubgoal* e1 e2 a s1 s2)
    e1 is a subgoal of e2 or a connected subgoal* of a subgoal of e2 for agent a, where
    e1 and e2 are connected by sugoals in s1 and subgoal relations in s2.

(plan p a g)
    p is a plan by agent a to achieve goal g.

(subgoalIn e p)
    e is a subgoal in plan p.

(subgoalsOf s p)
    Set s is the set of subgoals in plan p.

(subplan p1 p)
   Plan p1 is a subplan of plan p.

(planseq s a g)
   s is a sequence of plans by agent a to achieve goal g.

(desire a e)
   Agent a desires e.

(thePlan p a)
   p is the plan agent a is currently executing.

(thePlanseq s a)
   s is a sequence of plans agent a executes.

(intend a e)
   Agent a intends to do e.

(decideTo a e)
   Agent a decides to do e.

(planTo a g p)
   Agent a decides to achieve goal g by doing plan p.

(will a e)
   Agent a wills event e to happen.

(strategy p e)
   Plan p is a strategy for achieving goal e.

(tactic p e)
   Plan p is a tactic for achieving goal e.

(executable1 p a c t)
   Plan p is ultimately executable by agent a given constraints c at time t, perhaps
   with committed others.

(committed a e)
   Agent a is committed to doing e.

(completePlan p a e c)
   p is a complete plan by agent a for achieving goal e given constraints c.

(partialPlan p a e c)
   p is a partial plan by agent a for achieving goal e given constraints c.

(planInstance p1 p)
   Plan p1 is an instance of plan type p.

(planInstancePlus p1 p)
   Plan p1 is an instance of plan type p, perhaps with some subgoals elaborated into
   subplans.

(normalPlan p a g)
   Plan p is the normal way for agent a to achieve g.

(adversarialPlan p a a1 g)
   p is a plan by agent a to achieve g, which is the negation of a goal of agent a1.

(counterplan p p1 a a1 g)
   p is a plan by agent a to counteract an adversarial plan p1 by agent a1 to block
   a's goal of achieving g.

(competitiveGoal g a1 a2)
    g is a goal type, agents a1 and a2 both have instances of g as goals, and these
    instances are mutually exclusive.

(competitivePlan p a1 a2 g)
    p is a plan by agent a1 to achieve an instance of g, where g is a competitive goal
    between agents a1 and a2.

(assistivePlan p a a1 g)
    p is a plan by agent a to achieve agent a1's goal g.

(sharedPlan p s g)
    p is a shared plan by a group of agents s to achieve g.

(envisionedPlan p a a1 g)
    p is a plan by agent a that agent a1 envisions.

(unknownPlan p a a1 g)
    p is a plan that agent a has for achieving g that agent a1 does not know about.

(nonconsciousPlan p a g)
    p is a plan that a has for achieving g but does not know he or she has.

(reusedPlan p a g)
    p is a reusable plan that is actually reused.

(occasionalPlan p a g)
    p is a plan that a uses occasionally for achieving g.

(repeatedPlan p a g)
    p is a plan that a uses repeatedly for achieving g.

(periodicPlan p a g)
    p is a plan that a uses periodically for achieving g.

(continuousPlan p a g t)
    p is a plan that a executes continuously over interval t for achieving g.

(help0 e1 e2)
    e1 is in the causal complex for e2.

(help1 a a1 e)
    a does something to cause a1 to achieve e.

(help2 a a1 e)
    a does something to cause a1 to achieve e, for the purpose of a1's achieving e.

(help3 a a1 e)
    a and a1 engage in a shared plan to achieve a1's goal e.

32

Goal Management

32.1 ADDING, REMOVING, AND MODIFYING GOALS

In previous chapters we have discussed the desires agents have in terms of their
beliefs about the efficacy of certain actions for bringing about certain states; we have
discussed the goals and subgoals in "The Plan" the agents are continuously executing as they go through the world in a purposeful fashion; and we have discussed the
decisions that convert a causal belief into a subgoal. But in a way, this suggests too
simple a picture. The Plan is a very dynamic structure, and the goals in it can be
added, accomplished, abandoned, and modified. We define predicates for this aspect
of planning in this section. This requires being able to talk about manipulating goals
as independent entities and relating them to desires and to The Plan. In Chapter 31
we presented a very simplified picture of people as agents for whom a goal is either
in or not in The Plan. But reality is much more complicated than this. Some goals
are in The Plan and are actively being pursued at a given moment. Others have high
priority, even though they are not currently being pursued. In the second section
we characterize priority in terms of its determining factors, and then in the last section we talk about how priority influences which goals in The Plan are executed at
a given time. All of this presents a much more nuanced picture of how beliefs and
desires generate actions.

Agents can decide that a goal is worth pursuing, thereby adding it to their plan.

$$(forall \ (a \ g) \hspace{4cm} (32.1)$$
$$(iff \ (addGoal \ a \ g)$$
$$(exists \ (p \ e)$$
$$(and \ (thePlan \ p \ a)(subgoalIn' \ e \ g \ p)(changeTo \ e)))))$$

That is, agent a adds goal g if and only if there is a change to g being a subgoal in a's
plan.

Agents can remove goals once they are achieved.

$$(forall \ (a \ g) \hspace{4cm} (32.2)$$
$$(iff \ (removeAchievedGoal \ a \ g)$$
$$(exists \ (p \ e \ e1 \ e2)$$
$$(and \ (thePlan \ p \ a)(subgoalIn' \ e \ g \ p)(changeFrom' \ e1 \ e)$$
$$(changeTo' \ e2 \ g)(cause \ e2 \ e1)))))$$

That is, there is a change from g being a goal in agent a's Plan and this was caused by g becoming true in the real world.

Agents can decide that a goal is no longer worth pursuing.

```
(forall (a g)                                              (32.3)
   (iff (abandonGoal a g)
        (exists (p e)
           (and (thePlan p a)(subgoalIn' e g p)(changeFrom e)
                (not g)))))
```

That is, there is a change from g being a subgoal in agent a's Plan even though g is not true, or does not hold.

Agents can remove goals if they are thought to be unachievable. For example, suppose I have as a goal that a valuable vase not get broken. It breaks. This goal is no longer achievable, so I remove it from my Plan.

```
(forall (a g c)                                            (32.4)
   (iff (removeViolatedGoal a g c)
        (exists (p e e1 e2)
           (and (thePlan p a)(subgoalIn' e g p)(changeFrom' e1 e)
                (impossible' e2 g c)(cause e2 e1)))))
```

This is one kind of goal abandonment, where the goal's impossibility (with respect to constraints c) is what causes the goal to be abandoned. Resignation is ceasing to have a goal because of a realization or belief that it is impossible to achieve.

Agents can put off goals so they are no longer in pursuit of them. This involves changing temporal parameters on the goal so that there is no longer a necessity of pursuing them immediately.

```
(forall (a g)                                              (32.5)
   (iff (suspendGoal a g)
        (exists (p e1 e2 e3 e4 t1 t2)
           (and (thePlan p a)(change e1 e2)
                (subgoalIn' e1 e3 p)(subgoalIn' e2 e4 p)
                (atTime' e3 g t1)(atTime' e4 g t2)
                (before t1 t2)))))
```

Here e3 is g's occurring at time t1 and e4 is g's occurring at time t2. e1 is a's having e3 as a goal, and e2 is a's having e4 as a goal, where p is a's Plan. Thus, there is a change from a's wanting to do g at time t1 to a's wanting to do g at some later time t2.

Agents can modify their goals. This can be viewed as a change from having one goal to having another, where the two goals are somehow related. They may be closely related, for example deciding to go on vacation to Puerto Vallerta rather than Mazatlan. Or they could be less closely related, for example, as a change from planning an expensive vacation to a decision to buy a new car.

```
(forall (a g1 g2)                                          (32.6)
   (iff (modifyGoal a g1 g2)
        (exists (p e1 e2)
           (and (change e1 e2)(thePlan p a)
                (subgoalIn' e1 g1 p)(subgoalIn' e2 g2 p)
                (similar g1 g2)))))
```

That is, agent a modifies goal g1 into goal g2, where g1 and g2 are similar in that they share properties.

Agents can modify a goal to a more specific goal. The relation between the old and new goals is implication.

```
(forall (a g1 g2)                                        (32.7)
    (iff (specifyGoal a g1 g2)
        (and (modifyGoal a g1 g2)(imply g2 g1))))
```

Agents can modify a goal to a more general goal.

```
(forall (a g1 g2)                                        (32.8)
    (iff (generalizeGoal a g1 g2)
        (and (modifyGoal a g1 g2)(imply g1 g2))))
```

An agent is actually pursuing a goal if the agent is executing an action that is a subgoal of that goal, precisely because it is a subgoal, or if the agent is planning how to achieve the goal. But the first of these is the way we defined the predicate try in Chapter 28. To be pursuing a goal is to be developing or executing a plan for achieving it.

```
(forall (a g)                                            (32.9)
    (iff (pursueGoal a g)
        (exists (p)
            (or (and (plan p a g)(ecs p a))
                (planTo a g p)
                (try a g)))))
```

In line 4 the agent is just envisioning a plan, that is, planning. In line 5 the agent has decided on a plan to execute. In line 6 the agent is actually trying to achieve the goal.

32.2 PRIORITY

The order in which actions in a plan are carried out is usually underdetermined by the causal structure in the plan. A man may want to read a novel and go to the grocery store. There is no causal relation between these two actions that says one must be done before the other. Whether we execute an action at any given moment and the order in which we execute a set of actions are often determined by priority.

At least three factors play a role in determining the priority of an action, all of them scalar and two of them already explicated in previous chapters. The first is the importance of the action to the agent. This was introduced in Chapter 28 and constrained by its relation to the subgoal predicate – a goal is at least as important as its subgoals.

The more important an action is, the higher its priority.

The second factor is effort. We have not discussed this before. There is physical effort and mental effort. A commonsense theory of the human body and its activities would have to include an account of the intake and expenditure of energy, and physical effort would correlate with this. Mental effort is harder to characterize, but perhaps it could be explicated in terms of the time or number of mental operations required to integrate a proposition in the focus of attention into one's belief system. A closely related concept which we have explicated is difficulty, in Chapter 15. The more obstacles one must overcome to achieve something, the more difficult it is. Difficulty and effort roughly correlate: Usually the more difficult something is, the more effort it requires.

We would like to say that, defeasibly, the more effort something takes, the lower its priority. We tend to do the short and easy jobs before the long and hard ones. Here we will translate that into difficulty. The more difficult an action, the lower its priority.

The third factor, not unrelated to the second is the likelihood of success. If I learn that I am bound to fail when I attempt an action, I will become less likely to attempt it. Thus, the more likely something is, the higher its priority, other things being equal.

To deal with the "other things being equal" clause, we have to make the simplifying assumption that importance, difficulty and likelihood are the only factors in determining priorities, and even with that we can only place very loose constraints on what it means for an action to have a priority.

First, we introduce a priority scale for an agent.

```
(forall (s a)                                                    (32.10)
    (if (priorityScale s a)
        (and (agent a)(scale s))))
```

The axioms constraining the partial ordering on the priority scale are long, but not complicated, because the antecedent needs to establish labels and state the ceteris paribus conditions. But the key provision in the following axiom is that if the importance is less, then so is the priority. The axiom is defeasible.

```
(forall (p a g1 g2 g s1 s2 s3 s x11 x12 x2 x3 y1 y2)              (32.11)
    (if (and (thePlan p a)(subgoalIn g1 p)(subgoalIn g2 p)
             (importanceScale s1 a)(difficultyScale s2 g)
             (likelihoodScale s3)
             (instance g1 g)(instance g2 g)
             (priorityScale s a)
             (at g1 x11 s1)(at g2 x12 s1)
             (at g1 x2 s2)(at g2 x2 s2)(at g1 x3 s3)(at g2 x3 s3)
             (at g1 y1 s)(at g2 y2 s)
             (lts x11 x12 s1)(etc))
        (lts y1 y2 s)))
```

Line 2 says that g1 and g2 are subgoals in agent a's Plan; these are the goals whose priorities are being compared. Lines 3–6 say that s1 is the importance scale, s2 the difficulty scale, s3 the likelihood scale, and s the priority scale. Since difficulty is with respect to a class of eventualities, we posit an eventuality type g that subsumes both g1 and g2 (line 5). Line 7 labels g1's importance as x11 and g2's as x12. Line 8 says that g1 and g2 have the same difficulty and likelihood; these are the ceteris paribus conditions. Line 9 labels g1's priority as y1 and g2's as y2. Line 10, the significant part of the antecedent, says g1's importance is less than g2's. The conclusion, line 11, says that g1's priority is less than g2's priority.

To complete our constraints on the meaning of priority, we would need similar axioms relating difficulty and likelihood to priority, but because importance is probably the most important factor, we will leave it with that.

The priority of a goal is its location on the priority scale.

```
(forall (p g a)                                         (32.12)
    (iff (priority p g a)
        (exists (s)
            (and (priorityScale s a)(at g p s)))))
```

32.3 ASSESSING AND PRIORITIZING GOALS

Goals are justified by an agent's model of the world. A justification is a causal story relating the goal to some higher-level goal. The causal story is the product of an envisionment.

```
(forall (e g a)                                         (32.13)
    (iff (goalJustification e g a)
        (exists (p g1)
            (and (thePlan p a)(subgoalIn g1 p)
                (plan e a g1)(subgoalIn g e)))))
```

That is, a justification e for a goal g is a plan of which g is a part that links g with some goal g1 in the agent's Plan.

Agents can reconsider whether a goal is worth pursuing. This is a matter of envisioning to situations involving the costs, values, and feasibility constraints, thereby arriving at new priorities. To assess a goal is thus to envision to and from the goal and its priority, perhaps to modify its priority.

```
(forall (a g e p)                                       (32.14)
    (if (priority' e p g a)
        (iff (assessGoal a g)
            (or (envisionFrom a g)(envisionFrom a e)
                (envisionTo a g)(envisionTo a e)))))
```

That is, where e is the property of p being the priority of goal g, then to assess g is to envision causal chains from or to g or e, thus exploring the causes or consequences of the goal or its priority.

Two goals are in conflict if they cannot both obtain at the same time.

```
(forall (g1 g2)                                         (32.15)
    (iff (conflict g1 g2)
        (forall (t)
            (and (if (atTime g1 t)(not (atTime g2 t)))
                (if (atTime g2 t)(not (atTime g1 t)))))))
```

An agent can modify goals in order to resolve conflicts among them.

```
(forall (a g1 g2 g3 g4)                                 (32.16)
    (iff (resolveConflictingGoals a g1 g2 g3 g4)
        (and (modifyGoal a g1 g3)(modifyGoal a g2 g4)
            (conflict g1 g2)(not (conflict g3 g4)))))
```

Here goals g1 and g2 conflict with each other. Agent a modifies goal g1 to goal g3 and modifies goal g2 to g4, where g3 and g4 do not conflict.

An account of preference will be explicated in Chapter 37 on Planning Goals. The predication (prefer a x1 x2) says that agent a prefers x1 to x2.

Agents may prefer to pursue some types of goals over others. Goal preferences rely on properties of the goals; these properties of the goals determine which is preferred over the other.

```
(forall (a g1 g2)                                              (32.17)
   (iff (preferGoal a g1 g2)
        (exists (e0 e1 e2 e3 e4 e)
           (and (and' e0 e1 e2)(arg* g1 e1)(arg* g2 e2)
                (pursueGoal' e3 a g1)(pursueGoal' e4 a g2)
                (cause e0 e)(prefer' e a e3 e4)))))
```

Here e3 is agent a's pursuit of goal g1, e4 is a's pursuit of g2, and a prefers the former to the latter, because of properties e1 of g1 and e2 of g2.

Agents can reprioritize their goals.

```
(forall (a g)                                                  (32.18)
   (iff (prioritizeGoal a g)
        (exists (e1 e2 p1 p2)
           (and (goal g a)(change e1 e2)
                (priority' e1 p1 g a)(priority' e2 p2 g a)))))
```

Here p1 is the original priority of agent a's goal g, and p2 is the new priority.

A goal with a high priority will defeasibly be pursued.

```
(forall (g a p e1 s1 s)                                        (32.19)
   (if (and (goal g a)(priority p g a)(inScale' e1 p s1)
            (Hi s1 s)(priorityScale s a)(etc))
       (exists (e2)
          (and (pursueGoal' e2 a g)(cause e1 e2)))))
```

That is, if agent a has goal g with priority p, then that priority's being high will defeasibly cause the goal to be pursued. This is the chief effect of priorities, along with the next axiom.

A goal with a low priority will defeasibly not be pursued.

```
(forall (g a p e1 e2 s1 s)                                     (32.20)
   (if (and (goal g a)(priority p g a)(inScale' e1 p s1)(Lo s1 s)
            (priorityScale s a)(pursueGoal' e2 a g)(etc))
       (exists (e3)
          (and (not' e3 e2)(cause e1 e3)))))
```

A low enough priority can lead to the goal's being abandoned.

PREDICATES INTRODUCED IN THIS CHAPTER

(addGoal a g)
   Agent a adds goal g to his Plan.

(removeAchievedGoal a g)
   Agent a removes goal g from his plan because it has been achieved.

(abandonGoal a g)
   Agent a removes goal g from his plan even though it has not been achieved.

(removeViolatedGoal a g c)
    Agent a removes goal g from his plan because it has become impossible, given
    constraints c.

(suspendGoal a g)
    Agent puts off the time goal g must be achieved.

(modifyGoal a g1 g2)
    Agent a modifies goal g1 to goal g2.

(specifyGoal a g1 g2)
    Agent a replaces goal g1 by more specific goal g2.

(generalizeGoal a g1 g2)
    Agent a replaces goal g1 by more general goal g2.

(pursueGoal a g)
    Agent a is developing or executing a plan for achieving goal g.

(priorityScale s a)
    Scale s is the scale of priorities for agent a's goals.

(priority p g a)
    p is the priority of goal g for agent a.

(goalJustification e g a)
    e is a plan or causal system for realizing goal g of agent a's.

(assessGoal a g)
    Agent a considers the causes or consequences of goal g.

(conflict g1 g2)
    g1 and g2 cannot hold at the same time.

(resolveConflictingGoals a g1 g2 g3 g4)
    Agent a modifies goal g1 to g3 and goal g2 to g4 to resolve a conflict.

(preferGoal a g1 g2)
    Agent a prefers pursuing goal g2 to pursuing goal g2.

(prioritizeGoal a g)
    Agent a changes the priority of goal g.

In addition, we used the predicate prefer, explicated in Chapter 37 on Planning
Goals.

(prefer a g1 g2)
    Agent a prefers goal g1 to goal g2.

33

Execution Envisionment

33.1 EXECUTIONS AND THEIR ENVISIONMENT

We plan. We act. We assess whether our actions have achieved our goals. If they haven't, we replan. The expensive step in this process is the action. Fortunately there is a cheaper alternative. We can simply imagine carrying out our plan and assess the results of that. Its results are not as accurate as actually executing the plan, where we find out for sure what the results would be. But the cost of imagining is very low compared with the cost of acting, so the trade-off is worth it. We can also backtrack when imagining, whereas backtracking from an action gone amiss is often a real problem.

Moreover, it is important for us to predict and explain the behavior of other entities in our environment. Among those entities are intentional agents. The best way to predict or explain their behavior is generally to assume they are executing some plan. If we surmise what the plan is and we envision their execution of that plan, then we are often able to predict or explain their actions.

We will discuss the actual executions of plans in Chapter 44 and subsequent chapters. Here we consider envisioning the execution of plans, viewed as a special case of envisioning a causal system. First we need two useful concepts.

We will say that an action e by an agent a in a plan p of a's is an eventuality in which a is the agent of the action and that occurs because it is in the plan p.

```
(forall (e a p)                                          (33.1)
    (iff (actionIn e a p)
        (exists (g e1)
            (and (agentOf a e)(plan p a g)(subgoalIn' e1 e p)
                (cause e1 e)))))
```

Here e1 is the condition of eventuality e being a subgoal in plan p. It causes e to actually occur.

A side effect of an execution of a plan is an eventuality that is caused by the achievement of some subgoal in the plan but is itself not a subgoal of the plan.

```
(forall (e a p)                                                      (33.2)
    (iff (sideEffect e a p)
         (exists (e1)
             (and (subgoalIn e1 p)(not (subgoalIn e p))
                  (causallyInvolved e1 e)))))
```

The expression (sideEffect e a p) says that eventuality e is a side effect of agent
a's plan p.

To envision an execution is to envision a causal system whose elements are subgoals in a plan or side effects of subgoals in a plan. Thus, at one particular moment
we think about an agent executing some of the actions in a plan, possibly along with
computing the consequences of those actions, and at the next moment we extend or
contract that envisioned causal system incrementally.

```
(forall (a b s p)                                                    (33.3)
    (iff (envisionExecution a b s p)
         (exists (g)
             (and (ecsSeq s a)(plan p b g)
                  (forall (c1 e1)
                      (if (and (inSeq c1 s)(eventualityIn e1 c1))
                          (or (subgoalIn e1 p)(sideEffect e1 b p))))
                  (exists (c2 e2)
                      (and (inSeq c2 s)(eventualityIn e2 c2)
                           (actionIn e2 b p)))))))
```

The expression (envisionExecution a b s p) says that agent a envisions a
sequence s of executions of some agent b's plan p. This holds when s is a sequence of
causal systems that is envisioned by a ((ecsSeq s a) in line 4), when every element
c1 of the sequence consists of eventualities e1 that are either subgoals in p or side
effects (lines 5–7), and when at least one of those eventualities is an action by b (lines
8–10). The agents a and b may or may not be the same; we can envision our own acts
and the acts of others. Thus, the scenario described by this predicate is of an agent a
thinking about one fragment of b's plan occurring, and then thinking of an extended
or contracted fragment of b's plan occurring.

A very important special case of this is when an agent envisions the execution of
the agent's own plan.

```
(forall (a s)                                                        (33.4)
    (iff (envisionSelfExecution a s p)
         (envisionExecution a a s p)))
```

33.2 ENVISIONING SUCCESS AND FAILURE

An agent envisions success in an execution of a plan if the goal of the plan is one of
the envisioned eventualities.

```
(forall (a b s g)                                                    (33.5)
    (iff (envisionExecutionSuccess a b s g)
         (exists (p)
             (and (envisionExecution a b s p)(plan p b g)
                  (envisionedEv g s a)))))
```

The expression (envisionExecutionSuccess a b s g) says that agent a envisions a sequence s of ecs's of a plan p by agent b and the goal g of plan p is in one of those ecs's.

An agent envisions failure in an execution of a plan if the negation of the goal of the plan is one of the envisioned eventualities.

```
(forall (a b s g)                                          (33.6)
    (iff (envisionExecutionFailure a b s g)
         (exists (p e1)
            (and (envisionExecution a b s p)(plan p b g)
                 (not' e1 g)(envisionedEv e1 s a)))))
```

The expression (envisionExecutionFailure a b s g) says that agent a envisions an ecs sequence s of ecs's of a plan p by agent b and the negation e1 of goal g of plan p is in one of those ecs's.

Because causal systems can have branches in them, an agent can envision success and failure at the same time.

Agents can envision the side effects of plans.

```
(forall (a b s e p)                                        (33.7)
    (iff (envisionExecutionSideEffect a b e s p)
         (exists (g)
            (and (envisionExecution a b s p)(plan p b g)
                 (sideEffect e b p)(envisionedEv e s a)))))
```

Very often agents don't just envision the success or failure of executions of plans but also make judgments about their likelihood. We will define a predicate only for success. Recall from Chapter 20 that likelihood is with respect to a set of constraints.

```
(forall (d a b s g c)                                      (33.8)
    (iff (envisionedLikelihoodOfSuccess d a b s g c)
         (exists (e1)
            (and (envisionExecutionSuccess a b s g)
                 (likelihood' e1 d g c)(believe a e1)))))
```

The expression (envisionedLikelihoodOfSuccess d a b s g c) says that d is the likelihood (a point on the likelihood scale) that agent a envisions the ecs sequence s to contain the successful achievement of goal g by agent b, given constraints c.

An envisioned opportunity is an eventuality that is discovered in the course of envisioning the execution of a plan by an agent, that is not a subgoal in that plan, but that is a subgoal in another plan to achieve some goal of the agent's.

```
(forall (e a b s g)                                        (33.9)
    (iff (envisionedOpportunity e a b s g)
         (exists (p1 g1 p)
            (and (envisionExecution a b s p1)(plan p1 b g1)
                 (envisionedEv e s a)(not (subgoalIn e p1))
                 (plan p b g)(subgoalIn e p)))))
```

The expression (envisionedOpportunity e a b s g) says that eventuality e is an opportunity envisioned by agent a while envisioning a contiguous ecs sequence s for agent b to achieve some goal g of b's. It holds when a is envisioning the execution of a plan p1 by agent b to achieve goal g1 (line 4) and among the eventualities thought of is one which is not a subgoal in plan p1 (line 5) but would contribute to another plan p to achieve b's goal g (line 6).

Some execution envisionments have branch points that depend on the value of some parameter, in the sense that when the parameter is on one side of some value, the desired effect e occurs, and when it is on the other, it doesn't. That is, there is a scale s and a threshold t which is a point on s, and when some entity is greater than t, success will occur, and when it is less, failure will occur. For example, suppose someone wants to break a pencil. When force is applied up to a certain point, the pencil remains intact. When the force is just great enough, the pencil snaps. English expressions that make reference to this concept include "hang on by a thread," "breaking point," and "push one's luck."

```
(forall (t s0 a b s)                                              (33.10)
    (iff (thresholdOfFailure t s0 a b s)
        (exists (p g e e1 e2 x x1 x2 z e0)
            (and (envisionExecution a b s p)(plan p b g)
                 (inSeq x s)(inSeq x1 s)(inSeq x2 s)
                 (resolveBranch x e e1 e2 x1)
                 (resolveBranch x e e2 e1 x2)
                 (lts' e1 z t s0)(geqs' e2 z t s0)
                 (not' e0 g)(eventualityIn e0 x1)
                 (eventualityIn g x2)))))
```

The expression (thresholdOfFailure t s0 a b s) says that t is a threshold point on a scale s0 in agent a's envisionment s of b's plan. Line 4 says that the envisionment is of a plan p of agent b's. Lines 5–7 say that the envisionment contains a two-way branch point that is resolved in both ways in the envisionment. Line 8 says that the disjunction that is branched on is whether some entity z is less than, or greater than or equal to, the threshold. Line 9 says that failure to achieve goal g is in the less-than branch. Line 10 says that success is in the greater-than-or-equal-to branch. Every scale has a reverse, so we only need to define the case where less than the threshold represents failure.

33.3 SPECIFIC AND ARBITRARY CONTEXTS OF EXECUTION

We talk about a "specific" entity as though this were a property. But in fact it is a relation between the entity and a set. The entity is a specific member of the set. But a third argument is required as well, and we must be explicit about it if we are going to characterize what "specific" means. An entity is a specific member of a set with respect to some purpose. We can say that this holds if and only if there is some property of the entity that does not hold for any of the other members of the set, and that property is causally involved in the purpose. Since we already defined a predicate specific in Chapter 7, we will call this predicate specific1. Thus the axiom is as follows:

```
(forall (x s e)                                                     (33.11)
   (iff (specific1 x s e)
        (exists (e1)
            (and (member x s)(arg* x e1)(causallyInvolved e1 e)
                 (forall (y e2)
                     (if (and (member y s)(nequal y x)
                              (subst x e1 y e2))
                         (or (not e2)
                             (not (causallyInvolved e2 e)))))))))
```

The expression (specific1 x s e) says that entity x is a specific member of set s with respect to some purpose e. This holds when there is a property e1 of x that is causally involved in e (line 4), and when for all other members of the set, the corresponding property either does not hold or is not causally involved in e (lines 5–9).

When we think of a specific member of a set, we are thinking of one or more "identity" properties that distinguish it from all other members. For example, in the sentence "The course will be designed for each student's specific needs," the set s is the set of possible needs for all students, x is the typical need for a particular student, e is the learning that the course is intended to bring about, and e1 is a description of the need that impacts on the learning.

Something is an arbitrary member of a set if it is not specific. That is, if the arbitrary member has a property that impacts the purpose, then every other member has the corresponding property and it also impacts the purpose.

```
(forall (x s e)                                                     (33.12)
   (iff (arbitrary x s e)
        (forall (e1 y)
            (if (and (arg* x e1)(causallyInvolved e1 e)
                     (member y s))
                (exists (e2)
                    (and (subst x e1 y e2)
                         (causallyInvolved e2 e)))))))
```

The expression (arbitrary x s e) says that entity x is an arbitrary member of set s with respect to purpose e. This holds when for any property e1 that x has that impacts e (line 4), any other member y of the set has the corresponding property e2 and it also impacts e (lines 6–8).

English phrases such as "could be done anywhere," "works in any circumstance," and "applicable to any situation," make reference to the concept of an arbitrary execution context. In Chapter 24 we made explicit one kind of context for envisioning – the set of background propositions that are not negated in the envisionment. Combining this with the predicate arbitrary gives us the following axiom:

```
(forall (b e0 a a1 e)                                               (33.13)
   (iff (arbitraryExecutionContext b e0 a a1 e)
        (exists (s p e1 b1 s1)
            (and (envisionExecution' e0 a a1 s p)
                 (backgroundBeliefs' e1 b1 e0)(dset s1 b1 e1)
                 (arbitrary b s1 e)))))
```

The expression (arbitraryExecutionContext b e0 a a1 e) says that a set b of background beliefs is an arbitrary execution context for an execution envisionment event e0 by agent a, where the arbitrariness is with respect to purpose e. This holds exactly when e0 is an envisioning by a of a sequence s of executions of some plan p of agent a1's (line 4), and furthermore b is an arbitrary member of the set s1 of such sets b1 of background beliefs (lines 5–6).

The specificity or arbitrariness of a context of an envisioned execution is significant. The more specific the context is, the more precise the predictions will be. The more arbitrary it is, the more likely the conclusions will be correct in the variety of circumstances the real world poses against the agent.

33.4 ENVISIONED EXECUTIONS AND TIME

A moment in an envisioned execution is an instant in its time span. English expressions that make reference to moments in execution include "in the midst of" and "in the course of."

```
(forall (t0 x)                                                        (33.14)
    (iff (momentInExecution t0 x)
        (exists (t s) (and (timeSpanOf t s)(eventualitiesOf s x)
            (insideTime t0 t)))))
```

The phrase "any moment while doing" makes reference to an arbitrary moment in the execution of a plan.

```
(forall (t0 x e)                                                      (33.15)
    (iff (arbitraryMomentInExecution t0 x e)
        (exists (e1 t s)
            (and (momentInExecution' e1 t x)
                (arbitrary t0 s e)(dset s t e1)))))
```

An instant t0 is an arbitrary moment in an envisioned execution x if it is an arbitrary member of the set of such moments, given some purpose e.

The envisioned duration of an execution is the duration of an execution that is being envisioned. The English phrases "time needed to," "the time it takes to," and "manhours" make reference to this concept.

```
(forall (d x u a b)                                                   (33.16)
    (iff (envisionedExecutionDuration d x u a b)
        (exists (s p)
            (and (envisionExecution a b s p)(inSeq x s)
                (durationOf d x u)))))
```

That is, agent a envisions a sequence s of contiguous ecs's containing x, and d is the duration of x in units u.

PREDICATES INTRODUCED IN THIS CHAPTER

(actionIn e a p)
　　e is an action by agent a in a's plan p.

(sideEffect e a p)
　　e is a side effect of agent a's plan p.

(envisionExecution a b s p)
   Agent a envisions a sequence s of executions of plan p by b.

(envisionSelfExecution a s p)
   Agent a envisions a sequence s of execution of a's own plan p.

(envisionExecutionSuccess a b s g)
   Agent a envisions, in a sequence s of executions of agent b's plan, the achievement of the goal g of the plan.

(envisionExecutionFailure a b s g)
   Agent a envisions, in a sequence s of executions of agent b's plan, the failure to
   achieve the goal g of the plan.

(envisionExecutionSideEffect a b e s p)
   Agent a envisions a side effect e in the sequence s of executions of agent b's
   plan p.

(envisionedLikelihoodOfSuccess d a b s g c)
   d is the likelihood that agent a believes, in envisioning a sequence s of executions
   of agent b's plan, that goal g will be achieved, given constraints c.

(envisionedOpportunity e a b s g)
   e is an opportunity that agent a envisions in sequence s of executions of b's plan
   for b to achieve goal g.

(thresholdOfFailure t s0 a b s)
   t is the threshold point on scale s0 that a envisions, in sequence s of executions
   of agent b's plan, that determines success or failure.

(specific1 x s e)
   x is a specific member of set s, with respect to purpose e.

(arbitrary x s e)
   x is an arbitrary member of set s, with respect to purpose e.

(arbitraryExecutionContext b e0 a a1 e)
   b is a set of background beliefs for agent a's envisionment e0 of a plan by agent
   a1, where b is arbitrary with respect to purpose e.

(momentInExecution t0 x)
   t0 is a moment in the execution x.

(arbitraryMomentInExecution t0 x e)
   t0 is an arbitrary moment in the execution x, with respect to some purpose e.

(envisionedExecutionDuration d x u a b)
   d is the duration of execution x of agent b's plan, in temporal units u, envisioned
   by agent a.

34

Causes of Failure

34.1 INTRODUCTION

Often in life, things don't turn out the way we hope. Despite our best efforts to understand the world and plan a course of action that will achieve our goals, things go wrong somewhere along the way. When attempting to explain what went wrong, the explanations that people come up with are rarely very creative. It is much easier to rely on a certain pattern of explanation that is useful and satisfying across a wide range of failures than to understand really deeply the root of our problems. That is, it is easy to say that someone's plan didn't succeed because he or she didn't have the skills necessary to execute it properly or claim that the plan would have been successful if only there were a little more time, rather than deconstruct the myriad of causal influences that were factors leading to the failure to achieve a goal.

These patterns of explanation for failed plans received a significant amount of attention among Artificial Intelligence researchers in the 1990s, largely emanating from the Yale University / Northwestern University computer science labs led by Roger Schank. Schank (1986) elaborated the notion of an Explanation Pattern, and pushed a multiyear, multidissertation effort to author a cognitive model of case-based explanation built on this idea (Domeshek, 1992; Jones, 1992; Ram, 1989; Kass, 1990; Leake, 1990; Owens, 1990), summarized in (Schank, Kass, and Riesbeck, 1994). Within the context of this work, a significant amount of effort was put into authoring comprehensive taxonomies of the types of explanation patterns that people used in understanding failed plans. Primarily, elements in these taxonomies were used as indices for the retrieval of stored explanations in support of a case-based reasoning process. The aim was to develop an indexing vocabulary (or content theory) of plan failure explanation patterns with broad coverage and utility for both scientific and engineering goals.

In this chapter we develop a new taxonomy of plan failure explanation patterns by combining the best of the taxonomies that have been developed in the past, synthesizing a taxonomy that is more comprehensive and elegant than any of the individual taxonomies that have been proposed in the past, and integrate it into the overall framework of this book. We close the chapter with a discussion of the utility of our taxonomy in scientific and engineering research.

34.2 CONTRIBUTING SOURCE TAXONOMIES

The first source is the 1990 Ph.D. dissertation of Christopher Owens (1990), *Indexing and Retrieving Abstract Planning Knowledge*. Owens's thesis is remarkable in the scale of his analysis, which involved the consideration of the planning advice entailed in 1,000 English proverbs. In this work, Owens developed a high-level division of plan failure explanation patterns based on goals, tasks, resources, time, and information, and created an indexing vocabulary for these patterns consisting of fifty-nine labels. An example of one of these labels is "GLASS – failing to note obvious consequences of an action," used to label the proverbs "He that scattereth thorns must not go barefoot" and "People who live in glass houses should not throw stones."

The second source is a 1992 technical report by Roger Schank and Andrew Fano (1992), "A Thematic Hierarchy for Indexing Stories in Social Domains." This work aimed at developing a single taxonomy of all of the abstract points that can be expressed in stories, organizing 758 point indices into an abstraction hierarchy. Exactly 34 of these labels concerned plan failures, with 27 of these referring to points that indicated the causes of failure. An example of one of these points is "Plans may fail as a result of plan execution with opportunities that are misidentified."

The third source is the 2004 book by Andrew Gordon, *Strategy Representation: An Analysis of Planning Knowledge* (Gordon, 2004b). This work, around which the present work is organized, aimed at identifying all of the abstract concepts that were necessary to correctly develop formal representations of planning strategies, and resulted in a set of 988 concepts organized into 48 representational areas. One of the representational areas included in this organization consisted of 31 plan failure explanation patterns that were needed to represent strategies among the 372 that were analyzed. An example of one of these concepts is "False knowledge goal achievement: An execution failure caused by the achievement of a knowledge goal with information that is incorrect," which is needed for the representation of the anthropomorphic strategy of molecular mimicry in cellular immunology.

34.3 TAXONOMY OF PLAN FAILURE EXPLANATION PATTERNS

In developing a unified taxonomy of plan failure explanation patterns, we have tried to achieve a degree of breadth that is as large as the union of each of the three contributing source taxonomies and to retain the level of detail in discriminating between patterns as found in these earlier works. The plan failure taxonomy of Schank and Fano (1992) was used as the starting point for merging the other two, and the resulting taxonomy retains the structural form that they used. The thirty-one plan failures from Gordon (2004b) were first added to this base in places where no synonymous label already existed, followed by those from Owens (1990). The hierarchy was then reorganized with the aim of aligning it with the categories of cognitive functions explicated in this book.

The unified taxonomy can be summarized as follows: When things go wrong, it is either because the plan was flawed to begin with (type 1 failures in Section 34.4) or because of problems in the execution of a plan (type 2 and 3 failures). In the latter case, the reasons are because of the world (the resources, instruments, states, other agents) – type 2 failures – or because of the person executing the plan (knowledge, control, imagination, concurrently executing plans, time) – type 3 failures. We expand on this classification in Section 34.4.

Plans fail because

1. Characteristics in the execution environment
   (a) Are ignored
   (b) Are more negative than could have been predicted
2. Resources/instruments used in the execution
   (a) Are mismanaged
   (b) Are inappropriate
   (c) Are not available at execution
   (d) Are underestimated during planning
   (e) Are faulty
3. Agent interaction
   (a) Of competitors who achieve a competitive goal
   (b) Of adversaries who execute a successful counterplan
   (c) Of collaborators who fail
4. Knowledge
   (a) Is obtained that is in fact false
   (b) Was not obtained that should have been sought
   (c) That was sought could not be obtained
5. Causal reasoning about the world
   (a) Was based on faulty theories
   (b) Required more thought than was applied
   (c) Involves too much uncertainty
   (d) Is conducted with too narrow of a perspective
   (e) Fails to consider the obstacles
6. Goal management
   (a) Involves selecting goals that are already satisfactorily achieved
   (b) Has led to the pursuit of a goal of little importance
   (c) Has led to the pursuit of goals that would have been achieved anyway
   (d) Where goals are neglected
7. Threats and opportunities
   (a) Are missed
   (b) Are mistakenly identified during execution
   (c) Are mistakenly expected during planning
   (d) Are inappropriately assessed
8. Plan construction selects plans
   (a) That don't actually satisfy the goal
   (b) That are too excessive
   (c) That are insufficient
   (d) Where a different plan would have been better
   (e) That have a low probability of actually succeeding
   (f) That undo the progress made by other plans
   (g) With conditions for execution that cannot be met
   (h) Where the consequences of the plans are unforeseen

(i)   Where the costs of executing the plan are greater than the benefit
(j)   Where the risks of executing the plan are greater than the benefit
(k) That does not include adequate preparation
(l)   That does not include adequate follow-through

9. Plan adaptation
(a) Where an inappropriate base plan was selected for adaptation
(b) Fails in learning from errors that were made previously

10. Planning goals
(a) That lead to plans where resources are too conservatively utilized
(b) That lead to plans with actions that are to be executed in haste
(c) Inappropriately balanced the tradeoff between planning and execution

11. Decisions
(a) Where the wrong candidate was selected from a choice
(b) Where a candidate in a choice was overlooked

12. Plan scheduling
(a) Involves underestimating the amount of time necessary
(b) Involves incorrectly ordering parts of the plan
(c) Is mistaken such that it overlaps with other scheduled plans
(d) Cannot identify a time for the plan (full schedule failure)

13. Plan execution
(a) Includes mistakes in following the plan
(b) Requires a greater degree of ability
(c) Is uncoordinated with other collaborating agents
(d) Is inflexible to the characteristics of the execution environment
(e) Cannot be done without violating execution rules
(f) Is not done with sufficient intensity

14. Monitoring during execution
(a) Triggers an action when it shouldn't have
(b) Fails to trigger an action when the conditions are met

15. Body interaction
(a) Where undirected execution interferes with execution of the plan
(b) Where the mind–body state is impaired
(c) Where perceptions are misinterpreted

34.4 CAUSAL COMPLEXES AND FAILURE

When we try to achieve some goal state or event e, we find a causal complex s that we believe will result in e. We pick some element e1 of s that does not hold and we try to achieve that, in hopes that it bring us closer to causing e to hold as well. Very broadly speaking, this process can fail in one of three ways:

1. We can be wrong in our belief that s is a causal complex for e.
2. We can execute e1 but fail because other elements of s do not obtain.
3. Recursively, we can fail to achieve e1.

We can call these type 1, type 2, and type 3 failures.

To define these formally we need a strong notion of trying by some means, and a notion of failure defined in terms of that. We will say that for agent a to try to achieve e by doing e1 is for a to believe that e1 is in a causal complex s for e and for a to do e1 where a's having the goal e causes a to do e1.

```
(forall (a e e1 s)                                          (34.1)
    (iff (tryBy a e e1 s)
         (exists (e2 e3)
             (and (causalComplex' e2 s e)(member e1 s)(agentOf a e1)
                  (believe a e2)(goal' e3 e a)(cause e3 e1)))))
```

Then to fail when trying by some means can be defined as trying without the goal coming to exist.

```
(forall (a e e1 s)                                          (34.2)
    (iff (failBy a e e1 s)
         (and (tryBy a e e1 s)(not e))))
```

Then a type 1 failure can be defined as failing to achieve the goal e because s is not a causal complex for e.

```
(forall (a e e1 s)                                          (34.3)
    (iff (failType1 a e e1 s)
         (and (failBy a e e1 s)(not (causalComplex s e)))))
```

A type 2 failure happens when eventualities in s other than e1 do not hold.

```
(forall (a e e1 s)                                          (34.4)
    (iff (failType2 a e e1 s)
         (and (failBy a e e1 s)
              (exists (e2) (and (member e2 s)(not e2))))))
```

We did not stipulate in the definition of tryBy that the agent believes all the other eventualities in the causal complex hold. An important subcase of this is where the agent hopes that doing e1 will cause e and believes it is possible, but does not believe it is certain to, and may not even believe it is likely. An example of this is a "Hail Mary" pass. At the end of a football game when his team is less than one touchdown behind, the quarterback has nothing to lose by throwing a long pass and hoping his receiver will catch it in the end zone, unlikely as that may be. We can call this a type 2a failure, and define it as follows:

```
(forall (a e e1 s)                                          (34.5)
    (iff (failType2a a e e1 s)
         (and (failType2 a e e1 s)(hope a s)(not (believe a s)))))
```

That is, a fails to achieve e by means of e1 where a hopes but does not believe that s holds. The predicate hope is defined in Chapter 49 on emotions.

A type 3 failure is the recursive case. The agent a fails to achieve e by means of e1 because a fails to achieve e1.

```
(forall (a e e1 s)                                          (34.6)
    (iff (failType3 a e e1 s)
         (exists (e2 e3 e4 s1)
             (and (failBy' e2 a e e1 s)(failBy' e3 a e1 e4 s1)
                  (cause e3 e2)))))
```

The failure to achieve e1 could be a type 1, 2, or 3 failure.

The majority of the causes of failure in Section 34.3 are of type 1. The agent is wrong about the causal complex for causing e. For example, in cause 1a, "Plans fail because characteristics in the execution environment are ignored," the agent wrongly believes an incomplete causal complex will yield the effect. In cause 5a, "Plans fail because causal reasoning about the world was based on faulty theories," the faulty theories result in an incorrect belief that the causal complex achieves the goal. Similarly, cause 8a, "Plans fail because plan construction selects plans that don't actually achieve the goal," the plan chosen represents a hypothesized causal complex and the hypothesis is wrong. In cause 12a, "Plans fail because plan scheduling involves underestimating the amount of time necessary," the agent believes in a causal complex that contains incorrect temporal constraints.

A clear case of a type 2 failure is cause 1b, "Plans fail because characteristics in the execution environment are more negative than could have been predicted." Here the agent is correct about what causal complex will bring about the effect, but one or more of the necessary eventualities in the causal complex do not hold when one would normally expect them to hold. In cause 3b, "Plans fail because of agent interaction of adversaries who execute a successful counterplan," the agent is correct in the belief in the causal complex, but the adversary has changed the facts on the ground. In cause 4a, "Plans fail because knowledge is obtained that is in fact false," the agent is again correct in the belief of what causes what, but wrong about the actual state of the world. Other examples of type 2 failures are causes 2e, 3a, 3c, 4b, 4c, 8e, 13d, 14a, 14b, 15a, and 15b.

An example of a type 3 failure is cause 2a, "Plans fail because resources or instruments used in the execution are mismanaged." Using a resource or instrument is one element of the causal complex for achieving the goal. If it is mismanaged, that means that the agent fails in the task of using it. Two other examples of type 3 failures are causes 2c and 8g.

34.5 APPLICATIONS

A taxonomy of plan failure explanation patterns has three important applications in intelligent and knowledge based systems, namely, for case indexing, explanation generation, and explanation recognition.

Each of the source taxonomies of plan failure explanation patterns was developed for the purpose of case indexing or representation. This work was strongly rooted in the academic tradition of case-based reasoning, where cases are stored in an intelligent system's memory to be retrieved and adapted to achieve new reasoning goals. Case indexing/representation remains the most obvious utility of this taxonomy, particularly where cases are difficult to automatically process due to the media in which they are captured (e.g., videoclips, audio clips, or natural language text). The relative comprehensibility of the taxonomy itself lends itself to be used as a tool by human content analysts without extensive training in knowledge representation, or even as a browsing structure for untrained consumers of stories and cases in intentional domains. The simplest of applications would involve setting up a website where the taxonomy was used to organize a large collection of online stories of failed plans within a particular domain of practice.

A second application of this taxonomy is as a tool in the automated generation of explanations of failures in autonomous agent systems. Each of the plan failure explanation patterns in this taxonomy represents a sort of explanation that human users are likely to accept as reasonable (or at least coherent). By coupling each pattern with use-conditions and templates for natural language generation, a system for constructing explanations of failures from execution logs could be constructed. This would be particularly appropriate in simulation environments where the agents that are executing plans in the world are operating using control algorithms that are not reasonable to present to human users as explanations of behavior.

A third application of this taxonomy is as a set of classification targets for natural language explanations of plan failures. In this use, statistical machine learning techniques could be used to identify the words and phrases that are most predictive of a class of plan failure explanation patterns by analyzing a large collection of hand-classified training data. Compelling knowledge management applications could then be constructed that involve accepting a user-authored explanation for a plan failure, classifying the text as an instance of a particular pattern, and then retrieving some application-specific information to be presented back to the user as a response.

PREDICATES INTRODUCED IN THIS CHAPTER

(tryBy a e e1 s)
Agent a tries to achieve goal e by doing e1 in causal complex s.

(failBy a e e1 s)
Agent a fails to achieve goal e by doing e1 in causal complex s.

(failType1 a e e1 s)
Agent a fails to achieve goal e by doing e1 in causal complex s because a is wrong in the belief that s is a causal complex for e.

(failType2 a e e1 s)
Agent a fails to achieve goal e by doing e1 in causal complex s because an expected eventuality in s does not exist.

(failType2a a e e1 s)
Agent a fails to achieve goal e by doing e1 in causal complex s because a hoped for eventuality in s does not exist.

(failType3 a e e1 s)
Agent a fails to achieve goal e by doing e1 in causal complex s because a fails to do e1.

35

Plan Elements

Suppose we are watching a workman doing his job. He looks around for his toolbox, and when he finds it, he opens it and takes out a hammer and nails. He pounds one nail after another into boards. Each step in this repetitive action is itself a repetitive action, hitting the nail with the hammer again and again until it is flush with the wood. He sweats, and from time to time as the sweat drips into his eyes, he takes out a handkerchief and wipes his brow. Five o'clock comes, and he puts his tools away and goes home. He comes back the next morning at nine o'clock for a day of similar tasks.

The workman has a goal he is trying to achieve, and he breaks this into subgoals that eventually bottom out in individual actions and bring him closer to the satisfaction of the goals. He needs to have certain tools and resources to do his job, and to have these, he needs to know where they are – resource preconditions and knowledge preconditions. He generally engages in repetitive actions because each repetition brings him a little closer to his goal. Situations arise and have to be dealt with immediately. To do his job, he has to be able to see, and when something interferes with this, he must somehow counteract it. His job is embedded in a larger structure of plans for his life as a whole, and this has to be aligned with periodic regularities of his physical and social environment. Thus, the fine structure of his actions emerges from his manipulations of the causal structure of the world as organized in his plans.

We as observers see individual actions happening one after the other. We make sense of them in part by recognizing similarities in successive actions and thereby recognizing repetitions. We see an action happening occasionally and realize it happens only when some condition arises. We thereby recognize conditional events. We see that some actions happen only at particular times or for particular durations. By these means we recognize the temporal structure of complex events, but we have not really interpreted his actions until we understand the causal structure implicit in them, that is, until we have recognized the plan he is executing.

Not every repetitive sequence of actions has a larger causal structure it fits into. If someone is eating one piece of candy after another, he is probably not doing so in order to empty the bag or to fill his stomach. In fact, he may wish he had the strength to not take all the candy and not spoil his appetite. Each individual action is done for its own sake alone. But generally a "repeat until" structure has the goal of achieving the "until" condition, and a "while do" structure has the goal of negating the "while" condition. Each individual iteration may be supposed to cause the world to be a little closer to that goal state. Conditional actions are generally directed toward the goal of negating or exploiting the occurrence of the condition. By reasoning such as this, we infer the causal structure of events from their temporal structure.

We can capture some of these observations in several defeasible rules. The first says that if there is a conditional action by an agent a, then either the condition enables a goal of a's or the negation of the condition is a goal of a's. In the first case the agent is exploiting the occurrence of the condition. In the second he is escaping from the consequences of the condition. In either case, the condition is relevant to his goals.

```
(forall (e e1 e2 a)                                             (35.1)
    (if (and (cond e e1 e2)(agentOf a e2)(etc))
        (exists (g)
            (and (goal g a)
                (or (enable e1 g)(not' g e1))))))
```

The negation of the condition in a whileDo is defeasibly a goal of the agent's. That's why the agent keeps executing the body until the condition is gone.

```
(forall (e e1 e2 a)                                             (35.2)
    (if (and (whileDo e e1 e2)(agentOf a e2)(etc))
        (exists (e0) (and (not' e0 e1)(goal e0 a)))))
```

A similar rule holds for repeatUntil.

```
(forall (e e1 e2 a)                                             (35.3)
    (if (and (repeatUntil e e1 e2)(agentOf a e1)(etc))
        (goal e2 a)))
```

Suppose someone wants to relax, and their plan for doing so is to do nothing. This plan does not involve events; nothing changes. But the overwhelming majority of plans do involve changing the world somehow, and thus involve events, generally very complex events. We can superimpose plan structure onto event structure to characterize different varieties of plans, and thus different categories of explanations of behavior. In this chapter, we define a number of concepts connecting temporal event structure and causal structure.

We defined subplan in Chapter 31 as that part of a plan intended to achieve a subgoal in the plan.

A partial subplan is one in which the terminal nodes are not all executable, given a set of constraints c.

```
(forall (p1 p c)                                               (35.4)
    (iff (partialSubplan p1 p c)
        (exists (a g1)
            (and (subplan p1 p)(plan p1 a g1)
                (partialPlan p1 a g1 c)))))
```

Someone is a subplan agent if they are the agent of every action in the subplan.

```
(forall (a p1 p)                                          (35.5)
    (iff (subplanAgent a p1 p)
         (and (subplan p1 p)
              (forall (e)
                  (if (and (subgoalIn e p1)
                           (exists (a1) (agentOf a1 e)))
                      (agentOf a e))))))
```

That is, a is the agent of every subgoal in the subplan p1 that has an agent.

The termination of a plan is the final action in the plan, after which the goal is achieved.

```
(forall (e p)                                             (35.6)
    (iff (planTermination e p)
         (exists (a g)
             (and (subgoalIn e p) (plan p a g)
                  (forall (e1)
                      (if (subgoalIn e1 p) (not (before e e1))))
                  (causalComplex p g) (cause e g)))))
```

Two important varieties of preconditions or enabling conditions are knowledge preconditions and resource preconditions. They can be characterized as follows:

```
(forall (e1 e)                                            (35.7)
    (iff (knowledgePrecondition e1 e)
         (exists (a e2)
             (and (enable e1 e) (know' e1 a e2)))))
```

That is, a knowledge precondition is the eventuality of someone a knowing something e2 where that knowing is an enabling condition in the causal complex for e.

It is not easy to distinguish between a resource and a tool or instrument. Are nails tools or resources? What distinguishes both resources and tools is that they go through a change of state (perhaps location) and that change plays an intermediate causal role in the effect occurring. Having the resource enables the action. For "having" we will use the abstract predicate at – the agent has the resource at hand (in some system s).

```
(forall (e1 e)                                            (35.8)
    (iff (resourcePrecondition e1 e)
         (exists (a s x e2)
             (and (at' e1 x a s) (enable e1 e2) (changeIn' e2 x)
                  (causallyInvolved e2 e)))))
```

A plan consists of eventualities linked by subgoal relations. Thus, a plan can be viewed as an aggregate of eventualities (eventuality types), namely, the subgoals in the plan. So the variety of complex events we defined in Chapters 16 and 17 can be applied directly to plans. For example, a conditional plan is a plan whose corresponding event is a conditional event.

```
(forall (p a g)                                          (35.9)
    (iff (conditionalPlan p a g e)
         (exists (e1)
             (and (plan p a g)(cond p e e1)))))
```

That is, p is a plan of a's to achieve goal g, executed only when condition e occurs.

"Then" and "else" branches and branch points can be defined similarly. Reactive plans and their parts can be viewed as conditional plans, whose conditions are the eventualities the reactive plan is a reaction to.

A repetitive plan is a plan with a "while do" or "repeat until" structure.

```
(forall (p a g)                                          (35.10)
    (iff (repetitivePlan p a g)
         (exists (e1 e2)
             (and (plan p a g)
                  (or (whileDo p e1 e2)(repeatUntil p e1 e2))))))
```

Iteration quantities and termination conditions can be defined similarly.

Periodic subplans can be defined as plans whose time spans are periodic temporal sequences.

```
(forall (p1 p)                                           (35.11)
    (iff (periodicSubplan p1 p)
         (exists (t)
             (and (subplan p1 p)(timeSpanOf t p1)
                  (periodicTseq t)))))
```

A required precondition is an eventuality that is an enabling condition for a disjunctive effect. That is, it is a precondition of each disjunct.

```
(forall (e0 e)                                           (35.12)
    (iff (requiredPrecondition e0 e)
         (exists (e1 e2)
             (and (or' e e1 e2)(enable e0 e1)(enable e0 e2)))))
```

PREDICATES INTRODUCED IN THIS CHAPTER

(partialSubplan p1 p c)
    p1 is a subplan of p some of whose nodes are not executable, given constraints c.

(subplanAgent a p1 p)
    a is the agent of all the actions in subplan p1 of p.

(planTermination e p)
    e is the last action in a plan p for achieving a goal.

(knowledgePrecondition e1 e)
    e1 is a knowing event that enables e.

(resourcePrecondition e1 e)
    e1 is a having event that enables e.

(conditionalPlan p a g e)

    p is a plan of agent a's for achieving g that is only executed when eventuality e occurs.

(repetitivePlan p a g)

    p is a plan of agent a's for achieving g that has a repetitive structure.

(periodicSubplan p1 p)

    p1 is a subplan of p that is executed periodically.

(requiredPrecondition e0 e)

    e0 is a precondition for a disjunctive effect e, regardless of which disjunct is to hold.

36

Planning Modalities

36.1 THE ACTIVITY OF PLANNING

The process of achieving goals is in part a matter of using our causal knowledge to construct larger-scale causal knowledge. We then "decide" to use some bits of our causal knowledge, including this larger-scale causal knowledge, so they become part of The Plan we are actually executing. That is the source of our intentional behavior. We have called this whole process "pursuing goals," represented with the predication (pursueGoal a g). The processes of constructing plans or larger-scale causal knowledge, making decisions about which of these plans to execute, and executing them are all parts of goal pursuit. Goal pursuit is our top-level intentional behavior. It is what we are doing when we are just "going about our business."

We can define the activity of planning as an agent's sequence of envisionments of a causal system that is a plan for achieving one of the agent's goals.

```
(forall (e a g s)                                        (36.1)
   (iff (planning e a g s)
        (and (ecsSeq' e s a)(goal g a)(planseq s a g))))
```

The expression (planning e a g s) says that e is an activity by agent a to plan to achieve goal g, where s is the sequence of plans produced by this activity. This is true exactly when e is the envisioning of a plan sequence of plans to achieve g.

Goal pursuit has planning as a subevent.

```
(forall (e0 a g)                                         (36.2)
   (if (pursueGoal' e0 a g)
       (exists (e s) (and (planning e a g s)(subevent e e0)))))
```

Planning activity includes all types of planning, including plan adaptation, reactive planning, and constructing elaborate plans from scratch. People have an ability to construct, adapt, and modify plans.

```
(forall (a g)                                            (36.3)
   (if (and (person a)(goal g a))
       (exists (e s c)(and (able a e c)(planning e a g s)))))
```

36.2 PLANNING ACTIVITY AND OTHER AGENTS

People exist in a world populated by other agents with other goals, and these goals can coincide, merely coexist, or contradict each other. We can define predicates for planning activity in the various cases.

In cases in which the goals coincide and two agents collaborate with each other, we have collaborative planning.

```
(forall (e a1 a2 g s)                                           (36.4)
    (iff (collaborativePlanning e a1 a2 g s)
        (exists (e1 e2 s1 s2)
            (and (planning e1 a1 g s1)(planning e2 a2 g s2)
                 (and' e e1 e2)(doubleton a a1 a2)(goal g a)
                 (forall (p)
                    (iff (inSeq p s)
                        (or (inSeq p s1)(inSeq p s2))))))))
```

That is, collaborative planning activity by agents a1 and a2 is the conjunction of a1's planning to achieve goal g and a2's planning to achieve the same goal g, where the set consisting of a1 and a2 has g as a collective goal. Moreover, the plans in the joint sequence of plans come from one of the agents or the other.

Assistive planning is a slightly weaker notion. Here agent a1, who is assisting agent a2, does not necessarily have the goal that both agents achieve goal g, but only that agent a2 achieves g. Agent a1 is satisfied to accomplish a subgoal g1 of g.

```
(forall (e a1 a2 g s)                                           (36.5)
    (iff (assistivePlanning e a1 a2 g s)
        (exists (e1 e2 g1 s1 s2)
            (and (planning e1 a1 g1 s1)(planning e2 a2 g s2)
                 (and' e e1 e2)(subgoal g1 g)
                 (forall (p)
                    (iff (inSeq p s)
                        (or (and (assistivePlan p a1 a2 g)
                                 (inSeq p s1))
                            (inSeq p s2))))))))
```

Two agents can also be opposed in their efforts. Competitive planning is where two agents work toward goals that cannot both occur at once.

```
(forall (e a1 a2 g s)                                           (36.6)
    (iff (competitivePlanning e a1 a2 g s)
        (exists (e1 e2 s1 s2)
            (and (planning e1 a1 g s1)(planning e2 a2 g s2)
                 (and' e e1 e2)
                 (forall (p)
                    (iff (inSeq p s)
                        (or (and (competitivePlan p a1 a2 g)
                                 (inSeq p s1))
                            (and (competitivePlan p a2 a1 g)
                                 (inSeq p s2)))))))))
```

Adversarial planning is a stronger notion than this. It is when one agent a1 has as an active plan that another agent a2 not achieve a goal g.

```
(forall (e a1 a2 g s)                                    (36.7)
   (iff (adversarialPlanning e a1 a2 g s)
        (exists (e1 e2 s1 s2 g1)
           (and (planning e1 a1 g1 s1)(planning e2 a2 g s2)
                (and' e e1 e2)(not' g1 g)
                (forall (p)
                   (iff (inSeq p s)
                        (or (and (adversarialPlan p a1 a2 g)
                                 (inSeq p s1))
                            (inSeq p s2)))))))))
```

A stronger notion still is when active counterplanning goes on. Agent a1 tries to figure out a2's plan, and then tries to block its success. We can model this by saying that a1 strives to achieve (not g2) where g2 is a subgoal of a2's ultimate goal.

```
(forall (e a1 a2 g s)                                    (36.8)
   (iff (counterPlanning e a1 a2 g s)
        (exists (p2 g1)
           (and (plan p2 a2 g)(planning e a1 g1 s)(not' g1 g)
                (forall (p)
                   (if (inSeq p s)(counterplan p p2 a1 a2 g)))))))
```

36.3 COUNTERFACTUAL PLANNING

Suppose Pat imagines how she would achieve world peace if she were president. In her plan there is a proposition (President Pat) which enables a large number of actions, and consequently is a subgoal in the plan. If Pat really is president, this is an ordinary plan and the plan bottoms out in this subgoal, because it already holds. If she is not, she may develop a plan to become president – declare her candidacy, begin campaigning, and so on. In this case also we have an ordinary plan. Being president is a subgoal and she constructs a plan to achieve the subgoal. But if the subgoal does not hold and she does no planning to achieve the subgoal, but goes on planning anyway to achieve world peace as though she were president, then she is engaged in counterfactual planning.

We can say that a counterfactual plan involves a counterfactual subgoal. A counterfactual subgoal is one that does not hold and the agent engages in no planning to make it hold.

```
(forall (g1 g2 a)                                        (36.9)
   (iff (counterfactualSubgoal g1 g2 a)
        (and (subgoal g1 g2)(not g1)
             (not (exists (e s) (planning e a g1 s))))))
```

Counterfactual planning occurs when there is a counterfactual subgoal in the last plan in the sequence of plans that the planning activity produces.

```
(forall (e a g1 g2 s)                                    (36.10)
   (iff (counterfactualPlanning e a g1 g2 s)
        (exists (p)
           (and (planning e a g2 s)(last p s)(subgoalIn g1 p)
                (counterfactualSubgoal g1 g2 a)))))
```

A particularly common kind of counterfactual planning is imagining what we would do if we were a different person. For example, Pat might imagine what she would do if she were Barack Obama. Generally this means that there is some property of the other person that does not hold for the person doing the planning, and it functions as a counterfactual subgoal in the plan.

```
(forall (e a1 a2 g1 g2 s)                                (36.11)
   (iff (otherPersonPlanning e a1 a2 g1 g2 s)
        (and (counterfactualPlanning e a g1 g2 s)
             (exists (g3) (and (subst a2 g3 a1 g1)(Rexist g3))))))
```

The expression (otherPersonPlanning e a1 a2 g1 g2 s) says that e is the activity of agent a1 planning as though property g1, a property of a1, were true, even though it isn't, where the corresponding property g3 of a2 is true.

PREDICATES INTRODUCED IN THIS CHAPTER

(planning e a g s)
   e is activity by agent a of planning to achieve g, producing a sequence s of plans.

(collaborativePlanning e a1 a2 g s)
   e is activity by agents a1 and a2 of planning collaboratively to achieve g, producing a sequence s of plans.

(assistivePlanning e a1 a2 g s)
   e is activity by agent a1 of planning to achieve g and by agent a2 of assisting by achieving a subgoal of g, where s is the sequence of plans produced.

(competitivePlanning e a1 a2 g s)
   e is activity by agents a1 and a2 of planning to achieve for themselves an instance of goal g, to the exclusion of the other, producing a sequence s of plans.

(adversarialPlanning e a1 a2 g s)
   e is activity by agents a1 and a2 of planning to achieve for themselves an instance of goal g while actively planning to prevent the other from doing the same, producing a sequence s of plans.

(counterPlanning e a1 a2 g s)
   e is activity by agents a1 and a2 of planning to prevent the other from achieving an instance of goal g, producing a sequence s of plans.

(counterfactualSubgoal a g1 g2)
   g1 is a subgoal in a's plan for g2 where g1 is not true and a does not plan to make g1 true.

(counterfactualPlanning e a g1 g2 s)
  e is planning activity by agent a to achieve g2, producing sequence s of plans,
  where g1 is a counterfactualSubgoal.

(otherPersonPlanning e a1 a2 g1 g2 s)
  e is counterfactual planning activity by agent a1 where the counterfactual subgoal
  is a property agent a2 has that a1 lacks.

37

Planning Goals

37.1 CONSTRAINTS AND PREFERENCES

As we develop plans for achieving specific goals, especially where many possible plans will work, we often seek to optimize various extraneous factors. For example, we may want to buy a sandwich but do so in a way that takes the least time. We may want to drive to a friend's house, but in a way that avoids traffic jams. We may plan a hike but leave open until we are there exactly where we will stop for our picnic lunch. This chapter focuses on these influences and modifications on plans, such as including and avoiding certain actions, enabling or blocking certain events, minimizing or maximizing certain values, locating relevant instances for general parameters, and maintaining the progress of the planning and the execution of the plan.

First we need to characterize constraints and preferences.

It will be useful to define the action of adding a goal to a plan to form another plan.

$$
\begin{array}{ll}
\text{(forall (a g2 p1 p2)} & \text{(37.1)} \\
\quad \text{(iff (addGoalToPlan a g2 p1 p2)} \\
\qquad \text{(exists (g1 g)} \\
\qquad\quad \text{(and (plan p1 a g1)(plan p2 a g)(and' g g1 g2)} \\
\qquad\qquad \text{(subplan p1 p2)))))}
\end{array}
$$

The predication (addGoalToPlan a g2 p1 p2) says that agent a adds goal g2 to plan p1 to produce p2. This happens when p2 is a plan to achieve g2 in addition to p1's top-level goal g1 and when the original plan p1 is a subplan of the resulting plan p2.

People often have hard constraints for plans that they would consider to be successful. These constraints can be viewed as goals that are added to the plan.

$$
\begin{array}{ll}
\text{(forall (e1 a p)} & \text{(37.2)} \\
\quad \text{(iff (planningConstraint e a p)} \\
\qquad \text{(exists (p2) (addGoalToPlan a e p p2))))}
\end{array}
$$

This says that eventuality e is a constraint on agent a's plan p exactly when a adds e as a goal to p.

Soft constraints or preferences are more difficult to capture than hard constraints are. We would like to maximize the satisfaction of preferences as goals are being pursued, but allow the successful achievement of goals even if the preferences are not satisfied. Someone may prefer an aisle seat to a window seat, but she won't cancel her flight if no aisle seat is available. In a way, we can think of a preference as a kind of "pre-goal" or "pre-constraint." If possible, we will add the preferred eventuality to the plan, but if not possible, we will execute the plan without it.

Let us take prefer to be a relation among an agent a, two situations or eventualities e1 and e2, and a plan p. The predication (prefer a e1 e2 p) says agent a prefers eventuality e1 to eventuality e2 in carrying out plan p. It is certainly the case that we sometimes prefer one object over another, but we normally have some event in mind involving those objects. To prefer an apple to an orange is usually to prefer eating an apple to eating an orange.

```
(forall (a e1 e2 p)                                          (37.3)
    (if (prefer a e1 e2 p)
        (and (agent a)(eventuality e1)(eventuality e2)
            (exists (g) (plan p a g)))))
```

The two eventualities should be incompatible; otherwise there will be no reason to have to choose one over the other. You would not say you prefer walking to chewing gum unless you couldn't do both at once.

```
(forall (a e1 e2 p)                                          (37.4)
    (if (and (prefer a e1 e2 p)(etc))
        (exists (e)(and (not' e e1)(imply e2 e)))))
```

This says that, defeasibly, e2 implies the negation e of e1.

Preferences are in a sense "goals in waiting." They do not override real goals, but if they do not contradict any real goals and they are otherwise possible, they will normally be adopted as goals.

```
(forall (a e1 e2 p s1 s2 s3 s0)                              (37.5)
    (if (and (prefer a e1 e2 p)
            (cwu s1 a)(eventualitiesOf s2 s1)(subgoalsOf s3 p)
            (union s0 s2 s3)
            (possible e1 s0)(etc))
        (exists (p2)
            (addGoalToPlan a e1 p p2))))
```

Line 2 says that agent a prefers e1 to e2 while executing plan p. Lines 3 and 4 label the eventualities s2 in a's current world understanding, the subgoals s3 in plan p, and the union s0 of these two sets. Line 5 says that e1 is possible given s0 as constraints, that is, given the way the world is and given the plan. Line 7 says that under these conditions, the agent will incorporate e1 as a goal in the plan, producing a new plan p2.

Occasionally the dispreferred element e2 is a completely unacceptable state of affairs. Someone might say, "I prefer a meeting with George to a sharp stick in the eye," as a way of saying he doesn't want to meet with George. But this works as a joke precisely because in normal usage, we will adopt the dispreferred element if the preferred one is not possible. Hence, the following axiom:

```
(forall (a e1 e2 p s1 s2 s3 s0)                                    (37.6)
    (if (and (prefer a e1 e2 p)
             (cwu s1 a)(eventualitiesOf s2 s1)(subgoalsOf s3 p)
             (union s0 s2 s3)
             (not (possible e1 s0))
             (possible e2 s0)(etc))
        (exists (p2)
           (addGoalToPlan a e2 p p2)))))
```

Lines 1–4 are the same as in the previous axiom. Line 5 says e1 is not possible. Line 6 says that the dispreferred item e2 is possible. Line 8 says that in these circumstances, e2 will be incorporated into the plan. Both axioms are defeasible.

We can strengthen Axiom (37.5) in two ways. We often think of preferences as applying in forced choice situations, where both options are possible and one of the two options is going to occur anyway at some future time. We can encode these conditions in the antecedent.

Secondly, when neither option is very desirable, it seems strange that we adopt the less bad as a goal. Suppose you face the choice of having your leg amputated or dying of gangrene. You'll choose the first, but it seems wrong to say that you have the goal of having your leg amputated. Your goal is really not to die of gangrene, and losing your leg is just a side effect of that. We capture this by saying in the consequent that if the preferred option is bad for you, then the goal you add to your plan is the negation of the dispreferred option.

```
(forall (a e1 e2 p s1 s2 s3 s0 e3 t t1)                            (37.7)
    (if (and (prefer a e1 e2 p)
             (cwu0 s1 a t)(Now t)
             (eventualitiesOf s2 s1)(subgoalsOf s3 p)
             (union s0 s2 s3)
             (possible e1 s0)(possible e2 s0)
             (or' e3 e1 e2)(atTime e3 t1)(before t t1)(etc))
        (exists (p2 e4)
           (or (and (not (badFor e1 a))(addGoalToPlan a e1 p p2))
               (and (badFor e1 a)(not' e4 e2)(addGoalToPlan a e4 p p2)))))))
```

Line 6 says both options are possible. Line 7 says that one of them is going to happen anyway. In line 9 we add the preferred option if it is not bad for us. If it is, then in line 10 we add the negation of the dispreferred option.

Preference is a partial ordering. Hence, it is antisymmetric.

```
(forall (a e1 e2 p)                                               (37.8)
    (if (prefer a e1 e2 p)(not (prefer a e2 e1 p))))
```

Preference is also transitive.

```
(forall (a e1 e2 e3 p)                                            (37.9)
    (if (and (prefer a e1 e2 p)(prefer a e2 e3 p))
        (prefer a e1 e3 p)))
```

Since the conjunction of a preference and a goal is also a goal, we can apply these rules iteratively and satisfy many preferences in carrying out the plan p. Since the rule can be applied to any preference first, we can end up with any of many possible sets of preferences.

It will be convenient to have a predicate meaning that the agent prefers a situation e1 to its absence.

```
(forall (a e1 p)                                              (37.10)
    (iff (prefer0 a e1 p)
        (exists (e2) (and (not' e2 e1)(prefer a e1 e2 p)))))
```

A great deal of work has been done on preferences in artificial intelligence (cf. Brafman and Domshlak, 2009), philosophy (e.g., van Bentham, Roy, and Girard, 2009; Von Wright, 1963), and many other fields. Much of this research has concerned how to compare two complex entities given preferences among their properties. We will not pursue this issue.

A richer theory of preferences would explore what causes us to prefer one eventuality over another. For example, in general we will prefer options that require less effort. Perhaps we should have a rule saying that the effort to achieve e1 should be negligible relative to the effort required to achieve plan p's top-level goal. We might want to avoid traffic jams on our way to our friend's house, but not if it means driving ten miles out of the way. We have not spelled this out in greater detail axiomatically because we have not developed a theory of effort. We might also want a theory of the strengths of preferences that could adjudicate among conflicting strong preferences and weak goals, and could determine the level of effort the satisfaction of a preference might be worth.

We can say something about how preferences interact with value and cost. If e1 is more valuable than e2, then defeasibly a will prefer e1 to e2.

```
(forall (e1 e2 a p)                                          (37.11)
    (if (and (moreValuable e1 e2 a)(etc)) (prefer a e1 e2 p)))
```

If e1 is more costly than e2, then defeasibly a will prefer e2 to e1.

```
(forall (e1e2 a p)                                           (37.12)
    (if (and (moreCostly e1 e2 a)(etc)) (prefer a e2 e1 p)))
```

In the rest of this chapter we define a number of predicates related to planning goal preferences, to demonstrate the range of the vocabulary we have built up.

37.2 INCLUDING AND AVOIDING

One can prefer to include a particular action in a plan, as seen in the phrase "try to incorporate the step." This is just the predicate prefer0.

One can prefer to avoid including a particular action in a plan, as seen in the phrases "try to avoid" and "only as a last resort."

```
(forall (a e p)                                              (37.13)
    (iff (preferAvoidAction a e p)
        (exists (e1)
            (and (not' e1 e)(prefer0 a e1 p)))))
```

That is, an agent a prefers to avoid action e in plan p exactly when a prefers to include its negation in the plan.

37.3 ENABLING AND BLOCKING

One can prefer to work toward plans that enable an event to occur, as in "set the stage for."

```
(forall (a e p)                                          (37.14)
    (iff (preferEnableEvent a e p)
          (forall (e1)
              (if (enable e1 e)(prefer0 a e1 p)))))
```

One can prefer to work toward plans that prevent an event from occurring, as in "safeguard against."

```
(forall (a e p)                                          (37.15)
    (iff (preferBlockEvent a e p)
          (forall (e1)
              (if (prevent e1 e)(prefer0 a e1 p)))))
```

One can prefer to work toward plans that ensure a threat will actually occur, as in "set one up to fail."

```
(forall (a e p)                                          (37.16)
    (iff (preferEnableThreat a e p)
          (and (preferEnableEvent a e p)(threat0 e a))))
```

One can prefer to work toward plans that ensure a threat will not actually occur, as in "take preemptive action" and "alleviate the risk."

```
(forall (a e p)                                          (37.17)
    (iff (preferBlockThreat a e p)
          (and (preferBlockEvent a e p)(threat0 e a))))
```

One can prefer to work toward plans that allow a physical transfer through space, as in "clear the path" and "remove obstacles."

```
(forall (a e p)                                          (37.18)
    (iff (preferEnableTransfer a e p)
          (exists (x y z)
              (and (move' e x y z)(physobj x)
                  (preferEnableEvent a e p)))))
```

One can prefer to work toward plans that prevent a physical transfer through space, as in "obstruct" and "prevent from leaving."

```
(forall (a e p)                                          (37.19)
    (iff (preferBlockTransfer a e p)
          (exists (x y z)
              (and (move' e x y z)(physobj x)
                  (preferBlockEvent a e p)))))
```

One can prefer to work toward plans that enable a different agent to act, as in "make it possible for."

```
(forall (a b e p)                                              (37.20)
    (iff (preferEnableAgency a b e p)
        (and (agentOf b e)(preferEnableEvent a e p))))
```

One can prefer to work toward plans that block a different agent from acting, as in "paralyze" and "keep one on a short leash."

```
(forall (a b e p)                                              (37.21)
    (iff (preferBlockAgency a b e p)
        (and (agentOf b e)(preferBlockEvent a e p))))
```

One can prefer to work toward plans that enable others to achieve their goals, as in "make someone happy."

```
(forall (a b e p)                                              (37.22)
    (iff (preferEnableOtherAgentGoalSatisfaction a b e p)
        (exists (g1)
            (and (goal g1 b)(enable e g1)
                (preferEnableEvent a e p)))))
```

One can prefer to work toward plans that prevent others from achieving their goals, as in "thwart" and "derail."

```
(forall (a b e p)                                              (37.23)
    (iff (preferBlockOtherAgentGoalSatisfaction a b e p)
        (exists (g1)
            (and (goal g1 b)(enable e g1)
                (preferBlockEvent a e p)))))
```

37.4 MINIMIZING AND MAXIMIZING

One can prefer to try to minimize a value that is part of a plan, as illustrated in "less is more," "be conservative," and "frugal."

```
(forall (a v p)                                                (37.24)
    (iff (preferMinimizeValue a v p)
        (forall (e1 e2 x1 x2 s)
            (if (and (at' e1 v x1 s)(at' e2 v x2 s)
                    (lts x1 x2 s))
                (prefer a e1 e2 p)))))
```

Lines 4–7 specify conditions e1 and e2, saying that e1 is the eventuality of some value v being at point x1 on some scale s, e2 is the eventuality of v being at x2 on s, where x1 is less than x2 on the scale. Under these circumstances, agent a will prefer e1 to e2.

One can prefer to try to maximize a value that is part of a plan, as illustrated in the phrases "bigger is better," "as much as possible," and "be liberal with."

```
(forall (a v p)                                      (37.25)
   (iff (preferMaximizeValue a v p)
        (forall (e1 e2 x1 x2 s)
           (if (and (at' e1 v x1 s)(at' e2 v x2 s)
                    (lts x2 x1 s))
              (prefer a e1 e2 p)))))
```

This definition is the same as the previous one, except x1 and x2 are reversed in line 5.

Among the values one can seek to minimize or maximize are the durations of activities and events. Thus, one can prefer to try to minimize the overall duration of a plan, as in "time is of the essence" and "not waste time."

```
(forall (a p)                                        (37.26)
   (iff (preferMinimizeDuration a p)
        (exists (d u)
           (and (durationOf d p u)
                (preferMinimizeValue a d p)))))
```

One can prefer to try to maximize the overall duration of a plan, as in "prolong" and "make it last."

```
(forall (a p)                                        (37.27)
   (iff (preferMaximizeDuration a p)
        (exists (d u)
           (and (durationOf d p u)
                (preferMaximizeValue a d p)))))
```

37.5 LOCATING INSTANCES FOR PLANS

To instantiate an underspecified element in a plan is to add to the plan as a subgoal a property of that element that allows it to be identified. A context-dependent property of an entity that allows it to be identified is captured in the wh-words in English, for example, "I know who he is." In Hobbs (1985) the predicate wh is used for this. Thus, to know the identity of something x is to know an e such that (wh' e x p). The wh property is relative to a context, and in the planning realm, that can be specified by the plan p.

Sometimes unspecified things must be instantiated for plans to be complete, as in "locate," "search for," and "get one's hands on."

```
(forall (a x p)                                      (37.28)
   (iff (locateThing a x p)
        (exists (e p2 e1 g)
           (and (plan p a g)(addGoalToPlan a e p p2)(arg* x e)
                (imply e e1)(wh' e1 x g)))))
```

The expression (locateThing a x p) means that agent a instantiates unspecified entity x in plan p. Line 4 says that p is a plan for achieving g and agent a adds to that plan as a constraint a property e of x. Line 5 says that e implies a property e1 that enables x to be identifiedd.

Sometimes unspecified people must be instantiated for plans to be complete, as in "find someone to" and "fill the job."

```
(forall (a x p)                                          (37.29)
    (iff (locateAgent a x p)
        (and (person x)(locateThing a x p))))
```

Sometimes unspecified locations must be instantiated for plans to be complete, as in "find a place where."

```
(forall (a x p)                                          (37.30)
    (iff (locateLocation a x p)
        (exists (y s e)
            (and (atLoc y x s)(arg* y e)(subgoalIn e p)
                (locateThing a x p)))))
```

Note that there is no such thing as a location per se. Something is the location of something else, indicated by the atLoc relation. Thus, to identify a location crucial to the execution of a plan is to recognize or decide upon the location of an entity that is an argument of or is involved in one of the subgoals of the plan.

37.6 MAINTAINING PLAN PROGRESS

One can (and generally does) prefer to work toward plans that maintain the progress that has already been achieved. For example, if the top of a block is already clear and its being clear is necessary to achieve the goal, don't put something on top of it if you can help it. This is illustrated in the phrases "avoid backpedaling" and "keep moving forward."

```
(forall (a p)                                            (37.31)
    (iff (preferMaintainPlanProgress a p)
        (forall (e e1)
            (if (and (subgoalIn e p)(changeFrom' e1 e))
                (exists (e2)
                    (and (not' e2 e1)(prefer0 a e2 p)))))))
```

That is, if e is a subgoal of the plan, agent a prefers not to change it. In cases where a previously achieved state must be undone for the plan to succeed, the preference will be overridden.

PREDICATES INTRODUCED IN THIS CHAPTER

(addGoalToPlan a g p1 p2)
    Agent a adds goal g to plan p1, yielding plan p2.

(planningConstraint e a p)
    e is a constraint agent a wants to achieve in carrying out plan p.

(prefer a e1 e2 p)
    Agent a prefers achieving e1 to achieving e2 in carrying out plan p.

(prefer0 a e1 p)
    Agent a prefers achieving e1 to its absence in carrying out plan p.

(preferAvoidAction a e p)
    Agent a prefers to avoid e in carrying out plan p.

(preferEnableEvent a e p)
    Agent a prefers to enable e in carrying out plan p.

(preferBlockEvent a e p)
    Agent a prefers to block e in carrying out plan p.

(preferEnableThreat a e p)
    Agent a prefers to enable e in carrying out plan p, where e is a threat.

(preferBlockThreat a e p)
    Agent a prefers to block e in carrying out plan p, where e is a threat.

(preferEnableTransfer a e p)
    Agent a prefers to enable e in carrying out plan p, where e is a physical transfer.

(preferBlockTransfer a e p)
    Agent a prefers to block e in carrying out plan p, where e is a physical transfer.

(preferEnableAgency a b e p)
    Agent a prefers to enable another agent b's doing action e, in carrying out plan p.

(preferBlockAgency a b e p)
    Agent a prefers to block another agent b's doing action e, in carrying out plan p.

(preferEnableOtherAgentGoalSatisfaction a b e p)
    Agent a prefers to enable another agent b to achieve b's goal, by doing e in carrying out plan p.

(preferBlockOtherAgentGoalSatisfaction a b e p)
    Agent a prefers to block another agent b from achieving b's goal, by doing e in carrying out plan p.

(preferMinimizeValue a v p)
    Agent a prefers to minimize the value of v in carrying out plan p.

(preferMaximizeValue a v p)
    Agent a prefers to maximize the value of v in carrying out plan p.

(preferMinimizeDuration a p)
    Agent a prefers to minimize the duration of plan p.

(preferMaximizeDuration a p)
    Agent a prefers to maximize the duration of plan p.

(wh' e x p)
    e is a property that identifies x in the context of plan p.

(locateThing a x p)
    Agent a instantiates unspecified entity x in plan p.

(locateAgent a x p)
    Agent a instantiates unspecified other agent x in plan p.

(locateLocation a x p)
    Agent a instantiates unspecified location x in plan p.

(preferMaintainPlanProgress a p)
    Agent a prefers to maintain progress and not backtrack in plan p.

Plan Construction

38.1 THE PLANNING ACTIVITY

In Chapter 36 we introduced the predication (planning e a g s), meaning that e
is a planning activity by agent a to achieve goal g, where s is the sequence of plans
that result from this activity. For example, the first element of s may be the limiting
case of a plan, consisting of g alone, the second element might be that plus several
immediate subgoals, and the last a complete, executable plan that should achieve the
goal.

As agents goes through the planning process, there is a range of moves they may
use to develop their plans. At one end is instantiating an eventuality type in order to
produce a plan more specifically tailored to the immediate situation.

```
(forall (e a g s)                                                    (38.1)
    (iff (planningByInstantiating e a g s)
        (and (planning e a g s)
            (forall (p1 p2)
                (if (successiveElts p1 p2 s)
                    (planInstance p2 p1)))))))
```

That is, the only way we get from one plan to the next is instantiating entity and
eventuality types in the earlier plan. This kind of planning is seen, for example, when
we engage in the near habitual action of giving a waiter our order in a restaurant,
where we are taking the general restaurant-ordering script and instantiating it with
this waiter and the items on this menu.

At the other end of the spectrum is planning from scratch. Here we are not instantiating a well-worn script. Rather we are mining our knowledge of what causes what
and using the basic planning axioms to try to achieve our goal.

```
(forall (e a g s)                                                    (38.2)
    (iff (planningFromScratch e a g s)
        (and (planning e a g s)
            (forall (e0 p1 p2 s1 s2 r1 r2)
```

```
(if (and (successiveElts' e0 p1 p2 s)
         (eventualitiesOf s1 p1)
         (eventualitiesOf s2 p2)
         (relationsOf r1 p1)(relationsOf r2 p2))
    (exists (e1 e2 r r0 e3)
        (and (member e1 s1)(addElt s2 s1 e2)
             (causallyInvolved' r e2 e1)
             (subgoal' r0 e2 e1)
             (addElt r2 r1 r0)(believe' e3 a r)
             (cause e3 e0))))))))
```

Lines 5–8 of this definition label the sets s1 and s2 of subgoals in p1 and p2, the sets r1 and r2 of subgoal relations, and the succesiveElts relation e0 between p1 and p2. In lines 10–13 we say that p2 is constructed from p1 by adding a subgoal e2 to p1, on the basis of a belief e3 in r. that is, that e2 is causally involved in e1. The predication (cause e3 e0) in line 14 says the belief e3 in r is why p1 and p2 are successive elements of s.

We should point out that this definition does not really capture the complete idea of planning from scratch, because the belief that e2 is causally involved in e1 could have resulted from prior elaborate causal reasoning, including planning for other goals.

These two concepts delimit a range of types of planning processes, from routine to novel. Most planning is a combination of these types. In addition, in the next chapter we will introduce another way of developing plans – tweaking existing plans for related goals.

People can plan to achieve single goals.

```
(forall (e a g s)                                          (38.3)
   (iff (singleGoalPlanning e a g s)
        (and (planning e a g s)
             (not (exists (g1 g2) (and' g g1 g2))))))
```

People can plan to achieve multiple goals.

```
(forall (e a g s)                                          (38.4)
   (iff (multipleGoalPlanning e a g s)
        (and (planning e a g s)
             (exists (g1 g2) (and' g g1 g2)))))
```

People can develop solutions to problems of design. In Chapter 40 on Design, we define the action of designing.

38.2 PLANNING PROCESS CONTROL

A planning process is itself a plan-in-action, that is, a coherent sequence of actions that the agent carries out with the goal of coming up with a plan. Thus, it is subject to the same kinds of detailed characterization that other goal-directed behavior is. In particular, we can apply various aspectual predicates to it that we define in Chapter 45 on Execution Control.

People can suspend a planning process, as seen in the expressions "hold off on the details" and "put aside the plan."

```
(forall (a e)                                               (38.5)
    (iff (suspendPlanning a e)
        (exists (g s t)
            (and (suspend a e t)(Now t)(planning e a g s)))))
```

People can resume working on a plan after they have suspended the planning process, as seen in the expressions "finish the plan" and "take up the plan again."

```
(forall (a e)                                               (38.6)
    (iff (resumePlanning a e)
        (exists (g s t)
            (and (resume a e t)(Now t)(planning e a g s)))))
```

People can decide to abandon a planning process, as in "stop planning" and "give up on the plan."

```
(forall (a e)                                               (38.7)
    (iff (abortPlanning a e)
        (exists (g s t)
            (and (abort a e t)(Now t)(planning e a g s)))))
```

The planning process can be restarted, as seen in "start from scratch," "back to the drawing board" and "try a different approach."

```
(forall (e1 a p g)                                          (38.8)
 (iff (replan' e1 a p g)
      (exists (e s t)(and (planning e a g s)(restart' e1 a e t)(Now t)))))
```

Since a subplan of a plan, to achieve a subgoal, is itself a plan, this can also be restarted. We see this in the phrases "patch the plan," "fix part of the plan," and "rework a step."

```
(forall (e1 a p1 p g)                                       (38.9)
    (iff (replanSubplan' e1 a p1 p g)
        (exists (g1)
            (and (replan' e1 a p1 g1)(plan p a g)(plan p1 a g1)
                (subgoal g1 g)))))
```

38.3 PLANNING SUBPROCESSES

In this section we define a number of moves an agent can make in developing a plan, from one plan in the plan sequence to the next. All of these definitions involve two successive plans p1 and p2 and say how p1 and p2 differ.

During planning, people can add detail to a plan in development, as seen in the expressions "flesh out the details" and "be specific about the plan."

```
(forall (e a g s p1 p2)                                     (38.10)
    (if (and (planning e a g s)(successiveElts p1 p2 s))
        (iff (specifyPlan e a g s p1 p2)
            (planInstancePlus p2 p1))))
```

For example, we may have a plan to eat at McDonald's. When we walk into McDonald's, we make our plan more specific by choosing a specific register.

People can add a subplan to a plan, as in the expressions "add a step," "addendum to the plan," and "put a part in the plan."

```
(forall (e a g s p1 p2)                                         (38.11)
    (if (and (planning e a g s)(successiveElts p1 p2 s))
        (iff (addSubplan e a g s p1 p2)
            (exists (s1 s2 s3 g1 p3)
                (and (eventualitiesOf s1 p1)(eventualitiesOf s2 p2)
                    (setdiff s3 s2 s1)(subgoalIn g1 p1)
                    (plan p3 a g1)(eventualitiesOf s3 p3)
                    (forall (g2)
                        (if (member g2 s3)(subgoalIn g2 p3)))))))))
```

The expression (addSubplan e a g s p1 p2) says that in the planning activity e by agent a to achieve goal g, via plan sequence s, a has moved from plan p1 to the next plan p2 by adding a subplan (p3) to achieve a subgoal (g1) of g. Lines 5–7 label the sets s1 and s2 of eventualities in plans p1 and p2, the set difference s3 between these sets, and the subplan p3 that is in p2 but not in p1. Line 7 also stipulates that s3 is the set of eventualities in p3. Lines 8–9 say that the differences in the two plans are all in the subplan.

During planning people can remove a subplan from the plan in development, as in the expressions "remove a step" and "simplify the plan."

```
(forall (e a g s p1 p2)                                         (38.12)
    (if (and (planning e a g s)(successiveElts p1 p2 s))
        (iff (removeSubplan e a g s p1 p2)
            (exists (s1 s2 s3 g1 p3)
                (and (eventualitiesOf s1 p1)(eventualitiesOf s2 p2)
                    (setdiff s3 s1 s2)(subgoalIn g1 p2)
                    (plan p3 a g1)(eventualitiesOf s3 p3)
                    (forall (g2)
                        (if (member g2 s3)
                            (subgoalIn g2 p3)))))))))
```

This definition is like that for addSubplan, but with the arguments of setdiff in line 6 reversed.

During planning, people can notice that the goal or a subgoal has a precondition, as in "realize we first need to" and "see a necessary step."

```
(forall (e a g s p1 p2)                                         (38.13)
    (if (and (planning e a g s)(successiveElts p1 p2 s))
        (iff (identifyPrecondition e a g s p1 p2)
            (exists (s1 s2 s3 g1 g2)
                (and (eventualitiesOf s1 p1)(eventualitiesOf s2 p2)
                    (setdiff s3 s2 s1)(member g1 s1)(member g2 s3)
                    (enable g2 g1))))))
```

In lines 6 and 7 g2 is the new subgoal of g1 that was realized to be a precondition of g1 in p1.

During planning, people often make selections among alternative subplans. That is, they replace a disjunction with one of its disjuncts. This is seen in the expressions "choose a step" and "select an action."

```
(forall (e a g s p1 p2)                                      (38.14)
    (if (and (planning e a g s)(successiveElts p1 p2 s))
        (iff (selectSubplan e a g s p1 p2)
            (exists (s1 s2 e0 e1 e2)
                (and (eventualitiesOf s1 p1)(eventualitiesOf s2 p2)
                    (or' e0 e1 e2)
                    (or (replaceElt s2 s1 e0 e1)
                        (replaceElt s2 s1 e0 e2)))))))
```

Line 6 says e0 is a disjunction of eventualities e1 and e2, and lines 7 and 8 say the difference between the successive plans is that e0 is replaced by e1 or e2.

People often decide during planning what order they should achieve the subgoals in, as seen in the expressions "first things first" and "figure out the order." This amounts to adding temporal detail, that is, a before relation.

```
(forall (e a g s p1 p2)                                      (38.15)
    (if (and (planning e a g s)(successiveElts p1 p2 s))
        (iff (orderSubplans e a g s p1 p2)
            (exists (s1 s2 s3 g1 g2 e0)
                (and (eventualitiesOf s1 p1)(eventualitiesOf s2 p2)
                    (setdiff s3 s2 s1)(member g1 s1)(member g2 s1)
                    (before' e0 g1 g2)(member e0 s3))))))
```

In lines 6 and 7 g1 and g2 are subgoals in plan p1 and what is new in plan p2 is the before relation between them.

38.4 PLANNING PROBLEMS

An obstacle is something that causes a goal not to occur. Other words for this are "barrier," "impediment," and "impasse." This definition includes both conditions as obstacles and entities whose properties are obstacles.

```
(forall (x a g)                                              (38.16)
    (iff (obstacle x a g)
        (exists (e e1)
            (and (or (cause x e)(and (arg* x e1)(cause e1 e)))
                (not' e g)(goal g a)))))
```

The expression (obstacle x a g) says that entity x is an obstacle to agent a's achieving goal g. In line 4 it can either be x itself or one of its properties e1 that can cause the goal not to occur.

To overcome an obstacle is to cause it not to occur in a way that is consistent with the goal being achieved.

```
(forall (a x g)                                              (38.17)
  (iff (overcomeObstacle a x g)
       (exists (e0 e)
          (and (obstacle' e0 x a g) (cause a e) (not' e e0)
               (enable e g)))))
```

Essentially, the elimination of an obstacle is the satisfaction of a precondition. The agent causes the obstacle not to exist as an obstacle.

People see these obstacles as problems that must be overcome in their plans. The concept is exemplified in language in "challenge," "dilemma," "sticky situation," and "something must be done."

```
(forall (x a p g)                                            (38.18)
  (iff (planningProblem x a p g)
       (exists (e)
          (and (obstacle x a g) (overcomeObstacle' e a x g)
               (plan p a g) (subgoalIn e p)))))
```

One kind of planning option is the overcoming of an obstacle.

```
(forall (e p a x g e1)                                       (38.19)
  (if (and (plan p a g) (planningProblem x a p g)
           (overcomeObstacle' e a x g))
      (planningOption e p)))
```

38.5 SELECTING AMONG CANDIDATE PLANS

An agent may construct several possible plans to achieve a goal, and then must select among these candidate plans for a plan to execute. A candidate plan is a plan that the agent has in focus and is executable now with respect to a set c of constraints.

```
(forall (p a g)                                              (38.20)
  (iff (candidatePlan p a g)
       (exists (e s c t)
          (and (planning e a g s) (member p s) (inFocus p a)
               (executable p a c t) (Now t)))))
```

Agents can successfully construct a plan to achieve a goal.

```
(forall (a p g)                                              (38.21)
  (iff (successfulPlanning e a p g)
       (exists (e1 s)
          (and (planning e a g s) (cause e e1)
               (candidatePlan' e1 p a g)))))
```

Agents can fail to construct a plan to achieve a goal.

```
(forall (a p g)                                              (38.22)
  (iff (planningFailure e a g)
       (and (planning e a g s)
            (not (exists (p)
                   (and (member p s) (candidatePlan p a g)))))))
```

Agents can assess candidate plans to determine which are most likely to achieve the goal.

```
(forall (a p g d)                                                    (38.23)
    (iff (assessPlan a p g d)
         (exists (e e1)
             (and (cause' e p g)(gbel' e1 a e d)(changeTo e1)))))
```

That is, to assess a plan is to come to a belief about how certain the plan is to achieve the goal. The expression (assessPlan a p g d) says that agent a assesses plan p for achieving goal g and has degree of belief d in its success.

When they behave rationally, agents select from among the candidate plans the plan that is assessed to be the most likely to succeed.

```
(forall (a p g)                                                      (38.24)
    (iff (selectCandidatePlan a p g)
         (exists (d0)
             (and (assessPlan a p g d0)
                  (forall (p1 d1)
                      (if (and (candidatePlan p1 a g)
                               (assessPlan a p1 g d1))
                          (leq d1 d0)))
                  (decideTo a p)))))
```

A plan that is selected is scheduled, that is, is assigned a time to be executed.

```
(forall (a p1 g)                                                     (38.25)
    (if (selectCandidatePlan a p1 g)
        (exists (p2) (schedulePlan a p1 p2))))
```

The predicate schedulePlan is defined in Chapter 42 on Scheduling. The expression (schedule a p1 p2) says that agent a adds a schedule to plan p1, yielding plan p2.

Candidate plans that are not selected will not be executed.

```
(forall (p p1 a g)                                                   (38.26)
    (if (and (candidatePlan p a g)(candidatePlan p1 a g)(nequal p p1)
             (decideTo a p))
        (not (decideTo a p1))))
```


PREDICATES INTRODUCED IN THIS CHAPTER

(planningByInstantiating e a g s)
> e is a planning activity by agent a for achieving goal g, resulting in sequence s of plans, where each element of s is derived from the previous one by instantiating entity or eventuality types.

(planningFromScratch e a g s)
> e is a planning activity by agent a for achieving goal g, resulting in sequence s of plans, where each element of s is derived from the previous one by accessing a causal rule.

(singleGoalPlanning e a g s)
> e is a planning activity by agent a for achieving goal g, resulting in sequence s of plans, where g is not a conjunction.

(multipleGoalPlanning e a g s)
    e is a planning activity by agent a for achieving goal g, resulting in sequence s of
    plans, where g is a conjunction.

(suspendPlanning a e)
    Agent a suspends a planning activity e.

(resumePlanning a e)
    Agent a resumes a planning activity e.

(abortPlanning a e)
    Agent a aborts a planning activity e.

(replan' e1 a p g)
    Agent a restarts a planning activity e.

(replanSubplan a p1 p g)
    Agent a replans a subplan p1 within plan p to achieve g.

(specifyPlan e a g s p1 p2)
    e is a planning activity by agent a for achieving goal g, resulting in sequence s of
    plans, where plan p2 is derived from plan p1 by instantiating entity and eventu-
    ality types and by elaborating detail.

(addSubplan e a g s p1 p2)
    e is a planning activity by agent a for achieving goal g, resulting in sequence s of
    plans, where plan p2 is derived from plan p1 by adding a subplan.

(removeSubplan e a g s p1 p2)
    e is a planning activity by agent a for achieving goal g, resulting in sequence s of
    plans, where plan p2 is derived from plan p1 by removing a subplan.

(identifyPrecondition e a g s p1 p2)
    e is a planning activity by agent a for achieving goal g, resulting in sequence s
    of plans, where plan p2 is derived from plan p1 by adding a precondition to a
    subgoal in p1.

(selectSubplan e a g s p1 p2)
    e is a planning activity by agent a for achieving goal g, resulting in sequence s of
    plans, where plan p2 is derived from plan p1 by resolving a disjunction to one of
    the disjuncts.

(orderSubplans e a g s p1 p2)
    e is a planning activity by agent a for achieving goal g, resulting in sequence s
    of plans, where plan p2 is derived from plan p1 by adding temporal constraints
    between the achievement of subgoals.

(obstacle x a g)
    Entity x prevents a goal g of agent a's from being achieved.

(overcomeObstacle a x g)
    Agent a removes entity x as an obstacle to achieving goal g.

(planningProblem x a p g)
    Obstacle x constitutes a problem in agent a's plan p to achieve goal g.

(planningOption e p)
    Eventuality e is an option in plan p.

(candidatePlan p a g)
   Plan p is one of the candidates generated by agent a in a planning activity for achieving goal g.

(successfulPlanning e a p g)
   e is a successful planning activity by agent a for achieving goal g in that a resulting plan p achieves the goal.

(planningFailure e a g)
   e is a failed planning activity by agent a for achieving goal g in that no resulting plan achieves the goal.

(assessPlan a p g d)
   Agent a determines the degree d of belief in whether candidate plan p will achieve goal g.

(selectCandidatePlan a p g)
   Agent a selects candidate plan p to execute for achieving goal g.

The predicate schedule is defined in Chapter 42 on Scheduling:

(schedule a p t)
   Agent a schedules eventuality e for time t.

The following predicates are defined in Chapter 45 on Execution Control:

(suspend a e t)
   Agent a suspends process e at time t.

(resume a e t)
   Agent a resumes process e at time t.

(abort a e t)
   Agent a aborts process e at time t.

(restart a e t)
   Agent a restarts process e at time t.

39

Plan Adaptation

39.1 TWEAKING

One way people have for developing a plan to achieve a certain goal is to retrieve a known plan for achieving a related goal and tweaking it enough for it to achieve the desired goal. Suppose for example you go to a restaurant for the first time where you have to pay for your food before you eat rather than after; you retrieve your standard restaurant plan and tweak it by changing the order of events.

Tweaking occurs when an agent a takes a plan p1 for achieving goal g1 and forms a plan p2 for a similar goal g2 by replacing one step e1 in p1 with a similar step e2, yielding plan p2.

```
(forall (a p1 g1 p2 g2)                                          (39.1)
   (iff (tweak a p1 g1 p2 g2)
        (exists (e1 e2 s1 s2 e3 e4)
           (and (plan p1 a g1)(plan p2 a g2)
                (change e3 e4)
                (ecs' e3 p1 a)(ecs' e4 p2 a)
                (subgoalsOf s1 p1)(subgoalsOf s2 p2)
                (replaceElt s2 s1 e1 e2)
                (similar g1 g2)(similar e1 e2)))))
```

The expression (tweak a p1 g1 p2 g2) says that agent a tweaks plan p1 for achieving goal g1 into plan p2 for achieving goal g2. Lines 5 and 6 say there is a change in the plan that is envisioned from p1 to p2. Lines 7 and 8 say that the plans' subgoals differ by only one element. Line 9 says the goals of the plans are similar, and the new subgoal is similar to the one it replaced.

Perhaps the most interesting question with respect to tweaking is how we know what kind of similarity in e1 and e2 to look for given that we want to realize a similarity in g1 and g2.

Plan adaptation is then a planning activity in which every step is a tweak.

```
(forall (e a p1 g1 p2 g2 s)                                        (39.2)
   (iff (planAdaptation e a p1 g1 p2 g2 s)
        (and (planning e a g2 s)(plan p1 a g1)(plan p2 a g2)
             (first p1 s)(last p2 s)
             (forall (p3 p4)
                (if (successiveElts p3 p4 s)
                    (exists (g3 g4) (tweak a p3 g3 p4 g4)))))))
```

The expression (planAdaptation e a p1 g1 p2 g2 s) says that e is a planning
activity in which agent a adapts a plan p1 for achieving g1 into a plan p2 for achieving
g2, by producing a sequence of partial plans s. Line 3 says that e is a planning activity
and that p1 and p2 are plans for achieving g1 and g2, respectively. Line 4 says the
sequence s starts with p1 and ends with p2. Lines 5–7 say that successive elements in
the sequence are produced by tweaking.

In plan adaptation we retrieve a known plan from memory to the focus of attention. This could be a plan we have executed before, or a plan we have just thought
through but not executed before, or, as we will see later, we can extend this notion
to plans other agents have executed or thought up. The existing plan then is a large-
scale causal structure that we can envision. Then modifying the plan is performing
the substitution action in envisioning.

Expressions related to plan adaptation as a whole include "apply to this situation,"
"adapt to this case," "tweak to make it work," and "rethink the approach." Expressions related to tweaking individual steps include "tweak a step," "swap an action,"
"substitute a step," "amend a part of a plan," and "change it up a bit."

The first step of plan adaptation is retrieving the source plan from memory.
Phrases signaling the retrieval of a plan include "remember how to," "consider an
approach," "recall a technique," and "pull from the playbook."

```
(forall (e a p1)                                                    (39.3)
   (iff (retrievePlan' e a p1)
        (exists (g1) (and (plan p1 a g1)(retrieve' e a p1)))))
```

Once the plan is retrieved, it is in the agent's focus of attention, and being a causal
structure, it is envisioned. We can thus talk about its being tweaked one or more
times.

It could be that the plan the agent adapts is the plan currently being executed.

```
(forall (e a p1 g1 p2 g2 s)                                        (39.4)
   (iff (modifyCurrentlyExecutingPlan e a p1 g1 p2 g2 s)
        (exists (p)
           (and (planAdaptation e a p1 g1 p2 g2 s)(subgoalIn g1 p)
                (thePlan p a)))))
```

Recall from Chapter 31 on Plans that p is thePlan if it is the plan currently being
executed.

It could be that the plan the agent is adapting is a plan that has not yet begun to be executed.

$$
\begin{aligned}
&\text{(forall (e a p1 g1 p2 g2 s)} \qquad\qquad\qquad\qquad\qquad\qquad (39.5)\\
&\quad \text{(iff (futurePlanModification e a p1 g1 p2 g2 s)}\\
&\qquad \text{(exists (p)}\\
&\qquad\quad \text{(and (planAdaptation e a p1 g1 p2 g2 s)}\\
&\qquad\qquad \text{(not (subgoalIn g1 p))}\\
&\qquad\qquad \text{(thePlan p a)))))}
\end{aligned}
$$

That is, the goal that is the starting point of the adaptation is not a subgoal in the plan currently being executed.

39.2 TYPES OF PLAN ADAPTATION

We can think of a range of changes that fall under the heading of plan adaptation. Plan p1 may be our first attempt to achieve g1 but it failed; g2 is the same as g1; and p2 is the new plan with a modified step – e2 for e1 – in it. For example, p1 might involve trying to pick up something with one hand, p2 picking it up with two hands.

Goal g2 may involve nothing more than a change of time, so that only temporal parameters are involved in changing p1 into p2.

More parameters may be changed. For example, p1 can be the plan to go to a movie with a friend last Friday night, and p2 is the plan to go to a different movie this Friday night at a different theatre, with a different friend, and with someone else driving.

More substantial changes may be involved. Suppose someone hears of a strategy to control nervousness during a choir performance by focusing on the conductor. He is nervous about giving a lecture to an august group of scholars. He retrieves this plan, modifies the activity, and decides to focus on a friendly face in the audience.

Retrieved plans can be modified by changing values in a plan, as seen in the phrases "use more," "do it with more," "try increasing," and "correct for." This means that e1 and e2 are at relations of the same external entity v being at different points x1 and x2 in some system s.

$$
\begin{aligned}
&\text{(forall (a p1 g1 p2 g2)} \qquad\qquad\qquad\qquad\qquad\qquad\qquad (39.6)\\
&\quad \text{(iff (modifyPlanValue a v p1 g1 p2 g2)}\\
&\qquad \text{(exists (e1 e2 s1 s2 e3 e4)}\\
&\qquad\quad \text{(and (plan p1 a g1)(plan p2 a g2)}\\
&\qquad\qquad \text{(change e3 e4)}\\
&\qquad\qquad \text{(ecs' e3 p1 a)(ecs' e4 p2 a)}\\
&\qquad\qquad \text{(subgoalsOf s1 p1)(subgoalsOf s2 p2)}\\
&\qquad\qquad \text{(replaceElt s2 s1 e1 e2)}\\
&\qquad\qquad \text{(exists (x1 x2 s) (at' e1 v x1 s)(at' e2 v x2 s))}\\
&\qquad\qquad \text{(similar g1 g2)(similar e1 e2)))))}
\end{aligned}
$$

This is just the definition of tweak with line 9 particularizing subgoals e1 and e2 to being at relations.

Retrieved plans can be modified by changing the agent who executes a plan, as seen in the expressions "stand in for," "play the role of," "fill in for," "take over for," and "what would Jesus do?" This is an extension of the notion of tweaking. Before we tweaked only our own previous plans. Here we can tweak the plans of others.

```
(forall (a1 p1 g1 a p2 g2)                              (39.7)
    (iff (modifyPlanAgency a1 p1 g1 a p2 g2)
        (exists (e1 e2 s1 s2 e3 e4)
            (and (plan p1 a1 g1)(plan p2 a g2)
                 (change e3 e4)
                 (ecs' e3 p1 a)(ecs' e4 p2 a)
                 (subgoalsOf s1 p1)(subgoalsOf s2 p2)
                 (subst a s2 a1 s1)))))
```

Here the agent a1 in plan p1 is changed to a to yield plan p2.

In all of these cases of plan adaptation we are setting up a mapping between the two plans, where for the most part the mapping is identity, and the nonidentity parts of the mapping preserve causal relations.

39.3 OUTCOMES OF PLAN ADAPTATION

Sometimes plan adaptation is worth the effort. Sometimes it is quicker just to develop a plan from scratch. We must have some measure of plan adaptation effort to be able to judge this. People do, as illustrated by the expressions "difficult to apply," "complex application of," and "straightforward modification."

One measure of difficulty is the number of substitutions needed in plan p1 to arrive at p2. By the theory of envisioning, a substitution is one step in the envisioning process. Adding an eventuality to a plan, as we do in generating a plan de novo, is also one step. Thus, this view of difficulty assumes each step in the envisioning process costs the same. Hence, this notion of cost is rather crude.

```
(forall (c e)                                           (39.8)
    (iff (adaptationCost c e)
        (exists (a p1 g1 p2 g2 s)
            (and (planAdaptation e a p1 g1 p2 g2 s)(card c s)))))
```

Difficulty of adaptation is at least subset-consistent with the number of steps in the sequence of plans; adding one more step and leaving the rest of the process the same does not make the adaptation easier.

The process of plan adaptation is successful when a new plan is created. We see this concept in language in the expressions "successful application of" and "thoroughly reworked the plan." A successful adaptation is one in which the agent succeeds in finding a final plan that is executable by the agent.

```
(forall (e a p1 g1 p2 g2 s)                             (39.9)
    (iff (successfulAdaptation e a p1 g1 p2 g2 s)
        (exists (c t)
            (and (planAdaptation e a p1 g1 p2 g2 s)(succeed a e)
                 (executable p2 a c t)(cwu c a)(Now t)))))
```

The process of plan adaptation can fail when a new plan cannot be created from an old one. The expressions "not applicable here," "unsalvageable plan," and "not serve one's purposes" are about this concept.

```
(forall (e a p1 g1 g2 s)                                              (39.10)
    (iff (failedAdaptation e a p1 g1 g2 s)
        (not (exists (p2)
                (and (planAdaptation e a p1 g1 p2 g2 s)
                     (succeed a e)(executable p2 a c t)(cwu c a)(Now t))))))
```

PREDICATES INTRODUCED IN THIS CHAPTER

(tweak a p1 g1 p2 g2)
Agent a tweaks plan p1 for achieving g1 into plan p2 achieving g2.

(planAdaptation e a p1 g1 p2 g2 s)
Activity e is a planning activity by agent a for adapting plan p1 for achieving goal g1 into a plan p2 for achieving goal g2 by a series of tweaks, resulting in the sequence s of plans.

(retrievePlan' e a p1)
Event e is the retrieval by agent a of plan p1 from memory.

(modifyCurrentlyExecutingPlan e a p1 g1 p2 g2 s)
Activity e is a plan adaptation by agent a where what is being modified is part of the plan currently being executed.

(futurePlanModification e a p1 g1 p2 g2 s)
Activity e is a plan adaptation by agent a where what is being modified is not part of the plan currently being executed.

(modifyPlanValue a v p1 g1 p2 g2)
Agent a tweaks plan p1 for g1 into plan p2 for g2 by changing the value of v.

(modifyPlanAgency a1 p1 g1 a p2 g2)
Agent a tweaks plan p1 for g1 into plan p2 for g2 by changing the agent from a1 to a.

(adaptationCost c e)
Integer c is the cost in number of steps in the plan adaptation activity e.

(successfulAdaptation e a p1 g1 p2 g2 s)
Activity e is a successful plan adaptation by agent a of plan p1 for g1 into plan p2 for g2, in that p2 is executable.

(failedAdaptation e a p1 g1 g2 s)
Activity e is a failed plan adaptation by agent a of plan p1 for g1 into plan p2 for g2, in that no executable p2 achieving g2 was found.

Design

ARTIFACTS

Consider a simple artifact – the coffee cup. It reflects a plan. We wish to transport coffee; that's our highest-level goal. We do this by containing the coffee in a cup and then we transport the cup. One of the principal inferences about containment is that when the container moves, the substance that is contained also moves. Thus, transporting the cup transports the coffee. Similarly, when we attach a secondary entity to a primary entity, then moving the secondary entity causes the primary entity to move; this is one of the principal properties of attachment. Thus if we attach a handle to the cup and move the handle, the cup will also move, and so will the coffee. We can represent this plan for moving the coffee as follows:

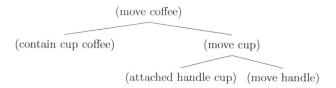

```
                          (move coffee)
              _____/_____
             /                                        \
    (contain cup coffee)                         (move cup)
                                        _____/_____
                                       /                  \
                          (attached handle cup)    (move handle)
```

As a composite entity, at this level of analysis, a coffee cup has as its components the cup and the handle, entities that occur in this plan. The relation between these two is the "attached" relation, which is a terminal node in the plan.

In general, we can say about artifacts that they are composite entities with a functionality. One can find a plan such that the components of the artifact are arguments of subgoals in the plan, and the relations among the components are subgoals in the plan. A further fact about artifacts, often taken to be their defining property, is that there is an artificer. There are agents who designed the artifact and agents, possibly the same, who brought it into existence.

```
(forall (x)                                                          (40.1)
   (if (artifact x)
      (and (compositeEntity x)
           (exists (f p a1 a2)
              (and (functionality0 f x)(plan p a1 f)(agent a1)
                   (planFor p x)
                   (cause a2 e0)(Rexist' e0 x)(agent a2)
                   (forall (y)
                      (if (componentOf y x)
                         (exists (e1)
                            (and (subgoalIn e1 p)(arg* y e1)))))
                   (forall (r)
                      (if (relationOf r x) (subgoalIn r p)))))))))
```

Line 3 says that the artifact x is a composite entity. Lines 4–7 say that there is a functionality f, a plan p to achieve f, and an agent a1 who does the planning, and an agent a2 who brings x into existence; line 6 labels the plan p as the planFor x. Lines 8–11 say that the components y of the composite entity x play a role in the plan. Lines 12 and 13 say that the relations among components are subgoals in the plan.

In the coffee cup example, x is the coffee cup, f is the eventuality type of moving coffee, p is the plan illustrated above, a1 is whoever first designed the coffee cup, a2 is the manufacturer, the components y are the cup and the handle, and the relation r is the "attached" relation between the cup and the handle. The coffee and the "contained" relation are part of the plan for the coffee cup, but not part of the coffee cup itself as a composite entity (although there would be no harm in viewing them that way).

Most artifacts have more complex plans. In fact, the plan for the coffee cup is more complex than the above picture. Another goal is for the hot coffee not to burn one's fingers. The functionality of the handle is to give one something to grasp to which only a tolerable amount of heat has been conducted.

We often talk about nonfunctional elements in an artifact, but having the artifact look good (according to some aesthetic) can be one of the goals in designing it, and that is the functionality of the purely decorative elements.

As it is defined here, an artifact can be a physical object, an organization, a theory, or any other kind of human-made functional composite entity. But usually when we talk about artifacts, we have in mind physical objects. We can define a more specialized predicate for this concept, artifact1.

```
(forall (x) (iff (artifact1 x)(and (artifact x)(physobj x))))   (40.2)
```

A broom can be used to sweep the kitchen floor. It can also be used to retrieve something in a hard to reach place, like behind the refrigerator. The first is its intended use, the second an unintended use. In general, an artifact can be used as intended.

```
(forall (e1 a x)                                                    (40.3)
   (if (intendedUse e1 x a)
      (exists (p e)
         (and (planFor p x)(subgoalIn e p)(instance e1 e)
              (agentOf a e1)(arg* x e1)))))
```

The expression (intendedUse e1 x a) says that e1 is an intended use of artifact x by agent a. This holds exactly when a is the agent of e1, e1 somehow involves x, and e1 is an instance of a subgoal e in the plan p for x.

An unintended use e1 happens when a is the agent of e1 and x is somehow involved in e1, but e1 is not the intended use.

```
(forall (e1 a x)                                                    (40.4)
    (iff (unintendedUse e1 x a)
         (and (agentOf a e1)(arg* x e1)(not (intendedUse e1 x a)))))
```

40.2 DESIGNS

A design is a pattern whose instances are artifacts, in the broad sense. We can design a teapot, a logo, a font, or a government. The two principal features of designs are that a design is intended to have instances and that a design and its instances are functional composite entities whose structure reflects a plan to realize the functionality. Thus, crucial to the design is the planFor the artifact. The plan behind the artifact is an instance of the plan for the design. In the same way that an artifact is a plan made concrete, a design is a specification of an artifact that concretizes a plan.

```
(forall (x)                                                         (40.5)
    (iff (design x)
         (exists (f p a)
             (and (pattern x)
                  (functionality0 f x)(plan p a f)(planFor p x)
                  (forall (x1)
                      (if (instance x1 x)
                          (exists (f1 p1)
                              (and (artifact x1)
                                   (functionality0 f1 x1)(instance f1 f)
                                   (planFor p1 x1)(instance p1 p)))))))))
```

Line 4 says that the design x is a pattern. Line 5 introduces and labels the functionality f of and the plan p for the design. Lines 6–9 introduce instances x1 of x and say that they are artifacts. Lines 10 and 11 say that the artifact's functionality f1 is an instance of f and its plan p1 is an instance of p.

A design is flawed if executing the plan for an artifact instantiating the design fails to achieve the functionality of the artifact. We first define what it means for a set s of eventualities to fail to achieve a goal e.

```
(forall (s e)                                                       (40.6)
    (iff (notAchieve s e)
         (and (Rexist s)(not e))))
```

That is, the eventualities in s happen or hold, but e does not result from that.

Let the terminal subgoals of a plan be those subgoals that have no subgoals of their own.

```
(forall (s p)                                                    (40.7)
    (iff (terminalSubgoalsOf s p)
        (exists (a g)
            (and (plan p a g)
                (forall (g1)
                    (iff (member g1 s)
                        (and (subgoalIn g1 p)
                            (not (exists (g2)
                                (and (subgoalIn g2 p)
                                    (subgoal g2 g1)))))))))))
```

That is, the set s is the set of subgoals g1 in the plan p that have no subgoals g2 of their own in p.

Then a flawed design is one in which for every instance, the set of terminal subgoals in the plan do not achieve the top-level goal.

```
(forall (x)                                                      (40.8)
    (iff (flawedDesign x)
        (forall (p p1 a e1 s)
            (if (and (planFor p x)(instance p1 p)(plan p1 a e1)
                    (terminalSubgoalsOf s p1))
                (notAchieve s e1)))))
```

Lines 4 and 5 say that p is the plan for the design x, p1 is an instance of p, e1 is the top-level goal in some agent a's plan p1, and s is the set of terminal subgoals in p1. If all of this holds and s fails to achieve e1, then the design x is flawed.

This is a strong notion of "flawed design," in which all instances of the design have to fail to achieve the goal. A weaker notion of "flawed design" would result if we were to replace forall in line 3 with exists. The truly useful notion would be somewhere in between these two definitions, which would allow for some random instances of the design to happen to achieve the top-level goal, but the design does not reliably produce instances that will achieve the goal.

40.3 DESIGNING

The activity of designing is a planning activity where all the plans in the sequence of plans are plans for a design.

```
(forall (e a x s)                                                (40.9)
    (iff (designing e a x s)
        (exists (f)
            (and (planning e a f s)(functionality0 f x)(design x)
                (forall (p)
                    (if (inSeq p s)(planFor p x)))))))
```

The expression (designing e a x s) says that e is a designing activity by agent a of design x through a sequence s of plans. Each plan p in the sequence is a plan for the design.

Reference to designing or generating a design is common in language, as seen in expressions like "think about the design," "working out the layout," "imagining the structure," "configure," and "arrange."

An artifact often has multiple intended uses. In these cases, the functionality of
the artifact is a set or conjunction of what might be called "design constraints."

```
(forall (e x)                                                      (40.10)
    (iff (designConstraint e x)
         (exists (f)
             (and (design x)(functionality0 f x)(member e f)))))
```

For example, when one designs an office layout, it is usually with respect to typical
office goals as the design constraints.

The creation of a design is successful if it satisfies design constraints.

We often talk about design adaptation, for example, "customize the design" and
"design inspired by." To adapt a design is to engage in a designing activity that is also
a plan adaptation.

```
(forall (e x)                                                      (40.11)
    (iff (designAdaptation e a x)
         (exists (s p1 g1 p2 g2)
             (and (designing e a x s)
                  (planAdaptation e a p1 g1 p2 g2 s)))))
```

A design failure is a designing activity that is a planning failure.

```
(forall (e a)                                                      (40.12)
    (iff (designFailure e a)
         (exists (x s g)
             (and (designing e a x s)(functionality0 g x)
                  (planningFailure e a g)))))
```

In this definition, e is the designing activity, a is the agent doing the designing, x is
the (nonexistent) design, g is the goal or functionality of the design, and s is the set
of plans the agent considers in the course of the planning activity.

For an entity to instantiate a design is for that entity to instantiate all the properties and relations in the design. It is possible for an entity to be a partial instantiation
of a design by instantiating only some of the properties and relations. Thus, there is
a partial ordering defined by the relation moreAdherentToDesign meaning roughly
that more of the relations and properties are instantiated. We cannot fully specify
what this predicate means, but we can constrain its meaning. We can say that if an
entity x1 instantiates all the design properties and relations that entity x2 does and
more, then it is more adherent to the design.

```
(forall (x x1 x2)                                                  (40.13)
    (if (and (design x)(incompleteInstance x1 x)
             (incompleteInstance x2 x)
             (forall (p p2)
                 (if (and (propOrRelOf p x)(patternInstance p2 p)
                          (propOrRelOf p2 x2))
                     (exists (p1)
                         (and (patternInstance p1 p)(propOrRelOf p1 x1)))))
```

```
(exists (p1 p)
    (and (propOrRelOf p x)(patternInstance p1 p)
         (propOrRelOf p1 x1)
         (not (exists (p2)
                 (and (patternInstance p2 p)
                      (propOrRelOf p2 x2)))))))))
    (moreAdherentToDesign x1 x2 x)))
```

Lines 2–3 introduce two incomplete instances x1 and x2 of design x. Lines 4–8 say that any design-relevant property or relation p that x2 has, x̄1 also has. Lines 9–14 say that x1 has a design-relevant property or relation that x2 lacks. Line 15 says that under these conditions, x1 is more adherent to design x than x2 is.

PREDICATES INTRODUCED IN THIS CHAPTER

(artifact x)
   x is an artifact.

(planFor p x)
   p is the plan realized in the structure of artifact x.

(artifact1 x)
   x is a physical artifact.

(intendedUse e1 x a)
   e1 is the intended use of artifact x by agent a.

(unintendedUse e1 x a)
   e1 is an unintended use of artifact x by agent a.

(design x)
   x is a design.

(notAchieve s e)
   The occurrence of the eventualities in s do not result in e occurring.

(terminalSubgoalsOf s p)
   The eventualities in s are the terminal subgoals in plan p.

(flawedDesign x)
   x is a flawed design.

(designing e a x s)
   e is a designing activity by agent a in designing x via a sequence s of designs.

(designConstraint e x)
   e is a design constraint design x satisfies.

(designAdaptation e a x)
   The designing activity e by agent a of design x is a planning activity by adaptation.

(designFailure e a)
   e is a designing activity by agent a that fails.

(moreAdherentToDesign x1 x2 x)
   Instance x1 adheres more closely to design x than instance x2 does.

Decisions

41.1 THE DECISION-MAKING PROCESS

In Chapter 31 on Plans we introduced the predicate decideTo, which describes a transition of an action or other eventuality from something that is merely thought about or entertained to something that is part of the plan (thePlan) that the agent is actually executing. It expresses the conversion of thoughts into intentions.

But in our thinking and in our discourse about decisions, we have a much richer model that we can appeal to concerning the processes involved in coming to a decision. We make decisions all the time and much of our mental life is wrapped up in how this is done.

When we go into a restaurant, we look at the menu to identify our choices, we think about those choices for a while, and then we select one of them. We can think about this as a general pattern for making decisions.

1. Identify choices ("think of the possibilities")
2. Deliberate about the choices ("think about the possibilities")
3. Select one of the choices ("settle on")

In our theory of decisions, we will take this as the basic process of decision making.

```
(forall (e0 a s e)                                          (41.1)
   (iff (decision e0 a s e)
        (exists (e1 e2 e3)
           (and (choiceEnumeration e1 a s)(deliberation e2 a s)
                (selection e3 a e s)(member e s)
                (before e1 e3)(before e2 e3)(subevent e1 e0)
                (subevent e2 e0)(subevent e3 e0)))))
```

The predication (decision e0 a s e) says that e0 is a decision-making process by agent a in which set s of alternatives are considered and e is chosen. The choice enumeration e1 and the deliberation e2 have to take place before the selection e3 of one of the alternatives, but e1 and e2 can be interleaved. In the course of deliberating about one member of s we might think of something else that should be considered. The choice enumeration, the deliberation, and the selection are all subprocesses of the decision-making process.

Here we will take the elements of s to be eventualities, generally, actions by the agent a. Of course, we often decide among members of a set of physical objects; we choose the cherry pie over the apple pie, and the Ford over the Chevrolet. This is true for abstract entities as well, as when we're asked to pick a number between 1 and 10 and we pick 5. Or a proposition, as when we decide that Pluto is not a planet. But where the options are not eventualities, there is an implicit action or relation we have in mind involving the physical or abstract object, such as eating, or owning, or committing to having in mind and reporting, or believing.

The first part of making a decision is to identify the set of choices. Identifying something in this sense is coming to think of it, or have it in focus, and recognizing that one of the set must be chosen.

```
· (forall (e1 a s)                                                    (41.2)
     (iff (choiceEnumeration e1 a s)
          (exists (e5 e)
              (and (changeTo' e1 e4)(thinkAbout' e4 a s)
                   (believe a e5)(decideTo' e5 a e)(member e s)
                   (before e4 e5)))))
```

The predication (choiceEnumeration e1 a s) says that e1 is the process by agent a of identifying a set s of options. In this case, e1 is a change to a situation in which a is thinking about the set of options, and a believes he will decide on some member e of s after thinking about s.

The second part of making a decision is deliberating over the choice set. This is a matter of thinking about the options with the goal of selecting one of them. That is, there is a plan p whose top-level goal is to select an option and thinking about the option constitutes the subgoal in the plan.

```
(forall (e2 a s)                                                      (41.3)
    (iff (deliberation e2 a s)
         (exists (p g e)
             (and (plan p a g)(selection g a e s)
                  (forall (e4)
                      (if (member e4 s)
                          (exists (e5)
                              (and (thinkAbout' e5 a e4)
                                   (subgoalIn e5 p)))))))))
```

The predication (deliberation e2 a s) says that e2 is a deliberation process by agent a in considering a set s of alternatives. Lines 3 and 4 say there is a plan p aimed at the selection g of one of the options e in s. Lines 5–9 say that for all the options e4 in s, there is an action e5 of thinking about e4 that is a subgoal in the plan p. That is, the thinking is in service of the selection.

The third part of making a decision is to select one option from the choice set, after deliberating.

```
(forall (e3 a e s)                                                    (41.4)
    (iff (selection e3 a e s)
         (and (decideTo' e3 a e)(member e s)
              (exists (e2)
                  (and (deliberation e2 a s)(before e2 e3))))))
```

The predication (selection e3 a e s) says that e3 is the act by agent a to select option e from set s. This amounts to deciding to do e after deliberating about the set s of options.

If one eventuality e3 is selected and another e4 is not, then we should expect the agent a to prefer e3 over e4 as goals to achieve (or actions to perform).

```
(forall (e e3 e4 a s)                                        (41.5)
    (if (and (selection e a e3 s)(member e3 s)(member e4 s)
            (nequal e3 e4)(etc))
        (preferGoal a e3 e4)))
```

Decision making is a process, and as a process it is subject to the same aspectual operators as other processes.

In some cases, a person may change his or her mind after making a decision ("renege on," "go back on"). A decision revision is a decision to choose an alternative once a decision has already been made.

```
(forall (e a e3 e4 s)                                        (41.6)
    (iff (decisionRevision e a e3 e4 s)
        (exists (e1 e2)
            (and (decision e1 a s e3)(decision e2 a s e4)
                (change' e e1 e2)))))
```

Like all processes decision-making can be suspended and resumed. In particular, people can suspend a decision before they make a selection ("sleep on it").

```
(forall (e0 e1)                                              (41.7)
    (iff (suspendDecision e0 e1)
        (exists (a s e e3 t)
            (and (decision e1 a s e)(suspend' e0 a e1 t)
                (selection e3 a e s)(subevent e3 e1)
                (before t e3)))))
```

Here, e0 is the suspend action applied to the decision-making process e1, e1 is a decision-making process by agent a in deciding on member e of set s of alternatives. The suspension e0 takes place before the selection subevent e3 of e1.

People can resume decision-making processes that they earlier suspended ("finish deciding").

```
(forall (e0 e1)                                              (41.8)
    (iff (resumeDecision e0 e1)
        (exists (a s e e2 t)
            (and (decision e1 a s e)(resume' e0 a e1 t)
                (suspendDecision e2 e1)(before e2 t)))))
```

Here e0 is the resume action applied to the decision-making process e1, where agent a is deciding among the set s of alternatives, eventually choosing e, and there was a suspend-decision action before the resumption.

Some sets of decisions are interrelated, in that the options chosen have a causal influence on the other decisions.

```
(forall (e1 e2)                                              (41.9)
    (iff (linkedDecisions e1 e2)
        (exists (a s1 s2 e3 e4)
            (and (decision e1 a s1 e3)(decision e2 a s2 e4)
                (causallyInvolved e3 e2)))))
```

Linked decisions can constitute a series of decisions.

```
(forall (s)                                                  (41.10)
    (iff (decisionSeries s e1)
        (exists (e2)
            (or (and (linkedDecisions e1 e2)(doubleton s e1 e2))
                (exists (s1)
                    (and (linkedDecisions e1 e2)
                        (decisionSeries s1 e2)
                        (addElt s e1 s1)))))))
```

The expression (decisionSeries s e1) says that s is a series of decisions beginning with e1. Line 4 says that a pair of linked decisions is a decision series. Lines 5–8 say that adding a decision at the beginning of a decision series results in a decision series.

41.2 CHOICES AND CHOICE SETS

For any decision there are a number of possible choices ("range of candidates"). This is the third argument of the predicate decision.

```
(forall (s e)                                                (41.11)
    (iff (choiceSet s e)
        (exists (a e1) (decision e a s e1))))
```

Any member in the choice set is a possible choice ("option," "prospect," "alternative").

```
(forall (e1 s)                                               (41.12)
    (iff (possibleChoice e1 s)
        (exists (e) (and (choiceSet s e)(member e1 s)))))
```

In Section 41.1 we said that when a selection is made, the agent prefers that option over the other options. Here we provide an explication of when one option would be a better choice than another option.

Decisions are made with respect to a complex of goals. As idealized in decision theory, decisions are made for choices that optimize the utility of the goals achieved and the probability of achieving them. We will not use this idealization, because it assumes more precise values of the measures than could ever be available in commonsense reasoning. But we will assume that the goal structure imposes a partial ordering or scale, against which possible choices are judged. Two relevant factors are just what is idealized in decision theory. All other things being equal, that choice is better that achieves a goal with higher utility, and that choice is better that achieves a goal with greater probability. These are very weak constraints on the partial ordering. To get very much more detailed would require the specifics of domain theories.

Constraints on the arguments of the predicate `betterChoice` are as follows:

```
(forall (e1 e2 s a e)                                          (41.13)
    (if (betterChoice e1 e2 s a e)
        (exists (e3)
            (and (decision e a s e3)(possibleChoice e1 e)
                 (possibleChoice e2 e)))))
```

The choice e3 that is actually selected may or may not be equal to e1 or e2.

A weak constraint on the `betterChoice` partial ordering, capturing something like utility, is that that choice that leads to achieving a more important goal is a better choice.

```
(forall (e1 e2 s a e e3 g1 g2)                                 (41.14)
    (if (and (decision e a s e3)
             (possibleChoice e1 e)(cause e1 g1)(goal g1 a)
             (possibleChoice e2 e)(nequal e1 e2)
             (forall (g2)
                 (if (and (cause e2 g2)(goal g2 a))
                     (moreImportant g1 g2 a))))
        (betterChoice e1 e2 s a e)))
```

In this axiom e is a decision-making process by agent a among a set s of alternatives. The ultimate choice e3 plays no role. Suppose eventuality e1 is a possible choice in e that causes some goal g1 of a's. Suppose e2 is another possible choice in e, and that every goal g2 of a's that is caused by e2 is less important to a than g1. In this case e1 is a better choice than e2.

Each of the possible choices has different characteristics that are relevant to the decision ("distinguishing features," "pros and cons"). These characteristics are properties of the possible choices that are relevant to the agent's goals.

```
(forall (e0 e1 e a)                                            (41.15)
    (iff (choiceCharacteristic e0 e1 e a)
         (exists (s e3)
             (and (decision e a s e3)(possibleChoice e1 e)
                  (arg* e1 e0)(goalRelevant e0 a)))))
```

The expression `(choiceCharacteristic e0 e1 e a)` says that e0 is some choice characteristic of possible choice e1 in a decision-making process e by agent a. It means essentially that e0 is goal-relevant to agent a.

After deliberation, one may be able to identify the best choice ("frontrunner," "cream of the crop," "leading candidate").

```
(forall (e1 s a e)                                             (41.16)
    (iff (bestChoice e1 s a e)
         (forall (e2)
             (if (possibleChoice e2 e)
                 (or (equal e1 e2)
                     (betterChoice e1 e2 s a e))))))
```

After selecting, one of the possible choices becomes the selected choice ("one's pick," "one's decision").

```
(forall (e3 e a)                                          (41.17)
    (iff (selectedChoice e3 e a)
         (exists (s) (decision e a s e3))))
```

After selecting, all but one of the possible choices become unselected choices ("not make the cut," "decided against").

```
(forall (e2 e a)                                          (41.18)
    (iff (unselectedChoice e2 e a)
         (exists (s e3) (and (decision e a s e3)(nequal e2 e3)))))
```

Suppose we let e in (decision e a s e1) be an event type, that is, the typical element of a set of decisions, where the choice set s in each is the same, but the selected choice may be different. When given the same choice set another time, there is a previously selected choice.

```
(forall (e3 e1 a s)                                       (41.19)
    (iff (previouslySelectedChoice e3 e1 a s)
         (exists (e2 e4)
            (and (decision e1 a s e3)(decision e2 a s e4)
                 (nequal e3 e4)(before e1 e2)))))
```

The expression (previouslySelectedChoice e3 e1 a s) says that item e3 was chosen by agent a out of set s in decision process e1. This holds when e1 is a decision process by agent a selecting e3 out of set s, when e2 is also a decision process by agent a selecting a different e4 out of the same set s, and when e1 is before e2.

41.3 THE PROCESS OF DELIBERATION

One way people come to their decisions is by predicting the outcome of a particular choice ("look before you leap"). We add a possible choice to our current world understanding and we envision from that to a set of consequences.

```
(forall (e3 e s1)                                         (41.20)
    (iff (envisionChoiceConsequences e3 e s1)
         (exists (a s e0 e1 e2)
            (and (decision e a s e1)(and' e2 e0 e1)(cwu e0 a)
                 (envisionFromTo' e3 a e2 s1)))))
```

The expression (envisionChoiceConsequences e3 e s1) says that e3 is the process of envisioning the consequences s1 of a particular choice in a decision process e. Line 4 labels the arguments of the decision process, so a is the agent and e1 is the choice that would be made. That is conjoined with agent a's current world understanding e0 to yield e2. The process e3 is then an envisioning by a from e2 to the set s1 of consequences.

One way people make decisions is by weighing the pros and cons. A pro is an envisioned consequence that is good for the agent. A con is an envisioned consequence that is bad for the agent.

```
(forall (e2 e1 e)                                              (41.21)
    (iff (pro e2 e1 e)
         (exists (e3 s1 a s)
             (and (envisionChoiceConsequences e3 e s1)
                  (decision e a s e1)(member e2 s1)
                  (goodFor e2 a)))))
```

The expression (pro e2 e1 e) says that consequence e2 of choice e1 in decision process e is a pro.

```
(forall (e2 e1 e)                                              (41.22)
    (iff (con e2 e1 e)
         (exists (e3 s1 a s)
             (and (envisionChoiceConsequences e3 e s1)
                  (decision e a s e1)(member e2 s1)
                  (badFor e2 a)))))
```

The expression (con e2 e1 e) says that consequence e2 of choice e1 in decision process e is a con.

A cost–benefit analysis by an agent is the agent's considering each alternative in the choice set and determining if it results in a pro or a con. (A cost is a con; a benefit is a pro.) Thus, a cost–benefit analysis is a set of envisionChoiceConsequences activities by the agent.

```
(forall (e e0 a s)                                             (41.23)
    (iff (costBenefitAnalysis e e0 a s)
         (exists (s1)
             (and (decision e0 a s e1)(subset s1 s)(not (null s1))
                  (forall (e3)
                      (iff (member e3 e)
                           (exists (e4 e5 e6)
                               (and (thinkOf' e3 a e4)(member e6 s1)
                                    (or (pro' e4 e5 e6 e0)
                                        (con' e4 e5 e6 e0)))))))))))
```

The expression (costBenefitAnalysis e e0 a s) says that process e is a cost–benefit analysis by agent a in decision process e0 involving choice set s. For this to hold there must be a non-null subset s1 of the set s of options for which the agent thinks of whether they are a pro or con. The set of these thinking-of actions constitutes the cost–benefit analysis. Line 4 labels e0 as the decision process, a as the agent, s as the choice set, and s1 as the non-null subset; the ultimate choice e1 is not relevant here. Lines 5 and 6 say essentially that the cost–benefit analysis e is a set of eventualities e3. Lines 8–10 say that these e3's are "thinking of" events by the agent where the content e4 of the thought is about either some consequence e5 of a member e6 of s1 being a pro or its being a con in decision process e0. Equivalently, we pick an element e6 of the subset s1 of the choice set s. We find an e5 that is a pro or con of choosing e6. We think about (e3) its being a pro or con (e4). A set of such thinking-about events is a cost–benefit analysis.

An agent can choose one option over another.

```
(forall (a e1 e2)                                                    (41.24)
    (iff (chooseOver a e1 e2)
        (exists (e0 s)
            (and (decision e0 a s e1)(doubleton s e1 e2)))))
```

That is, agent a chooses option e1 over e2 if and only if there is a decision process e0 in which the choice set consists of e1 and e2 and e1 is the option that is chosen.

People have criteria ("yardstick," "benchmark," "litmus test") by which they determine which possible choice is the best choice.

```
(forall (e p e0)                                                     (41.25)
    (iff (choiceCriterion e p e0)
        (exists (a s e1)
            (and (decision e0 a s e1)
                (forall (e2 e3)
                    (if (and (member e2 s)(member e3 s)
                            (subst e2 e4 p e)(Rexist e4)
                            (subst e3 e5 p e)(not e5))
                        (chooseOver a e2 e3)))))))
```

The expression (choiceCriterion e p e0) says that e is choice criterion for options p in decision process e0; p is a parameter. Line 4 labels e0 as a decision process by agent a with choice set s and ultimate choice e1. Lines 6–9 say that if e2 and e3 are options, and e is true of e2 but not true of e3, then a will choose e2 over e3. For e to be true of e2, line 7 says that there is an e4 in which e2 is substituted for the parameter p in e, and e4 really holds. Line 8 similarly says that e does not hold for e3.

After deliberation, people find that some decisions are obvious ("no brainer," "clear cut"). One way to characterize this is that one option is a much better choice than any other.

```
(forall (e)                                                          (41.26)
    (iff (obviousDecision e)
        (exists (a s e1 e0 e3 e4 s1 s2)
            (and (decision e a s e1)(betterChoice' e0 e3 e4 s a e)
                (scaleDefinedBy s1 s e0)(Hi s2 s1)(inScale e1 s2)
                (forall (e2)
                    (if (and (member e2 s)(nequal e2 e1))
                        (not (inScale e2 s2)))))))))
```

The expression (obviousDecision e) says that decision process e has an obvious outcome. Line 4 labels the agent a, choice set s and the best choice e1; it also labels e0 as the betterChoice partial ordering for decision process e. Line 5 says that s1 is the scale defined by that partial ordering, that s2 is the Hi region of that scale, and that e1 is in the Hi region of the scale. Lines 6–8 say that no other element of s is in the Hi region.

This definition may not capture all cases of obvious decisions, however. We haven't said anything about the internal structure of the scale defined by betterChoice. There should be enough structure that we can characterize the difference between where two choices lie on the scale and can say that one is very much better than another. One component of obviousness is the effort of deliberation required to make the decision unambiguously. One can imagine a choice that is very much better than all alternatives but requires a great deal of inference to figure that out; and a choice that is slightly better than the alternatives, but is obvious immediately.

After deliberation, people may not have any certainty about the best choice.

```
(forall (e)                                                    (41.27)
   (iff (uncertainDecision e)
        (exists (a s e1)
           (and (decision e a s e1)
                (not (exists (e2) (bestChoice e2 s a e)))))))
```

After deliberation, one may feel that it doesn't matter which choice is made ("inconsequential," "immaterial").

```
(forall (e)                                                    (41.28)
   (iff (insignificantDecision e)
        (exists (a s e1)
           (and (decision e a s e1)
                (forall (e2 e3)
                   (if (and (member e2 s) (member e3 s))
                       (not (betterChoice e2 e3 s a e)))))))))
```

Line 4 labels e as a decision process by agent a among choices in s, where e1 is the ultimate choice. Lines 5–7 say that no option in s is a better choice than any other.

41.4 JUSTIFICATIONS FOR DECISIONS

People have justifications for the choices that they select. A factor in a decision is a pro for the option selected or a con for an option not selected.

```
(forall (f e)                                                  (41.29)
   (iff (decisionFactor f e)
        (exists (a s e1 e2)
           (and (decision e a s e1)
                (or (pro f e1 e)
                    (and (con f e2 e) (member e2 s)
                         (nequal e2 e1)))))))
```

A decision justification is the set of decision factors. Thus, because of the definitions of "pro" and "con," it is the causal story built up by envisioning from the options during the course of deliberation.

```
(forall (j e)                                                  (41.30)
   (iff (decisionJustification j e)
        (forall (f) (iff (member f j) (decisionFactor f e)))))
```

Sometimes people have no justification for the decision they make ("whim," "impulsive decision," "crap shoot").

```
(forall (e)                                                    (41.31)
   (iff (arbitraryDecision e)
        (exists (j) (and (decisionJustification j e) (null j)))))
```

41.5 **CONSEQUENCES OF DECISIONS**

There can be decision processes that are not carried to completion. When they are, however, they have consequences. By making a decision, people make things happen in the world.

```
(forall (e2 e a)                                              (41.32)
    (iff (decisionConsequence e2 e a)
         (exists (s e1)
             (and (decision e a s e1)(causallyInvolved e1 e2)
                  (causallyInvolved e e2)))))
```

That is, eventuality e2 is a consequence of decision process e for agent a if the selected option e1 is causally involved in the occurrence of e2 and in addition the decision process itself is causally involved in the occurrence of e2.

Sometimes the effects of a decision are in accord with the agent's goals.

```
(forall (e2 e a)                                              (41.33)
    (iff (positiveDecisionConsequence e2 e a)
         (and (decisionConsequence e2 e a)(goodFor e2 a))))
```

Sometimes the effects of a decision are counter to people's goals.

```
(forall (e2 e a)                                              (41.34)
    (iff (negativeDecisionConsequence e2 e a)
         (and (decisionConsequence e2 e a)(badFor e2 a))))
```

PREDICATES INTRODUCED IN THIS CHAPTER

(decision e0 a s e)
  Eventuality e0 is a decision-making process by agent a among options in set s and resulting in the choice of option e.

(choiceEnumeration e1 a s)
  Eventuality e1 is the process by agent a of enumerating the set s of options in a decision-making process.

(deliberation e2 a s)
  Eventuality e2 is a deliberation process by agent a among a set s of options in a decision-making process.

(selection e3 a e s)
  Eventuality e3 is the action by agent a of selecting option e from a set s of options.

(decisionRevision e a e3 e4 s)
  Eventuality e is an action by agent a to select e3 from a set s of options after having already selected e4.

(suspendDecision e0 e1)
  Eventuality e0 is the action of suspending a decision process e1.

(resumeDecision e0 e1)
  Eventuality e0 is the action of resuming a decision process e1.

(linkedDecisions e1 e2)
  Decision processes e1 and e2 are causally linked.

(decisionSeries s e1)
    Series s of eventualities is a series of linked decision processes beginning with decision process e1.

(choiceSet s e)
    Set s is the set of options for decision process e.

(possibleChoice e1 s)
    Eventuality e1 is an element of the choice set s for a decision process.

(betterChoice e1 e2 s a e)
    Eventuality e1 is a better choice than e2 out of a set s of options for agent a in decision process e.

(choiceCharacteristic e0 e1 e a)
    Eventuality e0 is a property of option e1 in decision-making process e by agent a that is relevant to the decision.

(bestChoice e1 s a e)
    Eventuality e1 is the best choice from set s of options by agent a in decision-making process e.

(selectedChoice e3 e a)
    Eventuality e3 is the option selected in decision-making process e by agent a.

(unselectedChoice e2 e a)
    Eventuality e2 is an option not selected in decision-making process e by agent a.

(previouslySelectedChoice e3 e1 a s)
    Eventuality e3 is the option selected in decision-making process e by agent a, where a different item is selected out of the same set s of options subsequently.

(envisionChoiceConsequences e3 e s1)
    Eventuality e3 is the process of envisioning the consequences of selecting the items in set s in a decision-making process e.

(pro e2 e1 e)
    Consequence e2 of selecting e1 in decision-making process e is a pro, that is, good for the agent making the decision.

(con e2 e1 e)
    Consequence e2 of selecting e1 in decision-making process e is a con, that is, bad for the agent making the decision.

(costBenefitAnalysis e e0 a s)
    Process e is a cost–benefit analysis by agent a in decision-making process e0 of choosing among set s of options.

(chooseOver a e1 e2)
    Agent a chooses e1 over e2.

(choiceCriterion e p e0)
    Abstract eventuality e with parameter p is a choice criterion in decision-making process e0.

(obviousDecision e)
    Decision-making process e has an obvious result.

(uncertainDecision e)
    Decision-making process e has an uncertain result.

(insignificantDecision e)
   Decision-making process e has an insignificant result.

(decisionFactor f e)
   Eventuality f is a factor in decision-making process e.

(decisionJustification j e)
   Set j is the justification for the result in decision-making process e.

(arbitraryDecision e)
   The result in decision-making process e is arbitrary.

(decisionConsequence e2 e a)
   Eventuality e2 is a consequence in decision-making process e by agent a.

(positiveDecisionConsequence e2 e a)
   Eventuality e2 is a positive consequence in decision-making process e by
   agent a.

(negativeDecisionConsequence e2 e a)
   Eventuality e2 is a negative consequence in decision-making process e by
   agent a.

The following predicates are defined in Chapter 45 on Execution Control:

(suspend a e t)
   Agent a suspends process e at time t.

(resume a e t)
   Agent a resumes process e at time t.

42

Scheduling

42.1 SIMULTANEOUS ACTIONS

Scheduling is a problem because we cannot do very many things at once. Preconditions for the actions must be met before the action is performed. Actions take a certain amount of time, whose normal duration we can estimate. There are physical and cognitive limits on the number of simultaneous actions an agent can perform at one time. All of these facts entail that time is a limited resource. Time places limitations and constraints on what can be done. Scheduling is figuring out how to work around temporal limitations and constraints. It is planning to satisfy these constraints.

Gerald Ford purportedly could not walk and chew gum at the same time. We shouldn't talk while we are chewing, but we can interleave the activities and have a conversation over lunch. People cannot watch television, read the newspaper, and drive rapidly along a busy highway at the same time. It is difficult to do two unrelated actions with the same hand at the same time without substantial practice.

It is difficult to give precise conditions under which simultaneous actions can and cannot be performed. But a general rule schema that most such conditions instantiate is the following:

```
(forall (e1 e2 x)                                         (42.1)
    (if (and (p' e1 x)(q' e2 x))
        (not (exists (t)(and (atTime e1 t)(atTime e2 t))))))
```

That is, if e1 is a p-type action by x and e2 is a q-type action by x, then there is no time t such that both e1 and e2 are occurring at t. For example, p might be "walk" and q might be "chew-gum."

A less domain-specific but defeasible rule generalizing this is the following:

```
(forall (e1 e2 x)                                         (42.2)
    (if (and (agentOf x e1)(agentOf x e2)(etc))
        (not (exists (t)(and (atTime e1 t)(atTime e2 t))))))
```

That is, x cannot be the agent of two actions simultaneously. This may seem too strong, but we use something like it when we make sense of the text

Pat couldn't lift the grate; he was carrying a stack of books.

which we understand even if we have never before thought about the interactions of lifting grates and carrying books.

A more general, intermediate rule might be that some body part, like one's right hand, or some cognitive component, such as the focus of attention, cannot contain and/or process more than one or two entities at once.

42.2 SCHEDULES

A schedule is a mapping from a set of actions and other events into a set of temporal intervals or sequences. That is, it is a set of <event, interval> pairs. From a logical point of view, in a planning framework, we can view a schedule as a particular part of a plan, namely, those subgoals of the form (timeSpan t e) where t is an instant or interval and e is an action or other event in the plan. Thus, a schedule is an augmentation of a plan with temporal information. For example, a simple plan to drink coffee is the following:

```
             (and (drink' e1 i c)(coffee c))
            ╱‾‾‾‾‾‾‾‾‾‾‾‾‾‾‾‾‾‾‾‾‾‾‾‾╲
    (and (pourInto' e2 i c k)(cup k))   (liftToLips' e3 i k)
```

When we schedule these actions, we elaborate the plan by adding temporal information as a subgoal. Such a temporal relation is something else we expect to achieve in executing the plan.

```
             (and (drink' e1 i c)(coffee c))
          ╱‾‾‾‾‾‾‾‾‾‾‾‾‾‾‾‾‾╱‾‾╲‾‾‾‾‾‾‾‾‾‾‾‾‾╲
(and (pourInto' e2 i c k)(cup k))  (before e2 e3)  (liftToLips' e3 i k)
```

The sequentiality of the two actions is also something that has to be achieved in executing the plan, in addition to the pouring and the lifting.

Like all planning, scheduling must be done in a way that satisfies all the relevant constraints. The constraints on simultaneous actions and the constraint that preconditions need to be satisfied first are two kinds of constraints in scheduling, and in fact these give scheduling its unique flavor.

In Chapter 14 on Time we defined the predicate temporal to cover the relations atTime, during, timeSpanOf, happensIn, before and durationOf. Each of these predicates is a relation between an eventuality and a temporal entity, or in the case of before possibly another eventuality.

We can define the schedule for a plan as the set of temporal subgoals of the plan.

```
(forall (s p)                                                    (42.3)
    (iff (schedule s p)
        (forall (e)
            (iff (member e s)
                (and (subgoalIn e p)(temporal e))))))
```

That is, s is a schedule for a plan p if and only if it is the set of temporal properties e that are subgoals in the plan p.

A minimal sort of schedule might consist of one before relation – do one action before another. More elaborate plans may have dates and times associated with all its actions.

We can say that a subgoal e of a plan is scheduled for a temporal entity t if it can be inferred from the plan that e is at or during t.

```
(forall (e p t)                                                    (42.4)
    (iff (scheduled e t p)
        (and (subgoalIn e p)(temporalEntity t)
            (exists (e1 s1)
                (and (or (atTime' e1 e t)(during' e1 e t))
                    (subgoalsOf s1 p)(imply s1 e1))))))
```

The expression (scheduled e t p) says that subgoal e is scheduled for time t in plan p. In lines 5 and 6, e1 is the temporal relation and s1 is the set of subgoals in p. Subgoal e is scheduled for t exactly when s1 implies such a relation.

It is not enough to say that a temporal relation for e is in the schedule for p, because the temporal relation may not be explicit, but rather may follow from facts about the durations of events and about before relations.

We can define unscheduled time as the temporal sequence (tseq) of those intervals which have no associated action in the agent's schedule. We will relativize it to a larger containing interval that would normally be supplied by context. We all have unscheduled time in the next century, but it is never relevant. A time is unscheduled with respect to a plan if there is no subgoal of the plan which is scheduled for that time ("free time," "spare time").

```
(forall (t p t0)                                                   (42.5)
    (iff (unscheduledTime t p t0)
        (and (tseq t)
            (forall (t1)
                (iff (member t1 t)
                    (and (insideTime t1 t0)
                        (not (exists (e)
                            (and (subgoalIn e p)
                                (scheduled e t1 p)))))))))))
```

The expression (unscheduledTime t p t0) says that t is the unscheduled time in plan p, within larger interval t0. Line 3 says that t is a temporal sequence, that is, a set of instants and intervals ordered by time. Lines 5–9 say that a temporal entity is in t if and only if it is inside t0 and there is no subgoal of p that is scheduled for that time.

Because the duration of temporal sequences can be measured, we can talk about the duration of a plan's unscheduled time, relativized to a larger interval (t0) and to a unit (u) of temporal measure.

```
(forall (d p t0 u)                                                 (42.6)
    (iff (scheduleCapacity d p t0 u)
        (exists (t)
            (and (unscheduledTime t p t0)(durationOf d t u)))))
```

That is, duration d is the schedule capacity of plan p in interval t0 in units u if and only if there is a temporal sequence t that is the unscheduled time of p in t0 and d is t's duration in units u.

Durations constitute a scale; thus, so do schedule capacities. The partial ordering on these scales is lessDuration. The predicate lessDuration say that one temporal entity or eventuality has less duration than another. It is defined as follows:

```
(forall (e t1 t2)                                          (42.7)
   (iff (lessDuration' e t1 t2)
        (exists (d1 d2 u)
           (and (durationOf d1 t1 u)(durationOf d2 t2 u)
                (lt' e d1 d2)))))
```

A scale of "scheduled-ness" is one in which the elements are schedule capacities and the partial ordering is lessDuration.

```
(forall (s p t0 u)                                         (42.8)
   (iff (schedulednessScale s p t0 u)
        (exists (s1 t1 t2)
           (and (lessDuration' e t1 t2)
                (forall (d)
                   (if (member d s1)
                       (scheduleCapacity d p t0 u)))
                (scaleDefinedBy s s1 e)))))
```

The predication (schedulednessScale s p t0 u) says that scale s is a scale consisting of schedule capacities in units u (lines 5–7) and having partial ordering lessDuration (line 4).

Because we can make qualitative judgments about whether something lies in the high, medium or low region of a scale, we can talk about an agent's schedule being full, in terms of the duration of the agent's unscheduled time being in the low region of a scale. ("overbooked," "busy," "stretched thin"), with respect to a plan p and interval t0.

```
(forall (p t0)                                             (42.9)
   (iff (fullSchedule p t0)
        (exists (s d u s1)
           (and (schedulednessScale s p t0 u)
                (scheduleCapacity d p t0 u)
                (Lo s1 s)(inScale d s1)))))
```

The next unscheduled moment t for a plan p at time t0 is the first temporal entity in the unscheduled time for p for a postively infinite interval beginning at t0 ("soonest opportunity," "have a chance").

```
(forall (t p t0)                                           (42.10)
   (iff (nextUnscheduledMoment t p t0)
        (exists (s t1 t2)
           (and (unscheduledTime s p t1)(first t2 s)
                (posInfInterval t1)(begins t0 t1)
                (begins t t2)))))
```

In this axiom think of t0 as the present time. Interval t1 is the positive infinite interval beginning at t0, s is the temporal sequence of intervals that are not scheduled for actions in plan p, t2 is the first interval in s, and t is the instant that begins t2.

The last few predicates we have defined were done relative to a plan p. Often the relevant plan is The Plan to thrive that the agent is in the midst of and that defines intentional action. This can be expressed by conjoining (thePlan p a) to these predications. Thus, to represent the fact that Chris is busy, one can write

```
(and (fullSchedule p t0)(thePlan p C))
```

42.3 SCHEDULED AND PENDING PLANS

Concerning scheduled and pending plans, there is range of possibilities. Do we want to say that a plan is scheduled when every event and nontemporal state is anchored to a specific real time, and that it is pending otherwise? Or do we want to say that a plan is pending when no event or nontemporal state is anchored to a specific real time, and that it is scheduled otherwise? Do we want to count as scheduled a plan whose left fringe subgoals are anchored to a specific time, but not necessarily other subgoals? Do we want to count it as anchoring when we only know the order of subgoals but not their specific times?

We will rather arbitrarily say that a scheduled plan is a plan all of whose nontemporal subgoals are scheduled.

```
(forall (p)                                            (42.11)
    (iff (scheduledPlan p)
        (exists (a g)
            (and (plan p a g)
                (forall (e)
                    (if (and (subgoalIn e p)(nontemporal e))
                        (exists (t) (scheduled e t p))))))))
```

A pending plan is one that is not scheduled.

```
(forall (p)                                            (42.12)
    (iff (pendingPlan p)
        (exists (a g) (and (plan p a g)(not (scheduledPlan p))))))
```

The subgoals of a plan are eventualities. The set of subgoals of a plan can be viewed as a conjunction of eventualities, and hence as an eventuality. This has a time span, and we can define that to be the time span of the plan itself.

```
(forall (t p a g)                                      (42.13)
    (if (plan p a g)
        (iff (timeSpanOf t p)
            (exists (s) (and (subgoalsOf s p)(timeSpanOf t s))))))
```

The next scheduled event e2 after event e1 in a plan p is an event such that there is no event in the plan's schedule between e1 and e2.

```
(forall (e1 e2 p)                                       (42.14)
    (iff (nextScheduledEvent e1 e2 p)
        (exists (t1 t2)
            (and (scheduled e1 t1 p)(scheduled e2 t2 p)
                (before t1 t2)
                (not (exists (e3 t3)
                        (and (subgoalIn e3 p)(scheduled e3 t3 p)
                            (before t1 t3)(before t3 t2))))))))
```

That is, e2 is the next scheduled event in p after e1 if and only if the time t1 scheduled for e1 is before the time t2 scheduled for e2, and there are no subgoals e3 of p scheduled for a time t3 between t1 and t2.

The scheduled plan interval is the smallest interval that spans the entire scheduled plan. That is, it is the convex hull of the time span of the plan.

```
(forall (t p)                                                    (42.15)
    (iff (scheduledPlanInterval t p)
        (exists (t1)
            (and (scheduledPlan p)(timeSpanOf t1 p)
                (convexHull t t1)))))
```

The scheduled start time of an event in a scheduled plan is the time that that event is scheduled to begin.

```
(forall (t e p)                                                  (42.16)
    (iff (scheduledStartTime t e p)
        (exists (t1)
            (and (scheduledPlan p)(subgoalIn e p)
                (scheduled e t1 p)(begins t t1)))))
```

The predication (scheduledStartTime t e p) says that p is a scheduled plan and its subgoal e is scheduled for temporal entity t1, which begins at time t.

The scheduled end time of an event in a scheduled plan is the time that that event is scheduled to end.

```
(forall (t e p)                                                  (42.17)
    (iff (scheduledEndTime t e p)
        (exists (t2)
            (and (scheduledPlan p)(subgoalIn e p)
                (scheduled e t2 p)(ends t t2)))))
```

The predication (scheduledEndTime t e p) says that p is a scheduled plan and its subgoal e is scheduled for temporal entity t2, which ends at time t.

The reason for a plan is that it causes a goal to be satisfied. Sometimes this causality is time sensitive; if the plan is not executed by a certain time, it will no longer cause the goal to be satisfied. This certain time is *a* deadline. We can define the predicate aDeadline as follows:

```
(forall (t p)                                                    (42.18)
    (iff (aDeadline t p)
        (exists (a g t1 t2)
            (and (plan p a g)(timeSpanOf t1 p)(ends t2 t1)
                (if (before t t2)(not (cause p g)))))))
```

That is, t is a deadline for plan p if and only if whenever the end t2 of p's time span t1 is after t, it means that p will not cause or bring about the goal g that p was designed to achieve.

The deadline for a plan is the earliest such deadline.

```
(forall (t p)                                              (42.19)
    (iff (deadline t p)
        (and (aDeadline t p)
            (forall (t1)
                (if (aDeadline t1 p)
                    (or (before t t1)(equal t t1)))))))
```

There can be a deadline for starting a plan.

```
(forall (t p)                                              (42.20)
    (iff (aStartTimeDeadline t p)
        (exists (a g t1 t2)
            (and (plan p a g)(timeSpanOf t1 p)(begins t2 t1)
                (if (before t t2)(not (cause p g)))))))
```

That is, t is a start-time deadline for plan p if and only if whenever the beginning t2 of p's time span t1 is after t, it means that p will not cause or bring about the goal g that p was designed to achieve.

The start-time deadline for a plan is the earliest such start-time deadline.

```
(forall (t p)                                              (42.21)
    (iff (startTimeDeadline t p)
        (and (aStartTimeDeadline t p)
            (forall (t1)
                (if (aStartTimeDeadline t1 p)
                    (or (before t t1)(equal t t1)))))))
```

The amount of time between the end of a scheduled plan and the deadline for that plan occupies a significant share of people's thought. The expressions that refer to this duration include "finish in the nick of time," "finished with time to spare," "finish in plenty of time," and "finished at the very last second." We can call this interval the "slack" in a plan.

```
(forall (t p)                                              (42.22)
    (iff (slack t p)
        (exists (t0 t1 t2)
            (and (scheduledPlan p)(timeSpanOf t0 p)
                (ends t1 t0)(deadline t2 p)
                (begins t1 t)(ends t2 t)))))
```

That is, a slack t in plan p is a temporal interval that begins when the plan is to be completed and ends at the plan's deadline.

Slacks have duration and consequently can be located along a scale defined by durations. This scale can have high and low regions, corresponding to the slack being small or large. Consequently, we can define the following two predicates.

```
(forall (p)                                                          (42.23)
   (iff (scheduledCloseToDeadline p)
        (exists (s s0 e t2 t3 s1 t)
            (and (scaleDefinedBy s s0 e)
                 (forall (t1)
                     (if (member t1 s0)(exists (p1) (slack t1 p1))))
                 (lessDuration' e t2 t3)
                 (Lo s1 s)(slack t p)(inScale t s1)))))
```

That is, a plan p is scheduled close to its deadline if its slack is in the low region s1 of a scale s whose elements t1 are "slacks" and whose partial ordering e is lessDuration.

A predicate scheduledFarFromDeadline can be defined similarly; it picks out the high region of the scale.

```
(forall (p)                                                          (42.24)
   (iff (scheduledFarFromDeadline p)
        (exists (s s0 e t2 t3 s1 t)
            (and (scaleDefinedBy s s0 e)
                 (forall (t1)
                     (if (member t1 s0)(exists (p1) (slack t1 p1))))
                 (lessDuration' e t2 t3)
                 (Hi s1 s)(slack t p)(inScale t s1)))))
```

42.4 SCHEDULE PREFERENCES

In Chapter 32 on Goal Management we introduced the predication (preferGoal a g1 g2), meaning that agent a prefers to pursue goal g1 over pursuing goal g2. A schedule is a set and therefore a conjunction of the temporal subgoals of a plan. Thus, we can define a schedule preference in terms of goal preferences between schedules.

```
(forall (a s1 s2)                                                    (42.25)
   (iff (schedulePreference a s1 s2)
        (exists (p p1 p2 g)
            (and (plan p a g)(sameAbstractPlan p1 p2 p)
                 (schedule s1 p1)(schedule s2 p2)
                 (preferGoal a s1 s2)))))
```

The predication (schedulePreference a s1 s2) says that agent a prefers schedule s1 to schedule s2. The predication (sameAbstractPlan p1 p2 p), defined in Chapter 45, says that plans p1 and p2 are both instantiations of the same abstract plan p.

Examples of preferences are "Do the most interesting tasks first," and "Minimize or maximize the slack."

42.5 SCHEDULING ACTIONS

For an agent to schedule a plan is for there to be a change from a state in which one has a pending plan to one in which one has a scheduled plan, where the subgoals of the pending plan are all included in the subgoals of the scheduled plan.

```
(forall (e a p1 p2)                                         (42.26)
   (iff (schedulePlan' e a p1 p2)
        (exists (e1 e2 g e3)
           (and (change' e3 e1 e2)(gen e3 e)
                (plan' e1 p1 a g)(pendingPlan p1)
                (plan' e2 p2 a g)(scheduledPlan p2)
                (forall (s1 s2)
                   (if (and (subgoalsOf s1 p1)(subgoalsOf s2 p2))
                       (subset s1 s2)))))))
```

That is, there is a change from agent a having a pending plan p1 for achieving goal g to having a scheduled plan p2 for achieving g, where all the subgoals of p1 are also subgoals of p2.

In Chapter 31 we defined a periodic plan as one whose time span is a periodic temporal sequence.

To schedule a periodic plan is to schedule a plan that is periodic.

```
(forall (a p1 p2)                                           (42.27)
   (iff (schedulePeriodicPlan' e a p1 p2)
        (exists (g e3)
           (and (schedulePlan' e3 a p1 p2)(gen e3 e)
                (periodicPlan p2 a g)))))
```

For an agent to unschedule a plan is for there to be a change from a state in which there is a scheduled plan to a state in which there is a pending plan with all the same nontemporal sugoals.

```
(forall (e a p1 p2)                                         (42.28)
   (iff (unschedulePlan' e a p1 p2)
        (exists (e1 e2 g e3)
           (and (change' e3 e1 e2)(gen e3 e)
                (plan' e1 p1 a g)(scheduledPlan p1)
                (plan' e2 p2 a g)(pendingPlan p2)
                (forall (s1 g2)
                   (if (and (subgoalsOf s1 p1)(subgoalIn g2 p2)
                            (nontemporal g2))
                       (member g2 s1)))))))
```

The predication (unschedulePlan' e a p1 p2) says that e is the action by agent a of unscheduling a scheduled plan p1 resulting in a pending plan p2. Lines 7–10 say that the nontemporal subgoals of p2 are subgoals of p1. Thus, only temporal goals are changed in the process.

To reschedule a plan is to schedule a plan where there has been a previous unscheduling.

```
(forall (e a p2 p3)                                         (42.29)
   (iff (reschedulePlan' e a p2 p3)
        (exists (e1 p1 e2)
           (and (schedulePlan' e2 a p2 p3)(gen e2 e)
                (unschedulePlan' e1 a p1 p2)(before e1 e)))))
```

The predication (reschedulePlan' e a p2 p3) says that e is an action by agent a to reschedule a pending plan p2, resulting in scheduled plan p3. This holds when there was a previous unscheduling event e1 by agent a changing a scheduled plan p1 into the pending plan p2.

To indefinitely postpone a plan is to unschedule it and not reschedule it.

```
(forall (e a p1 p2)                                          (42.30)
   (iff (indefinitelyPostponePlan' e a p1 p2)
        (exists (e4)
           (and (unschedulePlan' e4 a p1 p2)(gen e4 e)
                (not (exists (e3 p3)
                        (reschedulePlan' e3 a p2 p3)))))))
```

To juggle a schedule is to change from a state in which one's plan is p1 to a state in which one's plan is p2, where the nontemporal subgoals of p1 and p2 are the same and the time spans of p1 and p2 are the same.

```
(forall (e a p1 p2)                                          (42.31)
   (iff (juggleSchedule' e a p1 p2)
        (exists (e1 e2 t e3)
           (and (change' e3 e1 e2)(gen e3 e)
                (plan' e1 p1 a g)(scheduledPlan p1)
                (plan' e2 p2 a g)(scheduledPlan p2)
                (forall (g)
                   (if (nontemporal g)
                       (iff (subgoalIn g p1)(subgoalIn g p2))))
                (exists (g1)
                   (and (not (subgoalIn g1 p1))(subgoalIn g1 p2)))
                (timeSpanOf t p1)(timeSpanOf t p2)))))
```

The predication (juggleSchedule' e a p1 p2) says that e is the action by agent a of changing scheduled plan p1 into scheduled plan p2, where p1 and p2 have all the same nontemporal subgoals (lines 7–9), where p1 and p2 differ in at least one temporal subgoal (lines 10–11), and where p1 and p2 have the same time spans.

Collaborative scheduling of a plan is the scheduling of a plan by a set of agents.

```
(forall (e s p1 p2)                                          (42.32)
   (iff (collaborativelySchedulePlan' e s p1 p2)
        (exists (e1)
           (and (schedulePlan' e1 s p1 p2)(gen e1 e)
                (forall (a) (if (member a s)(agent a)))))))
```

A scheduling failure is to fail to schedule a plan.

```
(forall (e)                                                 (42.33)
   (iff (schedulingFailure e a p)
        (exists (e1 p1)
           (and (fail' e a e1)(schedulePlan' e1 a p p1)))))
```

PREDICATES INTRODUCED IN THIS CHAPTER

(schedule s p)
   Set s of subgoals is a schedule for plan p.

(scheduled e t p)
   Subgoal e is scheduled for temporal sequence t in plan p.

(unscheduledTime t p t0)
  Temporal sequence t is the unscheduled time in plan p in interval t0.

(scheduleCapacity d p t0 u)
  Duration d is the schedule capacity of plan p in interval t0 in units u.

(lessDuration' e t1 t2)
  Eventuality e is the state of temporal entity t1 being of less duration than temporal entity t2.

(schedulednessScale s p t0 u)
  Scale s is a scale of durations in units u for the amount of time plan p takes in interval t0.

(fullSchedule p t0)
  Plan p is takes a lot of the time in interval t0.

(nextUnscheduledMoment t p t0)
  Instant t is the next unscheduled moment in plan p after time t0.

(scheduledPlan p)
  All of the subgoals in plan p are scheduled.

(pendingPlan p)
  Plan p is pending, i.e., not a scheduled plan.

(nextScheduledEvent e1 e2 p)
  Eventuality e2 is the next scheduled event in p after e1.

(scheduledPlanInterval t p)
  Interval t is the convex hull of the time span of scheduled plan p.

(scheduledStartTime t e p)
  Subgoal e in scheduled plan p is scheduled to begin at time t.

(scheduledEndTime t e p)
  Subgoal e in scheduled plan p is scheduled to end at time t.

(aDeadline t p)
  Instant t is *a* deadline for plan p.

(deadline t p)
  Instant t is *the* deadline for plan p.

(aStartTimeDeadline t p)
  Instant t is *a* deadline for plan p to start.

(startTimeDeadline t p)
  Instant t is *the* deadline for plan p to start.

(slack t p)
  A slack t in plan p is an interval that begins when the plan is to be completed and ends at the plan's deadline.

(scheduledCloseToDeadline p)
  Scheduled plan p is scheduled close to its deadline.

(scheduledFarFromDeadline p)
  Scheduled plan p is scheduled far from its deadline.

(schedulePreference a s1 s2)
  Agent a prefers schedule s1 over schedule s2.

(schedulePlan' e a p1 p2)
Eventuality e is the action by agent a of scheduling pending plan p1, resulting in plan p2.

(schedulePeriodicPlan' e a p1 p2)
Eventuality e is the action by agent a of scheduling pending plan p1, resulting in periodic plan p2.

(unschedulePlan' e a p1 p2)
Eventuality e is the action by agent a of unscheduling a scheduled plan p1, resulting in a pending plan p2.

(reschedulePlan' e a p2 p3)
Eventuality e is an action by agent a to reschedule a pending plan p2, resulting in scheduled plan p3.

(indefinitelyPostponePlan' e a p1 p2)
Eventuality e is the action by agent a to unschedule a scheduled plan p1, resulting in pending plan p2, without rescheduling it.

(juggleSchedule' e a p1 p2)
Eventuality e is an action by agent a to rearrange scheduled plan p1, resulting in scheduled plan p2.

(collaborativelySchedulePlan' e s p1 p2)
Eventuality e is the action by set s of agents of scheduling pending plan p1, resulting in plan p2.

(schedulingFailure e a p)
Eventuality e is the failure by agent a to schedule plan p.

In addition, the predicate sameAbstractPlan, defined in Chapter 45, is used.

(sameAbstratcPlan p1 p2 p)
Plans p1 and p2 are both instantiations of the same abstract plan p.

43

Monitoring

43.1 MONITORING PROCESSES

As we go through our daily lives, we are executing plans and continually monitoring their effects to make sure they are actually achieving our goals and to make sure nothing else arises that demands greater attention. In a way, it is difficult to see how to capture this aspect of our experience in computational terms. It seems that we would need to wrap all action in a huge conditional that would check at every instant for threats and opportunities before executing the next step in the ongoing plan. But in fact the top-level loop in our behavior is a kind of "Interpret–Act" cycle. We look at the world and figure out what is going on, and then we do the next thing. Most of the time this requires little computation, since what is going on is what was going on an instant before, just advanced a little bit. When something unexpected presents itself, we must do more computation. It is not so much a matter of checking every possible opportunity or threat at every instant as it is of interpreting what presents itself, be it threat, opportunity, or the next expected thing.

Monitoring as we conceive it is a conscious subprocess of this "Interpret" stage of the loop. It is thoroughly integrated with the steps in the ongoing plans agents execute. It involves those threats and opportunities we are especially attuned to, given the nature of our plans.

We will say that an agent a monitors a set s of eventuality types. When a goal-relevant instance of any of these is perceived, this causes the agent to focus on that instance. This axiom is defeasible because sometimes we miss significant threats and opportunities even though we are monitoring for them.

```
(forall (e a s e1 e2)                                              (43.1)
    (if (and (monitor' e a s)(member e1 s)(instance e2 e1)(perceive a e2)
             (goalRelevant e2 a)(etc))
        (exists (e3) (and (inFocus' e3 e2 a)(cause e e3)))))
```

In this axiom, e1 is the eventuality type that is being monitored for, and e2 is the eventuality token of that type that is actually perceived.

A weaker defeasible rule is that if we are monitoring for an eventuality type and a token actually occurs, then that will cause us to focus on it. This rule fails when something goal-relevant occurs and we don't perceive it.

```
(forall (e a s e1 e2)                                              (43.2)
    (if (and (monitor' e a s)(member e1 s)(instance e2 e1)(Rexist e2)
             (goalRelevant e2 a)(etc))
        (exists (e3) (and (inFocus' e3 e2 a)(cause e e3)))))
```

These are necessary conditions (modulo defeasibility) on monitoring. We can also give a (defeasible) sufficient condition. If an eventuality type has a goal-relevant instance, it should be monitored for.

```
(forall (a e1 e2)                                                  (43.3)
    (if (and (goalRelevant e2 a)(instance e2 e1)(etc))
        (exists (s) (and (member e1 s)(monitor a s)))))
```

A big reason for this defeasibility is that many goal-relevant phenomena are, at the least, very difficult to perceive, such as radiation, carcinogens in the environment, and bacteria in food.

Some monitoring is for events that happen to things. To monitor a thing is to monitor for events happening to the thing or states involving the thing.

```
(forall (a x)                                                      (43.4)
    (iff (monitorThing a x)
         (exists (s)
             (and (monitor a s)
                  (forall (e) (if (member e s)(arg* x e)))))))
```

Some monitoring is for events that happen to an agent.

```
(forall (a b)                                                      (43.5)
    (iff (monitorAgent a b)
         (and (monitorThing a b)(agent b))))
```

Some monitoring is for events that happen to one's own self.

```
(forall (a)                                                        (43.6)
    (iff (monitorSelf a) (monitorAgent a a)))
```

For example, an athlete will monitor his or her body for various conditions relevant to the performance.

People can stop monitoring some set of events after some time.

```
(forall (e0 a s)                                                   (43.7)
    (iff (terminateMonitor' e0 a s)
         (exists (e1 e2)
             (and (changeFrom' e2 e1)(gen e2 e0)(monitor' e1 a s)))))
```

43.2 CHARACTERISTICS OF MONITORING PROCESSES

When monitoring, people are looking for monitor trigger conditions. These are the eventuality types in the set s.

```
(forall (e)                                                    (43.8)
    (iff (monitorTriggerCondition e)
         (exists (a s)(and (monitor a s)(member e s)))))
```

We monitor for both threats and opportunities. The trigger condition can be either good for us or bad for us. In fact, it is a theorem that if an eventuality is goal relevant to an agent it is either good for or bad for the agent.

```
(forall (e a)                                                  (43.9)
    (if (goalRelevant e a)(or (goodFor e a)(badFor e a))))
```

A monitored trigger condition can be satisfied.

```
(forall (e)                                                    (43.10)
    (iff (monitorTriggerConditionSatisfied e)
         (exists (e1)
             (and (monitorTriggerCondition e)
                  (instance e1 e)(Rexist e1)))))
```

A monitored trigger conditions can remain unsatisfied.

```
(forall (e)                                                    (43.11)
    (iff (monitorTriggerConditionUnsatisfied e)
         (and (monitorTriggerCondition e)
              (not (exists (e1)
                  (and (instance e1 e)(Rexist e1)))))))
```

When one of the trigger conditions occurs, we typically execute some action in response. We can call this the triggered action.

```
(forall (e2 e1 a s)                                            (43.12)
    (iff (monitorTriggeredAction e2 e1 a s)
         (exists (e0 s1 g)
             (and (monitor' e0 a s)(member e1 s)
                  (cause e0 e2)
                  (agentOf a e2)(goal g a)
                  (causalComplex s1 g)(member e2 s1)))))
```

The predication (monitorTriggeredAction e2 e1 a s) says that action e2 is triggered by condition e1 while agent a is monitoring a set s of eventuality types. Condition e1 is one of the conditions being monitored for (line 4). The monitoring causes action e2 (line 5). Agent a is the agent of the action e2, and e2 is in a causal complex for some goal g of a's (lines 6–7). That is, action e2 somehow serves a's interests.

There is a time span during which monitoring is conducted.

```
(forall (t e0)                                                 (43.13)
    (iff (monitoringTimeSpan t e0)
         (exists (a s) (and (monitor' e0 a s)(timeSpanOf t e0)))))
```

There is a frequency at which monitoring is conducted. For example, when we drive down the freeway, we monitor our distance from the car in front of us on a

second-by-second basis. We monitor the presence of police cars at less frequent intervals, and we monitor our gas guage probably no more than every thirty or forty miles
in normal circumstances. We can estimate the speed of events and the distance we
are from certain expected trigger conditions. As we approach them, we take action to
monitor the trigger condition more frequently. If we have something planned for two
o'clock, we check our watch more frequently as the hour approaches. A basketball
referee will be more attuned to the ball's being out of bounds the closer the ball gets
to the line. Here we define the monitoring frequency.

```
(forall (r a s t)                                              (43.14)
    (iff (monitoringFrequency r a s t)
        (exists (s1)
            (and (forall (e1)
                    (if (member e1 s1)(monitor' e1 a s)))
                (tseq t)(rate r s1 t)))))
```

The predication (monitoringFrequency r a s t) says that r is the rate of occurrence in temporal sequence t of monitoring events by agent a of eventuality types
in set s. Set s1 is the set of monitoring events. r is the number of times such events
occur in each element of t.

Monitoring causes eventualities in the environment to be in focus. Monitoring can
fail if the triggering does not happen when the conditions are met – a false negative.
The event happens but the monitoring does not end up in focus. False positives are
also possible; the triggering event is believed to have happened, an instance of it is
in focus, but in fact the instance did not really happen.

```
(forall (a s)                                                 (43.15)
    (iff (monitoringFailure a s)
        (exists (e e1 e2)
            (and (monitor' e a s)(member e1 s)(instance e2 e1)
                (or (and (Rexist e2)
                        (not (exists (e3)
                                (and (inFocus' e3 e2 a)
                                    (cause e e3)))))
                    (and (not (Rexist e2))
                        (exists (e3)
                            (and (inFocus' e3 e2 a)
                                (cause e e3)))))))))
```

The predication (monitoringFailure a s) says that agent a has failed to monitor correctly for conditions s. Eventuality e is a's action of monitoring for s (line
4). Eventuality type e1 is one of the conditions being monitored for and eventuality token e2 is an instance of e1 (line 4). Lines 5–8 define the false-negative case.
Eventuality e2 really exists (line 5), but the monitoring did not cause e2 to be in
focus (lines 6–8). Lines 9–12 define the false positive case. The eventuality e2 does
not really exist (line 9), but the monitoring caused it to be in focus (lines 10–12).

PREDICATES INTRODUCED IN THIS CHAPTER

(monitor a s)
    Agent a monitors the environment for set s of eventualities.

(monitorThing a x)
   Agent a monitors the environment for eventualities involving x.

(monitorAgent a b)
   Agent a monitors the environment for eventualities involving agent b.

(monitorSelf a)
   Agent a monitors the environment for eventualities involving agent a.

(terminateMonitor a s)
   Agent a stops monitoring for conditions in s.

(monitorTriggerCondition e)
   Eventuality type e is a trigger condition in some agent's monitoring activity.

(monitorTriggerConditionSatisfied e)
   Monitor trigger condition e actually occurs.

(monitorTriggerConditionUnsatisfied e)
   Monitor trigger condition e doesn't occur.

(monitorTriggeredAction e2 e1 a s)
   Action e2 is an action by agent a caused by a's perception of trigger condition e1
   while monitoring for s.

(monitoringTimeSpan t e0)
   t is the time span of monitoring activity e0.

(monitoringFrequency r a s t)
   r is the number of times a monitoring action by a for conditions s occurs in each
   element of temporal sequence t.

(monitoringFailure a s)
   Agent a fails to monitor correctly for conditions s.

44

Execution Modalities

44.1 EXECUTIONS

A plan is a causal network that someone has in mind. Its actions may or may not actually happen in the real world. The plan may be designed to happen immediately or it may be designed with no intention of it ever happening. The plan, as a mental construct, is the same in either case. The two cases differ only in that in one the plan is executed, whereas in the other it isn't. For reasons like this it is useful to have as a distinct notion the "execution" of a plan. We will first define the execution of an action in a plan and then define the execution of a plan.

An agent a executes an action e in a plan p if and only if e is a subgoal of the plan, a is the agent of that action, and the fact that e is a subgoal in p plays a causal role in the occurrence of e.

```
(forall (e0 a e p)                                          (44.1)
   (iff (execute' e0 a e p)
        (exists (g e1)
           (and (plan p a g)(subgoalIn' e1 e p)(agentOf a e)
                (causallyInvolved e1 e)))))
```

We execute a plan by executing all of its subgoals. The first axiom for executePlan defines necessary conditions and introduces the subexecution relation.

```
(forall (e2 a p)                                            (44.2)
   (if (executePlan' e2 a p)
       (and (exists (g) (plan p a g))
            (exists (e) (and (subgoalIn e p)(agentOf a e)))
            (forall (e)
               (if (and (subgoalIn e p)(agentOf a e))
                   (exists (e0)
                      (and (execute' e0 a e p)
                           (subexecution e0 e2)))))))))
```

The expression (executePlan' e2 a p) says that e2 is the execution by agent a of plan p. If this is true, then p is a plan by a to achieve goal g (line 3), there is at least one subgoal e of p for which a is the agent (line 4), and for every subgoal e in p of which a is the agent, there is an execution e0 of e by a in the service of plan p (lines 5–8). Line 9 posits a subexecution relation between e0 and e2.

The next axiom gives sufficient conditions for executePlan.

```
(forall (a p g)                                                    (44.3)
    (if (and (plan p a g)
             (exists (e) (and (subgoalIn e p)(agentOf a e)))
             (forall (e)
                 (if (and (subgoalIn e p)(agentOf a e))
                     (exists (e0) (execute' e0 a e p)))))
        (exists (e2) (executePlan' e2 a p))))
```

The conditions in the antecedent of this axiom are just the same as the conditions in the consequent of the previous axiom.

We broke the definition of executePlan into two axioms in order to introduce the relation subexecution. An esoteric aside: Suppose we are able to prove the antecedent of Axiom (44.3). Then we can use that axiom to conclude that there is an executePlan. Then we can use Axiom (44.2) to establish the existence of subexecutions e0. But because we did not go to the trouble of stipulating the uniqueness of the subexecutions, we cannot guarantee that the subexecutions given to us in the consequent of Axiom (44.2) are the same as the executions of the subgoals we began with in the antecedent of Axiom (44.3). This should not cause difficulties, however.

These axioms tell us about the abstract concepts of execute and executePlan, but they do not tell us about their actual occurrence. Before addressing that, we need to introduce another concept.

In addition to actions by an agent, plans contain states and events that must hold or happen at the appropriate time. For example, it may be part of a plan for a picnic that the sun is shining. The predicate happensInTime says about such an eventuality in a plan that it actually does occur when it needs to.

```
(forall (e p)                                                      (44.4)
    (iff (happensInTime e p)
         (and (subgoalIn e p)
              (exists (s)
                  (and (subgoalsOf s p)
                       (forall (e1 t)
                           (if (and (atTime' e1 e t)(imply s e1))
                               (Rexist e1))))))))
```

The expression (happensInTime e p) says that subgoal e of plan p happens in time for the successful execution of the plan. Line 3 says that e is a subgoal in p. Line 5 labels the set s of subgoals of p. Lines 6–8 say that any atTime relation implied by the subgoals of p actually holds. That is, all temporal constraints involving e hold.

The following axiom says that an executePlan really exists exactly when all its subexecutions really exist and the other events in the plan happen at the appropriate times.

```
(forall (e2 a p)                                                (44.5)
    (if (executePlan' e2 a p)
        (iff (Rexist e2)
            (and (forall (e0)
                    (if (subexecution e0 e2)(Rexist e0)))
                 (forall (e)
                    (if (and (subgoalIn e p)(not (agentOf a e)))
                        (happensInTime e p)))))))
```

The temporal relations among subgoals are themselves subgoals that have to be satisfied, so this definition ensures that the subgoals will be executed in a legitimate order.

Partial executions of plans can be viewed as total executions of subplans.

In Chapter 17 on Event Structure we defined a number of ways in which one event can be a subevent of another. Being a subexecution is one way of being a subevent.

```
(forall (e2 e0)                                                 (44.6)
    (if (subexecution e0 e2)(subevent e0 e2)))
```

A person can execute the action of driving. It is strange to say that a person executes a semi-involuntary action like breathing; it is normally not a part of the agent's plan, although you sometimes breathe under voluntary control. We would not say you execute the action of your heart beating; your intention that your heart beat plays no causal role in your heart's actually beating.

44.2 MODALITIES OF EXECUTION

Executions of plans can have a number of properties involving the agents' cognitive stance toward the executions. In this section we define a number of these modalities that our investigations have shown to be frequent.

In some cases, the event being executed is consciously planned by the agent.

```
(forall (e a p)                                                 (44.7)
    (iff (plannedExecution e a p)
        (exists (e1 p0)
            (and (executePlan' e a p)(inFocus e1 a)
                 (subgoalIn' e1 e p0)(thePlan p0 a)))))
```

This says that e is a planned execution by agent a of plan p exactly when e is an execution by a of p, and the fact that the execution of the plan is a subgoal of The Plan p0 that defines a's intentional behavior is in a's focus of attention.

In some cases people do things spontaneously that they did not consciously plan to do.

```
(forall (e a p)                                                 (44.8)
    (iff (spontaneousExecution e a p)
        (exists (p0)
            (and (executePlan' e a p)(not (subgoalIn e p0))
                 (thePlan p0 a)))))
```

This says that e is a spontaneous execution by agent a of plan p exactly when e is an execution by a of p, but the execution of the plan is not explicitly a part of The Plan p0 that defines a's intentional behavior.

In some cases people do things they have no control over. These are cases where the person is the agent of the action but is not conscious of being the agent.

```
(forall (e a p)                                                    (44.9)
    (iff (nonconsciousExecution e a p)
        (and (executePlan' e a p)
            (forall (e1)
                (if (subgoalIn e1 p)
                    (not (exists (e2)
                        (and (agentOf' e2 a e1)
                            (inFocus e2 a)))))))))
```

A nonconscious execution e by agent a of plan p is an execution by a of p. Lines 4–8 say moreover that for all subgoals e1 of p, it never happens that a is aware of being the agent of e1.

For the next two concepts, we make use of the predicate externalTo defined in Chapter 10 on Composite Entities. Recall that an entity x is external to entity y if they share no components.

People do things, reacting to events in their environment. That is, some change of state external to the agent is causally involved in the execution of the action.

```
(forall (e a p)                                                    (44.10)
    (iff (reactiveExecution e a p)
        (exists (e1 x m)
            (and (executePlan' e a p)
                (changeIn' e1 x)(externalTo x m)(mind m a)
                (causallyInvolved e1 e)))))
```

Line 4 says that e is an execution by agent a of plan p. Lines 5 and 6 say that there is a change e1 in some entity x external to the agent's mind m that is causally involved in the execution.

People do things that only involve thinking in their heads; no change occurs in the external world as a result of the execution.

```
(forall (e a p)                                                    (44.11)
    (iff (mentalExecution e a p)
        (and (executePlan' o a p)(inFocus e a)
            (not (exists (e1 x m)
                (and (changeIn' e1 x)(externalTo x m)
                    (mind m a)(cause e e1)))))))
```

Execution e is a mental execution by agent a of plan p if it is an execution and it is in a's focus of intention (line 3), but there is no change in an entity external to a's mind that is caused by e (lines 4–6).

Some executions are made collaboratively with other people. A collaboration is the execution of plans by a set of agents.

```
(forall (e s p)                                                (44.12)
    (iff (collaborativeExecutuion e s p)
        (and (executePlan' e s p) (set s)
            (forall (a) (if (member a s)(agent a))))))
```

Some executions are constrained by execution rules that must be followed. These constraints can be viewed as properties of the subexecutions of the action that is being executed.

```
(forall (e a p s)                                              (44.13)
    (iff (followExecutionRules e a p s)
        (and (executePlan' e a p)
            (forall (c)
                (if (member c s)
                    (exists (e1)
                        (and (subexecution e1 e)(arg* e1 c)
                            (if (Rexist e1)(Rexist c)))))))))
```

The predication (followExecutionRules e a p s) says that e is an execution by agent a of plan p respecting the constraints c in set s. Line 3 says that e is an execution by a of p. Lines 4–7 say that every member c of s is a property of some subexecution e1 of the execution e. Line 8 says if that subexecution occurs then the corresponding constraint property also holds.

44.3 PLAN EXECUTION AND TIME

Executions of plans are often composite actions that can be classified by the structure of the action that is executed. Our theory of event structure (Chapter 17) has provided us with the appropriate predicates for defining these categories.

Some executions are for iterative plans. That is, the agent is iterating through some set of entities, the notion captured by the predicate iteration.

```
(forall (e a p s)                                              (44.14)
    (iff (iterativeExecution e a p s)
        (and (executePlan' e a p)
            (exists (e1 x)
                (and (iteration e e1)
                    (typelt x s)(arg* x e1))))))
```

The predication (iterativeExecutuion e a p s) says that e is an execution by agent a of plan p which iterates through the elements of set s. Line 3 says e is an execution of p. Line 5 says it is an iteration through instances of the event type e1. Line 6 says that the elements of s are all arguments of the corresponding instances of e1.

Some executions are for repetitive plans. That is, the action being executed is a repeatUntil.

```
(forall (e a p)                                                (44.15)
    (iff (repetitiveExecution e a p)
        (and (executePlan' e a p)
            (exists (e1 e2)
                (repeatUntil e e1 e2)))))
```

A periodic execution of a plan is is an execution whose time span is a periodic temporal sequence.

```
(forall (e a p)                                          (44.16)
    (iff (periodicExecution e a p)
         (and (executePlan' e a p)
              (exists (t)
                  (and (timeSpanOf t e)(periodicTseq t))))))
```

Some executions are continuations of the execution of a prior plan. That is, there is some larger plan the plan being executed is a subplan of, and the execution continues the execution of that larger plan.

```
(forall (e a p)                                          (44.17)
    (iff (continuingExecution e a p p0)
         (and (executePlan' e a p)(subplan p p0)
              (exists (e0)
                  (and (executePlan' e0 a p0)(subexecution e e0))))))
```

The predication (continuingExecution e a p p0) says that execution e by agent a of plan p is a continuation of an execution of the larger plan p0 of which p is a subplan.

Some executions are triggered by specific times. For example, someone leaves for work at 8:00 A.M. every morning.

```
(forall (e a p t)                                        (44.18)
    (iff (timeTriggeredExecution e a p t)
         (exists (t1 e1)
             (and (executePlan' e a p)(timeSpanOf t1 e)
                  (begins' e1 t t1)(causallyInvolved e1 e)))))
```

The predication (timeTriggeredExecution e a p t) says that e is an execution by agent a of plan p triggered by the fact that the time is t. Line 4 says that e is an execution of p whose time span is t1. Line 5 says that the property of t being the beginning of t1 is causally involved in the occurrence of the execution e.

Some plans are executed consecutively one after another. That is, the time spans of the executions constitute a temporal sequence.

```
(forall (e a s)                                          (44.19)
    (iff (consecutiveExecution e a s)
         (exists (t)
             (and (forall (p)
                      (iff (member p s)
                           (exists (e1 t1)
                               (and (executePlan' e1 a p)
                                    (timeSpanOf t1 e1)
                                    (member t1 t)))))
                  (tseq t)))))
```

The predication (consecutiveExecution e a s) says that e is an execution by agent a of a consecutive sequence s of plans. The temporal entity t is introduced in line 3. Lines 4–9 say that t consists of the time spans t1 of all the executions e1 of the plans p in the set s. Line 10 says that the t thus defined is a temporal sequence.

Some plans are executed concurrently with other plans.

```
(forall (e a s)                                                    (44.20)
    (iff (concurrentExecution e a s)
         (and (forall (p)
                  (if (member p s)(exists (e1) (executePlan' e1 a p))))
              (forall (p1 p2 e1 e2)
                  (if (and (member p1 s)(member p2 s)
                           (executePlan' e1 a p1)(executePlan' e2 a p2))
                      (intOverlap e1 e2))))))
```

The predication (concurrentExecution e a s) says that e is the concurrent execution by agent a of the plans in set s. Lines 3 and 4 say that each of the plans in s has an execution. Lines 5–8 say that these overlap pairwise.

Distinct agents can execute their plans simultaneously.

```
(forall (e a1 a2 p1 p2)                                            (44.21)
    (iff (simultaneousExecution e a1 a2 p1 p2)
         (exists (e1 e2)
             (and (executePlan' e1 a p1)(executePlan' e2 a p2)
                  (and' e e1 e2)(intOverlap e1 e2)))))
```

The predication (simultaneousExecution e a1 a2 p1 p2) says that e is the simultaneous execution by agent a1 of plan p1 and agent a2 of plan p2. This happens when e is the conjunction of executions of the two plans and the executions of the plans overlap.

PREDICATES INTRODUCED IN THIS CHAPTER

(execute a e p)
   Agent a executes action e as part of plan p.

(executePlan a p)
   Agent a executes plan p.

(subexecution e1 e2)
   Execution e1 is a subexecution of execution e2.

(happensInTime e p)
   Subgoal e of plan p happens in time for the successful execution of p.

(plannedExecution e a p)
   Eventuality e is a planned execution by agent a of plan p.

(spontaneousExecution e a p)
   Eventuality e is a spontaneous execution by agent a of plan p.

(nonconsciousExecution e a p)
   Eventuality e is a nonconscious execution by agent a of plan p.

(reactiveExecution e a p)
   Eventuality e is a reactive execution by agent a of plan p.

(mentalExecution e a p)
   Eventuality e is a mental execution by agent a of plan p.

(collaborativeExecutuion e s p)
Eventuality e is a collaborative execution of plan p by the agents in set s.

(followExecutionRules e a p s)
Eventuality e is an execution by agent a of plan p respecting the constraints in set s.

(iterativeExecution e a p s)
Eventuality e is an execution by agent a of plan p that iterates through the elements of set s.

(repetitiveExecution e a p)
Eventuality e is a repetitive execution by agent a of plan p.

(periodicExecution e a p)
Eventuality e is an execution by agent a of plan p where the time span of e is a periodic temporal sequence.

(continuingExecution e a p p0)
Eventuality e is an execution by agent a of plan p which is a continuation of an execution of a larger plan p0 of which p is a subplan.

(timeTriggeredExecution e a p t)
Eventuality e is an execution by agent a of plan p which is triggered by the fact that the time is t.

(consecutiveExecution e a s)
Eventuality e is a consecutive execution by agent a of the plans in set s.

(concurrentExecution e a s)
Eventuality e is the concurrent execution by agent a of the plans in set s.

(simultaneousExecution e a1 a2 p1 p2)
Eventuality e is the simultaneous execution by agent a1 of plan p1 and agent a2 of plan p2.

45

Execution Control

45.1 BEGINNING EXECUTIONS

In the previous chapter we defined the actions of executing a plan and executing a step in a plan, and we defined various concepts concerning external circumstances that might accompany such executions. In this chapter we will look at the internal structure of executions of plans, beginning with beginning.

The "left fringe" of a plan is the set of all those subgoals that can be done first, that is, those subgoals such that there is no subgoal that must be achieved before it.

```
(forall (s p)                                                      (45.1)
   (iff (leftFringe s p)
        (exists (a g s1)
          (and (plan p a g)(subgoalsOf s1 p)
               (forall (e t)
                 (iff (and (member e s)(begins t e))
                      (and (subgoalIn e p)(begins t e)
                           (not (exists (e1 t1)
                                  (and (subgoalIn e1 p)
                                       (begins t1 e1)
                                       (imply s1 b)
                                       (before' b t1 t))))))))))))
```

The expression (leftFringe s p) says that s is the left fringe of plan p. This holds when p is a plan by some agent a to achieve goal g with subgoals s1 (line 4), and s is the set of subgoals of p (lines 6–7) for which there does not exist another subgoal e1 in p which must occur before e (lines 8–12). The condition in lines 8–12 is that it does not follow from the structure of the plan (s1) that the beginning t1 of subgoal e1 occurs before the beginning t of subgoal e. (The predication (begins t e) occurs twice because the starting time of e has to be labeled on both sides of the biconditional.)

It is a theorem that if two subgoals of a plan must begin to be executed simultaneously, then either both or neither will be in the left fringe of the plan.

```
(forall (e1 e2 t p s)                                          (45.2)
    (if (and (begins t e1)(begins t e2)
             (subgoalIn e1 p)(subgoalIn e2 p)(leftFringe s p))
        (iff (member e1 s)(member e2 s))))
```

The top-level goal in a plan is a limiting case of a subgoal. Executing any of the subgoals of a goal entails that we are in the process of executing the goal. Thus, there cannot be any of its subgoals that must be executed before the goal. It is a theorem that the top-level goal is in the left fringe of the plan.

```
(forall (p a g s)                                              (45.3)
    (if (and (plan p a g)(leftFringe s p))
        (member g s)))
```

A precondition of a plan is a precondition of a subgoal in the left fringe of the plan.

```
(forall (e p)                                                  (45.4)
    (iff (precondition e p)
         (exists (s e1)
            (and (leftFringe s p)(member e1 s)(enable e e1)))))
```

Preconditions are not part of the plan. Otherwise e would be in the left fringe of the plan rather than e1.

Preconditions of plans may be satisfied at the time the plan is executed.

```
(forall (e p t)                                                (45.5)
    (iff (satisfiedPrecondition e p t)
         (and (precondition e p)(atTime e t))))
```

Preconditions of plans may be unsatisfied at the time the plan is executed.

```
(forall (e p t)                                                (45.6)
    (iff (unsatisfiedPrecondition e p t)
         (and (precondition e p)(not (atTime e t)))))
```

Satisfied preconditions can become unsatisfied during the execution of a plan.

```
(forall (e0 e p t)                                             (45.7)
    (iff (violatePrecondition' e0 e p t)
         (exists (e1 e2)
            (and (changeFrom' e2 e1)(gen e2 e0)
                 (satisfiedPrecondition' e1 e p t)
                 (atTime e0 t)))))
```

There is a subset of state characteristics that have a relationship to an execution. These are the states and events that are causally involved in the occurrence or nonoccurrence of the subgoals in the plan. We can call this the execution environment.

```
(forall (s p)                                                    (45.8)
  (iff (executionEnvironment s p)
       (exists (a g)
          (and (plan p a g)
               (forall (e)
                  (iff (member e s)
                       (exists (e1 e2)
                          (and (subgoalIn e1 p)(not' e2 e1)
                               (or (causallyInvolved e e1)
                                   (causallyInvolved e e2)))))))))))
```

In (executionEnvironment s p), p is a plan by agent a to achieve goal g (line 4), and s is the set of eventualities e which are causally involved in some subgoal e1 in p happening or not happening (lines 5–10).

A plan is enabled if all its preconditions hold.

```
(forall (p a g t)                                               (45.9)
  (iff (enabledPlan p a g t)
       (and (plan p a g)
            (forall (e) (if (precondition e p)(atTime e t))))))
```

To begin the execution of a plan is to execute an action in the left fringe of the plan.

```
(forall (a p)                                                   (45.10)
  (iff (beginExecute a p)
       (exists (g e s)
          (and (plan p a g)(member e s)(leftFringe s p)
               (execute a e p)))))
```

45.2 EXECUTIONS IN PROGRESS AND COMPLETED

The predicates execute and executePlan are defined in the abstract, without reference to specific times. At any given time t, an agent may be in the process of executing an action or a plan, and the agent may have completed an action or a plan. We will define time-dependent predicates using the present participle ("-ing") for the former (executing, executingPlan) and the past participle "-ed") for the latter (executed, executedPlan).

An agent is executing an action of a plan at time t if the execution takes place at that time.

```
(forall (a e1 p t)                                              (45.11)
  (iff (executing a e1 p t)
       (exists (e) (and (execute' e a e1 p)(atTime e t)))))
```

At any moment t an agent a can be executing one or more plans p. For a to execute plan p at time t is for a to be executing a subgoal of p at that time.

```
(forall (a p t)                                                 (45.12)
  (iff (executingPlan a p t)
       (exists (e1) (executing a e1 p t))))
```

We would like to be able to keep track of those parts of a plan that have already been completed. We can define a predicate executed saying that the execution of the action has already taken place by a particular time.

```
(forall (a e1 p t)                                              (45.13)
   (iff (executed a e1 p t)
        (exists (e t0)
             (and (execute' e a e1 p)(ends t0 e)
                  (before t0 t)))))
```

The purpose of the subgoals of a goal is to bring about the goal. Thus, a goal has been executed when all its subgoals have been executed and vice versa.

```
(forall (a e p t)                                               (45.14)
   (iff (executed a e p t)
        (forall (e1)
             (and (if (and (subgoal e1 e)(agentOf a e1))
                      (executed a e1 p t))
                  (if (and (subgoal e1 e)(not (agentOf a e1)))
                      (happensInTime e1 p))))))
```

The expression (executed a e p t) says that agent a has executed subgoal e of plan p by time t. Lines 4 and 5 say that a has executed all the actions a was agent of. Lines 6 and 7 say that all other events happened at the appropriate time.

Because of this rule, we can define an entire plan to have been executed when its top-level goal has been executed.

```
(forall (a p t)                                                 (45.15)
   (iff (executedPlan a p t)
        (exists (g) (and (plan p a g)(executed a g p t)))))
```

Now we can define the "remaining plan" p1 of plan p at time t as that part of p that has not yet been executed.

```
(forall (p1 a p t)                                              (45.16)
   (iff (remainingPlan p1 a p t)
        (exists (g s0 s s1)
             (and (plan p a g)(subgoalsOf s0 p)
                  (relationsOf s p)(relationsOf s1 p1)
                  (forall (e0)
                     (iff (subgoalIn e0 p1)
                          (or (and (subgoalIn e0 p)(agentOf a e0)
                                   (not (executed a e0 p t)))
                              (and (subgoalIn e0 p)
                                   (not (agentOf a e0))
                                   (exists (t1 e3)
                                        (and (begins' e3 e0 t1)
                                             (imply s0 e3)
                                             (before t t1)))))))
                  (forall (r e1 e2)
                     (iff (subgoal' r e1 e2)
                          (iff (member r s1)
                               (and (member r s)(subgoalIn e1 p1)
                                    (subgoalIn e2 p1)))))))))
```

The expression (remainingPlan p1 a p t) says that p1 is that part of agent a's plan p that remains to be done at time t. Line 4 says that p is a plan by a to achieve goal g; it also labels as s0 the set of subgoals of p. Line 5 labels the set of subgoal relations of p as s and the set of subgoal relations of p1 as s1. Lines 6–9 say that among the subgoals in p1 are the subgoals in p that have not yet been executed by a. Lines 10–15 say that among the subgoals of p1 are the subgoals of p that a is not the agent of and that must begin at some time t1 after t. Lines 16–20 specify the subgoal relations of p1 as those of p that are between subgoals that remain in p1.

There is a time that an agent begins the execution of a plan.

```
(forall (t1 e a p)                                              (45.17)
    (iff (executionStartTime t1 e a p)
         (and (executePlan' e a p)(begins t1 e))))
```

The expression (executionStartTime t1 e a p) says that t1 is the start time of execution e by agent a of plan p.

There is a time that an agent ends the execution of a plan. The definition is similar to that for executionStartTime.

```
(forall (t2 e a p)                                              (45.18)
    (iff (executionEndTime t2 e a p)
         (and (executePlan' e a p)(ends t2 e))))
```

There is a total duration for the amount of time that a plan has been being executed as of time t0.

```
(forall (d a p t0 u)                                           (45.19)
    (iff (executionDuration d a p t0 u)
         (exists (e t1 t)
             (and (executePlan' e a p)(executionStartTime t1 e a p)
                  (intervalBetween t t1 t0)(durationOf d t u)))))
```

The expression (executionDuration d a p t0 u) says that d is the duration in units u of agent a's execution of plan p as of time t0.

The concept of a deadline was defined in Chapter 42 on Scheduling. Agents can fail to execute a plan or subplan by its deadline.

```
(forall (a p)                                                  (45.20)
    (iff (missDeadline a p)
         (exists (t2)
             (and (deadline t2 p)
                  (not (exists (e t1)
                       (and (executePlan' e a p)
                            (executionEndTime t1 e a p)
                            (before t1 t2))))))))
```

That is, agent a misses the deadline for plan p if and only if there is a deadline t2 for p (line 4) and there is no execution e of the plan whose end time was before t2 (lines 5–8).

45.3 EXECUTION COSTS AND OUTCOMES

In Chapter 28 on Goals we developed a rudimentary theory of the cost of actions to an agent, in terms of what goals the action will force the agent to abandon. For example, if someone spends $30,000 on a car, he will not be able to spend that money on other things he wants. The cost scale we characterized is consistent with costs being amounts of money, but it is not restricted to that. We defined the predication (cost c e a) to mean "c is the cost of eventuality e to agent a."

The cost of an execution to an agent is easily expressed in terms of that predicate.

```
(forall (c e a p)                                        (45.21)
   (iff (executionCost c e a p)
        (and (executePlan' e a p)(cost c e a))))
```

The execution of a plan can result in the achievement of the goal.

```
(forall (e a p)                                          (45.22)
   (iff (executionSuccess e a p)
        (exists (g)
           (and (executePlan' e a p)(plan p a g)(cause e g)))))
```

The execution of a plan can fail to result in the achievement of the goal.

```
(forall (e a p)                                          (45.23)
   (iff (executionFailure e a p)
        (exists (g)
           (and (executePlan' e a p)(plan p a g)
                (not (cause e g))(not (Rexist g))))))
```

For the execution of a plan to fail, not only must the execution not cause the top-level goal to come about, the top-level goal also cannot come about for reasons unrelated to the plan.

45.4 ABSTRACT PLANS AND THEIR INSTANTIATIONS

Plans can be at various levels of specificity. In a more abstract plan the identity of some of the participants and props may be unspecified and the times of some of the actions may not be fixed. Once we add properties to the plan, by elaborating the subgoals of the plan, then we are creating a new plan that is an instantiation of the old plan.

```
(forall (p1 p)                                           (45.24)
   (iff (instantiatePlan p1 p)
        (exists (a g g1 s s1 r r1)
           (and (plan p a g)(plan p1 a g1)(imply g1 g)
                (subgoalsOf s p)(subgoalsOf s1 p1)
                (relationsOf r p)(relationsOf r1 p1)
                (subset s s1)(subset r r1))))))
```

That is, the goal g1 of the more specific plan p1 is something that entails the goal g of the more general plan p (line 4), and subgoals and subgoal relations in p are also in p1 (lines 5–7). Plan p1 fills in details of plan p, including possibly temporal constraints.

Two plans are the same abstract plan if all their nontemporal goals are the same. This means that they are both instantiations of the same nontemporal abstract plan.

This concept will allow us to talk about plans that are the same except that one is displaced in time with respect to the other.

```
(forall (p1 p2 p)                                              (45.25)
    (iff (sameAbstractPlan p1 p2 p)
         (exists (a g)
             (and (plan p1 a g)(plan p2 a g)
                  (instantiatePlan p1 p)(instantiatePlan p2 p)
                  (forall (e)
                      (if (subgoalIn e p)(nontemporal e)))))))
```

The expression (sameAbstractPlan p1 p2 p) says that plans p1 and p2 are instantiations of the same abstract plan p. Line 4 says that p1 and p2 have the same agent and the same goal. Line 5 says there is an abstract plan p that they both instantiate. Lines 6 and 7 say that abstract plan p has no temporal constraints.

People execute actions in plans.

```
(forall (a)                                                    (45.26)
    (if (person a)
        (exists (p e g)
            (and (plan p a g)(execute a e p)))))
```

People defeasibly execute the plans that they had scheduled to do.

```
(forall (a p g s e)                                            (45.27)
    (if (and (person a)(plan p a g)(scheduledPlan p)(leftFringe s p)
             (member e s)(etc))
        (execute a e p)))
```

This axiom only states that they defeasibly execute the left fringe of their scheduled plans, but once they do, they will defeasibly execute the left fringe of the remainder, so that defeasibly they will execute the entire scheduled plan.

A reusable plan is a plan that is sufficiently abstract that it can be instantiated at two different times.

```
(forall (p a g)                                                (45.28)
    (iff (reusablePlan p a g)
         (exists (p1 p2 t1 t2)
             (and (instantiatePlan p1 p)(instantiatePlan p2 p)
                  (timeSpanOf t1 p1)(timeSpanOf t2 p2)(nequal t1 t2)))))
```

An activity is an abstract plan that can be instantiated multiple times (i.e., is reusable) and is a plan that all members of a group s have.

```
(forall (p s)                                                  (45.29)
    (iff (activity p s)
         (exists (g)
             (forall (a)
                 (if (member a s)(reusablePlan p a g))))))
```

Executions of plans can be constrained by rules that agents are trying to follow. Where this is true, the instantiated rule can be included among the subgoals of the plan.

45.5 **PLANS AND ASPECT**

The ways in which eventualities can unfold in time often go under the name of "aspect." When we make aspectual statements about events, we look at the fine structure of the event as it is being executed and say something about that execution. The fine structure of events is captured in plans, or in an equivalent causal structure. Therefore, this is the place in a theory of commonsense knowledge where a theory of aspect goes. We have already laid out the necessary infrastructure, and we can define various aspectual predicates in terms of that. Here we define a number of concepts that relate the execution of plans to the passage of time.

To start a plan is to start to execute an action in its left fringe.

```
(forall (e0 a p)                                                    (45.30)
    (iff (start' e0 a p)
         (exists (e1 e s e2)
             (and (changeTo' e2 e1)(gen e2 e0)(execute' e1 a e p)(member e s)
                  (leftFringe s p)))))
```

Equivalently, to start a plan is to change to a state of executing the plan.

```
(forall (e0 a p)                                                    (45.31)
    (iff (start' e0 a p)
         (exists (e1 e2)
             (and (changeTo' e2 e1)(gen e2 e0)(executePlan' e1 a p)))))
```

To continue to execute a plan at time t is to execute an action in the left fringe of the remaining plan at time t.

```
(forall (a p t)                                                     (45.32)
    (iff (continue a p t)
         (exists (p1 s e)
             (and (remainingPlan p1 a p t)(leftFringe s p1)
                  (member e s)(executing a e p t)))))
```

Equivalently, to continue to execute a plan at time t is to be executing the plan at time t.

```
(forall (a p t)                                                     (45.33)
    (iff (continue a p t)(executingPlan a p t)))
```

To stop the execution of a plan is to change from executing it to not executing it.

```
(forall (e0 a p)                                                    (45.34)
    (iff (stop' e0 a p)
         (exists (e e1)
             (and (changeFrom' e1 e)(gen e1 e0)(executePlan' e a p)))))
```

To postpone the execution of a plan is to change the time at which the plan will start to be executed to a later time.

```
(forall (eo a p t1 t2)                                    (45.35)
   (iff (postpone' e0 a p t1 t2)
        (exists (e1 p1 e2 p2 e3 e4)
           (and (executePlan' e1 a p1)
                (executionStartTime t1 e1 a p1)
                (executePlan' e2 a p2)
                (executionStartTime t2 e2 a p2)
                (sameAbstractPlan p1 p2 p)
                (change' e3 e1 e2)(before t1 t2)
                (cause' e4 a e3)(gen e4 e0)))))
```

The expression (postpone' e0 a p t1 t2) says that e0 is the eventuality in which agent a postpones executing abstract plan p from time t1 to time t2. Lines 4–7 label the executions and start times of the two instantiations of plan p. Line 8 says these are both instantiations of p. Line 9 labels as e3 the change from one instantiation to the other, later one. Line 10 says that a's causing this change generates the postponing action.

To complete a plan is to cause a change into the state of having executed it.

```
(forall (e0 a p t)                                        (45.36)
   (iff (complete' e0 a p t)
        (exists (e1 e2 e3)
           (and (executedPlan' e1 a p t)(changeTo' e2 e1)
                (cause' e3 a e2)(gen e3 e0)))))
```

The completion of a plan and its success are independent notions. We can execute all the actions in a plan and yet have the plan fail for reasons beyond our efforts. We can also be in the midst of executing a plan and have the goal achieved, before we have actually performed all the actions in the plan that we thought were necessary.

To interrupt a plan is to cause the plan to stop without completing it.

```
(forall (e0 a p t)                                        (45.37)
   (iff (interrupt' e0 a p t)
        (exists (e1)
           (and (stop' e1 a p)(gen e1 e0)(atTime e0 t)
                (not (complete a p t))))))
```

To resume a plan is to start the remaining part of the plan after it has been interrupted.

```
(forall (e0 a p1 t2)                                      (45.38)
   (iff (resume' e0 a p1 t2)
        (exists (p2 t1 p3 p e1)
           (and (interrupt a p1 t1)(remainingPlan p2 a p1 t1)
                (sameAbstractPlan p3 p2 p)(before t1 t2)
                (start' e1 a p3)(gen e1 e0)(atTime e0 t2)))))
```

The expression (resume' e0 a p1 t2) says that e0 is the eventuality of agent a resuming original plan p1 at time t2. This holds if there was an interruption of p1 at time t1, before t2, where the remaining plan at that time was p2. There is a new instance p3 of the same abstract plan p as p2 that starts at time t2, and this starting generates the resumption.

To restart a plan is to start it from the beginning after having interrupted it.

```
(forall (e0 a p1 t2)                                        (45.39)
    (iff (restart' e0 a p1 t2)
        (exists (t1 p3 p e1)
            (and (interrupt a p1 t1)
                (sameAbstractPlan p3 p1 p)(before t1 t2)
                (start' e1 a p3)(gen e1 e0)(atTime e0 t2)))))
```

This definition differs from the definition of resume only in that the new plan p3 is an instantiation of the original plan p1 rather than of the remaining plan at the time of the interruption.

To pause in a plan is to stop and to resume. The stopping generates the pausing action, but the resuming has to occur at some subsequent point. It's possible to intend to pause but have it later turn out that it was merely a stopping because there was no resumption.

```
(forall (e0 a p t1)                                         (45.40)
    (iff (pause' e0 a p t1)
        (exists (t2 e1)
            (and (stop' e1 a p)(gen e1 e0)(atTime e0 t1)
                (resume a p t2)(before t1 t2)))))
```

The pause interval is the interval between the stop and the resumption.

```
(forall (t e1)                                              (45.41)
    (iff (pauseInterval t e1)
        (exists (a p t1 e2 t2)
            (and (pause' e1 a p t1)(atTime e1 t1)
                (resume' e2 a p t2)(before t1 t2)
                (forall (e3 t3)
                    (if (and (resume' e3 a p t3)(before t1 t3))
                        (or (equal e3 e2)(before t2 t3))))
                (intervalBetween t t1 t2)))))
```

The expression (pauseInterval t e1) says that interval t is the interval between the time t1 that a pause begins and the time t2 the execution of a plan resumes. Lines 4 and 5 label the pause event e1 and the resume event e2 and say that the former precedes the latter. Lines 6–8 say that e2 is the first such resume event.

The execution of a plan is ongoing for a time interval t if it is either being executed or there is a pause in its execution. That is, ongoing spans pauses.

```
(forall (a p t)                                             (45.42)
    (iff (ongoing a p t)
        (forall (t1)
            (if (insideTime t1 t)
                (or (executingPlan a p t1)
                    (pause a p t1))))))
```

That is, agent a's execution of plan p is ongoing during time interval t exactly when at all instants t1 inside t, there is an execution of p happening at t1 (line 5) or there is a pause happening at t1 (line 6).

Recall from Chapter 31 on Plans that to intend something is to have it as a subgoal in The Plan. To suspend the execution of a plan is to interrupt the execution of the plan with the intention of resuming it.

```
(forall (e a p t)                                           (45.43)
    (iff (suspend' e a p t)
        (exists (e1 t2 e2)
            (and (interrupt' e2 a p t)(gen e2 e)(intend a e1)
                (resume' e1 a p t2)))))
```

The distinction between pausing and suspending is that with suspending there is only the intention to resume. The plan may not actually be resumed. Something is not a pause unless the resumption actually happens.

To abort the execution of a plan is to interrupt the execution of the plan with the intention not to restart or resume it.

```
(forall (e0 a p t)                                          (45.44)
    (iff (abort' e0 a p t)
        (exists (e5)
            (and (interrupt' e5 a p t)(gen e5 e0)
                (forall (t2)
                    (if (before t t2)
                        (exists (e1 e2 e3 e4)
                            (and (intend a e1)(not' e1 e2)
                                (restart' e2 a p t2)
                                (intend a e3)(not' e3 e4)
                                (resume' e4 a p t2)))))))))
```

The expression (abort' e0 a p t) says that e0 is an aborting by agent a of the execution of plan p at time t. This holds if e0 is generated by an interruption by a of p at t (line 4) and for all subsequent times (lines 5–6), a intends not to restart (lines 7–9) or resume (lines 10–11) the execution of p.

A plan is terminated when it is completed or aborted.

```
(forall (e0 a p t)                                          (45.45)
    (iff (terminate' e0 a p t)
        (exists (e1)
            (and (or (complete' e1 a p t)(abort' e1 a p t))
                (gen e1 e0)))))
```

45.6 DISTRACTION

Distraction happens when there is a change for an agent from thinking of one thing x to thinking of another thing y, where some property of y (e.g., its proximity to the agent) plays a causal role in the change.

```
(forall (e a x y)                                           (45.46)
    (iff (distract' e a x y)
        (exists (e1 e2 e0 e3)
            (and (change' e3 e1 e2)(gen e3 e)(thinkOf' e1 a x)
                (thinkOf' e2 a y)
                (arg* y e0)(causallyInvolved e0 e3)))))
```

When someone is executing an action in the service of a plan, then defeasibly they are thinking of both the action and the plan.

```
(forall (a e1 p)                                          (45.47)
    (if (and (execute a e1 p)(etc))
        (and (thinkOf a e1)(thinkOf a p))))
```

It is a defeasible inference that if something distracts us while we are executing a plan, it will cause us to suspend that plan.

```
(forall (e1 a p y t)                                      (45.48)
    (if (and (executingPlan a p t)(distract' e1 a p y)
             (atTime e1 t)(etc))
        (exists (e2)
            (and (suspend' e2 a p t)(cause e1 e2)))))
```

The antecedent (lines 2–3) says that agent a is executing plan p at time t and is distracted by y at time t. The consequent (lines 4–5) says that this distraction e1 causes a's suspension e2 of the execution of plan p.

PREDICATES INTRODUCED IN THIS CHAPTER

(leftFringe s p)
 Set s is the left fringe of plan p, consisting of those subgoals that can be executed first.

(precondition e p)
 Eventuality e is a precondition of plan p if it must happen or hold before the execution of p begins.

(satisfiedPrecondition e p t)
 Precondition e of plan p holds at time t.

(unsatisfiedPrecondition e p t)
 Precondition e of plan p does not hold at time t.

(violatePrecondition e p t)
 There is a change at time t from precondition e of plan p being satisfied to its not being satisfied.

(executionEnvironment s p)
 Set s consists of the eventualities relevant to the achievement of the subgoals of plan p.

(enabledPlan p a g t)
 All of the preconditions of agent a's plan p to achieve goal g are satisfied at time t.

(beginExecute a p)
 Agent a begins to execute plan p.

(executing a e1 p t)
 Agent a is executing subgoal e1 in plan p at time t.

(executingPlan a p t)
 Agent a is executing plan p at time t.

(executed a e1 p t)
  Agent a has executed subgoal e1 of plan p by time t.

(executedPlan a p t)
  Agent a has executed plan p by time t.

(remainingPlan p1 a p t)
  Plan p1 is the part of agent a's plan p that remains to be done at time t.

(executionStartTime t1 e a p)
  Time t1 is the start time of execution e by agent a of plan p.

(executionEndTime t2 e a p)
  Time t2 is the end time of execution e by agent a of plan p.

(executionDuration d a p t0 u)
  The number d is the duration in time units u of the execution of agent a's plan p
  up until time t0.

(missDeadline a p)
  Agent a misses the deadline associated with plan p.

(executionCost c e a p)
  Cost c is the cost to agent a of execution e of a's plan p.

(executionSuccess e a p)
  Execution e of agent a's plan p brings about p's top-level goal.

(executionFailure e a p)
  Execution e of agent a's plan p was carried out, but the top-level goal did not
  come about.

(instantiatePlan p1 p)
  Plan p1 is a more specific version of plan p.

(sameAbstractPlan p1 p2 p)
  Plans p1 and p2 are instantiations of the same abstract plan p.

(reusablePlan p a g)
  Plan p is an abstract plan that can be reused at different times by agent a for
  achieving goal g.

(activity p s)
  Plan p is a reusable plan that can be executed by any agent in set s.

(start a p)
  Agent a starts the execution of plan p.

(continue a p t)
  Agent a continues the execution of plan p at time t.

(stop a p)
  Agent a stops the execution of plan p.

(postpone a p t1 t2)
  Agent a postpones the execution of plan p from time t1 to time t2.

(complete a p t)
  Agent a completes the execution of plan p at time t.

(interrupt a p t)
  Agent a interrupts the execution of plan p at time t.

(resume a p1 t2)
>   Agent a resumes the execution of plan p1 at time t2.

(restart a p1 t2)
>   Agent a restarts the execution of plan p1 at time t2.

(pause a p t1)
>   Agent a pauses at time t1 in the execution of plan p.

(pauseInterval t e1)
>   Time interval t is the time between a pausing event e1 and the end of the pause.

(ongoing a p t)
>   At time t, agent a's plan p is being executed or there is a pause in its execution.

(suspend a p t)
>   Agent a suspends the execution of plan p at time t.

(abort a p t)
>   Agent a aborts the execution of plan p at time t.

(terminate a p t)
>   Agent a completes or aborts the execution of plan p at time t.

(distract a x y)
>   Agent a is distracted from x by y.

46

Repetitive Execution

Many of the actions we perform in life have a repetitive structure. In this chapter we define a number of concepts related to repetitive executions of plans. Much of this depends on the event structures we developed in Chapter 17.

A composite execution e of a plan p is a repetition structure of the execution e1 of some subplan p1 of p if e has the structure of a repeatUntil, with e1 as its body. The repeatUntil also has a termination condition c.

```
(forall (a e e1 c p)                                        (46.1)
   (iff (repetition a e e1 c p)
        (exists (g p1 e3)
           (and (repeatUntil' e3 e1 c)(executePlan e a p)(gen e3 e)
                (plan p a g)(subplan p1 p)
                (forall (e2)
                   (if (executePlan' e2 a p1)
                       (instance e2 e1)))))))
```

The expression (repetition a e e1 c p) says that agent a's execution e of plan p is a repetition of executions e1 until condition c is satisfied. Line 4 says that e3 has the structure of a "repeat until" and generates the execution of plan p. Lines 5–8 say that there is a subplan p1 of p such that every execution e2 of it is an instance of e1.

Any instance of the body is "a repetition" of the process.

```
(forall (e2 e)                                              (46.2)
   (iff (aRepetition e2 e)
        (exists (a e1 c p)
           (and (repetition a e e1 c p)(instance e2 e1)))))
```

In executing a repetitive plan or process, the start of the process is the first execution of the body.

```
(forall (e2 e)                                              (46.3)
   (iff (startRepetition e2 e)
        (exists (a e1 c p)
```

478

```
        (and (repetition a e e1 c p)(instance e2 e1)
             (forall (e3)
                 (if (instance e3 e1)
                     (or (equal e3 e2)(before e2 e3)))))))))
```

The expression (startRepetition e2 e) says that execution e2 is the first repetition of the body of e.

In executing a repetitive plan or process, the termination of the process is the last execution of the body.

```
(forall (e2 e)                                                       (46.4)
    (iff (terminateRepetition e2 e)
         (exists (a e1 c p)
             (and (repetition a e e1 c p)(instance e2 e1)
                  (forall (e3)
                      (if (instance e3 e1)
                          (or (equal e3 e2)(before e3 e2))))))))
```

While executing a repetitive plan, an intermediate repetition is one that is not a start or terminate repetition.

```
(forall (e2 e)                                                       (46.5)
    (iff (intermediateRepetition e2 e)
         (exists (a e1 c p)
             (and (repetition a e e1 c p)(instance e2 e1)
                  (not (startRepetition e2 e))
                  (not (terminateRepetition e2 e))))))
```

Any repetitive event has a time span, and we can talk about the state of the repetition at any instant t within that time span. In particular, there are the executions of the body that have been completed and those remaining that have yet to be executed.

```
(forall (s e t)                                                      (46.6)
    (iff (completedRepetitions s e t)
         (and (repetition a e e1 c p)
              (forall (e2)
                  (iff (member e2 s)
                       (and (aRepetition e2 e)
                            (executed a e2 p t)))))))
```

```
(forall (s e t)                                                      (46.7)
    (iff (remainingRepetitions s e t)
         (and (repetition a e e1 c p)
              (forall (e2)
                  (iff (member e2 s)
                       (and (aRepetition e2 e)
                            (not (executed a e2 p t))))))))
```

There may or may not be a current repetition of the body at any given time t in the time span of the repetitive cycle.

```
(forall (e2 e t)                                                    (46.8)
    (iff (currentRepetition e2 e t)
        (exists (a e1 c p t1 t2)
            (and (repetition a e e1 c p)(aRepetition e2 e)
                (begins t1 e2)(before t1 t)
                (ends t2 e2)(before t t2)))))
```

At any given time after the first repetition, there is a previous repetition.

```
(forall (e2 e t)                                                    (46.9)
    (iff (previousRepetition e2 e t)
        (exists (a e1 c p t2 e0 t0)
            (and (repetition a e e1 c p)(aRepetition e2 e)
                (ends t2 e2)(before t2 t)
                (startRepetition e0 e)(ends t0 e0)(before t0 t)
                (not (exists (e3 t3)
                        (and (aRepetition e3 e)(nequal e3 e2)
                            (ends t3 e3)(before t2 t3)
                            (before t3 t)))))))))
```

The expression (previousRepetition e2 e t) says that e2 is the repetition of the body of repetitive execution e previous to time t. Line 4 states these constraints on e and e2. Line 5 says that e2 ends before t. Line 6 says that t comes after the first repetition. Lines 7–10 say that there are no intervening repetitions between e2 and t.

At any given time before the last repetition, there is a next repetition. The axiom for this predicate is similar.

```
(forall (e2 e t)                                                    (46.10)
    (iff (nextRepetition e2 e t)
        (exists (a e1 c p t2 e0 t0)
            (and (repetition a e e1 c p)(aRepetition e2 e)
                (begins t2 e2)(before t t2)
                (terminateRepetition e0 e)(begins t0 e0)
                (before t t0)
                (not (exists (e3 t3)
                        (and (aRepetition e3 e)(nequal e3 e2)
                            (begins t3 e3)(before t3 t2)
                            (before t t3)))))))))
```

At any given time, there is a quantity that is the number of times a repetitive event has been executed.

```
(forall (n e t)                                                    (46.11)
    (iff (repetitionsCount n e t)
        (exists (a e1 c p s)
            (and (repetition a e e1 c p)
                (completedRepetitions s e t)(card n s)))))
```

Sometimes in a repetitive process, the body is applied to every element of a sequence in turn. To apply an abstract event type with a distinguished abstract participant to a sequence of entities of the same type is to perform a substitution of the entities for the distinguished abstract participant.

```
(forall (e e1 x s s1)                                          (46.12)
   (iff (iterationThru e e1 x s s1)
        (and (arg* x e1)(sequence s)(sequence s1)
             (forall (y) (if (inSeq y s)(instance y x)))
             (forall (e2 n)
                (iff (nth e2 n s1)
                     (exists (y)
                        (and (nth y n s)
                             (subst x e1 y e2)))))))))
```

The expression (iterationThru e e1 x s s1) says that e is an iteration through the elements of sequence s, where the entity x plays a role in e1 and the sequence s1 consists of instantiations of e1 in which x's role is played by the successive elements of s. Line 3 says that x plays a role in e1 and that s and s1 are sequences. Line 4 says that s consists of instances y of x. Lines 5–9 say that s1 consists of the instances of e1 in which the role of x in e1 is played by the successive elements y in the elements e2 of s1. For example, suppose a father wants to kiss each of his four children. x is the generic child; the y's are the specific children, Matthew, Mark, etc., and s is the sequence of these children. e1 is the abstract act of kissing a child; the e2's are the four specific acts of kissing specific children, and s1 is the sequence of these specific acts.

In executing an iterative plan, one has to start at the beginning.

```
(forall (e2 e)                                                 (46.13)
   (iff (startIterationThru e2 e)
        (exists (e1 x s s1)
           (and  (iterationThru e e1 x s s1)(first e2 s1)))))
```

We can define completed iterations in the same way as we defined completed repetitions above.

```
(forall (s0 e t)                                               (46.14)
   (iff (completedIterationsThru s0 e t)
        (exists (e1 x s s1)
            (and (iterationThru e e1 x s s1)
                 (forall (e2)
                    (iff (member e2 s0)
                         (exists (t2)
                            (and (member e2 s1)(ends t2 e2)
                                 (before t2 t)))))))))
```

In executing an iterative plan, one can move on to the next iteration.

```
(forall (e3 a e t)                                             (46.15)
   (iff (doNextIterationThru' e3 a e t)
        (exists (e1 x s s1 p)
            (and (iterationThru e e1 x s s1)
                 (execute a e3 p)
                 (nextRepetition e3 e t)))))
```

The expression (doNextIterationThru' e3 a e t) says that e3 is the execution by agent a of the next iteration in the iterationThru e at time t.

In executing an iterative plan, one can abort before completely iterating through the entire set of values.

```
(forall (a e t)                                                    (46.16)
    (iff (abortIterationThru a e t)
        (exists (e1 x s s1 p)
            (and (iterationThru e e1 x s s1)
                 (executePlan' e a p)
                 (abort a p t)))))
```

The expression (abortIterationThru a e t) says that agent a aborts iteration e at time t before the entire sequence s of entities has been dealt with. Line 4 says e is an iterationThru. Line 5 labels the plan p that e is an execution of. Line 6 says that agent a aborts that plan at time t.

In executing an iterative plan, one can come to the end of the iteration. The axiom for this is similar to the previous one.

```
(forall (a e t)                                                    (46.17)
    (iff (completeIterationThru a e t)
        (exists (e1 x s s1 p)
            (and (iterationThru e e1 x s s1)
                 (executePlan' e a p)
                 (executedPlan a p t)))))
```


PREDICATES INTRODUCED IN THIS CHAPTER

(repetition a e e1 c p)
  Agent a's execution e of plan p is a repetition of executions of body e1 until condition c is satisfied.

(aRepetition e2 e)
  Execution e2 is an instance of the body of repetitive execution e.

(startRepetition e2 e)
  Execution e2 is the first instance of the body of repetitive execution e.

(terminateRepetition e2 e)
  Execution e2 is the last instance of the body of repetitive execution e.

(intermediateRepetition e2 e)
  Execution e2 is an intermediate instance of the body of repetitive execution e.

(completedRepetitions s e t)
  Set s is the set of repetitions of repetitive execution e that have been completed by time t.

(remainingRepetitions s e t)
  Set s is the set of repetitions of repetitive execution e that remain to be done at time t.

(currentRepetition e2 e t)
  Execution e2 is the current repetition in repetitive execution e at time t.

(previousRepetition e2 e t)

Execution e2 is the previous repetition in repetitive execution e at time t.

(nextRepetition e2 e t)

Execution e2 is the next repetition in repetitive execution e at time t.

(repetitionsCount n e t)

Integer n is the number of times the body of repetitive execution e has been executed by time t.

(iterationThru e e1 x s s1)

Execution e is an iteration through the elements of sequence s, where the entity x plays a role in the body e1 of e and the sequence s1 consists of instantiations of e1 in which x's role is played by the successive elements of s.

(startIterationThru e2 e)

Execution e2 is the first iteration in the iterationThru e.

(completedIterationsThru s0 e t)

Set s0 is the set of iterations through the iterationThru e that have been completed by time t.

(doNextIterationThru' e3 a e t)

Action e3 is agent a's execution of the next iteration of the iterationThru e at time t.

(abortIterationThru a e t)

Agent a aborts iterationThru e at time t before the entire sequence of entities has been dealt with.

(completeIterationThru a e t)

Agent a completes iterationThru e at time t when all the entities have been dealt with.

47

Mind–Body Interaction

47.1 INTRODUCTION

The English language is rich with words and phrases with meaning that is grounded in a commonsense theory of the interaction between the mind and the body. Concerning the mind's control of the body, we speak of motion that is dexterous, graceful, and nimble, or alternatively, awkward and clumsy. When the body moves without volition, we speak of spasms, reflexes, and stumbles. Concerning the perception of the world through the body to the mind, we speak of sensations and hallucinations. More subtly, we speak of the control that we have over our perceptions, as when we tune out distractions and pay attention to something. Conversely, we speak of the perception that we have of our own actions, when doing something feels unnatural or uncomfortable, or when we get the hang of doing something. When the normal functioning of the mind, the body, control, or perception is interrupted, we speak of being paralyzed, dazed, numb, asleep, knocked out, deaf, and tired, among a wide range of other mind–body states. In this chapter, our aim is to provide a theory that is rich enough to capture subtle differences in the meaning of these and other concepts.

Among the perils of formalizing a logical theory of mind–body interaction is the risk of trivializing the scholarship of generations of philosophers who have devoted their life's work to this topic, specifically within the field of philosophy of mind. Chalmers (2002) reviews the rich history of philosophical debate on this topic, and outlines the various positions that different philosophers have taken. The classic dualism offered in Descartes' *Meditations on First Philosophy* (2002) views a person as having both a physical body and a nonphysical mind. Descartes' views are further characterized as interactionalism, in that the mind and body interact in both directions. Huxley (1874) offers an alternative view of dualism, epiphenomenalism, where this interaction is only in the direction from the body to the mind. Ryle (1949) begins a philosophical shift away from dualism toward behavioralism, the view that the mind is not to be seen as something distinct from the body and steering it from inside, but as an aspect of the body's own activities. The influence of neuroscience can be seen in the Identity Theory, put forth by Place (1956) and refined by Smart (1959),

The chapter contains revisions of material published previously in Gordon and Hobbs (2011).

which holds that mental states are identical to their associated brain states: they are one and the same. Putnam (1973) argued against this view, noting that it is plausible that mental states are realizable by multiple brain states, and instead advanced the view of functionalism. Here mental states are seen as more abstract than their biological or mechanical realization, a view that has significant influence in contemporary artificial intelligence and cognitive science.

Our aim, however, is not to encode a theory that reflects contemporary scientific or philosophical views of the nature of mind–body interaction, but rather to explicate the commonsense theory that nonscientists use to make everyday inferences. The result is a theory that most resembles Descartes' dualism and interactionalism, where a physical body and a nonphysical mind interact in both directions.

47.2 MIND AND BODY

Recall from Chapter 19 that we said a person has a body and a mind, and that the body has body parts. We specified that the body is a physical object. It seems most congruent with common sense to say that the mind is not a physical object.

```
(forall (m p)                                              (47.1)
    (if (mind m p)
        (not (physobj m))))
```

Arms, legs, heads, ears, tongues, vocal cords, and so on are body parts. A detailed explication of the body would be a part of a commonsense theory of anatomy and will not be done here. Body parts are capable of actions, many of them under voluntary control. Most body parts provide sensory information to the mind, including kinesthetic, pressure, and temperature information. Some body parts such as the eyes provide other specific kinds of information. Thus, we need to explicate the relation of the mind to bodily actions and to sensory information from body parts.

We restrict our discussion to persons, rather than to agents more generally. So we do not include the wider range of nonhuman entities that are typically discussed in formalizations of agent-based theories, such as organizations and machines. Some of these agents may be seen as having minds and many certainly have various sensors and effectors. But all this would have to be axiomatized separately.

47.3 AWARENESS AND FOCUSING

In our theory of memory in Chapter 23, we distinguished between the focus of attention and the memory. Concepts pass back and forth between the two all the time. We are conscious of what is in the focus of attention.

It is sometimes convenient to distinguish a third, intermediate "region" of the mind, one's awareness.

```
(forall (m p)                                              (47.2)
    (if (and (person p)(mind m p))
        (exists (a)
            (awareness a m))))
```

Concepts that are merely in awareness will include those that we are only peripherally aware of. Someone typing at a terminal will be focussed on the text that he or she is typing, but merely aware of the overhead light. There is a distinction between being aware of something and being unconscious of it. Our typist will be aware of the light, but perhaps not aware of someone who has just slipped into the room.

As with the focus of attention and the memory, it is convenient to allow either awareness or the person to be the second argument of the predicate.

```
(forall (p m a)                                              (47.3)
   (if (and (person p)(mind m p))
       (iff (awareness a p)(awareness a m))))
```

In Chapter 21 we introduced the predicate inm for "mentally in." Concepts can be mentally in the focus of attention, awareness, or memory.

```
(forall (x y)                                                (47.4)
   (if (inm x y)
       (exists (p)
           (or (focusOfAttention y p)(awareness y p)(memory y p)))))
```

It seems reasonable to make the focus of attention a part of awareness.

```
(forall (x p)                                                (47.5)
   (if (inFocus x p)
       (exists (a)
           (and (awareness a p)(inm x a)))))
```

If a concept x is in focus, it is also in awareness.

In Chapter 24 on Envisioning we defined the predicate thinkOf to mean to have a concept in the focus of attention. People can, by simply willing it, cause themselves to think of a particular concept. We can call this concentration.

```
(forall (e p x)                                              (47.6)
   (iff (concentrate' e p x)
       (exists (e1 e2)
           (and (thinkOf' e2  p x)(gen e2 e)(will' e1 p e2)(dcause e1 e2)))))
```

Willing one's self to think of something directly causes it.

47.4 PERCEPTION

In Chapter 19 on Persons we introduced the predicate perceive and stated three of its properties: that what we perceive is external to the mind; that an entity's being near a person enables perception of the entity; and that intact sense organs enable perception.

Axiom 21.9 in Chapter 21 on Knowledge Management expresses the principal property of perception, that perceiving is defeasibly believing. Here we can state two similar, more fine-grained properties of perception. If something is perceived, that causes it to be in one's awareness.

```
(forall (e p x a)                                            (47.7)
   (if (and (perceive' e p x)(person p)(awareness a p))
       (exists (e1)
           (and (inm' e1 x a)(cause e e1)))))
```

If something is perceived, then defeasibly it is part of one's focus of attention.

```
(forall (e p x m a)                                    (47.8)
   (if (and (perceive' e p x)(person p)(etc))
       (exists (e1)
          (and (inFocus' e1 x p)(cause e e1)))))
```

Sense organs were introduced in Chapter 19 as a subset of body parts whose intactness enables perception (Axiom 19.12). We can also state a converse rule, namely, that all perception is enabled by the intactness of some sense organ.

```
(forall (e p x)                                        (47.9)
   (if (and (perceive' e p x)(person p))
       (exists (y)
          (and (intact' e1 y)(senseOrgan y p)(enable e1 e)))))
```

People have various senses, including vision, hearing, taste, and smell, and we can categorize the corresponding sense organs as sense organs.

```
(forall (y p) (if (eye y p)(senseOrgan y p)))          (47.10)
```

```
(forall (y p) (if (ear y p)(senseOrgan y p)))          (47.11)
```

```
(forall (y p) (if (tongue y p)(senseOrgan y p)))       (47.12)
```

```
(forall (y p) (if (nose y p)(senseOrgan y p)))         (47.13)
```

In the absence of a richer commonsense physics, we can distinguish among the types of sensations by the sense organ that perceives them.

Perception happens when the world's stimulation of the body through sense organs causes it.

```
(forall (e x p)                                        (47.14)
   (if (and (stimulate' e x p)(person p)(etc))
       (exists (e1)
          (and (perceive' e1 p x)(cause e e1)))))
```

The predicate stimulate is meant to connote events where the world activates some sensory capacity of a person, for example, when light hits their eyes, sound vibrates their eardrums, or objects pass across their skin. Elaborating on exactly what is sensed by each of the sense organs would take us into commonsense physics, so we will leave underspecified the sorts of states and events that can stimulate the body. A richer theory could distinguish between eventualities that are perceptible to people, for example, generating sounds loud enough to be heard or reflecting enough light into the eyes. Here we deal with perception at an abstract level and state what is common to all modalities. The advantage of having the predicate stimulate is that it can be explicated in terms external to the mind, that is, in terms of an object's location with respect to a person's body, and its visual and aural properties.

People can directly cause themselves, by an act of will, to focus on the sensations of a particular sense organ. For example, people can block out ambient noise and focus on the book in front of them.

```
(forall (e p y)                                                    (47.15)
   (iff (attendToSense' e p y)
        (exists (e1 x e2 e3 e4)
           (and (perceive' e1 p x)(person p)
                (senseOrgan y p)(intact' e3 y)(enable e3 e1)
                (will' e2 p e4)(dcause e2 e4)
                           (concentrate' e4 p x)(gen e4 e)))))
```

That is, the event e of a person p attending to sensory channel y is the act of concentration or focusing on x, the content of a perceiving via sensory channel y, where this concentration is caused by an act of will. The sensory channel y is the sense organ whose intactness plays a causal role in the perception occurring.

47.5 BODILY ACTIONS

A bodily action by a person is a movement of one or more of the person's body parts.

```
(forall (e p)                                                      (47.16)
   (iff (bodilyAction e p)
        (exists (x y z)
           (and (person p)(bodyPart x p)(move' e x y z)))))
```

There is a range in the voluntary character of bodily actions. If a car hits a man and he goes flying through the air, his body parts are moving from one place to another, so under our current definition it would be a bodily action. But all the causality is provided by the external world.

In a reflex action, such as a kick resulting from a tap on the knee or blinking caused by a sudden flash of light, the external world provides some of the causality and the body provides the rest, but the conscious mind is not involved. It is directly caused by a stimulation from the environment, that is, by the motion of some entity (a hammer, a beam of light) from somewhere outside a body part to the body part, where some property of the body part enables the bodily action. (This last condition rules out being hit by a car as a reflex.) But the action is not willed.

```
(forall (e p)                                                      (47.17)
   (iff (reflex e p)
        (exists (e1 x1 y1 z1 s e2)
           (and (bodilyAction e p)(move' e1 x1 y1 z1)
                (not (at y1 p s))(bodyPart z1 p)(cause e1 e)
                (arg* z1 e2)(enable e2 e)
                (not (exists (e3)
                           (and (will' e3 p e)(dcause e3 e)))))))))
```

The expression (reflex e p) says that event e is a reflex action by person p. Lines 4 and 5 say that there is the motion e1 of some entity x1 from some external point y1 to one of p's body parts z1 which causes the reflex action e. Line 6 says there is some property e2 of z1 that enables the reflex action. Lines 7 and 8 say that there is no action e3 of p willing e to happen that directly causes the reflex action.

In the case of a twitch or a tic, the body is providing all the causality, and there is no external stimulation, but the mind is not involved. The person does not will the bodily action to occur. Let us call such an action a "tic."

```
(forall (e p)                                              (47.18)
   (iff (tic e p)
        (exists (b e2)
            (and (bodilyAction e p)(not (reflex e p))
                 (body b p)(arg* b e2)(enable e2 e)
                 (not (exists (e3)
                       (and (will' e3 p e)(dcause e3 e))))))))
```

The expression (tic e p) says that bodily action e is a tic (or involuntary movement) by person p. Line 4 says e is not a reflex (i.e., it does not have a cause external to the body). Line 5 says that there is some property e2 of p's body b that enables the tic to occur. Lines 6 and 7 say that there is no act of the will e3 that directly causes e.

The most interesting case of bodily actions is the voluntary actions. These constitute, after perception, the second principal channel between the body and the mind. They are how the mind controls the body. A voluntary action is one in which an act of will plays a direct causal role in the occurrence of the action.

```
(forall (e p)                                              (47.19)
   (iff (voluntaryAction e p)
        (exists (e3)
            (and (bodilyAction e p)
                 (will' e3 p e)(dcause e3 e)))))
```

Defeasibly, a voluntary action is an execution of a plan.

```
(forall (e p)                                              (47.20)
   (if (and (voluntaryAction e p)(etc))
       (exists (q)
          (executePlan' e p q))))
```

That plan is defeasibly a subplan of a larger plan.

```
(forall (e p)                                              (47.21)
   (if (and (voluntaryAction e p)(etc))
       (exists (e0 q)
          (execute' e p e0 q))))
```

In this axiom q is larger plan the voluntary action e is in the service of, and e0 is the subgoal in q that e accomplishes.

An involuntary bodily action is a bodily action that is either a reflex or a tic. The body plays a causal role in the action, but an act of will does not.

```
(forall (e p)                                              (47.22)
   (iff (involuntaryAction e p)
        (or (reflex e p)(tic e p))))
```

To control the body is to engage in voluntary bodily actions.

```
(forall (p b)                                            (47.23)
  (iff (controlBody p b)
       (and (person p)(body b p)
            (exists (e)
                (voluntaryAction e p)))))
```

People are capable of coordinated action of various body parts. Coordination involves the motion of more than one body part where the time of occurrence of the motion of one part plays a causal role in the time of occurrence of the motion of another.

```
(forall (e p)                                            (47.24)
  (iff (coordinatedAction e p)
       (exists (e1 e2 e3 e4 t1 t2)
           (and (bodilyAction e1 p)(subevent e1 e)
                (atTime' e3 e1 t1)
                (bodilyAction e2 p)(subevent e2 e)
                (atTime' e4 e2 t2)
                (causallyInvolved e3 e4)))))
```

The expression (coordinatedAction e p) says that e is a coordinated bodily action by person p. Lines 4–7 identify two subevents e1 and e2 of e and the properties e3 and e4 of their occurring at particular times t1 and t2. Line 8 says that e1's happening at the right time is causally involved in e2's happening at the right time.

Bodily actions generally involve the contraction of muscles, as when someone clenches their fist to squeeze a sponge. However, this action may not result in motion of the hand, e.g. if instead one tries to squeeze a rock. In this theory, the bodily action (squeezing the rock) occurs in accordance with a person's will even if the intended result of the action (crushing a rock) fails to occur. But we can classify voluntary actions as successes or failures.

Bodily actions can fail in one of two ways. First, the willing can fail to directly cause the body part to move, as when one tries to move a paralyzed limb.

```
(forall (e p e1)                                         (47.25)
  (if (and (will' e1 p e)(bodilyAction e p)(not (dcause e1 e)))
      (failedBodilyAction e p)))
```

The second way a voluntary bodily action can fail is for the willing to succeed in causing the body part to move, but some higher-level goal that the bodily action was supposed to be in service of is not thereby brought about.

```
(forall (e p e1 e2)                                      (47.26)
  (if (and (will' e1 p e)(bodilyAction e p)(dcause e1 e)
           (subgoal e e2) (not (cause e e2)))
      (failedBodilyAction e p)))
```

Line 2 says that the act of will e1 directly causes bodily action e. Line 3 says that the goal e2 failed to be brought about by e.

A successful bodily action is one that is successfully willed and succeeds in achieving its purpose.

```
(forall (e p e1 e2)                                      (47.27)
    (if (and (will' e1 p e)(bodilyAction e p)(dcause e1 e)
            (subgoal e e2)(cause e e2))
        (successfulBodilyAction e p)))
```

Line 2 says that the act of will e1 directly causes bodily action e. Line 3 says that the goal e2 was brought about by e.

A voluntary action is fluent if it is skilled. The predicate skilled is defined in Chapter 48 on Observation of Plan Executions.

```
(forall (e p)                                            (47.28)
    (iff (fluentAction e p)
        (exists (q)
            (and (voluntaryAction e p)(executePlan' e p q)
                (skilled e q)))))
```

Here q is the plan (or subplan) that the action e is executing.

A voluntary action is awkward if it is in the low region of the skill scale.

```
(forall (e p)                                            (47.29)
    (iff (awkwardAction e p)
        (exists (q s s1)
            (and (voluntaryAction e p)(executePlan' e p q)
                (skillScale s q)(Lo s1 s)(inScale e s1)))))
```

In this axiom, e is a voluntary action by person p. Scale s is the skill scale for the plan q that e is the execution of, s1 is the scale's low region, and e is in that region.

47.6 PERCEIVING BODILY ACTIONS

Among the phenomena we can perceive are some of our own bodily actions. Our kinesthetic sense enables awareness of the position and movement of parts of the body by means of proprioceptors in the muscles and joints. Certainly there are some bodily actions we are not aware of, such as the normal working of our digestive systems or our heart, or the circulation of the blood in our cardiovascular system.

We will say that a bodily action defeasibly causes a person to perceive it.

```
(forall (e p)                                            (47.30)
    (if (and (bodilyAction e p)(etc))
        (perceive p e)))
```

If it is a voluntary action, we can state a nondefeasible rule.

```
(forall (e p)                                            (47.31)
    (if (voluntaryAction e p)(perceive p e)))
```

The kinesthetic sense provides feedback as to the extent to which the actual bodily action matches the intended bodily action.

The resulting perception can often be characterized in a variety of ways, for example, as fluent, awkward, dexterous, uncomfortable, and so on. Sometimes, people just feel that a bodily action "feels weird." We began to characterize these states above in terms of a person's skill in carrying out voluntary action.

47.7 CONTROLLING PERCEPTION

Among the body parts that can be moved in a voluntary action are the sense organs. We can direct our gaze and focus our eyes onto a particular object in the environment, or we can look away from it. We can touch something to see how it feels, or retract our hand if it feels slimy. We can cup our ears to hear something better, or change the orientation of our head to determine the direction of a sound better, or plug up our ears with our fingers to avoid hearing the sound. We can flare our nostrils to smell something better or hold our noses to not smell it. The purpose of all these actions is to perceive something we would not otherwise perceive or to avoid perceiving something we would otherwise perceive. We can call these actions "sense organ actions."

```
(forall (e p)                                                    (47.32)
   (iff (senseOrganAction e p)
        (exists (x y z e1 w)
           (and (person p)(senseOrgan x p)(move' e x y z)
                (or (and (enable e e1)(perceive' e1 p w))
                    (and (enable e e2)(not' e2 e1)))))))
```

The expression (senseOrganAction e p) says that e is a bodily action by person p of moving a sense organ x from y to z, where in line 5 that action enables p to perceive something w, or in line 6 to not perceive it.

It is not always by changing the location or orientation of a sense organ that we control what we perceive. We are often able to perceive more or less by a sheer act of will. We may notice previously unseen things in our environment simply because we have a heightened awareness. We can listen intently to a distant conversation, blocking out ambient noise. We can try to ignore a pain. We can sometimes shut out annoying sounds. We can "tune" things in and out. Probably when we do this, the perceptions are always in our awareness, but we are moving them in and out of our focus of attention.

To tune into a perception is to cause it to be in the focus of attention by an act of will.

```
(forall (p s)                                                    (47.33)
   (iff (tuneIn p x)
        (exists (e1 e2)
           (and (person p)(perceive p x)
                (will' e1 p e2)(inFocus' e2 x p)(dcause e1 e2)))))
```

The action of "tuning out" a perception is causing it not to be in one's focus of attention by an act of will.

```
(forall (p s)                                                    (47.34)
   (iff (tuneOut p x)
        (exists (e1 e2 e3)
           (and (person p)(perceive p x)
                (will' e1 p e3)(not' e3 e2)(inFocus' e2 x p)
                (dcause e1 e3)))))
```

Unfortunately tuning in and tuning out do not always work.

47.8 LEVELS OF CAPABILITY AND ACTIVITY

In Chapter 28 on Goals we defined what it is for a functional composite entity to be intact, namely, for each of its functional components to be able to execute its function. Such an entity is "impaired" when some of its functional components are not able to achieve their functionality.

```
(forall (x)                                                    (47.35)
    (iff (impaired x)
        (exists (e1 y e e2 e3)
            (and (functionality e1 y e x)
                (arg* y e2)(not' e3 e1)(cause e2 e3)))))
```

This says that an entity x is impaired if there is some functionality e1 of one of its components y, relative to the functionality e of the whole, which is not being achieved (e3) because of some property e2 of y.

A very strong sense of "destroyed" is that none of a functional entity's functional components achieve their functionality.

```
(forall (x)                                                    (47.36)
    (iff (destroyed x)
        (forall (e1 y e)
            (if (functionality e1 y e x)
                (exists (e2 e3)
                    (and (arg* y e2)(not' e3 e1)
                        (cause e2 e3)))))))
```

Lines 4–7 say that for every functional component y with functionality e1, there is some property e2 of y that causes e1 not to be achieved (e3).

The human body can be viewed as a functional composite entity, whose function is to thrive physically, which includes feeding itself, growing when appropriate, fighting off disease, predators and other dangers, and so on. A very abstract and noncommittal way of putting this is that the functionality of the body, relative to the functionality of thriving of the person, is to thrive physically. Exactly what counts as thriving physically is a matter for a commonsense physiology to spell out.

```
(forall (p b e1)                                               (47.37)
    (if (and (person p)(body b p)
            (thrive' e1 p)(functionality0 e1 p))
        (exists (e2)
            (and (thrivePhysically' e2 b)
                (functionality e2 b e1 p)))))
```

Lines 2 and 3 say that the thriving e1 of a person p with body b is p's absolute functionality. Lines 4–6 say there is a physical thriving e2 of p's body that is its relative functionality with respect to the person's thriving.

A person is a functional composite entity, and a person's body is a functional component of the person. The body is thus itself a functional composite entity, and as such can be intact, impaired, or destroyed. In fact, it follows from our axioms that one of these three states must be the case.

```
(forall (b p)                                               (47.38)
    (if (body b p)
        (or (intact b) (impaired b) (destroyed b))))
```

The components of the body are of course the body parts, the overwhelming majority of which are functional. For example, the function of the hands is to manipulate the environment and the function of the heart is to cause nutrition to be circulated to all the cells of the body. Since the body parts are themselves functional composite entities, we can also characterize each of them as intact, impaired, or destroyed.

```
(forall (x p)                                               (47.39)
    (if (bodyPart x p)
        (or (intact x) (impaired x) (destroyed x))))
```

The mind and the channels of sensation and control do not have as clearcut a structure as the body, so it is harder to characterize their impairment. But we can do so in terms of their principal functionalities. First consider the mind. When it is fully active, thoughts are in the focus of attention and reasoning is taking place. There are many aspects of reasoning, some of which have been explicated in previous chapters. Here we will axiomatize two for illustrative purposes. The first is that if one is envisioning, then one is reasoning.

```
(forall (s p) (if (ecs s p) (reasoning p)))                 (47.40)
```

The second is that if one is doing some simple kind of logical operation, such as modus ponens, one is reasoning.

```
(forall (p e1 e2 e3 e4 e5 e6)                               (47.41)
    (if (and (person p) (imply' e1 e2 e3) (and' e4 e2 e1)
            (inFocus' e5 e4 p) (inFocus' e6 e3 p) (cause e5 e6))
        (reasoning p)))
```

That is, suppose that in one's focus is the conjunction of e2 and "e2 implies e3" and suppose that causes one to have e3 in focus. Then one is reasoning.

We can say that the mind is active when there are thoughts in focus and when the person is reasoning.

```
(forall (p m)                                               (47.42)
    (if (and (person p) (mind m p))
        (iff (active m)
            (exists (x)
                (and (inFocus x p) (reasoning p))))))
```

A perhaps too crude definition of the mind's being impaired is that there are thoughts in focus, but the person is not reasoning. For example, a drunk person has thoughts, but they are not coherent.

```
(forall (p m)                                               (47.43)
    (if (and (person p) (mind m p))
        (iff (impaired m)
            (and (exists (x) (inFocus x p))
                (not (reasoning p))))))
```

Finally, a mind is inactive when one does not have thoughts in focus.

```
(forall (p m)                                               (47.44)
    (if (and (person p)(mind m p))
        (iff (inactive m)
             (not (exists (x) (inFocus x p))))))
```

It follows from all this that the mind is either active, impaired or inactive.

```
(forall (m p)                                               (47.45)
    (if (and (person p)(mind m p))
        (xor (active m)(impaired m)(inactive m))))
```

We can posit channels of sensation and control.

```
(forall (p)                                                 (47.46)
    (if (person p)
        (exists (s c)
            (and (sensationChannel s p)(controlChannel c p)))))
```

We can define what it means for them to be active, impaired, or inactive. When working correctly, the channel of sensation consists of an external entity impinging on a sense organ and having that cause the perception to be in one's awareness. Furthermore, when one perceives something, it actually exists. If all of this is true, the sensation channel is active.

```
(forall (p s o e1 x s1)                                     (47.47)
    (if (and (person p)(sensationChannel s p)(senseOrgan o p)
             (near' e1 x o s1)(spatialSystem s1))
        (iff (active s)
            (and (exists (e2)
                     (and (perceive' e2 p x)(cause e1 e2)))
                 (forall (y) (if (perceive p y)(Rexist y)))))))
```

This axiom encodes two properties of an active sensation channel. Lines 3 and 5–6 say that one perceives things nearby because they are nearby. Line 7 says that if one perceives something, it actually exists.

If the second of these two conditions fails to hold, the sensation channel is impaired. We perceive things that aren't there. For example, we may dream, or hear voices, or have a tingly feeling.

```
(forall (p s)                                               (47.48)
    (if (and (person p)(sensationChannel s p))
        (iff (impaired s)
            (exists (y)
                (and (perceive p y)(not (Rexist y)))))))
```

The sensation channel is inactive if the first condition does not hold. We fail to perceive something altogether.

```
(forall (p s)                                                   (47.49)
    (if (and (person p)(sensationChannel s p))
        (iff (inactive s)
            (forall (o x s1)
                (if (and (senseOrgan o p)(near x o s1)(spatialSystem s1))
                    (not (perceive p x)))))))
```

It follows from these definitions that the sensation channel is either active, impaired, or inactive.

```
(forall (s p)                                                   (47.50)
    (if (and (person p)(sensationChannel s p))
        (xor (active s)(impaired s)(inactive s))))
```

We can similarly define the three states of active, impaired, and inactive for the control channel. When the control channel is working properly, one wills a bodily action to take place and that exact bodily action takes place.

```
(forall (p c)                                                   (47.51)
    (if (and (person p)(controlChannel c p))
        (iff (active c)
            (forall (e1 e)
                (if (and (will' e1 p e)(voluntaryAction e p))
                    (cause e1 e))))))
```

In this axiom the person wills a voluntary action e (line 5), and that willing actually causes e to occur (line 6).

When the control channel is impaired, as when one is tired or drunk, a voluntary action can be willed, and it causes some bodily action, but not the one that was willed.

```
(forall (p c)                                                   (47.52)
    (if (and (person p)(controlChannel c p))
        (iff (impaired c)
            (exists (e e0 e1)
                (and (will' e1 p e)(voluntaryAction e p)
                    (cause e1 e0)(bodilyAction e0 p)
                    (not (equal e0 e)))))))
```

In this axiom the person wills a voluntary action e (line 5), and that causes some bodily action e0 (line 6), but that action is not the one intended (line 7).

The control channel is inactive either when the willing of a voluntary action causes no bodily action at all, as when one is paralyzed, or when willing cannot take place, as when one is unconscious.

```
(forall (p c)                                                   (47.53)
    (if (and (person p)(controlChannel c p))
        (iff (inactive c)
            (or (not (exists (e1 e) (will' e1 p e)))
                (forall (e1 e)
                    (if (will' e1 p e)
                        (not (exists (e0)
                            (and (bodilyAction e0 p)
                                (cause e1 e0)))))))))))
```

Line 4 covers the case where the person does not will any bodily actions. Lines 5–9 cover the case in which the person does will bodily actions but the willing fails to cause any actual motion.

It follows from these three axioms that the control channel is either active, impaired, or inactive.

```
(forall (c p)                                                        (47.54)
    (if (and (person p)(controlChannel c p))
        (xor (active c)(impaired c)(inactive c))))
```

We could define scales of capability and activity in which active or intact is higher than impaired, which is higher than inactive or destroyed. We could even identify each of these states with the Hi, Md, and Lo regions of the scale.

47.9 STATES OF CONSCIOUSNESS

The theory of mind–body interaction presented here postulates that a person has both a mind and a body, which are connected by the two channels of sensation and control. The mind, the body, the sensation channel, and the control channel each have a three-valued state, namely, they are active, impaired, or inactive, or in the case of the body, intact, damaged, or destroyed. The normal sensation channel operates to translate the stimulation provided by the world to beliefs in the mind. The normal control channel translates the will to do an action into the performance of the action in the world.

We can elaborate our theory with an account of action and perception that is dependent on the status of the mind, the body, control, and sensation. Under this account, the mind's perception of the world is a consequence of the world stimulating the body, and is influenced by the channel of sensation. With an intact body, an active mind, and active sensation, this perception yields beliefs; that is, seeing is believing. Likewise, the body's actions are a consequence of the mind's will, influenced by the channel of control. With an active mind, an intact body, and active control, will yields action.

States of consciousness are bundles of inferences we can draw about the control a person's mind has over his or her body and the influence perception can have on the mind. That is, a state of consciousness is a quality we hypothesize of a person that then allows us to draw many inferences about how he or she is likely to behave. Some states of consciousness, such as being drunk, have identifiable causes, while others, such as sleep and dreaming, normally do not.

When somebody is "fine," his or her body, mind, and sensation and control channels are all intact or active.

```
(forall (p b m s c)                                                  (47.55)
    (if (and (person p)(body b p)(mind m p)(sensationChannel s p)
             (controlChannel c p)(fine p))
        (and (intact b)(active m)(active s)(active c))))
```

There are various altered states, including dreaming, being drunk, under the influence of cocaine, marijuana, morphine, LSD or some other drug, having hallucinations, feeling phantom limb pains, being exhausted, being blind, being in religious ecstasy, and so on. Each of these altered states would have to be axiomatized

Table 47.1 Mind–body states

State	Body	Mind	Control	Sensation
Fine	+	+	+	+
Sore	/	+	+	+
Wounded	/	+	+	+
Tired	+	/	/	+
Numb	+	+	+	−
Blind/deaf	+	+	+	−
Tingly	+	+	+	/
Paralyzed	+	+	−	−
Dazed	+	/	+	+
Schizophrenic	+	/	+	/
Drunk	+	/	/	/
Dreaming	+	/	−	/
Sleeping	+	−	−	/
Unconscious	+	−	−	−
Brain dead	/	−	−	−
Dead	−	−	−	−

(+ = active or intact, / = impaired or damaged, − = inactive or destroyed)

separately according to their causes, if known, and their effects. The axioms in the previous sections postulate the separation of the mind and the body, and identify the channels of control and sensation between them. Each of these four components is given a three-valued state. The mind, control, and sensation can be active, impaired, or inactive, and the body can be intact, damaged, or destroyed. Different combinations of these possible values each yield different mind–body states, each with their own set of inferred consequences. For example, when one is unconscious, one's body is intact, but one's mind, sensation channel, and control channel are all inactive.

```
(forall (p b m s c)                                              (47.56)
    (if (and (person p)(body b p)(mind m p)(sensationChannel s p)
             (controlChannel c p)(unconscious p))
        (and (intact b)(inactive m)(inactive s)(inactive c))))
```

With analogous axioms, a wide variety of mind–body states can be described by varying these three values for these four components. Table 47.1 lists several of these mind–body states with their corresponding properties. Each of the rows in this table corresponds to axioms like (47.55) and (47.56).

Table 47.1 also serves to highlight some of the places where the theory needs to be elaborated. Here, the states of being numb, blind, and deaf have identical properties, each with an intact condition of the body, and an active mind and control, but inactive sensation. To distinguish these, we would need to formulate a theory of the sense organs and perhaps other body parts and to assign senses of touch, taste, smell, hearing, and sight as appropriate. Such an extension would also improve inferences about damage to the body, for example, how damage to sense organs might affect the sensory modalities.

In many respects, the theory of mind–body interaction presented here is more complicated than previous formalizations of action or perception. For example,

Davis's high-level theories of visual perception (Davis, 1988) and hand–eye coordination (Davis, 1989) are extremely compact, introducing only a handful of new predicates to articulate key axioms. In contrast, we have posited dozens of axioms and predicates, including the predicates and axioms implicit in Table 47.1. Rather than focusing our effort as Davis does on a few difficult puzzles, our work is primarily motivated by a need for a deeper lexical semantics for natural language, where the logical formalizations are themselves rich enough to characterize differences in meaning at varying degrees of subtlety. With this aim in mind, the theory presented here is successful inasmuch as it affords distinctions in meaning, for example, between dexterous action and reflexes, or between sleep and unconsciousness. There remain many aspects of the theory that need elaboration. As mentioned previously, our treatment of perception does little to distinguish between sensory modalities, or recognize that sensations have degrees of clarity. As a consequence, the theory as developed so far cannot distinguish between seeing clearly and faintly hearing.

In Chapter 30 we developed a rudimentary theory of pleasure and pain. These often result from bodily sensations, and a more complete theory would elaborate on that here.

Our treatment of bodily actions mentions but does not explore in detail how different body parts move separately in coordinated action.

Our treatment of control of perception is only at a very high level (tuning in and out), and fails to distinguish between the ways in which the mind controls different sensory modalities. For example, the eye tracks moving objects, focuses on distant and close objects, closes before sleeping, and blinks while awake. The theory as developed so far does not specify which types of sensations can be easily tuned out, for example, that people might find it easy to tune out the gentle sound of rain while reading a book, but not loud conversations.

Our treatment of the perception of action would also benefit from elaboration of the subjective types of sensations created by bodily actions. This would enable richer interpretations of language related to ergonomics, for example, distinguishing painful from natural body motions, or characterizing comfortable grips on handles and handholds.

As mentioned previously, the theory does not distinguish between certain mind–body states. The differences between deaf, blind, and numb require (at least) distinctions in sensory modalities. This would also improve the interpretation of states such as sleeping, and how you can be awakened by a loud noise, but not by a horrific photograph.

Nevertheless, the theory presented here moves us toward a deeper lexical semantics for the language of mind–body interaction, more so than any previous formalization effort. Our approach was to adopt a strong view of mind–body dualism, following the original two-way interactionalism of Descartes' *Meditations*. Alternative formulations of the same content based on different philosophical perspectives are certainly possible. As extensions and alternative theories are put forth, it will be necessary to consider the criteria by which content theories such as this are to be evaluated and compared. Ultimately, theories of this sort should be evaluated by both breadth and depth, that is, by their capacity to encode the meaning of natural language words and phrases (coverage), and their ability to generate correct inferences based on these encodings (competency).

PREDICATES INTRODUCED IN THIS CHAPTER

(awareness a m)
 a is the mind m's "region" of awareness.

(concentrate p x)
 Person p concentrates on concept x.

(eye y p)
 Sense organ y is person p's eye.

(ear y p)
 Sense organ y is person p's ear.

(tongue y p)
 Sense organ y is person p's tongue.

(nose y p)
 Sense organ y is person p's nose.

(stimulate x p)
 Entity or event x stimulates person p.

(attendToSense p y)
 Person p focuses on the input from sense organ y.

(bodilyAction e p)
 Event e is a bodily action by person p.

(reflex e p)
 Event e is a reflex action by person p.

(tic e p)
 Event e is an involuntary bodily action by person p that has no cause external to
 the body.

(voluntaryAction e p)
 Event e is a voluntary action by person p.

(involuntaryAction e p)
 Event e is an involuntary action by person p.

(controlBody p b)
 Person p controls his or her body b.

(coordinatedAction e p)
 Event e is a coordinated action by person p.

(failedBodilyAction e p)
 Event e is a failed attempt at a bodily action by person p.

(successfulBodilyAction e p)
 Event e is a successful attempt at a bodily action by person p.

(fluentAction e p)
 Event e is a fluent action by person p.

(awkwardAction e p)
 Event e is an awkward action by person p.

(senseOrganAction e p)
 Event e is a bodily action by person p to change the quality of perception by a
 sense organ.

(tuneIn p x)
> Person p focuses on perceived entity x.

(tuneOut p x)
> Person p stops focusing on perceived entity x.

(impaired x)
> Functional composite entity x is impaired.

(destroyed x)
> Functional composite entity x is destroyed.

(thrivePhysically b)
> Body b thrives physically.

(reasoning p)
> Person p is engaged in reasoning.

(sensationChannel s p)
> s is person p's sensation channel.

(controlChannel c p)
> c is person p's control channel.

(active x)
> Mental capability x is active.

(inactive x)
> Mental capability x is inactive.

(fine p)
> Person p is fine.

(unconscious p)
> Person p is unconscious.

48

Observation of Plan Executions

OBSERVING THE PLAN EXECUTIONS OF OTHER AGENTS

In the previous several chapters we have addressed issues involving agents executing plans to achieve goals and monitoring these executions to make sure they do advance toward the goal. We have also gone deeper into the possible states of an agent's perception of the world. Among the events an agent will perceive are the efforts of other agents to achieve *their* goals, and that is the focus of this chapter. This will take us into issues of instruction, performance, skill, and evaluation. This topic lies at the edge of commonsense microsociology, as interactions among agents crucially involve their observations of each other's purposeful actions.

People can observe some aspects of the execution of plans by other agents.

```
(forall (e b c)                                              (48.1)
   (iff (observableExecution e b c)
        (exists (a p e0 e1 e2)
           (and (executePlan' e a p)(execute' e1 a e0 p)
                (not (agentOf b e))
                (possible e2 c)(perceive' e2 b e1)))))
```

The expression (observableExecution e b c) says that e is an execution of a plan that is observable by agent b given constraints c. (The "-able" in "observable" tells us the concept is relative to a set of constraints.) In the definition e is the execution of the entire plan p by agent a, and e1 is the execution of a subgoal e0 that can be perceived by b.

There are some parts of the execution of plans by other agents that are not observable.

```
(forall (e b c)                                              (48.2)
   (iff (unobservableExecution e b c)
        (exists (a p)
           (and (executePlan' e a p)(not (agentOf b e))
                (forall (e0 e1 e2)
                   (if (and (execute' e1 a e0 p)
                            (perceive' e2 b e1))
                       (not (possible e2 c)))))))))
```

The expression (unobservableExecution e b c) says that e is an execution of a plan that is not observable by agent b given constraints c. That means it is not possible to perceive any execution e1 of a subgoal e0 of the plan.

Of the observable executions of plans, some are actually observed by another person.

```
(forall (e b)                                                (48.3)
   (iff (observedExecution e b)
        (exists (a p e0 e1 e2)
            (and (executePlan' e a p) (execute' e1 a e0 p)
                 (not (agentOf b e))
                 (perceive b e1))))))
```

The expression (observedExecution e b) says that e is an execution of a plan that is actually observed by agent b.

Some executions are not observed by a given agent.

```
(forall (e b)                                                (48.4)
   (iff (unobservedExecution e b)
        (exists (a p)
            (and (executePlan' e a p) (not (agentOf b e))
                 (forall (e0 e1)
                     (if (execute' e1 a e0 p)
                         (not (perceive b e1))))))))
```

The expression (unobservedExecution e b) says that e is an execution of a plan that is not actually observed by agent b. This means that no execution e1 of a subgoal e0 of the plan is perceived.

Some executions are unobserved by anyone but the agent of the execution.

```
(forall (e)                                                  (48.5)
   (iff (observedByNoneExecution e)
        (forall (b)
            (if (not (agentOf b e)) (unobservedExecution e b)))))
```

Two trivial theorems are that observed executions are observable and that unobservable executions are unobserved.

```
(forall (e b)                                                (48.6)
   (if (observedExecution e b)
       (exists (c)
           (and (observableExecution e b c) (Rexist c)))))
```

If e is actually observed, then constraints c must hold under which e is observable.

```
(forall (o b c)                                              (48.7)
   (if (and (unobservableExecution e b c) (Rexist c))
       (unobservedExecution e b)))
```

If the conditions c under which e is unobservable actually hold, then e is not observed.

48.2 INSTRUCTIONS

In a previously developed theory of information structure (Hobbs and Mulkar-Mehta, 2013), communication is characterized as the presentation by one agent (the speaker) of a symbol x to another agent (the hearer), causing the second agent to think of a corresponding concept y, where the mapping from x to y is a result of conventionalized rules in a social group s that both agents belong to. This is encapsulated in the predication

(mean x y s): Symbol x means concept y to members of group s.

The symbol x can be a physical object, like a billboard, or a transient event, like a spoken word, or even the absence of an event, like a pregnant silence. The concept y can be propositional or an image or a remembered odor or any number of other mental entities. The symbol and the concept can be "atomic" with no meaningful internal structure, such as the letter "I" or a remembered smell of burning autumn leaves. Or they can be large complex composite entities with a great deal of structure, like the novel *War and Peace* or the theory of quantum mechanics.

We will understand a document broadly to be a symbolic object, something that has meaning, of any degree of complexity.

```
(forall (d)                                              (48.8)
    (iff (document d)
        (exists (y s) (mean d y s))))
```

That is, a document is any meaning-bearing object.

Instructions are a document whose content is a plan.

```
(forall (d g)                                            (48.9)
    (iff (instructions d g)
        (exists (p s a)
            (and (document d)(mean d p s)
                (member a s)(plan p a g)))))
```

The expression (instructions d g) says that d is a set of instructions for accomplishing goal g. This is true when d is a document that means p to members of group s, where p is a plan by some member a of s to achieve g.

A plan is based on causal relationships. Doing the body of a plan causes the goal to be achieved. So instructions are a statement of a causal relationship: Doing e1; e2; e3; ... will cause g. The consumer of the instructions may know the details of that causality, that is, why it follows from more basic causal principles, or may not know, in which case this becomes an unanalyzed principle in one's causal knowledge. For example, for instructions that state "Add salt to improve taste," few of us understand this causal relation at a deeper level.

Agents can execute plans that are explicitly specified, that is, for which there is a document, broadly construed, whose content is that plan.

```
(forall (p a g)                                          (48.10)
    (iff (explicitPlan p a g)
         (exists (d s)
             (and (instructions d g)(mean d p s)
                  (member a s)(plan p a g)))))
```

48.3 PERFORMANCES AND THEIR SPECIFICATION

A performance is the execution of an explicit plan before an audience.

```
(forall (e a p s)                                        (48.11)
    (iff (performance e a p s)
         (exists (g)
             (and (explicitPlan p a g)(executePlan' e a p)
                  (forall (b) (if (member b s)(perceive b e)))))))
```

The expression (performance e a p s) says that eventuality e is a performance by agent a of plan p before audience s. It holds when e is an execution of the plan and the members of the audience see it happening,

The instructions for a performance can be called the "performance specification."

```
(forall (d a g)                                          (48.12)
    (iff (performanceSpecification d a g)
         (exists (e p s)
             (and (instructions d g)(performance e a p s)
                  (explicitPlan p a g)))))
```

The expression (performanceSpecification d a g) says that document d is a specification for a performance by agent a aimed at achieving goal g. This holds when d is instructions for a's performance of plan p to audience s for achieving g.

When learning how things are to be done, people may have some idea. A candidate performance specification is one that the agent believes may achieve the goal.

```
(forall (e d a g)                                        (48.13)
    (iff (candidatePerformanceSpecification' e d a g)
         (exists (e1 e2 c e3)
             (and (believe' e3 a e1)(gen e3 e)(possible' e1 e2 c)
                  (performanceSpecification' e2 d a g)))))
```

The expression (candidatePerformanceSpecification' e d a g) says e is the eventuality of d being a candidate performance specification for agent a to achieve goal g. This holds when a believes d is possibly a performance specification.

People generate ideas about how things should be done.

```
(forall (e a d g)                                        (48.14)
    (iff (generateCandidatePerformanceSpecification' e d a g)
         (exists (e1 e2)
             (and (changeTo' e2 e1)(gen e2 e)
                  (candidatePerformanceSpecification' e1 d a g)))))
```

The expression (generateCandidatePerformanceSpecification' e d a g) says
there is a change e into the state e1 in which document d is a candidate performance
specification for agent a to achieve goal g.

When an idea for how something is to be done is found to be wrong, it can be
modified.

```
(forall (e a d1 d2 g)                                              (48.15)
    (iff (modifyCandidatePerformanceSpecification' e d1 d2 a g)
        (exists (e1 e2 e3)
            (and (change' e3 e1 e2)(gen e3 e)
                (candidatePerformanceSpecification' e1 d1 a g)
                (candidatePerformanceSpecification' e2 d2 a g)))))
```

The expression (modifyCandidatePerformanceSpecification' e d1 d2 a g)
says that e is a change from document d1 to document d2 being a candidate performance specification for agent a to achieve goal g.

When an idea for how something is to be done is found to be wrong, it is invalidated.

```
(forall (e a d g)                                                 (48.16)
    (iff (invalidateCandidatePerformanceSpecification' e d a g)
        (exists (e1 e2 e3 e4)
            (and (change' e4 e1 e2)(gen e4 e)
                (candidatePerformanceSpecification' e1 d a g)
                (believe' e2 a e3)(not' e3 e1)))))
```

The expression (invalidateCandidatePerformanceSpecification' e d a g)
says that e is the eventuality of document d ceasing to be believed as a performance
specification for agent a to achieve goal g.

When an idea for how something is to be done is found to be correct, it is
validated.

```
(forall (e a d g)                                                 (48.17)
    (iff (validateCandidatePerformanceSpecification' e d a g)
        (exists (e1 e2 e3)
            (and (change' e3 e1 e2)(gen e3 e)
                (candidatePerformanceSpecification' e1 d a g)
                (performanceSpecification' e2 d a g)))))
```

The expression (validateCandidatePerformanceSpecification' e d a g) says
that e is the eventuality of document d being promoted from a candidate performance specification to a performance specification.

48.4 SKILL

Ideally when we attempt to carry out a plan, we do it the right way. The "way" a goal
is achieved is simply by executing the subgoals and having that cause to goal to come
about, that is, by executing the plan.

```
(forall (e a p d)                                                 (48.18)
    (iff (rightWay e a p d)
        (exists (s)
            (and (executePlan' e a p)(mean d p s)))))
```

That is, e is the right way for agent a to carry out plan p according to instructions d if e is an execution of p and d describes p.

A plan consists of a set of subgoals. Thus, the execution of a plan consists of a set of subevents of that execution. A sad fact about the world is that there is not always an identity between these two sets. Some lower level actions may be missed, meaning that higher level actions are not performed in the right way, meaning that even higher level subgoals are not achieved at all.

We can define an attempted execution of a plan p as an execution of a plan p1 intended to achieve the same goal.

```
(forall (e1 a p p1 g)                                          (48.19)
   (iff (attemptExecute' e1 a p p1 g)
        (exists (e e2 e3)
           (and (executePlan' e3 a p1)(gen e3 e1)(plan p a g)(plan p1 a g)
                (goal' e2 e a)(executePlan' e a p)
                (cause e2 e1)))))
```

The expression (attemptExecute' e1 a p p1 g) says that e1 is an attempted execution by agent a of plan p, actually instantiating plan p1, in service of goal g. Line 4 says that e1 is generated by an execution of plan p1, and that plans p and p1 are both aimed at achieving goal g. Lines 5 and 6 say that a's goal of executing plan p caused the execution e3 of plan p1. That is, wanting to execute plan p causes a to execute plan p1.

Where there is a right way to do something and people can fall short, we can introduce the notion of "skill." We can define "more skilled" as a partial ordering between two executions of the same explicit or ideal plan, based on the extent to which they match it. This partial ordering defines a scale on which we can locate various executions of the same plan, and we can define "skilled" to be the Hi region of that scale.

We cannot provide necessary and sufficient conditions for "more skilled," but we can impose constraints on the possible interpretations of the predicate. Specifically, suppose we have two attempted executions e1 and e2 of the same plan p. Plan p has its set of subgoals s, and e1 and e2 are actually executions of plans p1 and p2, respectively, which have their sets of subgoals s1 and s2. Execution e1 is a more skilled execution of plan p than e2 is if s1 overlaps more with p than s2 does and underlaps less.

Our first axiom says that, other things being equal, if e1 has all the correct subgoals that e2 has, and then some, e1 is more skilled than e2.

```
(forall (e1 e2 a p p1 p2 s s1 s2 s3 s4 s5 s6)                  (48.20)
   (if (and (attemptExecute' e1 a p p1 g)
            (attemptExecute' e2 a p p2 g)
            (subgoalsOf s p)(subgoalsOf s1 p1)(subgoalsOf s2 p2)
            (setdiff s3 s1 s)(setdiff s4 s2 s)
            (intersection s5 s1 s)(intersection s6 s2 s)
            (subset s3 s4)(properSubset s6 s5))
      (moreSkilled e1 e2 p)))
```

The expression (moreSkilled e1 e2 p) says that execution e1 was a more skilled execution of plan p than execution e2. Plans p1 and p2 are the actual plans that are executed in e1 and e2, and s1 and s2 are their sets of subgoals. The set s consists of the subgoals of the ideal plan p. Line 5 defines s3 and s4 as the sets of extraneous subgoals executed in e1 and e2. Line 6 defines s5 and s6 as the correct subgoals in e1 and e2, those that the agents were supposed to perform in executing plan p. Line 7 is the constraint of the "more skilled" partial ordering. It says that if e1 had fewer extraneous subgoals and did not have fewer correct subgoals than e2, then e1 is more skilled than e2.

The second axiom says that, other things being equal, if e2 has all the extraneous subgoals that e1 has, and then some, e1 is more skilled than e2.

```
(forall (e1 e2 a p p1 p2 s s1 s2 s3 s4 s5 s6)                    (48.21)
    (if (and (attemptExecute' e1 a p p1 g)
             (attemptExecute' e2 a p p2 g)
             (subgoalsOf s p)(subgoalsOf s1 p1)(subgoalsOf s2 p2)
             (setdiff s3 s1 s)(setdiff s4 s2 s)
             (intersection s5 s1 s)(intersection s6 s2 s)
             (properSubset s3 s4)(subset s6 s5))
        (moreSkilled e1 e2 p)))
```

These two axioms differ only in the placement of the predicate properSubset in line 7.

We can now define a "skill scale" as one whose elements are attempted executions of a plan and whose partial ordering is moreSkilled.

```
(forall (s p)                                                   (48.22)
    (iff (skillScale s p)
        (exists (s1 a g e1 e2)
            (and (scaleDefinedBy s s1 e)(plan p a g)
                (forall (e0)
                    (if (member e0 s1)
                        (exists (a1 p1)
                            (and (plan p1 a1 g)
                                 (attemptExecute' e0 a1 p p1 g)))))
                (moreSkilled' e e1 e2 p)))))
```

The expression (skillScale s p) says that s is the scale for skill at carrying out plan p. Line 4 says that s is the scale defined by set s1 of entities and partial ordering e, and that p is a plan to achieve goal g. Lines 5–9 say that the elements of s1 are attempted executions of plan p to achieve goal g. Line 10 says that the partial ordering is the moreSkilled relation.

Finally we can stipulate that an attempted execution is "skilled at p" if it is in the Hi region of a skill scale for p.

```
(forall (e p)                                                   (48.23)
    (iff (skilled e p)
        (exists (s s1)
            (and (skillScale s p)(Hi s1 s)
                 (inScale e s1)))))
```

The expression (skilled e p) says that attempted execution e was a skilled attempt to carry out plan p. Line 4 says that s is the skill scale for plan p, and that s1 is its high region. Line 5 says that e is in that high region.

For any skill scale for a plan p, we can designate some or all of the possible attempted executions of p as "skill levels" against which other attempted executions of p can be compared. The primary constraint on skill levels is that they have to be consistent with the moreSkilled relation.

```
(forall (y e1 e2 p)                                              (48.24)
    (if (and (skillLevel y e1 p)(skillLevel y e2 p))
        (and (not (moreSkilled e1 e2 p))
             (not (moreSkilled e2 e1 p)))))
```

This axiom says that if two executions e1 and e2 of plan p have the same skill level, then neither is more skilled than the other. The converse is not necessarily true since moreSkilled is only a partial ordering.

The skillLevel relation is an at relation, so we can talk of an attempted execution being at a particular skill level.

```
(forall (s y e p)                                               (48.25)
    (if (and (skillScale s p)(skillLevel y e p))
        (at e y s)))
```

This defines skill levels for individual agents. We can extend the skill scale to other agents by stipulating that where an execution of a plan lies on the skill scale is independent of the agent. Two agents doing the same thing will be judged to have been equally skillful.

```
(forall (e1 e2 a1 a2 p p1 p2 g s)                              (48.26)
    (if (and (attemptExecute' e1 a1 p p1 g)
             (attemptExecute' e2 a2 p p2 g)
             (skillScale s p)
             (subst a1 e1 a2 e2))
        (forall (y)
            (iff (skillLevel y e1 p)(skillLevel y e2 p)))))
```

Lines 2 and 3 define e1 and e2 as two attempted executions of the same plan p by agents a1 and a2. Line 4 defines s as the skill scale for plan p. Line 5 says that a1 plays the same role in e1 as a2 plays in e2; that is, the executions differ only in the agents performing the actions. Lines 6 and 7 say that e1 and e2 exhibit the same skill level.

48.5 EVALUATION

To evaluate a performance is to come to a belief about where that performance lies on a skill scale for such performances, as a result of witnessing the performance.

```
(forall (e b e1 p y)                                           (48.27)
    (iff (evaluate' e b e1 p y)
        (exists (a p1 g e2 e3 s e4 e5)
            (and (attemptExecute' e1 a p p1 g)
                 (changeTo' e5 e2)(gen e5 e)(believe' e2 b e3)
                 (skillLevel' e3 y e1 p)
                 (perceive' e4 b e1)(cause e4 e5)))))
```

The expression (evaluate' e b e1 p y) says that e is the eventuality of agent b
evaluating a performance e1 of plan p, resulting in judgment y. Line 4 says that e1 is
an attempt by agent a to execute plan p, actually instantiating plan p1. Lines 5 and
6 say that e is generated by a change to the eventuality of b's believing that e1 is at
some skill level y on the skill scale for p. Line 7 says that that change is caused by the
agent's having perceived the execution.

The value on the scale is the evaluation result.

```
(forall (y e)                                                      (48.28)
    (iff (evaluationResult y e)
        (exists (b e1 p)
            (evaluate' e b e1 p y))))
```

It is a defeasible inference that if someone witnesses an attempted execution of
a plan, they will evaluate it as a result of the witnessing.

```
(forall (a b e1 e4 p p1 g)                                         (48.29)
    (if (and (perceive' e4 b e1)
            (attemptExecute' e1 a p p1 g)(etc))
        (exists (e y)
            (and (evaluate' e b e1 p y)
                (cause e4 e)))))
```

People use certain criteria to judge a performance. An evaluation criterion is a
property of the thing being evaluated that is causally involved in the result of the
evaluation.

```
(forall (e0 p)                                                     (48.30)
    (iff (evaluationCriterion e0 p)
        (exists (e b e1 y e2)
            (and (evaluate' e b e1 p y)(evaluationResult' e2 y e)
                (arg* e1 e0)(causallyInvolved e0 e2)))))
```

The expression (evaluationCriterion e0 p) says that e0 is a criterion for evaluating executions of plan p. Lines 4 and 5 say that there is an evaluation e by agent
b of execution e1 of plan p, resulting in skill level y, that e0 is a property of e1, and
that e0 is causally involved in the result being what it is.

PREDICATES INTRODUCED IN THIS CHAPTER

(observableExecution e b c)
   e is an execution of a plan that is observable by agent b given constraints c.

(unobservableExecution e b c)
   e is an execution of a plan that is not observable by agent b given constraints c.

(observedExecution e b)
   e is an execution of a plan that is actually observed by agent b.

(unobservedExecution e b)
   e is an execution of a plan that is not actually observed by agent b.

(observedByNoneExecution e)
    e is an execution of a plan that is not actually observed by anyone.

(mean x y s)
    Symbol x means concept y to members of group s.

(document d)
    d is a document, that is, a meaning-bearing object.

(instructions d g)
    Document d is a set of instructions for accomplishing goal g.

(explicitPlan p a g)
    Plan p is an explicit plan by agent a for accomplishing goal g.

(performance e a p s)
    Eventuality e is a performance by agent a of plan p before audience s.

(performanceSpecification d a g)
    Document d is a specification for a performance by agent a aimed at achieving goal g.

(candidatePerformanceSpecification' e d a g)
    e is the eventuality of d being a candidate performance specification for agent a to achieve goal g.

(generateCandidatePerformanceSpecification' e d a g)
    There is a change e into the state in which document d is a candidate performance specification for agent a to achieve goal g.

(modifyCandidatePerformanceSpecification' e d1 d2 a g)
    There is a change e from document d1 to document d2 being a candidate performance specification for agent a to achieve goal g.

(invalidateCandidatePerformanceSpecification' e d a g)
    e is the eventuality of document d ceasing to be believed as a performance specification for agent a to achieve goal g.

(validateCandidatePerformanceSpecification' e d a g)
    e is the eventuality of document d being promoted from a candidate performance specification to a performance specification.

(rightWay e a p d)
    e is the right way for agent a to carry out plan p according to instructions d.

(attemptExecute' e1 a p p1 g)
    e1 is an attempted execution by agent a of plan p, actually instantiating plan p1, in service of goal g.

(moreSkilled e1 e2 p)
    e1 is a more skilled execution of plan p than e2 is.

(skillScale s p)
    s is the scale for skill at carrying out plan p.

(skilled e p)
    Attempted execution e was a skilled attempt to carry out plan p.

(skillLevel y e1 p)
    y is the skill level of attempted execution e1 of plan p.

(evaluate' e b e1 p y)
   e is the eventuality of agent b evaluating a performance e1 of plan p, resulting in judgment y.

(evaluationResult y e)
   y is the result of evaluation e.

(evaluationCriterion e0 p)
   Property e0 is a criterion for evaluating executions of plan p.

Emotions

EMOTIONS IN GENERAL

To paraphrase the Dick and Jane primers of an older generation, we see, think, and do. Intelligent agents perceive the environment around them, they consider how that environment will impact what they seek to achieve and modify their plans accordingly, and they execute actions that will achieve their goals in this environment. Their actions alter the environment, and possibly their own and others' beliefs and goals, and the cycle begins again. This is the basic cycle of cognition.

Emotion can be viewed similarly. We see, feel, and do. One view of emotion is that it is leftover reptilian cognition. It is a system of cognition that enables rapid and usually appropriate responses to threats and opportunities. In any case, it is best to view emotion, not as it is sometimes viewed, as opposed to or an alternative to cognition, but as a special variety of cognition.

Emotions, like cognition, mediate what happens to us and how we respond to it, but generally in a much more direct way than cognition. We can analyze the internal structure of emotions to some extent, in terms of the accompanying cognitive elaborations and in terms of levels of arousal. But for the most part the important facts about emotions involve their relations to the outside world. Specifically, to understand the role of emotion in human life, one has to know what kinds of things cause various emotions, and what kinds of things are caused by various emotions. We are all able to fake emotions, and the way we fake them is by knowing and using these two categories of causal facts.

A number of different theories of emotions have been proposed in the psychological literature (e.g. Scherer, 2010). One of the most popular is the so-called "appraisal" theory. Appraisal is the combination of "see" and "think"/"feel." We perceive our environment and we judge how it relates to our beliefs and goals, in order to operate in this environment in the optimal way. The patterns of appraisal in appraisal theories are the specific causal rules associated with different emotions, telling us what classes of event cause which emotions.

This chapter contains revisions of material published previously in Hobbs and Gordon (2008).

The patterns of appraisal, or their associated emotions, trigger specific coping strategies, or physiological, behavioral, or cognitive reactions. In our terms, these links are the rules about what classes of actions by the person are caused by the emotions. Emotions exist because these responses usually have adaptive value.

"Dimensional" theories of emotion posit two or more dimensions along which affective states can be characterized. In a dimensional theory, the external environment causes the person to be in a particular state, fully characterized by an n-tuple of the values along each of the dimensions. This state then induces various behaviors. The problem with dimensional theories is that in mapping the environmental stimulus into such an n-tuple, the specificity of response is lost and must be recovered by cognitively assessing the cause of the particular state. For example, you see a bear in your path as you are hiking through the woods. You feel a generalized fear state, rather than specifically being afraid of the bear. Then you have to assess your situation to figure out what it was that triggered your fear state and thus, what an appropriate response would be. Such an account may in fact be true. It may be true that being afraid of the bear is an after-the-fact interpretation of a subconsciously produced state of generalized fear. But this is decidedly not the commonsense view of how emotion operates. Moreover, it would be counter to the whole approach of this book, based on first-order logic, to arbitrarily lose track of arguments of predicates in the middle of a psychological process. Dimensional theories are fundamentally propositional – FEAR rather than (fear I bear).

Nevertheless, the dimensions that dimension theorists propose are aspects of emotions that we need to take into account. Three commonly proposed dimensions are pleasure or valence, arousal or intensity, and dominance. We specify for the emotions we characterize whether or not they are varieties of happiness or unhappiness, as our way of capturing pleasure or valence. We discuss and partially characterize the scalar notion of intensity. Dominance concerns the person's ability to deal with the environmental stimulus, and can thus be characterized in terms of the response that particular emotions trigger.

"Anatomic" theories of emotion focus on the physiological changes that are triggered by stimuli, rather than actions that result from deliberation. We do not deal with these aspects of emotion, as we have not explicated a commonsense theory of anatomy and in any case commonsense approaches to emotion deal with physiological effects only at a very coarse level, for example, an association of anger with being hot.

"Communicative" theories of emotion view emotions as states that we display for the purpose of communicating beliefs and likely actions to others, thereby facilitating social interaction. This perspective is especially relevant to computational work on emotion in human-computer interaction, where the whole point of emotional displays by the computer is to elicit particular social responses. Our view of this is that of course people exploit displays of emotion to convey things to or infer things about other people. People can exploit virtually anything they perceive or experience for communicative purposes. But this is parasitic on an emotion system that evolved for independent reasons. By knowing what class of actions is caused by a particular emotion, as we explicate in our axioms, observers of a person's action can work backwards from the action to the emotional state, and from there back to possible causes or forward to other possible actions. The person has thereby communicated all this information to the observer, whether intentionally or unintentionally.

We can identify five events involved in a specific emotional response:

1. Some external (or internal) event or trigger occurs.
2. It is perceived and evaluated with respect to the person's possibility of attaining his or her goals, for example, survival.
3. There is a subjective feeling, for example, anger, fear, or happiness.
4. There are various physiological manifestations, for example, a smile or grimace, dilation or contraction of the pupils, and dilation or contraction of the blood vessels.
5. The person takes some external (or internal) action in response to the emotion, for example, fight or flight.

In 1 and 5 we normally think of the event and action as external, but it could be internal. Suddenly thinking of an old friend who died can trigger sadness, and the response to an emotion might be a change of belief.

William James (1890, Chapter 25) argues, contra a naive view that 3 causes 4, that 3 in fact just *is* 4. That is, 3 is the way we experience subjectively the physiological effects in 4, in the same way that "tired" is the way we experience a high concentration of lactic acid in our muscles. It's just two different levels of description. They can be viewed as identical, or we can say that there is a kind of "how to" or "how did" causal relation between them – 4 is the way 3 is "implemented."

In any case, we do not need to concern ourselves with this issue, as we are not explicating the physiological accompaniments of emotion.

In addition to the mediating role emotions play in causal knowledge, all emotions have an associated level of intensity. This interacts with the causal facts. In general, the more important the goals involved, the more intense the emotion. The more intense the emotion, the greater the effect of the responses. Because intensity applies to all emotions, we will discuss this first.

It has been argued that there are a small number of basic emotions. A common proposal identifies five – happiness, sadness, anger, fear, and disgust. We will consider these first in the list of emotions we discuss. The first two are relatively long-term moods that result from one's general success or failure and result in characteristic patterns of behavior. Happiness is caused by one's goals being satisfied, and promotes further action. Sadness is caused by one's goals not being satisfied, and suppresses further action.

Then as a way of demonstrating the nuances of meaning that we can capture in the framework we have built up, we examine a number of synonyms and near synonyms of "happy."

The other three basic emotions – what we call "the raw emotions" – are specific responses to specific events. These are discussed next.

Many other emotions, if not all, can be seen as cognitive elaborations on these basic five. Thus, resentment is a kind of anger. We next axiomatize the emotions characterized by Ortony, Clore, and Collins (1990), and relate them to the basic emotions, insofar as appropriate.

49.2 INTENSITY AND AROUSAL

Intensity of emotion is a scalar notion that is probably impossible to define precisely. But we can delimit its interpretation by means of two of its properties, both defeasible, one relating to what causes the emotion and one relating to what the emotion causes.

The first property is that, defeasibly, the more important the goal involved in the emotion, the more intense the emotion. Fearing that your life is in danger is usually more intense than fearing that you might stub your toe.

In Chapter 28 we explicated a moreImportant relation between eventualities in terms of an agent's goal hierarchy – supergoals are more important than subgoals. Toward the end of this chapter we label various emotional states *as* emotional states, by the predicate emotionalState, which takes an eventuality and a person as its arguments.

$$
\begin{aligned}
&\text{(forall (e p)} &&(49.1)\\
&\quad\text{(if (emotionalState e p)(and (eventuality e)(person p))))}
\end{aligned}
$$

Also in the rest of this chapter, we will identify various classes of causes for the various emotional states. Then we can constrain the moreIntense relation as follows:

$$
\begin{aligned}
&\text{(forall (p e1 e2 e3 e4)} &&(49.2)\\
&\quad\text{(if (and (emotionalState e1 p)(emotionalState e2 p)}\\
&\qquad\text{(cause e3 e1)(cause e4 e2)}\\
&\qquad\text{(moreImportant e3 e4 p)(etc))}\\
&\quad\text{(moreIntense e1 e2 p)))}
\end{aligned}
$$

That is, if e1 is an emotional state in p caused by e3, e2 is an emotional state in p caused by e4, and e3 is more important to p than e4, then defeasibly e1 is more intense than e2.

Thus, we would find it strange for someone to grieve deeply after hitting a bird with his car and then feel no emotion whatever when his mother died.

A second property of moreIntense with respect to the cause of the emotion is that an event that is in some sense "bigger" than another will defeasibly cause a more intense emotion. Your fear will be more intense if you are being chased by two bears than if you are being chased by only one. It is difficult to say what makes one action "bigger" than another, but one obvious constraint is that an event is "bigger" than its subevents. As this is the only property that we will consider for the "bigger" relation, we can just state the constraint in terms of the subevent predicate.

$$
\begin{aligned}
&\text{(forall (p e1 e2 e3 e4)} &&(49.3)\\
&\quad\text{(if (and (emotionalState e1 p)(emotionalState e2 p)}\\
&\qquad\text{(cause e3 e1)(cause e4 e2)}\\
&\qquad\text{(subevent e4 e3)(etc))}\\
&\quad\text{(moreIntense e1 e2 p)))}
\end{aligned}
$$

That is, if e1 is an emotional state in p caused by e3, e2 is an emotional state in p caused by e4, and e4 is a subevent of e3, then defeasibly e1 is more intense than e2.

The third property of moreIntense concerns the effect of the emotion. Defeasibly, the more intense the emotion, the "bigger" the response to it. For example, someone learns she won $100 in the lottery, and she smiles; she learns she won $1,000,000, and she dances with joy and shouts the news to all her friends.

Here also we will express the constraint only with respect to the subevent relation. If the response to emotional state e2 is only a subevent of the response to emotional state e1, then, defeasibly, e1 is more intense than e2.

```
(forall (p e1 e2 e3 e4)                                        (49.4)
    (if (and (emotionalState e1 p)(emotionalState e2 p)
             (cause e1 e3)(cause e2 e4)
             (subevent e4 e3)(etc))
        (moreIntense e1 e2 p)))
```

That is, if e1 is an emotional state in p that causes e3 (dance with joy), e2 is an emotional state in p that causes e4 (smile), and e4 is a subevent of e3, then defeasibly e1
is more intense than e2.

Axioms (49.3) and (49.4) are only defeasible, in part, because the superevent may
include mitigating eventualities.

We can define an emotional state as being intense if it is in the Hi region the
moreIntense scale, where Hi is determined by distributions, functionality, and contextual factors.

```
(forall (p e0 e1 e2 s0 s s1)                                   (49.5)
    (if (and (forall (e) (if (member e s0)(emotionalState e p)))
             (moreIntense' e0 e1 e2 p)(scaleDefinedBy s s0 e0)(Hi s1 s))
        (forall (e) (iff (intense e p)(inScale e s1)))))
```

Here s0 is a set of person p's emotional states, and e0 is the moreIntense partial
ordering.

Very often events involve some other qualitative or quantitative scale, such as a
pain lasting for a length of time, one's child performing in a school play with some
degree of proficiency, and one's winning a certain amount of money is the lottery.
In these cases there is often a monotonic, scale-to-scale causal relation between a
change in the scalar quantity and a change in the intensity of the emotion. Raising
the value of the scalar raises the intensity, and lowering the value lowers it. One
would have to spell these out on a case by case basis, but many of these rules could
be subsumed under the moreImportant Axiom (49.2) earlier.

Now we can explicate to some extent the notion of arousal. It often correlates
with the intensity of an emotional state, but only certain emotional states. We will
say that when there is such a correlation, there is a causal relation from the intensity
to the arousal. Of the five basic emotions, it seems that happiness, anger and fear lead
to a higher level of arousal. Hence the following defeasible axioms:

Intense happiness causes arousal.

```
(forall (e1 p)                                                 (49.6)
    (if (and (happy' e1 p)(intense e1 p)(etc))
        (exists (e2) (and (aroused' e2 p)(cause e1 e2)))))
```

Intense anger causes arousal.

```
(forall (c1 p)                                                 (49.7)
    (if (and (angry' e1 p)(intense e1 p)(etc))
        (exists (e) (and (aroused' e2 p)(cause e1 e2)))))
```

Intense fear causes arousal.

```
(forall (e1 p)                                              (49.8)
    (if (and (afraid' e1 p)(intense e1 p)(etc))
        (exists (e2) (and (aroused' e2 p)(cause e1 e2)))))
```

Intense sadness in general does not cause arousal. Quite the opposite. Intense disgust seems to be neutral with respect to arousal.

The converse of these rules is weaker. If we know someone is in an aroused state, we can't necessarily say which particular emotion caused it. But we can say, defeasibly, that *some* intense emotional state caused it.

```
(forall (e2 p)                                              (49.9)
    (if (and (aroused' e2 p)(etc))
        (exists (e1) (and (emotionalState e1 p)(intense e1 p)
                          (cause e1 e2)))))
```

Another important property of states of arousal is one that gives arousal its selective advantage. When we are aroused, we are generally more able to cope with unexpected events. We are ready for anything. One aspect of this is that we are very focused on what is going on in our environment. In terms of concepts we have explicated already in this book, arousal defeasibly causes us to have the current state of the world in focus.

```
(forall (e1 p)                                              (49.10)
    (if (and (aroused' e1 p)(etc))
        (exists (e2 e)
            (and (inFocus' e2 e p)(cwu e p)(cause e1 e2)))))
```

49.3 HAPPINESS AND SADNESS

Specific emotions can in part be characterized by what abstract classes of eventualities cause them. Happiness is normally caused by the belief that one's goals are being satisfied.

```
(forall (e1 p)                                              (49.11)
    (if (and (goal e1 p)(etc))
        (exists (e2) (and (happy' e2 p)(cause e1 e2)))))
```

That is, if eventuality e1 is a goal of person p's, then defeasibly e1, should it actually occur, will cause p's happiness e2.

Tense is significant here. One can be happy because in the distant past one's goals were satisfied, but there has to be some relevance to the present. You can be happy you earned your Ph.D. thirty years ago, but it is probably because it enabled you to be in your present, pleasant situation. It is less likely that you are happy you won your third-grade spelling bee. Whatever influence that had on your self-esteem has long since vanished.

Happiness is not caused exclusively by one's goals being satisfied. A belief that your goals *will* be satisfied can also result in happiness. You can be happy while you imagine what you will do with lottery winnings and how they will solve all your problems; it is a curious feature of human cognition that imagination has this causally disconnected effect.

```
(forall (p e e1 e2 e3 t1 t2)                              (49.12)
    (if (and (atTime' e1 e t2)(goal e1 p)(believe' e2 p e1)
             (atTime' e3 e2 t1)(before t1 t2)(etc))
        (exists (e4 e5)
            (and (happy' e4 p)(atTime' e5 e4 t1)(cause e3 e5)))))
```

In this axiom, e1 is the occurrence of eventuality e at time t2, and this is a goal of p's. Eventuality e2 is p's belief in e1, that is, that e will hold at time t2. Eventuality e3 is the belief's holding at some earlier time t1. Then, defeasibly, there is an eventuality e4 of p's being happy, and an eventuality e5 of that happiness e4 holding at time t1. Furthermore, e3 causes e5. In simpler terms, anticipating satisfaction of our goals makes us happy.

One can feel happy for no particular identifiable reason. One can be made happy by taking the right sort of medications. And one can have one's goals satisfied without feeling happy about it. The causal inferences associated with emotions are at best defeasible. But when they don't hold, this is an occasion of note. ("You got everything you wanted. Now why aren't you happy?")

We can introduce a more specific predicate "happyThat" that includes as one of its arguments the occasion that resulted in the happiness.

```
(forall (e1 p)                                           (49.13)
    (if (and (goal e1 p)(etc))
        (exists (e2) (and (happyThat' e2 p e1)(cause e1 e2)))))
```

That is, if eventuality e1 is a goal of person p's, then defeasibly e1, should it actually occur, will cause p's happiness e2 that e1 occurred.

"Happiness that" implies "happiness."

```
(forall (p e) (if (happyThat p e)(happy p)))             (49.14)
```

An inference that one can draw from one's success in satisfying one's goals is that the rules or beliefs that generate one's behavior are correct, or at least functional. They are the right rules. The person has the right beliefs. Therefore, there are two conclusions with respect to the person's actions. Because the rules are correct, there will be a reluctance to change one's beliefs; the current beliefs are doing a good job. And one will be inclined to act on one's current beliefs; one will exhibit a greater level of activity.

Happiness tends to cause one to not change one's beliefs.

```
(forall (e1 p e2 s1 s2)                                  (49.15)
    (if (and (happy' e1 p)(changeBeliefSet' e2 p s1 s2)(etc))
        (exists (e3) (and (not' e3 e2)(cause e1 e3)))))
```

That is, if p is happy, this will tend to cause p not to change his or her beliefs.

A more precise formulation of this would be to say that one is reluctant to change one's beliefs in a knowledge domain relevant to the goals whose achievement made the person happy.

If we had a theory of energy, we could say that being happy causes one to have more energy. We can state what should be a corollary of this theory, namely that happiness tends to cause one to do things in accordance with one's beliefs.

```
(forall (p e1 e2 e3 e4)                                          (49.16)
    (if (and (happy' e1 p)(goal e2 p)(believe p e3)
             (cause' e3 e4 e2)(agentOf p e4)(etc))
        (cause e1 e4)))
```

In this axiom, e1 is p's happiness, e2 is a goal of p's, p believes e3 which is the proposition that e4 causes e2, and p is the agent of e4. Then defeasibly the happiness e1 causes p to do e4.

Sadness is the other side of happiness. One is sad when one's goals are not being satisfied. This means that the rules or beliefs one is operating under are not to be trusted. Therefore, sadness should result in a lower level of activity, that is, the person should be reluctant to act on those distrusted beliefs. Moreover, the person should be more susceptible to changes in beliefs.

Absence of goal satisfaction tends to cause sadness.

```
(forall (e1 p e2)                                                (49.17)
    (if (and (goal e1 p)(not' e2 e1)(etc))
        (exists (e3) (and (sad' e3 p)(cause e2 e3)))))
```

That is, if eventuality e1 is a goal of person p's and e2 is its negation, then defeasibly e2 will cause p's sadness e3.

Anticipating a failure to reach one's goals makes one sad.

```
(forall (p e e0 e1 e2 e3 t1 t2)                                  (49.18)
    (if (and (atTime' e1 e t2)(not' e0 e1)(goal e1 p)
             (believe' e2 p e0)(atTime' e3 e2 t1)
             (before t1 t2)(etc))
        (exists (e4 e5)
            (and (sad' e4 p)(atTime' e5 e4 t1)(cause e3 e5)))))
```

This axiom is similar to the corresponding axiom for happiness.

We could sharpen the conditions on this. Generally, there should be some expectation that the goal will be satisfied, and there may be some effort involved in trying to achieve the goal, although we can be sad about occurrences over which we have no control.

Sadness suppresses the urge to action.

```
(forall (p e1 e2 e3 e4)                                          (49.19)
    (if (and (sad' e1 p)(goal e2 p)(believe p e3)(cause' e3 e4 e2)
             (agentOf p e4)(etc))
        (exists (e5) (and (not' e5 e4)(cause e1 e5)))))
```

In this axiom, e1 is p's sadness, e2 is a goal of p's, p believes e3 which is that e4 causes e2, and p is the agent of e4. Then defeasibly there is a negation e5 of e4 that is caused by the sadness e1. That is, if p is sad, then even though p believes there is some action e4 that would cause the goal to hold, the sadness tends to cause p not to do the action.

Sadness opens one to a change of beliefs.

```
(forall (e1 p)                                                    (49.20)
   (if (and (sad' e1 p)(etc))
      (exists (e2 s1 s2)
         (and (changeBeliefSet' e2 p s1 s2)(cause e1 e2)))))
```

That is, if p is sad, this will tend to cause p to change his or her beliefs.

Unhappiness is not a single emotion. There are many ways one can be unhappy. One can be irritated, afraid, anxious, disgusted, remorseful, and so on. The predicate unhappy is essentially an indicator of negative polarity. One thing unhappiness for sure is not is happiness. We state this as follows:

```
(forall (p) (if (unhappy p)(not (happy p))))                     (49.21)
```

The converse of this is not true; there is a neutral region between being happy and being unhappy.

Sadness is one way to be unhappy.

```
(forall (p) (if (sad p)(unhappy p)))                            (49.22)
```

49.4 SHADES OF HAPPINESS

We have rich and nuanced emotional lives. We can be glad that something happened without being cheerful about it. We can be elated without being euphoric. We can be happy because we feel gratitude, gloating, vindication, or pride. In this section we give characterizations of several synonyms and near synonyms of "happy," as a way of demonstrating the scope of the theories we have developed.

We characterized happiness in terms of its causes (goals being satisfied) and its effects (higher level of activity). Sometimes in discourse the cause of the happiness is focused on. In

The docents were very happy that we chatted with them.

the chatting is the cause of the happiness. Sometimes the effects are focused on. In

The staff were happy and helpful.

the helpfulness is implicitly an effect of the happiness.

A number of near synonyms of "happy" are characterized as variants of happiness where certain constraints are placed on the cause. In Section 49.6 we characterize the emotion terms "grateful," "gloat," and "proud" in terms of the circumstances that triggered the happiness.

Another example in this class is the word "joyful," which is most often used to describe a happiness that results from long-term goals or high-level values such as being with one's friends and family. We can begin to capture this in the following axiom:

```
(forall (e p)                                                    (49.23)
   (if (and (joyful' e p)(etc))
      (exists (e1)
         (and (cause e1 e)(longTermGoal e1 p)))))
```

That is, if e is a state of p's being joyful, then there is likely to be a long-term goal e1 of p's whose actual occurrence would cause e.

A long-term goal is a goal that is likely to persist through time. So if e is a goal of p's at time t1, then defeasibly it will be a goal of p's at a later time t2.

```
(forall (e p e1 t1 t2)                                            (49.24)
    (if (and (longTermGoal e p)(goal' e1 e p)(atTime e1 t1)
            (before t1 t2)(etc))
        (atTime e1 t2)))
```

That is, if e is a long-term goal of p's, e1 is the eventuality of its being a goal of p's, and e1 holds at time t1, then e1 will probably hold at any later time t2 as well.

Another, fairly complex synonym of "happy" is "vindicated." It also focuses on the cause of the happiness. Specifically, if one commits to an action that others believe will lead to something bad and in fact it leads to something good, then one will feel vindicated. Hence, the following axiom:

```
(forall (p x e1 e2 e3 e4 e5)                                      (49.25)
    (if (and (agentOf p e1)(cause' e4 e1 e2)(believe x e4)
            (badFor e2 p)(cause' e5 e1 e3)(goodFor e3 p)(etc))
        (exists (e6)
            (and (vindicated' e6 p e1)(cause e5 e6)))))
```

In this rule e1 is the action p performs, e2 is its bad possible consequence, e3 is its good possible consequence, e4 is the causal relation between e1 and e2, and e5 is the causal relation between e1 and e3. Someone x believes e1 will cause the bad outcome e2. But if in fact e1 causes the good outcome e3, that causal relation e5 will cause p to feel vindicated (e6) about performing e1.

Vindication is a kind of happiness.

```
(forall (p e1)                                                    (49.26)
    (if (vindicated p e1)(happy p)))
```

The words "pleased" and "glad" are almost interchangeable. They both focus on the cause of the happiness. Their principal complements name causes. To be pleased or glad that something happened is to have that something cause one's happiness. To be pleased with something is for some property or event involving that something to be the cause.

The word "glad" seems a little bit stronger than the word "pleased." In

> I'm pleased that my second cousin, whom I've never met, was elected to his city council.

the relationship alone seems sufficient explanation, whereas in

> I'm glad that my second cousin, whom I've never met, was elected to his city council.

we expect a little more by way of explanation, for example, I'll get more access to the wheels of government.

We can approximate this subtle difference f by saying that being pleased only defeasibly implies happiness, whereas being glad always does.

```
(forall (p e)                                                    (49.27)
    (if (and (pleased p e)(etc))(happyThat p e)))
```

```
(forall (p e)                                                    (49.28)
    (if (glad p e)(happyThat p e)))
```

The words "cheerful" and "jubilant" focus on the effects of happiness. We said that one of the principal effects of happiness is a higher level of activity. For the words "cheerful" and "jubilant," this is specialized to higher levels of social activity. Cheerfulness is manifested mostly in interactions with others, and in discourse most uses of the word occur near a mention of the social group the person is interacting with.

In other work (Hobbs, 2005a) we presented an account of communication consisting of an axiomatization of Gricean nonnatural meaning of atomic symbols and an axiomatization of how simple meanings compose into complex meanings. In another paper (Hobbs, Sagae, and Wertheim, 2012) we defined a social interaction as a set of one or more of these communicative actions. The predication (interaction p1 p2) says that agents p1 and p2 interact in this sense.

Then the following axiom says that one's cheerfulness causes one to interact with others.

```
(forall (e1 p1)                                                  (49.29)
    (if (and (cheerful' e1 p1)(etc))
        (exists (e2 p2)
            (and (interact' e2 p1 p2)(cause e1 e2)))))
```

The word "jubilant" also focuses on social interaction and is often associated with making lots of noise together. It is a more intense form of happiness than cheerfulness, and hence has more obvious manifestations. We can capture this by saying that being jubilant is an intense form of cheerfulness.

```
(forall (e p)                                                    (49.30)
    (if (jubilant' e p)
        (and (cheerful' e p)(intense e p))))
```

The words "pleased" and "glad" focused on the cause of the happiness. The words "cheerful" and "jubilant" focus on the effects of happiness. Our next pair of words, "elated" and "euphoric," focus on the feeling itself. Both mean "intensely happy." But consider

I was elated, but not euphoric.
? I was euphoric, but not elated.

The first sentence sounds okay; the second sounds strange.

The word "elated" refers to the Hi end of the intensity scale. It means "intensely happy." The word "euphoric" refers to the Hi end of the Hi end of the intensity scale. It means "very intensely happy."

The axiom for "elated" is

```
(forall (e p)                                          (49.31)
   (if (elated' e p)
       (and (happy' e p)(intense e p))))
```

The scale for "elated" is happiness in the high region of intensity, so we can define "euphoric" as being in the high region of the scale for "elated."

```
(forall (p e e0 s0 s1)                                 (49.32)
   (if (and (elated' e0 p)(scaleFor s0 e0)(Hi s1 s0)
            (euphoric' e p))
       (exists (e1)
           (and (happy' e1 p)(gen e1 e)(inScale e1 s1)))))
```

Line 2 defines s1 to be the Hi region of the "elated" scale. Line 3 says that e is p's euphoria. Then lines 4 and 5 say that the euphoria is generated by p's happiness that lies in the Hi region of the elated-ness scale and hence in the Hi region of the Hi region of the intensity scale.

49.5 THE RAW EMOTIONS

What we are calling the raw emotions are ones that are generally in anybody's list of the basic emotions. There are three. The raw emotions are fear, anger, and disgust.

Unlike happiness and sadness, they are specific responses to specific threats, and the actions they trigger have immediate survival value. They are deeply biological. For sure, reptiles do not feel such complex emotions as vindication or resentment. But we can easily imagine reptiles feeling something like fear, anger, and disgust.

We can give a very coarse-grained, primitive, "reptilian" characterization of the raw emotions in the form of a schema. Threats are of two kinds – the kind that eats you and the kind that you eat that then kills you from inside. Disgust is the response to things that you eat. It triggers efforts to eject the threat. Anger and fear are responses to things that eat you, and correspond to the fight-or-flight responses. In general, if the threat is something you can defeat or cope with, you get angry and fight. You attempt to move it to a place where is is no longer a threat or to destroy its capacity to do you harm. If it is something that can defeat you or that you can't cope with, you become afraid and flee. You cause yourself to move to where it is no longer a threat.

Of course, these emotions extend beyond culinary concerns. As with all emotions, we can characterize abstract situations in which they arise, and abstract responses we have to those situations.

The person is embedded in an environment. Something in the environment poses a threat, that is, there is the possibility that one or more of the person's goals, such as survival, is going to be defeated. The first question is where the threat is located. If it is in the external environment the emotion triggered will be fear or anger. If it is literally or metaphorically "inside" the person, it will trigger disgust. The response to disgust is to eject the threat. The response to fear is to remove one's self from the threatening environment. The response to anger is to remain in the environment and to modify it so that the threat no longer exists.

To formalize the account of anger, we first define the notion of eliminating a threat to one's goals.

```
(forall (p x g)                                                (49.33)
    (iff (eliminateThreat p x g)
         (exists (e0 e1 e2 e3)
             (and (threat' e0 x p g)(cause p e1)(changeIn' e1 x)
                  (cause e1 e2)(changeTo' e2 e3)(not' e3 e0)))))
```

That is, person p eliminates a threat x to goal g if and only if there is the eventuality e0 that is x's threatening p's goal g, and p causes a change e1 in x, which in turn causes a change into the negation e3 of e0. In simpler terms, to eliminate a threat posed by entity x in the environment is to change some property of x so that it is no longer threatening. For example, chasing x away or disarming x would both be ways of eliminating the threat.

Anger is triggered by a threat that the person believes he or she can eliminate.

```
(forall (x p g e1 e2 e3 c)                                     (49.34)
    (if (and (threat' e1 x p g)(believe p e2)(possible' e2 e3 c)(cwu c p)
             (eliminateThreat' e3 p x g)(etc))
        (exists (e4)
            (and (angry' e4 p)(cause e1 e4)))))
```

That is, if e1 is a situation in which something x threatens a goal g of person p's and p believes it is currently possible (e2) that p can eliminate (e3) the threat, then e1 will defeasibly cause p to become angry (e4).

We can characterize `angryAt` and `angryThat` predicates similarly. The threat x can be anything – a concrete entity, another agent, or an eventuality – and we can be angry at any of them. We can be angry only that a situation holds, and if x is not an eventuality, we must find some situation involving x (arg*) that itself consitutes a threat to p.

```
(forall (x p g e1 e2 e3 c)                                     (49.35)
    (if (and (threat' e1 x p g)(believe p e2)(possible' e2 e3 c)(cwu c t)
             (eliminateThreat' e3 p x g)(etc))
        (exists (e4 e5 e6)
            (and (angryAt' e4 p x)(cause e1 e4)
                 (or (and (eventuality x)(angryThat' e5 p x)
                          (cause e1 e5))
                     (and (not (eventuality x))(arg* x e6)
                          (threat e6 p g)(angryThat' e5 p e6)
                          (cause e1 e5)))))))
```

Lines 1–5 are as in axiom (49.34). Lines 6 and 7 take care of the case where x is an eventuality. In lines 8–10, if x is not an eventuality, we need to find an eventuality e6 involving x that is a threat to p. The person p is then angry that that situation holds.

We are angry that the situation e1 obtains, and we are angry at the principal agent x in that situation.

We have placed no constraints on what x can be. Ortony et al. (1990) argue that there has to be an entity x that is the target of the anger. But it seems to us that, for example, a bride can be angry at the rainy weather on the day of her outdoor wedding, without necessarily blaming it on some agent.

The principal consequence of anger is an attempt to eliminate the threat.

```
(forall (x p g e1 e2)                                           (49.36)
    (if (and (angry' e1 p)(threat' e2 x p g)(cause e2 e1)(etc))
        (exists (e3 e4)
            (and (try' e3 p e4)(eliminateThreat' e4 p x g)
                (cause e1 e3)))))
```

If a person feels anger at a threat, this is likely to trigger an attempt to eliminate the threat that caused the anger.

Anger is a form of unhappiness.

```
(forall (p) (if (angry p)(unhappy p)))                          (49.37)
```

To formalize fear, we first define the notion of avoiding a threat.

```
(forall (p x g)                                                 (49.38)
    (iff (avoidThreat p x g)
        (exists (e0 e1 e2 e3)
            (and (threat' e0 x p g)(cause p e1)(changeIn' e1 p)
                (cause e1 e2)(changeTo' e2 e3)(not' e3 e0)))))
```

That is, person p avoids a threat x to goal g if and only if there is the eventuality e0 that is x's threatening p's goal g, and p causes a change e1 in p, which in turn causes a change into the negation e3 of e0. In simpler terms, to avoid a threat posed by entity x in the environment is to change some property of one's self p so that x is no longer threatening. Thus, the only difference between eliminating a threat and avoiding a threat is in what is changed. To eliminate a threat, change the properties or location of the threat x. To avoid a threat, change your own properties or location. For example, running away or acting submissive might both be ways of avoiding the threat.

Fear is triggered by a threat that the person believes must be avoided.

```
(forall (x p g e1 e2 e3 e4 c)                                   (49.39)
    (if (and (threat' e1 x p g)(believe p e2)(not' e2 e3)
            (possible' e3 e4 c)(cwu c p)(eliminateThreat' e4 p x g)(etc))
        (exists (e5)
            (and (afraid' e5 p)(cause e1 e5)))))
```

That is, if e1 is a situation in which something x threatens a goal g of person p's and p believes it is currently not possible (e2) that p can eliminate (e4) the threat, then e1 will defeasibly cause p to become afraid (e5).

The principal consequence of fear is that the person attempts to avoid the threat.

```
(forall (x p g e1 e2)                                        (49.40)
    (if (and (afraid' e1 p)(threat' e2 x p g)(cause e2 e1)(etc))
        (exists (e3 e4)
            (and (try' e3 p e4)(avoidThreat' e4 p x g)
                 (cause e1 e3)))))
```

We are reluctant to say that fear is a variety of unhappiness. In many cases it is. But we often seek out experiences that will evoke a kind of unthinking fear out of proportion to its real danger. For example, we take amusement park rides, skydive, and go to horror movies. Fear seems to be different in this; we rarely seek out experiences we believe will make us disgusted or angry. (Seeing movies about injustice may be an exception to this.)

We can be disgusted at the thought of eating snakes. But we can also be disgusted, perhaps metaphorically, at our own or someone else's behavior. The thing that disgusts has to be "interior" in some sense. Snake meat in the stomach is literally interior. But the bad behavior of someone in our in-group is also in a way interior – interior to the group. We can be disgusted at the actions of an uncle who molests our sister. If a total stranger does it, it will make us angry, but perhaps not disgusted. A Democrat or an American citizen may be disgusted at Bill Clinton's affair with Monica Lewinsky. Clinton was a part of the in-group, and threatened long-standing goals of the in-group by his behavior, evoking a reaction of members wanting to eject him. We are unlikely to have the same reaction if a married oil company executive has an affair with an intern; he is not part of our in-group. Some behavior, such as murdering and cannibalizing people, is so heinous that it goes beyond what we feel is remotely acceptable in human beings; we are viewing the whole human species as our in-group.

To characterize disgust formally, we first posit a notion of an entity being interior to a person. One way of being interior is being inside. (It is beyond the scope of this book to define `inside`.) Another is to be a member of the same in-group.

```
(forall (x p) (if (inside x p)(interior x p)))              (49.41)
```

```
(forall (p1 p2 s)                                           (49.42)
    (if (and (person p1)(member p1 s)(person p2)(member p2 s))
        (interior p2 p1)))
```

The second axiom says that if persons p1 and p2 are both members of the same group s, then p2 is interior to p1 in the sense of "interior" that we need here.

To eject a threat is to cause the threat to be no longer interior.

```
(forall (e1 p x g)                                          (49.43)
    (iff (ejectThreat' e1 p x g)
        (exists (e2 e3)
            (and (threat x p g)(interior' e2 x p)(cause p e3)
                 (changeFrom' e3 e2)(gen e3 e1)))))
```

That is, p ejects an interior threat x by causing x's location to change from "interior" to p to some other place that is not interior to p, thereby causing x not to be a threat. Vomiting and ostracizing are examples.

Disgust is triggered by an interior threat.

```
(forall (x p g e1)                                            (49.44)
    (if (and (threat' e1 x p g)(interior x p))
        (exists (e2)
            (and (disgusted' e2 p)(cause e1 e2)))))
```

That is, if e1 is a situation in which something x interior to person p threatens a goal g of p's, then e1 will defeasibly cause p to become disgusted (e2).

If a person feels disgust from a threat, this is likely to trigger an attempt to eject the threat that caused the disgust.

```
(forall (x p g e1 e2)                                         (49.45)
    (if (and (disgusted' e1 p)(threat' e2 x p g)(cause e2 e1)(etc))
        (exists (e3 e4)
            (and (try' e3 p e4)(ejectThreat' e4 p x g)
                 (cause e1 e3)))))
```

Disgust may be a variety of unhappiness.

```
(forall (p) (if (disgusted p)(unhappy p)))                    (49.46)
```

49.6 BASIC EMOTIONS COGNITIVELY ELABORATED

49.6.1 Happiness and Sadness for Others

There are hundreds of words and phrases in English that describe emotional states, each conveying slightly different shades of meaning from the others. Ortony et al. (1990) give schematic definitions of several dozen of these terms, and in the next few sections we show how they can be formalized within our theory. Most of them can be characterized as one of the basic emotions in which constraints are placed on their causes. For example, happiness is caused by one's goals being satisfied. Gloating is a very particular kind of happiness that is caused by one particular kind of goal being satisfied, namely, by one's enemy or competitor not achieving his or her goal. We first consider happiness and sadness for others.

One can have an emotional reaction to someone else's success or failure in reaching goals. There are two relevant dimensions in this. The other person can be someone with whom one empathizes, because he or she is in the same group or involved in some collaborative activity, or someone with whom one does not empathize, because he or she is in some "countergroup" or is involved in an adversarial or competitive relationship with one. We will call the points on this dimension "in-group" and "out-group." The other dimension is whether the other person is succeeding or failing in achieving the goals, that is, whether events are "good for" or "bad for" the other person.

We first need to define in-groups and out-groups. We will do so in terms of shared, competitive and adversarial goals. We will say that a person p2 is in one of p1's in-groups if there is a goal they share.

```
(forall (p1 p2)                                           (49.47)
    (iff (inGroup p1 p2)
         (exists (s g)
             (and (member p1 s)(member p2 s)(sharedGoal g s)))))
```

The set s is a set consisting of at least the two persons p1 and p2.

We will say that person p2 is in one of p1's out-groups if p1 and p2 have competitive or adversarial goals.

```
(forall (p1 p2)                                           (49.48)
    (iff (outGroup p1 p2)
         (exists (g1 g2)
             (or (competitiveGoals g1 g2 p1 p2)
                 (adversarialGoals g1 p1 p2)))))
```

Something is good for someone if it causes one of their goals to hold, and something is bad for someone if it causes one of their goals not to hold.

Then we can fill the 2×2 matrix with emotion terms as in the following table:

	good-for	bad-for
in-group	"happy for"	"sorry for"
out-group	"resent"	"gloat"

Something good for someone in our in-group tends to cause us to be happy for that person.

```
(forall (e1 p1 p2)                                        (49.49)
    (if (and (goodFor e1 p2)(inGroup p1 p2)(etc))
        (exists (e2) (and (happyFor' e2 p1 p2)(cause e1 e2)))))
```

Eventuality e1 is the good thing that happened to person p2, and e2 is person p1's happiness for p2.

"Happiness for" is a kind of happiness.

```
(forall (p1 p2) (if (happyFor p1 p2) (happy p1)))         (49.50)
```

Something bad for someone in our in-group tends to cause us to be sorry for that person.

```
(forall (e1 p1 p2)                                        (49.51)
    (if (and (badFor e1 p2)(inGroup p1 p2)(etc))
        (exists (e2) (and (sorryFor' e2 p1 p2)(cause e1 e2)))))
```

One can argue that being sorry for someone is a kind of sadness, and hence a way of being unhappy.

```
(forall (p1 p2) (if (sorryFor p1 p2) (sad p1)))           (49.52)
```

If something good happens for someone in an out-group, it tends to cause us to resent that person, according to Ortony et al. (1990).

```
(forall (e1 p1 p2)                                            (49.53)
   (if (and (goodFor e1 p2)(outGroup p1 p2)(etc))
       (exists (e2) (and (resent' e2 p1 p2)(cause e1 e2)))))
```

Resentment seems more like anger than like sadness. Because we are in a competitive or adversarial relationship, the other person's success is a threat to our own success.

```
(forall (p1 p2) (if (and (resent p1 p2)(etc)) (angry p1)))    (49.54)
```

In any case, resentment is a kind of unhappiness.

```
(forall (p1 p2) (if (resent p1 p2) (unhappy p1)))             (49.55)
```

If something bad happens for someone in an out-group, it tends to cause us to gloat about that person.

```
(forall (e1 p1 p2)                                            (49.56)
   (if (and (badFor e1 p2)(outGroup p1 p2)(etc))
       (exists (e2) (and (gloat' e2 p1 p2)(cause e1 e2)))))
```

Gloating is a (rather pitiful) kind of happiness.

```
(forall (p1 p2) (if (gloat p1 p2) (happy p1)))               (49.57)
```

49.6.2 Hope and Fear-2

Fear is ambiguous between the senses illustrated in

I fear bears.
I fear we will be late for the meeting.

The first (fear-1) is a raw emotion, and is dealt with above. The second (fear-2) is a cognitive attitude or a belief about the likelihood of an event together with an evaluation, perhaps with an emotional accompaniment. The emotion associated with fear-2 is certainly a form of unhappiness, but it is not necessarily a form of fear-1.

Hope and fear-2 are both concerned with eventualities that are anticipated. We can define "anticipate" as a nonzero graded belief that something will happen in the future, where the belief results from envisioning courses of events from the current world understanding.

```
(forall (p e)                                                (49.58)
   (iff (anticipate p e)
        (exists (e1 e2 e3 d)
            (and (gbel' e1 p e d)(gt d 0)
                 (envisionFromTo' e2 p e3 e)(cwu e3 p)
                 (cause e2 e1)))))
```

That is, for person p to anticipate situation e is for p to envision from p's current world understanding e3 to situation e and have that cause a nonzero graded belief that e will happen.

The graded belief in anticipation has to be nonzero. You can hope that you will win this week's lottery, but you can't really hope that someday you will flap your arms and fly.

Hope and fear-2 are varieties of anticipating. Hope is when you anticipate something good for you. Fear-2 is when you anticipate something bad for you.

```
(forall (p e)                                              (49.59)
    (iff (hope p e)
         (and (anticipate p e)(goodFor e p))))
```

```
(forall (p e)                                              (49.60)
    (iff (fear2 p e)
         (and (anticipate p e)(badFor e p))))
```

It is debatable whether hope is a kind of happiness, so let's make the rule defeasible.

```
(forall (p e) (if (and (hope p e)(etc))(happy p)))         (49.61)
```

At least we can say that hope, for some reason, tends to suppress unhappiness.

```
(forall (e1 p e)                                           (49.62)
   (if (and (hope' e1 p e)(etc))
        (exists (e2 e3)
            (and (not' e2 e3)(unhappy' e3 p)(cause e1 e2)))))
```

That is, hoping (e1) causes one not (e2) to be unhappy (e3).

Fear-2 is at least sometimes a kind of raw fear.

```
(forall (p e) (if (and (fear2 p e)(etc))(afraid p)))       (49.63)
```

Fear-2 is certainly a kind of unhappiness.

```
(forall (p e) (if (fear2 p e)(unhappy p)))                 (49.64)
```

49.6.3 Reactions to Goals Realized and Frustrated

Circumstances that are anticipated eventually either happen or don't happen, and these possibilities have their own set of emotions. In these emotions an event and its nonoccurrence are both anticipated, the event either occurs or not, and the event is either good for or bad for the person. The terms for these emotions are indicated in the following table:

	good-for	bad-for
happens	satisfaction	fears confirmed
doesn't happen	disappointment	relief

Satisfaction results when an event and its negation are both anticipated, the event is good for the person, and the event actually occurs.

```
(forall (p e e1)                                              (49.65)
    (iff (and (anticipate p e)(anticipate p e1)(not' e1 e)
              (goodFor e p)(etc))
         (exists (e2)
            (and (satisfied' e2 p e)(cause e e2)))))
```

That is, if person p anticipates both e and its negation e1, where e is good for p, then e actually occurring will cause p to be satisfied that e.

Satisfaction is a kind of happiness.

```
(forall (p e) (if (satisfied p e)(happy p)))                 (49.66)
```

Disappointment results when an event and its negation are both anticipated, the event is good for the person, and the event does not actually occur.

```
(forall (p e e1)                                              (49.67)
    (iff (and (anticipate p e)(anticipate p e1)(not' e1 e)
              (goodFor e p)(etc))
         (exists (e2)
            (and (disappointed' e2 p e)(cause e1 e2)))))
```

That is, if person p anticipates both e and its negation e1, where e is good for p, then e1 actually occurring, that is, e not occurring, will cause p to be disappointed that e did not occur.

Disappointment is a kind of sadness.

```
(forall (p e) (if (disappointed p e)(sad p)))                (49.68)
```

A confirmation of one's fears results when an event and its negation are both anticipated, the event is bad for the person, and the event actually occurs.

```
(forall (p e e1)                                              (49.69)
    (iff (and (anticipate p e)(anticipate p e1)(not' e1 e)
              (badFor e p)(etc))
         (exists (e2)
            (and (fearsConfirmed' e2 p e)(cause e e2)))))
```

That is, if person p anticipates both e and its negation e1, where e is bad for p, then e actually occurring will cause p to feel that fears that e were confirmed.

Confirmation of fears is at least defeasibly a kind of sadness.

```
(forall (p e) (if (and (fearsConfirmed p e)(etc))(sad p)))   (49.70)
```

Confirmation of fears is certainly a kind of unhappiness.

```
(forall (p e) (if (fearsConfirmed p e)(unhappy p)))          (49.71)
```

Relief results when an event and its negation are both anticipated, the event is bad for the person, and the event does not actually occur.

```
(forall (p e e1)                                              (49.72)
    (iff (and (anticipate p e)(anticipate p e1)(not' e1 e)
              (badFor e p)(etc))
         (exists (e2)
             (and (relief' e2 p e)(cause e1 e2)))))
```

That is, if person p anticipates both e and its negation e1, where e is bad for p, then e1 actually occurring, that is, e not occurring, will cause p to feel relief about e.

Relief is a kind of happiness.

```
(forall (p e) (if (relief p e)(happy p)))                    (49.73)
```

49.6.4 Reactions to Achievements and Failures

The emotions explicated in the last two sections have to do with whether or not good or bad things happen. But there is no role played by agency in those emotions. However, some emotions crucially depend on the agency of ourselves or others. Here we have a $2 \times 2 \times 2$ array of possibilities. First, is the agent of the action one's self or an other? Second, is the action good for or bad for one? Third, was the action merely attempted or did it actually succeed? This defines a space of eight emotional states and their corresponding terms, as indicated in the following table:

	Attempts		Succeeds	
	good-for	bad-for	good-for	bad-for
self	pride	self-reproach	gratification	remorse
other	appreciation	reproach	gratitude	anger-2

According to Ortony et al. (1990), we feel pride when we attempt to achieve a goal that is difficult to achieve. If we succeed, we feel gratification. There is a similar distinction between three other pairs of emotions. Self-reproach results when a person attempts something that is bad for the person; remorse results from the success of such an action. Appreciation results when someone else attempts to achieve our goals for us; gratitude results when he or she succeeds. Reproach results when another person attempts to bring about an outcome that is bad for you; what we will call "anger-2" results when he or she succeeds.

We distinguish between the raw emotion anger, discussed earlier, and the concept explicated here, anger-2, which has a specific kind of cause. Anger-2 can be a kind of anger, but it does not encompass all kinds of anger.

Before examining each one of these in turn, we need to consider how the self-based emotions extend beyond the self to one's in-group. We feel pride in our own attempts and achievements. But we can also feel pride in the achievements of others, provided they are a part of what we consider to be one of our in-groups. We are proud of the accomplishments of our children; here there may be a strong component of self-congratulation – we played a significant role in their success by raising them right. But we might be proud of the achievement of a cousin or a grandparent where we played no causal role. We might be proud when a countryman wins a gold medal in the Olympics; the entire citizenry of the country is the in-group. We might be proud that the human race is capable of discovering the theory of quantum mechanics; the entire human race is the in-group in pursuing the goals of scientific knowledge. On the other hand, where there are adversarial goals, we do not feel pride. A USC football fan might admire the play of the Texas quarterback Vince Young as he single-handedly beats USC, but the fan is unlikely to feel pride in it. To make the statement of the axioms easier, we will say that a person is in his or her own in-group.

$$\text{(forall (p) (if (person p)(inGroup p p)))} \tag{49.74}$$

Pride in this schema occurs when a person or someone in the person's in-group attempts to achieve something good for the person, generally something difficult.

$$\begin{aligned}
&\text{(forall (e p1 p2 e1)} \tag{49.75}\\
&\quad\text{(if (and (inGroup p1 p2)(goodFor e p1)(difficult e p2)}\\
&\qquad\qquad\text{(agentOf p2 e)(try' e1 p2 e)(etc))}\\
&\quad\text{(exists (e2) (and (proud' e2 p1 e)(cause e1 e2)))))}
\end{aligned}$$

That is, if person p2 is in an in-group of p1's, and action e by p2 is good for p1 but difficult for p2, then p2's trying e1 to do e causes p1 to feel proud (e2). In this axiom p1 can equal p2, so one may be proud of one's own accomplishments.

This sort of pride is a kind of happiness.

$$\text{(forall (p e) (if (proud p e)(happy p)))} \tag{49.76}$$

Gratification results when the attempt actually succeeds. Gratification also extends from the self to in-groups.

$$\begin{aligned}
&\text{(forall (e p1 p2 e1)} \tag{49.77}\\
&\quad\text{(if (and (inGroup p1 p2)(goodFor e p1)(difficult e p2)}\\
&\qquad\qquad\text{(agentOf p2 e)(succeed' e1 p2 e)(etc))}\\
&\quad\text{(exists (e2) (and (gratified' e2 p1 e)(cause e1 e2)))))}
\end{aligned}$$

That is, if person p2 (possibly the same as p1) is in an in-group of p1's, and action e by p2 is good for p1 but difficult for p2, then p2's succeeding e1 at doing e causes p1 to feel gratified (e2).

Since succeeding implies trying, if one is gratified, one is also proud (and consequently, happy).

$$\text{(forall (p e) (if (gratified p e)(proud p e)))} \tag{49.78}$$

Appreciation occurs when someone other than the person attempts to achieve something good for the person, generally something difficult.

$$\begin{aligned}
&\text{(forall (e p1 p2 e1)} \tag{49.79}\\
&\quad\text{(if (and (nequal p1 p2)(goodFor e p1)(difficult e p2)}\\
&\qquad\qquad\text{(agentOf p2 e)(try' e1 p2 e)(etc))}\\
&\quad\text{(exists (e2) (and (appreciative' e2 p1 e)(cause e1 e2)))))}
\end{aligned}$$

That is, if person p2 is someone other than p1, and action e by p2 is good for p1 but difficult for p2, then p2's trying e1 to do e causes p1 to feel appreciative (e2). Note that if p2 is in an in-group of p1's, p1 can feel both proud and appreciative of the attempt.

Appreciation is at least defeasibly a kind of happiness.

```
(forall (p e) (if (and (appreciative p e)(etc))(happy p)))        (49.80)
```

Gratitude results when the attempt actually succeeds.

```
(forall (e p1 p2 e1)                                             (49.81)
   (if (and (nequal p1 p2)(goodFor e p1)(difficult e p2)
            (agentOf p2 e)(succeed' e1 p2 e)(etc))
       (exists (e2) (and (grateful' e2 p1 e)(cause e1 e2)))))
```

That is, if person p2 is not the same as p1, and action e by p2 is good for p1 but difficult for p2, then p2's succeeding e1 at doing e causes p1 to feel grateful (e2).

Since succeeding implies trying, if one is grateful, one is also appreciative (and consequently, defeasibly, happy).

```
(forall (p e) (if (grateful p e)(appreciative p e)))             (49.82)
```

Self-reproach occurs when a person attempts to achieve something bad for himself or herself.

```
(forall (e p e1)                                                 (49.83)
   (if (and (badFor e p)(agentOf p e)(try' e1 p e)(etc))
       (exists (e2) (and (selfReproachful' e2 p e)(cause e1 e2)))))
```

That is, if an action e by a person p is bad for p, then p's trying e1 to do e causes p to feel self-reproach (e2).

Self-reproach is often a kind of anger at one's self, and hence a kind of unhappiness.

```
(forall (p e) (if (and (selfReproachful p e)(etc))(angry p)))    (49.84)
```

Remorse results when the attempt actually succeeds.

```
(forall (e p e1)                                                 (49.85)
   (if (and (badFor e p)(agentOf p e)(succeed' e1 p e)(etc))
       (exists (e2) (and (remorse' e2 p e)(cause e1 e2)))))
```

That is, if a person p's action e is bad for p, then p's succeeding e1 at doing e causes p to feel remorse (e2).

Since succeeding implies trying, if one is remorseful, one also feels self-reproach.

```
(forall (p e) (if (remorse p e)(selfReproachful p e)))           (49.86)
```

Remorse can certainly have a component of anger at one's self, as we would expect from axioms (49.84) and (49.86). But remorse often also has a component of sadness.

```
(forall (p e) (if (and (remorse p e)(etc))(sad p)))              (49.87)
```

Embarrassment is a kind of remorse, where the person believes others in an in-group disapprove of the action.

```
(forall (p1 p2 s e1 e2)                                        (49.88)
    (if (and (succeed' e1 p1 e)(badFor e p1)(nequal p1 p2)
            (inGroup p1 p2)(doubleton s p1 p2)(believe p2 e2)
            (badFor' e2 e s)(etc))
        (exists (e3)(and (embarrassed' e3 p1 e)(cause e1 e3)))))
```

That is, if a person p1 "succeeds" in doing something bad for p1 and at least one other person p2 in an in-group of p1's believes that it is bad for the set s of the two of them, that tends to cause p1 to be embarrassed about e. The implication in Axiom (49.88) leaves open the possibility of other causes of embarrassment.

Reproach occurs when someone other than the person attempts to achieve something bad for the person.

```
(forall (e p1 p2 e1)                                           (49.89)
    (if (and (nequal p1 p2)(badFor e p1)
            (agentOf p2 e)(try' e1 p2 e)(etc))
        (exists (e2) (and (reproachful' e2 p1 e)(cause e1 e2)))))
```

That is, if person p2 is someone other than p1 and action e by p2 is bad for p1, then p2's trying e1 to do e causes p1 to feel reproachful (e2).

Reproach is often felt as a kind of anger.

```
(forall (p e) (if (and (reproachful p e)(etc))(angry p)))      (49.90)
```

When the attempt to do something bad to another agent actually succeeds, the victim often feels a kind of anger, which we will call anger-2.

```
(forall (e p1 p2 e1)                                           (49.91)
    (if (and (nequal p1 p2)(badFor e p1)
            (agentOf p2 e)(succeed' e1 p2 e)(etc))
        (exists (e2) (and (angry2' e2 p1 e)(cause e1 e2)))))
```

That is, if person p2 is not the same as p1 and action e by p2 is bad for p1, then p2's succeeding e1 at doing e causes p1 to feel angry-2 (e2).

Since succeeding implies trying, if one is angry-2, one is also reproachful.

```
(forall (p e) (if (angry2 p e)(reproachful p e)))             (49.92)
```

Therefore, anger-2 defeasibly implies the raw emotion of anger.

Sanders (1989) presented a logic of emotions focusing on some of these emotions, including anger (our anger-2), gratitude, and shame. Her definitions, in addition to goals, make appeal to notions of right and wrong, which we have avoided as concepts from a commonsense theory of microsociology and hence beyond the scope of this book.

49.7 ENVY AND JEALOUSY

Envy and jealousy are closely related and are often used interchangeably. Envy is displeasure resulting from seeing the success of others, and is very much related to the particular success. Jealousy seems to be more directed toward the person.

Suppose an athlete about to receive an Olympic gold medal is told that he must share it with a rival. He will not feel envious, because his rival has nothing that he doesn't have. But he may well feel jealous.

One possible characterization of envy and jealousy is that in envy we feel resentment over a nonexclusive goal that the other person has and we don't, whereas in jealousy, we feel resentment over a mutually exclusive goal that someone else has. We are more likely to label our feelings jealousy when someone has an exclusive relationship with someone we secretly admire. Our feelings toward someone who is very wealthy is more likely to be described as envy.

The following axiom says that if one person achieves one of a pair of mutually exclusive goals, it can cause jealousy in the other person.

```
(forall (p g p1 g1 p2 g2)                                    (49.93)
    (if (and (person p1)(person p2)(arg* p g)
             (subst p1 g1 p g)(subst p2 g2 p g)
             (competitiveGoals g1 g2 p1 p2)(etc))
        (exists (e1) (and (jealous' e1 p1 g2)(cause g2 e1)))))
```

In this axiom, g is an abstract eventuality involving a parameter p. Eventuality g1 results from instantiating g with person p1, and eventuality g2 results from instantiating g with person p2, where g1 and g2 are conflicting goals that cannot both be satisfied. Then if goal g2 actually comes about, that will cause p1 to feel jealous (e1) about g2. So g might be winning first prize, g1 is my winning it, and g2 is your winning it. If g2 is what actually comes about, then, defeasibly, I will feel jealous of your victory.

Envy, on the other hand, results from your success in the presence of my lack of success. Our goals are not necessarily mutually exclusive; they just don't happen to both hold.

```
(forall (p g p1 g1 p2 g2)                                    (49.94)
    (if (and (person p1)(person p2)(arg* p g)
             (subst p1 g1 p g)(subst p2 g2 p g)
             (goal g1 p1)(goal g2 p2)(not g1)(etc))
        (exists (e1) (and (envious' e1 p1 g2)(cause g2 e1)))))
```

This axiom differs from the axiom for jealousy only in line 4: Goals g1 and g2 do not have to be conflicting; it's just that goal g1 does not happen.

Quite often jealousy is associated with anger, consistent with the idea that p2's success was a threat to p1's achievement of a goal.

```
(forall (p e) (if (and (jealous p e)(etc))(angry p)))        (49.95)
```

Envy could be associated with anger, but more often it is closer to sadness, consistent with the idea that sadness results from goals not being satisfied.

```
(forall (p e) (if (and (envious p e)(etc))(sad p)))          (49.96)
```

Envy and jealousy are certainly both varieties of unhappiness.

```
(forall (p e) (if (jealous p e)(unhappy p)))                 (49.97)
```

```
(forall (p e) (if (envious p e)(unhappy p)))                 (49.98)
```

49.8 LIKING AND DISLIKING

As Heider (1958, p. 140) points out, liking and disliking are not so much emotions as dispositions to feel particular emotions in specific circumstances.

We like a state or event if it makes us happy, defeasibly of course.

```
(forall (e e1 e2 p)                                    (49.99)
    (if (and (eventuality e)(cause' e1 e e2)(happy' e2 p)(etc))
        (exists (e3) (and (like' e3 p e)(cause e1 e3)))))
```

That is, the causal relation e1 between e and p's being happy (e2) causes the eventuality e3 of p's liking e.

If a person likes an eventuality, then the eventuality defeasibly causes the person to be happy.

```
(forall (p e)                                          (49.100)
    (if (and (eventuality e)(like p e)(etc))
        (exists (e1) (and (happy' e1 p)(cause e e1)))))
```

We like an entity if there is an eventuality that makes us happy in which the entity plays a role.

```
(forall (p e x)                                        (49.101)
    (if (and (eventuality e)(like p e)(arg* x e)(etc))
        (like p x)))
```

The converse isn't true, even if x plays a causal role in the event. You can like people without liking everything they do. Your spouse can do things you dislike without causing you to dislike him or her. On the other hand, as instances accumulate, the balance can tip.

We dislike an eventuality if it tends to cause us to be unhappy.

```
(forall (e e1 e2 p)                                    (49.102)
    (if (and (eventuality e)(cause' e1 e e2)
             (unhappy' e2 p)(etc))
        (exists (e3) (and (dislike' e3 p e)(cause e1 e3)))))
```

That is, the causal relation e1 between e and p's being unhappy (e2) causes the eventuality e3 of p's disliking e.

If a person dislikes an eventuality, then the eventuality defeasibly causes the person to be unhappy.

```
(forall (p e)                                          (49.103)
    (if (and (eventuality e)(dislike p e)(etc))
        (exists (e1) (and (unhappy' e1 p)(cause e e1)))))
```

Defeasibly, we dislike an entity if there is an eventuality that makes us unhappy in which the entity plays a role.

```
(forall (p e x)                                        (49.104)
    (if (and (eventuality e)(dislike p e)(arg* x e)(etc))
        (dislike p x)))
```

Liking something and having it tends to make one happy. Liking it and not having it often makes one have its acquisition as a goal.

There is probably no word whose meaning is more a topic of discussion than the word "love." Probably no serious relationship escapes such a discussion. We will avoid this quagmire, and simply say, as a very rough first approximation, that love and hate are intense versions of liking and disliking.

```
(forall (e p x)                                          (49.105)
    (if (and (love' e p x)(Rexist e)(etc))
        (and (like p x)(intense e p))))
```

That is, if e is p's love for x and e really exists, then p likes x and the emotional state e is intense for p. We make the axiom defeasible to leave room for the song lyrics,

I don't like you, but I love you.
Seems like I'm always thinking of you.

Hate can be similarly characterized.

```
(forall (e p x)                                          (49.106)
    (if (and (hate' e p x)(Rexist e)(etc))
        (and (dislike p x)(intense e p))))
```

Heider (1958, Chapter 7) examines liking and disliking under the heading of positive and negative sentiment, and attempts to develop an algebra of associations for how our sentiment toward things spreads among closely related entities. ("Love me. Love my dog.")

49.9 EMOTIONAL STATES AND TENDENCIES

It is sometimes convenient to talk about emotional states in general, independent of their particular content. Insofar as the five purportedly basic emotions cover the field, we can characterize emotional states by five axioms.

```
(forall (e p)                                            (49.107)
    (if (happy' e p)(emotionalState e p)))
```

```
(forall (e p)                                            (49.108)
    (if (sad' e p)(emotionalState e p)))
```

```
(forall (e p)                                            (49.109)
    (if (angry' e p)(emotionalState e p)))
```

```
(forall (e p)                                            (49.110)
    (if (afraid' e p)(emotionalState e p)))
```

```
(forall (e p)                                            (49.111)
    (if (disgusted' e p)(emotionalState e p)))
```

If person p is happy, sad, angry, fearful, or disgusted, that is an emotional state of p's.

It's possible for someone to be feeling no emotion at all.

```
(forall (p)                                             (49.112)
    (iff (noEmotion p)
        (not (exists (e) (and (emotionalState e p)(Rexist e))))))
```

But normally at any given moment, a person will have an emotional state.

```
(forall (p t)                                           (49.113)
    (if (and (person p)(instant t)(etc))
        (exists (e) (and (emotionalState e p)(atTime e t)))))
```

It is unclear whether we want to say that different emotional states are incompatible, for example, that one cannot feel happy and sad at the same instant. There are certainly bittersweet emotional experiences, for example, the emotions felt when one recalls happier times in the past, or when one felt gratified that the Civil Rights Bill of 1964 was passed as a legacy to John Kennedy but sad about his death. It is probably better not to stipulate any mutual exclusivity conditions. It is one of the features of the rich human emotional life that we often feel several emotions at once.

People usually have explanations for their emotional states, that is, there is some eventuality that they believe causes them.

```
(forall (e p)                                           (49.114)
    (if (and (emotionalState e p)(etc))
        (exists (e1 e2)
            (and (believe p e2)(cause' e2 e1 e)))))
```

People's emotional states can change.

```
(forall (e e1 e2 p)                                     (49.115)
    (iff (emotionalStateChange e e1 e2 p)
        (and (change' e e1 e2)
            (emotionalState e1 p)(emotionalState e2 p))))
```

People often have tendencies to experience one emotion or another. Some have dispositions to be happy, some unhappy, some fearful, and so on. These are not necessarily mutually exclusive. A strong version of this is to say that at any given time the person is defeasibly in that emotional state.

```
(forall (p e t)                                         (49.116)
    (if (and (emotionalTendency p e)(instant t)(etc))
        (exists (e1)
            (and (subst p e1 p e)(emotionalState e1 p)
                (atTime e1 t)))))
```

The expression (emotionalTendency p e) says that person p has a tendency to be in an instance of the abstract emotional state e. For example, e might be defined by the expression (happy' e p). e1 is a particular instance of that abstract state, and line 5 says that it holds at time t.

49.10 **APPRAISAL AND COPING**

People's emotions are generally caused by their appraisal of the situation, that is, by their coming to believe something about the environment. An emotional appraisal happens when a change in belief causes an emotional state.

```
(forall (p e1 e)                                               (49.117)
    (iff (emotionalAppraisal p e1 e)
         (exists (e2)
             (and (changeTo e2)(believe' e2 p e1)(cause e2 e)
                  (emotionalState e p)))))
```

The expression (emotionalAppraisal p e1 e) says that person p appraises situation e1 resulting in emotional state e. In line 4, e2 is p's belief that e1. There is a change into that belief state, and that belief state causes the emotional state e.

An emotional state is usually caused by an emotional appraisal.

```
(forall (e p)                                                  (49.118)
    (if (and (emotionalState e p)(etc))
        (exists (e1) (emotionalAppraisal p e1 e))))
```

This says that if e is an emotional state of p's, then there is some situation e1 whose appraisal caused e.

A coping strategy is a strategy people have for making them become happy in the presence of an unhappy emotional state.

```
(forall (e1 p e2)                                              (49.119)
    (iff (copingStrategy e1 p e2)
         (exists (e3 e4 e5)
             (and (unhappy' e2 p)(believe p e3)(cause' e3 e1 e4)
                  (change' e4 e2 e5)(happy' e5 p)))))
```

The expression (copingStrategy e1 p e2) says that e1 is a strategy, or a set of actions, that person p can perform to deal with p's unhappiness e2. Eventuality e3 is the causal relation between the strategy e1 and a change e4 from the unhappiness e2 to a state e5 of happiness.

A weaker version of this rule would have e5 be not a state of happiness, but only the negation of the unhappiness.

To cope is to employ a coping strategy to deal with an emotion.

```
(forall (p e2)                                                 (49.120)
    (iff (cope p e2)
         (exists (e1 e3)
             (and (unhappy' e2 p)(copingStrategy e1 p e2)
                  (cause e1 e3)(changeFrom' e3 e2)))))
```

Here person p copes with a state e2 of unhappiness by employing coping strategy e1 and having that cause a change out of the state of unhappiness.

PREDICATES INTRODUCED IN THIS CHAPTER

(emotionalState e p)
    Eventuality e is an emotional state in person p.

(moreIntense e1 e2 p)
　　Emotional state e1 is more intense than emotional state e2 for person p.

(intense e p)
　　Emotional state e is intense for person p.

(aroused p)
　　Person p is aroused.

(happy p)
　　Person p is happy.

(happyThat p e)
　　Person p is happy that eventuality e holds.

(sad p)
　　Person p is sad.

(unhappy p)
　　Person p is unhappy.

(joyful p)
　　Person p is joyful.

(longTermGoal e p)
　　Eventuality e is a long-term goal of person p's.

(vindicated p e)
　　Person p feels vindicated about doing e.

(pleased p e)
　　Person p is pleased that eventuality e occurred.

(glad p e)
　　Person p is glad that eventuality e occurred.

(cheerful p)
　　Person p is cheerful.

(interact p1 p2)
　　Person p1 interacts with person p2.

(jubilant p)
　　Person p is jubilant.

(elated p)
　　Person p is elated.

(euphoric p)
　　Person p is euphoric.

(eliminateThreat p x g)
　　Person p eliminates threat x to p's goal g.

(angry p)
　　Person p is angry.

(angryAt p x)
　　Person p is angry at entity x.

(angryThat p e)
　　Person p is angry that eventuality e occurred.

(avoidThreat p x g)
  Person p avoids threat x to p's goal g.

(afraid p)
  Person p is afraid.

(inside x p)
  Entity x is inside person p.

(interior x p)
  Entity x is interior to person p.

(ejectThreat p x g)
  Person p ejects threat x to p's goal g.

(disgusted p)
  Person p feels disgusted.

(inGroup p1 p2)
  Person p2 is in one of person p1's in-groups.

(outGroup p1 p2)
  Person p2 is in one of person p1's out-groups.

(happyFor p1 p2)
  Person p1 is happy for person p2.

(sorryFor p1 p2)
  Person p1 is sorry for person p2.

(resent p1 p2)
  Person p1 resents person p2.

(gloat p1 p2)
  Person p1 gloats about person p2's situation.

(anticipate p e)
  Person p anticipates eventuality e.

(hope p e)
  Person p hopes for eventuality e.

(fear2 p e)
  Person p fears that eventuality e will occur.

(satisfied p e)
  Person p is satisfied that eventuality e occurred.

(disappointed p e)
  Person p is disappointed that eventuality e occurred.

(fearsConfirmed p e)
  Person p's fears that eventuality e would occur are confirmed.

(relief p e)
  Person p is relieved that eventuality e occurred.

(proud p e)
  Person p is proud that eventuality e occurred.

(gratified p e)
  Person p is gratified that eventuality e occurred.

(appreciative p1 e)
  Person p is appreciative that eventuality e occurred.

(grateful p e)
  Person p is grateful that eventuality e occurred.

(selfReproachful p e)
  Person p feels self-reproach that eventuality e occurred.

(remorse p e)
  Person p is remorseful that eventuality e occurred.

(embarrassed p e)
  Person p is embarrassed that eventuality e occurred.

(reproachful p e)
  Person p is reproachful that eventuality e occurred.

(angry2 p e)
  Person p is angry at eventuality e done by someone else which is bad for p.

(jealous p e)
  Person p is jealous of situation e.

(envious p e)
  Person p is envious of situation e.

(like p x)
  Person p likes entity or eventuality x.

(dislike p x)
  Person p dislikes entity or eventuality x.

(love p x)
  Person p loves entity or eventuality x.

(hate p x)
  Person p hates entity or eventuality x.

(noEmotion p)
  Person p feels no emotion.

(emotionalStateChange e e1 e2 p)
  Eventuality e is a change of person p's emotional state from e1 to e2.

(emotionalTendency p e)
  Person p has a tendency to be in emotional state e.

(emotionalAppraisal p e1 e)
  Person p appraises situation e1, resulting in emotional state e.

(copingStrategy e1 p e2)
  e1 is a strategy, or a set of actions, that person p can perform to deal with p's unhappiness e2.

(cope p e)
  Person p copes with emotional state e.

APPENDIX A

First-Order Logic

A.1 PREDICATE-ARGUMENT RELATIONS

This book is necessarily heavy in logic, but we would like it to appeal to a wide audience, including those who have not studied logic. Fortunately, the logic we use here is neither deep nor complicated. In this appendix we assume nothing more than a vague memory of high school algebra, and present all of the logic the reader needs for understanding the formulas in this book.

The two headlines

Dog Bites Man

and

Man Bites Dog

both convey the same lexical content. In both situations there are a dog, a man, and a biting event. The two situations differ in the respective roles of the dog and the man in the biting event. We can represent the situations formally by positing a "predicate" – bite – that takes two "arguments" – a biter and a bitee. Then if a dog named D1 bites a man named M2, we can represent the first situation by the expression

    (bite Biter: D1 Bitee: M2)

Suppose we know that for the predicate bite the Biter argument always comes first and the Bitee second. Then we can dispense with the labels and write more economically

    (bite D1 M2)

A variant of this notation puts the left parenthesis after the predicate and separates the arguments with a comma.

    bite(D1,M2)

In this book we use the first notation.

We generally try to have the order of the arguments be the same as in the simplest English sentence that would express its meaning. Thus, this expression means

D1 bites M2.

(A linguist one of the authors once worked with was intimidated by logic at first, until he realized, as he put it, "Logic is English in Verb-Subject-Object order.")

Each predicate has a fixed number of arguments. For example, we might say

    (sleep M2)

to mean M2 sleeps, and

    (give M2 D1 W3)

to mean that M2 gives D1 to W3. As we are using them, the predicate sleep always takes one argument, and the predicate give always takes three. If a predicate takes n arguments, we call it an "n-ary predicate." The number of arguments a predicate takes is called its "arity."

The term in logic for a predicate applied to the appropriate number of arguments is "positive literal." but this is very unintuitive terminology for the nonlogician. In this book we will refer to such an expression as a "proposition" or a "predication."

A proposition can be true or false. If we are able to identify the dog D1 and the man M2, then the expression (bite D1 M2) is true exactly when D1 bites M2.

A.2 LOGICAL CONNECTIVES

Propositions can be combined by what are called "logical connectives." The logical connectives we use in this book are and, not, or, if and iff (pronounced "if and only if"). These connectives are, in a sense, cleaned-up versions of the corresponding word(s) in English. In logic, they are given precise definitions. The connective and is used to combine two or more propositions, and the resulting expression is true exactly when all of the propositions it combines are true. Thus, the expression

    (and (bite D1 M2)(bite M2 D1))

is true exactly when D1 bites M2 and M2 bites D1. This semantics of and can be expressed in a truth table as follows:

P	Q	(and P Q)
T	T	T
T	F	F
F	T	F
F	F	F

That is, if P and Q are both true (T), then so is (and P Q). Otherwise, (and P Q) is false.

In ordinary English "and" usually means "and then," as in

Pat opened the window and a bird flew in.

or "and similarly," as in

Sugar is sweet and lemons are sour.

The two propositions being linked generally have something to do with each other. But in logic this is not necessary. The sentence

Sugar is sweet and Los Angeles is diverse.

is a bit strange, but from the point of view of logic, it is simply true.

The other connectives can be defined similarly.

P	Q	(not P)	(or P Q)	(if P Q)	(iff P Q)
T	T	F	T	T	T
T	F	F	T	F	F
F	T	T	T	T	F
F	F	T	F	T	T

Several things should be pointed out about these definitions. In English, the word "or" can be the exclusive "or," where both P and Q can't be true, or the inclusive "or," where they can. Our logical connective or is the latter. If both P and Q are true, then so is (or P Q). (A few axioms have the operator xor, meaning exclusive "or.")

The connectives and and or can link two or more propositions. The expression (or P Q R) is just an abbreviation for (or P (or Q R)). It's true when at least one of the three propositions is true.

The connective if differs the most from standard English usage. In ordinary English, the two propositions joined by "if" usually have some causal connection, as in

If Pat goes to the party, Chris will go too.

In logic there's no such requirement. The connective if is defined in strictly logical terms. If P and Q are both true, then (if P Q) is true, just as we'd expect. If P is true and Q is false, then (if P Q) is false, again just as we'd expect. But if P is false and Q is false, we might be inclined to call (if P Q) true, or we might call it nonsense. If P is false and Q is true, we would probably call the sentence either deceptive or nonsense. But in logic, in the latter two cases, that is, when P is false, we say that (if P Q) is true. For example, by our definition the sentences

If salt is sweet, then sugar is bitter.
If salt is sweet, then sugar is sweet too.

are both true, even though most of us would say they are nonsense. But we can perhaps see the motivation in this move from sentences like

If salt is sweet, then I'll eat my hat.

in which P and Q are both false and the sentence as a whole strikes us as true. You're safe – since salt isn't sweet, you don't have to eat your hat.

We call (and P Q) a conjunction and P and Q its conjuncts. We call (or P Q) a disjunction, and P and Q its disjuncts. We call (if P Q) an implication, P its antecedent, and Q its consequent. The connective iff is sometimes called an "equivalence" or a "biconditional."

Expressions with logical connectives can be embedded arbitrarily deeply in other expressions, and their truth or falsity can be determined from the truth tables. For example, the following expression is true:

```
(iff (or P (and Q R))(and (or P Q)(or P R)))
```

Just plug in all eight possible combinations of values T and F for P, Q, and R, and use the tables to compute the truth value of the expression. They all turn out to be true.

The expression (iff P Q) is equivalent to the expression

```
(and (if P Q)(if Q P))
```

as the reader can verify from the truth tables.

A.3 VARIABLES AND QUANTIFIERS

In Section A.1 we used the "names" of the dog and the man as arguments of predications. In logic, those are called "constants." We can also use variables as arguments. In high school algebra, variables stood for numbers. In logic, variables can stand for any kind of entity.

In high school algebra, there were two distinct uses for variables. We saw them in equations that had to be solved, as in

$$x^2 - 7x + 12 = 0$$

where x has to be 3 or 4. We also saw them in identities, such as

$$(x + y)(x - y) = x^2 - y^2$$

which is true for any x and y. The first formula is to be read as saying, "There exists an x such that . . . ." The second formula is to be read as saying, "For all x and y, ..."

In logic, we say the first formula is "existentially quantified," and the second is "universally quantified." We represent this by means of two "quantifiers" called exists and forall. A quantified expression begins with a quantifier and is followed by a list of variables and then the expression that the variables occur in. Thus,

```
(exists (x y) (p x y))
```

says that there exist entities x and y such that the predicate p is true of x and y. The expression

```
(forall (x y) (q x y))
```

says that for all entities x and y, the predicate q is true of x and y. In this book we do not use variables that are not within the "scope" of a quantifier that tells how they are to be interpreted.

These expressions can be embedded in other logical expressions, arbitrarily deeply. Suppose we want to say that cars have engines. Then we can write

```
(forall (x) (if (car x) (exists (y) (engineOf y x))))
```

This says that for all entities x, if x is a car, then there exists an entity y such that y is the engine of x. If there is more than one car, or even if not, there can be more than one engine.

A.4 RULES OF INFERENCE

The principal use of logic is for reasoning. Suppose we know some propositions to be true. Then logic provides the means for deriving other true propositions. The means are "rules of inference." The two most important rules of inference are Modus Ponens and Universal Instantiation.

Modus Ponens is the rule

```
P, (if P Q) ⊢ Q
```

That is, if we know P and we know (if P Q), then we can conclude Q.

Universal Instantiation can be illustrated by the following rule, where A is a constant:

```
(forall (x) (p x)) ⊢ (p A)
```

This says that if we know that p is true of x for all x, then p must be true of A, where A can be any constant. In the general version of the rule, A is substituted for all occurrences of x in the expresssion that forall scopes over. The "Universal" in Universal Instantiation is because of the universal quantifier on the left side of the rule. The "Instantiation" is because the right side of the rule is one instance of the general pattern expressed on the left side.

Suppose we know that all persons are mortal.

```
(forall (x) (if (person x)(mortal x)))
```

and we know about an entity Socrates (S), that he is a person.

```
(person S).
```

Then by Universal Instantiation we can conclude

```
(if (person S)(mortal S))
```

and by Modus Ponens we can conclude

```
(mortal S).
```

That is, Socrates is mortal.

A.5 AXIOMS AND LOGICAL THEORIES

An axiom is a logical expression that we stipulate to be true. A theorem is a logical expression that we can derive from axioms by means of rules of inference.

A logical theory is characterized by a set of predicates and a set of axioms in which the predicates occur. We can also talk about the theorems of a logical theory as the set of theorems derivable from its axioms.

A simple example of a logical theory is one that contains the predicates car, engineOf and vehicle, plus the two axioms

```
(forall (x) (if (car x) (vehicle x)))
```

```
(forall (x) (if (car x) (exists (y) (engineOf y x))))
```

That is, cars are vehicles and have engines.

In this book we construct a much much bigger logical theory for commonsense psychology, but like this simple example, the theory consists of a set of predicates and a set of axioms involving the predicates.

A.6 MODELS

A English description of a landscape is an object in a symbolic system (English) being used to characterize some part of the world (the hills, bushes and trees). Similarly, a realistic painting of a landscape is an object in a symbolic system (paintings) being used to characterize some part of the world. We can look at the description or the painting and at the hills, trees and bushes, and we can decide how accurately the symbolic object corresponds to reality. Suppose the English description says "There is a bush next to the tree." We can check whether there really is a bush next to the tree. Similarly, if there is a bush next to the tree, we can check whether the painting depicts that.

Logic is also a symbolic system, and logical theories are objects within that system. We can ask about a logical theory, does it give a true description of that part of the world it purports to describe? To answer this, we first have to say what set, or "domain," of entities in the world the variables are intended to range over. We have to say what the predicate symbols in the theory mean. That's called an "interpretation." Then we have to check the world to see if the axioms thus interpreted are really true. If they are, the interpretation is a "model."

For example, consider the logical theory consisting of the predicates tree, bush, and nextTo, and the single axiom

```
(forall (x) (if (tree x) (exists (y) (and (bush y)(nextTo y x)))))
```

That is, every tree has a bush next to it. Let's say the variables x and y range over all physical objects in Los Angeles. Suppose I've decided a variable x denotes a particular tree. The interpretation of x is easy enough: It's just the tree. But what about predicates? How do I say what the interpretation of the predicates tree and nextTo are? For this we use set theoretic constructions. We will say that the meaning of tree is the set of all those physical objects that happen to be trees and similarly the meaning of bush is the set of all the bushes. The meaning of nextTo is the set of all ordered pairs of physical objects in Los Angeles such that the first is next to the second. Now suppose we know what physical object we want x to correspond to; then we will say that (tree x) is true exactly when that physical object is in the interpretation of tree. That is, when it is in the set of all trees in Los Angeles. That is, when it is in fact a tree. Similarly, if we know what two physical objects we want x and y to correspond to, we will say (nextTo x y) is true exactly when the ordered pair of those two physical objects is in the interpretation of nextTo, that is, exactly when the first of those physical objects is next to the second. Now we have our interpretation. We can now check if it is a model by seeing if the axiom holds. We do this by looking at every tree in Los Angeles and checking whether it has a bush next to it. If so, we have a model. If not, we don't.

In general, an interpretation of a theory is a set of entities, called a "domain," together with a mapping from every n-ary predicate in the theory to a set of n-tuples of the entities, for all n, namely, the n-tuples of arguments for which the predicate is true. If the axioms of the theory hold in the interpretation, it is a model.

Suppose we have a predicate sum with three arguments. We intend the expression (sum w x y) to mean that w is the sum of x and y. We posit two axioms involving sum. The first is the Associative Law.

```
(forall (x y z w)                                          (A1)
    (iff (exists (u) (and (sum u y z)(sum w x u)))
         (exists (v) (and (sum v x y)(sum w v z)))))
```

The second line says that u is the sum of y and z and w is the sum of x and u. That is, we add y and z together first and add x to the sum of those. The third line says that v is the sum of x and y and w is the sum of v and z. That is, we add x and y together first and add the sum of those and z. The fact that the same variable w, the sum of all three, occurs in both lines says that we get the same answer either way we do it.

The second axiom is the Commutative Law.

```
(forall (w x y)                                            (A2)
    (iff (sum w x y)(sum w y x)))
```

This says that if we take the sum of x and y, we get the same answer w as when we take the sum of y and x. Order doesn't matter.

We said we intend sum to mean addition. Let's consider the theory consisting of the predicate sum and the axioms (A1) and (A2). For our domain, we pick the nonnegative integers. The interpretation of the predicate sum is the set of all triples <w,x,y> such that w = x + y. Thus, the set would include triples such as <4,2,2> and <10,4,6> but not triples such as <1,1,1> or <2,5,3>. The two axioms are true under this interpretation, so the interpretation is a model.

But addition is not the only model. These two axioms are true for multiplication as well. We could also say that (sum w x y) is true whenever w is the *product* of x and y. Multiplication is also associative and commutative, so multiplication of nonnegative integers is also a model.

We can think of models of a theory as examples of the theory.

Two uses of models are in establishing the consistency of a theory and in establishing the independence of axioms from each other.

A theory is inconsistent if one can prove a contradiction from its axioms. It is a theorem in logic that if a theory has a model, then it is consistent. So suppose we want to know if the theory of sum with Axioms (A1) and (A2) is consistent. We could try to prove a contradiction from the axioms. We would fail to do so, but that wouldn't tell us the theory is consistent. Maybe we needed to try harder to prove a contradiction. But we do know the theory is consistent, because it has a model – addition. Multiplication as well.

Two axioms are independent if you can't prove either from the other. So we can ask, are Axioms (A1) and (A2) independent? We try to prove (A2) from (A1). Then we try to prove (A1) from (A2). We fail at both. But that doesn't allow us to conclude they are independent. Maybe we needed to try harder.

But it is a theorem of logic that two axioms are independent if there are interpretations that are models of each but not the other. Suppose we interpret sum as concatenation of strings. Axiom (A1) holds under this interpretation, since concatenation is associative. If we concatenate "ab" with "cd" yielding "abcd" and then concatenate that with "ef," we get "abcdef." If we concatenate "cd" with "ef," yielding "cdef," and then concatenate "ab" with that, we again get "abcdef."

But Axiom (A2) does not hold under this interpretation. If we concatenate "ab" with "cd" we get "abcd," whereas if we concatenate "cd" with "ab," we get "cdab," a different result. Axiom (A1) is true under this interpretation while Axiom (A2) is false. There are also interpretations under which Axiom A2 is true and Axiom A1 is false. Therefore the two axioms must be independent.

A.7 DEFINITION AND CHARACTERIZATION

The definition of a concept is an "if and only if" statement. If we want to define person as a featherless biped, the axiom would be

```
(forall (x) (iff (person x) (and (biped x)(featherless x))))
```

That is, x is a person if and only if x is a biped and x is featherless.

In commonsense knowledge very few concepts can be defined precisely. For example, by the above definition a plucked chicken is a person. The most we can hope to do is characterize the predicates by means of axioms that involve them and thereby constrain what they can mean.

With no axioms, the predicate person can mean anything – person, dog, bird, telephone, and so on. Suppose we have the axiom

```
(forall (x) (if (person x) (biped x)))
```

where the predicate biped has been constrained to mean having exactly two legs. Then person can no longer mean "dog" or "telephone," because they do not have exactly two legs. But it can still mean "bird." By adding the axiom

```
(forall (x) (if (person x) (featherless x)))
```

we rule out normal birds as persons. We have thus further constrained the meaning of the predicate person by adding an axiom involving it.

The role of axioms in constraining predicates can be illustrated by an example from an early version of a well-known ontology. The predicate near was characterized by two axioms:

```
(forall (x y) (if (near x y) (not (equal x y))))
```

```
(forall (x y) (if (near x y) (near y x)))
```

The first axiom says something cannot be near itself. The second says that near is symmetric; if x is near y, then y is near x. Because of the first axiom, near cannot mean "equal." Because of the second, it cannot mean "less than"; if x is less than y, then it is not the case that y is less than x. But near can still mean "far"; both axioms are still true if we substitute far for near.

In general, increasing the number of axioms reduces the set of models. If we have only Axiom (A1), we have ruled out interpreting sum as subtraction; subtraction is not associative. But we have not ruled out addition, multiplication, or the concatenation of strings. They are all associative. When we add Axiom (A2), we can still interpret sum as addition or multiplication, but it can no longer be concatenation.

Concatenating "ab" and "cd" does not give the same result as concatenating "cd" and "ab." We have added an axiom and thereby eliminated some of the models.

Where we have an axiom of the form

```
(forall (x) (if (p x) (q x)))
```

we say that (q x) is a necessary condition for (p x). If p is true of x, then q is necessarily true of x as well. Where we have an axiom of the form

```
(forall (x) (if (q x) (p x)))
```

we say that (q x) is a sufficient condition for (p x). q being true of x is sufficient for making p be true of x. Where we have an axiom of the form

```
(forall (x) (iff (p x) (q x)))
```

we say that (q x) is a necessary and sufficient condition for (p x).

For most interesting concepts in commonsense knowledge, we will not have necessary and sufficient conditions, but we will have lots of necessary conditions and lots of sufficient conditions. Even if we cannot state precisely the meaning of near, we can state enough axioms involving near to rule out its being interpreted as "far."

The idea of characterizing concepts rather than defining them contrasts with the "Euclidean" program familiar from geometry and set theory. There we take certain predicates to be primitive, and define all other predicates, ultimately, in terms of these. For example, in set theory, we take the predicate member to be primitive; we don't attempt to say formally what it means. Then we define a more complex concept like subset in terms of this.

```
(forall (s1 s2)
   (iff (subset s1 s2)
        (forall (x) (if (member x s1)(member x s2)))))
```

That is, a set s1 is a subset of another set s2 if and only if every member of s1 is also a member of s2.

In our approach it is as if nearly every predicate is a primitive. But the set of axioms they participate in constrain their possible interpretations more or less tightly. If we have only a small number of axioms constraining our predicates, we may be able to invent some bizarre interpretation in which the axioms are true. But the more axioms we add, the more likely it is that the only model we can find is the interpretation we intend.

A.8 COMMON PATTERNS IN AXIOMS

Some of the axioms in this book can appear very formidable, being ten or more lines long and having a large number of embeddings. But most axioms can be seen as examples of a fairly small number of patterns. Here we point out some of the most common patterns.

Let's start off with the simplest pattern. Suppose we want to say a car is a vehicle. We can write

```
(forall (x) (if (car x) (vehicle x)))
```

That is, if x is a car, it's also a vehicle.

If we are able to state that two conditions are equivalent, we use iff in place of if.

```
(forall (x) (iff (car x) (automobile x)))
```

That is, x is a car if and only if it's an automobile.

Often there will be conjunctions of conditions in the antecedent and consequent of if or iff. For example, the axiom

```
(forall (x) (if (and (car x)(intact x))
                (and (vehicle x)(motorized x))))
```

says that an intact car is a motorized vehicle.

Suppose we want to say a car has an engine. We might take engineOf to be a two-place predicate – "y is the engine of x." Then the axiom would be

```
(forall (x) (if (car x)
                (exists (y) (engineOf y x))))
```

That is, if x is a car, there is a y that is the engine of x. Or we could say that engine is a one-place predicate describing the kind of thing y is, and there is another predicate in that will be used to say the engine is in the car.

```
(forall (x) (if (car x)
                (exists (y) (and (engine y)(in y x)))))
```

That is, if x is a car, there is a y that is an engine, and y is in x.

In general, when you see a universal quantifier, you should expect to see an if (or iff) as the next logical operator.

```
(forall (x ...) (if ...))
```

Very few if any properties are true of every thing in the universe, so the antecedent of the if operator constrains the universal quantifier to only those things that we think should have the property. This will be the top-level structure of almost every axiom.

When you see an existential quantifier, you will often see an and as the next logical operator.

```
(exists (x ...) (and ...))
```

When we posit the existence of something, we generally have more than one property in mind that we want it to have.

Now suppose we want to say a car has four wheels. There is a set s. The set has four members; this will be represented by the predication (card 4 s), that is, 4 is the cardinality of s. Each member of s is a wheel. The following axiom expresses this.

```
(forall (x)
     (if (car x)
         (exists (s)
             (and (set s)
                  (card 4 s)
                  (forall (y) (if (member y s)
                                  (and (wheel y)(part y x))))))))
```

Line 2 introduces a car x. Lines 3 and 4 posit the existence of a set s for that car. Line 5 says that 4 is the cardinality of that set. Lines 6 and 7 say that every member y of s is a wheel and a part of x.

In general, when we posit the existence of a set, we will see an `exists` quantifier and a variable (s) standing for the set. Then there will usually be a conjunction (`and`) of properties of s, and a `forall` expression that says something about all the members of s.

Sometimes we want to overload a predicate and have it mean something slightly different for different kinds of arguments. For example, we may make use of the two-place predicate `part` in several different contexts. A member or subset is a part of a set. A component is part of a device, for example, a wheel is a part of a car. A bit of material is a part of the larger bit of material it is embedded in. There may be other uses we want for `part` as we develop an ontology. Let us define the predicate just for sets.

```
(forall (x s)
   (if (set s)
      (iff (part x s)
         (or (member x s)(subset x s)))))
```

That is, if s is a set, then x is part of s if and only if x is a member or subset of s. Line 2 of this axiom has the effect of restricting this definition of `part` to only those cases where the second argument is a set. The general pattern is

```
(forall (...)
   (if <Constraints on Arguments>
      <Definition or Rule>))
```

The predicate of interest is then available to be defined in different ways for different types of arguments.

These patterns, together with the glosses we give for nearly every axiom, should be enough to enable the reader to understand the axioms in this book, though sometimes with a little bit of effort.

References

Carlos E. Alchourrón, Peter Gärdenfors, and David Makinson. On the logic of theory change: Partial meet contraction and revision functions. *Journal of Symbolic Logic*, 50(2):510–530, 1985.

James Allen and George Ferguson. Actions and events in interval temporal logic. In O. Stock, editor, *Spatial and Temporal Reasoning*, pp. 205–245. Dordrecht, the Netherlands: Kluwer Academic, 1997.

James F. Allen. Maintaining knowledge about temporal intervals. *Communications of the ACM*, 26(11):832–843, 1983.

James F. Allen and Henry A. Kautz. A model of naive temporal reasoning. In Jerry R. Hobbs and Robert C. Moore (eds.), *Formal Theories of the Commonsense World*, pp. 251–268. Norwood, NJ: Ablex, 1985.

Michael C. Anderson and Collin Green. Suppressing unwanted memories by executive control. *Nature*, 410(6826):366–369, 2001.

Janet W. Astington. *The Child's Discovery of the Mind*. Cambridge, MA: Harvard University Press, 1993.

Angeliki Athanasiadou and Elzbieta Tabakowska. *Speaking of Emotions: Conceptualisation and Expression*. Berlin: Walter de Gruyter, 1998.

Jeremy Avis and Paul L. Harris. Belief-desire reasoning among Baka children: Evidence for a universal conception of mind. *Child Development*, 62(3):460–467, 1991.

Emmon Bach. On time, tense, and aspect: An essay in Englipagessh metaphysics. In P. Cole (ed.), *Radical Pragmatics*, pp. 63–81. New York: Academic Press, 1981.

Simon Baron-Cohen, Alan M. Leslie, and Uta Frith. Does the autistic child have a "theory of mind"? *Cognition*, 21(1):37–46, 1985.

Karen Bartsch and Henry M. Wellman. *Children Talk About the Mind*. Oxford: Oxford University Press, 1995.

Lawrence Birnbaum. Rigor mortis: A response to Nilsson's "Logic and Artificial Intelligence." *Artificial Intelligence*, 47(1):57–77, 1991.

Paul Bloom and Tim P. German. Two reasons to abandon the false belief task as a test of theory of mind. *Cognition*, 77(1):B25–B31, 2000.

Ronen I. Brafman and Carmel Domshlak. Preference handling—an introductory tutorial. *AI Magazine*, 30(1):58–86, 2009.

Michael E. Bratman. *Intention, Plans, and Practical Reason*. Cambridge, MA: Harvard University Press, 1987.

Donald Brown. *Human Universals*. New York: McGraw-Hill, 1991.

Jerome R. Busemeyer and Joseph G. Johnson. Computational models of decision making. *Blackwell Handbook of Judgment and Decision Making*, pp. 133–154. Malden, MA: Blackwell, 2004.

Josep Call and Michael Tomasello. A nonverbal false belief task: The performance of children and great apes. *Child Development*, 70(2):381–395, 1999.

Josep Call and Michael Tomasello. Does the chimpanzee have a theory of mind? 30 years later. *Trends in Cognitive Sciences*, 12(5):187–192, 2008.

David J. Chalmers. Foundations. In David J. Chalmers (ed.), *Philosophy of Mind: Classical and Contemporary Readings*, pp. 1–9. Oxford: Oxford University Press, 2002.

Paul M. Churchland. Eliminative materialism and the propositional attitudes. *The Journal of Philosophy*, 78(2): 67–90, 1981.

Paul M. Churchland. *Scientific Realism and the Plasticity of Mind*. Cambridge: Cambridge University Press, 1986.

Herbert H. Clark. *Arenas of Language Use*. Chicago: University of Chicago Press, 1992.

John Clement. A conceptual model discussed by Galileo and used intuitively by physics students. In Dedre Gentner and A. Stevens (eds.), *Mental Models*. Mahwah, NJ: Lawrence Erlbaum Associates, 1983.

Paul Cohen and Hector Levesque. Intention is choice with commitment. *Artificial Intelligence*, 42:213–261, 1990.

Paul J. Cohen. *Set Theory and the Continuum Hypothesis*. New York: W. A. Benjamin, 1966.

Philip R. Cohen and C. Raymond Perrault. Elements of a plan-based theory of speech acts. *Cognitive Science*, 3:177–212, 1979.

Gregg Clinton Collins. *Plan Creation: Using Strategies as Blueprints*. PhD thesis, Yale University, 1987.

Blandine Courtois. Dictionnaires électroniques DELAF anglais et français. In C. Leclère, É. Laporte, M. Piot, and M. Silberztein (eds.), *Lexique, Syntaxe et Lexique-Grammaire/Syntax, Lexis and Lexicon-Grammar, Papers in Honor of Maurice Gross*, pp. 113–123. Amsterdam: John Benjamins Publishing, 2004.

William Croft and D. A. Cruse. *Cognitive Linguistics* (Cambridge Textbooks in Linguistics). Cambridge: Cambridge University Press, 2004.

Donald Davidson. The logical form of action sentences. In N. Rescher (ed.), *The Logic of Decision and Action*, pp. 81–95. Pittsburgh: University of Pittsburgh Press, 1967.

Ernest Davis. Inferring ignorance from the locality of visual perception. In *Proceedings of the Seventh National Conference on Artificial Intelligence*, pp. 786–790. Palo Alto, CA: AAAI Press, 1988.

Ernest Davis. Reasoning about hand–eye coordination. In *Proceedings of the IJCAI-89 Workshop on Knowledge, Perception, and Planning*. San Francisco, CA: Morgan Kaufmann, 1989.

Ernest Davis. The kinematics of cutting solid objects. *Annals of Mathematics and Artificial Intelligence*, 9(3–4):253–305, 1993.

Ernest Davis. Knowledge preconditions for plans. *Journal of Logic and Computation*, 4(5):721–766, 1994.

Ernest Davis. Naive physics perplex. *AI Magazine*, 19(4):51, 1998.

Ernest Davis. Knowledge and communication: A first-order theory. *Artificial Intelligence*, 166(1):81–139, 2005.

Ernest Davis and Leora Morgenstern. Introduction: Progress in formal commonsense reasoning. *Artificial Intelligence*, 153(1):1–12, 2004.

Ernest Davis and Leora Morgenstern. A first-order theory of communication and multi-agent plans. *Journal of Logic and Computation*, 15(5):701–749, 2005.

Daniel C. Dennett. *The Intentional Stance*. Cambridge, MA: Bradford Books, 1989.

Daniel C. Dennett. Two contrasts: Folk craft versus folk science, and belief versus opinion. In John D. Greenwood (ed.), *The Future of Folk Psychology: Intentionality and Cognitive Science*, pp. 135–148. Cambridge: Cambridge University Press, 1991.

René Descartes. Meditations on first philosophy. In David J. Chalmers (ed.), *Philosophy of Mind: Classical and Contemporary Readings*, pp. 10–21. Oxford: Oxford University Press, 2002.

Eric Andrew Domeshek. *Do the Right Thing: A Component Theory for Indexing Stories as Social Advice*. PhD thesis, Yale University, 1992.

Jon Doyle. A truth maintenance system. In G. F. Luger (ed.), *Computational Intelligence*, pp. 529–554. Palo Alto, CA: AAAI Press, 1995.

Rolf A. Eberle. A logic of believing, knowing, and inferring. *Synthese*, 26:356–382, 1974.

Albert Einstein and Leopold Infeld. *The Evolution of Physics: The Growth of Ideas From Early Concepts to Relativity and Quanta*. Cambridge: Cambridge University Press, 1938.

Ronald Fagin and Joseph Y. Halpern. Belief, awareness, and limited reasoning. *Artificial Intelligence*, 34:39–76, 1988.

Ronald Fagin, Jeffrey D. Ullman, and Moshe Y. Vardi. On the semantics of updates in databases. In *Proceedings of the 2nd ACM SIGACT-SIGMOD Symposium on Principles of Database Systems*, pp. 352–365. New York: Association for Computer Machinery, 1983.

Brian Falkenhainer, Kenneth D. Forbus, and Dedre Gentner. The structure-mapping engine: Algorithm and examples. *Artificial Intelligence*, 41(1):1–63, 1989.

Christiane Fellbaum. *WordNet*. Wiley Online Library, 1998.

Richard E. Fikes and Nils J. Nilsson. Strips: A new approach to the application of theorem proving to problem solving. *Artificial Intelligence*, 2(3-4):189–208, 1971.

Garth Fletcher. *The Scientific Credibility of Folk Psychology*. Mahwah, NJ: Lawrence Erlbaum Associates, 1995.

Jerry A Fodor. *Psychosemantics: The Problem of Meaning in the Philosophy of Mind*. Cambridge, MA: MIT Press, 1987.

Jerry A. Fodor and Zenon W. Pylyshyn. Connectionism and cognitive architecture: A critical analysis. *Cognition*, 28(1):3–71, 1988.

Dedre Gentner. Structure-mapping: A theoretical framework for analogy. *Cognitive Science*, 7(2):155–170, 1983.

Dedre Gentner and Kenneth D. Forbus. MAC/FAC: A model of similarity-based retrieval. In *Proceedings of the Thirteenth Annual Conference of the Cognitive Science Society*, Volume 504, p. 509. Mahwah, NJ: Lawrence Erlbaum, 1991.

Dedre Gentner and Arthur B. Markman. Structure mapping in analogy and similarity. *American Psychologist*, 52(1):45, 1997.

Edmund L. Gettier. Is justified true belief knowledge? *Analysis*, 23(6):121–123, 1963.

Alvin I. Goldman. Interpretation psychologized. *Mind & Language*, 4(3):161–185, 1989.

Alison Gopnik and Andrew N. Meltzoff. *Words, Thoughts, and Theories*. Cambridge, MA: MIT Press, 1997.

Alison Gopnik and Henry M. Wellman. Why the child's theory of mind really is a theory. *Mind & Language*, 7(1-2):145–171, 1992.

Andrew S. Gordon. Strategies in analogous planning cases. In *Proceedings, Twenty-Third Annual Conference of the Cognitive Science Society*, pp. 370–375. Mahwah, NJ: Lawrence Erlbaum, 2001.

Andrew S. Gordon. The representation of planning strategies. *Artificial Intelligence*, 153(1):287–305, 2004a.

Andrew S. Gordon. *Strategy Representation: An Analysis of Planning Knowledge*. Mahwah, NJ: Lawrence Erlbaum Associates, 2004b.

Andrew S. Gordon. Language evidence for changes in a theory of mind. In Michael A. Arbib (ed.), *Action to Language via the Mirror Neuron System*, pp. 374–393. Cambridge: Cambridge University Press, 2006.

Andrew S. Gordon and Jerry R. Hobbs. Coverage and competency in formal theories: A commonsense theory of memory. In *Proceedings of the 2003 AAAI Spring Symposium on Logical Formalizations of Commonsense Reasoning*, pp. 24–26. Palo Alto, CA: AAAI Press, 2003.

Andrew S. Gordon and Jerry R. Hobbs. Formalizations of commonsense psychology. *AI Magazine*, 25:49–62, 2004.

Andrew S. Gordon and Jerry R. Hobbs. A commonsense theory of mind-body interaction. In *Proceedings of the 2011 AAAI Spring Symposium on Logical Formalizations of Commonsense Reasoning*, pp. 36–41. Palo Alto, CA: AAAI Press, 2011.

Andrew S. Gordon and Anish Nair. Literary evidence for the cultural development of a theory of mind. In *Proceedings of the 25th Annual Meeting of the Cognitive Science Society*, pp. 468–473. Boston, MA: The Cognitive Science Society, 2003.

Andrew S. Gordon and Anish Nair. Expressions related to knowledge and belief in children's speech. In *Proceedings of the 26th Annual Meeting of the Cognitive Science Society*, pp. 476–481. Boston, MA: The Cognitive Science Society, 2004.

Andrew S. Gordon, Abe Kazemzadeh, Anish Nair, and Milena Petrova. Recognizing expressions of commonsense psychology in English text. In *Proceedings of the 41st Annual Meeting on Association for Computational Linguistics*-Volume 1, pp. 208–215. Association for Computational Linguistics, 2003.

Robert M. Gordon. Folk psychology as simulation. *Mind & Language*, 1(2):158–171, 1986.

Delia Graff. Shifting sands: An interest-relative theory of vagueness. *Philosophical Topics*, 28(1):45–81, 2000.

Jonathan Gratch. Emile: Marshalling passions in training and education. In *Proceedings of the Fourth International Conference on Autonomous Agents*, pp. 325–332. New York: ACM, 2000.

John D. Greenwood, ed. *The Future of Folk Psychology: Intentionality and Cognitive Science*. Cambridge: Cambridge University Press, 1991.

Jean Harkins and Anna Wierzbicka. *Emotions in Crosslinguistic Perspective*, Volume 17. Berlin: Walter de Gruyter, 2001.

Paul L. Harris. *Children and Emotion: The Development of Psychological Understanding*. Oxford: Basil Blackwell, 1989.

Patrick J Hayes. Naive physics I: Ontology for liquids. In Jerry R. Hobbs and Robert C. Moore (eds.), *Formal Theories of the Commonsense World*, pp. 71–108. Norwood, NJ: Ablex, 1985.

Jane Heal. Replication and functionalism. In J. Butterfield (ed.), *Language, Mind, and Logic*. Cambridge: Cambridge University Press, 1986.

Fritz Heider. *The Psychology of Interpersonal Relations*. Mahwah, NJ: Lawrence Erlbaum Associates, 1958.

Fritz Heider and Marianne Simmel. An experimental study of apparent behavior. *The American Journal of Psychology*, 57(2):243–259, 1944.

Jaakko Hintikka. *Knowledge and Belief*. Ithaca, NY: Cornell University Press, 1962.

Thomas Hobbes. Leviathan. www.gutenberg.org, 1651.

Jerry R. Hobbs. Coherence and coreference. *Cognitive Science*, 3:67–90, 1979.

Jerry R. Hobbs. An improper treatment of quantification in ordinary English. In *Proceedings of the 21st Annual Meeting on Association for Computational Linguistics*, pp. 57–63. Association for Computational Linguistics, 1983.

Jerry R. Hobbs. Ontological promiscuity. In *Proceedings of the 23rd Annual Meeting on Association for Computational Linguistics*, pp. 60–69. Association for Computational Linguistics, 1985.

Jerry R. Hobbs. Monotone decreasing quantifiers in a scope-free logical form. In K. van Deemter and S. Peters (eds.), *Semantic Ambiguity and Underspecification*, pp. 55–76. Stanford, CA, CSLI Publications, 1995.

Jerry R. Hobbs. The logical notation: Ontological promiscuity, 1998. www.isi.edu/hobbs/disinf-tc.html. Chapter 2 of *Discourse and Inference*.

Jerry R. Hobbs. Half orders of magnitude. In *Papers from the KR-2000 Workshop on Semantic Approximation, Granularity, and Vagueness*, pp. 28–38, 2000.

Jerry R. Hobbs. An ontology of information structure. In *Proceedings of the 7th International Symposium on Logical Formalizations of Commonsense Reasoning*, Corfu, Greece, pp. 99–106, 2005a. Available at http://commonsensereasoning.org/2005/

Jerry R. Hobbs. Toward a useful concept of causality for lexical semantics. *Journal of Semantics*, 22(2):181–209, 2005b.

Jerry R. Hobbs and Andrew S. Gordon. Encoding knowledge of commonsense psychology. In *7th International Symposium on Logical .org/2005/ Formalizations of Commonsense Reasoning, May 22–24, 2005*, Corfu, Greece, 2005. Available at http://commonsensereasoning

Jerry R. Hobbs and Andrew S. Gordon. The deep lexical semantics of emotions. In *Workshop on Sentiment Analysis: Emotion, Metaphor, Ontology and Terminology (EMOT-08), 6th International Conference on Language Resources and Evaluation (LREC-08)*, Marrakech, Morocco, 2008. Available at www.lrec-conf.org/proceedings/lrec2008/

Jerry R. Hobbs and Andrew S. Gordon. Goals in a formal theory of commonsense psychology. In *Proceedings of the 6th International Conference on Formal Ontology in Information Systems (FOIS-2010)*, Toronto, Canada, pp. 59–72. Amsterdam: IOS Press, 2010.

Jerry R. Hobbs and Andrew S. Gordon. Axiomatizing complex concepts from fundamentals (invited paper). In *Conference on Intelligent Text Processing and Computational Linguistics (CICLing 2014)*, Kathmandu, Nepal, pp. 351–365. Heidelberg, Germany: Springer, 2014.

Jerry R. Hobbs and Andrew Kehler. A theory of parallelism and the case of vp ellipsis. In *Proceedings, 35th Annual Meeting of the Association for Computational Linguistics*, Madrid, Spain, July 1997, pp. 394–401. San Francisco: Morgan Kaufmann, 1997.

Jerry R. Hobbs and Vladik Kreinovich. Optimal choice of granularity in commonsense estimation: Why half-orders of magnitude. In *IFSA World Congress and 20th NAFIPS International Conference, 2001. Joint 9th*, Volume 3, pp. 1343–1348. IEEE, 2001.

Jerry R. Hobbs and Rutu Mulkar-Mehta. Toward as formal theory of information structure. In Bernd-Olaf Küppers, Udo Hahn, and Stefan Artmann (eds.), *Evolution of Semantic Systems*, pp. 101–126. Berlin: Springer-Verlag, 2013.

Jerry R. Hobbs and Feng Pan. An ontology of time for the semantic web. *ACM Transactions on Asian Language Information Processing (TALIP)*, 3(1):66–85, 2004.

Jerry R. Hobbs, Mark E. Stickel, Douglas E. Appelt, and Paul Martin. Interpretation as abduction. *Artificial Intelligence*, 63(1–2):69–142, October 1993.

Jerry R. Hobbs, Alicia Sagae, and Suzanne Wertheim. Toward a commonsense theory of microsociology: Interpersonal relationships. In *Proceedings of the Seventh International Conference (FOIS 2012)*, Graz, Austria, pp. 249–262. Amsterdam: IOS Press, 2012.

Keith J. Holyoak and Paul Thagard. Analogical mapping by constraint satisfaction. *Cognitive Science*, 13(3):295–355, 1989.

Thomas H. Huxley. On the hypothesis that animals are automata, and its history. *Fortnightly Review*, 16:555–580, 1874.

International Organization for Standardization. Common logic (CL): A framework for a family of logic-based languages. *ISO/IEC IS*, 24707, 2007.

William James. *The Principles of Psychology*. New York: Henry Holt and Company, 1890.

Julian Jaynes. *The Origin of Consciousness in the Breakdown of the Bicameral Brain*. Boston: Houghton-Mifflin, 1976.

Edward E. Jones and Keith E. Davis. A theory of correspondent inferences: From acts to dispositions. *Advances in Experimental Social Psychology*, 2:219–66, 1965.

Edward E. Jones and Victor A. Harris. The attribution of attitudes. *Journal of Experimental Social Psychology*, 3(1):1–24, 1967.

Edward E. Jones and Richard E. Nisbett. *The Actor and the Observer: Divergent Perceptions of the Causes of Behavior*. Morristown, NJ: General Learning Press, 1971.

Eric Jones. *The Flexible Use of Abstract Knowledge in Planning*. PhD thesis, Yale University, 1992.

Alex Kass. *Developing Creative Hypotheses by Adapting Explanations*. PhD thesis, Yale University, 1990.

Daniel Kayser and Farid Nouioua. From the textual description of an accident to its causes. *Artificial Intelligence*, 173(12):1154–1193, 2009.

Harold H. Kelley. Attribution theory in social psychology. In *Nebraska Symposium on Motivation*. University of Nebraska Press, pp. 192–238, 1967.

Ami Klin, Warren Jones, Robert Schultz, and Fred Volkmar. The enactive mind, or from actions to cognition: Lessons from autism. *Philosophical Transactions of the Royal Society of London B: Biological Sciences*, 358(1430):345–360, 2003.

Kurt Konolige and Martha E. Pollack. A representationalist theory of intention. In *International Joint Conference on Artificial Intelligence*, pp. 390–395. San Francisco: Morgan Kaufmann, 1993.

George Lakoff and Mark Johnson. *Metaphors We Live By*. Chicago: University of Chicago Press, 2008.

Ellen J. Langer. The illusion of control. *Journal of Personality and Social Psychology*, 32 (2):311, 1975.

David Leake. *Evaluating Explanations*. PhD thesis, Yale University, 1990.

Douglas B. Lenat. Cyc: A large-scale investment in knowledge infrastructure. *Communications of the ACM*, 38(11):33–38, 1995.

Douglas B. Lenat and Ramanathan V. Guha. *Building Large Knowledge Bases*. Reading, MA: Addison-Wesley, 1990.

Hector J. Levesque. A logic of implicit and explicit belief. In *Proceedings of the National Conference on Artificial Intelligence (AAAI'84)*, pp. 198–202. Palo Alto, CA: AAAI Press, 1984.

Beth Levin. *English Verb Classes and Alternations: A Preliminary Investigation*. Chicago: University of Chicago Press, 1993.

David K. Lewis. *Counterfactuals*. Cambridge, MA: Harvard University Press, 1973.

Angeline Lillard. Ethnopsychologies: cultural variations in theories of mind. *Psychological Bulletin*, 123(1):3, 1998.

Brian MacWhinney. *The CHILDES project: The Database*, Volume 2. New York: Psychology Press, 2000.

Bertram F. Malle. The actor-observer asymmetry in attribution: A (surprising) meta-analysis. *Psychological Bulletin*, 132(6):895, 2006.

John C. McCarthy. Programs with common sense. In *Proceedings of the Teddington Conference on the Mechanization of Thought Processes*, pp. 75–91, London: Her Majesty's Stationary Office, 1959.

John C. McCarthy. Epistemological problems of artificial intelligence. In *Proceedings, International Joint Conference on Artificial Intelligence*, pp. 1038–1044. San Francisco: Morgan Kaufmann, August 1977.

John C. McCarthy. Ascribing mental qualities to machines. In Martin Ringle (ed.), *Philosophical Perspectives in Artificial Intelligence*. Harvester Press, 1979.

John C. McCarthy. Circumscription – A form of non-monotonic reasoning. *Artificial Intelligence*, 13:27–39, April 1980.

John C. McCarthy and Patrick J. Hayes. Some philosophical problems from the standpoint of artificial intelligence. *Readings in Artificial Intelligence*, pp. 431–450, 1969.

L. Thorne McCarty. Ownership: A case study in the representation of legal concepts. *Artificial Intelligence and Law*, 10(1–3):135–161, 2002.

Michael McCloskey. Naive theories of motion. In Dedre Gentner and A. Stevens (eds.), *Mental Models*. Mahwah, NJ: Lawrence Erlbaum Associates, 1983.

Charles Moore. *Daniel H. Burnham, Architect, Planner of Cities*, Volume 1. Boston: Houghton Mifflin, 1921.

Leora Morgenstern. Mid-sized axiomatizations of commonsense problems: A case study in egg cracking. *Studia Logica*, 67(3):333–384, 2001.

Leora Morgenstern. A first-order axiomitization of the Surprise Birthday Present problem: Preliminary report. In *Seventh International Symposium on Logical Formalizations of Commonsense Reasoning (Commonsense-2005)*, Corfu, Greece, 2005. Available at http://commonsensereasoning.org/2005/

Adam Morton. Frames of mind: Constraints on the common-sense conception of the mental, 1980.

Bernhard Nebel. Base revision operations and schemes: Representation, semantics and complexity. In *Proceedings of the 11th European Conference on Artificial Intelligence (ECAI'94)*, pp. 341–345. Hoboken, NJ: John Wiley & Sons, 1994.

Shaun Nichols, Stephen Stich, Alan Leslie, and David Klein. Varieties of off-line simulation. In *Theories of Theories of Mind*, pp. 39–74. Cambridge: Cambridge University Press, 1996.

Nils J. Nilsson. Logic and artificial intelligence. *Artificial Intelligence*, 47(1–3):31–56, 1991.

Andrew Ortony, Gerald L. Clore, and Allan Collins. *The Cognitive Structure of Emotions*. Cambridge: Cambridge University Press, 1990.

Christopher C. Owens. *Indexing and Retrieving Abstract Planning Knowledge*. PhD thesis, Yale University, 1990.

Charles Sanders Peirce. Abduction and induction. In Justus Buchler (ed.), *Philosophical Writings of Peirce*, pp. 150–156. New York: Dover Books, 1955.

Elizabeth Pennisi. Social animals prove their smarts. *Science*, 312(5781):1734–1738, 2006.

Pavlos Peppas. Belief revision. In Frank van Harmelen, Vladimir Lifschitz, and Bruce Porter (eds.), *Handbook of Knowledge Representation*. Amsterdam: Elsevier, 2008.

John Perry and Jon Barwise. *Situations and Attitudes*. Cambridge, MA: MIT Press, 1983.

Jean Piaget. *The Construction of Reality in the Child*. New York: Basic Books, 1954.

Martin Pickering and Nick Chater. Why cognitive science is not formalized folk psychology. *Minds and Machines*, 5(3):309–337, 1995.

Ullin T. Place. Is consciousness a brain process? *British Journal of Psychology*, 47:44–50, 1956.

Carl Pollard and Ivan A. Sag. *Head-driven Phrase Structure Grammar*. Chicago: University of Chicago Press, 1994.

David Premack and Guy Woodruff. Does the chimpanzee have a theory of mind? *Behavioral and Brain Sciences*, 1(04):515–526, 1978.

Hilary Putnam. The nature of mental states. In *Art, Mind, and Religion*, pp. 37–48. Pittsburgh: University of Pittsburgh Press, 1973.

Zenon Walter Pylyshyn. *Computation and Cognition*. Cambridge: Cambridge University Press, 1984.

Ashwin Ram. *Question-driven Understanding: An Integrated Theory of Story Understanding, Memory, and Learning*. PhD thesis, Yale University, 1989.

Anand S. Rao and Michael P. Georgeff. Modeling rational agents within a BDI-architecture. In *Proceedings of the 2nd International Conference on Principles of Knowledge Representation and Reasoning*, pp. 473–484. Burlington, MA: Morgan Kaufmann, 1991.

Byron Reeves and Clifford Nass. *The Media Equation: How People Treat Computers, Television, and New Media Like People and Places*. Stanford, CA: CSLI Publications, 1996.

Raymond Reiter. *Knowledge in Action: Logical Foundations for Specifying and Implementing Dynamical Systems*. Cambridge, MA: MIT Press, 2001.

Ivor Richards. *The Philosophy of Rhetoric*. Oxford: Oxford University Press, 1937.

Gilbert Ryle. *Concept of Mind*. London: Hutchinson, 1949.

Peter Salovey and Daisy Grewal. The science of emotional intelligence. *Current Directions in Psychological Science*, 14(6):281–285, 2005.

Kathryn E. Sanders. A logic for emotions: A basis for reasoning about commonsense psychological knowledge. Technical report, Brown University, Providence, RI, 1989.

Roger C. Schank. *Explanation Patterns: Understanding Mechanically and Creatively*. Mahwah, NJ: Lawrence Erlbaum Associates, 1986.

Roger C. Schank and Robert P. Abelson. *Scripts, Plans, Goals and Understanding: An Introduction into Human Knowledge Structures*. Hillsdale, NJ: Lawrence Erlbaum, 1977.

Roger C. Schank and Andrew Fano. A thematic hierarchy for indexing stories in social domains. Technical Report 29, Institute for the Learning Sciences, Northwestern University, 1992.

Roger C. Schank, Alex Kass, and Christopher K. Riesbeck (eds.). *Inside Case-based Explanation*. Mahwah, NJ: Lawrence Erlbaum Associates, 1994.

Klaus R. Scherer. Emotion and emotional competence: Conceptual and theoretical issues for modeling agents. In *A Blueprint for Affective Computing: A Sourcebook and Manual*, Affective Sciences. Oxford: Oxford University Press, 2010.

Yoav Shoham. Nonmonotonic reasoning and causation. *Cognitive Science*, 14(2):213–252. Amsterdam: IOS Press, 1990.

Max Silberztein. Text indexation with INTEX. *Computers and the Humanities*, 33(3):265–280, 1999.

Munindar P. Singh and Nicholas M. Asher. A logic of intentions and beliefs. *Journal of Philosophical Logic*, 22(5):513–544, 1993.

John Jamieson Carswell Smart. Sensations and brain processes. *Philosophical Review*, 68: 141–156, 1959.

Jan Smedslund. What is measured by a psychological measure? *Scandinavian Journal of Psychology*, 29(3-4):148–151, 1988.

Jan Smedslund. The pseudoempirical in psychology and the case for psychologic. *Psychological Inquiry*, 2(4):325–338, 1991.

Jan Smedslund. *The Structure of Psychological Common Sense*. Mahwah, NJ: Lawrence Erlbaum Associates, 1997.

Jan Smedslund. From hypothesis-testing psychology to procedure-testing psychologic. *Review of General Psychology*, 6(1):51, 2002.

Bruno Snell. *The Discovery of the Mind. The Greek Origins of European Thought*. Oxford, 1953. Translated by Thomas Gustav Rosenmeyer.

Stephen P. Stich. *From Folk Psychology to Cognitive Science: The Case Against Belief*. Cambridge, MA: MIT Press, 1983.

Reid Swanson and Andrew S. Gordon. Automated commonsense reasoning about human memory. In *AAAI Spring Symposium: Metacognition in Computation*, pp. 114–119. Palo Alto, CA: AAAI Press, 2005.

Helen Tager-Flusberg. Evaluating the theory-of-mind hypothesis of autism. *Current Directions in Psychological Science*, 16(6):311–315, 2007.

Kentaro Toyama and Drew McDermott. An interview with drew mcdermott. *Crossroads*, 3(1):3–4, 1996.

Alan M. Turing. Computing machinery and intelligence. *Mind*, LIX(236):433–460, 1950.

Amos Tversky. Features of similarity. *Psychological Review*, 84(4):327, 1977.

Johan van Bentham, Oliver Roy, and Patrick Girard. Everything else being equal: A modal logic for ceteris paribus preferences. *Journal of Philosophical Logic*, 38(1):83–125, 2009.

Giambattista Vico. *The New Science of Giambattista Vico*. Ithaca, NY: Cornell University Press, 1744. Translated by T. Bergin and M. Frisch (1968).

Eduard von Hartmann. *Philosophy of the Unconscious (1869)*. Translated by William Chatterton Coupland. New York: Harcourt, 1931.

George Henrik Von Wright. *The Logic of Preference*. Edinburgh: Edinburgh University Press, 1963.

Henry Wellman. *The Child's Theory of Mind*. Learning, Development, and Conceptual Change. Cambridge, MA: MIT Press, 1990.

Henry M. Wellman, David Cross, and Julanne Watson. Meta-analysis of theory-of-mind development: The truth about false belief. *Child Development*, 72(3):655–684, 2001.

Lancelot Law Whyte. *The Unconscious Before Freud*. New York: St. Martin's Press, 1978.

Janyce Wiebe, Theresa Wilson, and Claire Cardie. Annotating expressions of opinions and emotions in language. *Language Resources and Evaluation*, 39(2-3):165–210, 2005.

Anna Wierzbicka. *Emotions Across Languages and Cultures: Diversity and Universals*. Cambridge: Cambridge University Press, 1999.

Heinz Wimmer and Josef Perner. Beliefs about beliefs: Representation and constraining function of wrong beliefs in young children's understanding of deception. *Cognition*, 13(1):103–128, 1983.

Marianne Winslett. *Updating Logical Databases*. Cambridge: Cambridge University Press, 1991.

Ludwig Wittgenstein. *Tractatus Logico-Philosophicus*. London: Routledge & Kegan Paul, 1974. Translated by D. F. Pears and B. F. McGuinness.

Christian Wolff. *Preliminary Discourse on Philosophy in General.* Indianapolis, IN: Bobbs-Merrill, 1963. Translated by R. J. Blackwell. Originally published in 1728.

Michael J. Wooldridge. *Reasoning about Rational Agents.* Cambridge, MA: MIT Press, 2000.

Shali Wu and Boaz Keysar. The effect of culture on perspective taking. *Psychological Science*, 18(7):600–606, 2007.

Index

abandoning, 317, 367, 409
abduction, 135, 237, 240, 243
Abelson, Robert, 68
ability, 170
abnormal (logic), 136
aborting, 474, 482
abstract plans, 469
achieving, 316, 366
action, 166
activities, 470
actor-observer asymmetry, 7
adapting plans, 416–420
addition, 151
adherence to designs, 425
adversarial goals, 319
adversarial planning, 394
adversarial plans, 359
agents, 166
aggregates, 127
AGM postulates, 230
Alchourrón, Carlos, 230
Allen, James, 46, 184
allowing, 169
analogies, 40, 202, 266, 267
anatomic theories of emotion, 514
anger, 517, 524, 525, 533
animal behavior strategies, 42
anthropomorphic computing, 18, 22, 24, 25
anthropomorphism, 17, 22
anticipation, 530
applicability, 377
appraisal of emotions, 513, 541
appreciation, 533, 534
arbitrary contexts, 377
arguments (logic), 95, 545
arithmetic, 150–157
arity, 97
arousal, 517
artifacts, 421
Asher, Nicholas, 30
aspect, 471
assistive planning, 393
assistive plans, 360

associations, 273, 281
assumptions, 235
at (preposition), 130
attribution theory, 7
autism, 9
auxiliary goals, 317
avoiding an action, 400
awareness, 485
awkward actions, 491
axiom of comprehension, 111
axiom of infinity, 100
axiom schema, 94

Bach, Emmon, 93, 98
background theories, 54
BDI agents, 30
before in a sequence, 124
beginning, 464, 471, 478, 481
belief revision, 228
beliefs, 224
blind, 498
blocking, 401
bodies, 207, 485
bodily actions, 492
body parts, 208, 485, 488
bottom of a scale, 142, 146
brain dead, 498
Bratman, Michael, 30
Burnham, Daniel, 70
business strategies, 42

candidate plans, 412
case roles (linguistics), 167
case-based reasoning, 380
causal complexes, 163, 283, 383
causal systems, 283
causality, 163–176
causally involved, 168
causes of failure, 53, 380–386
Chalmers, David, 485
change of state, 158–162
characterization (logic), 552
Chater, Nick, 27

cheerful, 523
children's speech, 58
chimpanzee studies, 10
choices, 428, 430
Churchland, Paul, 15
circumscriptive logic, 136
Clark, Herbert, 251
Clore, Gerald, 52, 515, 526, 528, 530, 533
cognitive modeling, 26
Cohen, Philip, 30
collaborative executions, 460
collaborative planning, 393
collaborative scheduling, 448
collective action, 168
Collins, Allan, 52, 515, 526, 528, 530, 533
common logic interchange format, 55
commonsense sociology, 47, 502, 536
communicative theories of emotion, 514
comparisons, 267
competitive goals, 318
competitive planning, 393
competitive plans, 359
completing, 472, 482
complex events, 200
components, 126
composite entities, 126–134, 421
composite scales, 145
computational cognitive models, 26, 29
concentrating, 486
concern, 344
concurrent executions, 462
conditional events, 198
conditionals, 388, 390, 453
conflicting goals, 317
conjunction, 116, 546
consecutive executions, 461
consequences, 432, 436
constraints, 397, 425
continuing, 471, 479, 481
continuing executions, 461
continuous plans, 362
control, 490, 492
control channels, 495
coordinated actions, 490
coping with emotions, 541
correspondent inference theory, 7
cost, 322, 469
cost–benefit analysis, 433
counterfactual planning, 394
counterfactuals, 164
counterplanning, 394
counterplans, 359
counting strategies, 42
counts, 480
Courtois, Blandine, 57
covariation model of attribution, 7
criteria, 434, 510
cultural differences, 10
current world understandings, 295
curvilinear momentum error, 13
CYC knowledge base, 36, 98, 202

Davidson, Donald, 98
Davis, Ernest, 31, 499
dazed, 498
dead, 498

deadlines, 444, 468
deaf, 498
decisions, 427–438
decrease, 161
deduction, 240
defeasibility, 135–138
definitions (logic), 552
delayed gratification, 337
deliberating, 428, 432
Dennett, Daniel, 16, 18
Descartes, René, 485
designing, 421–426
designs, 423
desires, 351
desktop metaphor, 20
destroyed functionality, 493
difficulty, 173, 369
dimensional theories of emotions, 514
directly cause an event, 172
disappointment, 531, 532
discordant computers, 22
disgust, 524, 527
disjoint scales, 142
disjoint sets, 103
disjunction, 118, 546
disliking, 538
distance, 203
distractions, 474
documents, 504
doing an action, 167
domains (logic), 550
doubleton set, 101
dreaming, 296, 498
drunk, 498
durations, 187, 190, 468

Eberle, Rolf, 30
education strategies, 42
effort, 369
Einstein, Albert, 40
elated, 523
eliminative materialism, 15
Eliot, George, 12
embarrassment, 536
emotional states, 539
emotional tendencies, 539
emotions, 52, 513–544
enabling, 401
enabling conditions, 168, 173, 314
end times, 444, 468
English expressions, 47, 60–88, 484
envisioned causal systems, 289, 374
envisioning, 280–298, 373–379
envy, 536
epistemic logic, 30
et cetera literals, 135
evaluation of performances, 509
Evans, Mary Ann, 13
event sequences, 198
events, 196–201
eventualities, 93–99
executability, 172, 173, 357
execution, 373–379, 456–463, 464–477, 478–483,
    502–512
expectations, 306–308
expertise, 248

explanation failures, 303
explanation patterns, 380
explanations, 282, 299–305, 380–386

Fagin, Ronald, 230
failure, 303, 320, 374, 380–386, 448, 454, 469, 490
false-belief task, 8
Fano, Andrew, 53, 381
fear, 518, 524, 526, 530, 531, 532
Ferguson, George, 184
figure-ground relationship, 130, 161
Fikes, Richard, 169, 314
fine, 497, 498
finite-state transducers, 57
first in a sequence, 123
first-order logic, 53, 226, 545–555
flawed design, 424
fluent actions, 491
focus of attention, 23, 238, 239, 270, 280, 451, 458, 485, 487, 488
Fodor, Jerry, 15
forgetting, 276
fractions, 153
frequency, 193, 454
Freud, Sigmund, 12, 14, 58, 277
functional dependencies, 111, 122
functionality, 321
functions, 121
fundamental attribution error, 7

Gaussian distributions, 147
generation of eventualities, 98
Gentner, Dedre, 266
Georgeff, Michael, 30
gestalt psychology, 4
Gettier, Edmund, 244
gladness, 522
gloating, 529, 530
goal of an action, 167
goal themes, 332–340
goals, 312–331, 366–372
good and bad, 322
Gosford Park, 164
graded beliefs, 231, 292
gratification, 533, 534
gratitude, 533, 535
greater than, 140
Gärdenfors, Peter, 230

half orders of magnitude, 156
Halpern, Joseph, 30
happiness, 517, 518, 529
hate, 539
head-driven phrase structure grammar, 98
Heider, Fritz, 3, 5, 35, 171, 538, 539
Heider-Simmel film, 3
helping, 362
high on a scale, 146
Hintikka, Jaakko, 30
historical change, 10
hope, 530

identity function, 155
image schemas (linguistics), 203
immunology strategies, 42
impaired functionality, 493

implication, 118, 546
importance, 272, 322, 345, 368, 516
in-groups and out-groups, 527, 528, 529, 534
inactive functionality, 495
including an action, 400
increase, 161
induction, 240, 243
Infeld, Leopold, 40
inference, 239, 549
inferential theories, 28
insignificant decisions, 435
instances, 113, 132
instantiation, 407, 425, 469
instants in time, 177
instructions, 504
instrument of an action, 167
intact functionality, 493
intelligence, 245
intended use, 422
intensity, 516
intentional stance, 18
intentions, 353
interpretations (logic), 550
interrupting, 472
intersection of sets, 103
interval relations, 183
intervals of time, 177
introspection, 310
involuntary actions, 489
iterations, 199, 481
iterative executions, 460

James, William, 515
Jaynes, Julian, 11
jealousy, 536
Johnson, Mark, 202
joyful, 521
jubilant, 523
juggling schedules, 448
justifications, 242, 307, 370, 435

Kautz, Henry, 184
kinesthetic sense, 491
knowledge, 223–255, 389
knowledge domains, 248
knowledge goals, 315
Konolige, Kurt, 30

Lakoff, George, 202
Langer effect, 14
last in a sequence, 124
law of the excluded middle, 109, 110, 225, 247
learning, 245
left fringe of a plan, 464, 471
length of sequences, 123
less than, 140
Levesque, Hector, 30
Levin, Beth, 51
likelihood, 170, 215, 232, 345, 369, 375
liking, 538
locating, 403
locations, 205
logical formalization, 29, 34, 53, 549
logical omniscience, 225, 229
long-term goals, 336

love, 539
low on a scale, 146

macaroni defense, 44
Machiavelli, Niccolo, 42
Machiavellian strategies, 43
Makinson, David, 230
maximizing, 403
McCarthy, John, 31, 136
McDermott, Drew, 28
meaning, 504
means-end planning, 407
measures, 154
memory, 47, 52, 270–279, 485
mental executions, 459
middle on a scale, 146
Mill on the Floss, 12
mind–body interaction, 484
mind-body interaction, 501
minds, 207, 238, 270, 485, 494
minimizing, 402
modalities of eventualities, 211–219
models (logic), 550
Modus Ponens, 119, 213, 225, 237, 549
monitoring, 451–455
Morgenstern, Leora, 31
movement, 161
multiplication, 151
multitasking, 23
mutual belief, 250
mysteries, 299

Nass, Clifford, 19
natural language understanding, 24
nearness scale, 204
Nebel, Bernhard, 230
necessity, 214
negation, 117, 213, 546
Nilsson, Nils, 169, 314
nonconscious executions, 459
nonconscious plans, 361
nonmonotonic reasoning, 135
normal plans, 358
now (time), 212
null set, 101
numb, 498

object of an action, 167
observable executions, 502
observation, 502–512
obstacles, 401, 411
obvious decisions, 434
OCC emotion categories, 52, 515, 528
occasional plans, 362
ongoing executions, 473
opportunities, 375, 451, 453
Ortony, Andrew, 52, 515, 526, 528, 530,
    533
other agent reasoning, 309–311, 361
Owens, Christopher, 53, 381
OWL-Time, 46, 177, 178, 184, 188

pain, 333
pairs, 121, 129
paralyzed, 498
partially cause, 169

pattern recognition, 267
patterns, 132
pausing, 473
Peano axioms, 150
Peirce, Charles, 237
pending plans, 443
people, 207–210, 485
perception, 208, 226, 233, 245, 251, 280, 295, 451,
    484, 486, 491, 495, 497, 502
performance strategies, 43
performances, 505
periodic executions, 461
periodic plans, 362
periodic temporal sequences, 190, 390
Perrault, C. Raymond, 30
persistent goals, 316
physical objects, 203, 401, 485
Pickering, Martin, 27
Place, Ullin, 485
planning, 392–396, 397–406, 407–415, 416–420
planning domain, 41
planning goals, 397–406
plans, 348–365, 387–391
Plato, 61
pleased, 522
pleasure, 333
Pollack, Martha, 30
positive modalities, 213
possibility, 170, 213
postponing, 448, 471
power sets, 103
pre-Freudian shift, 58
preconditions, 168, 389, 465
predicate index, 55
predicates, 96
predicates (logic), 545
predictions, 281, 294
preferences, 398, 446
preservation goals, 315
preventing, 169
pride, 533, 534
primate studies, 10
primed predicates, 93, 211
priority, 368
probability, 169, 215
progressing, 404
properties of composite entities, 127
proportion, 155
propositions, 95, 116, 223, 247, 546
proverbs, 381
Psychologic, 31
psychology, 13
Psychophrase!, 49
pursuing goals, 392
Putnam, Hilary, 485

qualitative probability, 215
qualitative scales, 145, 156
quantified variables, 106, 112, 548

Rao, Anand, 30
rates, 191
rational numbers, 153
raw emotions, 524
reactive executions, 459
real existence, 211

realizing, 245
reasoning, 494
Reeves, Byron, 19
reflexes, 488
reification, 93, 112, 116–120
relations of composite entities, 128
relationship strategies, 43
relief, 531, 533
remembering, 274, 277
remorse, 533, 535
repeatability of methodology, 58
repeated plans, 362
repetitions, 388, 390, 478
repetitive executions, 460, 478–483
repressing memories, 277
reproach, 533, 536
requirements, 390
rescheduling, 447
resentment, 529, 530
resignation, 367
resources, 389
rest of a sequence, 124
restarting, 473
resuming, 472
reusable plans, 361, 470
reverse of a scale, 142
risk aversion, 344
roadrunner physics, 13
rule-following, 460
Russell's paradox, 111
Ryle, Gilbert, 485

sadness, 518, 520
Sanders, Kathryn, 31, 536
satisfaction, 531, 532
scale-to-scale functions, 143
scales, 139–149
Schank, Roger, 53, 68, 380, 381
scheduled plans, 443
schedules, 440
scheduling, 439–450
schizophrenic, 498
science strategies, 43
self-reproach, 533, 535
sensation channels, 495
sense organs, 208, 487, 492
sentences, 247
sequences, 123, 129
seriousness, 345
sets, 100–104, 129
shared goals, 318
shared plans, 360
Shoham, Yoav, 165
short-term goals, 336
similarity, 256–269
Simmel, Marianne, 3
Simulation Theory, 14
simultaneous actions, 439
simultaneous executions, 462
Singh, Minindar, 30
singleton set, 101
situation calculus, 98
skill, 506
skolem functions, 112, 122
slack, 445
sleeping, 498

Smart, John, 485
Smedslund, Jan, 31
sore, 498
sorrow, 529
source of an action, 167
space, 202–206
spatial systems, 203
spontaneous executions, 458
start times, 444, 468
states of consciousness, 497
stimulation, 487
stopping, 471
strategies, 39, 41, 355, 381
STRIPS planning, 169, 314
structure mapping, 266
subconscious desires, 12, 14
subevents, 196
subgoals, 313, 324, 349, 353, 356, 443, 458, 464, 469, 507
subplans, 388
subscales, 142
subscripted predicates, 109
subsets, 103
substitution, 105
success, 320, 374, 469, 491
successive formalization, 56
successive formalization methodology, 38
successive in a sequence, 124
successor (integer), 150
Sun Tzu, 42
surprises, 308
suspending, 474

tactic, 355
tall on the height scale, 146
temporal logic, 46
temporal ordering, 183
temporal sequences, 179
tendency to cause, 169
terminating, 389, 474, 479
termination conditions, 199, 478
Thackeray, William Makepeace, 58
Theaetetus, 61
Theory of Mind, 8, 310
Theory Theory, 8
thinking of, 280
thinking that, 239
threat detection, 343
threats, 341–347, 451, 453, 524
thriving, 322, 324, 332, 350, 352, 493
tics, 489
time, 45, 177–195, 211, 378
time-triggered executions, 461
tired, 498
top of a scale, 141, 146
truth-maintenance systems, 230
trying, 319
tuning into and tuning out, 492
Turing Test, 21
Turing, Alan, 20
Tverksy, Amos, 264
tweaking, 416
typical elements, 106

Ullman, Jeffrey, 230
uncertain decisions, 435

unconscious, 498
unconscious state, 498
unhappiness, 526, 527, 528
union of sets, 102
Universal Instantiation, 549
unknown, 227
upper ontologies, 202
user modeling, 23

value, 322
Van Hartmann, Eduard, 13
Vanity Fair, 58
Vardi, Moshe, 230
vindication, 522
voluntary actions, 489

warfare strategies, 43
weighted abduction, 135
will, 172, 209, 226, 354, 486, 488, 492
Winslett, Marianne, 230
Wittgenstein, Ludwig, 48
Wolff, Christian, 237
Wooldridge, Michael, 30
word processing, 23
WordNet, 51, 52, 57, 275, 276
wounded, 498

Xerox PARC, 21

Zermelo-Fraenkel set theory, 100
zero (integer), 150